ALSO BY BRUCE COOK

The Beat Generation

LISTEN TO THE BLUES BY BRUCE COOK

Charles Scribner's Sons, New York

FOR ROBERT NEAL COOK
1906-1956

Printed in the United States of America
Library of Congress Catalog Card Number 72-11126
SBN 684-13376-8 (cloth)

On this and page V, which constitute an extension of the copyright page, permission to quote from the following sources is gratefully acknowledged:

Satchmo: My Life in New Orleans by Louis Armstrong. Copyright © 1954 by Louis Armstrong. Used with permission of the publisher, Prentice-Hall, Inc., Englewood Cliffs, N.J.

Spirituals and the Blues by James H. Cone. Copyright © 1972 by James H. Cone. Used by permission of Seabury Press.

"Take My Hand, Precious Lord" by Thomas A. Dorsey. Copyright 1938 by Hill and Range Songs, Inc. Copyright renewed 1965 and assigned to Hill and Range Songs, Inc. Used by permission.

CONTENTS

PART ONE

CHAPTER ONE

"SWEET HOME CHICAGO"

MY FATHER was a jazz musician who could never make a living at it. He tried a couple of times. The first was when he came to Chicago from Iowa in the late twenties and began to jam around the speakeasies and roadhouses that were going full blast just then. But he got married after a while, bowed to his responsibilities, and settled down to his job as a railroad telegrapher, sneaking out only occasionally to play a gig when somebody got sick on bad gin and they needed a cornet man in a hurry.

He lost the railroad job in 1932, a couple of months before I was born, and from that time until he got it back in 1934, about the only work that came his way during those Depression years was as a musician. But you couldn't really say he made a living at it even then. People ask me who he played with, as if in this way to establish just how good he was. Well, I don't know how good he was exactly. But I do remember him mentioning Chet Roble, who became fairly well known as a piano player and bandleader in Chicago during the thirties and forties, Boyce Brown, an alto saxophonist who played with various Eddie Condon units before going into a monastery (that's right, he

3

became a monk), and the best known of them all, a guitar player named Lester Polfus. Is that a frown? Well, when my father was playing around in a little band with him in taverns on the north side of Chicago, Lester was also singing hillbilly as Rhubarb Red on station WJJD. But if Rhubarb Red doesn't help either, the year he left Chicago Lester Polfus shortened his name to Les Paul and did well as a jazzman and finally as a kind of combination pop guitarist-electronic wizard.

For years, whether he was playing regular dates or not, my father kept at his music. I think it gave him a sense of identity and purpose that the job he did for money never could. He thought of himself as a "jazzman." It was a word he used a lot. To be ready to play every date every now and then he would practice for at least an hour every day "just to keep the lip up." Practice consisted of scales, a bit of reading, and lots of jamming—that is, improvising along with records by the jazzmen he respected most: Bix Beiderbecke, Louis Armstrong, and Red Nichols.

Yes, those records—they are just the point, for I grew up hearing them over and over again. I got to know them so well that to this day I can hear solos and even whole records through in my mind's ear. And I am sure that on the day I die, whether it be tomorrow or forty years from tomorrow, I shall be able to hum, whistle, or pick out on a piano that marvelous trumpet fanfare that begins Louis Armstrong's "West End Blues."

Those were the records my father played, and while he was scrupulously careful of them himself it was always understood that if I were careful of them, too, I could play them when I wanted. And when I grew old enough to be curious about them —say, at the age of ten or eleven—I began to do just that, digging through the drawer in which they were kept, looking over those blue-label Vocalions and the red-label OKehs, playing one or two as I continued on down to those odd items at the bottom of the drawer. These were the records he didn't play, and when I asked him about them he shrugged and said, sure, he listened to them once in a while. They were just sort of . . . different from the Louies and the Bixes. Of course I could play them if I wanted to. He said he'd like to know what I thought of them, indicating by the tone of his voice and the expression on his face that he didn't think I'd like them much.

Well, I was of such an age and turn of mind that that was all I needed to like them a lot. With him away one afternoon I began playing those records at the bottom of the drawer. My mother passed through the room several times, making awful faces of disapproval, all but holding her nose. Yet I pretended not to notice and just sat there listening to them one after another. There was a scratchy old thing on the Paramount label, a piano solo that was unmistakable boogie, called "Cow Cow Blues," by one Cow Cow Davenport. There was a crazy Tampa Red record on Bluebird, "Stop Truckin' and Suzy-Q," and others on the same label by Memphis Slim and Jazz Gillum. And then there was some fascinating moaning and groaning by ladies whose very names stirred my imagination—Victoria Spivey, Hociel Thomas, Mamie Smith, and Bessie Smith. Well, let me qualify that last—Bessie's name, powerful voice and unmistakable style were known to me from her record of the "St. Louis Blues," which was one my father played often, chiefly because Louis Armstrong played back-up trumpet on it. But here were others by her: "One and Two Blues," "Down-Hearted Blues," and a couple of others.

It was quite an afternoon. I sat, if not quite amazed then deeply impressed by this new sound I heard coming through the speaker. For it was a new sound to me. The voices changed from disc to disc, but there was a unity of style and feeling in all of them that told me that this was a separate musical idiom. It was very *like* the jazz I had grown up listening to, but at the same time it was different—somehow more basic and more direct. There were strong echoes of this music through all those Louis Armstrong Hot Five recordings that I knew so well, but it was there not so much perhaps in Satchmo's flashing horn work as in his groaning, scatting vocals, and particularly in the doleful smears of Kid Ory's Creole trombone. But I heard some of it in Bix and Red Nichols, too. I had the feeling that even though some of these records at the bottom of the drawer were fairly recent, I had found on them a music that was older than the jazz on which I had been brought up.

And in a way, I *had* found something older, for I had discovered the blues. It was funny. It seemed I was hearing it for the first time then, yet at the same time I was vaguely aware that there were hints, bits, and pieces of it in nearly all the music

I heard all around me—certainly in the big-band stuff that was so popular in the forties, but even dimly in some of the most banal of the popular music that spewed forth endlessly from the radio.

Yes, the radio. It suddenly became interesting again when, not long after my first afternoon with the blues, I found out that if you fooled around with the dial far to the right of the network stations you could catch an approximation of that same blues sound in the twanging guitars and the down-home moans of the one or two black stations then broadcasting in Chicago. I became a special fan of a disc jockey named Al Benson—or that's not quite right, for the old swing-master, as Benson called himself, actually put me off a bit with his Jamaican accent and his corny line of jive. What I liked was the music he played. Some of it, though not enough, was straight blues, but most shaded into what they soon began calling rhythm-and-blues. There was something nice called "Drifting Blues," by Johnny Moore's Three Blazers, a kind of funkier version of the King Cole Trio; there were various pieces by Ivory Joe Hunter; something lusty by Helen Humes called "Ee-Bobba-Lee-Bob"; and a delicate, confidential bluesy thing by one Cecil Gent called "I Wonder," which I can hear in my head to this day.

Hearing blues on the radio this way was particularly good for me, for it saved me from the error of supposing that all the blues that was worth listening to was on those few discs at the bottom of the record drawer. I don't mean that quite as facetiously as it may sound, for there are blues scholars today that will tell you that the only true blues was played in the Mississippi Delta during the second and third decades of this century, or that no authentic blues has been recorded since Robert Johnson died in 1938, or that once the blues moved north of Memphis it stopped being blues. Tuning it in on the radio every night and listening in as I did saved me from such dogmatic certainties —and a good thing, too. I knew that blues were still being written and sung. I knew that the form was being bent and squeezed to fit personal styles and particular audiences. I realized— though I would have been hard put to articulate it at the age of twelve—that the blues was a living tradition and not some dead and ancient form fit only for the attention of folklorists and musical antiquarians.

Any vague doubts I may have had about all this were quickly dispelled the moment I set eyes and ears on my first bluesman. His name was Lonnie Johnson, and he was the real thing. I came upon him almost by accident at a jazz concert—my first —to which my father had taken me probably sometime in 1944. It was a session sponsored by a group that called itself, I think, the Hot Club of Chicago, and it was a program of traditional jazz in the old New Orleans style. The front-line men were all excellent New Orleans musicians—Lee Collins, trumpet; Preston Jackson, trombone; Tony Parenti, clarinet—all of whom would have been better known if they had recorded more. Also from there was the drummer Warren "Baby" Dodds, who did record a lot and was very well known; he was the drummer on all those Louis Armstrong Hot Five records I knew so well.

But Lonnie Johnson—what about him? When he was introduced, it turned out that, whether by the intention of the program planners or merely by coincidence, he was from New Orleans, too, one of the few blues *singers* to come out of the Crescent City. Lonnie Johnson was born there in 1894, and although he became best known when he left home, he is well remembered by the early Storyville musicians as one of the most talented members of a large musical family. In his autobiography, New Orleans bassist Pops Foster speaks of Johnson playing guitar on street corners along with his father, an excellent violinist, for whatever change came their way. In 1917 he went overseas with a troupe to entertain American soldiers in France. While he was there, the deadly influenza epidemic of that year hit New Orleans and killed nine members of his family, leaving only one older brother.

There was nothing to hold him there after that, and so he left New Orleans for good and started to ramble with his guitar, playing and singing the blues wherever he could gather a crowd to listen—through Texas, up and down the Mississippi on riverboats, gradually working his way farther north. In St. Louis, in 1925, he won a blues-singing talent contest at a theater that brought him a seven-year recording contract with OKeh Records. He became one of the most prolific of all the recording bluesmen, playing and singing his own fine songs, playing backup guitars for others, and even doing a series of excellent guitar duets in which he took great pride with the white jazz guitarist Eddie Lang. By the time I saw and heard him, he had been active in Chicago for a number of years, playing at the old 3 Deuces and other clubs and recording for Decca and Bluebird. He was to fall on hard times in a few years, but the afternoon I listened to him Lonnie Johnson, at the age of fifty, must have been close to his prime.

He had to be! I remember my own impression in listening to him was that it would be hard to imagine anybody playing better. There is a quality that the real virtuoso communicates, an added dimension to his playing, that makes it immediately and recognizably distinct from that of one who is merely proficient. Lonnie Johnson had it that day, and he may always have had it, for Pops Foster, though then hardly more than a boy, remembered him as "the only guy we had around New Orleans who could play jazz guitar. He was great on guitar. Django Reinhardt was a great jazz player like Johnson." And here he was, at fifty, playing deep rolls and treble runs that he extended with amazing subtlety, torturing out the last nuance of melody from those simple blues chords.

But the blues is essentially a vocal art, and Lonnie Johnson was pre-eminently a blues singer. I remember his voice as hushed and rather insinuating in tone; he was a singer with a style that managed to say more than words alone might allow. He was a dapper man, light-complexioned, with a pencil mustache, and dressed in a careful and precise way that reminded me a little of my father. (I remember he kept his hat on as he played and sang, and that struck me as odd.) He was the very picture of the urban bluesman, and that was the image he projected as he sang—knowing, world-wise, a man who had no illusions left but who still had pride in himself, a kind of played-out masculinity that you might associate with Bogart. All that was Lonnie Johnson. I won't pretend to remember what he sang. Diligent digging and listening have turned up any number, from "Backwater Blues" and "Falling Rain Blues" to "Careless Love" and "When You Fall for Someone That's Not Your Own," that he *might* have sung. But what seems important as I look back now is that he presented me with a figure, a living, breathing person to go with the brooding music I had started to listen to. I could see it as well as hear it: I knew it was real.

My father's attitude about all this was interesting. I remember asking him on the way home what he thought of Lonnie Johnson. He said he was a good guitar player, one of the best he had heard—and that's all he would say. I tried to draw him out on the blues we had heard, the odd, hushed style in which they'd been sung: I asked him what he thought of the blues and how come he didn't play them more himself. He just smiled, and shrugged, and changed the subject. It was only gradually, over a period of years, that I got the kind of answers I was looking for, and even then I apprehended rather than heard them from him. I came to understand that he, like most of the white jazzmen of his generation—and many of the black, too— was a little ashamed of the music's primitive beginnings. The juke joints and whorehouses from which jazz had sprung represented a world he had not known and one he would just as soon not know. The blues were much closer to this world, closer to the beginnings, and I think he (quite rightly) perceived them as the dark underside of jazz, the music he played and loved. Still, there were those records at the bottom of the drawer: they were his; he had chosen them and yes, he did listen to them from time to time. What about them? Well, I can only say that his attitudes in this were complicated and for the most part undefined, even to himself. There was a contradiction there, and he knew it, but he managed to live with it.

And that was how I grew up—or at least one of the ways I grew up—listening to jazz and blues, hearing the former more and more on records and the latter on the radio. I would go to jazz concerts when I could and I started collecting records on my own, buying a few of the modern things that my father didn't go for at all, by Dizzy Gillespie and Charley Parker. But as for blues, I found those records couldn't be bought at the North Side record shops I patronized. I remember being annoyed by that but not especially troubled: I was quite willing to listen to what Al Benson played every night on the radio.

Back in the late forties and early fifties in Chicago you were never really very far from the blues anyway. Get off the El at any stop between Cermak and Sixty-third, walk down the stairs, and you'd hear the music rise up to meet you. For a white kid from the North Side there was always a thrill in going into the South Side, as if traveling to another country—and in the cultural sense, that is what it was. Not an unfriendly country, just a place where people walked and talked a little differently and where you might keep an eye and an ear open for the unusual. I remember taking a State Street streetcar clear across town once when a blind street singer got aboard with his dog around Thirty-first Street. He sat down near the front of the car, unslung his guitar, and began serenading us all with blues and gospel songs. Everybody liked it just fine, and he collected a fair share of change before he got off someplace in the Fifties.

Time passes. Think of me as in college now, and still right in the city. I was acting hip, going to jazz spots mostly—the Bee Hive, the Streamliner, the Rag Doll—until I started working at a Michigan Avenue bookstore, Werner's. The porter at the bookstore was named Ernest Crawford, and portering was just something he did for money; in real life he was "a old ham-fat bass player" (in his own phrase). I used to sell the paperbacks downstairs, which left me more or less alone with Ernest, whose domain was the shipping room next door. When no customers were around, and I was supposed to be dusting the shelves, I was usually hanging out in the shipping room, talking to Ernest, asking him questions about his music. He liked to talk about the time he went on tour with Nellie Lutcher, that lusty, shouting two-handed piano lady from Kansas City. That was his taste of the big time, I guess, and he never forgot it.

I asked who he was playing with right then, and he just shrugged and said, "Muddy and Slim mostly." That turned out to be Muddy Waters, his steady gig, and Memphis Slim, for whom he played occasionally at Sylvio's. I extracted a kind of halfhearted invitation from him to come up and listen to him play sometime, and I think I astonished him when I actually did show up one Friday night around midnight. He was with Muddy then at a place on Forty-third Street that must have been Pepper's Lounge. I was with a friend, and I remember I was slightly intimidated by the place at first. The crash and holler of the music was something I wasn't quite prepared for. The Chicago blues sound, electrified and fully amplified, would shake an auditorium; inside a place as small as that one it seemed almost to explode around you, bouncing off the walls and punishing your ears. Or that's how it seemed at first. As my friend and I settled in to listen, we found that we were able to take it pretty well by the end of a set, we felt a little easier about having come to listen.

I went back to Pepper's a couple of times after that. Ernest decided he didn't mind at all having me come by. He even had me out one weeknight when he sat in with Memphis Slim at Sylvio's, on Lake Street. But I never went back. The place had a kind of forbidding atmosphere that made me uncomfortable. The West Side made me uneasy, and the South Side never did. I hit the blues spots pretty regularly out there the year that I was a senior in college. That was when Willie Mabon's "I Don't Know" was such a big hit, and I remember catching him at a big loud bar on Forty-seventh Street. I went to the Crown Propeller Lounge often to hear the brand of jazz and slick-blues they dished out there. And farther up Sixty-third Street, at the corner of Cottage Grove, there were spots on each corner that were worth hitting any weekend. I remember hearing Big Joe Williams at one of them. Across the street from it was a place I kept going back to again and again. Eddie Vinson was there —"Mr. Cleanhead," the Houston alto sax player and blues singer whom I had heard years before at the Oriental Theater when he was with the Cootie Williams big band. Yes, I remember sitting there when it was close to 4:00 a.m. on a Saturday morning, listening to Eddie Vinson sing "Juice-Head Baby" for the third time that night, looking in the long bar mirror and realizing mine was the lightest face in the place: there hadn't been any of those white guys in since one o'clock or so.

IF I SEEM to dwell a bit on these memories of all those years of listening in Chicago, it is because I am trying to establish my credentials for what will follow. It is not a question of knowledge. There is plenty of that around, for the blues has become a whole field of scholarship all its own. Serious young fellows with tape recorders have been combing the Mississippi Delta for the last dozen years or more looking for blues singers who might still be active in the territory, or maybe just for people who still remember the ones who were. The oral history thus amassed is impressive enough—and I'll admit I've made plenty of use of it myself in gathering facts, information, and opinions in my own research—but it all seems to have more to do with anthropology than with music. This "folklore" approach to the blues tends, ultimately, to diminish it, for it isolates the form, defining it all too narrowly and delimiting it to a style and an era that are for the most part long gone, and to a locale from which it has since gone forth, spreading its influence wide and deep throughout the world into all sorts and styles of music.

The blues is a living tradition. It has changed a time or two in the recent past and will probably change again. It has had a shaping influence on *all* native American music of this century—from jazz to country and western, and to rock-and-roll. You could even call it the *fundamental* American music. It is the tough, hard, durable stuff that all our styles and genres have in common. If a particular kind of music should lose contact with its origins in the blues it will go into an at least temporary decline. This is what happened to jazz in the forties and fifties, when musicians who had gained greatly in musical sophistication began emphasizing non-native elements more and more so that what was promised as jazz by some—the Dave Brubecks, the John Lewises, and the Lennie Tristanos—was delivered as a kind of hybrid, half-European form that may have intrigued some but excited none. The more arid and intellectual the music became, the smaller was its audience. It looked for a while as though jazz would lose its popular audience altogether, until some black jazzmen began injecting certain down-home blues and gospel elements into the music, and a little later on blues-based rock became an important element in jazz. And now, little by little, the audience is being won back.

If in that last paragraph you seem to detect the suggestion of a kind of musical chauvinism from me, then you are only partly wrong. I did, of course, contrast European music with American music. The difference between the two, I think, is self-evident. The point is that they can and should be compared—and they have been by the music critic Henry Pleasants. In three books—*The Agony of Modern Music, Death of a Music?,* and *Serious Music—and All that Jazz*—he has developed a thesis that has put the music world on its ear, infuriating some (Mark Schubart, dean of the Juilliard School of Music called his first book "scurrilous, unfair, destructive, and specious"), but gradually winning over others with the force of his argument (Erich Leinsdorf called it "frighteningly sound and logical").

Put briefly, Henry Pleasants' thesis is this: To remain vital and to continue to grow, a music must be sustained by popular taste and living popular music traditions. But toward the end of the nineteenth century, following the great explosion of harmonic innovation that began with Beethoven and ended roughly with Wagner, gradually music began to lose the support of popular taste, was no longer fed by the streams of popular music that had nourished it in the past. The reason for this is that European music became technically exhausted: there were fewer and fewer new tricks to pull. But because composers felt themselves in a sort of competition with the innovators of the past, they felt obliged to keep right on trying. The result of their efforts—atonality, serial and twelve-tone composition —only served to alienate what popular support they had left. It is significant that all this came to a crisis at just about the time that American music had established a separate identity of its own. As Henry Pleasants writes in *The Agony of Modern Music:*

> This time factor is essential to the critical comprehension of what has happened to serious music. Technical exhaustion coincided with sociological obsolescence and esthetic decay. All coincided with the ultimate agony of the nineteenth century on the battlefields of Europe in the First World War. Until then Western music had been a European affair in a European culture. Thereafter cultural leadership passed to America. Western civilization is now well into its American phase, and its music is the popular music of America.

So that today European music—and this, of course, includes all music by American composers in the European idiom, all "serious" music—is at a dead end. It has no popular appeal and it has no relation to any spontaneous popular tradition. Today the new music—the music that has supplanted the European idiom—is American music.

Now, what does Henry Pleasants mean by "the popular music of America"? In the beginning—say, at the time he wrote *The Agony of Modern Music*—he would have answered forthwith "jazz," yet (as he himself later indicated) he would not have been entirely sure what he meant by it—that is, how broadly or narrowly he would have defined the term. The reason for that is that he is himself a product of that European tradition whose agonized end he has described so well. He studied voice and piano at the Curtis Institute and went on to become the regular classical music critic of the Philadelphia *Eve-*

ning Bulletin from 1930 to 1942 and was subsequently a musical correspondent and critic for the *New York Times*. The point in delving into his *curriculum vitae* is to demonstrate how firmly he was at one time attached to the musical tradition he has now to some extent rejected.

His theory on the death of European music and the new dominance of American music was developed inductively, step by step—that is, he seemed to know that European music was in trouble and what the trouble was before he was really very intimate with American music. As his familiarity with this music grew, he sensed it offered the way out—and today he is the only music critic around who can speak with real authority on both; he had actually broadened his notion of the American musical idiom, which he contrasts with the European. In *Serious Music—and All That Jazz* he included rhythm-and-blues, country and western, rock, and pop along with jazz, remarking on the diversity of Afro-American music as a clear sign of its vitality. He would say that all these are elements in the new idiom that is American music. And I would add, of course, that blues is the element common and basic to them all.

My reason for presenting Pleasants' view at such length is twofold. First, I think he is right and that his theory deserves to be widely known and accepted. Second, I think it is terribly important that he is right, for it is a rare thing when such an epoch is begun in the history of music; the last such, which has been called the harmonic era by Pleasants, began about 1600 with the development and use of the musical key. But this is also notable as an important phenomenon of American culture —probably the *most* important because the most far-reaching in its implications. In a way, what is remarkable about American music is that it came to be at all. To call it Afro-American music, as is done so often today, is merely to acknowledge its dual nature. It is not to say that it is African music that is made in America—although for reasons that don't have much to do with music some seem to believe it is just that. No, American music is distinctive and separate. If it is different from European music, it is perhaps even more different from African music. It is a new music, an idiom, a whole new language that represents a synthesis of the two. Having written that, my immediate impulse is to go back and alter that last sentence to remove the word "synthesis"; it sounds programmatic, tendentious. But a synthesis is what it is, and the analogy to language in that same sentence is exactly to the point. For it is a synthesis in the same way that English is also one: that is, a whole new language that cannot be reduced to its original constituents of Anglo-Saxon and Norman French. That is how the American musical idiom has developed: as a language will—organically, naturally, and popularly with no special respect for what is "high" or "low," what is acceptable usage or unacceptable, or which of the original elements came from which group. It would be easy enough to dispose of the problem if one could say that American music combined European harmony with African rhythm—as it does more or less—but this would be to generalize our way too quickly through a vast complex of musical borrowing, trades, and thefts that went back and forth between white and black over a couple of centuries.

But if it is a music apart and a true synthesis of separate idioms, it is so not because anybody planned it that way but because in one of the more abominable episodes of history the black man was brought to America by the white man and kept here for centuries—in captivity but not in isolation. For the process of musical exchange and assimilation that ultimately brought forth American music as a separate idiom began very early. A change of sorts could be perceived in our folk and popular music during the first half of the nineteenth century. What this means is that even in slavery days a kind of cultural exchange was under way. American culture—the musical part of it, anyhow, which may well be the part that matters most—was even then being shaped by the black man.

There wouldn't be an American music if African culture had not had that prolonged encounter with the European down there in the American South. That was how the process began. The black man provided its essential element, the fuel for this engine of change. This is not quite the same thing as saying he is responsible for creating the music. So what is it exactly that I'm trying to sidestep here? Fundamentally, these are rhetorical evasions of the old nature-versus-nurture question, which is, of course, the root of the problem: Was it the peculiar genius of the black man that was responsible? Or the environment— slavery, Christianity, European music, and all—into which he

was thrust? Flip Wilson caps his routine, "The Blues Singer,"
with an exchange that catches the essentials of this dilemma:
The earnest young white blues singer tells the black lady who
owns the club at which he has been playing, "You should be
very proud because everybody knows the Negro gave the blues
to America." She replies: "Just a minute, honey. The Negro
didn't give the blues to America. America gave the blues to the
Negro."

And perhaps took it away from him again when it began to
look as though he had made a pretty good thing of it. Because
when we talk about a synthesis we are using a nice neutral
term that clouds an untold number of plagiarisms, a good deal
of outright cheating on copyright material, and a general pattern according to which the black man makes the music and
the white man makes the money.

And one of the ways that the white man makes the money is by
writing *about* the music the black man makes—as, of course, I
am doing now. Yes, I know full well that I myself am caught up
in the ironies of this situation. And that, fundamentally, is why I
took the time and space to go into my own early relations with
the blues. I wanted to show that I have a personal, emotional
investment in what I'm writing about here. For in criticism
generally, and particularly in the critcism of something as wide
open as popular music, it seems to me that this sort of personal
investment is really the authority that matters most. This is my
stake in all that follows.

But back to Chicago, that city so fabulous to southern black
people in general and to bluesmen in particular. Only a place
with a potent myth could have attracted such gifted people
from Louisiana, Mississippi, Texas, and Tennessee. All along
the Illinois Central right-of-way, clear down to New Orleans,
people must have responded with a kind of longing to Robert
Johnson's erroneous exhortation:

Oh, baby, don't you want to go
Back to the land of California,*
To my sweet home, Chicago?

*Don't laugh too hard: Remember, Keats attributed the discovery of the Pa-
cific to Cortex 3 in a sonnet.

And so it was more or less in that spirit, objectively—as a kind of pilgrimage to the single Northern city that had sustained and extended the blues tradition—that I returned not long ago to my sweet home, Chicago, and looked for some blues to listen to.

I had been primed for the visit when a little while before I met Bruce Iglauer, a young man from Louisville who came to Chicago because he is a passionate blues fan and stayed to edit a magazine, *Living Blues,* and founded a blues record label, Alligator. I had come to know about him through the first release on that label, a good album by a bluesman named Hound Dog Taylor. Talking to Iglauer once at a concert at Notre Dame, I had heard from him where I might catch Hound Dog. "If you go on a Monday," he had told me, "you'll be able to hear anybody who's in town. They all come out and jam. Blue Monday, they call it—at Pepper's and Theresa's."

When it came time to start, though, I found out that Pepper's had moved from Forty-third Street to what was considered a "safer" location on Michigan Avenue just south of Roosevelt Road. The idea, it turned out, was to be in a location that was still south yet close enough to the Loop that it would be easily accessible to the white college-age kids who have taken up Chicago blues as a kind of crusade.

I met one of these young aficionados only minutes after I had stepped inside the place. His name was Wesley Race, and he was, coincidentally, co-producer with Bruce Iglauer of that Hound Dog Taylor LP that had started me out on my Blue Monday quest. Hound Dog was there, too—just setting up with the drummer, apparently waiting around for a musician or two more before starting the jam.

Wesley Race told me he was from Wichita, Kansas, "where all they play is country music." How did he get into blues, then? "Well, when I was thirteen," he said, "my mother bought me a Bessie Smith album and said, 'Here, get off that rock-and-roll stuff.' She did me a favor, all right. I was hooked from then on."

That, he said, was how he happened to come to Chicago: "It was either here or Houston, and Chicago had more of what I wanted. You think it's so unusual for somebody to come here to live just to hear the blues? There are people here from England who came here just to listen to the music. I know twenty or thirty people who moved here just for that reason."

The place was beginning to bustle and fill up a bit. It was still early, they said, only ten o'clock, and Junior Wells would be in any minute. A few of the tables were a little loud, shouting to compete with the all-soul jukebox. This one didn't look a thing like the old Pepper's. It is dark and sort of Moorish, with a whole wall of mirrors to make it look twice its modest size.

Suddenly, a tall young black man strode up to the stand, a guitar under his arm, and from a table or two away Wesley Race signaled me they would soon be starting. He was right. After a bare moment given to the preliminaries of plugging in and tuning up, the trios—two guitars and drums—began in earnest. They swung beautifully through a couple of Hound Dog's own slow blues, which the man himself shouted with authority, looking black and haughty, as he told Baby just what she could do when she cried his name. And they played breakdowns—boogies to you—on which, in the absence of a bassman, Hound Dog played the bass line on his guitar with a funny kind of bloop-bloop-bloop inflection due to the higher pitch of his instrument.

The surprise was the late arrival; he played a good strong lead throughout, more than holding up his own, and soloed fluently in a somewhat more modern style than Hound Dog's. At the end of the set he sat down with Wesley Race. I was called over then and introduced to young Lefty Diz, a twenty-four-year-old guitar man out of Kankakee, Illinois, who had started out playing jazz and rock-and-roll. "But I'm into this Delta blues thing all the way now. Maybe I had to learn it, but it's me. This is what I feel."

Lefty Diz clearly has a lot of respect for Hound Dog Taylor, but he would rather talk about Junior Wells, the brilliant young harp player who, with guitarist Buddy Guy, leads the boss Chicago blues band. There are elder statesmen around, like Muddy Waters and Howlin' Wolf, but Buddy and Junior are the movers today on the Chicago blues scene. Lefty Diz told me a little about the tour he had made with their band in Africa and ended his encomium by urging me to stick around until Junior came. "We'll do a few of his things then because I know his music," he assured me.

I did wait through a couple of sets but then ducked out and

headed for Theresa's, telling myself I could look in at Pepper's on the way back. It's out south on Indiana Avenue, an inconspicuous little walk-down right on the corner of Forty-eighth Street. At this point Indiana is a dark, mean street, and just a little scary. I parked directly across the street from Theresa's, locked up tight, and went inside. The band at the far end of the club was grinding out "Hoochie-Koochie Man," laying it down with that electric panache and verve that when heard is quite unmistakably Chicago blues. There was a somber-looking individual at the door, holding a cord and looking over the customers as they entered. And beyond him, greeting those deemed worthy of admission, was Junior Wells.

Although he owns no part of the club, you get the sense that he is presiding there, almost holding court—if not quite a king, then a reigning prince of the realm. Junior Wells is a quick, shrewd, intelligent young man, one who has learned a good deal from his travels and social contacts. It was one of these contacts, a mutual friend, whose name I tossed to him as we shook hands. "Sure, man! You know him? We're like *that!*"

Junior has the natural host's ability to concentrate fully on whomever he is talking to. He called the bartender over and told him to set me up and listened attentively to my questions about his beginnings in the blues. He told me he is originally from Arkansas and learned to play harp there, listening to Sonny Boy Williamson on the old King Biscuit show, so he knew a little when he came. I asked him if he started playing clubs right away. "At my age then? Oh, man, I was twelve!" No, what he used to do was to play riding the streetcars and set up on the street corners. "Me and Earl Hooker, we'd do that. We'd catch those streetcars at one end and ride them clean on through to the other, just playing and singing all the way.

"My first band? You mean in a club? They're right over here —well, two of them are anyway. Come on, let me introduce you." And in another moment he had guided me artfully down the bar and passed me on to a couple of friendly and slightly older men, Louis Myers and Freddy Bellow—and then Junior was gone, back to his post near the door. The perfect host.

I had heard about both Myers and Bellow, a guitarist and drummer of some standing. They had a nice way of listening and talking in a completely relaxed way so that they were able to divide their attention between what was being said and the music that was being played, dropping a remark in response after a pause as they listened to a chorus or two of a solo. Or to a vocal. I remember we were listening to a young man in a visored cap delivering an impassioned "Every Day I've Got the Blues." I asked who he was.

"Him? That's B. B. King," said Louis Myers.

"B. B. *King?*" I repeated skeptically. It seemed unlikely that B.B. would jam in such an informal way anywhere.

"B. B. King, *Junior,*" Fred Bellow clarified.

"His son?"

"Well, he looks a lot like him, doesn't he?"

Well, it was true enough: he did look like the Blues Boy. When he came down off the stand and mixed with the crowd, I noted the resemblance—though as it turned out, the two are not actually related. I was just shaking hands with him there at my place at the bar when a party of four young white kids entered rather hastily and were ushered to an empty table that had suddenly come vacant directly in front of the stage. I asked if many white kids came to Theresa's.

"Some do," said B.B., Jr. "Usually just Mondays and the weekends."

I said in a kind of neutral way to the group at large that I was about that age when I started going out to listen to the blues bands around town. There was some interest in that, and so I added that I had started because somebody I knew used to play bass with Muddy Waters.

"Yeah?" Louis Myers leaned forward with interest. "Who was that?"

"Ernest Crawford," I said. "I used to work with him at a bookstore."

"Sure, Big Crawford! I remember that bookstore job of his. So you used to work with him there?" I could tell I had gained a bit of stature in his eyes.

"Yeah. You remember him?"

"Remember him?" said Myers. "Man, I used to *play* with him. Yeah, him and me used to gig at the 108 Club on Forty-seventh. That's closed now. I closed that place up with Otis Rush in 1958."

"That must have been just before he died," I prompted.

"Yeah, must have been. Doesn't seem that long ago I was gigging with Big Crawford, though," he mused. "He was some bass player, he was, on that upright bass of his. He was the onliest cat I ever heard play who could get a real big sound on an upright bass."

In the world of the blues, where competition is tough and memories are short, Louis Myers' tribute to Big Crawford qualifies as high praise indeed. Ernest would have been pleased to hear himself talked about that way. And listening to it made me glad I had come out that night to make the old scene. It made up for the uneasy feeling I had that things had changed on the South Side, perhaps permanently, that the four white kids who now sat up front near the stage digging the sounds were a bit braver and more aware of what they were doing than I had ever been.

Junior Wells came back over to me and said he had just been wondering where I had parked. I told him I had parked directly across the street.

"Uh-oh. Wrong side of the street. I think B.B. should walk you to the car whenever you think you want to go." I protested, told him I was quite capable of taking care of myself, but he dismissed all this with a shake of his head. "No," he said, "listen, when you go to a place you always want to park right by the club and not on a side street and not across the street or down the street, either. And don't go for any walks."

I felt intimidated. It was hard to listen to the music after that. Had I been invited to leave? I didn't think so. Was Junior Wells trying to scare me? No, he seemed genuinely concerned for my . . . what? Safety, I guess.

I finished my drink after a while and decided to leave. With goodbyes and shakes all around, I made for the door and found B. B. King, Jr., already there ahead of me, leading the way. Outside it seemed a little colder than when I had come in. Just as we were about to start across Indiana a cab pulled right up to the door and another couple of white kids jumped out and scurried for the shelter of Theresa's.

"We call cabs for them when they go," said B.B., Jr., without my asking.

We walked across the street then, and I stood for a moment with the car door open as we tried to make small talk and act casual. And then I left the scene.

Things sure have changed there.

CHAPTER TWO

IN SEARCH OF A DEFINITION

OFTEN PEOPLE seem not quite sure what you mean when you talk about the blues. They may have the general idea without getting the particulars down quite right—sometimes without being sufficiently aware that there are particulars of any sort to settle.

"The blues? That's black music, isn't it?"

Yes, that's right, but not all American black music is blues. And it may be, too, that not all blues are black, a proposition that we shall examine briefly a few chapters from now.

"The blues is soul, right? James Brown, Chuck Berry, Bo Diddley, and all the rest?"

That's a big hasty, too. When we talk about soul music, we're talking about a wide spectrum of styles that would include singers and shouters as different as James Brown, Otis Redding, Aretha Franklin, Wilson Pickett, the old Supremes, and on high up into that rarefied atmosphere where only songbirds such as Diana Ross and Dionne Warwick seem to survive. Soul has blues in it—as nearly every variety of American popular music does today—but its line of descent is circuitous and rather complicated. On the other hand, the line from blues to what was called rhythm-and-blues—Chuck Berry, Bo Diddley, Little Richard, and all the rest—is straight and direct. In point of time, the difference between the two is a matter of a generation (Bo Diddley, for instance, played guitar for Muddy Waters early in his career). In style, it is a matter of tempo and attack. But perhaps the real significance of rhythm-and-blues is as a station on the way from blues to white rock-and-roll. Which is just the sort of complication this book is all about.

"All right then, what about this? Blues is that old-time music that the jazz bands used to play, like the 'St. Louis Blues' and 'The Birth of the Blues' and so on."

The relationship of the blues to jazz was, it is true, simple and straightforward back in the beginning. They were more or less different styles of the same music: jazz chiefly instrumental (heavy on the brass), and blues chiefly vocal (usually with string accompaniment). As jazz developed, however, and became the virtuoso music it was even by the 1920s, its relationship to the blues became tenuous, but more complex and even symbiotic. Jazz needed the blues. That's where the roots were, and that's where they are to this day.

"St. Louis Blues," a jazz standard if there ever was one, is an example of the sort of blues that gave jazz its foundation. It is a true blues. Although it is credited to W. C. Handy, it may only have been adapted by him from one or more folk blues that he heard in his travels from Memphis; certainly lines in the lyrics are interchangeable with those in many others that came from as far away as Texas. I suspect that W. C. Handy's chief contribution was the interpolation of the bridge between the basic blues figures, which in this case came, oddly enough, in the form of a tango. (Just listen to Louis Armstrong's early recording of it, where this is unmistakable.) It may have made it a little less a blues in the bargain, but it introduced the "Spanish tinge" that Jelly Roll Morton used to claim was absolutely essential to jazz.

You may have heard "The Birth of the Blues" played *ad nauseam* down in New Orleans, but that doesn't make it a blues; it is still just a popular song *about* the blues. In this case, when we talk about a popular song, we are not implying one of those tired value judgments that exalts true folk art over what is merely manufactured for public consumption. No, we mean something much more specific. It is in the thirty-two-bar form in which nearly all American popular songs have been written up to and even into the rock-and-roll era. It consists of an eight-bar figure that is repeated once before a new eight-bar figure is introduced as a "bridge" to the original eight-bar figure, which is then repeated to conclude the chorus. That is the form of "The Birth of the Blues," just as it is the form of "Stardust," "Up, Up and Away," and countless other songs.

But it is not the form of the blues. Although simpler, the blues chorus is just as precise in formulation. Examples of short eight-bar chorus blues can be cited, and there are extended sixteen-bar blues choruses, as well. But the most common—no, call it the classic—blues chorus consists of twelve bars that are divided in an interesting way that is just right for the easy improvisation of lyrics. In it, a four-bar line is stated:

> *When a woman gets the blues she wrings her hands and cries.*

Then it is repeated with the addition of a pickup word or phrase:

> *I said, when a woman gets the blues she wrings her hands and cries.*

And then the final "answering" line comes, concluding the chorus and completing the rhyme:

> *But when a man gets the blues he grabs a train and rides.*

Each of the three lines consists of four bars, giving us the standard twelve-bar blues chorus. Yet it is no more than a couplet stretched to three lines, simply by repeating the first line before following through with the second. This gives the singer, if he happens to be making up his words as he goes along, a little extra time to come up with the last line. In almost any folk blues the figure that carries each line fills its allotted four bars rather slackly, so that, again, there is room for both musical and verbal improvisation. All this emphasizes the blues as vocal art.

Harmonically, blues was—at least in the beginning—a very simple form, but one that had a trick or two in store for the performer who thought he could pick it up just by reading the right notes. Most of the early bluesmen began by learning three common chords on the guitar; they could sing a lot of songs just knowing these chords alone. (Many, of course, have gained overwhelming skill on this difficult instrument—Lonnie Johnson, Scrapper Blackwell, and Shirley Griffiths, for example— but a few talented shouters—John Lee Hooker, for one—have never gotten much beyond that basic primitive skill.) The trick in blues harmony is in the so-called "blue notes." The third, fifth, and seventh notes of the major scale are flatted, diminished to produce chords that can only truly come together in quarter tones. The human voice can sing a quarter tone; horns and stringed instruments can "bend" into them; but a piano can only suggest it with a dissonant chord, for the true quarter tone lies, as they say, "between the keys." These "blue notes" are now heard in American music of all kinds, not just in the blues. They and certain distinctive elements of rhythm have given American music its distinctive sound. And the blue notes were there even before the blues—well back in the nineteenth century, when all this was taking shape. Some say these quarter tones were brought from Africa; they are the black contribution to Western harmony.

And so if, in the blues scale, we drop certain tones from major to minor, the effect is basically a *sad* sound. And that, of course, is what the blues is all about: sadness, despondency. Just look in the *Oxford English Dictionary,* and you can see such a definition taking shape as far back as the sixteenth century. Blue was the color of the Devil; candles were said to burn blue when he was near (probably because blue flame was associated with brimstone). From this came the expression "blue devils"—a man who was plagued by them was despondent, felt a depression of spirits. And as early as 1807, Washington Irving could dispense with the devils entirely and remark that he was "in a fit of the blues," and have it perfectly well understood that he felt depressed.

It may well be that I am making too much of something simple, for elementary color psychology designates blue as the color of melancholy. And whenever it has been used in a figurative or poetic sense in the past it has carried this meaning, though sometimes with connotations that shaded into fear and anxiety (all of which goes well enough with the music). And when this melancholy music began to be heard as something in itself, it may only have seemed the natural thing to call it "blue" music, or, simply, the blues.

When was this? When did blues first come to be perceived as a distinctive style or form? If we were to go by copyrights, dates of publication, and so on, we would mark the beginning at 1912, for that's when something called "Baby Seals Blues" was published in St. Louis, "Dallas Blues" was published in Oklahoma City, and "Memphis Blues" was published in Memphis. But actually, of course, the form was well set years before. In New Orleans, that black-hearted cornet man who is said to have led the first real jazz band used to play his "Buddy Bolden Blues" as a kind of musical signature as early as 1897. And Big Bill Broonzy recorded something he called "Blues in 1890," actually a version of the old "Joe Turner Blues," which he said his uncle used to play and sing back then; this, to Big Bill, was the "first" blues.

It was something different, a sad and personal kind of music. Once you heard it you knew it was different and you remembered it. And right from the start, the people who played it knew there was something special about it, too.

> . . . I think that the blues is more or less a feeling that you get from something that you think is wrong, or something that somebody did wrong to you, or something that somebody did wrong to some of your own people or something like that . . . and the onliest way you have to tell it would be through a song, and that would be the blues . . . but the blues is really aimed at an object of some kind or an indirect person. It's not aimed at the whole public; the blues cannot be aimed at the whole public.

That's Li'l Son Jackson, quoted in *The Blues Line*, an anthology of blues lyrics. It is a huge collection, 270 songs that fill well over 400 pages. There is not a note of music. The lyrics are laid out on the pages like so many pieces of verse. Read through them this way, and you will be struck again and again, I think, by the points cited by Li'l Son Jackson in that modest little commentary quoted above. He's saying it's trouble-music, sad music, but there is nothing abstract about it; no, its miseries are specific and personal, and the way they come out best is in a song.

And it's true enough, for just look how specific the songs are in *The Blues Line*. Place names and personal references abound. In many, experiences are described with the kind of precise detail that has to come straight from life. Take Li'l Son Jackson's own "Charlie Cherry":

> *If the shack get raided*
> > *ain't no body run*
> *If the shack get raided*
> > *ain't no body run*
> *You stay right here till*
> > *Charlie Cherry come*
> *Well he cut you if you stand*
> > *shoot you if you run*
> *Well he cut you if you stand*
> > *shoot you if you run*
> *You better stay right here*
> > *till Charlie Cherry come*
> *Now he arrested my brother*
> > *tied him to a tree*
> *Well now he arrested my brother*
> > *tied him to a tree*
> *You could hear him crying,*
> > *Please don't murder me*
> *Well now Charlie Cherry*
> > *meanest man I know*
> *Well it's Charlie Cherry*
> > *meanest man I know*
> *Well now you meet him in the morning*
> > *you don't know which-a-way*
> > > *to go*
> *Well now where was you baby*
> > *when the wind blowed cold*
> *Well now where was you*
> > *when the wind blowed cold*
> *Well now you was in the bottom*
> > *by the red hot stove*

There are no notes here to inform us who Charlie Cherry was, but it seems fairly obvious that he was a sheriff against whom Li'l Son Jackson brushed a time or two, and it is just as evident that Charlie Cherry was a mean son of a bitch ("You could hear him crying, Please don't murder me"—that says it pretty well). It kind of calls to mind that picture of Sheriff Jim Rainey (who was tried and acquitted for the murder of civil-rights workers James Chaney, Michael Schwerner, and Andrew Goodman in

Philadelphia, Mississippi), chewing on that gob of tobacco and smirking in the courtroom.

Turn the pages of this or any other blues collection, read through the lyrics, and you will be impressed by the evocative and very specific quality of the language. You will note a limited but sometimes very compelling use of metaphor, as here in Blind Lemon Jefferson's stanza:

> *Blue jumped a rabbit, run him one solid mile*
> *Blue jumped a rabbit, run him one solid mile*
> *This rabbit sat down, crying like a natural child.*

Or the sort of resonant images that say more than words can tell:

> *Well the sun's gonna shine in*
> > *my back door some*
> > *day*
>
> *Well the sun's gon' shine*
> > *in my back door some*
> > *day*
>
> *Ahhhh it's one more drink*
> > *gonna drive these*
> > *blues away*

What I am saying, in effect, is that the more we read of blues lyrics the more we are struck by their poetic qualities. It is not just seeing the songs set down in printed lines that persuades us. You can look at rock lyrics presented in the same way in any number of collections, then read through them quickly, and be impressed merely by how pitifully they are diminished, languishing there on the page without music to support or charisma to sustain them. The poetic qualities of the blues are right there in the lines.

Does this mean that the blues is poetry? There has been a tacit assumption that it is since the time—late in the 1920s— when white intellectuals first began to listen seriously to the music that blacks were singing. And, indeed, the blues have been emulated in imagery and diction by some black and white poets ever since then. But does this make it poetry? Samuel Charters takes up the matter in a book that seems to beg the question in its very title, *The Poetry of the Blues*.

And yet though Charters notes the poetic qualities of the

blues early in his little book, just as I have done here, he seems to withhold final sanction on what for him seems to be no less than a point of doctrine. The question is one of authorship. He says even in a note on sources preceding his text, "Most of the verses of the blues are used by every singer, and they have become the root language for the more personal singers like John Estes and Robert Johnson. I have not mentioned a particular source for these verses, since this would tend to imply that there is someone who could be thought of as having written them." Does Charters really mean this? It seems to me that it comes awfully close to saying that the blues were not written but, instead, they just happened. This may make a case for the blues as folk art of a kind, but it doesn't really convince us that it is poetry, for poetry implies single authorship, a direct expression of individual human experience.

And this seems to be exactly what Samuel Charters is saying, because a little later in the text, where he ought to be talking about the bluesman writing a song, he speaks of him "creating a verse pattern." And then he goes on to say: "Because so much of the blues is concerned with the disappointments of love there are hundreds of verses using this idea, and a singer can simply put four or five of these second-hand verses together and have a blues that will have little individuality but will give him something to sing without much effort involved." As an alternative to this, he goes on to extoll not authorship, but the arrangement of verses by "an emotional association." He stops just short of insisting that there are no original lines in the blues, but he strongly suggests that the best one can hope for from any bluesman is good editorial work of the scissors-and-paste sort.

Why? Why is Samuel Charters so determined to reduce the poetry of the blues to mere folklore? What does he hope to prove by generalizing authorship in this way? Not to belabor this, but it seems self-evident that blues are and have been written. Pushed back to their sources, stanzas and whole songs had to have come from specific composers, even if we are unsure of their identity (and in most cases we know precisely who wrote them). No, the beginnings of the blues are not shrouded in quite the obscurity that Charters pretends. But it suits his purposes to present the blues as folklore, for—and here we come to that point of doctrine that he tacitly defends—group authorship of the kind he seems to insist upon implies that the music could only have come out of a very specific set of conditions and circumstances. For Samuel Charters, as for a number of others who have written on the subject, the blues is purely a product of the black man in the rural South—more specifically, a product of the black in the Mississippi Delta region. Its origin, he insists in *The Poetry of the Blues* and elsewhere, is social, growing directly out of racial segregation: "From this separateness of white and Negro there have come not only differences in social attitude, but also in social expression. The lives of the two groups are so insistently kept apart that there has grown up within the Negro society its own artistic self-expression."

And while there is no disputing that the blues is essentially Negro music, we can certainly question the implication that it was cut from whole cloth (or at least that the cloth was quite so black in color). And we are hardly giving the music its due if we allow to go unchallenged the tacit assumption that the only true blues is that which came from a limited territory and time; the corollary to this is that whatever may follow in time, or derives from it in style or is adapted from it, is unauthentic and probably debased. Such a purist's position reduces ultimately to the stubborn insistence that the blues is what *I* say it is.

But because blues is what it is—a *living* tradition—there are still blues being made today in just about the same way they always were. Muddy Waters, Willie Dixon, and Sunnyland Slim still *write* them, of course. They are blues composers; they write them (often in far more interesting and subtle patterns than that of the old three-line couplet of the classic blues form), and record them, and play and sing them ever after in just about that way. Fine. Theirs is an important, respectable, and certainly vital part of the blues tradition today. But travel down to the blues country, take a look around, and, above all, take a listen, and you will find that there are bluesmen who survive even now in the backwaters of the South, not just playing the blues but *making* them, too. Blues-makers, if you will, innovators, improvisors of the word, poets: most of them are conscious artists who can and do draw from their own experience and intense personal feelings the very stuff of their music.

Let me tell you about one of them.

IN 1958, a folklorist named Harry Oster, who was then a member of the English Department at Louisiana State University, visited the state prison farm at Angola, Louisiana, and with the permission of the warden began holding auditions among the prisoners. He was collecting songs and looking for singers for a series of field recordings that he would be undertaking under university auspices. But once made, these recordings were eventually released commercially (they are, in fact, still available). Dr. Oster got more than he bargained for. Two of the men he found there at Angola—Mathew "Hogman" Maxey and Robert "Guitar" Welch—were more or less conventional bluesmen who had learned most of their material from recordings and from itinerant singers like themselves. But the third was an exceptional man named Robert Pete Williams, then thirty-five and serving a life sentence for murder.

Robert Pete could and did play some familiar material— "Levee Camp Blues" and "Motherless Children"—but he showed himself as something special when Richard Allen, who was assisting Oster in recording the material, asked if he knew a blues about doing time in prison. Robert Pete said that he did not, but he could make up one for him. And with that, he began picking away and singing the blues that appears on the recording, *Angola Prisoner's Blues,* as "Some Got Six Months." This is how it goes:

> *Some got six months, some got a solid year.*
> *But me and my buddy we got life time here.*
> *Some got six months, some got one solid year,*
> *But me and my buddy we got life time here.*
>
> *Six months, oh baby, let me go to bed,*
> *I've drunk white lightnin', gone to my head . . . it*
>   *gone to my head.*
>
> *I've got so much time, darlin',*
> *It worryin' me, oh babe,*
> *You know this time killin' me,*
> *But I just can't help it, darlin', I just got to roll.*
>
> *You know that old judge must been mad.*
> *Yeah, hey, that old judge must have been mad,*
>   *darlin',*
> *When he gave me my sentence,*
> *He throwed the book at me.*

First time in trouble, I done get no fair trial at all,
Oh Lord, seem like to me, baby, they locked the poor
boy in jail.

It's kind of ragged. The inequality of lines in the stanzas are not quite as noticeable on the recording as they are here on the page, for the lines are chanted, almost spoken, against a steady guitar rhythm. The effect is something slightly closer to a spoken poem than to a sung blues. And that is why, too, the imperfections in the rhymes seem less obvious as we listen to Robert Pete Williams' improvised rendition. What is sung may be expected to rhyme; what is spoken may not.

And yet what cannot be denied and what need not be excused is the simple, direct power of these lines. If it is not poetry, than it is something very close to it, for this sort of eloquence born of experience raises the simple blues as far above the level of the ordinary popular song as Grünewald's *Crucifixion* stands above a Hallmark Easter card. It is a kind of talent for truthsaying that Robert Pete Williams has. He possessed it, has developed it, and uses it just as any other artist might—with the difference that his poems are sung and spoken against the rhythm of a guitar and within the loose conventions of the blues form.

This ability of his to extemporize poetry is shown even more impressively in another number recorded by Oster and Allen at Angola, listed in the album as "Prisoner's Talking Blues." Although too long to quote here, it is worth searching out and listening to. For that matter, it is only that way—actually hearing it spoken and sung—that you can perceive the real power of it. His blues, like that of any original bluesman, is essentially oral poetry; it must be heard to be truly appreciated. Shadings of tone and enunciation, the interplay of the musical background with spoken and sung phrases—these are what make "Prisoner's Talking Blues" the moving experience it is.

Dr. Harry Oster knew that he had found someone special in Robert Pete Williams. He not only came back to Angola to record him again—one full album, *Those Prison Blues,* was recorded while Robert Pete was still there at the prison farm— but he set about to see what he could do to secure his release. Oster sent letters and copies of the albums on which Robert

Pete had appeared to Governor Russell Long and members of the Louisiana pardon board; and in December, 1959, parole was granted.

Even then it was not easy for Robert Pete Williams, for he had been released to a farmer in Denham Springs, Louisiana, for whom he worked about eighty hours a week during the seven years of his parole period. He could not travel outside the state, so he was unable to make appearances as a blues singer in the North, where he had been invited on the strength of his prison albums. He continued to be recorded by Oster, however, and just as his Angola recordings mirror his prison experiences, so his first album afterward (*Free Again*) is filled with material—"Hay-Cutting Song," "Hobo Worried Blues," and "A Thousand Miles from Nowhere"—drawn from his life as a farmhand.

Eventually, he was permitted to travel, and the first trip that he made was up to the Newport Folk Festival, where he was well received—although what he offered was not quite what the crowd there was used to. He is not essentially a performer. Before going to jail, he had only played for family and friends in a small hometown circle. Even when he recorded in prison and afterward, there were only himself, the tape recorder, and one or two others present to run it. In the beginning he had trouble coping with a crowd as immense as the one that looked up at him the afternoon he made his debut as a professional bluesman, and it is only gradually that he has learned a few of the tricks that most real performers seem born with. He is still uncertain of himself on stage, and the best possible place to hear him—as I discovered—is in his own living room in Rosedale, Louisiana, where he now makes his home.

Robert Pete Williams was born not far away, in Zachary, and before going to prison he farmed in Scotlandville. All the towns in which he has resided during his lifetime are within a few miles of one another and lie on the outskirts of Baton Rouge. In fact, on the day I set out to find him, driving through intermittent rain along Route 190, I passed through Denham Springs, where he had served his parole, and it seemed almost suburban compared to the raw, rural communities I had just driven through.

There had very recently been trouble in Baton Rouge. You

may remember it: A rally led by newcomers to the city who claimed to be Black Muslims (Elijah Muhammed subsequently denied knowledge of them) erupted into a shoot-out with the local police. They were burying the dead that day; I was just as glad to be skirting the city rather than driving through it. And apparently I was not the only one made uneasy by the situation. I remember pulling up behind an International pickup truck, noting the two very red necks displayed in the rear window of the cab—and just behind the seat, trigger up, was a Browning semiautomatic shotgun. Memories flashed through my head of the last few minutes of *Easy Rider*. I cut out around the pickup at the earliest opportunity, and quickly put some distance between me and it.

Rosedale lies northwest of Baton Rouge at the end of a back-country road. Robert Pete had given me explicit directions to the town, but because I had never driven there before it seemed to take a little longer than it should. The rain was gone and the sky was clear by the time I got to Rosedale—a good omen, I thought—and I turned in at the crossroads post office and got further directions from a helpful white postal clerk. And finally, I checked at the black general store off on a sideroad, and I was told precisely where I might find the house. They said to keep an eye open for the red truck—that I couldn't miss Robert Pete's house if I just kept an eye open for that truck with "Williams" on the side.

It is with this truck that he plies the scrap-iron trade. He makes rounds of the farms and businesses in the area, collecting what he can and then taking it in to Baton Rouge to sell. He also does a bit of light farming out the back door of his house —chickens, a few hogs, and a vegetable garden. This, combined with the money he makes from the few personal appearances he makes each year at colleges and coffeehouses around the country, gives him and his family a pretty good living. He works hard and is conscientious about his responsibilities.

He met me at the door of the single-story house that he and his wife built together when they moved to Rosedale from Denham Springs. It is not only well kept but well constructed: he pointed out to me that it is put together in "the old way," with joists at the corners, and has stood up through hurricanes without so much as a wobble. As Hattie, his wife, was preparing what turned out to be quite a feast, Robert Pete and I broke out a bottle and sat down in the living room. Although he is not a hard drinker, he likes a taste now and then, and as he drinks the only real change to be noted is that he becomes more relaxed and outgoing.

Assuming I'd like to hear him play something, he went into the bedroom and brought out a guitar. It was a narrow-necked, slightly undersized affair that he said was given to him by a fellow once in Bertrand (Berkeley) "just because he liked me." It is one of two guitars he owns. This one he keeps for bottle-neck work. He produced a piece of conduit that was just about finger-sized, and I asked him when he had started to use that.

"That would be about 1964, I guess, or after that," he said, "when I met Fred McDowell at Newport. He was the first man I saw with one of these on his fingers." Robert Pete held up the piece of conduit, which he had now attached to the little finger of his free hand. "Around here they always use a pocketknife for a slide. But I sure like the sound he got with this, so I been practicing."

He demonstrated what he had picked up on his own of the bottle-neck technique—the Delta style of guitar, in which notes are bent or flattened by touching the strings with metal or glass (bottle necks were first used) as they are struck for a whining, nasal sound that is oddly appealing. I had never heard him play bottle-neck on records and was surprised at the facility he had developed with it. He is a good, if unorthodox, guitarist—one with quick, caressing fingers, who is far more daring harmonically than others who are more polished musicians.

He sang nothing, merely played for a few minutes and talked sporadically in phrases that were loosely timed to the music. He talked about his travels. Something like: "Yessir, I been to Bertrand. . . . Been to Europe, too, in Germany. . . . Yessir, played in England and Czechoslovakia. . . . Played at Newport and got five hundred at Ann Arbor. . . . Cut a tape, and I got five more hundred. . . ."

I asked him about his first guitar. When had he gotten it? When had he started playing and singing the blues?

"I made my first guitar," he said. "I made it out of a cigar box and a good stout long board, and it had five strings of baling wire. Hurt my fingers on it. That was when I was just a farm boy." Robert Pete stopped playing, set down the guitar, and started remembering: "That was right here in Louisiana. We made cotton, corn, potatoes, and raised hogs and chickens. We worked on the halves back then. The boss man got half of everything, all but the peanuts. I was just a kid of fifteen then and I took care of my mother. Back then, see, my mother had parted from my father, and she made me work for the milk dairy to take care of the family. I'd get up, oh, at two a.m. and had to milk seventy-five head of cattle.

"I have all those old-country talents. I can cook and milk cows, and all. And I'm going to tell you something, I learned all that by *doing* it. Why, I picked moss to fill a mattress, and learned how to skin cows and mules so I could sell bones for fertilizer. And I did all that to take care of my mother and sisters and brothers. They were all dead on my father's side, so there was no one but me to take care of them."

He glanced up and smiled then, remembering my question. "Now, you asked me when did I start. That must have been in 1943, when I was about twenty years old. That was when I first started looking at men playing the blues. I remember back then was Walter Green, Eddie Ticette, and Bill Chaney. I'd listen to them and beat on the bucket—that was my style. Good rhythm! But then I built this old cigar-box guitar I'm telling you about, and this fellow Walter Green he showed me a few things. He started me out with something sound like this—" Robert Pete picked up his guitar again and played a simple bass pattern, kind of a walking boogie. "Then he showed me how to add this." He added a treble line to it, and he called it "this little bumble-bee thing."

But, he reminded me, this was just a homemade guitar, and he wasn't able to do much with it. "But finally one day a colored lady working for a white lady, she told me to go over there because they had a guitar, a Simon, that might be for sale. So I went over like she said and I knocked on the door—knock-knock-knock—and the white lady comes, and I say to her, 'Yes, ma'am, I heard you had a guitar here.' And she looks at me, and she says, 'Yes, we do, and it's a mighty good one, a real eighty-five-dollar box.' Then she looks at me again, and she says, 'Do *you* have any money?' And I say, 'Yes, ma'am, but I only have four dollars.' And she says, 'I bought this for my son to learn, and he just wasn't interested, so I believe I'll teach him a lesson and sell you that guitar for four dollars.' And that was it. She got it, and I gave her the four dollars, and I got an eighty-five-dollar guitar.

"And that was my first real guitar. Pretty soon I was playing those country suppers for the colored people. And white folks would hear me playing, and they'd get me to come to their parties and play for them. I'd get a kazoo and blow on that, and they'd say, 'Come on, Pete! Come on, Pete!' Everywhere I play there's white folks there."

He looked up at me and smiled. There is this that is disturbing to me, a city-bred white from the North with the usual liberal responses: As Robert Pete Williams talks with me, I notice that whenever there is eye contact between us, he smiles automatically. It is a reflex that must have been developed long before he was an adult and must have helped him immeasurably in getting along with white people. Yet, as at least one story he told convinced me, he is not to be dismissed as anybody's "good nigger." His relations with white people have been very complicated, and still are. He is interested in getting along, but not in getting along at any price.

He was chuckling now. "Before I had trouble with my throat, I used to whoop and holler when I sang the blues, and I'd get quite a crowd around me among the colored, too. They got a man over there, his name was Willie Hudson. He was a great guitar player, too. But when I got started, he was trying to learn from me. I was a kid, and he knew I play, and he was looking at what I play and making notes on it, then he'd go out do the same thing his own self."

Robert Pete shook his head and laughed, remembering. Then he picked up the guitar and began playing softly. "I didn't have no picks," he remarked. "I had to have tough fingers." He found his way into a steady rhythm, a figure repeated. "Hear that?" he asked. "That's something like Lemon used to play, you know?" And then he began to sing against that rhythm, crooning softly as he looked out the door:

Why you treat me so mean?
Way you treat me, yeah, baby, ooh yeah.
I'm a long way from home.
I'm a stranger here, baby.
Please don't treat me wrong.

It didn't rhyme, as many of his lines do not, but that didn't matter, for again it was almost spoken against the guitar accompaniment. The steady rhythmic figure was almost a setting for the lines that came from him. And then he added, as an afterthought:

I'm gonna leave.
I'm gonna leave, baby, oh yeah.

Then he played a little swinging ride on the guitar, an improvisation on that same rhythmic pattern he had set down before, and stopped suddenly and looked up with a smile. "With the blues you make your own beat," he said.

I asked him where he got his songs, how his blues came to him. "It's just air music," he answered. "It just comes to me, is all. When I ride in a car or I'm in a field working I might begin to hear sort of an echo, as an echo of singing, like. And then maybe I start to sing with the echo, or maybe I just keep it on my brain until I get home and then pick up my guitar and start to play those blues. Yessir, it's just air music, but I remember it."

What about a blues he might want to write to say something in particular? "Oh, I write them, too. I sit here and look at you from the head on down, and I could make a song of you. Or say you misuse and scold me, I could make a record of that." He began playing idly at the guitar once more, picking with his fret hand as well as the other in a little virtuoso touch.

He continued to pick as I asked him if that is what the blues is—a song about being misused and scolded. "Well, sure," he said with an easy nod of his head. "Like me and my wife. If she's mad at me and get to fussin', then I just get my guitar and sit down like I am now, and I just pick it off. Just pick those blues away. It'll be all right then."

There was an uneasy laugh from farther in the house, and Robert Pete turned and smiled and must have realized that what he had just said embarrassed his wife, Hattie. She was setting the table now, working quietly and efficiently, eyes downcast.

"She never gives me trouble I don't deserve, though," he added after a moment. "This child I got here for a wife, she's my third wife. See, I'm the father of eight head of boys and two girls, and if I live to see this March come I'll be fifty-eight years old. But Hattie, I'll tell you, I been in love with her since the first day I met her. And I'll tell you something else, if you knock me down in a ditch, she'll pull me out—that's how she sticks by me. When we got married I was on parole and making fifteen dollars a week, had to live on grits and cheap rice and all, but she stuck by me, even though she knowed I was a convict. This was on that farm I worked when I was on parole that I met her.

"I had some trouble on that farm, too, and she stuck by me in that. Somebody there, one of the white folks, put it out to the parole officer that I was throwing wine and whiskey bottles around, and this same somebody he start giving orders to my son, who was with me then. So I tell him, 'You want my boy to do something you ask me. I'm the father.' And he gets upset then and real nasty, and he comes down on me and says, 'Why don't you thus-and-so,' and with Hattie standing right there he sort of run out of words and say, 'Aw, shit!' And I shake my finger at him then, and I say, 'Now, watch your mouth. Hattie is a black woman, and your wife, she's white, but I think I respect Hattie just like I respect your wife, and I think you should, too.'" He paused with a sober nod to let that sink in.

What happened then? I asked him.

"Well, then I was call up to the parole man and had to defend myself. And I found then that that white man had changed his story. He said no, Robert Pete didn't throw bottles, but he was waving a gun around at a party. Well, now, that wasn't true. I didn't have no gun then, and they knew that, but it was hard to get the parole man on my side. Oh, I'll tell you, parole is hard to be!"

With that, Hattie called us to the table to sit down to lunch. It was good, and there was a lot of it—pork chops, peas, and mashed potatoes, with a real country taste to the peas that said ham fat to me. Hattie seemed to do more serving than eating. We got to talking about the blues again over coffee. I think it began with a question of mine about his unusual style—the sort of setting in which he can talk the blues or chant them freely. Had he known any bluesmen earlier who played the way he does?

"Well, I'll tell you," pausing to light the filter cigarette he had pulled out of the pack on the table. "I'm just a straight-out bluesman. I'm a finger man, a picker. Fred [McDowell], he'll use that slide, and he's not too much with his fingers. A lot of people like slide and a lot don't. It's best to learn both ways. You never know. You may get in a place where you want to use it. That's why I been practicing slide.

"Let me tell you some more about the blues."

He started talking then in the rhythmic way he had earlier —but this time without his guitar. The phrases came with slight pauses between them; imagine them that way.

"The blues is something gonna tame your mind. You got a girl friend. She's in New York. Say you left her, and she wants to see you. She may start moanin' and whistlin'. She got you on her mind. *You* is the blues. I is the blues. Hattie is the blues. Say Hattie is gone. I take a few drinks and start to sing. Got Hattie on my mind. Don't help me to talk to other people. I just start to pick the blues. You got your wife on your mind. No woman you can pick up can satisfy your mind. Ain't gonna be satisfied until you get back to her."

It was a kind of recitation. He concluded it with a nod and took a puff of the cigarette, satisfied that he had had his say.

"You know," he began in a more conversational manner, "I was raised up with a white boy. He didn't have no experience of life. He was rich and married rich where what you should do is marry somebody that love you." Robert Pete told the story, a sordid one, that had involved him indirectly as an observer. The young husband bullied his wife and beat her when he suspected her of infidelity, and finally she left him. When she returned with her mother the next day for her things, he was waiting for her; he shot his wife and then himself.

"Love *means* something," said Robert Pete, commenting on his story and returning to that measured, rhythmic style of speech. "It makes you do anything. Love means a whole lot. Love makes the blues." He nodded for emphasis, and then repeated: "Love makes the blues. That's where it comes from. There wouldn't be no love and there wouldn't be no blues if there was just men. Men shootin' bull. Men shootin' dice, wrestlin'. Men don't mean nothin' together. The blues is not there. They don't have time to make the blues. The most blues you can make is when you go out with another man's wife. When a man want to see a woman he want to *see* her. Man thinks the sweetest woman is another man's wife. He want to *see* that woman —he can't help himself. . . ."

He might have continued on this subject for a while, but suddenly he started coughing. And what began as a mild smoker's hack developed into a fit. Hattie brought a glass of water, and finally it passed. "Can't get to talk like I want to," he said unhappily with a shake of his head.

It was clear he attributed to love and to the blues a kind of occult power. This got him talking specifically about occult powers—spells and the like, of the power of a black hen's egg. "If I get your name, Mr. Cook, and write it seven times across a black hen's egg, then you leave here and go to Washington, I can draw you right back to this house in three days' time. That's why it never pays to give people your full name."

He suddenly broke off and stood up, assuming a dramatic posture. "How did you think I kept those people from executing me?" he asked. Then he went on to explain: "When I knew the names of the jury, I took their names and wrote them down on a piece of paper just like that, see, and then I covered them over with my name and folded it real tight, and then I breathed my breath of life on it. So then what happened? I got up in court and I told them, 'You can send me to your prison, but I won't be there long.' This confounded the jury. I said, 'You can't kill me because I got help from somebody.' And then they want to know from where, and I tell them, 'I got help from God.'"

They took him to Angola on April 6, 1956, he said, and then he stopped, realizing perhaps just where he had come in his story and what really needed telling now.

"All my life," he began, "I been just like you see me around here. I been a humble man and a good man all days. You ask colored and white, and they tell you, 'That's a good man.' But I got in this trouble, not for being biggety and not for being bad. That was back in Scotlandville. I used to carry a gun then. I had a big family and I used to take them to the picture show and go to the store and drink a beer and then bring them home when the show was out. That was how it was that one night. I was just there drinking my beer, and there was these two men standing up against the bar, one of them I knew. The other was a stranger, just a huge man, he was.

"I say to the one I know, 'Hello, Lee.'

"He say, 'Hey, Pete.'

"And the other man, the big man, he say to me, 'Where you from?'

"I say, 'I'm from Zachary.'

" 'You're a lyin' son of a bitch.'

"And I just look at him, see, and I say, 'I wouldn't call you that.'

"Then this big man act real mean to me, and he says, 'Why don't you go back there to Zachary and pick cotton?'

"And all I said to him was 'I don't need to do that.'

"And what does he do? He hauls out this knife, and he says, 'See that, motherfucker?'

"I start moving out, and I say, 'I'm goin', you all.' He had this big hook-'n'-bill knife, and he's coming at me, and then I find my way behind is barred by that other man, the one I knew. But I had a gun in my pocket, so what could I do? I pulled it out, and still he kept on coming at me, and so I told myself, 'Shoot at the navel, and he'll live,' and so I did that, and he kept coming, so I shot him in the heart."

Robert Pete said he fled for home then and declares that the two officers who apprehended him there lied when they said he resisted arrest. Their testimony hurt him, as did that of another at the scene of the shooting who took the knife out of the hand of the man he had shot and threw it away. Robert Pete sighed. "The jury sent me up for my natural life," he said.

He had not done badly at Angola, where his skill as a dairyman had soon earned him respect on the prison farm. And then one day: "The captain tell me to get down on that guitar and pick those blues." With that, Robert Pete went over to the seat near the door where he had left the guitar. He took it up, sat down, and started picking an intricate line, as if in demonstration of what he had played there for the captain the day that the folklorist Harry Oster came to Angola.

He sat and played for several minutes there by the door without singing a line. He just looked out the front door of his house and listened to the sounds of the late Louisiana afternoon. But more than the sounds I remember the smell. There was a thick smell of mud and wet emanating from the line of trees across the field we were facing. It was almost as though we were smelling the country right down to the roots.

"There was not a lot who played and sang there at Angola," he explained. "The onliest ones were Hogman Maxey and Guitar Welch and me. Us three met up there and made the music there. And that Dr. Oster was there to record us. And he handed me a twelve-string guitar, and I never seen no twelve-string guitar before, but I played it for them, and they say to me, 'Can you make up a talkin' blues about your family?' And so that was what I did for them."

And this was how he got out of jail. They made him a guard shortly after that, handed him a gun, and told him to shoot any prisoner who stepped over the line. He was in the guard tower quite alone one night he says, when suddenly a voice behind him—"no voice I knew"—said, "Don't worry. You'll be home for Christmas with your family." He looked around and found nobody there, and he told himself, "God is talking to me." He said a prayer right then and there, kneeling as he held onto his gun.

"And then three days later my parole came through. A man came for me and took me to Denham Springs, where I met Hattie."

He had stopped playing momentarily, but he had now come to the end of the story, more or less, and so he resumed his playing once again, and he began to chord softly through a walking blues, singing as he played.

It's a mean old world, mean, mean, mean
Been livin' awful alone by myself
This is a mean old world, woman. . . .
You know the way the world run, woman,
Sometimes I wish I was dead and gone.
The way the world run, mama,
I wish I was dead and gone.

That's the blues. These casual improvisations of Robert Pete Williams that he calls "air music" conform to no established definition, yet in context they seem to capture the very essence of the music. The operative phrase here is "in context," for what I have tried to do in providing as many details as I have is to convey something of the quality of his life. Because it is out of the totality of his experiences, beliefs, and fears that he creates his music. He may, of course, have created more impressively on other occasions than he did that afternoon I spent with him at his home in Rosedale. Some of his records have some very interesting material, and I commend them to you, but listening to them over and over again, as I have since, they seem to lack the immediacy and impact of Robert Pete in his living room. Which isn't really surprising. Hear him in live performance, and you will perceive the difference, too, I think.

And if Robert Pete Williams has created his blues out of the whole of his life, so has every other bluesman worthy of the name. Disappointment in love is cited by him and so many others as the purest sort of blues experience, yet Bukka White put it to me with that special sort of wry eloquence of his that "the blues was born behind a mule." Don't forget, in other words, that life isn't all how-I-miss-you-baby and mean-mis-treatin'-mama; most of it is spent behind a mule, or washing dishes, or working on the line in some factory—if you're lucky enough to have a job at all. This is what I mean about the blues coming from the *totality* of a man's experience. In Robert Pete Williams' case, his imprisonment and subsequent parole were the shaping experiences of his life. That is why so much of his music seems to express a kind of nameless and absolute loneli-ness, a sense of isolation that is distinctive in the music created by American bluesmen.

CHAPTER THREE

THE BIRTH
OF THE
BLUES

THE DIFFICULTY in talking about the origins of the blues is that so much of what anyone might say on the subject must necessarily be guesswork—and this, of course, includes what I might have to say, as well. Not that this has discouraged debate. They keep right on telling us how it all began in tones that seem increasingly louder and more strident. Theories have been tossed up as though they were facts, and a good deal of instant erudition has been used to shore them up before the structures collapse. Actually, much of what has gone down as scholarship in this area in the past is really not much more than foggy second- and third-hand pedantry meant not so much to inform as to choke off further discussion.

The big problem is Africa. Clearly, blues and jazz and the whole world of popular music that they have produced all find their source in the American Negro and his culture. Since he came from Africa and must have brought his music with him, reason seems to dictate that we have only to go back to Africa, or to those parts of Africa from which the slaves were shipped, and listen closely to hear the roots of the music that came to bloom over here. As a result, nearly every book on blues and jazz—particularly jazz—has had its obligatory first chapter on African origins. *Shining Trumpets,* by Rudi Blesh, a very thorough book on early jazz, was one of the first to go into this at length and in detail. Marshall Stearns' *The Story of Jazz* has a good three chapters to what he calls "The Prehistory of Jazz," taking the music from Africa to the New World by way of the West Indies. And a recent book, *Black Music in America,* by John Rublowsky, a much less imposing volume than its title would indicate, devotes fully a third of its 150 pages to the music of West Africa.

This music of West Africa—specifically that from Dahomey, Ghana, Guinea, and even from down in Nigeria—was distinguished for the sophistication of its rhythm. It is essentially percussion music in which melodies are done for the most part in leader-chorus, call-and-response style. Since jazz is rhythmically different from European music, it was easy and convenient to cite Africa as the source for this new rhythm. Appropriate passages were quoted by jazz historians reminding readers of Congo Square in Old New Orleans, where slaves spent their days off, listening to the drums and the chants and dancing to them with all the energy and abandon they might have shown if they were back in Africa. And they managed to suggest that a straight line could be drawn from eighteenth-century Dahomey, that would pass through Congo Square and lead right to Warren "Baby" Dodds, the best and most inventive of all the old New Orleans drummers.

Well, fine. Surely the subtle and impressive percussive effects of the native African drummers must have had some sort of ethnic or perhaps even genetic influence on the black innovators of jazz. But a couple of things—objections, if we must call them that—should be mentioned before conceding the point. First of all, rhythm does not serve at all the same function in West African music that it does in jazz. Percussion is much more prominent in native African music and more complex, too. Not only might there be four or five percussion instruments going at any given moment, but these five will probably all be playing in as many different rhythmic patterns. The subtle blending that Westerners think of as characteristic of advanced music is there in African music, all right, but it is in the rhythm rather than the harmony.

Jazz, by contrast, developed through much simpler and more strictly defined use of rhythms. Except for the occasional wild, go-go-go drum solo, the rhythm section has traditionally restricted its activities to time-keeping. In this, jazz is somewhat closer to its European than its African roots. In fact, time signatures in jazz are adapted from those used in European music, the chief differences lying in syncopation, the contrasting use of strong accents, and the "flow" of the rhythm. As a result of all this, American music and African music clearly sound quite different. They are not the same music at all; a much more profound and complete metamorphosis took place here in America during the nineteenth century (perhaps starting even before then), producing a music that was more singular in nature than the historians of jazz and American popular music are willing to allow. Latin-American music—and particularly that of Brazil—is much closer to pure West African music than is our own.

The English blues critic and historian Paul Oliver recently raised another objection in his little book *Savannah Syncopators,* which he subtitles "African Retentions in the Blues." He notes, as I have above, the usual line of the jazz historians that associates jazz rhythms with the percussion music of West Africa. But what may or may not be true for jazz, which is largely instrumental music, he says, is almost certainly not true for the blues

> Largely a vocal music, it is also one which was, in its formative years, created by solo artists, or by pairs of musicians. The "blues band" is seldom of more than four or five pieces at any event, and even when it is as large as this it is dominated by stringed instruments. . . . When blues instrumentation, improvisation, rhythm and use of vocals are compared with the music of the rain forest [West African] drum orchestras they seem even further removed than jazz from the African tradition.

Because he had been troubled by this difficulty for a while, Oliver became quite excited when, on a visit to Africa, he came upon a pair of native musicians in the village of Nangodi, in Ghana, considerably inland from the West African coastal belt that has traditionally been designated as the root source of jazz. This was savannah land, the long plain that gives way to the north and east to the Sahara Desert. And just as the country was different, so also was the music played there. The two Oliver heard in Nangodi were professional, traveling singer-musicians (a class he says is largely unknown among the tribes outside the savannah regions); they played stringed instruments and sang plaintive songs that seemed—to his ear, at least —to bear some rudimentary resemblance to the American blues he knows so well.

> For here was the combination of vocal, rhythm and stringed instrument which hinted at a link with the blues; here, too, I heard in person for the first time an African music which could be said to "swing" in the jazz sense, where the singer and his accompanist seemed free to improvise and where the combination of instruments had a certain feeling of syncopation.

Paul Oliver builds on this and further experiences listening to the "savannah syncopators" a fairly convincing case for these native musicians—*griots,* as they are called—as the African ancestors of American music. (To anticipate your question: Yes, slaves were taken from the sub-Saharan plain, as well as from the west coast of Africa.) And in this, Oliver has one terrific advantage over others who have written with great authority in this area: He has actually been to Africa; so many others have not.

Yet firsthand experience alone does not make an expert. And while Oliver knows his blues, he admits he is an amateur on African music. There is a bona-fide expert in this area, however, one whom Oliver acknowledges and quotes on at least one point in his short book. His name is Richard A. Waterman (not to be confused with Dick Waterman, whom we shall meet later on), and he is an ethnomusicologist with a wide and detailed knowledge of African music; he also knows a good deal about related Latin-American music, and something of Afro-American music as well. The paper that he wrote in 1952, *African Influences on the Music of the Americas,* has, yet to be superseded.

Dr. Waterman was interviewed in the magazine *Living Blues* not long ago. And because the Oliver thesis on the savannah music and the blues had just recently appeared, the interviewer questioned him closely on it. What he had to say must have given very little comfort to Paul Oliver and those to whom his thesis on the African origins of the blues made good sense. Waterman is quite devastating. Let me give a few specific examples selected from his responses.

> There are no African retentions, as such, in the blues. But undoubtedly influence was great in determining the form the blues was to take. Just how far we can go in specifying the extent of this influence is a question still open to debate. . . .

> . . . I don't think the savannah music bears particular resemblance to blues.

> . . . I think there's just as much of the roots of this blues stuff in the traditional African thing on the coast, as in Senegal and Gambia, which is where he [Oliver] is talking about. I think you probably find more of the materials that went into the blues on the coast. Although superficially the fact that you do something plunking like a guitar makes it sound a little bit like it, I think his hunch is wrong.

And so on. Yet what should probably be emphasized here since I have quoted Dr. Waterman in rebuttal, is that while he is certainly an expert on African music, Paul Oliver is no less an expert on American music—or on the blues, at least. There is —at least at the moment—no single "right" answer to be chosen from these opinions.

I am not sure that all this says much more than that the question of African origins of the blues, jazz, and American popular music is one on which reasonable men—and reasonably well-informed men—may differ. And that may indeed be all that should be said about it.* There is no better way to emphasize this than to cite an interview of guitarist Buddy Guy in another issue of that same magazine, *Living Blues.* He had just been on an African tour and had come back vaguely disappointed. He kept asking to hear some "real true African music," and then they would play imitation Buddy Guy for him, for this

---

*I cannot resist adding at this point, in support of Paul Oliver, that the bottleneck guitar sound, so popular among Delta blues performers, has no equivalent in the Western musical tradition and must surely be an attempt to duplicate an African sound resting in the racial memory.

was what the Africans were most enthusiastic about. But he kept insisting, and so at last they gave him some records and tapes. The interviewer then asks him, "Do you see any relation between African music and blues?" He says:

> No, don't start me to lyin', because I don't. Not of what I've heard yet. No, I mean, I met some people there and they told me that this is where it all came from, you know, and I haven't found anything yet. I mean, they playin' this South American beat, and the blues is a different thing, man. I mean, ain't no sense of me lyin', 'cause you know better. The blues is, you know, a feelin'. You got to feel it to play it.

What is lurking just beneath the surface here is Buddy Guy's suspicion that because his music is different from that of the blacks whom he encountered in Africa, he might well be different from them, too. It must indeed be a shocking realization, yet it is one experienced by hundreds, perhaps even thousands, of American Negroes who go to Africa each year. Many have come back to comment on it, often dismayed and disappointed to discover that they seem American rather then simply black to Africans. And perhaps they are also secretly surprised to learn that their acculturation has been so complete: They never knew quite how American they were until they went to Africa. (A common-enough discovery—sort of the immigrant son's equivalent of "You can't go home again.")

IN THE INTRODUCTION to another book of his, *Blues Fell This Morning,* Paul Oliver has a nice neutral statement on the blues as the music of the American Negro. Let me quote it.

> ... If there is one simple common denominator in all these aspects of the music it is that the blues is a folk form of expression that is by superficial appearance the product of a racial group, the Negro in America; although the Negro stock has been so reduced through intermarriage and miscegenation during the centuries that it is doubtful if pure African blood can be found to any great extent in the United States, and the features of African cultural origin have been so modified and altered during that passage of time, ousted by compulsory and later voluntary absorption of a new culture, that their remains—if they exist—are vestigal.

I think that statement is notable for what it does not—indeed, what it refuses to—say. It does not say, to underline the point, that the blues is absolutely and only the expression of the American Negro. Nor does it say that its origins are exclusively, or even especially, African.

But I would like us to take that "softer," more neutral, expression of the relation of the blues to the American Negro as a starting point in this discussion of how the blues came to be here in America. This way we can begin a little more lightly. We won't find ourselves quite so weighted down with the assumptions, conclusions, and prejudices of Paul Oliver and others as we try to sort out the influences that helped shape this distinctive music.

I believe, as I said earlier, that the blues is the fundamental American music. This makes it something more than merely the music of the American Negro, though I believe it was through and because of him that that music came to be. He was the agent of change, working continually from as early as the eighteenth century upon the music that he heard around him, shaping and reshaping it, giving it back to the culture as something ever more distinct. When he began on it, there was nothing unique about that music; it was simply that which colonists and emigrants had brought over with them from various corners of Europe—though chiefly, of course, from the British Isles. By the turn of the century, however, when the Negro brought blues, ragtime, and jazz into flower, the foundation of the new idiom—American music—was complete.

And so, far from being an expression of the cultural isolation of the American Negro, the music that he produced gave him the opportunity to participate in that culture and subsequently to play a dominant role in it. From very early on, long before the Civil War was fought and the slaves were freed, the blacks in America had begun to exert a subtle but very powerful influence on the Anglo-Saxon majority culture by their very presence. A sort of symbiotic relationship grew up between the two, one which nourished both more than they would ever know or recognize. I would go so far as to say that the influence of the American blacks has been the most profound of any minority on the American culture and character: It is the Negro who has given form to the Anglo-Saxon matter and created that new

Adam they talk about in the American Studies books. To the extent that we are American, we are all part black. It's what makes us what we are.

Why? Why has the *American* Negro had this distinct identity and this strong shaping influence on the majority culture? Melville Herskovits, one of the earliest and best-informed students of American Negro culture, points out that contact between American Negroes and whites from the earliest days in the slavery period was much closer than in the West Indies and South America. As a result, Africanisms persisted in both areas in a purer form—in music, certainly, and in other areas as well. "In the earliest days," Herskovits writes of America, "the number of slaves in proportion to their masters was extremely small, and though as time went on thousands and tens of thousands of slaves were brought to satisfy the demands of southern plantations, nonetheless the Negroes lived in constant association with whites to a degree not found anywhere else in the New World." It was in LeRoi Jones' book *Blues People* that I first found Melville Herskovits cited. And it is worth noting that the militant Mr. Jones not only accepts Herskovits' authority in this, but goes on to add:

> Some of this "constant association" between the white masters and the black slaves that took place in this country can be explained by comparing the circumstances of the slaves' "employment" in America with the circumstances of their employment in the rest of the New World. It was only in the United States that slaves were used on the smaller farms. Such a person as the "poor white" was a strictly American phenomenon.

The acculturation of the Negro in America, that first stage of the symbiosis between the races, was accomplished by the poor white. He was the dirt farmer in Tennessee or Kentucky or frontier Mississippi who went out and sweated in the field alongside the black man, who unbent to talk and laugh with him and who first began to sing with him. And those first songs were very likely Isaac Watts hymns or those of the Wesleys, for the first real cultural contact of the black with the white world came through religion. This—the late eighteenth and early nineteenth centuries—was the time of the Great Revival in America. The evangelical spirit of the Baptists and Methodists, which was particularly strong in the frontier West and South, knew few limits—certainly not, to their credit, those of race. It was their enthusiasm and fervor that overcame the objections of the large plantation owners (most of whom were Episcopal, Presbyterian, or—less often—Catholic) and saw to it that the good news of the Gospel was passed on to the Africans in their midst.

That old-time religion made an immediate and a lasting impression on the blacks to whom it was preached. To this day, and in spite of the proliferation of Pentacostal and fundamentalist sects, more American Negroes are members of the Baptist and Methodist churches than of all other denominations. And of all hymns and gospel songs, the favorite of blacks is still probably that familiar one from the early nineteenth century, sung by Baptists and Methodists alike in the South, "Amazing Grace."

But no matter how enthusiastically the slaves may have sung that hymn and all the others, and no matter how profoundly they may have welcomed the instruction of the missionaries who preached to them, the chief cultural importance of all this was that it soon gave them their first opportunity to work on the material of the white man's religion and begin reshaping it, just as they have reshaped, to a greater or lesser extent, other institutions here in America. For the blacks were left more or less on their own soon enough in matters of religion, and instruction fell to black preachers—the "nigger preachers" of jokes and folklore. Were they truly such figures of fun? No, for most had been given at least a fundamental education and some could lay a claim to eloquence and were the natural leaders of their slave communities—Nat Turner was such a one.

Most knew enough, in any case, to let the natural preference of their congregations for sacred music carry the burden of teaching and testifying. By most accounts, hymn-singing played an even greater part in black Baptist and Methodist church services than in the white. And soon black Christians had their *own* hymns—and what hymns they were!

Were you there when they crucified my Lord?
Were you there when they crucified my Lord?
Oh! Sometimes it causes me to tremble, tremble,
*   tremble!*
Were you there when they crucified my Lord?

There are a number of remarkable and curious things about these Negro spirituals, as they came to be known. The first is that they came into being so early. Well before the Civil War, the black church and its music were well known in the South and were known, at least as a phenomenon, in the North and in England, too. Since the ministry to the slaves did not really get under way until fairly late in the eighteenth century, it seems to have taken the blacks no more than about fifty years to master the style of the white man's hymns, alter it, and develop a whole body of their own sacred music.

Secondly, it was *their* music—that is to say, it was quite proper and accurate to speak of these as Negro spirituals, and not the spirituals of the Negroes in one particular section of the South or another, much less to speak of them as the spirituals of the slaves on a specific plantation. No, these hymns were spread from farm to farm and state to state so thoroughly that we must revise our notions of the isolation of groups of slaves, one from the other. Communication, at least in the form of music, seems to have been complete and fairly common among them.

It might well be that there was a special sense of urgency in the way these hymns were passed from one black congregation to another, owing to what they said, the "secret" message of protest they contained. For it has come to be rather generally recognized that when the slaves sang, "Let my people go," they were thinking less of the Israelites in captivity in Egypt than of themselves in captivity in America. A black theologian, James H. Cone, has put it quite directly in his book, *The Spirituals and the Blues*.

> The basic idea of the spirituals is that slavery contradicts God; it is a denial of his will. To be enslaved is to be declared *nobody,* and that form of existence contradicts God's creation of people to be his children. Because black people believed that they were God's children, they affirmed their *somebodiness,* refusing to reconcile their servitude with divine revelation.

With this firmly in mind, it is really rather remarkable how frequently this theme of protest against slavery and the yearning for freedom does recur in the old spirituals. Here is an example:

My Lord delivered Daniel,
My Lord delivered Daniel,
My Lord delivered Daniel,
Why can't He deliver me?

And another:

We'll soon be free,
We'll soon be free,
We'll soon be free,
When de Lord will call us home.

If you know lines and verses from the old spirituals—and it is interesting how widely they are known, even today—you can probably supply more examples from your own memory.

And finally, what must be commented on is the remarkable quality of the spirituals. Nobody who heard them could ignore them. Their emotional appeal was almost palpable in its intensity. And as music, they were something different—in ways, like the old Isaac Watts hymns from which they derived, yet with qualities of their own that suggested the forms that were to follow. There were blue notes in the spirituals, swinging tempos, and some syncopation, all of which anticipated blues, jazz, and especially gospel singing. But there were differences, too. The spirituals were ceremonial in nature, as is most African music (most *West* African music, anyway). It was choral music, too, in which a leader might sing a line and ask for a response, but in which the soloist, as such, was quite unknown. And finally, along this same line, it was also the sort of music in which the role of the individual was subjugated almost totally to that of the group—the congregation. It was "we," not "I," music.

So were the work songs, chants, and field hollers that the slaves sang. These are often cited by historians and anthropologists as sources for the blues. And at least one bluesman—Son House—agrees. He is quoted in Samuel Charters' *The Bluesmen* as supporting this notion when he says, "People keep asking me where the blues started and all I can say is that when I was a boy we always was singing in the fields. Not real singing, you know, just hollerin', but we made up our songs about things that was happening to us at that time, and I think that's where the blues started. . . ."

This is, in a way, rather convincing testimony, certainly enough to sell blues historians and scholars who seem eager to discount the importance of the spirituals as a source for the blues. Why this prejudice? It may be a sort of vague Marxist bias, a grudge against the old Negro church and the quietism that it stood for during the many decades when it served as the opium of the black people. Or it may be simply a matter of taste: remembered nausea from early exposure to the Hall Johnson Choir or a memory of Marian Anderson singing "Swing Low, Sweet Chariot." It was actually rather insidious the way that the spirituals were used *against* black people back in the thirties and forties, promoting an image of black submission that was even less accurate than when the hymns were created in the days of slavery. Among whites, it encouraged a complacency and an attitude of self-satisfied paternalism toward the blacks that prevailed until by some sort of rough justice that mood was shattered by a black churchman, Martin Luther King, Jr., in the middle fifties.

But what about those old field hollers? What relation have they to the blues? Not a very direct one, I think. I'm talking now about those wordless moans, trilling cries, and brief comments and messages that were given out in a kind of black style close to plainchant. When whites first became aware of all this back in the nineteenth century, they referred to it as Negro yodeling. Blacks themselves simply called it loud-mouthing, whooping, or just plain hollering. But it all seems to have less to do with the music that followed than with that which went before. In their rawest form, the field hollers seem a genuine and fairly pure survival from the African tradition. Harold Courlander, a widely traveled folklorist, has described in his *Negro Folk Music, U.S.A.* how he heard what seemed about the same cries in Nigeria, Haiti, and Matanzas Province, Cuba, as he had heard earlier in the American South. Probably so, but they are not heard here much today. Even a generation ago, you had to go pretty deep into the country to catch those haunting, pleasantly weird sounds, most of which were sung in modal scales. The closest most of us ever came was hearing the similar cries of the black peddlers and street merchants. New Orleans and Charleston are famous for these street cries even now, but they could be heard as far north as Chicago before the war.

Work songs are something else again. They are the rhythmic,

sometimes highly syncopated melodies and chants that are sung to provide the proper work beat for a gang of men as it toils together. The lead singer—usually the work-gang leader— in this way controls the pace of their labor. Now, there is nothing new about work songs of this sort. They probably go back to the building of the pyramids or the Babylonian temples, or before; whenever men have had to pull or strike together, songs in one style or another have helped them do it right. Nor is there anything peculiarly African about the work songs sung in America by black laborers. Many of them, in fact, sound as though they may have been derived from Irish sources, for indeed the blacks and the Irish worked side by side in the beginning on railroad and river-boat gangs even before the Civil War. In his 1876 sketch, "Levee Life," Lafcadio Hearn gives a fascinating account of the musical subculture of the black and white roustabouts who worked the Cincinnati river front, and he remarks in passing: "One fact worth mentioning about these Negro singers is, that they can mimic the Irish accent to a degree of perfection which an American, Englishman, or German could not hope to acquire." He goes on to tell of "a very dark mulatto," who sang for them "The hat me fahther worrre," and was joined by another black on the chorus:

'Tis the raylics of ould decency,
The hat me fahther wor-r-re.

And at least one of the many work songs that Hearn has transcribed from the stevedores working on the dock has a rollicking and distinctly Irish quality:

Molly was a good gal and a bad gal, too.
Oh Molly, row , gal.
Molly was a good gal and a bad gal, too,
Oh Molly, row, gal.

I'll row dis boat and I'll row no more,
Row, Molly, row gal.
I'll row dis boat, and I'll go on shore,
Row, Molly, row gal.

Captain on the biler deck a-heaving of the lead,
Oh Molly, row, gal.
Calling to the pilot to give her "Turn ahead,"
Row, Molly, row, gal.

But even among those ditties and work songs quoted in "Levee Life," you can discern a kind of black style emerging— Hearn, a good reporter, notes this at the time. And it became more and more distinct in the decades that followed—more complex in its rhythms, closer and closer to true syncopation. A few of these songs—"Grizzly Bear," "Take This Hammer," and "Told My Captain"—are still remembered and are in the repertoire of just about every folkie who has ever twanged a guitar. Another, probably the best known of them all, is not so much a work song as a work ballad. The ubiquitous "John Henry" may not even be of black origin, but it was enthusiastically taken up and sung by the black steel drivers and gandy dancers who worked the railroads throughout the South. It tells, of course, of the giant steel-driving champion (traditionally, a Negro) who takes on a steam-driven pile driver in a competition, wins over it handily, proving "A man ain't nothin' but a man." Yet in winning, he overtaxes his poor heart and dies at the moment of his triumph.

The tradition of ballad-making, which was so strong among the English-, Scotch-, and Irish-Americans, was taken up by the American Negroes in the latter part of the nineteenth century, probably sometime in the seventies or eighties. It is significant, though not really surprising, that the first of these black ballads should have come in the bad-man ballad tradition. There were plenty of white ballads describing the deeds of desperadoes, such as "Jesse James," "Sam Bass," and "Tom Dooley." There was also at least one, "John Hardy," which was a white ballad about a black murderer. But it wasn't long before the blacks themselves began telling stories in song of their own bad men, such as "Stackerlee," the Memphis gambler who shot down poor Billy Lyons in a senseless dispute over a Stetson hat. And then, of course, there were "Frankie and Albert," those ill-starred St. Louis lovers, whose tragic story became one of the best known in America (though in the bargain was changed somehow to the tale of "Frankie and Johnnie").

The underworld milieu of gamblers, gunmen, and whores that produced "Stackerlee" and "Frankie and Albert" is the same one that brought forth the earliest urban blues in cities up and down the Mississippi. Anyone who doubts the origins of blues and jazz in the world of vice has only to look at a few of the frank memoirs of the period—Louis Armstrong's *Satchmo: My Life in New Orleans* and Pops Foster's *The Autobiography of a New Orleans Jazzman* tell the story quite graphically—to find out what things were really like in Storyville. One of the denizens of that district, Jelly Roll Morton made a series of recordings for the Library of Congress in his later years under the direction of Alan Lomax, who was then Folk Music Curator. He talked and sang his way through a series of reminiscences of life in the Storyville district of New Orleans, and among the songs he recorded was an interesting one about a New Orleans bad man of the 1900s named Aaron Harris. He did not claim to have written it (which alone is remarkable, for he claimed to have written and even copyrighted many that he stole from others), but it is the sort of ballad a bluesman might write. In fact, it is a sort of merger of the two—a bad-man ballad in classic twelve-bar blues form.

Aaron Harris was a bad bad man. (twice)
He was the baddest man who ever was in this land.

He killed his sweet little sister and his
* brother-in-law.* (twice)
About a cup of coffee he killed his sister and his
* brother-in-law.*

He got out of jail every time he would make a kill.
* (twice)*
He had a hoodoo woman—all he had to do was pay
* the bill.*

All the policemen on the beat, they had him to fear.
* (twice)*
You could always tell when Aaron Harris was near.

He pawned his pistol one night to play in a
* gambling game.* (twice)
Well, old Four-Horn shot him—that blotted out his
* name.*

There were a number of songs that were first heard in the 1890s and 1900s in which blues and ballad elements were mixed. "Betty and Dupree" was one, a murder ballad somewhat in the "Frankie and Albert" vein that is told in three-line couplet blues stanzas. "Boll Weevil" was another, the ballad about that little bug who came up from Mexico, "just lookin' for a home, just lookin' for a home." In addition, there were songs like the old New Orleans parade classic, "Didn't He Ramble," and the blues W. C. Handy claimed, "Careless Love," which had their origins in English folk songs. And the one that Big Bill Broonzy called the first blues, "Joe Turner Blues," dated in 1890 on the advice of his uncle (Big Bill himself was born in 1893), a haunting story-song about a white man who goes about helping the blacks, in which the refrain is repeated:

> They tell me Joe Turner been here and gone
> Lord, they tell me Joe Turner been here and gone
> They tell me Joe Turner been here and gone

In all of these and others, as well, the elements merge and mix so that it is difficult to tell quite where the ballads left off and the blues began.

In case you don't recognize it as such, that last sentence—with its implication that the blues derive directly from certain ballad sources—would qualify as the rankest sort of heresy in many circles. For those who believe intensely in the segregation of black music from white will never allow that both races continued their musical commerce right up to and including the time, just about the turn of the century, when the creation of the new musical idiom had been finally and certainly accomplished. Some adhere almost fanatically to the notion of parallel musical streams moving along through the decades right up to the present. In reality, however, while the streams certainly did originate from separate sources—Europe and Africa—they crossed and recrossed again and again, meandering tortuously, until at last they flowed together into that wide mainstream sound that we all now recognize instinctively as American.

YOU HAVE ONLY to listen to someone like John Jackson to realize of what little moment are the fine musical distinctions on which blues scholars stake their reputations. He is by classification a songster and not a bluesman, although he will play and sing more blues on a good night's parlor concert than some Delta bluesmen may have known in a lifetime. The difference is that except for an occasional extra verse or two, or new words to an old song, John Jackson doesn't write music, he collects it.

He, of course, doesn't think of himself as either a collector *or* a songster, but simply as a guitar player and country singer who happens to know a lot of songs. That is his reputation in Fairfax, Virginia, in the suburbs of Washington, D.C., where he has lived with his family since 1949.

The funny thing is that by the time you get out there just beyond Fairfax it doesn't seem like suburbs at all: it seems like country. It may have been owing to the time of year that I drove out—early spring—but there wasn't much traffic on the road. And the deep, heavy humus smell that I sniffed as soon as I stepped out of my car was a country smell. It had been raining recently, and there was a damp chill in the air, so that the effect was a little like having driven far to the west, out to the Blue Ridge country, where John Jackson had been born and where, even then, there was still snow on the mountaintops.

Met at the door by one of his children, I was ushered into the house quickly and seated in the living room by John's wife, Cora. I had been misinformed about her. Someone who should have known better told me that she was a white woman. She is not—at least not in the sense that this is generally meant. But it is worth reflecting, on meeting someone like Cora Jackson, just how little these designations of race really mean. Although her hair is auburn and her face a ruddy pink, she was born and raised a Negro in rural Virginia. And is proud of it.

She told me that Johnny had been called out to do a little job. He expected to be back by the time I arrived. "But he shouldn't be long now, because he only has one grave to dig." One of the many ways John Jackson keeps busy and supports his family is as a gravedigger in Fairfax. He has also worked as an agricultural laborer, has done a little farming himself, has pumped gas, and has a good reputation as a handyman in his neighborhood.

He provides very well for his family. They live in a comfortable single-story house of cinder-block construction on a good-sized plot of land that lies just off the highway. As Cora Jackson excused herself to go back to the kitchen—"I'm baking, and the bread won't wait once it's in the pan"—I looked over the living room and noticed a kind of antique country-parlor look to it that I liked. There were two portraits, both of them old etchings, over the fireplace. One I recognized instantly as George Wash-

ington, but the bearded face next to his called for a closer look
—it was Robert E. Lee. The fire in the fireplace felt good. Warming my hands and listening to Cora Jackson sing in the kitchen
as she worked the bread, I happened to notice the eighteenth-
century andirons that supported the blazing logs. They were
cast in the shape of coachmen, complete with tricorn hats,
breeches, and cutaway coats—white coachmen.

John Jackson came in apologizing. Not just for being late, he
said, "but because there's a whole bunch of boys following me
down from the cemetery." They were coming to hear him play
and sing a little, and I got the idea that this was a regular thing
on Sundays. He wasted no time hauling out his guitar, and by
the time he was tuned up, the boys had arrived and had taken
places around the living room. Introductions were quite informal, but I found out that one of the visitors—two of them white
and two black—was John's brother Freddy.

"Well," John Jackson said with a smile, "what would y'all
like to hear?"

" 'Wildwood Flower,' " called out one of his visitors.

John nodded pleasantly, just to show he understood, but
promptly launched into another song, "Rattlesnakin' Daddy,"
one that he has recorded and sings with a lot of verve and spirit.
And he sings it in a voice that might confuse the casual listener,
for he sounds "white." Most of us are so used to hearing black
Southerners talk and sing in that Deep South accent that when
we hear something else from them it confuses us just a little.

And John Jackson talks the way everybody does up in the
mountains of Virginia. He is from Rappahannock County, up
in the mountain country, hard by the West Virginia line. He is
the son of a tenant farmer and one of thirteen children. He tells
of how he started guitar under his father's instruction but then
got a real education on the instrument when a fancy guitar
player came through on a chain gang. It was from him, he will
tell you, that he really learned how to play.

And you don't have to listen to him long on the guitar to
realize that he is really an accomplished musician. "A real
country picker," as they say down there. He can play those
double lines on guitar, and make it sound almost like a piano.
These were improvisations and variations that he interpolated
between verses in a style that was something between early

jazz and country music. He was having fun with it, you could tell. He finished with a smile on his face. He smiles a lot. He has a good time.

"Those at the end were my own verses," he explained. "I write my own verses sometimes. I heard the song off Blind Boy Fuller's record that my Daddy had, but I added to it."

I asked if he had learned most of his songs that way, from records, and he said that he had, and then went on to tell how his father had come to buy a record player in the first place. It seems a couple of salesmen for whom his father had little use came by one day with something in a big box to show him. His father told them in no uncertain terms that they were to get out, with which they drove up on the hill overlooking the Jackson place, wound up the box, and music began to issue forth from it. "Gawd a'mighty," said his father, and he beckoned them down from the hill. He and the family listened to it on the front porch for the better part of the afternoon and decided to buy it.

"We'd get the small records for ten cents then or the big ones for twenty-five. We must have had about 500 of them when we moved to Fairfax, but most of them got broke. But I'd learned them all by then."

"Blues, too?" I asked.

"Oh, sure. Blind Boy Fuller and Blind Lemon Jefferson, all of them fellas. Jimmie Rodgers, too."

"The hillbilly singer?"

"Jimmie Rodgers sang blues!" John Jackson declared. He seemed slightly vexed at the way I had so quickly classified the Singing Brakeman from Meridian, Mississippi, as a "hillbilly." "He's the onliest man I ever did hear singing the 'TB Blues,' and that was a good blues. He used to sing this one, too—" And he launched into the traditional "T for Texas, T for Tennessee," with its refrain, "I'm gonna drink muddy water, sleep in a hollow log." But only about a chorus of that—just enough to show which one he meant. "Jimmie Rodgers got that from Lemon Jefferson. He learned a lot of songs from him and some others when he used to work through Texas and Louisiana on the railroad."

"Play 'Wildwood Flower,' Jack." It was one of the men who had come in with Freddy Jackson who kept asking for "Wildwood Flower." He was white and about half-drunk.

"Please call me John," he answered mildly in reproof.

"Yeah," Freddy Jackson urged the man. "Call him John or Johnny. Jack isn't his name."

Cora came out from the kitchen. "Y'all gonna play together?" she asked, meaning the two Jackson brothers.

"Well, we just might do that," said John, obviously pleased at the idea. Freddy ran into another room and came out with a guitar which he had tuned in a moment. They sat down together, began picking around, and seeming to know just where they were headed, they began "Nobody's Business." This is a song he has recorded, and he does a fine version of it, but one much different from the one he did that day with his brother. Freddy played and sang the lead, John playing backup guitar and coming in on the choruses. The two like singing together, you can tell. Freddy's voice is thinner but a little more "black" in timbre. The two finished the song, nodded their mutual approval, and went right into the old hymn, "When the Roll Is Called Up Yonder." John harmonized on this, and everybody in the room joined in on the refrain, Cora Jackson carrying the high notes. It sounded nice, very nice, the way we all imagine it might have sounded in a living room like this a hundred years ago.

As soon as they finished, there was a general murmur of approval through the room, and the white man produced his bottle and started it around. They sang another hymn then— "one of those *old* hymns," said Freddy—called "Farther Along." And then, ready to swing a bit once more, John said, "Let's play 'Step It Up,'" and to me, in explanation, "That's kind of a ragtime song."

"You take the lead," said Freddy.

John did more than sing it. He did some real swinging on it. And what he had called "kind of a ragtime" turned out to be a highly syncopated blend of country and jazz styles that would demand a lot of any guitar player. He had it to give, though, and had the knack of keeping good time for himself on the bass line as he improvised some good licks on the treble. After a little of this Freddy just put down his own guitar and listened.

"Play another one, Johnny," his brother urged as soon as he had finished.

"Okay, how about this 'Guitar Rag'? I know a little bit of that."

And he took off once again, delivering a solid walking bass. It was just about the old "trucking" tempo, and Freddy found it irresistible. In a moment he was up, hopping around from foot to foot, shaking his finger in the air. Everybody laughed and applauded—everybody, that is, except the "Wildwood Flower" man. He was suddenly and very loudly asleep.

"Cora, you and Fred do a dance," said John. "Do the 'Flat-foot.' " He explained to me: "This is one of my songs I used to do at dances." The two of them started side by side through a kind of tap-and-clog routine that seemed to go over pretty well.

"Come on, Freddy!" somebody shouted.

"Well, I'm gettin' old." And then, cutting a particular caper, he cried out, "I'm from Rappahannock County. You can't mess with me!"

Through it all, John beat a pleasant, light rhythm on his guitar and kept things moving along just as though he were a whole rhythm section. "I love to play dances," he declared when he finished, "and I used to play a lot of them, too. But it was playing a dance that quit me playing music altogether." I asked him to explain, and he told me about playing a date in Slate Mill, Virginia, one night when a drunk came along in an evil mood. He sat down and didn't say a word for fifteen minutes, just glowered at John, who was playing the guitar. "Finally," said John, "he jumped up and said, 'You stole my guitar. Now give it here.' He was determined to fight me, but I sure wasn't going to let him have that guitar. So I just told him no, I didn't steal his guitar, and I took Cora and the kids and we headed out the door. Just as we hit outside he threw this jug at us he'd been carrying, and it hit a tree just ahead of us and broke into a hundred pieces. But we made the car and got out of there. Oh, I didn't like that at all, neither did Cora." It wasn't long before they moved to Fairfax, and because of that incident, he just decided to give up music for a while. "I really didn't play any more until 1964 or 1965."

Nobody said anything for a moment, and it may have seemed to John that things had gone a bit too solemn, for he suddenly said, "How about this?" And without further introduction, he set his guitar flat on his lap, Hawaiian-guitar style, produced a pocketknife, and did a real virtuoso slide-guitar performance of "The Wabash Cannonball."

"Hey! I know that one!" shouted the drunken sleeper, now suddenly awake. "That's the 'Wabash Cannonball.' Ain't it?"

John nodded as he continued to chord idly on the guitar.

"Now play 'Wildwood Flower.' "

"Oh, I played that one," said John with a wink to me. "Didn't you hear?"

"No, doggone it. I was asleep. I guess I slept right through it."

"Maybe next time."

Everybody laughed, but the guy never figured out why.

IT MIGHT be possible, and even desirable, to separate very precisely those elements that have shaped American music if it were dead, fixed, something in the past. But it is alive. The whole tradition lives in a good country picker like John Jackson. He will play an old hymn, such as "When the Roll Is Called Up Yonder," do a good old blues, and then cap the set with something like "Blue Suède Shoes." He knows them all. They are all real to him. They seem to him almost like pieces of the same long song.

Maybe they are.

B. B. KING.

"Ron Rogers"

MANCE LIPSCOMB and SON HOUSE at the Newport Folk Festival, 1965.

Dick Waterman

SKIP JAMES

SON HOUSE, SKIP JAMES, and JOHN HURT at the Newport Folk Festival, 1965.   *Dick Waterman*

SON HOUSE and DICK WATERMAN.   *Baron Wolman*

BUKKA WHITE.

Baron Wolman

FRED McDONELL.   *Baron Wolman*

ROBERT PETE WILLIAMS

BABE STOVALL

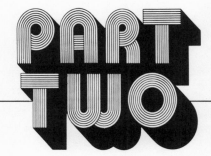

CHAPTER FOUR

DELTA BEGINNINGS: "GO BACK TO THE COUNTRY"

THERE IS one generalization that has been made about relations between blacks and whites in America that seems to me just about as valid today as it did when I first came across it late in the fifties. I remember reading it in an essay by S. I. Hayakawa; he offered it as a bit of folk wisdom that he felt summed up the situation pretty well: In the South (goes the analysis), they don't care how close a nigger gets as long as he doesn't get too high. In the North, they don't care how high a Negro gets as long as he doesn't get too close.

I recall with some slight chagrin that at the time I thought the North won on points in this sort of comparison. I no longer think that. I have seen too much in the intervening years of the going style of administering racial justice at arm's length from the White House, Gracie Mansion, and other Northern centers of power and influence. It has soured me a little on the liberal passion for the abstract—that de-personalizing, anyplace-but-here method of dealing with human problems of every sort: by appropriate programs, funded by sufficient money, and run by competent professionals.

That's not the South. It might well be argued that a bit more

69

of this approach early in the game might have saved Southern whites much of the pain they experienced during the past decade in the process of being dragged into the twentieth century. But nevertheless a change has been worked, and is being worked still, down there in that region where change once seemed impossible. And it is even more profound because, in those towns and small cities where the Southern experience is shaped daily, the change is being worked on a personal level. The South is a more personal place. That is its misery and its glory; it may ultimately be its damnation or its salvation. Injustice, when it comes there (which is still far too frequently), is not so often attributable to some abstract entity such as the System or the Man, but more likely to that damn peckerwood cracker down the road. Let a man know his antagonist, give him some focus for his rage, and he may not be able to overcome, but at least he can hold onto his sanity.

A black man named Albert Murray described his own long voyage home in a fine book called *South to a Very Old Place*. In it, he remarks, "Somebody once declared that when you come right down to intimate personal contacts, the Southerner is likely to be lying when he says he is a racist and the Northerner is likely to be lying when he professes not to be one." Which is a kind of restatement of the theme with which we began this discussion.

But what is the point of this discussion, after all? Where is it leading us? To the South, on this blues trip, down to the deepest, darkest part of it, the Mississippi Delta, down where the blues was born. But I think you should know that you'll be traveling in the company of one—myself—who has had only limited experience of the region. I tend to be suspicious of knowledge that does not have some basis in firsthand experience. Mine was gained on reporting trips, visits, and a couple of tours gathering information for this book. I was more certain what the South was and what I thought of it before I had been there than I am today. I seem to have fewer and fewer preconceptions each time I go down.

What do *I* know about the South? I know, as I have said, that it is a very personal place. I also know, with a nod to Albert Murray, who framed the quality well in the title of his book, that the South is a very old place. You sense that even as you drive along the sterile Interstate routes that everywhere else tend to obscure the qualities of the country through which they pass, rather than reveal them. Here, something of the land shows through. It is there in the somber green of the rolling countryside, and in the shacks that seem to pop up each mile or so on the horizon. Travel in the winter, as I did down through the Delta land, and you will be struck by the odd quality of the daylight filtering down through the pearly skies, enough like Ireland or Scotland at that time of year so that you might unconsciously begin to look for castle ruins and flocks of sheep along the way. Take a turn off the Interstate, however, and drive into one of the little towns along the way—Como, Askew, or Itta Bena—and then get out and walk around. As that raw Mississippi wind whips through you, any romantic memories you may have had of Ireland or Scotland will be blown away in an instant. No, this is down-home country, all right, the American South—but even so, the "old" quality of the country hereabouts should be immediately apparent as you walk through one of these Delta towns, for it is like taking a stroll back into the last century. The pace is altogether slower. No building in the center of town seems to have gone up since 1900. Everything is so specific, there is such a quality of place here, that you may have the feeling that you have wandered by mistake onto some elaborately constructed and perfectly authentic Hollywood set, one that might have been kept ready on the back lot as the "Turn-of-the-Century Southern Street." *Or whatever.*

Where is the Delta country? In his book *Country Blues,* Samuel Charters quotes some anonymous source to the effect that it "begins at the lobby of the Peabody Hotel in Memphis, Tenn.," and goes all the way down to Natchez, or "just about as far south as you want it to go." A less generous, though probably more precise measure would take in everything between the Yazoo and the Mississippi rivers. Since the Yazoo flows into the Mississippi at Vicksburg, that gives us a precise southern limit. Fixing the northern limits of the Delta is not quite so easy, for the Tallahatchie flows into the Yazoo up near Greenwood, and tradition puts most of the country watered by the Tallahatchie within the realm—Clarksdale, certainly, and Cleveland, Mississippi, off straight to the west, are pure Delta.

YES, ANY MAP of the blues country of Mississippi must include Cleveland, for it was just outside there on the Dockery Plantation that Charley Patton grew up, the first of the Delta bluesmen to emerge from the anonymity of the folk blues tradition. He was born farther south, just east of Vicksburg, in the little town of Edwards, in about 1885. A small man of frail physique, he was not really built for the back-breaking work in the fields, and he managed to escape it through most of his life because of his skill with a guitar, his deep, strong voice, and his remarkable ability to make original songs from the raw material of the life he saw around him.

If not unique, he was at least unusual because of the indelible stamp of authorship he put on so many of his blues. They belonged to him and not to some vague tradition. You knew they were Charley Patton's songs because specific references abounded in them to himself, his friends, their adventures and mishaps, and the local disasters they lived through together. In this, it is interesting that the first Delta bluesman of reputation worked in a kind of transitional idiom. His songs were much more closely related to the ballads than were those of the bluesmen who followed him. More often than not, they told a story or announced an event. In "High Water Everywhere," for example, he presents the drama of the Mississippi flood of 1927, marking the progress of the rising water town by town as it moves on down the river. The song is as effective a piece of *reporting* as you will find in all of the blues, but in a way it is closer to Woody Guthrie's ballads of the dust bowl disaster than to the work of any other black blues writer.

Using that simple three-line couplet, Charley Patton could tell a pretty good story, too. His "High Sheriff Blues" tells a tale that is obviously his own, naming names and locating it very specifically in the town of Belzoni, Mississippi. But it is not really a ballad because it lacks the objectivity of a ballad. The blues spirit is there, the emotion, for it is a story told from the inside.

> *When the trial's in Belzoni ain't no use in screaming*
> *   and crying* (twice)
> *Mister Webb will take you back to Belzoni jailhouse*
> *   flying.*

Let me tell you folkses how he treated me (twice)
And he put me in a cell there it was dark as it could
be.

It was late one evening Mr. Purvis was standing
'round (twice)
Mr. Purvis told Mr. Webb to let poor Charlie down.

It takes boozey booze, Lord, to carry me through
(twice)
Thirty days seem like years in a jailhouse where
there is no booze.

I got up one morning feeling mighty bad (twice)
And it must not of been them Belzoni jail blues I had

While I was in trouble ain't no use a-screaming and
crying (twice)
Mr. Purvis on his mansion he doesn't pay no mind.

In addition to the ballad-related blues that he wrote, he recorded a number of straight ballads—a version of the old Boll Weevil song, which he called "Mississippi Boll Weevil Blues," and "Frankie and Albert" among them.

Yes, he recorded a good deal before his death in 1934. In just five years, beginning in 1929, he cut something like sixty sides for Paramount and Vocalion; about half were blues and the rest were ballads and religious songs. He would only be a legend today if it were not for this recorded legacy he left behind. He barely strayed from his native Delta country except to make these trips north to Richmond, Indiana, Chicago and New York to record. Otherwise his life was the sort of endless round of nights spent at country dances and juke joints, and days at weekend picnics and fish fries, that was the pattern for all the itinerant bluesmen of the region.

And if Charlie Patton is important as an innovator with a direct relationship to the kinds of music that preceded the blues—to the ballads and the ur-blues that came out of the work songs and field hollers—he is just as important as a link to the music that followed. He traveled with the younger Son House, tutored a youngster named Chester Burnett who later made it big as Howlin' Wolf, and inspired Bukka White, who as a kid used to follow him around their hometown of Cleveland. Although it would be wrong to call him the originator of the Delta blues style, Patton was the earliest practitioner to send it via recordings outside the region.

IF ROBERT JOHNSON had not existed, they would have to have invented him. His is the most potent legend in all the blues— that of the gifted young artist, driven by his hunger for life and his passion for music to excesses that killed him at the age of twenty-four. Yet he left behind him a treasure of blues record- ings that have inspired collectors and musicians alike for decades since. He is the Shelley, Keats, and Rimbaud of the blues all rolled into one. If any bluesman is assured of immor- tality it is this little drifter-with-a-guitar who may never have left the South.

Nobody seems to know where or precisely when he was born, but by subtraction, the date comes out to sometime in 1914, and the place was probably in the vicinity of Robinsonville, Missis- sippi, for that was where he grew up. He showed up there, just a kid in short pants, with a harmonica, one night at a juke joint where Son House and Willie Brown were playing and asked if he could join them. He was pretty good with the harp, but it turned out that what he really wanted was to have them teach him guitar. Before they could settle down to that, though, Son and Willie moved on to another town down the river. It was six months later when they got back. They found that Robert John- son had not only taught himself how to play guitar in the in- terim, but, still only a boy, he had become a bluesman of some reputation in the area.

But he didn't stay around there long. In the next few years, he was constantly on the move through the South. It must have started for him as a kind of hegira to the great cities—he got to Memphis and St. Louis early—but soon he was rambling just to ramble—Helena, Arkansas, Itta Bena, Mississippi, and on down through the Delta to Louisiana, and then west to Texas. "I got to keep moving," he sang in one song, and in another he told them,

> You may bury my body, ooh, down by the highway
>   side,
> So my old evil spirit can get a Greyhound bus and
>   ride.

Sometime during this period of wandering Robert Johnson was heard by a local record salesman of the American Record Corporation (the kind who used to fill up the car trunk with "Race" records and go out to the crossroads in black communities to peddle them). He was recommended to A.R.C.'s Don Law, who had come south to record local artists for the Vocalion label. The sessions that Johnson recorded for Law in November, 1936, and June, 1937, are among the richest in the history of the blues. Not only did they leave a permanent record of his skill with a guitar and his extremely subtle and flexible vocal style, but they also established a fund of original blues material on which the younger generation has drawn liberally ever since. For example, Cream recorded his "Crossroads Blues" as "Crossroads," Paul Butterfield adapted his "Walking Blues," The Rolling Stones included "Love in Vain" on their *Let It Bleed* album, and Taj Mahal recently cut a fine version of Johnson's "Sweet Home Chicago."

What sort of man was he? He had a reputation as a hellion, and Don Law's experiences with Johnson on their first session in San Antonio, Texas, prove the point. (I've stooped to quoting liner notes here, but the story is too good to pass up.) Frank Driggs, who produced a Columbia reissue of Johnson material, tells it this way:

> ... A country boy in a moderately big town, Johnson found trouble within hours after he arrived. Don Law considered himself responsible for Johnson, found him a room in a boarding house and told him to get some sleep so he would be ready to begin the recording at ten the following morning. Law then joined his wife and some friends for dinner at the Gunter Hotel. He had scarcely begun dinner when he was summoned to the phone. A policeman was calling from the city jail. Johnson had been picked up on a vagrancy charge. Law rushed down to the jail, found Johnson beaten up, his guitar smashed; the cops had not only picked him up but had worked him over. With some difficulty, Law managed to get Johnson freed in his custody, whisked him back to the boarding house, gave him forty-five cents for breakfast, and told him to stay in the house and not go out for the rest of the evening. Law returned to the hotel, only to be called to the phone again. This time it was Johnson. Fearing the worst, Law asked, "What's the matter now?" Johnson replied, "I'm lonesome." Puzzled, Law said,

"You're lonesome? What do you mean, you're lonesome?" Johnson replied, "I'm lonesome and there's a lady here. She wants fifty cents and I lacks a nickel. . . ."

He was a man of contradictions. Perhaps if he had lived longer he might have reconciled some of them and settled down to a longer, steadier, more productive career. Instead, he settled for genius. On the one hand, he was shy. Law tells of asking him to show his stuff on guitar to a group of Mexican musicians and seeing Johnson so overcome with embarrassment that he was only able to play after he had turned away from them. On the other hand, he could be bold to the point of foolhardiness. Son House says he was surprised that Johnson lived as long as he did because of the young bluesman's way of moving in on any woman who caught his eye, whether or not a husband or a boy friend were in sight. In the end, it seems to have been jealousy that did him in. He died mysteriously and violently. Some say he was stabbed and some say he was poisoned. He died, in any case, early in 1938.

Because Robert Johnson was such a complex and ultimately mysterious personality, I decided to seek out the one man left who remembers him well and can comment with authority on him. His name is Johnny Shines. He met Johnson sometime in the middle thirties in Helena, Arkansas. At that time, Shines had the beginning of a reputation himself. They were calling him "Little Wolf," because one night he had picked up Howlin' Wolf's guitar and started playing his stuff. "Suddenly everything Wolf was doing fell into place, and so I started laying it out. When he got back, the joint was rocking." And so, when Johnny Shines met Robert Johnson they were more or less on even terms—and that was how they traveled together off and on over a period of a couple of years. They are no longer on even terms, though, for while Shines could hold his own with Johnson the man, he can't compete with the legend—and I sense he has grown tired of trying.

After nearly thirty years in Chicago, he has returned to the South and lives comfortably in a suburb of Tuscaloosa, Alabama. He is a sensitive, intelligent man, somewhat disenchanted with his long career as a bluesman. If not wasted, the time he gave to it (he seems to feel) was misspent. Although he looks younger, he is now in his fifties. He is trying to make sense of his life, as a man will at that age, and is engaged in the writing of his autobiography.

"Then when I finish that," he told me, "I got another book I want to write, and the name of it is *Success Was My Downfall.* What's it about? Well, it's about all of us who want success and maybe get a little of it and are not able to cope with it."

Who and what does he have in mind? "Well, that Robert Johnson, the boy I played along with so long. If I'd been a success like him I might not have been able to handle it any better than he could. He couldn't stand the success—it was his downfall. They talk about liquor and women, but that wasn't it. It was the success did him in."

Still, Johnny Shines isn't bitter. He has a good band going now—the best in his part of the South—and a decent life for himself, his wife, and the houseful of grandchildren who are with them. If he hasn't made it big, as have Muddy Waters and Howlin' Wolf and one or two others, nevertheless he has a respectable reputation with blues aficionados around the country and plays the festivals and the blues clubs on the two coasts.

It's just that after all these years he seems haunted by the memory of his old blues buddy. This happened, no doubt, partly because writers, researchers, and the merely curious keep annoying him with questions about Robert Johnson (I plead guity on all counts) and won't let him forget. But only partly because whenever he speaks of him he seems truly baffled by this episode. Even after this lapse of years, he seems to regard his time with Johnson as his encounter with genius. Robert, as he calls him, is still a mystery to Johnny Shines.

I asked him what Johnson was like, and he took it that I meant physically. "Oh, he was a good-looking-enough fellow, but little, no size to him at all. It's what made him look like a kid to everyone."

"Was he about my height?"

"Might be, but you'd make two of him across." (I'm about five-nine, 160.)

"What kind of person was he?"

"That was just it. You couldn't figure him. Now, I mean we were together off and on a long time and did a lot of traveling together, but he never would say much except what do you think of this guitar man or that girl over there, stuff like that. And you might be playing with him someplace, and he'll say, hey, I'm gonna go out and take a leak—then that would be the last you'd see of him for two weeks until he'd show up again looking like he'd really been through it." Johnny Shines shook his head, remembering.

"But Robert was good, really good. If you want to take rock-and-roll, he was the beginning of it. When he was playing guitar he never left his tonic so far he couldn't get back, but he was so inventive that he would play with variety just within these limits. I don't think he knew one chord from another. But still, he had this great talent, he could take a broken chord and make a natural chord out of it. He was just a man who was born to do this thing of playing and singing, and he did it well."

I asked if Shines had taught him anything on the guitar, and he smiled and shook his head. "You know," he said, "I hear other guys talk about when Robert learned to play the guitar, but I don't think he ever learned. He was *doing* it when they thought he was learning. They don't talk about a duck learning to swim, do they?"

TALK ABOUT GENIUSES of the Delta blues and you must mention Nehemiah "Skip" James. He was born in the heart of the Delta country, Bentonia, Mississippi, on June 9, 1902. The son of a preacher, he attended four years of high school in Yazoo City and got a musical education by hook or by crook from local musicians. He played good guitar but wanted most to learn how to play the piano. As a young man, he traveled as far west as Texas, taking any sort of day labor he could get, and then wound up working in a sawmill job in a little Mississippi town just south of Memphis. There, he met up with an old-time bar-relhouse piano player named Will Crabtree who taught him what he knew. Later he came to know Little Brother Montgomery, perhaps the best of all the blues pianists, who also became a kind of mentor to him; Skip even learned Little Brother's signature tune, "Special Rider," and adapted it for guitar. And although this was about the extent of his musical education— a little guitar picked up at home and some piano learned out on the road—it was far more than most had—and what he did with it must have surprised even him.

While staying in Jackson, Mississippi, he came to the attention of one H. C. Spears, a music-store proprietor who doubled as a talent scout for the Paramount Record Company of Grafton, Wisconsin. He sent Skip north, where he recorded some twenty-six sides for the label in about two days during February, 1931. Only seventeen were finally released, but they were among the most distinctive ever done by any blues performer during the twenties and thirties. His knowledge of the piano and his adventurous spirit led him to experiment in scales in which nobody before had ever tried to play the blues. These old Paramount sides are only partly successful—"Devil Got My Woman" and "22–20" are quite good—but nobody before had ever recorded anything like them. Hear his weird falsetto vocal style once, and you will never forget it. The voice and the far-out harmonies together must have been a little too much for the conservative blues-record-buying public. None of the Paramount records cut by Skip James sold exceptionally well. He was never invited back to record in Grafton again, and he swore later that he only made forty dollars from the two-day session.

He became discouraged, quit thinking of himself as a bluesman at all, and turned a year or two later to gospel music. He moved to Dallas, where his father had a church, and organized a quartet, the Dallas Texas Jubilee Singers. He toured with this group for about ten years, working at various jobs on the side, and was finally ordained a minister himself. He had been out of music for about twenty years when three enterprising young bluesologists—Bill Barth and guitarists John Fahey and Henry Vestine (the latter now lead guitarist with Canned Heat)—tracked him down in a hospital in Tunica, Mississippi. They convinced him that it was time to end his retirement and arranged for him to appear at the 1964 Newport Folk Festival.

His was one of the great personal triumphs in the Newport year that was probably the greatest ever for blues. Son House, Mississippi John Hurt, and Robert Pete Williams were all there, but Skip James came close to stealing the show. Although he remained active in music during the five years he had left to live, he never again achieved the sort of popular success he did that year at Newport. There were a couple of reasons for this. The first is simple: He was a sick man. They found him in a hospital with a respiratory ailment. He left it to play at the Folk Festival. And in a short time he was back in the hospital again, this time in Washington, D.C.; this last stay provided the inspiration for one of the finest of his latter-day blues, "Washington D.C. Hospital Center Blues."

The second reason is much more complicated; it is, in fact, a whole complex of reasons that add up to Skip James' unique personality. I once had an interesting conversation about this with Dick Waterman, who had served as Skip's manager during his last years and had seen to it that he was well recorded during that final period. I remember asking Waterman, innocently enough, what it was like working with Skip James then, and getting more than I bargained for in the way of an answer.

"He was a true genius, and he knew it," said Waterman. "He had a manner toward everyone that was aloof, condescending, and patronizing. And a *strong* mind. He would make demands, personal demands on people—on me. I would draw his baths for him, carry his guitar, hold the doors, everything. I know it was silly, but I felt sorry for him because by this time he had alienated a lot of people, and I felt, 'Well, I'm one of the few friends he's got.' And that was true, but he had this sort of control over a great many people."

Waterman remembered how he would appear for an engagement at a club or coffeehouse and there might be only forty or fifty people present. But to Skip James it might as well have been a concert at Carnegie Hall. He would appear in a tuxedo —not quite the picture of the Delta bluesman—and carefully shoot his cuffs before settling down on a stool and accepting his guitar from his assistant—who was Dick Waterman, of course. The trouble was that he was just as condescending toward the audience. He would lecture them on his music and its complexities.

"And that," said Waterman, "never worked, either, because Skip would use a lot of musical terms, but I always had the impression he was dropping them from a book he had read once. Very often he would refer to himself in the third person, and he would say, 'Mr. James will not play in triplicates,' and what he would play would be far out, but it wouldn't be triplets.

"And he'd play kitsch, too. I have tapes of him doing Hoagy Carmichael's 'Lazy Bones,' with all this shut-my-mouth stuff on it—but also a very interesting rolling left hand on piano that was not quite stride-style but was something all its own. But when he did material like this, he would send blues purists into agonies.

"He was a genius, all right," concluded Dick Waterman, "but he was strictly a *natural* genius."

The best kind.

FOR YEARS, Waterman was also associated with another Mississippi bluesman, Fred McDowell, who was as easygoing and unassuming as Skip James was haughty and cantankerous. Mississippi Fred McDowell, as he was known, was probably also the greatest living bottle-neck guitarist. But now he is no longer living. He died as this was being written, and the time he spent talking with me in a Batesville, Mississippi, hospital —"I got one of them ulcers," he told me—may well have been the last he was able to give to any of us who would pursue him so eagerly with pencils poised and cassettes running.

He was a pushover for note-takers such as myself because he was by nature cooperative and was quite generous with his time. At nearly every festival and concert at which he appeared he seemed to trail a wake of questioners and eavesdroppers whenever he was offstage. That was one of the reasons he was so popular with the young crowds he played for: He made himself so completely available. And the other, of course, was the glorious thing he did onstage. He would sit out there in front of the microphone, just Fred and his guitar, and with that length of copper conduit glinting on the little finger of his fret hand, he would do the most amazing things with his instrument, extracting whines and twangs from it that Andrés Segovia would never have dreamed were there. Bottle-neck guitar is its own strange sort of art. It's not just bending and sustaining those thirds and sevenths to make blue notes out of them; it's also putting it all together with the right licks and laying it down with a good steady beat. Fred McDowell played amazingly subtle music; the variety of his fillips and phrases was endless, it seemed. To be frank, many bluesmen are indifferent guitarists at best, repetitious, dull, and uninventive, and often without much sense of rhythm. But not Fred McDowell. He did it all as it was supposed to be done, giving audiences who would listen some sense of the blues guitar as it could and should be played.

And he could sing, too. He had the sort of hushed, slightly

nasal style that was just right for the sort of Delta blues material he sang. Not much of it was his, so technically he was a songster, a collector of songs. Some of the blues and sacred songs he did were his own, but most were learned—from itinerant singers (Fred stayed put for forty years) and from phonograph records.

It was after I had heard him one night at a blues festival that I made a date to talk to him. I told him I was going south on a trip and would like to look in on him if I could. He was insistent: by all means, I *had* to come by. He gave me a phone number and very precise directions to his home in Como, Mississippi (I still have them tucked away in a notebook somewhere). But when the time came, some months later, to leave on that trip, I had not received an answer to the letter I had sent him telling him when I would be coming. So, from Memphis, I called the number in Como he had given me and found out that he was in the hospital in Batesville and that I could visit him there.

Not knowing quite what to expect, I went to see him there. Batesville is one of those sleepy Delta towns, a bit bigger than most and the only one with a hospital of any size in Panola County. It is white-run and not segregated, as near as I could tell. The morning I went to visit Fred McDowell, they told me where I could find him, and a nurse even went half the distance down the hall with me to point out his room.

He seemed pretty well, and he said he was, too. Just an ulcer. They were taking care of it pretty good here, he declared, and he would be up and around soon. I asked how old he was, and he said he was sixty-eight. That surprised me, for he looked a good fifteen years younger. There were only a few gray hairs on his head, and the black pencil mustache that he maintained so carefully seemed to belong on a much younger man. Occasionally, as we talked, he seemed to be in some pain, but he kept right on talking, apparently glad to have some company.

I remember asking him if he had been born in the Delta. "No," he said, "I was born and raised east of Memphis, in Rossville, Tennessee, there in Fayette County. My father and mother didn't raise me. My uncle raised me, and to tell you the truth, I didn't ever know much about my father."

Did he learn to play guitar there? "Yes, but that wasn't anything exceptional. You take a man in my home, youngsters or old people, there wasn't hardly any seen who couldn't play guitar. There were some who were pretty good, though—Van D. McKenna, and Raymond Payne, and Jake Owens. They're all dead now. I'm about the onliest one of those Fayette County players still alive. That Raymond Payne, he was the one who taught me. It's too bad he didn't have time to record.

"Yeah, I stayed in Rossville, Tennessee, until I was grown, just farming then—that's what I did all my life. But after my uncle passed on, I had a sister who was married here in Mississippi, and so I came down here to live around her. That was around Lamar, Mississippi, and when I got down to there I found out there was a few guitars in the neighborhood, and I got acquainted with them. I remember I went to a dance one night, and there were two brothers playing, a violin and a guitar. I sat down and played, and I pulled the people away from them. I got their fans from them, and that's how I got to know them. That was kind of like one night in Cleveland, Mississippi, when Bukka White was playing for them, and then I started playing and the crowd commenced applauding me. And Bukka, he came up to me real tough, and he said, 'I don't need no goddam help from you here.' He was real tough then, but I get along pretty good with him now.

"I played a lot of dances in the country back then. I had the knack of the guitar, and everybody wanted to have me play for them. Sure, we used to play a lot of what they call blues now, only when we played it they didn't call it the blues—they called it 'the reel.' But when Blind Lemon and Charley Patton started recording, they started calling it the blues. I remember I was in Cleveland, Mississippi, in 1928 when Charley Patton put out that song "Pea-Vine Railroad." That was the first song he put out, and I remember I sure thought it was something."

When I asked Fred McDowell what occasions he played for, he carefully reminded me that times were different then from what they are today. "You want to remember," he said, "that back in the twenties and thirties, they didn't have nothin' to do but farm and nowhere to go on a Saturday night but to what you'd call a fish fry. There was no picture show or TV or nothin', just nowhere else to go. Of course, it ain't the case today. People down here got other things to do, and it's the ones from outside who come looking for the blues players in the Delta."

Did he do any traveling? "Oh, some. Just right around here to play those old juke houses in the Delta. They had to have some entertainment in them because they didn't have no record player or anything. We'd just play and they would dance. That was Eli Green and me. We did a lot of playing all around the Delta together—in Cleveland and Rosedale, towns like that. But I never did any real far traveling. I never did much hoboing. I tried it, but I didn't like it. I was scared of it."

He paused, then added with evident pride, "Of course, I've done a lot of traveling lately. The first tour I ever went on I went to Europe and I went to Germany, Denmark, and Switzerland. The blues gets through to all different kinds of people. Then I play the colleges and the clubs. I like colleges best. I even play Ole Miss around here. All this started happening after I did my first recording, though."

I asked him how that came about.

"Well, that was after I came down here to Como from Lamar in 1940. It was a good long time after that. You could check the dates on the records I made and find out for sure. [I did, and it was 1959.] Alan Lomax recorded me for the first time. I remember he was at the Pretcher brothers' house doing some recording, and somebody sent for me and said I should bring my guitar along. I did come by and played a little for Lomax, and he asked, could he come to my house on Saturday night to record, and I said, sure. So come that Saturday night the house is just full of people come to hear me recording and wanting to record, too. But right away Lomax said, 'I'm not interested in nobody but Fred.' And that discouraged a lot of them, and they left. The few of them that stayed didn't stay the whole time because he kept me going from eight o'clock in the evening to seven o'clock on Sunday morning. He'd say, 'Let me hear that one one more time.' Or, 'Do you know any songs about a mule?' He made me sing every song I knew. I played all that night, and I didn't get a motherfucking dime. Well, I did get seventy-five dollars from him later on, and then seventy dollars another time.

"I remember I was in Newport when I met him there next. He got me to come, sent me a little expenses and all. Then he said, 'All right, you all give me your address, and I'm going to mail you a check.' I ain't seen a check yet. He did the same thing with the Sea Island Singers. That Lomax, you'd think he was a millionaire the way he wear these big, rich-looking suits down here. But at those workshops at Newport, he wore these old clothes, overalls and all."

Fred McDowell broke off momentarily, shook his head in disgust, and lit up a cigarette. He had smoked more or less steadily through the hour or so I had been with him. It didn't seem to hurt him, but I wondered if it was the right thing to do with an ulcer.

"You take Chris and Dick, though," he continued, referring to Chris Strachwitz (of Arhoolie Records) and Dick Waterman. "They're the best somebodies I ever worked with. Dick has brought me to where I am now—why, I was still farming until I hooked up with him. Every time he sends for me I'm willing to go. Matter of fact, you going to be talking to him soon?"

I said I expected I would be.

"Well, I want you to tell Dick I'll be ready to go. I'll be out of the hospital soon, and I'll be ready next job he has for me. See, I can't get a job—a regular working job—now because of my age. But it works out pretty good now, because both Chris and Dick stick right with you and see you get your money."

About that time his wife and other members of his family showed up at the door to his hospital room, and I started to say my goodbye. He reiterated that he would like me to tell Dick that I had seen him and that he was all right now and ready to go. He was so insistent that I did call Waterman while I was still out on the road and found that he had not known that Fred McDowell was in the hospital; he had tried to reach him at Como a couple of times and had had no luck. I gave him Fred's message, told him it was supposed to be an ulcer, and that he seemed pretty well.

And that was the last I heard about it for a couple of months, when I got a call from Waterman who was changing planes in Washington; he had been down to help Fred McDowell settle his affairs. It was stomach cancer, he explained, and just a matter of time.

Mississippi Fred McDowell died in Baptist Hospital, in Memphis, on July 3, 1972, less than five months after I talked with him.

CHAPTER FIVE

"I THOUGHT I HEARD BUDDY BOLDEN SAY..."

From about 1900 on, there were three types of bands around New Orleans. You had bands that played ragtime, ones that played sweet music, and the ones that played nothin' but blues. A band like John Robichaux's played nothin' but sweet music and played the dicty affairs. On a Saturday night Frankie Dusen's Eagle Band would play the Masonic Hall because he played a whole lot of blues. A band like the Magnolia Band would play ragtime and work the District. They'd play *Bag of Rags, Frog Leg Rag, Maple Leaf Rag, Champagne Rag,* and ones like that; they were all dance numbers. All the bands around New Orleans would play quadrilles starting about midnight. When you did that nice people would know it was time to go home because things got rough after that. The rough guys would come about midnight. They were pimps, whores, hustlers, and that bunch. They'd dance with no coats on and their suspenders down. They'd jump around and have a bunch of fun. They wanted you to play slow blues and dirty songs so they could dance rough and dirty.

The speaker here is George "Pops" Foster, the New Orleans bassist. Born in 1892, he began playing more or less professionally around town in 1906 and had one of the longest playing careers in jazz. It ended only with his death in 1969. I'm calling him as an expert witness here because his classification of the three kinds of music played in New Orleans at the time jazz was taking shape has a lot to say about the part played by the blues in its development.

Although elsewhere in his autobiography Pops Foster draws the line of development from New Orleans ragtime to jazz ("What's called jazz today was called ragtime back then . . ."), in that passage just quoted he makes a point of mentioning Frankie Dusen's Eagle Band as the one that played the blues during that seminal period. And the Eagle Band had been taken over by Dusen from the legendary Charles "Buddy" Bolden, the New Orleans cornetist who is invariably cited as the first real jazz player, if not the man who started it all. The history of jazz goes back no further than Buddy Bolden.

The New Orleans barber, who was born in 1868, put together a six-piece band in 1895 to play in a dance pavilion at a private park. He was an immediate sensation. Everyone seems to agree that he could not read a note of music and had only the crudest sort of technique on his instrument, but the spirit was there— and the power. Yes, on that they are unanimous: Buddy Bolden was just about the *strongest* hornman who ever put mouthpiece to lip. Jelly Roll Morton called him that and said that when Buddy Bolden played a dance it was unnecessary to advertise it; all he had to do was point his cornet up at the sky and let loose a few well-chosen licks and he could be heard for ten miles around. And Louis Armstrong had something to say about Bolden's power, too. In his unghosted autobiography, *Satchmo: My Life in New Orleans,* he tells of living down the street as a kid from the Funky Butt Hall, where this first jazzman held forth nightly. "Old Buddy Bolden blew so hard that I used to wonder if I would ever have enough lung power to fill one of those cornets. All in all Buddy Bolden was a great musician, but I think he blew too hard. I will even go so far as to say that he did not blow correctly. In any case he finally went crazy. You can figure that out for yourself."

It's true, Buddy Bolden went crazy. That happened in 1907. He was playing a street parade with Allen's Brass Band when he suddenly flew into a berserk rage, broke ranks, and began to wield his cornet as a weapon, striking out wildly at bystanders and fellow bandsmen. When they overcame him, he was carted off to jail, pronounced insane, and shipped off to the East Louisiana State Hospital at Angola. There his illness was diagnosed as "dementia praecox, paranoid type," and, showing no signs of recovery, he died in the asylum in 1931.

It had been a long time coming. He was notorious as a heavy drinker and when, early on, he would become abusive and quarrelsome with people around the bandstand, and generally erratic in his behavior, people assumed he was drunk. His paranoid mutterings may well have inspired that strange blues about him, with its odd refrain:

I thought I heard Buddy Bolden say,
'Dirty, nasty stinky butt, take it away.'

After a while—this would have been around 1900—he was unable to get along even with the members of his own band, and one night he walked off the stand in a fury. That was when the Buddy Bolden Band became Frankie Dusen's Eagle Band. Dusen was his trombone player, just as funky as Bolden, but a lot more dependable. He hired another cornet player, Joe Howard, to take his place, then let Buddy come back when he promised to be good. That was how the Eagle Band happened to have *two* cornetists, the first of the New Orleans bands to double the lead.

What kind of music did this mad first king of jazz play? Although Buddy Bolden never recorded, Martin Williams, in his book *Jazz Masters of New Orleans,* has come up with a few titles that go a long way toward suggesting the peculiar sweaty, low-down quality of it. Buddy Bolden's Greatest Hits? How about "If You Don't Like My Potatoes Why Do You Dig So Deep," "All the Whores Like the Way I Ride," and "Make Me a Pallet on Your Floor." You get the idea, I'm sure. It was rough, tough music of a particular sort. And just what sort that was, Pops Foster makes most clear in his autobiography. He writes, "I only saw Buddy Bolden's band play once at Johnson's Park. That's where the rough people went. I knew all the guys in the band and later on played with them. Buddy played very good for the style of stuff he was doing. He played nothing but blues and all that stink music, and he played it very loud."

Blues is the point: ". . . nothing but blues and all that stink music . . ." The musician who is generally credited with putting together the first jazz band, and was acclaimed the first "king" of jazz (King Bolden became his nickname), was essentially a bluesman. No single fact that I have come across makes quite so clear the debt of jazz to the blues. Blues must have been there in some crude shape before Buddy Bolden picked it up and started blowing it on his horn. And to the extent that he influenced other musicians in New Orleans—and they all agree he was a moving force there in the music—jazz derived from the blues. The roots of jazz are stuck deep in that older, cruder, more basic music.

And what about ragtime? What influence had it? Probably a great deal, for this lively, complex, and subtle music was sweeping the country at just about that time. It was originally, and remained largely, the creation of itinerant black piano men. In the 1890s, one of them, Scott Joplin, got musical learning enough to begin to set down on paper what had by then become the prevailing style in St. Louis and on down the river. When his "Maple Leaf Rag" was published in 1899, the new music was formally launched, and Joplin himself became, for a while at least, a kind of celebrity.

Fundamentally, ragtime was a strong two-handed piano style in which the left hand beat out a steady 2/4 rhythm while the right hand executed a highly-syncopated eight beats to the bar. There were about as many variations of this as there were ragtime tunes, but this at least was the point from which most of the variations began. In the hands of men like Tom Turpin and Eubie Blake, who were skilled improvisers, the style began to shade subtly into jazz. But even early on, in the compositions of Scott Joplin, you could hear echoes of the blues. Just catch them* in his early composition (1902), "The Entertainer," which, to me at least, is the most beautiful and haunting of them all.

Given the nature of ragtime, it was almost inevitable that the New Orleans musicians would be drawn to it, for its basic 2/4 rhythm was march tempo, and the brass band tradition among

*An excellent selection of Scott Joplin compositions is available in two volumes on Nonesuch Records, beautifully recorded by a classical pianist named Joshua Rifkin, who is largely responsible for the recent revival of interest in Joplin and his music.

blacks in that city went far back into the nineteenth century. (Some say there were colored parade bands there well before the Civil War; New Orleans had the largest free black and mixed population of any Southern city during slavery days.) The challenge for groups like the Magnolia Band, mentioned by Pops Foster earlier, was to adapt a music that was essentially pianistic—ragtime—to the instrumentation and style of a brass band. They managed it well, if we are to judge from all reports of the music that evolved from that experiment. But, in his own way, Buddy Bolden was engaged in a similar experiment, for he was adapting what was essentially string and vocal music—the blues—to the brass band style. Eventually—or perhaps, more accurately, immediately—there began a pattern of borrowing back and forth, and the process of musical amalgamation began, so that by the time jazz came to be known as jazz (in 1917—fairly late in the game), there were elements of parade music, ragtime, and blues in it.

One peculiarity of those early New Orleans bands—including the Bolden Band, the Eagle Band, the Magnolia Band, and most of the rest—is that they did not carry piano players. It wasn't because they were trying especially to maintain the brass band instrumentation; all of them were hybrid organizations that used at least some stringed instruments—bass and guitar were the usual thing, but violins were also known. Why no piano, then? One very logical and simple explanation has been offered for this: None of the piano men who were good enough to play that early jazz wanted or needed to play with the bands because they could make far more playing in the big brothels in the Storyville District. These whorehouse "professors" of infamous legend were skillful, all right—Tony Jackson and Jelly Roll Morton were among the best of them—and they played a lot of blues and ragtime, if we are to judge from the repertoire that Jelly Roll carried with him into the recording era.

Ferdinand "Jelly Roll" Morton was, in almost every way, a remarkable man. What was most remarkable about him, however, is that with all the other things he was—pimp, con man, and pathological liar among them—he was nevertheless also a considerable musician. Jelly Roll could play a mean piano; he has left recorded evidence of that. He could sing. He could lead a band. He did not, however, "invent jazz," as he told Alan Lomax at a Library of Congress recording session once. Neither was he much of an influence in New Orleans jazz, for he left the city far too early for that. He began traveling as early as 1904, when he was only nineteen, but he would return from time to time, catch up on what was happening musically, and throw his weight around a bit. But he began to see more and more of the world, and his returns to New Orleans became more infrequent and brief. He traveled up to St. Louis and made friends among the ragtime players there, he cut quite a figure himself down in Memphis, and he became one of the first to bring jazz and the blues out to the West Coast. He saw more of the country in those few years as an itinerant piano player than any contemporary Delta bluesman would have seen in his whole lifetime. Yet he had not much more to show for it all than that famous gold tooth he sported with the diamond mounted in it. It was not until later, when he was in Chicago during the twenties, that he made the records that assured him his niche in jazz history.

Jelly Roll never lost his feeling for the blues. It is the essential element that is constant in nearly all his best recorded work. It provided the emotional basis and the source—as Martin Williams suggests—for his music. He borrowed freely from folk sources and occasionally he stole—but always to good purpose. For that quality of giddy, jittery euphoria that makes so much of the music of the so-called "Jazz Age" sound silly today was, for the most part, blessedly absent from the music of Jelly Roll Morton. There was substance and depth to it, which came from the blues sources from which so much of it was directly derived.

Pops Foster talked about another brand of music that was dished out regularly in New Orleans—not blues and not ragtime. He cited John Robichaux's band as an example of the sort that "played nothin' but sweet music and played the dicty affairs." Robichaux himself was a light Negro, a Creole, who was well schooled in music and insisted that all those who played with him be able to read his arrangements note for note. Some jazzmen played jobs with the band—Pops Foster was one —and most of the material they played was jazz or ragtime in style. But Robichaux's band played a music apart, for it was carefully orchestrated and had to be played with a precision that utterly throttled spontaneity. Whitney Balliett speaks of jazz as "the sound of surprise"—and that inspired phrase defines the difference between real jazz and the kind of music that John Robichaux's band played. In that brand of sweet music there were no surprises.

I may seem here to be trying to pass myself off rather shamelessly as an expert on the music of a band long gone and little recorded. Yet I'll confess that my impressions of the band are based on secondhand evidence—of a most intriguing sort. A contemporary group that calls itself the New Orleans Ragtime Orchestra has recently recorded whole albums precisely in the manner of the old Robichaux band. They were able to do it because the complete Robichaux repertoire—its "book" of arrangements—had been discovered not long ago and was donated to the Archive of New Orleans Jazz at Tulane University, in New Orleans. A young man named Lars Edegran, who works as a researcher there, came across the Robichaux arrangements, realized their value, and got permission to have them copied. With these in hand, he organized the New Orleans Ragtime Orchestra to play them. It proved worthwhile. The band has been in existence since 1967, and it has made a couple of records on the Pearl and Arhoolie labels. Chiefly because of them, the New Orleans Ragtime Orchestra has been invited to play at a couple of New Orleans jazz festivals and in 1970 journeyed north to the Newport Jazz Festival. It has been very well received wherever it has played, for if the group lacks something in fire—these are, after all, society band arrangements, which are played note for note here—it does offer a lot in nostalgia. The thin, treble sound of its violin-trumpet-clarinet lead gives a kind of wistful quality to the music. It is dated, even rather corny, but that somehow is its special charm. It is a valid re-creation of the popular style of another era.

WHEN I CAME to New Orleans, I had with me a kind of informal introduction to Lars Ivar Edegran, the leader of the New Orleans Ragtime Orchestra. He turned out to be a quiet and precise young man, with a conservative mien, a clean jaw, and a short haircut. We went off together to a nearby restaurant for coffee. There we talked about how and why he had come over, and it turned out that his father had been a musician in Sweden, and that Lars had gotten started listening to jazz at home —mostly records. He got started playing in Sweden, and one year he came to New Orleans to listen and stayed on to play. "In the beginning it was with string bands and jug bands, and so on," he told me, "but I got to know the local musicians better, and soon I was sitting in with them. It didn't take long, really."

He began asking me questions. He wanted to know what I was looking for in New Orleans, whom I wanted to hear, and so on. He told me then what everyone else I talked to in New Orleans would later confirm: that there really is not much blues to be heard in the town. Never was. "Oh," he added with a shrug, "there's Babe Stovall, but he's—well, you can decide for yourself about him."

What Edegran had hesitated to say about Babe Stovall was that he is an evident alcoholic. Over in nearby Jackson Square we found him, a tall, loose man who looked to be in his fifties (but, born in 1907, he was well into his sixties). He was standing at a junction of walks in the park whanging away at a steel-bodied guitar and singing sacred songs, with no one around but us to listen. He was sweating hard and blinking painfully in the bright sun, but he kept right on singing. It was "Do, Lord, Remember Me" when we walked up. Then, sensing us there, he began to run through a few tricks for us; almost mechanically he twisted the guitar around behind his back and began to strum it that way—the rankest sort of old-time showboating. His voice came out a querulous cry, squawking on almost tunelessly until at last the song ground to a halt. He mumbled something to Edegran that I couldn't understand—and he did so without quite looking at him; Stovall just kept blinking those watery, red-rimmed eyes as though they wouldn't focus. Then he launched into "May the Circle Be Unbroken."

Edegran pulled me a couple of steps back and said into my ear that this was no time to talk to Babe Stovall. "When he drinks, the booze goes to his brain. He's not bad when he's sober. But the drunker he gets, the more commerical he is—that picking the guitar behind his back, it's stupid isn't it?"

I shrugged, and asked if he thought it would be better to come back tomorrow. Would Stovall be here then?

"Sunday? Always. It's the big day here in the park. He'll be in better shape to talk then." Edegran suggested we walk around a little, and so we left Babe Stovall, still blinking. I dropped some money into the peaked cap by his foot.

Circulating around the curving walks of Jackson Square, we encountered an old banjo picker, who Edegran said was Ernest Roubleau, and listened to him do "Sweet Georgia Brown" and "Mississippi Mud" before we went on. We also met a friend of Lars', an English trumpet player named Clive Davis, whose story was quite similar; his love of New Orleans jazz had brought him to the city and he had stayed on to make a little of it himself. We didn't get much beyond this when Lars asked him how his lip was, and Davis said he thought he would be able to play again soon. I noticed the jagged scar on Davis' lip then, and when we left him, I asked Edegran what that was about.

He explained that Davis had been following one of those traditional New Orleans funeral parades through a black district of New Orleans when suddenly, and for no reason, someone heaved a brick at him, and it hit him squarely in the mouth; the damage it did to his lips had kept him from playing his trumpet for well over a month. "That was near the Lucianne Avenue Project, where they had all that trouble with the Panthers—the shoot-out, you remember? There's been a lot of trouble here. At that same parade, an Irish couple who had just come to New Orleans to hear the music were beaten with chains by blacks. And not long after that, a friend of mine from Sweden was on the Magazine Avenue Bus—the only white— and they took his glasses away from him and broke them and threatened his life." Lars hesitated, then blurted out suddenly, as though it were something that had been eating at him a long while, "What's the matter with those people anyway? They must know people who come out to listen like that are not racists, or they wouldn't be there. What's the matter with them?"

We wound up the afternoon at Lars Edegran's very nice and comfortable loft apartment on Charter Street. He played records from his extensive collection of blues and jazz, and, as I remember, Lee Collins, the trumpet player, was on one of them. It was an LP of European issue, and it was about the only time I had heard that skilled second-generation New Orleans trumpeter recorded to good advantage. I mentioned to Edegran that I had heard Collins once as a kid (at that concert in Chicago I described earlier), and he was interested in that. I told him about the session, as I recalled it, and I added that another New Orleans musician had been there—Tony Parenti, the clarinet player. He made a face at the mention of his name. What was the matter with Tony Parenti? I wanted to know. (I happened to think he was pretty good.) "Typical white musician," Edegran said, with a dismissive flick of his hand. "He lacked the *true* feeling." Then he added, by way of general explanation, "Most Europeans like only Negro music. I don't know why this is—not for racial reasons. We respond to it better, though. I wonder why." And that was about all, except that he added later in the afternoon—I forget the context exactly—"Some Europeans may hate everything about America except the Negroes and the Negro music." I got the idea that Lars Edegran considered himself one of these Europeans.

That night I went out and listened to jazz in New Orleans, such as it is. The reality is bound to disappoint, for it must contend with wild expectations conjured up by our fantasy. We know what New Orleans jazz *should* sound like; it should sound like King Oliver, Alphonse Picou, Kid Ory, Louis Armstrong, and all the rest from that pantheon of pioneers. And it isn't like that at all.

It is by now a fairly slick commercial routine, a product offered to satisfy the expectations of tourists and drinking residents. On any given night, wandering up and down Bourbon Street, you are likely to hear "When the Saints Go Marching In," "High Society," and "The Birth of the Blues," each about a dozen times. Neither the repertoire, the ensemble style, nor even the solos seem to vary much from place to place. The band that Lars Edegran was with at the Paddock Club was just about the best of them. Between sets he shrugged off my praise and said it was just a gig, but that I should be sure to hear his friend and fellow countryman Orange Kellin, up the street at the Hurricane. I did, and it was worth the visit. Kellin himself is a fine, fluent clarinetist who sounded a lot like Tony Parenti to me; the band was good enough, too—at least it didn't hold him back.

Finally, I ended the evening at Preservation Hall, which has become more or less the official sanctuary for traditional jazz in the city. The title it carries makes it sound a grander spot than it is. The place is on a French Quarter side street, a narrow little ground-floor room through which tourists are shunted at quick-step to squat on the floor and listen to a crew of grizzled old-timers push and grunt their way through a two- or three-tune set (which must necessarily include the ubiquitous "When the Saints Go Marching In"). The eager all-white crowd reacted with wild applause when occasional flashes of competence would pierce the dismal air of mediocrity that smothered the proceedings. But no more of that. Enough. About the music played at Preservation Hall, the less said the better.

The next day, sometime early in the afternoon, I started for Jackson Square, and walking through the Quarter I chanced to meet Lars Edegran and a young lady he introduced as his girl friend. They were standing at the corner of St. Peter and Royal listening to a street gospel trio preaching away at a song:

Ninety-nine-and-a-half won't do!
Lord, I'm prayin' and tryin' to make a hundred
Ninety-nine-and-a-half won't do. . . .

I asked who they were, and Edegran said the woman playing the guitar with the broken strings was Idelle Williams. When I started to ask something more, he said, "Ssshhh. Don't talk too loud. I've got a cassette going." He indicated the wrapped package in his hand from which protruded an amorphous dark shape that had to be a microphone; I would never have guessed.

For some reason, that bothered me a little. I stood around a few moments more, then indicated with gestures I was going on to Jackson Square. Lars Edegran waved me on my way with a quick motion of his free hand and gave me an abstracted smile.

It was easy to find Babe Stovall, even though the park was teeming with Sunday loungers and dotted with sidewalk entertainers of one kind or another. Stovall was right there in the middle of a big crowd, sounding a lot better than he had the day before but still indulging in the same sort of horseplay. He picked the guitar upside down, and then twisted it behind his back to play it. And again those sacred songs he had done before —"Do, Lord, Remember Me," "May the Circle Be Unbroken," and "When the Saints Go Marching In"—but he was in better voice and seemed generally healthier: alert, and none of that troublesome blinking.

Babe Stovall has recorded once. A session for Verve was arranged by local jazz enthusiasts, and an LP of traditional blues and folk material came out of it which bears listening to. It is difficult to praise him, though, for there is so little variety and subtlety to his performances that the best one can call them is spirited. Words are bawled out street-corner style, so that he is seldom, if ever, on pitch.

He is, however, a better guitar player than I had at first thought. I gradually became aware of the good things he was doing as I listened to him that Sunday in Jackson Square picking with some precision through "See, See Rider" and "It Takes a Worried Man," and I later confirmed it listening to his record. Yes, the licks are there, all right. He plays a kind of ragtime style that is highly syncopated and that, on that National guitar of his, gives a real banjo sound to his music.

Later, when I talked with him, I asked him why he played that steel-bodied guitar. They are as rare as can be now, and he must have been tempted many times to sell his and buy one of the standard wooden sort. "Oh, yeah," he told me, "that's right. You can't buy them no more. Why do I like it? That's because it gives me a sound 'twixt a guitar and a banjo." If that is what he is trying for, that is what he is getting, all right.

He kept right on playing through the afternoon, carelessly mixing the sacred songs with the most secular material—from "Jesus Is the Captain" to "Salty Dog." And as he serenaded the crowd around him, two or three white guys, hard cases all, circulated through the audience first asking, then demanding, money. They were out to get as much for Babe Stovall's efforts as they could. They were his bottle gang, drinking buddies who would share the bottles of wine that his concert would buy. Stovall has ten kids.

As the sun slanted down and dusk began to fall, the park custodians called out that they would be closing the gates soon. Babe Stovall began to pack up, and I stepped forward—rather aggressively, I'm afraid—and started to ask him questions.

He told me he was from Tylertown, Mississippi, "way down between McComb and Columbia," and that he had come to New Orleans in 1964.

I asked him how many songs he knew—none of his material seemed to be original—and he said he didn't know how many exactly, but it was a gang of them. "I just pick up anything I hear. If I like it, I learn it and start playin' it."

Was that the way it had been for him here in New Orleans? How many had he learned here? He looked at me kind of funny then, shook his head, and said, "No, I brought all my songs with me from Mississippi. I never learned none of them here in New Orleans. Ain't none of them here to learn."

I hesitated, and Babe Stovall asked, "You done now? My buddies is calling me. They want me to come with them."

IF, AS Babe Stovall says, there were no songs to learn there, how did the blues ever get to New Orleans in the first place? How did Buddy Bolden happen to learn them? Pops Foster answers colorfully, "Most of the guys you heard singing down there [in New Orleans] were guys who came out of the woods somewhere with a guitar playing and singing the blues." Guys, in other words, not much different from Stovall himself, who may have found their way into the city from the surrounding provinces bearing with them the heavy message of the blues. They unburdened themselves on street corners from Storyville to the Irish Channel.

But there were a few who themselves emerged from the alleys and back streets of New Orleans, bluesmen who were among the first to translate the urban experience into twelve-bar terms. The best of them, and the only real first-rank interpreter of the blues to come out of New Orleans, was Lonnie Johnson, of whom I spoke earlier. But I knew there were others, and to find out who they were and something about them I traveled out to the Archive of New Orleans Jazz at Tulane University, and with the help of the Archive director, Richard B. Allen, I managed to learn a little about a couple.

Lemon (born Lemoine) Nash, who died in 1969 without ever having recorded, was born in upcountry Lakeland, Louisiana, in 1898, but he lived in New Orleans from the time he was two months old. In his time he saw a bit of the world—hoboing, working the medicine shows and circuses, and even putting in a wartime stretch in the merchant marine. But what he was, for the most part, was a musician, a singer, a serenader. There were string bands of these so-called serenaders who used to roam the streets, playing the bars and the brothels one by one as they came to them and even holding forth on the street corners if that was where the action was. You had to play a lot of different instruments to be a serenader, and in his time Nash had played guitar, mandolin, ukelele, and even a little banjo. But he liked ukelele best, believe it or not, and from all reports he was about as skilled as one could be on the instrument. Was Lemon Nash a bluesman? Well, he knew a lot of blues, and by definition would probably have qualified as a songster, but he must have thought of himself chiefly as a performer. What he did with his material was terribly important to him. He knew medicine show routines, vaudeville routines, and lines of patter that he stuck between all the songs he did. It was show business of the neighborhood, down-home sort. All Lemon knew was that his audience sure did dig those blues, so that was what he played.

Richard "Rabbit" Brown was an altogether different sort. Allen played for me one of the two records he had made and showed me an early article by Abbe Niles from a 1928 issue of *The Bookman,* which contained a review of the record and some additional information on the artist. It was, Allen said, just about the first *serious* attention ever given to a bluesman in a national magazine. Niles told in the article how Rabbit Brown, when not out singing on the street corners, would hire himself as a kind of New Orleans singing gondolier, offering a rowboat ride into Lake Ponchartrain for a fee, during which he would haul out his guitar and give his passenger a short blues concert.

Lemon Nash had little use for Rabbit Brown. The two came from the same neighborhood, a particularly tough part of town known as the Battleground (Louis Armstrong grew up there, too). Nash had played with him a couple of times and claims that Brown knew only three chords on the guitar. According to Nash, Rabbit "would just hit the guitar and yell. He was what you call a clown man." But "clown man" or no, Rabbit Brown used to sing the blues, and on that recording session he had in 1927, just ten years before his death, he did the "James Alley Blues," a song about his street in the Battleground. It begins,

Times ain't now, nothing like they used to be,
   (twice)
And I'm telling you all the truth, oh, take it from me.

And if he could sing that then about New Orleans, he would shout it at the top of his voice if he were to see the old town today.

CHAPTER SIX

"T FOR TEXAS"

Huddie Ledbetter was the first bluesman of note to show up in Texas, and he came there from Louisiana in 1909. This is not to say he brought the blues with him. The music was already there, existing in a sort of state of potential, because, after all, the blacks who worked the cotton fields of east Texas were essentially the same blacks who picked cotton and corn in the Mississippi Delta and jived all night long in the juke joints; and they were ethnically the same as those who were at that moment creating a new kind of music in New Orleans that would later come to be known as jazz. The same music was there in east Texas, too, in the form of ballads, breakdowns, and early barrelhouse music, all of which were popular even then in the region. The blues was taking shape about this time in this westernmost sector of the old South, and it was following the same, if slightly retarded, pattern of development. It grew out of local circumstances. For some reason, the music of the Texas jails and chain gangs—such songs as "Ain't No More Cane on This Brazos," "Another Man Done Gone," and "The Midnight Special," for example—were especially rich and were certainly the kind of music that deepened and helped extend the blues tradition in Texas.

Huddie Ledbetter himself is credited by some with "The Midnight Special." It may well be that Leadbelly wrote the song, too, for he served time twice in Texas, on the first occasion for assault on a woman said to be a prostitute, and on the second for murder. He had always been a violent man, quick to anger and eager to punish, and there seems no doubt that he killed a man in the Texas town of New Boston during a quarrel. He was sentenced to thirty-five years and wound up at Sugar Land, a work camp outside Houston that was located alongside tracks of the Southern Pacific Railroad. There was a superstition among the Sugar Land inmates that if the light of the Midnight Special, the fast train to Houston, were to shine its light on an inmate, he could expect to be released in a short time. This is the sense of the song's plea, then, that the Midnight Special should shine its "ever-lovin' light on me." If Leadbelly didn't write it, he certainly sang it often, and he may even have included it in his program at that most famous concert of his, the one before the governor of Texas, Patrick Morris Neff, in 1924, during which he sang his way to a pardon. The Governor was so impressed with Leadbelly's sincerity and his progress in rehabilitation that he declared him sufficiently punished for the offense committed and set him free in January, 1925.

Within a short time, he was back in Mooringsport, Louisiana, near Shreveport, where he came from, and within three years he was up before a judge again for murder. Again it was in a brawl, and again there seems little doubt that Huddie Ledbetter actually committed homicide; the only real question was whether he had or had not started the fight. He was given a sentence of from six to ten years at hard labor at the Angola, Louisiana, prison farm. In 1933, when Leadbelly had been there five years, two men—John Lomax and his teen-age son, Alan—showed up with permission to record songs by the inmates for the Library of Congress. Not many could or would record for them, but Leadbelly, of course, was eager to perform from the moment he heard about their project. He saw a chance to repeat his previous feat of singing his way to a pardon. And that, in effect, is what he did. For he not only impressed the Lomaxes with his songs, he also laid down a steady barrage of entreaties, pleading that they do what they could to help him get out. In fact, they did just that. John

Lomax interceded in his behalf with Governor O. K. Allen of Louisiana, and Huddie Ledbetter was granted a commutation of sentence in 1934.

In effect, Leadbelly was paroled in the custody of Lomax, for he was taken north to Washington, D.C., by him, and then to New York. There he was unveiled to the public, presented at cocktail parties, brought around to play at a few colleges and universities, and finally recorded. He became a kind of trained bear for the Lomaxes, performing in convict stripes before their friends, running through his routine on command. Just how original some of his material may have been is, as I suggested earlier, open to doubt. Although he claimed to have written a good many songs, including one or two that he almost certainly did *not* write ("See, See Rider" and "Black Snake Moan") and a few others that are doubtful ("Goodnight Irene" and "Midnight Special"), there are some, nearly as good ("Mister Tom Hughes Town," for one), that Leadbelly very probably did write, for they tally with what we know of his personal experience. Paul Oliver indicates he was not an original bluesman and says flatly, "Leadbelly was a songster, and he had the songster's pride in the breadth of his repertoire."

He wasn't much of a musician, either. We have this on testimony from bassist Pops Foster, who recorded with him a number of times. "Willie [the Lion Smith] and I used to play with Leadbelly. I think we were the only two guys who could play with him. Leadbelly didn't know which key he was going to play in. He'd play in all naturals and sharps. We'd have to listen to him, then search around to find the key. Then when we found it, we'd take off. . . . When Leadbelly would get mad, he'd just sit and grit his teeth. One time I told him he'd have to play a chord up on his guitar or we couldn't make no record. He just set and started gritting his teeth. I told him he could grit his teeth all day, but if he didn't play the chord, we couldn't play with him. He finally played it."

What sort of singer was he? One whose virtues and limitations seemed to match those of the whole man almost perfectly. He had an enormously powerful voice, one to go with his immense physical strength. Yet there was no subtlety to it, just a kind of direct bellow that seemed an expression of the rage he carried with him always. He seemed to exercise as little control in phrasing and modulation over that voice as he did in keeping his physical strength in check when he lost his temper.

If his claims as a songwriter are open to dispute, if he lacked even rudimentary skill as a musician, and hadn't much to offer as a singer, then why is Huddie Ledbetter such an important figure in American music? What claim has he on our attention? He was the first backwoods black music maker to gain national prominence. Before Leadbelly, blacks who gained the attention of whites with their music were all professional enough to at least put a show-business shine on their presentation; they were sophisticated enough to choose material they thought might please this different audience. But not Leadbelly. He went at it like the country man he was, shouting out the songs just as he had on Shreveport's rough Fannin Street, hollering the blues in the same rough tones he had used on Dallas street corners. His introduction to the white intellectual community of the thirties by the Lomaxes marked the beginning of widespread serious interest in the black ethnic underpinnings of American music. He gave white intellectuals their first shot of the real hard stuff.

During the years Leadbelly was on the loose in Texas, he played and sang through the streets of Dallas with a bluesman ten years his junior named Lemon Jefferson, a better bluesman in nearly every way. Jefferson was born blind in 1897 near Wortham, Texas—hence, *Blind* Lemon Jefferson, as this widely-traveled singer came to be known all through the South. He made it one of the most famous names in the blues, working through that tough street-corner apprenticeship and going north to Chicago with a recording contract in 1925. There he became the most prolific of all early blues recording artists. Before he died in 1929, he had recorded seventy-nine pieces for the Paramount label and two for OKeh. He even managed to make some money at it, but except for a car he bought and a chauffeur he kept on salary during the last years of his life, he squandered nearly all of it on liquor and women.

And liquor and women were what he sang about in so many of his blues. A lot of the blues he recorded were not especially original—a tune borrowed, lines cribbed here and there—and many of them were derived from that rich repertoire of Texas prison songs, though Blind Lemon had never done time as

Leadbelly had. But the best of them clearly came from his own experience. If you've ever wondered, for example, what a blind street singer feels out there on the corner all day, it's right here in his "Tin Cup Blues":

I was down and I cried, my suitcase was down the line (twice)
Ain't it tough to see a man go to wreck and almost fall and die

I stood on the corner and almost bust my head (twice)
I couldn't earn enough money to buy me a loaf of bread

Baby, times is so hard I almost call it tough (twice)
I can't earn money to buy no bread and you know I can't buy my snuff

My gal's a house maid and she earns a dollar a week (twice)
I'm so hungry on payday I can't hardly speak

Now gather 'round me people and let me tell you a true fact (twice)
That tough luck has sunk me and the rats is getting in my hat.

The very specific details of that song ("My gal's a house maid and she earns a dollar a week" and "the rats is getting in my hat") are the source of its real power. This is so with so many of Blind Lemon Jefferson's songs that it may seem somewhat ironic that his most famous blues, "Black Snake Moan," is noted for its sexual symbolism. The moan is precisely that—a kind of extended groan with which he begins the first lines of every chorus. But the black snake of the title seems rather more Freudian than real.

Ummmmh oh ain't got no mama now (twice)
She told me last night you don't need no mama no how

Mmmmmm mmmm black snake crawling in my room (twice)
And some pretty mama had better come and get this black snake soon

Ummmmuh that must have been a bed bug baby, a
chinch can't bite that hard (twice)
Asked my baby for fifty cent she said, Lemon, ain't a
dime in the yard

Mmmmama that's all right, mama that's all right for
you (twice)
Say baby, that's all right most any old way you do

Mmmmmm mmmm honey, what's the matter now?
(twice)
Tell me what's the matter, baby. Don't like no black
snake no how
Mmmmmmm mmmm wonder where is my black
snake gone (twice)
Black snake, mama, done run my darling home.

But a transcription of the text does no justice to it, for "Black Snake Moan" is, after all, a song. What cannot be conveyed on paper is the eloquence of Blind Lemon Jefferson's strong but surprisingly light voice and the deft figures that he interpolates on his guitar. His was one of the great primitive talents in the blues, but only by searching out and listening to his recordings, many of which are still available in reissue, can you begin to realize just how great that talent was.

Recording was his life. All that was best in him is on those eighty-one sides he cut. In fact, he died just after his last recording session in Chicago in the dead of winter. He left the studio intending to go to a party. He was to be picked up by his car, but somehow the driver just didn't show up, and so Lemon started out into the snow, convinced that he could make it alone. He didn't. They found him the next morning frozen to death in the gutter. Paramount Records shipped his body home, and Blind Lemon Jefferson was buried under the warm Texas sun.

Another bluesman of note who emerged from Texas in the twenties was Alger "Texas" Alexander. He is about the only male blues singer of note, except for the modern pop blues phenomenon Bobby Bland, who played no instrument. That being the case, he owes at least some of his early success to his accompanist, who was none other than Lonnie Johnson. When the great New Orleans guitarist set off on his rambles just after World War I, Dallas was his first stop. Johnson hooked up with

Alexander there and helped him give a little polish to a style that remained pretty rough throughout his career. And when Lonnie Johnson traveled north and started to record, Texas Alexander followed him up and began a modest recording career of his own for the OKeh label.

A Dallas piano player named Alex Moore, who was born in 1899 and is still alive today, gained some reputation around town as a soloist and accompanist. The shrill whistling that he did when playing solo earned him the nickname "Whistlin'" Alex Moore, and it was under it that he did all his recording—not much—during the twenties and thirties. He was recently rediscovered and recorded, however, on the Arhoolie label.

Alex Moore is worthy of note as one of the few surviving members of a whole school of piano playing that had quite an influence both on jazz and the blues. The Texas "barrelhouse" piano style was an intricate blend of blues and ragtime delivered with a strong left hand, which anticipated boogie-woogie by about a decade. Among those remembered as barrelhouse men are Robert Shaw, who has also been recorded by Arhoolie, Frank Ridge, and R. L. McNeer. Pete Johnson, a traveling Kansas City pianist, is the direct link between these Texas players and exponents of the boogie-woogie style that he himself helped perfect.

Most of these musicians and singers seem to have been located in or near Dallas, but in Texas today Houston is the big blues town. Musicians and singers break in there every year, but one of the top performers among those who stay on permanently is Eddie "Cleanhead" Vinson, the blues-singing alto-saxist whom I used to listen to out on the South Side of Chicago. He has set the level of competition there in town, uncomfortably high for many of the country boys coming off the farms in east Texas hoping to find fame and fortune with their guitars. Vinson, who was not only a good singer but also a competent soloist by big band jazz standards (he spent years with trumpeter Cootie Williams' orchestra), could certainly work outside Houston again if he chose to, but he has decided he likes it where he is.

Sam "Lightning" Hopkins was for years the real boss in Houston, though. It was probably because of his continued presence there that it became the blues town it is. Samuel

Charters calls him the last of the old country bluesmen, and that seems about right, for although he has had a world of experience, Lightning remains as rough and unsophisticated in his style as when he first began. He has the old country intensity in his voice: While it may at first sound casual, there are subtle tensions in it and tricks with dynamics that would be remarkable in a singer of any sort. The total effect is a style that is personal and confidential, a tone that is almost insinuating in quality.

As a writer of blues, he produces work that is extremely spotty. He can come up with good lines and occasionally a whole song—"Black and Evil" is, in its rough way, very powerful—but too often he falls back on the old traditional lines and verses that seldom follow in logical sequence. He has recorded something like 600 times; no bluesman has that much original material in him—or not Lightning Hopkins, at any rate. His musicianship is also rather slapdash. He plays a little piano—*very* little, as the old joke goes—but guitar is his instrument. And characteristically, we see in his playing style the triumph of the instinctive musician over the unskilled instrumentalist. For his choruses are sometimes of uneven length, and in improvising he gets into such weird harmonies that one can only conclude he has hit a wrong note or two and is trying to work his way out of it as best he can. But working on familiar material, he can play licks and get effects that would be the envy of much better guitarists. The resonant, dramatic single-string style that he uses is actually beyond him technically, but he pulls it off somehow and gives the general impression that he is a much better guitarist than he really is.

Perhaps he has always had his troubles with the guitar. Samuel Charters tells a story in *The Country Blues* about the time Lightning drove with his father from his hometown of Centerville, Texas (he was born there in 1912), to nearby Buffalo for a picnic. Although just a boy, Lightning had his guitar with him, and so he headed quite naturally for the musician who was holding forth before a good-sized crowd; he was a fat blind man who turned out to be Blind Lemon Jefferson. Never one to hang back, Lightning came up behind him and began to pick along, annoying Lemon greatly, who assumed someone was moving in on his territory. Lemon shouted out critically, "Boy, you got to play it right." Young Lightning said something back, and Lemon realized he was just a boy and let him stay and play.

Lightning Hopkins' first professional experience came a few years later, during the thirties, with another established blues singer, Texas Alexander, who happened to be his cousin. Alexander had established himself by then, gone North and recorded, and come back to Texas; he was a little down on his luck by the time the two got together. As Lightning tells it, Alexander was so desperate for an accompanist (remember, he played no instrument) that he used to carry a guitar in a case around with him on the off-chance that he might meet up with someone who could play it for him. Lightning, of course, turned out to be that someone. They began traveling together and even made it to Houston. But this was the Depression era, and times were especially tough in the Southwest. Lightning decided to return to the farm.

He didn't try Houston again until just after the war, and this time it went fairly well for him. He hooked up temporarily with a barrelhouse piano man named "Thunder" Smith, and the two caught the attention of a scout from Aladdin, a West Coast label, now defunct. The two recorded as a duo, and that was when Sam Hopkins became Lightning (Thunder Smith and Lightning Hopkins), the name under which he has recorded ever since. As I indicated earlier, he has recorded a phenomenal number of sides, many of them for small blues labels such as Gold Star in Houston, TNT in Harlem, and Ace in New York.

Lately, however, he has been most active playing dates for the blues collector labels, such as Arhoolie. The finest introduction to this unusual singer, who is indeed sort of a survivor from an earlier era, is avilable on Poppy Records. The two-record album was produced by Arhoolie's Chris Strachwitz, and it offers Lightning at his relaxed best. He frequently plays concerts at colleges and universities, too, and sometimes dismays his audiences by being as irascible, cantankerous, and downright mean onstage as he is known to be off.

THE SONGSTER TRADITION has also been very strong in Texas— perhaps partly because a good many Texas bluesmen were secret songsters. A lot of what they claimed as original material was actually borrowed or adapted. But why not? No great store was put on private property among bluesmen, copyrights were virtually unknown, and singers were expected to know a lot of songs. At least one well-known Texas singer—Henry "Rambling" Thomas—laid no claims to originality. He was a songster with a vast repertoire, and he recorded only a bare fraction of it on the Vocalion label when he went north to Chicago in the twenties.

Mance Lipscomb is the leading representative of the Texas songster tradition today. He knows and sings many blues, but he is also fond of ballads, sacred songs, and even old popular songs from his youth. He is a walking mountain of folklore material and has been interviewed, pumped, and taken through his repertoire so often that it is remarkable that he remains so easygoing and cheerful when questions are put to him. Once he was asked how many songs he actually knew, and Mance replied, giving a very specific number in the hundreds, then explained: "That's how many Paul Oliver said I know." Mance's implication was that the English blues historian would know more about that than an old sharecropper from Navasota, Texas.

That's where he is from, a little town in the southeastern part of the state, seventy-two miles north of Houston and 200 miles south of Dallas. Born in 1895, he farmed around Navasota for most of his life, worked hard, and gained a reputation for steadiness and reliability that he is proud of today. "Ain't paid a fine in my life," he will tell you. "The first thing you hear in Navasota is that Mance don't drink. I take a little sniff of it now and again, but I don't get drunk." He was a sharecropper, and as hard as it is to survive under that damnable system, Mance Lipscomb actually prospered most years by working harder than anyone else; he is proud of that. In 1956, at the age of sixty, he suffered an accident that brought him a modest insurance settlement. And because his legs had been troubling him with varicose veins, he decided simply to retire. He took his settlement, bought a small piece of land, and built a two-room house on it.

That might be all there is to tell about him if it were not for his music. He came by it naturally, growing up a member of a big musical family (there were eleven children). His father was an old country fiddler who used to play at breakdowns and taught Mance how to play, too. Then, some years after he quit fiddling, "I took up the guitar," he remembers. "That was along about 1918, when everybody started getting guitars. They were getting these old pine guitars back then."

It was about that time, too—he places it at about 1917, although he is not entirely reliable on dates—that he encountered Blind Lemon Jefferson on the streets of Dallas. Until he was well into his sixties, that was the farthest he had ever traveled from home. He was there to pick cotton, and he remembers coming into Dallas on a Saturday and hearing a blind man on a corner playing something powerful. Was that the first blues he heard? "Oh, well, you know the blues was around a long time before that. People been playing blues or something like it from pretty far back."

Once Mance took up the guitar he began playing country dances and picnics, picking up songs everywhere. He had soon committed to memory just about everything anyone in town knew. "Then I learned songs off records, too," he adds. "You know that old Bessie Smith song?"—he half hums, half sings a little of it ("This house is so haunted, I can't move"; it is "Haunted House Blues")—"I learned that song off the Victrola. I used to lay down in the cotton patch and listen to Bessie Smith on records." And did he learn any songs from singers who traveled through Navasota? "Oh, yes, some. There was this fella Blind Willie Johnson. He was a songster, but not much of a guitar player until I tuned his guitar for him. I remember I learned 'Motherless Children' and 'God Moves on the Water' off of him when I tuned his guitar." He sums up: "Oh, I just learned my songs from all over."

Well, wherever he learned them, and no matter how many he knows, Mance Lipscomb certainly sings his songs well. There is nothing flashy—or even, in the usual way, very professional —about his presentation. He simply sits down in front of the microphone, wearing his hat, as he always seems to do, and plays his guitar and sings in a kind of reedy, high baritone. Nothing extraordinary about that at all, until you begin to notice that he really is getting around the guitar awfully well for such an old man, and there is something in his voice, a kind of sober dignity, that seems altogether distinctive and has the effect of elevating some of the rather ordinary popular song material that he includes in nearly every set he sings. When, for instance, I listened to him launch into "You Are My Sunshine" one afternoon before a Midwest college audience, I heard a few sounds of annoyance around me. "Come *on!*" somebody groaned out loud. Mance followed that up with "I Ain't Got Nobody" and "Alabama Jubilee," and just when he seemed to have his young blues audience pushed to the point of exasperation with this little Hit Parade medley, he cut loose with some of the good stuff: "Can't Do Nothing for Me," "Baby, Please Don't Go," "Truckin'," "See, See Rider," "T for Texas," "You'll Be Sorry That You Done Me Wrong." But then came a rendition of that hoary superauthentic folk blues, "Shine on, Harvest Moon." Well, that really upset the audience; a few got up and left, and those who stayed began shifting noisily in their seats. A shame, really, for those who walked out missed the really first-class work he did on "Motherless Children" (complete with bottle-neck guitar effects) and "When the Saints Go Marching In."

Such a set is typical of Mance and characteristic of the entire songster tradition. You never know quite what you are going to hear when a songster sits down to strum. Nevertheless, those who can appreciate the range of musical interest and enthusiasm that goes into such a performance are themselves a long way toward understanding how the many loose ends in our music may be tied into some sort of comprehensive knot.

I had made a date to talk with Mance following his set. It was easy to arrange. He was eminently approachable. In fact, I had almost bumped into him coming through a door, recognized him instantly, and put out my hand to shake. "Howdy doo," he said to me. "Mance Lipscomb's the name." Just like that. When I asked about talking with him afterward, he nodded vigorously and said, "Oh, sure. I'm getting rid of my bad habits as I grow older, but interviews—that's a good habit to get into." He was openly pleased by this sort of attention.

Something struck me in that first moment of meeting with Mance, and it stayed with me as I listened to him up on the stage and later settled down to talk with him. It is worth mentioning only because it made me feel somewhat more personally close toward him: He reminds me of my grandfather, whose name, should it matter, was Elmer Moon and who was also a farmer or a farm laborer nearly all his life. There is a distinct physical resemblance between the two and also a similarity in their personalities: a kind of upright, hard-necked quality that comes, I think, from a certain feeling of self-satisfaction in a life spent at hard physical labor. That old phrase from a country and western song says it: "Pride in what I am."

"You can't just pick up a song and talk it," he told me when I asked him about what he had been singing a little while before. "You got to think how it was when it was written, got to think what it means. Yes, I make up my own songs, too. I read people's appearance and fix my mind on them, and then I make up the words to fit." Some, he indicated, were verses and stanzas added to the songs he regularly sang, but others are his alone. " 'What You Gonna Do When Death Comes Creepin' at Your Room'—that's mine. I sold that song for $500."

I asked about the sort of playing and singing he did around Navasota before he began recording and going around the country to play at colleges and universities. He shrugged deprecatingly as if to indicate that it didn't amount to much and said it was "Saturday night parties mostly." But then he went on to describe them: "They were something, though. People had a lot of fun at them. You could buy yourself some lemonade and dance and tromp all night. I played parties and breakdowns where they'd kill a hog and serve it up with beans and people would dance all night. They had a custom then, you paid five cents to dance with a partner. If you was a good dancer you'd fill up a handkerchief with nickels. And even fifty cents would buy a lot in those days.

"That's how Arhoolie found me, from those old dances I used to play. It was a surprise. Mack McCormick and Chris Strachwitz, they didn't know who they was lookin' for when they set out from Houston, but they was lookin' for anyone who could sing and play music. They got my reputation around Navasota and quite naturally they came to me. They recorded me the same night. That was the number one time I recorded."

Was he surprised when they showed up so unexpectedly? "Oh, you bet I was. I didn't like it. I came in one evening, and they made themselves known by their truck in my yard. I didn't know what these two men on my porch were up to. They ask me, 'Can I play?' And I say, 'A little bit.' And then they asked would I play a little for them now, and I said I would if they'd let me go in there and clean up, take the grease off me. I said, 'You're blockin' the way. I can't get aroun' y'all.' So I came out on the porch with my guitar, and I played the worst one I could think of just to get rid of them. And then they said to me, 'Play us one of those old blues like you play in the country.' And so I did, and they carried on like they liked it a real lot. They said they'd be back in an hour or two, and then they left.

"Now, what they did was go after the recording equipment, only I didn't know. I thought they were trying to run a trick on me. So I think to myself, 'I can whip that little one, and maybe I can knock the big one down with a chair.' But when they got back, they had all this equipment, so I guessed that they was all right. I sat down and played about an hour for them, and they took the best of that and gave me fifty dollars for my work. That was more money than I ever got. But my wife, she was still suspicious. She thought maybe there was something wrong about making money that easy. She lay across the bed chewing me out, saying she was sorry she ever married a guitar-picker. Then I got a long letter from Chris with $300 in it telling me to come on out to Berkeley and record some more. She changed her mind after that."

Mance Lipscomb's circumstances have changed quite a lot since then. For a man who had never gone farther from his home than Dallas, 200 miles away, he has adapted remarkably well to a life that calls for him to travel great distances across the country, often on a rather tight schedule. But he is obviously enjoying himself. "That's what I've been doing ever since that first time, just traveling and recording, and going to play for people at shows like this. Two weeks out of the month I'm out, it seems like. My wife never has gone anyplace with me. I think she's afraid to travel, but I kind of like it myself. I like to get with people and let them know what I'm doing, then we can communicate. You've got to combine yourself with people some kind of way."

He now owns a six-room house in Navasota, where he lives with his wife and one of his grandchildren. Apparently referring to the white people in that Texas farm town, Mance remarks wryly, "It's funny. They didn't know me in my own hometown for sixty or seventy years, until the publicity started. Now they all do."

Traveling around, playing at festivals and colleges, Mance has met a lot of songsters and bluesmen, and has become well known himself. He cheerfully gives estimates of any and all. Of Sam Hopkins, who now lives about a hundred and fifty miles away, in Centerville, he says, with a shake of his head, "I can't get along with Lightning. Very few people can. You have to handle him like a soft-boiled egg. And that Howlin' Wolf, he's another one. He's got that mean look. He talks mean, too."

But the one he likes to talk about most is Mississippi John Hurt, the great old songster who died in 1966. "I met him at Newport in 1965. Everybody was saying to me, 'You ought to hear that John Hurt. He sounds a lot like you.' He came on right after I left the stage, so I walked right around and leaned up against a tree and listened to him. He played 'Candy Man'—you ask me, that's one of his best songs, that and 'Stagolee'—and ooooh, he sounded good. We were big friends from then on, him and me. He was about my biggest fan. Course, he died a couple of years ago."

Mance got to talking again about all the traveling he had done in the past few years, and I remember suggesting he must be the most widely traveled seventy-six-year-old man in the state of Texas. He allowed that that might be so, and then went on to say something that summed up his last ten years rather eloquently. "Yes," he said, "here I was an old farmer with his head down, given up on things, and these people come along and gave me a whole new life with my music."

CHAPTER SEVEN

"T FOR TENNESSEE"

HERE'S FURRY. A little man nestled on top of his bed and hunched over his guitar. He spends a lot of time on that bed, which, oddly enough, is stuck up against the wall next to the front door of his house on Mosby Street in Memphis. He keeps his bed in the living room because he finds it a little hard to get around now. He lost a leg in a railway accident over fify years ago. It didn't bother him too much for most of his life—in fact, he got around on his artificial leg well enough to work as a street cleaner for the city for forty-four years. But now he's seventy-eight, and he spends most of the day with the leg off, hopping around the room when he has to, and waving the stump about without embarrassment.

Furry Lewis is whipping that old guitar of his, not artfully perhaps, but very enthusiastically. Sitting on the bed, he can reach over and open the door for the visitors that stream in to listen. Every morning there is a little party at Furry's house that may last into afternoon, depending on whether or not somebody has brought a bottle along. Today somebody has.

"Don't forget to put in your book that this is the first time old Furry ever see whiskey," he says as he gulps down another slug.

"Don't forget to put in he can lie, too!" hoots one of his guests.

He is a mailman, as are a couple of others there that day. For some reason Furry's house is a gathering place for the men in gray in that section of town. I get the idea that they rush through their routes and then go over to Furry's to hide out. A couple of ladies are there, too. Modishly dressed and self-possessed. They laugh a lot at Furry and seem to regard him with indulgence.

Furry delivers a rather broad wink and says for their benefit, "A lady asked me two weeks ago, she say to me, 'As long as you been around, Furry, you never took a wife. How come?' And I say to her, 'What do I need with a wife as long as the man next door got one?' " He gives a great cackle at that, and the mailmen take it up.

And in between he sings. Blues mostly. Something he calls "Furry's Blues"—the idea being that he has a woman for every day in the week, a recitation of what he does with his Monday woman, and his Tuesday woman, and so on. It's one those bold, bragging songs that a Muddy Waters or a Howlin' Wolf might be able to pull off but not little Furry Lewis. Somehow he seems to know this, too, and he tries to distract our attention by playing little tricks with his guitar, elbowing his fretboard—"I'm just a crazy man," he calls out to nobody in particular—and beating on the body of his guitar as if it were a tom-tom. This goes over pretty well with the crowd in Furry's living room. They laugh, nod, do everything but applaud. And Furry cackles again, delighted with himself. He is the consummate entertainer; he lives for an audience.

"I'm gonna pick you some blues again," he announces, and he begins to tune up. He has a little trick with this. Like most guitarists, he has a little tune-up tune; his is "Taps." And then, just so he can be sure that we appreciate what he was up to, he picks "Reveille" for us very carefully. "Okay now, here we go. Here's a blues that I wrote."

Well, there's one kind favor I ask of you,
One kind favor I ask of you,
Lord, there's one kind favor I ask of you,
Please see that my grave is kept clean.

Lord, it's two white horses in a line,
It's two white horses in a line,

Lord, it's two white horses in a line
To take me to the burial ground.

Oh, dig my grave with a silver spade,
Dig my grave with a silver spade,
Yes, dig my grave with a silver spade.
Just let me down with a golden chain.

It is a good song—haunting and ominous in its overtones, dark and tragic in outlook—but it is Blind Lemon Jefferson's song and not Furry Lewis'. He seemed willing to claim just about anything he played or sang that day. He went on to do "Brownsville Blues," which has been credited to Willie Newbern but is more likely the work of Sleepy John Estes—and is not, in any case, that of Furry Lewis, as he claimed it to be.

I doubt if his audience there that morning—which by then had become afternoon—really cared if Furry had written any of the blues he played. They were there to enjoy themselves, relaxing in the parlor of the neighborhood's most colorful character. Nobody expects too much of him in the way of variety, and that's just as well, too, for old Furry only has one performance in him. He plays and sings the same songs whenever he squats down on that bed. His audiences come and go, but Furry just keeps singing the old songs that he learned a generation or more ago.

He no longer even sings them very well. He recorded back in the twenties, and held onto a good reputation then for years. People in Memphis tell me that he could sit down and do a pretty good set of blues until not so very long ago. But age seems to have caught up with him; years of jiving and shucking have taken their toll. Furry still goes out to play now and again. He was invited down to Preservation Hall in New Orleans for a session recently. He has even gone on tour with a rock road show, the Alabama State Troupers, that features him right up there with Don Nix, Jeanie Greene, and Brenda Patterson. His audiences are seldom disappointed, for he puts on a pretty good show. It's just that he can't play or sing much any more.

Still, he has been a part of the musical history of this very musical city for more years than many better bluesmen have lived. Born in Greenwood, Mississippi, in 1893, Walter "Furry" Lewis came up to Memphis with his family in 1899. He was hardly grown, he says, before he took up the guitar and started playing with various bands around town. "I played with W. C. Handy and Will Shade and the Memphis Jug Band, too. Handy gave me a guitar, I remember. It was the best guitar I ever had, too." When was that? He frowns and shakes his head. "That's kinda hard to answer," he says. "I don't remember as good as I used to. If Will Shade was still around you could ask him. He's dead two years now, though.

"No, I don't know any of the old-time musicians today but Gus Cannon. He still plays banjo some, but he won't go out in public, and he won't talk to anybody, either. Oh, he's *old,* older than I am, probably ninety or something. But him and me, we used to play a lot together, you know. We played those doctor shows, medicine shows *you* call them. We traveled through Arkansas, Louisiana, Mississippi, all over. Sure, we was selling Jackrabbit Syrup and Corn Salve."

THAT WAS the Dr. Willie Lewis Show. At one time or another most of the top Memphis bluesmen and street singers worked the medicine shows. Among them were Jim Jackson, oldest of them all; Robert Wilkins, who subsequently became a preacher in Memphis and gave up blues singing altogether; and Gus Cannon and Will Shade. The idea was that the medicine show used the bluesmen to gather a crowd at the little crossroads in the rural South where patent medicine pitchmen like Dr. Lewis would step up while the music was still ringing in the air and sing the praises of Jackrabbit Syrup or some similar preparation that was guaranteed to cure just about everything from snakebite to acne.

That was what the bluesmen did for fun. Furry and the others considered life out on the road with the medicine shows a kind of paid vacation from the rigors of town life. Town was Memphis, and Memphis was Beale Street, and there wasn't a tougher, more swinging and wide-open street in any city in the country during the first two and a half decades of the twentieth century. Beale Street grew up around an Italian-American saloon keeper and gambler who went by the name of Pee Wee. He came to Memphis in the 1880s, gravitated to the black gambling action in town, and won consistently and heavily enough so that he was soon able to buy into a saloon. He showed he had just the sort of dubious talents it took to run a honky-tonk, and it wasn't long before he had one of his own—Pee Wee's—going full blast on Beale. His place set the tone and the pace for the entire street. The tone? Anything goes. The pace? Fast and ragged, to a heavy blues beat. Pee Wee liked the music. He knew it was good for business; it brought the crowds in to drink and gamble. The better the bands, the bigger the crowds—it was as simple as that—and so there was a lot of competition among saloon keepers up and down the street to bring in the swingingest jug bands and the howlingest bluesmen. And that was how Beale Street happened to become America's Main Street of the blues.

Walk down it today, and you will be disappointed. Urban renewal has swept away all but a block or two. And on what is left, all you will see are pawnshops and cut-rate clothing stores. Most of the blacks have moved out from that section of downtown Memphis—Furry Lewis himself lived at Beale and Fourth until a few years ago, but decided to go because there was nothing doing on Beale Street any more. But in its day it teemed with life and echoed with song. It was a good-time district, noted particularly throughout the South for its good-time women. Their praises were sung up and down the river in tones of good-natured lust:

I'm gonna stay around this town
Where the gals won't allow me to walk around
  Ain't Nobody's business but mine
I'm gonna stay in Memphis, Tennessee
Where the gals in Memphis take a liking to me
  Now ain't nobody's business but my own

And wherever there are women there are bound to be plenty of blues. Out on one corner of Beale Street you might hear that blind man W. C. Handy wrote about moaning "See, See Rider," "Careless Love," "Joe Turner Blues," and most of the other old standard folk blues. On the other corner, competing with him lustily, you might hear a couple of country boys from some-

And down the street, in Pee Wee's, you might catch the Memphis Jug Band, which made quite a name for itself locally and then went on to gain national recognition recording for Victor. Will Shade, the leader of the group, was himself practically a one-man band, playing guitar, harmonica, jug, or tub bass when the occasion demanded. Mostly he sang, however, for there were always good stringmen in the group to back him up —and he specialized in little blues duets with his wife, Jennie Mae Bofors.

The Memphis Jug Band was the first of all the Beale Street string bands, and it stayed together in one shape or another until well into the thirties. But just as good was Cannon's Jug Stompers. Led by Gus Cannon, who went by the nickname of "Banjo Joe," the Jug Stompers was a trio composed of Cannon, a harmonica player named Noah Lewis, and a guitarist named Ashley Thompson. The three got together in the outlying rural area, and played country dances and picnics for a couple of years before they tried out on Beale Street. They went over big in Memphis, however, and Gus Cannon, one of the few bluesmen to play banjo, has lived there ever since.

There were other jug bands working up and down Beale at this time. Note, too, that they were *jug* bands—that is, they all honored the local preference for a bass line supplied by puffing into an empty gallon jug. It made an explosive tubalike sound that was especially effective against the strings. If, with a nod to the hype-artists at Stax Records, there really is such a thing as the "Memphis Sound," then it originated with the rhythmic rumbles that issued forth from those Beale Street jugs.

One solo performer who deserves special mention is Minnie Douglas. She was married for a while to bluesman Joe McCoy and was remembered by some (including Big Bill Broonzy) as Minnie McCoy, but she was known to the world at large as "Memphis Minnie," the name under which she recorded a number of fine blues. She was not a native of the city but was born farther south, in Algiers, Louisiana, on June 24, 1900, and grew up in a little town in Mississippi just over the line from Memphis. She early became such an accomplished performer on guitar that by the time she was fifteen she was singing on the streets of the city. She worked in and out of the saloons and up and down Beale Street, just as her brother blues singers did. In fact, she was still singing the streets when a scout for Columbia heard her, signed her up, and brought her north to Chicago to record. That was where Big Bill Broonzy met up with her and had the famous 1933 blues contest that he described in *Big Bill Blues*. What happened? He lost! When she got the joint rocking with "Me and My Chauffeur" and "Looking the World Over," Bill declares, he just didn't stand a chance with the audience or the judges (who were, incidentally, Tampa Red, Sleepy John Estes, and Richard Jones). His considered opinion: "Memphis Minnie can make a guitar cry, moan, talk, and whistle the blues." Coming from Broonzy, who was a fair guitarist himself, that's quite a tribute.

W. C. HANDY WAS once closely associated with Memphis, Beale Street, and the beginnings of the blues—far *too* closely to suit most blues historians and critics. They have been justifiably annoyed at the way he was billed as "the father of the blues." Handy, of course, was not the music's father; the most that can be said for him is that he was its rich uncle. But having been denied paternity, he has virtually been made into a nonperson: His name barely appears in the blues histories; he and the important part he played in popularizing the music have been all but ignored. Since he has lately been neglected somewhat, let us look at what he did and did not do and decide for ourselves just what sort of recognition he deserves—perhaps none at all, perhaps a little more than he has lately been allowed.

He was born into a fairly prosperous, landowning Negro family in Florence, Alabama, in 1873. He grew up there, constantly urged upward by his father, always admonished to improve himself. It was, in fact, because music was not "steady work" and not because young Handy lacked talent that his father forbade him to pursue it as a career. But he went against his father's wishes, bought a cornet, learned to play it in secret, and was well on his way before anyone was the wiser. One of the musicians with whom he played around Florence when he was little more than a boy was a violinist named Jim Turner, a drunken refugee from Beale Street. It was from him that Handy heard tales of that street that never shut down.

W. C. Handy spent his life in music and gives a fascinating account of it in his autobiography, *Father of the Blues*. Even if the title puts your teeth on edge, don't be put off by the book, for it contains, among much else that is good, a remarkable description of just what show business was like for blacks around the turn of the century. He went out on the road with Mahara's Minstrel Men, an all-black minstrel troupe that covered the entire country from top to bottom and one corner to the other. Touring with a tent show of any kind was no picnic; for blacks there was the very real danger of offending a hostile local populace in some way or other and having the show shot up or one of their number seized and lynched. It happened during Handy's years with Mahara's Minstrel Men. He paid his dues.

Handy was a legitimate musician, an excellent cornet player, and a good bandmaster. A theme running through his autobiography is the conflict in his life between strait-laced respectability, to which he was born and ultimately returned, and the keen attraction that he felt to the vulgar, the common, which the blues represented to him. He was excited by it because he was a good musician and saw the very real possibilities it offered. There is a key passage in the book in which he tells of the moment when he first realized that the music he had been hearing around him might be translated into something with wider appeal. He had been working as the leader of the local Knights of Pythias band in Clarksdale, Mississippi. Returning to the town one night, he had a long wait in the Tutwiler railroad station. He dozed off only to be awakened by a Negro next to him, who began playing a guitar and groaning out his intention: "Goin' where the Southern cross the Dog." Just a traveling song, as it turned out—nothing special, but it stuck in his mind, and Handy began wondering if music of this sort, music that he heard all around him in the Delta country, might not be written down and orchestrated for the band he led.

Well, that is just what he did, and suddenly he found his Knights of Pythias band the most popular in the region. It wasn't long until he was summoned to Memphis to take over a bigger band there. They played picnics, dances, and for special occasions up and down Beale Street, too. The Handy band was soon the toast of Memphis, playing for the white gentry at the city's Alaskan Roof Gardens, where it was billed as "The Best Band in the South." Which, remembering New Orleans down the river, was probably not true.

The great success of Handy and his band was due in large

measure to the special material that he wrote for it. He did an election song for E. H. Crump, the notorious boss of Memphis, which he titled respectfully, "Mr. Crump." After Crump's election—the issue was never in doubt—Handy decided to do something more with the tune, which had become enormously popular around town. He had it published at his own expense, but when it appeared that the sheet music was not moving he allowed himself to be persuaded to sell the rights to the song for a small figure (probably about $100). He saw it become a national hit as "The Memphis Blues"—and though he was not a cent richer, he was much, much wiser. He formed his own publishing company, and wrote and published in quick succession, "St. Louis Blues," "Yellow Dog Blues," "Joe Turner Blues," "Hesitating Blues," and "Beale Street Blues." All were hits. Blues was the new craze in popular music, and because he had written them all, he was hailed as "the father of the blues."

And yes, he *had* written them—not just taken them down, note for note, from that "blind man on the corner." As a trained musician, Handy had a grasp of what was going on musically when a Delta man sat down with his guitar and began hollering out his miseries. And nobody better than he was equipped to translate the folk idiom into something with a broader, more popular appeal. He selected, chose, and borrowed from the blues—but he never simply stole. He took the trouble, in his book *The Father of the Blues,* to make a detailed demonstration in one chapter what and how he had borrowed from folk sources. He concludes very candidly: "There are those who wish me to approach the subject of blues as though this type of music should be shrouded in mystery. Thousands have heard the material which went into the making of the blues . . . but they didn't write it down. I formed the habit of writing down ideas from watching my father." The combination of his systematic middle-class habits and the low-down black blues proved quite unbeatable.

No, you can't ignore William Christopher Handy. The job of bringing the blues and blues-based material to the vast American listening public was one that had to be done; only an anthropologist could wish that this great music be kept a secret.

IN A WAY, Memphis has continued to be a good blues town, even though Beale Street went into a steep decline following the war years. The city is still the first stop for the boys who emerge from the Delta with guitars in their hands. An inexhaustible supply of talent seems to lie all around it in the small towns and rural areas of Mississippi, Tennessee, and Arkansas. The last real superstar the city produced first surfaced as a disc jockey —that was Riley B. King, "the Beale Street Blues Boy," who kept up a line of patter and jive between the blues records he played until he started listening to them a little closer and decided he could do better himself if he put his mind to it. He clipped his DJ tag to initials only, and began touring the South as B. B. King.

It may have been inevitable, considering all the talent from around the area, that Memphis should have become a record-ing center. It started with Sam Phillips, a white radio engineer from Florence, Alabama, who set up a recording studio in Memphis in 1950. Although the label that he founded, Sun Rec-ords, became best known for the rockabilly-sound white sing-ers such as Elvis Presley, Jerry Lee Lewis, and Carl Perkins singing black material—Phillips started out by recording black singers in the Memphis and mid-South area. For its first few years, Sun was a black blues label and featured one local heavy in particular named James Cotton, who went on to make a name for himself first as Muddy Waters' harp player and then leading his own blues band.

Stax, the white-owned, black-managed Memphis recording company, is now just about the top soul label in the country. Nearly all of its top attractions come from Memphis or very nearby—including Isaac Hayes, David Porter, Carla Thomas, and the company's famous house rhythm section, Booker T. and the M.G.s. The only real blues singer on Stax is Albert King, who comes from just up the river in Osceola, Arkansas, a few miles from Johnny Cash's hometown, Dyess. Stax has made a star of King, the burly ex-bulldozer driver, and has given him a national following on the white rock circuit in addition to his loyal black audience. He had to work hard to get where he is. His success, which began when he started recording for Stax in 1966, was preceded by about twenty years of trying. But Albert King has a lot to offer, too—a good, rough, husky voice that sounds as though it belongs to a man who has experienced all the bad times the world has to offer and a style that blends country feeling with city sophistication in a rather subtle way.

On top of all this, he has one of the most distinctive electric-guitar styles in the blues: when he really gets going on a solo, he bends practically *every* note that he plays so that he makes it twang and whine through the amplifier, making it sound like an old Delta bluesman working a steel-bodied National with a length of tubing capped on the little finger of his fret hand.

If I seem suddenly quite specific, it is because I have a particular afternoon with Bukka White in mind. That was in Memphis, too, on Dunlap Street, not far from Furry Lewis' place. Bukka—the name is a corruption of Booker (he was born Booker T. Washington White in 1909)—is a tough-looking, though fairly genial, individual whose daughter calls him "big Daddy," and whose neighbors seem to give him a wide berth. They treat him as though he were a pretty tough customer, and they have good reason to, for he not only boxed professionally back in the thirties, but also did time for murder in Mississippi's notorious Parchman Prison Farm.

Bukka is probably Parchman's most famous alumnus. He had already recorded the first of his famous Vocalion sessions in 1937 when he was involved in the incident that sent him to jail. According to Paul Oliver in *The Story of the Blues*, it was a shooting fracas outside a Mississippi roadhouse. A man was killed, but there must have been extenuating circumstances, for Bukka was released in three years' time. It's no use asking him, though, for he won't talk about it, except to say, "Yeah, I cut some time down there, but I'll tell you this—I was just as innocent as you are, sittin' there right now. What was it like? Oh, it wasn't any too tough for me. I was lucky. They set me playin' instead of workin'. Just playin' for the big rich folks was all I was doin' there."

And though he would discuss the experience in terms no more specific than those, he was glad to sing his song about it to me, his famous "Parchman Farm Blues." He took a moment to set the National into rough tune, then launched into the driving, relentless, and, finally, monotonous rhythm against which he began groaning out his blues.

Judge gave me life this morning down on Parchman
  Farm (twice)
I wouldn't hate it so bad, but I felt my wife in
  mourn.

Oh, goodbye wife, oh you have done gone (twice)
But I hope someday you will hear my lonesome song.

Oh, listen you men, I don't mean no harm (twice)
If you wanna do good you better stay off of
   Parchman Farm.

We go to work in the morning just at dawn of day
   (twice)
Just at the settin' of the sun, that's when the work is
   done.

I'm down on old Parchman Farm, but I wanna go
   back home (twice)
But I hope some day I will overcome.

Of all the Mississippi bluesmen still singing today, Bukka's style is the most primitive, the least affected by all that has happened in music in the years since he started singing and shouting his way up from Mississippi in 1929. His intonation and his phrasing are virtually unchanged from what you will hear on those famous Vocalion blues sides that he made in 1937 and 1940. He had a way then of connecting lines and stanzas with a kind of nasal drone, and he still uses it today. This, together with the constant rhythm that he churns out monotonously as he declaims his lines, gives his performances a peculiar chanting quality.*

That rhythm he uses is especially interesting. It varies hardly a stroke from song to song, pulsing and driving along. Fundamentally, it is train rhythm; he seems to rock on and on at express tempo all afternoon. I asked him about this, and I could tell from the odd expression that came to his face that I had hit something sensitive.

He grinned almost slyly. "How you tell that?" he said. "You know, I live around trains all my life when I was a boy, so that's bound to be in my music, now ain't it?" I agreed that it was, and he went on to say, "My father, John White, was a railroad man from New York. He come down to work as a fireman. Oh, he was a huge man. He musta weighed about 286 pounds, and he

---

*I would speculate, purely on the basis of the striking similarity of their styles, that Richie Havens has consciously imitated and adapted mannerisms of Bukka White's.

worked all his life on the railroad—first for the M & O, and then he went to the Frisco. I got the trains from him, and I got the music from him, too. He played violin, and he gave me my first guitar. He died in 1930—that's the year I came to stay in Memphis."

I asked him if he had lived there ever since. He shrugged, not much interested in the question. "Oh, on and off, in and out, you know. I used to hobo a lot when I was young. But when I settled down, I settled down here. 'Course, there was that bad time down in Mississippi, but that's long in the past." He meant the Parchman Farm episode, of course.

How had he come to record those sides for Vocalion? Had he been discovered by someone? Gone up North to look for work?

"Oh, that was Lester Melrose come and find me. A lot of fellas they had trouble with him, but I never did. He nice to me till he die, and his daughter, she still send me money. I remember Melrose came down to Mississippi. He left the Delta and came up to the hills, and that's where he found me with my guitar in my hand. He say to me, 'This is what I been wantin'.' And he give me a railroad ticket taller than you to take me up to Chicago to play for him there. I was two weeks in Chicago that first time. He gave me a meal ticket, and I just stayed there right in the hotel. He brought whiskey to me. I wouldn't fool with it then, though. I'd just taste it then. Now I swallow it." He exploded suddenly in laughter at the little joke he had just made.

As nearly as I could remember, he did only original material. Where did he get his songs?

"I only do about three songs that ain't mine. I do St. Louis Slim's 'Please Write My Mother,' and 'Baby Please Don't Go,' by Big Joe Williams, and 'John Henry,' too. I don't know who wrote that. It's about 200 years old. Except for them, I pulled all my songs out of my brain. When I come to the point when I want to do it, then I'll do it. They just come."

Does he see any of the other old-time bluesmen around Memphis?

"Oh, sure. Some. You know. I see little old Furry. He lives pretty close here. And I see Memphis Minnie sometimes, too. She's in a nursing home now, and I went with a white boy from Washington to see her not so long ago. You know, she got fat as a butterball, that woman did, and all she do is sit in her wheel-

chair and cry and cry. But in her time she was really something. She was about the best thing goin' in the woman line.
And then my cousin, of course."

His cousin?

"B.B! B. B. King. He ain't no real *old-time* bluesman, but he's
pretty good at the blues, ain't he? He's my first cousin, and I give
him some tips every once in a while. He was startin' to play too
loud, too, like that band the Grateful Dead in San Francisco. So
I just told B.B. to cut it out because he was putting more racket
in it than solid music. And he just said, 'Okay, cuz, you know
best.'

"B.B.'s okay. They all are. I met some pretty good people in
this business to tell you the truth. And I think I did pretty good
in it, too. I been blessed. I never run up again too many bad
people to take advantage of me and all.

"And that's more than most can say."

CHAPTER EIGHT

"GOIN' TO CHICAGO— SORRY BUT I CAN'T TAKE YOU"

CHICAGO IS the home of the blues today. It is its own dark place and has its own wild style. They started out calling that style urban blues to distinguish it from the more primitive old country blues that was played in the juke joints of the South. But now they call it *Chicago* blues, because that's where the urban blues is at today: just plain Chicago. And how did it get there? Because that's where the blues was recorded. When Blind Lemon came north to record, it was to Chicago he came. When Sleepy John Estes and Hammie Nixon hoboed north to cut for Decca, they found the freight trains stopped at suburban Markham, Illinois, and they hitchhiked in from there. And when McKinley Morganfield came up from Stovall, Mississippi, looking for fame and fortune, he found it as Muddy Waters at the end of a phonograph needle out on the South Side of Chicago.

This story begins, as all too many Chicago stories do, in New York. It was there in February, 1920, that a plump *café au lait* contralto named Mamie Smith recorded a couple of songs, "That Thing Called Love" and "You Can't Keep a Good Man Down." They were neither blues nor jazz, but vaguely "jazzy" numbers with a kind of old-time show-business bounce to them. And Mamie Smith wasn't a blues singer, either—just a girl who had paid her dues in vaudeville. She did the job, though—and that was to break the color ban in recording. For over a year a little Harlem hustler named Perry Bradford had been pitching all the New York recording companies on that vast, untapped Negro phonograph-record market out there. "There's fourteen million Negroes in our great country," he told them, "and they will buy records if they are recorded by one of their own." Well, nobody paid much attention to him until he went to OKeh, then an aggressive independent company that was a bit more willing to take chances. They recorded Mamie Smith early in 1920, and then had a few months of misgivings before they finally released her record in August of that year. And although she was not advertised as black, Negro newspapers let out the news, and the record took off and sold an estimated 75,000 copies. The lesson was not lost on OKeh: they got Mamie Smith into a recording studio immediately, cut another record, and released it, this time proclaiming her as black in advertisements. It went over even better than they had hoped—and all of a sudden the "Race" race was on.

There was suddenly terrific competition among record companies to sign and record black artists—blues singers they were called, whether they sang blues or not. Few of them did. But as the black audience became more discriminating, the record companies, which with one exception (Black Swan) were white-owned and run, had to come up with real down-home funky blues singers doing real black blues. It wasn't long until it took such as Alberta Hunter, Bessie Smith, Clara Smith (no relation to Bessie), Ida Cox, Ma Rainey, Blind Lemon Jefferson, and Lonnie Johnson to satisfy them.

They were listed in the catalogs as "Race" artists, meaning, simply, Negro. (It was a term used by blacks themselves at the time and in the twenties had a great vogue in the black press.) No matter what they were called, their records sold phenomenally. Perry Bradford, who subsequently did well for himself as a songwriter and entrepreneur, had been proven right. There *was* a black audience out there, and they were willing to pay plenty. Those first records by Mamie Smith on the OKeh label, for example, cost a dollar each. Bessie Smith records on Columbia toward the end of the twenties went at seventy-five cents each and sold better than 20,000 each.

(But careful. Don't jump to conclusions. In his book *Screening the Blues,* Paul Oliver does just that when he observes,

Five or six million Race records sold annually at a time when the total Negro population in the United States was only double that amount meant that a very large proportion of the Negro world must have been hearing the music; a single record could be familiar in the lives of half a dozen people and many a young Negro grew up with the phonograph blues always in his ears. The colossal output indicates irrefutably the important part played by the gramophone in the spread of Negro musical culture and gives some indication of its potential strength in directing and forming Negro taste.

Most of which is true enough, but Oliver does seem to assume rather blindly here that *all* Race records were bought by blacks —and this was simply not the case. Records by Negro jazzmen were also listed in the Race category, and these included artists such as Louis Armstrong, Duke Ellington, Fats Waller, and others who were nationally popular with whites; of the blues singers, Bessie Smith, at least, and probably Ida Cox, too, had plenty of white record-buying fans. Taste is not and was not ever as neatly segregated in America as all that.)

From early on, Chicago had a big piece of the recording action. Paramount, especially, with a big mail-order and "drummer" trade in the South, was eager to record authentic black music that the country audience would buy. The man in charge of the company's Race recording operations in Chicago was J. Mayo Williams, himself a Negro; he brought Blind Lemon Jefferson up from Texas to cut records as early as 1926. After a brief and unsuccessful venture on his own, Williams joined Vocalion as a talent scout and began recording everyone from the old Memphis bluesman Jim Jackson (his "Kansas City Blues" was a big hit) to Tampa Red (Hudson Whittaker) and Georgia Tom (Thomas Dorsey). And later, when English Decca opened an American office in Chicago in 1934, they engaged J. Mayo Williams as scout, and he built up an impressive roster of black talent in a year's time.

Not surprisingly, the Depression hit the record industry hard, and that part of it supplying black music was hit hardest of all. Paramount folded. Field trips to various sectors of the South for on-the-spot recording, which had become standard procedure for some companies, were discontinued in the interest of belt-tightening. But somehow Chicago held on—perhaps because by this time there was in the city a kind of resident blues nucleus, some of them bluesmen who had come or been brought up north to record for one label or another and had simply stayed on to play at some of the many South Side bars as they waited for their next recording date to come up. It was in those South Side clubs that the country blues style of the Deep South was metamorphosed into what they would soon call urban blues. How was it different? It was music to be performed, music to dance to, music that had to compete with the jazz bands that were then so popular with blacks and whites alike in Chicago. And in competing, it became more than a little like jazz in the bargain—a little less personal and a little more structured. Johnny Shines, who started out country and wound up urban, explains the difference this way: "You take a man playing the country blues, he plays just what he feels because he's playing the country blues, he plays just what he feels because he's playing all by himself nine times out of ten, and he don't have to cooperate with nobody. But you take Chicago blues style, when you get up there with a band, you have to play together real tight just like it was any other arrangement. It was different, of course, with country blues, because there wasn't any arrangement. If your bluesman felt like holding a note for nine beats, he held it for nine. He didn't know nothin' about any one-two-three-four."

One of the originators of this urban style in Chicago was a William Lee Conley Broonzy, nicknamed "Big Bill," who was born in Scott, Mississippi, on June 26, 1893. He came to Chicago on his own, he says in his autobiography, *Big Bill Blues,* in 1920, and started playing for chicken and chittlin's at those Saturday-night rent parties. It took him a while, however, to convince somebody that he was ready to record—and that somebody was J. Mayo Williams, who was running things at Paramount. Bill did indifferently well. Of the four sides he cut, only one—"House Rent Stomp"—was released, and that after a delay of some months, in 1927. But he was available—very much on the scene in Chicago—and so he continued to record, usually in solo but sometimes backing up other singers. Although he was not above lifting material, most of what he recorded was his own, or at least freely adapted.

Most of his early recorded work shows him to be playing country blues of more or less the old sort. But gradually, in the early thirties, a change became perceptible. Perhaps influenced by the popular LeRoy Carr-Scrapper Blackwell duo, or swayed by the things that Tampa Red was doing with Georgia Tom Dorsey, Big Bill teamed up with a piano player named Joshua Altheimer, added rhythm and a saxophone-clarinetist named Buster Bennett—and out came Big Bill Broonzy's Memphis Five. What they played was a kind of good-time style that mixed blues with dance music. Through the thirties, as he began warming up to that Memphis Five band of his, he became more and more proficient as a guitarist. He could hold a good, steady beat as a rhythm guitarist, and as a soloist he was fluent, if not always very imaginative. It was largely because of his skill on the instrument and because of his wide contacts among Chicago bluesmen and black musicians that he became associated with Lester Melrose, a white blues entrepreneur on the order of an independent producer who worked with both Vocalion and Bluebird. He seems to have had a much freer hand and been more active for the Bluebird label. Bill recorded for both labels under Melrose's auspices, but for Bluebird he became a sort of house guitarist, putting together backup groups to record behind such favorites as Washboard Sam (whose real name was Robert Brown and who was actually Big Bill's half-brother), and later with a first-rate female vocalist named Lil Green who sang a lot of blues.

By and large, the Chicago blues sound began with these Bluebird sessions of the thirties and early forties. The talent on them was impressive. In addition to those already named, Bluebird artists included Lonnie Johnson, Tampa Red, and blues harp blower and shouter John Lee "Sonny Boy" Williamson (the *original* Sonny Boy, and not Rice Miller, who later took his name). It wasn't just the emphasis on groups—on blues bands and the bigger sound for dancing—that made the urban blues what it was; it was because it was about those *Chicago* miseries —and the lyrics complained of Depression unemployment, tough cops, and freezing cold, and sang their longing for the South, not because it was better but just because it was home. By and large, at least during this early period, it was a blues of exile made by exiles from the blues country.

Blues recording divides sharply into prewar and postwar periods. Wartime shellac restrictions went into force early in 1942, and the cutback hit blues record production hardest of all. And if things weren't bad enough, James C. Petrillo, president of the American Federation of Musicians, became disturbed at about this time about the impact of jukeboxes on the employment of musicians for live entertainment, and he called for a strike. It took two years to hammer out an arrangement on royalties, and during that time—from 1942 to 1944—no recording was done by AFM musicians. And although not all bluesmen were union musicians, the effect of the recording ban was to shut off what little wartime activity there was left. When the ban ended, there was some effort to revive Race recording activity within the limitations imposed by the shellac restrictions. But nothing much happened, because they brought back the old prewar favorites. And by that time, there was a new cast on the Chicago scene. A new era had begun.

Nineteen forty-two was also the year that Albert Luandrew came north to Chicago to stay. He had been up once before. "Yeah, I came to Chicago first time in 1933. I was like everybody else in the country during the Depression, running around without no job. I took a look around up here and figured it would be easier to get by in the country, so I went back. That was my first try at Chicago."

Like so many Chicago bluesmen, Luandrew, who is known universally as "Sunnyland Slim," is a country boy from the Mississippi Delta. He was born in Vance, Mississippi, in 1907, grew up and learned to play the piano there. He went rambling then, sitting down at any place along the way that offered a piano and a stool. He played and shouted the blues in jukes, levee and highway camps, and sawmills. He played the good-time towns like West Helena, Arkansas, and became one of the mainstays on old Beale Street in Memphis. Along the way, he jammed with the legendary Robert Johnson and told the kid to mind the beat. And he saw his competitors among all those down-home piano men, Little Brother Montgomery and Roose-velt Sykes, go up North to Chicago and make it pretty big. He traveled up for that look-around in the Depression that he men-tioned, got cold feet, and took the next train back to Memphis.

What happened then? "Oh, you know. I played those little old jobs in the country from around Vance and Longstreet. They got a lot of piano men from around there but I'm tops among them. Come right down to it, me and Roosevelt Sykes and Little Brother, we're the only ones living of that whole bunch of piano players and we're all up here in Chicago."

We were talking together in Slim's living room on East Sev-enty-ninth Street in Chicago. It is a small, comfortable apart-ment, a walk-up over a cleaning shop. It shows his wife's hand: The place is spotlessly clean, even *smells* clean—or is that the cleaning-fluid odor from downstairs? Bric-a-brac and figurines cover all available surfaces, and pictures crowd the walls. The television is on—one of those morning game shows. Slim ig-nores it, but his wife watches from a chair close by in rapt concentration.

He explains to me that when he came up in 1942 there was plenty happening in the music line but no recording because of the ban. He didn't like that, because it was in hopes of cutting some records that he had come up North. Everybody else he ever knew down there in the Delta had gone to Chicago and gotten a record contract, so why not him? Well, eventually he did—but not until 1947, when he cut some sides as "Dr. Clayton's Buddy." Who was Dr. Clayton? An old Delta blues singer-comedian who had cut quite a figure when Slim traveled with him on the chittlin' circuit—but that was years before, and here he was still just Dr. Clayton's Buddy.

What bands was he playing with during this time? Did he have his own group? "Naw, I didn't have my own group. I was just doing, you know, backup work. I was able to get Wolf and Muddy jobs pretty regular. They came up about this same time I did, and we always got along pretty good, I guess. That Muddy, I'll tell you, he's a good person. Always was. He's the goodest person you could meet."

He was playing with Howlin' Wolf's band the last time I had seen him, and that had not been long ago. Was he still? He nods. "Yeah," he says, "but I'm not going stay with Wolf. People come up to me and they say, 'Man, I'm surprised to see you with Wolf.' Nobody in his band doing anything but Hubert [Sumlin] and me. See, I do it a little different from Wolf personally. I don't do no slow four-five stuff. I lay it down *hard* on the piano. The way I do it I get a person to tap his foot just like a Baptist preacher."

Sunnyland Slim still has hopes of getting his own group together and playing the colleges and the festivals the way that Muddy and Buddy Guy and Junior Wells are doing—and he may make it yet. Nobody deserves it more than Slim, for nobody has worked harder than he has in the dives of the West Side and South Side of Chicago in bands headed by this guitar man or that harp blower. He is a sideman. He has recorded plenty for one label or another, but nearly all that he has done has been in a backup capacity. He sings well enough and he plays good piano—all he lacks is . . . what? A certain authority, perhaps, or the kind of personal magnetism that today passes for charisma. But Slim still makes plans for that band he's going to have— musicians, instrumentation, and the kind of material they will play—and in the meantime he keeps on taking those jobs with Wolf and may do a little session work with Willie Dixon to pay the rent.

His affairs are in a mess. He brings out a handful of letters and documents, spreads them out on the sofa between us, and begins a long, complicated, and somewhat rambling explanation of his problems. He has written songs, others have recorded them, and he feels he has not been paid as he should have been. Ideas, he says, have been stolen from him. In general, he seems to feel a sense of frustration and depletion as he sifts through the papers, and at one point he explains, "That's what my whole life is," and sweeps a big hand forward and back as though it were all laid out between us. "After fifty years of playing I ain't got nothin' to show for it. I mean, if anybody ought to be gettin' money in this business it's Brother, Sykes, and me."

And then, perhaps thinking to make his case stronger by repetition, he starts through it all once again, but breaks off suddenly. "I don't know," he says. "Maybe I messed up a little, I don't know. Some damn thing sure went wrong, though." Albert Luandrew, a.k.a. Sunnyland Slim, shakes his head and groans eloquently.

THE CHEAP BLUEBIRD LABEL on which the early urban blues came to be heard back in the thirties was dropped by Victor in 1950. Nobody really noticed, for by that time about all that appeared on it were reissues from earlier, livelier times. Robert Brown, who as Washboard Sam had been Bluebird's top star for nearly a decade, had by this time dropped out of the music business entirely and become a Chicago policeman.

With the war over and the blues business in full swing, records of the new Chicago sound began to pour forth plentifully —but from the oddest sources! For the most part, the major companies got out of blues recording just as the music was going into this new phase, and so it was cut on a score or more of fly-by-night labels—marks such as Tempo Tone, Ora Nelle, Chance, Keyhole, VeeJay, and J.O.B. Many of them were "club" labels, run by the manager or maybe just the bartender of some blues club where the groups were appearing. The boys might get together on their day off for a recording session, and the record would be pressed in limited quantity and then sold across the bar along with "Slitz" and watered-down rotgut.

That was how the Aristocrat label got started. If that name doesn't ring any bells, it may help to learn that it became Chess in 1950, the year Bluebird was discontinued. Yes, it was as neat as that, for Chess became just as important as Bluebird had ever been. Just look who they recorded: Muddy Waters, Howlin' Wolf, Little Walter, Buddy Guy, and just about everybody who was anybody in Chicago blues. And in the mid-fifties, with Chuck Berry and Bo Diddley under contract, Chess was one of the first to put on records that new sound that they first called rhythm-and-blues, and then rock-and-roll.

The Chess brothers, Leonard and Phil, owned a club in Chicago called the Macambo Lounge. As night-club owners, they got into the record business more or less by accident, according to Peter Guralnick in his book *Feel Like Going Home.* A talent scout came there to check out a singer named Andrew Tibbe at their club. On the spot, they decided that if he was good enough for somebody else to record he was good enough for them to do it, too. But whether they entered by accident or not, once in, the Chess brothers stayed in the business and worked hard at it, too. Where, for instance, others who ran club labels were satisfied to sell them across the bar and at a few shops in

Bronzeville, Leonard Chess took their records out and placed them with distributors and directly in record shops, especially around the South. It paid off, too, for first Aristocrat and then Chess were more than just Chicago labels; it wasn't long before they were running a national operation.

And if there ever was a time when exciting things were happening in Chicago blues, it was in the late forties and the fifties decade, when the Chess brothers hit their peak as recorders of the music. They made more money later on. In 1963 they paid a cool million for a radio station in Chicago—and converted it into WVON, soon the top black station in all of mid-America. By the sixties, there was a clutch of separate labels under the Chess umbrella: Argo (a jazz label, later discontinued), Checker, Cadet, and, of course, Chess. By this time, too, young Marshall Chess, Leonard's son, was getting into the business with a lot of new ideas for some of the label's old talent, mixing Muddy with acid rock, and Howlin' Wolf with howling feedback—with generally disastrous results.

If Chess was in large measure responsible for getting the Chicago blues sound out for the rest of the world to hear during its most exciting period, then the Chess brothers are, of course, to be commended. They kept a lot of blues fans happy and, moving into the sixties, helped reach a whole new audience of young whites with the music. And so, admittedly, they did a lot for the blues, but what did they do for the bluesmen? Charles Keil, in his excellent sociological study *Urban Blues,* had this to say about the Chess operation in 1966:

> Standards of honesty and integrity seem to be high, considering the industry as a whole. One arrives at an appraisal of this kind with mixed emotions. Stories circulate in the Chicago blues community that are not very flattering. At the same time, most of the performers currently under contract seem to be reasonably well satisfied with the arrangement. Muddy Waters, for example, has been with the company almost from its inception in the late 1940s *without* a contract. In a sense, this mutual trust in a highly competitive field speaks well for both Waters and Leonard Chess. Yet the arrangement also smacks of the old plantation and paternalism. I suspect that Waters can go to the Chess family with big dental bills or overdue car payments and receive a sizable "advance on royalties" on the spot, with no

LISTEN TO THE BLUES   140

questions asked. On the other hand, if Muddy were to become "uppity," it is possible that his career might be seriously disrupted. "We're just one big happy family here,"
say the Chess men when asked about management problems, and I am almost persuaded that they believe it.

That "almost" speaks volumes. For, yes, there have been stories
about the Chess operations in the past and a good deal of grum-
bling about the practices of Willie Dixon, bassist, songwriter
(or song copyrighter anyway), Chess A & R man, and kickback
artist extraordinaire. But all that talk has now subsided to a
mere whisper, for the situation there has been altered considerably in the last few years.

There is still a Chess Records, although it was bought in 1969
by the GRT Corporation, a recording-tape manufacturer, and
has subsequently been moved to New York. Leonard Chess died
not long ago at the age of fifty-two. His son Marshall and his
brother Phil stayed on briefly with GRT, but both are now completely out of the organization. Phil Chess runs WVON, and
Marshall Chess is now connected with the Rolling Stones' business organization. Willie Dixon continues as an independent
producer in Chicago with occasional forays into New York and
Memphis, although today he lacks the considerable clout he
once had as the black knight on the Chess board.

ALTHOUGH THE BLUES recording done in Chicago is very important and, I think, offers a key to the dissemination of that blues
style which has been so influential in American music of the
past two decades, nevertheless none of it would have worked if
there had not been an abundance of blues talent on the scene
in Chicago, clubs for them to play in, and fans to come, drink,
and listen. But all the elements were there. There was a big
active blues scene in Chicago for many years after the war. The
city became a kind of blues mecca, drawing the faithful from
close by and from every corner of the South. They went to the
clubs and they bought the records. It was a loyal and enthusiastic audience, just the kind of following the bluesmen needed to
keep them cooking.

But gradually that audience disappeared. Blame it on television, the coming of soul music, or any of a dozen other factors,
but the fact of the matter is that at the end of the fifties there

were blues bars all over the South and West sides of the city—
one on every block, it seemed—and through the decade that
followed they began to shut down at a dismaying rate. Most of
those that stayed open made do with jukeboxes. It was the end
of an era, though the survivors may have thought it just a
wrinkle in taste, a temporary difficulty to be endured somehow
until times got better. For some of them things never really did
pick up again. There have been an astonishing number of
deaths among this group of bluesmen in the last decade or so
—many of them young men and none of them old: Little Walter
Jacobs, Magic Sam Maghett, Earl Hooker, Otis Spann, James
Cotton, J. B. Lenoir, and Junior Parker, to name just a few
casualties of the era. As clubs shut down, competition for jobs
became intense and waits between them longer and longer. But
a few of those hearty enough to weather this period of adversity
were finally rewarded with salvation of sorts. For beginning
about 1967 that vast, young white rock audience out there discovered blues in the persons of B. B. King, Albert King, and
Muddy Waters, and by 1968 most of the top Chicago blues bands
were getting at least a few bookings at colleges, universities,
and rock clubs. And once given a bit of exposure, a few of the
lesser-known bluesmen have begun to pull and hold audiences
all around the country—have become, in short, bigger names
away from home than they had been back in Chicago.

J. B. Hutto is a case in point. The short-statured Chicagoan
who was born in 1929 in Augusta, Georgia, has been seeing a lot
of the country lately. I caught him in Los Angeles at the Ash
Grove on the last night of his engagement there. We talked
briefly, and he told me he would be coming East pretty soon, so
why couldn't we get together then? And sure enough, in a couple of months' time he showed up at Mr. Henry's on Capitol Hill
in Washington, D.C. His manager is a Washingtonian named
Topper Carew, a promoter active in a number of the arts and
an outspoken controversialist on a variety of issues. He has
given J. B. Hutto a solid home base at Mr. Henry's, the club at
which Roberta Flack held forth for a couple of years, and is
getting him bookings in and out of colleges throughout the
East. And all this has been accomplished without benefit of any
special record successes to back J.B. up—he himself is painfully aware of this, as we shall see.

Once you see him onstage in front of a group it is easy to understand how he has managed it. A mild, shy man in conversation, he is transformed before an audience into a sort of roaring, howling Mr. Hyde, big-mouthing his blues in memorably earthy style as he plays a slide electric guitar better than anyone else has managed to do since his mentor, the great Elmore James. He is a great, driving performer who leads a band—he is always billed as "J. B. Hutto and the Hawks"—with great authority. But oddly enough, although I found J.B. the same from the Ash Grove to Mr. Henry's, the Hawks were metamorphosed utterly. It was a big black blues band in Los Angeles of about the same instrumentation as the one Muddy Waters tours with—including French harp (harmonica) and piano. But in Washington, he had three white long-haired rockers with him, all quite proficient but not one of them over twenty-two. I asked J.B. about this when I sat down to talk with him in Washington.

He explained that when he had gone to the West Coast to play that date at the Ash Grove, he had worked with local musicians. They had had some good rehearsal time beforehand, so it had gone pretty well. This new group? Yeah, they were local, too, but he liked working with them, and since he was going to be playing a lot of dates in the East for Topper, he was hoping to keep them together. "My white boys really play the blues," he concluded brightly.

We were in Topper Carew's apartment in Northwest Washington. J.B. was all alone there on a bright autumn afternoon, just waiting for the day to end so that his could begin. He asked me if I would like some tea. "That's what I usually drink," he explained. When I said yes, he went at it efficiently like a man who had had some practice at it—no "flow-thru" teabags for him.

Bands, he continued, are always a problem, even back in Chicago. "You'd get a good group together and maybe get a job out of town not too far, and one or two would say no, they didn't want to play anyplace but just in Chicago. There always seemed to be something to hinder them from traveling. But I can't be too hard on them, though, because I've had some pretty good years, and it's because I've had some good bands. I mean I been fortunate enough to play a lot with good musicians like Big Walter Horton, the harmonica man—you know him?" I nodded. "Well, so I can't complain. But I guess most of those real good bands were in the old days."

"When were the good old days in Chicago?"

"For the blues? Well, you go back to 1945 to 1960, along about in there, and there was really a lot of young talent around. Everywhere you went there was some kind of club with a band or something or other. I don't know what happened then, but things got pretty tight. All these old musicians around town started retiring, dropping out—you know. I never had to. I was lucky. I stayed with it. But it was pretty bad for a while there. People would hear you start playing the blues and they'd walk out. Right there on the South Side, too, where the blues was home!

"But I stuck it out. I hoped it would come back, and it did. Right there around 1968 and 1969 people began hiring back blues bands again. Now even the young ones are starting to enjoy the music. I would say the people are getting re-educated to the blues. The younger people are getting into it. Right now I got a good public. The fans follow you. They say, 'Oh, when you coming back?' Yeah, it's building up pretty good."

I asked him to tell me how he happened to get started in the blues life. "Me? Oh, I was just a kid, but I'd sneak in those places like Sylvio's, and I remember one night I had a long talk with old Memphis Slim, and that got me decided that playing the blues was what I wanted to do. So I took up the drums, and I fooled around with that for a while until one night I heard Elmore James someplace around in Chicago. He was just getting started and he was real heavy, you know. He played it different from anybody. Old bottle-neck guitar had died out by then, nobody played it any more. And Elmore was the first I ever heard go at an electric guitar with a bar. Well, I never heard anything like that before. So I got me a guitar and a piece of pipe, and I went to work with the two of them. And oh, yeah, I suppose I ought to say, too, that T-Bone [Walker] was around then, and I started to listening to him, too. I learned from those I was listening to at the time.

"And then I tried putting my first little band together. And that's the problem, then, getting known. You got to work all those little clubs so long and work with different people and all. But most of what we played in the beginning wasn't even clubs, it was just most of them parties—basement jumps, they call them. And somehow or other when I was playing them I started calling my band J. B. Hutto and the Hawks, just because some-body told me the group needed some kind of odd name. I just came to me—J.B. and the Hawks—and so I stuck with it.

"I mean, it wasn't always so great after that. I've had my troubles, but they weren't music troubles, they were troubles with companies. Yes, those companies have given me some *hard* problems. On records, I stayed on one man's* contract for five years. I cut records, and they were supposed to sell here, but instead they sold them overseas. You know how much I made off that contract? Two hundred and fifty dollars in five years' time. I wouldn't have known what he did with the stuff I cut at all except I got three or four letters from overseas telling me how much they liked my record."

You could tell that it troubled him just to think about it. We were sipping tea now, and he sat staring down darkly into the tea leaves at the bottom of his cup. For a moment I caught a glimpse of that angry Mr. Hyde he becomes when he steps onstage.

At last he continued: "I've got Topper working on this now. We're trying to get a contract with the *right* record company now, one that will distribute my stuff. Get it out so the people who come to hear me can buy it when they want to."

I asked him if he had ever been tempted to get out of music altogether when things got tough back in Chicago. A few of them dropped out back then. Had he ever thought of quitting?

J.B. shook his head. "No," he said, "blues is my bag. Singing the blues—let me put it this way—you get the chance to tell the public what you're thinkin' and what you're doin'. See, you catch the heart of the public with the music. One of the verses you sing might catch somebody just right, tell him about his feelings or problems. Like my song, 'Now She's Gone,' well, every man has got a woman gone on him sometime—well, I'm *talkin'* to that man. And 'Alcohol'—I had to do that three or four times at Henry's the other night. A lot of people have that kind of problem. You get with a band that's good and you got a good voice, then you can handle it. Singing the blues is always just talking to somebody. That's how I see it."

*Not Chess or any of its affiliates.

CHAPTER NINE

TRANSATLANTIC BLUES

"THE AMERICAN DARKY is the performing fool of the world today. He's demanded everywhere. If I c'n only git some a these heah panhandling fellahs together, we'll show them some real nigger music. Then I'd be sitting pretty in this heah sweet dump without worrying ovah mah wants. That's the stuff for a live nigger like me to put ovah, and no cheap playing from café to café and a handing out mah hat for a lousy sou."

These are the thoughts of one Lincoln Agrippa Daily, nicknamed "Banjo" for the instrument he carries with him from one bar to the next on the Marseilles waterfront. He picks and sings for whatever francs come his way, telling himself that he is just between berths as a merchant seaman. In the meantime, he and his multinational black buddies—Bugsy, Malty, Ginger, and Dengel—laze about the beach, scrounge food where they can, live off the generosity of the girls in the quarter, and panhandle the American tourists when all else fails.

But Banjo has a talent and a dream. And he comes close to realizing that dream when a flute player named Goosey (an American black) and a Nigerian guitarist named Taloufa show up on the same boat ready to jam. That's what they do one glorious night when Banjo takes them around to his favorite hangout, and they play and sing for the dancers for hours until a casual shooting scatters the crowd. And although it goes well that night, the three never really get it together quite the same way again. The group is riven by controversy. The two newcomers deplore Banjo's easygoing ways and bemoan his lack of racial consciousness. At one point they fall into argument, and Goosey tells him: "Banjo is bondage, It's the instrument of slavery. Banjo is Dixie. The Dixie of the land of cotton and massa and missus and black mammy. We colored have got to get away from all that in these enlightened progressive days. Let us play piano and violin, harp and flute [Goosey's instrument]. Let the white folks play the banjo if they want to keep on remembering all the Black Joes singing and the hell they made them live in." It is talk like that which splits up Banjo's little band, and all eventually go their separate ways.

If you have not recognized it already, the book I have been talking about is a novel titled *Banjo,* by Claude McKay, a Negro novelist and poet of Harlem's Black Renaissance, which was published in 1929. It is a lively and engaging book that is interesting in a number of ways. First of all, it presents a remarkable picture of life on the Marseilles waterfront—no French novel that I know of offers anything as graphic. Secondly, it discusses questions of race more frankly and honestly and in greater depth than do most black novels, even today. Finally, it is (as far as I know) the first personal account of what it is like to be an American black in Europe—and in particular, an American black musician. Even when Claude McKay wrote about it, Banjo's experience was certainly not unique. It might well have been generalized from scores who were around the Continent by the end of the twenties. They were known chiefly for their music, their song and dance. The queen of the Paris music halls just then was a twittering yellow-skinned girl named Josephine Baker, whom the French (in their confusion) regarded as a jazz singer. During the mad, manic phase of European culture that followed World War I, black music was regarded with immense enthusiasm but little understanding. Banjo was right: the American darky *was* the performing fool of the world in that particular day and age.

It wasn't so in the beginning. As closely as I have been able to ascertain, the earliest firsthand experience Europe had of black music was provided by the Fisk Jubilee Singers, a choir of four men and five women who sang a repertoire of spirituals, during their tour in the late 1870s. They did well enough. Audiences turned out in good numbers all over the Continent; they may have come out of curiosity, but they were charmed by what they heard. However, the European musical establishment was not especially impressed. A German musicologist named Richard Wallaschek dismissed the spirituals as "mere imitations of European compositions which Negroes have picked up and served up again with slight variation." And the composers themselves, who were caught in the last harmonic throes of the Romantic movement, were not about to have their attention diverted from the serious matters at hand by this musical oddity from Nashville, Tennessee.

Gradually, however, black American music did come to have some effect on European composers, if only superficial and temporary. Ragtime was what caught their fancy first. Starting in the 1890s, the compositions of Scott Joplin, Tom Turpin, and Eubie Blake began to find their way across the ocean. The lovely, lively syncopated rhythms of the music fell on the ears of modernists such as Camille Saint-Saëns and Claude Debussy and convinced them that this was just the stuff with which to mock the stuffy old Romantics—hence those novel and essentially meaningless compositions such as the ricky-ticky little *Golliwog's Cakewalk*. None of which really proved anything.

The first real inkling of jazz that Europe got came from a couple of tours by bands led by a black man whose name was, appropriately enough, James Reese Europe. The first band he brought over, which was known as the Tennessee Students, played vaudeville theaters in London, Paris, and Berlin in 1905. It was essentially a show band that specialized in big orchestral arrangements of solo ragtime material and syncopated popular songs. Traditionally, the United States Army entertaining band he brought over in 1917 has been cited as the first real jazz group to be presented on the European continent. However, because the band never recorded and boasted no soloists of special note, its credentials as a jazz organization are slightly suspect. It did catch the interest of Europe, however—particularly France— and readied the way for the real jazzmen, who began to find their way over starting just after the war.

Will Marion Cook brought a big orchestra to London in 1919

that seems to have been about the same sort of show band as the one Jim Europe had had in France—except that Cook's New York Syncopated Orchestra, as it was know, featured the clarinet of jazzman Sidney Bechet, and there is no denying that Bechet is as authentic a jazzman as New Orleans produced. There were others—enough real, if minor, jazzmen who traveled over to give Europeans a general idea of what the music was all about. By this time, too, American records were starting to get wide distribution overseas and were getting through to the relatively few listeners and musicians in France, England, and elsewhere who were deeply interested in American music and regarded it as something more than a fad.

The man who really turned Europe on, however, was Louis Armstrong. He made it over first in 1932 without a band, where he had been preceded only by a couple of white groups—who had played there years before. He was booked into the London Palladium and brought over a pickup band from Paris, mixed French and expatriate-black. He rehearsed them, played a fabulously successful two-week engagement, and sent them back to Paris (the tough British musician's union forbade them to stay longer). Then, with an English band, he started a tour of England and Scotland which, with return engagements, lasted the better part of five months. This in the bottom year of the Depression. Louis was most gratified.

According to Armstrong himself, he picked up his famous nickname over in England on that trip. Heretofore he had been known as Gatemouth or Dippermouth (Dipper for short), because of his colossally large mouth. For some reason, Percy Mathison Brooks, editor of the English publication *Melody Maker,* got the nickname wrong and greeted Armstrong as he came down the gangplank with a rousing "Hello, Satchelmouth!" Louis loved it, shortened it to "Satchmo," and kept it in the act.

It was on his second trip to England the following year that there occurred another one of those incidents that has now become one of the chief features of the Armstrong legend. It was at a command performance, again at the Palladium, and with King George V up in the royal box, Satchmo thought it might be proper to dedicate his finale to him. And so, wiping his sweating face with that omnipresent handkerchief, he grinned and said, "This one's for you, Rex."

That trip to Europe, which began in 1933, lasted a full eighteen months. It included another tour of England, a radio broadcast from the Netherlands (a rare and grand thing for a jazz performer at that time), and a continental tour that took him through Scandinavia, France, Belgium, Switzerland, and Italy. But more important than where he went was how he was received. And audiences all over Europe were wildly enthusiastic for Armstrong, the trumpet player, the groaning, bluesy singer, and most of all, for Armstrong the performer. In those eighteen months he had done more to further the cause of American music in Europe than the small army of musicians who had preceded him there. By the time he left, Duke Ellington and his Orchestra, Coleman Hawkins, and Fats Waller had all come on their first visits. But Louis paved the way for them. He made all Europe jazz-conscious.

Traffic increased. Many others made it across. Louis himself came back a time or two before World War II began. The war put an end to things temporarily, of course. Only not really, for even during the war, in Germany and Italy, where American music had been banned, there existed an underground of jazz fans and record collectors who kept up their keen interest in the music and looked forward to the day when they could get back to the things that mattered. In his book *The Story of Jazz,* Marshall W. Stearns has some funny stories about a Lieutenant Schulz-Kohn, an avid jazz fan who kept a kind of Schweikian resistance to Hitler's jazz ban. During the occupation, he managed to get himself posted to Paris, where he searched out the French jazz critic Charles Delaunay. The two worked together on the 1943 edition of Delaunay's *Hot Discographie,* and it later turned out that the Frenchman was active in the Resistance. Later he was transferred, but he surfaced again rather surprisingly during surrender negotiations at St. Nazaire. At a lull, a German lieutenant suddenly piped up and asked in English if any of the Americans there collected Benny Goodman records. It was Schulz-Kohn.

After the war it *was* different. The late forties saw an explosion of interest in all things American among Europeans, and a passion for American music in particular. Things were helped along considerably by the postwar emigration of American jazzmen to Europe. The smoke had barely settled on the Continent when Sidney Bechet grabbed a boat back. The late

Don Byas, a superior tenor saxophonist who cut a groove somewhere between Lester Young and Coleman Hawkins, was another early émigré; he married there and started a new life for
himself. Many others did—clarinetists Mezz Mezzrow and Albert Nicholas, saxists Ben Webster and Phil Woods, trumpeter
Art Farmer, bassist Red Mitchell, and on and on. The names
are too numerous to list here; most of them came to stay more
or less permanently; even those who eventually returned, such
as trumpeter-arranger Quincey Jones, did so after lengthy residence, renewed as musicians.

Few came earlier and none have stayed longer than drummer Kenny Clarke. He was well established in America as the
originator of the bop drumming style and was working regularly in New York with such performers as Dizzy Gillespie,
Charlie Parker, and Tadd Dameron. But suddenly he decided to
leave all that and showed up one day in Paris. He just gigged
around the city for a while, playing jazz at the clubs and working with French show bands and recording orchestras; there
was always plenty of work for American jazz musicians there.
But from a quartet that Clarke put together for a 1961 date in
Cologne grew the mighty Kenny Clarke-Francie Boland Big
Band, possibly the best band of its kind in the world and certainly the best in Europe. The seventeen-piece organization
plays concert dates and festivals all over the Continent; its presence there has helped immeasurably to keep Europeans enthusiastic for jazz. Among the most enthusiastic, of course,
have been the many native Europeans who have made careers
for themselves as jazz musicians—Clarke's co-leader pianist-
arranger Francie Boland, German trombonist Albert Mangles-
dorf, French pianists René Utreger and Martial Solal, and, of
course, the Scandinavian contingent—but again the list is too
long.

The Clarke-Boland Band is a true European band, for their
musicians are settled in cities all over the Continent; they as-
semble to play concerts and then disperse to their local scenes
and gigs. But Paris, as you may have guessed from what has
been said thus far, is the center of most of this activity. This is
partly because it is such a pleasant place that it attracted many
just after the war who simply stayed on. It is partly, too, because
local authorites there have—at least, until recently—been far

more liberal than elsewhere in permitting foreign musicians to work. It must be admitted finally that the French have long made a display of enthusiasm for jazz, and, indeed, for all American music. But I, from two army years in Europe and a few visits to France, am inclined to view such enthusiasm rather skeptically. Europeans in general, and especially the French, seem terrifically excited about our music without ever really understanding what it is about. The composer and critic Ned Rorem, who knows the French so well, seems to agree with me in this: "Rightly or wrongly the French have always conde-scended to cultures beyond their frontiers. Before the New Wave of 1960 they admitted to no American influence, since what, after all, beyond our 'barbarism,' did we have to offer? Surely not so-called Serious Music. Except for Gershwin's, names like Copland or Harris or Sessions were merely names when I first arrived here, and are still merely names. The 'bar-barism' of jazz, which they respected (or rather were dazzled by), they quickly mistranslated into Ravel or Josephine Baker."

I like that; there is a world of wicked understanding in it.

IF IN THE last few pages I seem to have talked a lot about jazz and not much about blues, it is not because I am trying to pretend they are precisely the same, but because until fairly recently the Europeans had no firsthand experience of the mu-sic from the men who made it, the bluesmen themselves. Oh, they would hear plenty from jazzmen like Louis Armstrong; he sang a lot of blues, no mistaking, but he was chiefly a per-former, a great solo musician, and certainly not a bluesman of the old sort. Except through phonograph records, the pure blues style was virtually unknown in Europe until Big Bill Broonzy made his way over in the early fifties. He did a short tour on the Continent but enjoyed his greatest success in Great Britain, where he not only played to interested and receptive (though never especially large) audiences, but also was taken up by a group of intellectuals, including the then quite young Paul Oliver, all of whom were most encouraging. They made him feel so welcome there that he stuck around long enough to do an "as-told-to" autobiography, which he called *Big Bill Blues,* with one Yannick Bruynoghe.

Ultimately, Big Bill returned to Chicago—he died there in

1958—and told a friend of his, Peter Chatman, that they sure liked listening to those old blues over in Europe. And who is Peter Chatman? He is a piano-playing bluesman who was born in Shelby County, Tennessee, in 1915—that's Memphis. And when he first began playing and singing around the South, he took the city's name as his own and began calling himself Memphis Slim. It wasn't until he came North, to Chicago, in 1937 that Slim really hit his stride, though. After he had been there a while, he hooked up with Big Bill, who encouraged him to drop the style he had developed (which Slim admits today was highly derivative of Roosevelt Sykes') and develop his own. He did, and he has done well ever since—with Broonzy, and subsequently as one of the house rhythm section for blues recording sessions on Bluebird in Chicago.

Memphis Slim did a lot of writing, too. He estimates that he must have composed about 300 songs in his lifetime, and these include a couple that would classify as classics on just about any list: "Feel Like Screamin' and Cryin' " and "Every Day I Have the Blues." In addition, he is one of the ablest of the blues pianists, right up there with that paragon of the two-handed style, Little Brother Montgomery. And he sings in good, full voice and shows an ability to phrase that not many of the older singers can match.

In other words, he was far better equipped than most of the blues practitioners in his little circle in Chicago, and when Big Bill Broonzy came back from his successful sojourn in Europe telling all about it, Slim was one of the top bluesmen in town. And although Europe sounded pretty good to him, he had too much work to consider a trip then. Just a couple of years after that, however, something called rock-and-roll blew the bottom out of things there in Chicago, and before he knew it Peter Chatman was just another bluesman looking for a gig.

More resourceful than most, Memphis Slim managed to work his way into the folk-concert-and-coffeehouse circuit. He played the Newport Festival in 1959, was picked up by Joe Glaser, Louis Armstrong's manager, and was booked the following year for a European tour.

"Yes," says Slim, "that was 1960, but I wasn't over long then —just three months, and all that was in England and Belgium and Denmark. It wasn't until 1962 that I came back and hit Paris for the first time. I haven't really left since."

And how has it been for him in Paris? "Oh, it's been fantastic. I've got more peace of mind over here. There's less discrimination, so to speak. Although you get a certain amount of prejudice all over the world, here they let me do my thing. I've found here what practically every man is looking for—a lovely wife, a darling daughter."

It was his wife, Christine, with whom I had talked on the telephone and arranged the interview. "Are you sure it will be all right?" I asked, for I had not written and asked beforehand.

"Oh, yes," she assured me. "I make these appointments for him all the time." Her English is good, but, as one might expect, she has a heavy and rather charming French accent. She is attractive, dark-haired, precise. There is something almost shrewd in her manner. It later came as no surprise to learn that Slim has given her a great deal of credit for his success in Europe, pointing to the good advice she has given him in career matters and the managing of his money.

Signs of that success are evident everywhere. The Chatman's big, plush, and beautifully furnished apartment is located in a big elevator building on the Boulevard Suchet, near the Bois de Boulogne. It is one of Paris' most luxurious districts. His Rolls-Royce Silver Cloud is parked out on the street, and her Cadillac is in the garage.

Europe paid for all this. For quite some time he held forth with great success at Les Trois Mailletz, a left-bank club, traveling out of Paris from time to time to do concert dates all over Europe. But for the past few years now the more lucrative concerts have predominated. He ranges wide across the Continent, calls himself "the ambassador of the blues," and presents a unique show which he calls *The Story of the Blues*. It's just Memphis Slim and his piano up there on the stage in a kind of lecture-concert of nearly three hours' duration. He plays and sings the songs, traces the development of the music chronologically, and strings it all together with anecdotes, personal reminiscences, and his own knowing brand of black-belt humor. Whether they understand precisely or not, audiences in just about every European country have responded warmly to him.

When one meets him in person, it is easy to understand why. For one thing, he is a very impressive man physically. About six-feet-five or six-feet-six in height, he is very dark in complexion, with what may be a birthmark patch of white in his

closely-cropped black hair. As I shake hands with him, it occurs to me that mine has probably never been gripped by one
quite as large. His hands are nearly twelve inches in length, but
because of his long, tapering, narrow fingers, they seem almost
delicate. But physical presence aside, Memphis Slim exudes a
kind of confident warmth that is quite infectious.

I guess it was because of the frank, direct quality that I perceived in him that I felt encouraged to ask him the sort of
personal questions that are best left to the end of any interview.
I remember inquiring if he thought his lengthy stay in Europe
had changed him much.

"You mean as a man? Oh, yes, I've changed quite a bit. I've
stopped drinking—just mineral water and some Coke, you
know. No vices to speak of now. I'm a typical family man in the
way I never expected to be. But you know how it is, it's about
time. I've done everything else that a man *shouldn't* do, so I
guess it's time that I was decent for a change."

And as an artist? Has he changed that way, too? "I think, yes,
I am different as an artist. I've learned a lot over here. I'm more
relaxed and confident. I really know about audiences now. But
I've worked at it, the way I never really did back home the way
I should. You know, I've seen just about all my old friends at one
time or another since I settled over here—either they're passing
through here or I catch them on these short trips I take back to
the States. And they want to know, you know, how it's done over
here. How did I get all this? And I'm not sure just what I can
tell them. I guess I should say it's not so easy to make it over
here as it looks. Partly it's a question of being in the right place
at the right time. And partly, too, it's a matter of having the
right sort of character to know how to get along. One thing I
found out right away, for instance, is you can't come here and
tell them we do it this way back home, and so that's the way you
ought to do it here. They're proud, these people, and they don't
like to be told."

"You do get back to the United States every once in a while
then?"

"Oh, sure. I was back and did Newport in 1965, and then the
next year I did the Monterey Festival." That was in 1966. He was
booked down to play in the Ash Grove in Los Angeles, and he
found it quite an experience. "Oh, they liked me pretty good,

but I was shocked at them—acting so goofy and dressed so funny. The girls were wearing old evening gowns and going around barefoot. I guess you'd call them early hippies."

Slim says that what he would really like to do is play concerts like the ones he does at colleges and universities across Europe. "Give my wife a chance to see America and get some idea of it. She'd really like to do that. But I know we'd go back to Paris, because this is home to us."

Bad experiences in the past have convinced him, too, that he doesn't want to get deeply involved in business dealings back in America. "Oh, man, it was a rat race, I'll tell you. Those companies I recorded for, they made so much money off of us that we never saw. It was always like that. You'd call up and try to get some kind of explanation out of them, and unless you were riding on top with a hit record just then they wouldn't even talk to you. *That's* the rat race I'm talking about. I fought this shit a long time, and then I got out of it just the way I wanted to by coming over here. I don't know if I would even have survived if I'd stayed there.

"It's entirely different here. They treat you like you're some-body. I've been on television so many times and in so many countries I can hardly keep count. This fellow, Jean-Christophe Verte, he helped introduce me with his television show. I was on it a lot—1962 and 1963, that was Memphis Slim year on French TV. But then I've been on television in all those other countries, too—Rumania, Yugoslavia, Italy, Belgium, England, Germany, Holland, Poland, Austria, Switzerland—and concerts there and other places, too. So, you see, I really keep pretty busy over here. And oh, yeah, a little movie work, too. I had a small singing part in that American movie they shot over here, *The Sergeant.* And then I did the music for this one French film, *Femme Noire, Femme Nue,* and I'm going to do another one."

"What about European audiences?" I ask. "Are they different from American"

He nodded emphatically. "Yes, I think European audiences in general are more appreciative than in America. In America, see, they think they know all about it, and they almost let it get away from them. Over here they give you the same attention they would give any classical artists. They really *study* the blues when I talk to them about it. I tell them, you know, 'The blues is not so bad. The blues is part of life.' And they're really listening to you, see.

"I don't know, they're all good, I guess. But I like playing for French audiences because they may not know what you're saying about blues being a spiritualistic thing, but they go for it anyway. I get through to them. I feel it. I know I'm getting the same reaction from them here as in the Baptist Church, where they cry and shout. Well, they don't do that here, but they understand. They may not know English, but they like the music.

"Germany? You get a good audience there, too. Jazz is quite new in Germany, and they're still learning. *Very* attentive, you know? I remember I was onstage at a concert in Germany when the news came about President Kennedy being killed. The concert ended right then. The people started crying and walked out. The Germans would come up to me then on the street, guessing I was American, and they'd say to me that it was a shame and all because Kennedy was such a president for the black people. Oh, he was loved by the people in Europe and loved here in France, I'll tell you he was.

"Then just a little while ago, when there was all that rioting and stuff, people here in Europe they'd come up to me and say, 'What's the matter? Is America falling apart?' And I'd say, 'Hell, that's how America was built.' You know how it is. Just because we're over here doesn't mean we stop being Americans. Us musicians, we talk like hell about America, but we don't want a foreigner saying anything bad about it. If they do, then we jump all over them. But I guess that's just the natural way to be."

MISSISSIPPI JOHN HURT. *Dick Waterman*

MISSISSIPPI FRED McDOWELL, LUTHER ALLISON, J. B. HUTTO, and BUDDY GUY.

Joseph J. S

MUDDY WATERS.   *Betty Lane*

SON HOUSE. *Joseph J. S*

MANCE LIPSCOMB.

Baron Wolman

BIG BOY CRUDUP. *George Wilkinson*

LIGHTNING HOPKINS. *Dick Waterman*

BUKKA WHITE.   *Baron Wolman*

FURRY LEWIS.   *Dick Waterman*

PART THREE

CHAPTER TEN

"NASHVILLE STONEWALL BLUES"

HAVING GONE to such lengths earlier to try to prove mutual influence between white music and black as early as the nineteenth century, I am obliged to explain—or explain away—the determined survival of a brand of music that proponents insist is *pure* white. But "survival" is all wrong; it is far too weak a word. Right now there is no form of popular music in America that shows quite such vigor and activity as that of the Southern whites—call it hillbilly music, country and western, or anything you like, it is where a lot is happening right now.

Does this contradict my contention that the blues is the *fundamental* American music, that it has given shape and substance to all our music in the twentieth century? I don't think so. For although Merle Haggard is proud to be an Okie from Muskogee, and although all the country music cats in Nashville went for George Wallace in 1968, and although there really was a hillbilly hit a few years back by a character who called himself Johnny Rebel titled, "Nigger Hatin' Me"—nevertheless this music that has been extolled as racially pure was actually about octoroon at the outset and is now of such mingled parentage that it is a kind of miracle of musical miscegenation. The miracle is that, in spite of all evidence to the contrary given us by our ears, country and western continues to "pass" as white.

Like every other form of American music, country and western is an amalgam of styles. Musical influences from all over have come together to make the music what it is today. However, as the now widely accepted label—country and western—indicates, two strains predominate, and they survive even today, certain performers emphasizing one or the other or perhaps bringing them both together into a kind of neutral Nashville style.

Country music came first. It is probably what people mean when they talk about hillbilly music, for a lot of the first country performers came from the southern Appalachian belt and carried the old mountain balladeering and country-dance styles into the recording studios with them when, in the early twenties, the first samples of rural Southern white music were put on wax. Among many of them, too, there was a great preference for old songs—popular hits of the 1890s that perhaps had just worked their way up into the remote mountain recesses from which some of the best singers and pickers had come. This may have been why country music was never referred to as hillbilly music (a slang term with pejorative overtones) in the early record catalogues, but as "old-time music."

Just how "white" was it? Not very. The popular music of the 1890s and the first decade of the twentieth century was all ajump and aquiver with ragtime—America's first black music craze. And ragtime breaks and devices, as well as its distinctive tempo can be heard in country tunes like "Ain't Nobody's Business" and "Bully of the Town." There were also the so-called "coon songs," nearly all of which were written and sung by whites and were what was left of the old black-face minstrel tradition of the mid-nineteenth century. It may have been a poor imitation of black music, but nevertheless it *was* an imitation that was based on something real.

By the time the ballad tradition had merged into country music, it was a long way from the pure English style that the first rural settlers had brought with them. These were American ballads that were recorded by the early performers—"The Wreck of the Old 97" (Vernon Dalhart), "Buddy, Won't You Roll Down the Line" (Uncle Dave Macon), and "Wabash Cannon

Ball" (The Carter Family)—some of which were derived from Negro sources and all of which contained those subtle black rhythms, licks, and harmonies that even by the late nineteenth century had permeated nearly all American music.

And country dance? The instrument that made it what it was, that gave its distinctive ticky-ticky sound, was the banjo. They call it the only native American instrument—but how American was it, really? Musicologists trace it back in its fundamental form (strings stretched across a drumhead) to an African instrument called the *bania*. Even the white country guitar style, which expanded the player's range beyond old-fashioned strumming, was widely known as "nigger-picking," a clear nod to the black's superior technique on the instrument as source and inspiration.

But this talk of influences and sources is all pretty vague. It may give the erroneous impression that all this took place in two or three thick-walled chambers where from time to time wisps of melody managed to penetrate and were sometimes picked up. The reality was much different, of course. Music was in the air all the time. Even in medium-sized cities in the South like Atlanta, Charleston, and Richmond there would be buskers on every corner, white and black, singing out and trading songs with one another. Music was a matter of direct face-to-face encounter. You get an idea of this from what Bill Monroe told James Rooney in the latter's book, *Bossmen*. Monroe, of course, is the champion of bluegrass, which comes down to us as a direct and fairly pure survival of the old country style. The question was how he got started, and answering it, Monroe began talking about a black man back in Kentucky.

> The first time I think I ever seen Arnold Schultz . . . this square dance was at Rosine, Kentucky, and Arnold and two more colored fellows come up there and played for the dance. They had a guitar, banjo, and fiddle. Arnold played the guitar but he could play the fiddle—numbers like "Sally Goodin." People loved Arnold so well all through Kentucky there; if he was playing a guitar they'd go gang up around him till he would get tired and then maybe he'd go catch a train. . . . I used to listen to him talk and he would tell about contests that he had been in and how tough they was and how they'd play these two blues numbers and tie it up. And they had to do another number and I remember him

saying that he played a waltz number and he won this contest. . . . There's things in my music, you know, that come from Arnold Schultz—runs that I use in a lot of my music. I don't say that I make them the same that he could make them 'cause he was powerful with it. In following a fiddle piece or a breakdown, he used a pick and he could just run from one chord to another the prettiest you've ever heard. There's no guitar picker today that could do that. I tried to keep in mind a little of it—what I could salvage to use in my music. Then he could play some blues and I wanted some blues in my music too, you see. Me and him played for a dance there one night and he played the fiddle and we started at sundown and the next morning at daylight we was still playing music—all night long—that was about the last time I ever saw him. I believe if there's ever an old gentleman that passed away and is resting in peace, it was Arnold Schultz—I really believe that.

Bear in mind that's Bill Monroe talking, foremost exponent of the style that is thought by some to be the purest "white" music played in America today.

The "western" component of the country and western label is, in some sense, a misnomer. By and large, it is that only by comparison to the "eastern" country music, which seemed to emanate originally and almost exclusively from the Southeast. All the early stars of country music were from well east of the Mississippi, but the music's first real superstar, Jimmie Rodgers, was born in Meridian, Mississippi, right in the heart of blues country, in 1897. Rodgers' mother died when he was only four years old, and his father, a gang foreman on the Mobile and Ohio Railroad, began taking the boy out on the line with him. It was a rough way to grow up, knowing no real home, sleeping in bunk cars and cheap hotels throughout the Delta country. But he saw a lot of the world that way. His father worked in and out of the cities of the mid-South, and as a boy, Jimmie Rodgers had a chance to hear every sort of music the region had to offer; and this included a liberal education in the blues. In fact, when they returned to Meridian, when he was still a boy, he began to earn money of his own by carrying water to the black work gangs there in the yards. The black men taught him songs and gave him his first lessons on guitar and banjo.

He kept right on playing and singing when he went to work for the New Orleans and Northeastern Railroad as a brakeman, carrying his guitar with him, as legend has it, learning songs up and down the line from blacks as well as whites. And at the same time he had a little combo with which he played dances, picnics, and rallies around Meridian. He loved music, but would probably have continued indefinitely as a railroad man, except that in 1925 he showed up with tuberculosis and the railroad doctors forced him to retire. Left with no livelihood, he decided to try the only other thing he knew: He joined a medicine show that was touring the area, and because of his singing style and repertoire, he did his act in blackface. While he was out on the road, however, his health deteriorated, and he decided he might be better off breathing mountain air. He moved to Asheville, North Carolina, organized a little hillbilly band, and began to make a local reputation for himself playing around town and on the local radio station.

That was what he was doing when he was discovered in 1927 by a scout for the Victor Talking Machine Company. He signed a contract and began recording immediately. On his first session he cut a ballad and an old-time popular song; when released the record did well enough to let the Victor people know they had a potential winner in Jimmie Rodgers. Before the year was out they had him up to the big studio in Camden, New Jersey, for another session—and he came well stocked, bringing a lot of original material with him to record. Among these songs was his first big hit. Here's how it went:

T for Texas, T for Tennessee (twice)
T for Thelma, that gal that made a wreck of me.

If you don't want me, mama, you sure don't have to call (twice)
'Cause I can get more women than a passenger train can haul.

I'm gonna buy me a pistol just as long as I'm tall (twice)
I'm gonna shoot poor Thelma just to see her jump and fall.

I'm goin' where the water tastes like cherry wine (twice)
'Cause the Georgia water tastes like turpentine.

And so on. Pure blues—some trace it back to Blind Lemon Jefferson—with this difference: Between phrases, Rodgers would put his head back and wail out a yodel. This was the famous "Blue Yodel," which he was to repeat in a numbered series of blues all the way up to the thirteenth, which was known as "Jimmie Rodgers' Last Blue Yodel" and recorded just two days before his death from tuberculosis in 1933. Rodgers' yodel was something different. In intonation and phrasing it was far removed from the Swiss yodel, which was the presumed model. It was almost closer to the falsetto cry used by certain Delta bluesmen. But there was also a lot that was original in it, too, and it became Rodgers' signature as he became better and better known throughout the South.

He recorded many other blues without the yodel during the six and a half years that he had left in his career. Some of them were original and some simply cribbed from local bluesmen whom he had followed around as a boy and younger man. Although the yodel and his cowboy ways (he made his home in Texas) were what his fans remembered, his lasting contribution to country music was the blues. If ever a white man could sing them, it was Jimmie Rodgers. He introduced the raw black strain into Southern white music, and because he was its biggest star (only Hank Williams since has even come close) and an enormous, lasting influence, it has flourished there ever since. The western component in country and western, then, is essentially and most importantly the introduction of pure blues and blues elements into the music.

Inevitably, Jimmie Rodgers had imitators. Some of them, like Gene Autry, Hank Snow, and Ernest Tubb, became stars in their own right, chiefly by emphasizing the cowboy image even more strongly than had Rodgers. Although he is not quite so well remembered today as a country and western performer, Jimmie Davis was certainly the most interesting of them all. When he was at the top of his musical career, he was best known as a songwriter—his "Nobody's Darlin' but Mine" and "You Are My Sunshine" became national favorites. In fact, by the end of the thirties, Jimmie Davis was riding so high that he decided to run for governor of his home state of Louisiana. He was better qualified than you might suppose. With a B.A. from Louisiana College and an M.A. from Louisiana State University, he had taught history and social science at Dodd College before he had decided that he might, after all, be able to do better as an entertainer. Running against the tough Louisiana Long machine, he beat Huey's brother and the incumbent governor, Earl Long, in the Democratic primary of 1944 and became governor of the State of Louisiana until 1948. Beaten out by Earl then, he returned for another four years in 1960. What kind of governor was Jimmie Davis? Not bad, even by national standards. He was, of course, a Populist—since Huey Long every Deep South governor must be a Populist—but unlike some others, he was notably liberal toward his black constituents; he came as close as any for a long time to being a governor for *all* the people of Louisiana.

If he had not, he would have been an awful hypocrite, for Jimmie Davis, the country and western performer, owed southern blacks a great debt, greater perhaps than that of anyone since Jimmie Rodgers. Davis was from Shreveport, Leadbelly's stamping grounds, an old blues town that was blessedly free of Cajun, zydig, and jazz influences. The future governor grew up listening to the blues, and that was what he poured into his music time and time again, on record after record. The material he became known for first was distinctly black in tone, much of it in the blues form and nearly all of it downright bawdy: "She's a Hum Dum Dinger from Dingersville," "Triflin' Mama Blues," and "Sewing Machine Blues." Not only that, but he recorded with black musicians, a practice that was virtually unknown in the South during the thirties. And if he sought out such musical associations, it was because they were natural to him. Jimmie Davis had a keen appreciation of black music in general, and of the blues in particular.

Are there any other white singers who continue to extend the sound and spirit of the blues into country and western music? There are at least a few. First of all, there are the many who have worked their way in through rock-and-roll. Nashville called it "nigger music" when Elvis Presley first exploded out of Memphis in 1954, and wanted nothing to do with it. At that time they wouldn't even allow drums to be played on the stage of the Grand Ole Opry. But gradually the entrepreneurs of country and western were won over. There was no arguing with the fact that the kids liked the music, was there? And, well, it might not really *hurt* to have a couple of them around, like this Conway Twitty and this piano player from Louisiana—what was his name?—Jerry Lee Lewis, that was it. After all, they were all good country boys at heart, and maybe they might have a little something to offer.

Right on both counts. They were good country boys at heart —and Conway Twitty proved it by immersing himself completely in a sweet country style that has all but obliterated traces of the old rock-and-roller. And Jerry Lee? Still hangin' in like Gunga Din, he hasn't changed himself or his style to suit anybody, but he has certainly had an effect on the music. He opened up country and western, "modernized" it (though I'm not sure what that means in this context), and gave it a harder sound. He and the Elvis Presley influence (which has been terrific in the mid-South) helped pave the way for exciting young performers like Jerry Reed.

But there are also a couple of others who, like Jimmie Rodgers, seem to carry in them the old blues spirit. Do they sing the blues? Sure, every singer in country and western today has some blues or blues-derived material in his repertoire. But more important, these two have the old blues feeling—the bitter knowledge of disaster and personal misery that may be there waiting for us on this day or the next. They've been there and back; they know the score. And ask any bluesman what the blues is all about, and they'll begin, "Well, the blues is a feeling. . . ."

Merle Haggard has it. He's lived the life everyone seems to think that Johnny Cash has. He was born the son of an Oklahoma migrant in California at the end of a long trek not unlike that of the Joad family in *Grapes of Wrath*. Times were hard for them. His father died early, and Merle got in trouble—burglary and jailbreak kind of trouble—and wound up doing three years in San Quentin. That was the first time Merle Haggard ever heard Johnny Cash—at a concert when Cash drove in and drove out of the state prison on the same afternoon. It looked to Merle like a better way to make a living than the one he had tried, and so when he got out he gave it a whirl. It worked out well for him because even by then—and he was only in his mid-twenties—he had amassed enough bitter experience to make those tough songs he sang—"Lonesome Fugitive,"

"Mama Tried," "They're Tearing the Labor Camps Down," and "Hungry Eyes"—practically quiver with authenticity. It was inevitable, too, that Haggard would be drawn to Jimmie Rodgers, and he has become the old Singing Brakeman's greatest modern interpreter. The two-record album of Rodgers' songs that Haggard recorded a few years ago comes as close to being a top country and western classic as anything—well, as close as anything since Jimmie Rodgers himself died, choking on blood, just after his last recording session.

Waylon Jennings is not nearly as well known, nor has he led the sort of hard life that may be equated directly with the groaning miseries of which he sings. Oh, there were the usual troubles with the pills (as booze to bluesmen, as heroin to jazzmen, so amphetamines to country and westerners), but they were par for the course. Somehow all the disappointments, difficulties, and agonies he has ever had are right there in his voice, though, transmuted into something beyond sadness—a kind of infinite weariness that seems to say he is ready to endure anything life might have in store. Although he is not a prolific writer of songs, as is Merle Haggard, Jennings has shown excellent taste in choosing material; you don't find the usual minimum of 25 percent of sentimental trash on his albums that nearly all other country and western performers seem to carry on theirs. He has been far more venturesome in picking his songs, too. Not only has he recorded work by the top young writers in the field—Kris Kristofferson, Mickey Newbury, and Haggard, to name a few—he has gone beyond it and sought out songs by Bob Dylan, John Lennon and Paul McCartney, Jim Webb, Gordon Lightfoot, Mick Jagger and Keith Richard, and even Chuck Berry. You get the sense of the larger idiom in all this, an awareness of just how closely related are the genres and styles of music represented by these various writers.

WHAT ABOUT black performers in country and western? Over the years, there have been a few. Even in the early thirties, the Mississippi Sheiks, a hot black string band that was made up of members of the very musical Chatman family, were pushed on OKeh records in both the blues and country categories. One of the original performers on the Grand Ole Opry was a black harmonica virtuoso named DeFord Bailey, who cut the first records ever made in Nashville—eight masters for Victor in 1928. Although he stayed on for years, he became increasingly bitter at the second-class treatment and payment given him on the Opry, and so he quit, and he has remained out of music— white or black—ever since. He runs a shoeshine stand in the black district of Nashville.

Lately, others have fared better. Country and western impresario Shelby Singleton has been pushing a Negro vocalist named Linda Martell; she has recorded and been on the Opry a number of times. Stoney Edwards is a much bigger name. He has had one superhit in "Odd-Job Dollar Bill Man," about a hard-working guy who makes his money any way he can (or however the rhyme goes). At this writing Edwards has had three albums issued by Capitol, and his audience is still growing; he has a real future in country and western music. This is so chiefly because he has a fine voice, a good style, and a real country feel for a song. But clearly a bit of thought and conscious image-building has gone into his selection of material. He seems to present himself as an industrious and dependable individual ("Odd-Job Dollar Bill Man") who piously honors his parents and his God ("Daddy Did His Best"), yet he also takes pains to remind his white listeners that he shares a lot with them in attitudes and country heritage ("You Can't Call Yourself Country"). It's a good image, anything but Stepin Fetchit: self-respecting, upright . . . and square. What is lacking—by intention, surely—is any suggestion of sexuality; he is strictly a steady family man in his songs ("A Kingdom I Call Home"). And this is rather rare in the country field, where many male singers play the tomcat onstage and do some rather frank sexual boasting in their material. Edwards has very wisely declined this role. A black man's position in country and western music is precarious at best; it is best not to tempt the white country audience into the sort of neurotic fear of black sexuality that has riven the South for a couple of centuries.

In this, as in much else, Stoney Edwards is simply following the lead of Charley Pride—and a good thing, too, for there is no arguing with the phenomenal success achieved by country and western's one and only black superstar. Those outside the field don't know quite what to make of Pride. Some seem content to

shrug him off as an anomaly, just the sort of oddity that pops
up now and again in any field to let us know there are rules
operative that we might otherwise have overlooked. Others dismiss him as a kind of imitation white man, an Uncle Tom at
worst and an Oreo at best.

But all you have to do is watch him in live performance to
know that his success is no accident. There is something curiously and singularly personal in his appeal to the white audiences who flock in huge numbers to see and hear him. And talk
to him for a little while, and you will realize that he is not an
imitation anything, but the absolutely genuine Charley Frank
Pride from Sledge, Mississippi. That's right. The name that
sounds like a publicity agent's brainstorm is the one he was
born with thirty-odd years ago in that little Delta cotton-and-
corn town just south of Memphis off Highway 61.

Mention that name today in any city in the South—even one
on the border, like Baltimore—and you will get the kind of
immediate attention that any self-respecting name-dropper
feels is his due. That was the sort of treatment I got, anyway,
at the downtown Holiday Inn there when I asked if Charley
Pride had registered. The girl behind the desk said no, there
were no rooms reserved in his name, but added confidentially
that they were sort of expecting him because there was to be a
reception later on that night following his show at the huge
Civic Center across the street. I knew he would be arriving
shortly, for I had made a date to talk with him.

And just as I turned away from the desk, I spotted him coming in the door in the company of his manager, Jack D. Johnson,
and his second-line singer, Johnny Duncan (both white). They
caused quite a stir. But in the few minutes it took for Charley
Pride to work his way clear of the little crowd that congregated
around him at the desk, I managed to introduce myself and get
invited upstairs.

On the way he was spotted through the coffeeshop window by
a waitress. He smiled and gave her a wave, but before we had
reached the elevator she had overtaken him and asked for his
autograph. In the elevator I asked him if he grows tired of
shaking hands and signing autographs. "No," he said, "I love
being recognized. I don't think I'll ever get tired of that. As a
matter of fact, I wish I could have more contact with people

than I do. I'll tell you, what I really miss is being able to come off the stand and sit down in back and just talk to people, the way I used to when I first started out. They treat me like a star now, and that makes it hard to talk to anybody."

In the room he tossed himself down on the bed, propped a pillow behind his head, and continued in the same vein, explaining that he is a Pisces. "Very talkative. That's my nature —just the way I happen to be. I don't believe in planning your life by your sign, but I think it helps in understanding yourself and other people. I didn't even know what my sign was until about six months ago, when I read a book on astrology somebody gave me."

Anybody whose life has changed as dramatically as has Charley Pride's might well be interested in astrology or any other system that would offer him some hint as to what fate has in store for him next.

Born the son of a farmhand, he grew up with seven brothers and three sisters in the rural South and had logged plenty of hours in the cotton fields before he had even finished his education at Sledge Junior High. Nights were spent close to the radio, listening to the little radio stations around them on which he heard music of all kinds. "But the music I, personally, chose to listen to was country music," he emphasizes.

"I don't know why it was exactly. People are always saying to me, 'Why don't you sing this way or that way?' You know, as a matter of my pigmentation. Like whether you were pink or purple or whatever really should determine in some kind of absolute way the kind of music you like. That's kind of silly, isn't it? I mean it's all American music, anyway. And besides, I've always been an individualist—and that's how I try to fit into society—as an individual, and not as a pink or purple. I eliminated those skin hangups a long time ago."

But as for music in his youth, he says, he just listened and liked. Who in particular? "Oh, the whole country spectrum from the 1940s when I was growing up—Ernest Tubb, Eddy Arnold, and Hank Williams, all of them. I just loved the hits and learned them all." He had also picked up a little guitar, but insists he is no musician, and he is only embarrassed when he is described, as he has been in an article or two, as "an excellent

He had no special musical ambitions, but ambition he had aplenty. "It looked to me when I was growing up that the way out of the cotton field was baseball." With blacks permitted in the major leagues for the first time during those years, he determined he would play major league baseball himself one day. And he did eventually—during a few weeks in 1961 for the then Los Angeles Angels. This was the culmination of a career that began when he left Sledge at the age of seventeen to join the old Negro American League. He played first for Detroit and then for the Memphis Red Sox. Following a stretch in the army, when he married his wife, Rozene, he got the break that landed him on the Angels. Trying too hard to please, he soon developed a sore arm and one day was taken aside and given his walking papers. They told him he just didn't have a "major league arm."

Eventually, he wound up in Helena, Montana, where he worked in a smelting factory and played semipro baseball for the Amvets. "I remember where I was living in Helena, I was working the swingshift, and I would lay down on those off-hours trying to sleep, and I couldn't because there was this country group practicing next door. Well, I figured, if you can't beat 'em, join 'em, so I went over with my old Sears Silvertone guitar and began making some music with them. That started things. We played around Helena a little, and I began singing before the ball games. One day I sang and then had a pretty good day at the plate, and they wrote me up in the papers. And all of a sudden I was a local celebrity." One thing led to another then, and people started urging him to try for the big time, and so he headed for Nashville.

An audition before Chet Atkins, the top country guitarist who bosses RCA's Nashville operation, brought Charley Pride an immediate long-term recording contract. But the question was, how could he be sold to white country and western audiences? To be honest, he wasn't so much sold as put over on them. RCA released three singles by their new artist over the course of several months—yet there was not a word of publicity on him and not a single picture. All three records hit well up on the country and western charts, purely because of Pride's fine voice and his ability to sell a song. And so by the time they got around to letting people know what he looked like he was well established as a new star in the field.

Still, when he began making personal appearances there were some awkward moments. People were always asking him embarrassing things like, "How come you don't sound like you look?" And then there was the woman who came to hear him sing his first big single, "Just Between You and Me," and took one look at him when he came on stage and groaned loudly, "No, no, it can't be!" Then he started singing her favorite song, and she began shrieking ecstatically, "It's true! It's true!" Yes, every time he opened his mouth and started singing those hits of his—songs like "The Snakes Crawl at Night," "Does My Ring Hurt Your Finger?," and "Before I Met You"—he picked up more fans and became a little less an oddity and a lot more a star.

Right now, with sixteen albums and about as many hit singles to his credit, he's in the superstar class, right up there with Johnny Cash and Glen Campbell. Interestingly enough, however, Charley Pride is purer country, both in style and appeal, than either of those two giants in the field. He sings a sweet song—much of his material is unblushingly sentimental—in a rich baritone that throbs with feeling.

He's aware of where he is in the country and western field today and what it took to get him there—and he seems to have no regrets, for fundamentally Charley Pride is a very competitive individual. "Yeah, see, we live in a world of comparison and competitiveness. And since I started out from behind right from the git-go—I don't have any harsh feelings about this, I'm just trying to be realistic—what this means is that when an opportunity comes my way I have to work three or four or five times as hard as the next guy in order to take advantage of it. This is what I've done all my life—been in competition with people, trying to learn the knack of things.

"Why, I remember once I told my Dad I could beat him picking cotton, and I did, going down the rows—but when we weighed up, he had more poundage. So he went back and showed me all I'd missed, showed me the *right* way to do it. Eventually I did it right and beat him, though."

He smiled then, summing up: "Come right down to it, I guess that's my story. I'm just an old cotton picker doing the best he can."

And that best is impressively good. It more than satisfied his sell-out audience that night at Baltimore's Civic Center. Admittedly he had some help. George Jones and Tammy Wynette, who usually headline their own show, performed like the pros they are before intermission, yet failed to cause much excitement. The audience was obviously impatient for the headliner, Charley Pride.

When, after a couple of warm-up acts, he at last appeared, the crowd (virtually all-white) went absolutely wild. The electricity generated among them fairly crackled in the air as he sang many of his old favorites and new hits—among them Kris Kristofferson's "Me and Bobby Magee" and his great recent hit, "Kiss an Angel Good Morning." But make no mistake. Charley Pride wasn't fooling anybody in the Civic Center that night— and he wasn't trying to. They knew he was a black man, and just to make sure they did, he sang Leadbelly's "Cotton Fields" and the song he says is his personal favorite, "I'm Just Me" ("It answers a lot of questions for me," he says), with its refrain:

I'm just born to be exactly what you see
Hey and every day, I'm just me.

And just being Charley Pride seemed to be quite enough for everybody there that night.

CHAPTER ELEVEN

"ROCK ME, MAMA"

How to begin? With that old and oft-quoted formula, "Blues plus country equals rock"? But we have already seen that country and western music is so thoroughly saturated with blues feeling that this is a little like saying that blues plus blues equals rock. Which may not, after all, be far wide of the mark but seems a little like double-talk.

And if I am to indulge in that sort of phrasemongering, what about this one, short and to the point, lifted from Michael Lydon: "Rock 'n' roll was . . . blues with a beat"? Better, for it helps remind us that back before they had even thought to call it rock-and-roll, they were calling the same music rhythm-and-blues. It was the operative phrase for *any* sort of black music that, because of some trick of tempo or style, was not instantly classifiable as blues. It was only when white kids started playing the music in the early fifties that they began calling it something else.

In a way, it all happened the way it did because there grew up after the war a solid young white audience for black music across the country. We could probably go through a record-by-record analysis as some have done (the most exhaustive and

impressive of them is Charlie Gillett's *The Sound of the City*)
that would show conclusively that there was a kind of a growing rebel minority out there. They were tuning into these black
stations at the wrong end of the radio dial and really flipping
for Ivory Joe Hunter, Hank Ballard, Lavern Baker, and maybe
Muddy Waters, too. And all the while snickering contemptu-
ously at their older brothers and sisters who sat in the next
room mooning away at those sweet romantic sounds on "Your
Hit Parade." This is not some retrospective fantasy of the way
it *might* have been; that was the way it *did* happen with thousands of young people of high school age from Tallahassee,
Florida, to Oakland, California. Why this preference for black
music? It seemed funkier, earthier to them; it spoke to them of
violent emotions and more direct attitudes to life and seemed
free of the evasions of the romantic popular music of the period. The difference then was the vast distance that separated
the raunchy hedonism of Hank Ballard's "Work with Me, Annie" from the puerile euphemism of Doris Day's "My Foolish
Heart."

In its own way, of course, this sort of preference for the black
"hit parade," which so often had less to do with the quality of
the music than with its "outlaw" appeal, may have been simply
another brand of romanticism. There was a separate, though
oddly similar, development in relation to jazz and the growth
of the hipster cult of "cool" and emotional detachment; it, too,
had more to do with milieu than music. The two are so closely
parallel in time and attitude that there is almost a high culture-
low culture aspect to the phenomenon, as though the white
rhythm-and-blues audience (which was the one that welcomed
rock-and-roll, after all) were populist hipsters.

But when we look at those musicians and singers who were
directly responsible for the rock-and-roll phenomenon, we find
them much more certain of where their music came from and
what it was all about. Elvis Presley, to start at the top, was from
Tupelo, Mississippi, and had been turned on to the blues long
before he started to record. He told one English interviewer
that he "dug the real low-down Mississippi singers, mostly Big
Bill Broonzy and Big Boy Crudup, although they would scold
me at home for listening to them." And when he was working
as a truck driver in Memphis and wanted to record, he gravi-

tated almost naturally to Sam Phillips' Sun Records, a white-run independent label that had been active up until then recording black bluesmen from the Memphis and Delta areas. Phillips tried Presley on a country and western tune, and neither of them was happy with the results. It wasn't until Elvis started clowning around in the studio doing Arthur Crudup's "That's All Right, " the kind of music he had grown up on in Mississippi, that Phillips really got interested. He had Presley record it just as he had done it during the coffee break—and they had their first big hit. That, in fact, set the pattern, for Elvis Presley first became known in the business as a white singer of black material. His big hits for Sun and most of the best things he did for Victor were black and blues-based. "Milk-cow Blues Boogie," his third release on Sun, was an old Sleepy John Estes tune. "Mystery Train," which followed it, came from blues singer Little Junior Parker. "My Baby Left Me," for Victor, was another Arthur Crudup tune from one of the Mississippi bluesman's Bluebird sessions from early in the forties. He did a couple of Little Richard tunes, too, "Tutti-Frutti" and "Lawdy, Miss Clawdy," and one by Ray Charles, "I Got a Woman." But what about the energetic "Hound Dog"? Although a couple of whites wrote that one, the redoubtable Jerry Lieber and Alvin Stoller, they had handed it over first to Willie Mae "Big Mama" Thornton. Forget about the movie star and the crooning balladeer, it was the Elvis who sang black that his real fans would remember best.

Carl Perkins? He told Michael Lydon that when he was growing up in Tiptonville, Tennessee, he used to listen to the radio a lot. "White music, I liked Bill Monroe, his fast stuff; for colored, I liked John Lee Hooker, Muddy Waters, their electric stuff. Even back then I liked to do Hooker songs Bill Monroe style, blues with a country beat." Jerry Lee Lewis, they say, was influenced by Little Richard during his early Memphis period. And Buddy Holly's favorite guitarist was Lonnie Johnson.

When rock-and-roll came along it subsumed rhythm-and-blues completely. Suddenly performers such as Bo Diddley, Chuck Berry, and Little Richard Penniman found themselves playing to white audiences, and to mixed audiences, and sharing the bill with white performers. They were instant rock-and-roll stars, and in a year's time—say, by the beginning of 1957—

nobody even remembered what rhythm-and-blues was any more.

What about their roots in the blues? They were deep and strong. Ellas McDaniel, who was known universally and apparently only by his nickname, "Bo Diddley," came up to Chicago to make it big and did just that. After playing the blues clubs for a while in the early fifties he hooked up with Muddy Waters and played guitar in his group for a while. When he made his move, it was with Muddy's blessing; he signed a contract with Chess and began recording on the company's affiliate, Checker.

With Chuck Berry the story was similar. He was from East St. Louis, Illinois, where he had a heavy local reputation. One weekend he decided to see how far it would get him in Chicago. He made the rounds of the blues clubs until he found Muddy. When he marched in with his guitar, he was invited to sit in. Muddy liked what he heard and told him to "go see Leonard" (Chess) on Monday. When he showed up at the Chess office, he had with him a tape of a tune he had written—a little number called "Maybellene." Leonard listened. Leonard liked. Leonard signed him up on the spot. And recording in Chicago, as he did, Chuck Berry would often end a day's studio work by jamming in the blues clubs. He loved that scene and was fond of referring to himself—stretching just a little—as a bluesman.

What becomes plain here, as we sift through the beginnings of rock, may not need saying at all—and that is that rock is a direct, straight-line development from the blues. Just listen to any record by Muddy, B.B., or Wolf, and then vote for the rock record of your choice. You'll find they're all running on the same ticket. It is not just that any authentic piece of rock music is almost certain to be based on blues chords (today that is probably true of *most* American music), but also that the instrumentation of the band that plays on that record will be a development of the old Chicago blues band lineup. And that guitar solo in the middle?—the one that really makes it for you? —chances are it's pure blues, strictly Buddy Guy out of Elmore James. The whole idea of rock guitar came out of Chicago, where the blues went electric. Jazz guitar, which, by the time the rock style was being shaped had been developed to almost surgical sharpness, simply had no influence whatever in the development of the rock guitar style. Plenty of accomplished rock guitarists were aware of jazz guitar, but that just wasn't where it was at as far as they were concerned.

Prove the point with any album by Jimi Hendrix, as accomplished a soloist, as certain a virtuoso, as any rock has produced. The Seattle-born guitarist died in 1970 at the age of twenty-eight. What made his death seem especially sad at the time was his great potential—he had only just begun. Nobody seemed better prepared—musically, at least—for a long career than did Hendrix. He had put in a solid apprenticeship and learned his craft well, touring with Little Richard, among others. According to legend, he had turned a feedback problem with a faulty amplifier into one of the most sophisticated techniques used by modern electric guitarists. And that, in a way, was typical of his remarkable ability to make the best of whatever he had at hand. What Jimi Hendrix had at hand when he started was the blues. He began with that. Whatever background in music he had was solid blues. He cited Albert King as the guitarist to whom he had listened longest and from whom he had learned the most. If Hendrix had had the same sort of solid background in jazz to build on, he might have been a much different sort of player, but he would not likely have been a better one. For it was his special genius as a soloist to push blues guitar to its limits, to show just how much could be done melodically and harmonically and still remain within the fairly narrow confines of the old blues structure.

The only other rock instrumentalist around today who even comes close is English guitarist Eric Clapton, fluent, inventive, flashy, and with a strain of that nonstop sitar in his style. What are his blues credentials? Clapton told *Rolling Stone* editor Jann Wenner that Little Walter Jacobs had been one of his big influences, that he had made a conscious effort to translate what Little Walter was doing on harmonica to the guitar. And others?

At first I played exactly like Chuck Berry for six or seven months. You couldn't have told the difference when I was with the Yardbirds. Then I got into older bluesmen. Because he was so readily available I dug Big Bill Broonzy; then I heard a lot of cats I had never heard of before: Robert Johnson and Skip James and Blind Boy Fuller. I just finally got completely overwhelmed and listened to it and went right down in it and came back up in it. I was about seven-teen or eighteen. When I came back up in it, turned on to B. B. King and it's been that way ever since. I still don't think there is a better blues guitarist in the world than B. B. King.

It wasn't long, incidentally, until such generous praise in interviews by rock disciples such as Eric Clapton began to pay off for B. B. King, Albert King, and a couple of other bluesmen. They were suddenly hot on the rock circuit. Their bookings jumped, and their record sales increased.

So it goes. There is no real point, however, in overemphasizing these tributes in print by some young rock superstar or other to certain fairly obscure black bluesmen. For let's face it, it's hip for some young fugitive from the middle-class to say, "All that I am or hope to be I owe to Howlin' Wolf." It lends a certain legitimacy to his efforts and suggests an authenticity that—who knows?—his music may lack. We could multiply such quotations endlessly, but unless there is a real blues quality to the music made by these young performers (as I honestly think there is with Eric Clapton and certainly was with Jimi Hendrix), what they say proves nothing. Honoring that, there are still a few left to talk about.

It should come as no surprise that the first of them is Janis Joplin. Yes, the late rock shouter carved a niche for herself as a sort of latter-day Bessie Smith. She never claimed the title; it was awarded her by such critics as Nat Hentoff and Ralph Gleason, who heard in her a continuation and extension of the old classic blues tradition. And sure, why not? There was a quality of utter abandon to her delivery that no white woman before or since has ever matched. It's true, too, that Bessie Smith was the model she chose. She told David Dalton, "When I first started singing I was copping Bessie Smith records. I used to sing exactly like Bessie Smith, and when I started singing with Big Brother that was the only thing I knew how to do. . . ." Well it would be wrong to pretend that she ended her short career singing "exactly like Bessie Smith." No, she was her own woman, had gone her own way, and chosen her own style by then. It was as pure, authentic, and funky as anybody's, without regard to color. Any record by Janis should be an argument-clinching affirmative to that old pain-in-the-ass question: Can white folks sing the blues? The answer is, "Sure they can, if they got 'em." And Janis Joplin sure had them. She died of them.

I am not, however, so superstar-struck as to pretend that she was absolutely unique in this. She was the best of the blues-influenced young white singers, but there are others—Ida Coxes and Alberta Hunters—to her Bessie. Tracy Nelson of Mother Earth has it all: phrasing, intonation, and feeling, and it all seems as natural—or *authentic,* if you prefer the solid-gold adjective—as can be. Bonnie Raitt is perhaps a bit more studied in her delivery, more consciously a *singer* of songs in a particular style than either of the other two, but she is such a fine singer with such good taste that she never seems to disappoint. Her choice of material is impeccable, and she is a remarkably good guitarist.

Others? Bonnie Bramlett, of Delaney and Bonnie, and Rita Coolidge—down-home girls both. And that brings up a whole category in rock that cannot be neglected even in a survey as cursory as this one, for it is steeped in the old blues tradition and saturated with the feeling. Call it down-home style, for its practitioners are young Southern whites who have listened to black music and country and western all their lives and may have sung "sanctified" in church, as well. You can hear it all there in the music of Delaney and Bonnie, Johnny Winter, and Tony Joe White—three quite different performers, admittedly, but as honest and country as they come.

And then there's Canned Heat. It is a group perhaps most important for what it was and wanted to be than for what it became. It was a white *blues* group—very committed in that—and while the band was whole it did some fine things: "Bullfrog Blues" from their first album, and "Pony Blues," "One Kind Favor," and "Refried Boogie," all from their best album, *Livin' the Blues.* The album they did with John Lee Hooker, however, *Hooker 'n' Heat,* was pure gold. It is more his album than theirs. He sings on every cut and re-establishes himself as a real force in the blues. He was a Detroit bluesman—big frog in a little pond—born in Clarksdale, Mississippi. It seems that about all that I have said about Johnny Lee, as he called himself, up to this point is that he wasn't much of a guitar player. Well, he isn't. But he surely can sing. There is that marvelous, hushed urgency in his voice that is pure Delta, and if he hasn't much guitar technique, he certainly knows how to use the little he possesses to good advantage. Canned Heat deserves a great deal of credit for presenting him as it has on this two-record album. The mood is relaxed, and they give him space enough to stretch out; and what he does on the set more than justifies the time and trouble. The credit should probably go to Alan Wilson, who played guitar and harp with the group and was acknowledged as its "musical director." He and Henry Vestine, the lead guitarist, were both out of the Boston folk blues scene, both had pursued bluesmen in the Deep South (Vestine was along when Skip James was tracked down in Tunica, Mississippi), and the two had been playing blues from high school on. Wilson died of one of those barbiturates-and-booze accidents the same month in 1970 that Janis Joplin and Jimi Hendrix died. *Hooker 'n' Heat* was the last Canned Heat album on which he appeared. And although the group has striven mightily since, they still miss him. Maybe when Henry Vestine and Big Bear Hite and the rest get it together again they'll be able to pick up where Wilson left them.

But when you talk about blues and rock you find that Muddy Waters' name is the one that comes up most. That's right, old Muddy, the alias under which McKinley Morganfield has played ever since he left Clarksdale in 1943 and came North to try his luck in Chicago. Never mind, for the moment, what he did for Chicago blues (which was to take the style that was then still in metamorphosis and shape it into the glorious, whooping electric thing it is now). What has he done for rock?

Plenty. No single bluesman has had more direct nor more personal influence on the development of rock music in America and in England than has Muddy Waters. He dates his "discovery" by the young white audience in America from the moment the Rolling Stones appeared on the scene. They had, after all, taken the name for the group from one of Muddy's tunes, and when their first LP appeared, it had one of his songs, "Just Make Love to Me." And when the Beatles came to America for the first time they told everyone they wanted to see Muddy Waters and Bo Diddley.

"Muddy Waters?" said one reporter. "Where's that?"

Paul McCartney laughed at him and said, "Don't you know who your own famous people are here?"

Muddy, as we shall see, is terribly sensitive about this. He

cannot understand how and why it should be that he has become a rock-and-roll star because of the endorsement of young
English performers.

But even if Mick Jagger, Paul McCartney, Keith Richards,
and George Harrison had never heard of him, Muddy would
still be a star to the young rock audience today, thanks to the
earnest efforts of Paul Butterfield and Mike Bloomfield in his
behalf. The leader of the Paul Butterfield Blues Band and his
erstwhile sideman have made no secret of their personal debt
to Muddy Waters. In the early sixties the two were down on the
South Side of Chicago nearly every night digging the blues—
and Muddy most of all. Butterfield, who had been a student at
the University of Chicago and lived nearby, began making the
blues scene with Nick Gravenites (now a songwriter and man-
about-music in San Francisco) as early as 1957. Mike Bloomfield, years younger and a nervy young guitarist in suburban
rock-and-roll groups, began on his own sometime later. Mike
Bloomfield learned a lot of guitar out there at the wrong end of
town and got what no amount of practice or instruction could
have given: a real feeling for the blues. It is there in everything
he plays today. Paul Butterfield? Tough and durable, one of the
few fixed stars in the blinking firmament of rock; he knows
what he does best, and that is what he does most—play the
blues. He learned his harmonica style from Muddy's harp man
Little Walter and from Rice Miller, and his love for the blues
first from Muddy.

Thus Muddy Waters has become the black stepfather to them
all, the putative parent of a whole generation of young blues-
loving white rockers. This was made more or less official a few
years ago when he got together with his half-brother, Otis
Spann (who had played piano brilliantly in Muddy's blues band
but died later that same year), and with Paul Butterfield, Mike
Bloomfield, and a rock rhythm section; and this generation-
spanning all-star group recorded an album that is easily the
most successful of any such experimental session ever done.
This time it really jelled. Listen to the two records in the album
—all of it quite rightly Muddy's material—and you'll agree that
for once the title fits: *Fathers and Sons.*

That was in April, 1969, the high point of a bad year for
Muddy Waters. He had gotten out of Chicago and was doing a

lot of touring with his band. It was a tough schedule of one-nighters they played, mostly at colleges and universities, with monster jumps in between, and it left little time for them at home. One night in October they were in central Illinois heading north for Chicago when they were involved in a high-speed highway collision. Muddy's driver was killed, and he himself was so badly injured that the rumor was out for a while that he would never make it back. But somehow he did. More than a year later he began playing on crutches, sitting down at the microphone when it got to be too much for him. He kept right on playing and singing those blues until he was soon able to shed the crutches and shout and pick just about as he always had.

He is a big man, a durable man, and when one meets him and talks with him, it seems that his success over the years in this grueling business may be due in no small measure to his considerable physical strength. Those old Delta cotton-field muscles have put him back on his feet again. Not long ago they took him into New York, where he played an engagement at the Village Vanguard and set a new house record. The audience was so young that it seems that a new generation may have come along to claim him as grandfather. Whatever the relationship, however, it was one that clearly pleased Muddy. He sang as well as ever, with the same deep, authoritative tone and the constant laconic half-smile that has fascinated his listeners for years.

It was in New York that I saw him—at the Albert Hotel in the Village, that favorite downtown warren of rock musicians and their followers. His room was no better and no worse than any of the rest in the Albert, yet he seemed to pay no special attention to the dismal surroundings; he carries his dignity with him and needs no fancy furnishings to tell him who he is. He holds nothing back, but he volunteers little. He sits attentively and never hesitates on an answer, but at the same time seems oddly removed from what he is saying.

I remember asking him first about the playing he had done down in Mississippi before he came to Chicago. I had heard him on an album of material originally recorded in the field for the Library of Congress by Alan Lomax. He said that was the first recording he had ever done and was just a matter of being in the right place at the right time. What year was that? The flicker of a frown comes to his face. In 1942, he says after a moment's reflection.

McKinley Morganfield was born in Rolling Fork, Mississippi, in 1915, and he told Paul Oliver that he got his unusual nickname when he was just a baby from playing in a creek that ran just behind the two-room shack where he lived. Muddy's mother died when he was quite young, and he was taken in by his grandmother in Clarksdale. "That was where she raised me," he says, "and that was where I started in to singing the blues."

"How old were you then?"

"Oh, I been singing the blues since I was fourteen. You might say I started *playing* the blues when I was thirteen, though. But I was playing harp when I started, so I didn't sing. Had my mouth full of harp all the time. I started to fool with guitar at the age of seventeen. Scott Bowhandle, who I used to play with, was teaching me. Oh, you know, there wasn't much teaching to it. We would play those parties on a Saturday night, fish fries, where there was dancing and drinking. And Scott might show me a little something on guitar when we was playing. Those were great times. I didn't have no money in my pocket, but I had a ball.

"Influences? Yeah, I was influenced by Son House. I guess he made one or two records back then, but I knew him as a kid. He was all through the Delta back then, and I used to love to hear him play guitar. He had that bottle-neck thing, and he could make the guitar real whiny."

I ask Muddy if playing the blues was how he made his living then.

"You mean down there in the Delta? Around Clarksdale?" I nodded, and he shook his head deprecatingly and said, "Not down there. I worked hard growing cotton and corn. That's some of the hardest work you can get. That'll make a good man out of you. *Had* to work hard. See, I got married down there when I was just seventeen or eighteen. I figured I was wasting my blues talent driving a tractor. So I took my wife and went up North. She came up with me to Chicago. We didn't have no kids then. Do now, though. Got grandkids now."

That was after he had cut those records for Alan Lomax down

on Stovall Plantation. The idea of recording, as he had then, seems to have given him some sense of the greater world that lay beyond the Delta. He knew he had talent. He could play good bottle-neck guitar, and everybody liked the way he sang, and so he decided to take the gamble. He and his wife moved from Clarksdale to Chicago in 1943. It was during the war, and he had no trouble finding a job for himself—in a paper factory —but he remembered why he had come North, and he began playing those house parties right away.

"I don't know," says Muddy with that mysterious smile of his, "I made Chicago like a blues city when I started playing around there. I changed the style. I think it was 1945 when I got my first electric guitar. I was playing in the clubs then. And you can't hear an acoustic in a liquor club. There's just too much noise."

In 1946, he recorded commercially for the first time. He was recommended by Sunnyland Slim to the Chess brothers, and they recorded him on their Aristocrat label. "Rolling Stone" (sound familiar?) was on that first session. Did it move? "It went straight to the market," Muddy says with dramatic emphasis. "Why, by Friday there were 5,000 records out, and on Sunday you couldn't go anyplace without hearing it all over the South Side. And it just kept right on from there."

Success in the Chicago blues world meant working regularly enough so that you didn't have to have a day job. It meant having hit records (probably selling under 100,000) so the people came to see you. Muddy Waters was a success by these standards. And yet he seldom traveled out of Chicago, because he didn't have to. Chicago was where the blues scene was. That was where the people came to see him.

I asked about Paul Butterfield and Mike Bloomfield. Did he remember them coming by to see him?"

"Sure," he says, "sure I do remember them. Why, Paul blowed on my stand many times. He plays good. Both those boys are good white musicians. Did you hear that record I made with them?" I said I had. "Was good, wasn't it? I tell you, they can *play,* those boys can. But of course they can't *sing* the blues the way we can. We are the best blues singers in the world. We— I mean the black man. Most all the white kids play good, but they can't sing the blues like we can."

I ask Muddy why that was.

"Well, that's because we *had* the blues down there. I worked as low as fifty cents a day, seventy-five cents a day, a dollar a day, from sunup right on through. And that will *give* you the blues. If that don't give you the blues, *nothin'* will."

What about the English groups? Were they playing the blues?

"Sure, same thing. They playin' them, but we singin' 'em. I will tell you one thing about those Rolling Stones and Beatles over there. They woke up our white kids over here. They got them listening to the blues. They love the blues in England. Loves to listen to it. I been there four times, and the first was in 1958."

"Muddy," I say to him then, "everybody says you're tops in blues, just the king of them all. Why? What do you suppose you've got the others don't?" I deliver the question with a wink and a grin. I suppose I had some idea of jiving him.

But you don't jive Muddy—not about that, anyway. He shakes his head solemnly and says, "I musta been born with it, I guess. Everybody says I'm tops in blues, so it must be so. Sometimes it scares me. I really don't know why it is—just a way I have with the words in a song and having a good strong voice. Oh, when I was younger I really had a voice. I could go up and down and do anything with it.

"But I don't think I'm slowing down none. Not even that auto wreck did that to me. No, I don't have no intention of giving up. I just want to stay healthy. I just want to blow until I get to be a real old man."

"Why is that?"

"Why?" The smile. "I love what I'm doing, that's why."

CHAPTER TWELVE

"JAZZ ME, BLUES"—AND VICE VERSA

THERE WAS a period in the twenties when the blues and jazz were just about synonymous. Jazz bands, white and black, recorded blues that weren't blues. Harlem honeys who had never been south of Newark suddenly found fame as blues singers when all they knew about it was that they sang the words and notes just as they appeared on the page.

This was the time that they would later label the "classic blues" period, although nobody thought of it quite that way at the time. All they knew was that everybody was suddenly crazy about the music. If you put "blues" or "blue" in the title of almost anything you could be reasonably certain of selling it to the public. The backgrounds for such early recordings were of varying quality. They were usually provided by a full jazz band, though sometimes—as on many of the early Bessie Smith records—the singer made do with just piano accompaniment. Guitar recorded badly under the early primitive conditions and was not often heard until so-called "electric recording" came in toward the end of the twenties. In any case, it was all jazz as far as the public was concerned—for after all, this was the Jazz Age, wasn't it? And if somebody black opened his mouth and sang, then it had to be the blues that came out. Or so they supposed.

With a few exceptions—most of them jazz instrumentalists who also sang—the voices heard during this classic blues period were female. They were selling sex.

If you don't like my ocean, don't fish in my sea
   (twice)
Stay out of my valley and let my mountain be.

I ain't had no loving since God knows when (twice)
That's the reason I'm through with these no good
   trifling men.

And the public—black and white—was buying. For the first time the myth of Negro sexuality was openly and hotly celebrated—hence the women sang; it was more provocative and less threatening to the white segment of the audience that way.

The first who were recorded could hardly be considered blues singers at all, although occasionally they did sing material in the old blues form against warm jazz backgrounds. Mamie Smith and Lucille Hegamin came out of vaudeville and returned to it, more or less, when the craze died down. Edith Wilson came out of show business, did some revues—*Hot Chocolates, Blackbirds,* and *Rhapsody in Black,* that sort of thing—and went on to become Aunt Jemima in the commercials for Quaker Oats. Ethel Waters was certainly an impressive singer, though what she did had not much relation to blues or jazz; she was an actress, as she proved subsequently in *Mamba's Daughters* and *Member of the Wedding,* and it was as an actress she used her voice.

The record companies were not looking beyond New York for talent. They had to go down South to get real blues singers, and eventually that is just what they did. One of the first they brought back was one of the best: a round, homely, hoyden of a woman named Gertrude "Ma" Rainey. In her own way, her background was just as much show business as Mamie Smith's or Edith Wilson's. But she had put in her time in tent shows on the Southern circuits—the Silas Green Show, the Rabbit Foot Minstrels, and even two years with the Tolliver Circus.

She was born Gertrude Pridgett in Columbus, Georgia, in 1886. As early as 1900 she was appearing in local shows, and it wasn't long before she was out on the road learning the trade that was to be hers for thirty-five years. In a few years she married a singing comedian named William Rainey who carried the nickname "Pa," and that was how, at the age of twenty, she became Ma Rainey. They were billed as "Rainey and Rainey, Assassinators of the Blues," and that puts her pretty firmly in the showbiz context in which she worked for years under the tents.

In a way, it is remarkable that she managed to break away at all, but she did briefly when she began recording for Paramount in 1923. In a modest way she became a kind of national attraction then, playing theaters in Chicago and a few other cities in the North for the first and only time. For the most part, her appeal was to those Southern black audiences to whom she had been singing her blues for years before she was invited up North to record. And the South was in her voice. It was rough, expressive, and dramatic without ever being really a "good" voice by conventional standards. She had not much range, and even within her limits her pitch was not always good, yet she did good things with it. Even when she was unsure of her material—as she seemed to be whenever she strayed from pure blues—her experience as a performer would see her through. When she wound up talking her material, as she did from time to time, she never lost the intensity that made her a real blues singer.

She recorded a lot of traditional Delta blues material— "Levee Camp Moan," "Bo-Weevil Blues," and "Stack o' Lee Blues" among others—and she does it well in a kind of masculine style that was really natural to her. Jazz critics seem to prefer the three sides she cut with Louis Armstrong backing her up, in 1925, her "See, See Rider" usually cited as the best of all her recordings. My own preference, however, is for her last recordings in 1928, with Tampa Red and Georgia Tom Dorsey. Her "Sleep Talking Blues" and "Runaway Blues"—the same tune with different words—are as good as anything she ever recorded. Her voice is rich and full; she really sounds like the "Mother of the Blues." Those sessions in the fall of 1928 were her last. She continued to play throughout the South for five more years, however; then she retired to run the two theaters she had bought in Rome, Georgia. She died in 1939 at the age of fifty-three.

Ida Cox is harder to fix. Her style is someplace between that of vaudevillians such as Mamie Smith and hard blues shouters like Ma Rainey. She was certainly a performer in her own right; she toured the top black theaters in the country as the top attraction in her own revue—chorus girls, comedians, and second-line singers. But her voice, as it survives on records, establishes her as a much stronger and more authentic-sounding singer than you might suppose from this background. She wrote most of her own material, chose her backup groups carefully, and is easier to listen to today than most of the classic singers. She had a longer professional life than most, too, working intermittently right through the thirties and recording as late as 1961, six years before her death.

There were innumerable others—Victoria Spivey, Alberta Hunter, Martha Copeland, Clara Smith, Sara Martin, to name just a few worth attention. But the queen of them all, the Empress of the Blues, as she chose to call herself, was Bessie Smith, of course. She is one of the few of the legendary blues figures whose performances can stand up absolutely to careful listening today. If anything, she sounds even better on the recordings she made—all 160 of them have been reissued on Columbia—than one has any right to expect. There is drama and a subtlety of expression that come out in repeated listenings to them. And that in itself may seem surprising, for on first exposure what is sure to strike the listener is the raw power of the woman's voice. It practically assaults the ear, matching in strength the crudity of the lyrics she sang. She put more of herself on records than had most singers of any period up to the present. It is not just that she cut more than most, but that throughout her ten-year career as a recording artist she seemed to take more care in her performances before the microphone and the recording horn than most—she would do take after take on a session until she came up with one that satisfied her. Ma Rainey, Clara Smith, and many of the rest were very careless about what they laid down on wax; it is commonplace to hear of them that in person they were far more exciting than the recordings they have left behind indicate. Nobody has said that of Bessie Smith—not because she was an indifferent performer onstage (by all accounts she was sensational!), but because she was just as good on records. It was as though she believed that any sort of immortality she achieved would have to be through mechanical means.

She was a big woman—tall, abundant, statuesque as she struck her dramatic poses before audiences—every inch the empress she claimed to be. At the peak of her career, in 1927 and 1928, she toured with her own show and pulled close to a thousand a week for the entire package. Yet she began humbly enough down in the tent shows of the Deep South just as Ma Rainey did. In fact, she and the great Ma (who was twelve years her senior) worked together at one time in Tolliver's Circus. But she had split from it and was working theaters and bars when she was heard one night in Alabama by a scout named Frank Walker. He liked what he heard, remembered, and when he was put in charge of Columbia's Race recording operations, he searched her out and signed her up. That was in 1923. On her first session for Columbia she cut "Down-Hearted Blues," with just Clarence Williams' piano accompaniment. The song had already been recorded by Alberta Hunter, who had written it with blues accompanist Lovie Austin, so that it was just a "cover" recording, a safe choice of pretested material. But she did so well on it that, by the time it was released four months later, Walker had recorded her eighteen more times. His faith in her was more than justified: "Down-Hearted Blues," a great song with a great line—"I've got the world in the jug, got the stopper in my hand"—sold about 800,000 copies.

She was an immediate star. With her records coming out monthly, Bessie started touring through the Midwest and South, drawing huge crowds at theaters in the major cities and playing the whistlestops in between from a railroad car. She was in demand by whites as well. She did special shows for whites only in the South and played to mixed audiences in the North. As early as 1924, interest in her was so keen that the white-owned radio station WGM in Memphis (in 1924 all radio was white-owned) did a rare and expensive remote broadcast from a black theater, the Beale Avenue Palace, presenting Bessie Smith to the mid-South radio audience.

She recorded with top jazz musicians of the day. Fletcher Henderson and later the great James P. Johnson took over successfully as her accompanists. Joe Smith, Don Redman, Coleman Hawkins, and Buster Bailey all played behind her at one session or another. In 1925, Louis Armstrong did a session with her that really should have gone better than it did. On "St. Louis Blues," for instance, on which Bessie should have sung well, they switched Fred Longshaw, a pianist, to harmonium; he wheezes along behind her, nearly covering up her own strong voice and baffling Louis Armstrong completely. In general, she was better than the material she sang. It was only in the beginning and middle of her career that she did many true blues; toward the end she sang popular songs and lot of suggestive and downright raunchy material. The songs that she herself wrote were no closer to real blues than others she did, but a couple of them were good. Her "Blue Blue" was good and done in a spirited rendition in 1931; her "Spider Man Blues," which is a blues truly enough, is darkly paranoid in its expression, an altogether odd song.

The Depression came, and things got very tough for Bessie Smith. Columbia went bankrupt, and she did not record for the label after 1931. She was brought back by jazz critic and A & R man John Hammond in 1933, however, for a session that was cut for OKeh, which was by then Columbia's Race label. Her voice was rough—she even seems to be growling unnaturally on most of "Gimme a Pigfoot"—and there is not a blues among the four tunes recorded at the session. This seems fairly typical of what she was doing during her last years, though, for she was trying to "modernize"—keep up with the new trends in popular music. She was back to doing one-nighters in the South at the end. That came for her one night in 1937 in an auto accident outside Clarksdale, Mississippi. She was horribly mangled, an arm almost severed from her body. That was how a white doctor from Memphis found her, lying in the road. He saw her into the hospital in Clarksdale, but it would be difficult, he later said, to determine whether she died there or in the ambulance. There is no basis in fact, it seems, for the popular story that she was refused admission to a hospital because of her color.

A lot of singers were left behind in the era that followed the classic blues period. Times were hard. The Depression cut sharply into the music business at every level. Musicians and singers were playing for tips at cabarets around the country, and recording all but came to a standstill at the bottom of the slump. Because the black audience was hit hardest of all, black performers suffered most.

But tastes were changing, too. Jazz was becoming more and more distinct, a music apart from that rough-and-ready combination of blues and ragtime whence it had sprung. What was taking shape in the beginning of the thirties was a phenomenon called swing. By the end of that decade it had saved the music business. Thanks to bands like Benny Goodman's, Artie Shaw's, and those of the Dorsey Brothers, by 1939 kids around the country were dancing, swinging, and buying records as never before. But nearly all those big bands that made Swing Era history were white bands. And those few black bands that did make it then did so by managing to sound more or less "white"—Jimmie Lunceford's Orchestra is a good example of this sort of "mulatto jazz."

This trendy de-emphasis of the "blackness" of jazz was especially pronounced among the black singers. The blues was something old-fashioned or low-down. It was something they used to sing back in the twenties or maybe still did in the remote reaches of the Deep South. But the going style became gentlemanly and ladylike—they were "vocalists" who sang "ballads," but never blues singers. Ivie Anderson and Joya Sherrill of the Duke Ellington Orchestra, Maxene Sullivan with the John Kirby Sextet, Dan Grissom of the Jimmie Lunceford band—there was no black quality to their singing at all.

And there was also very little to Billie Holiday's. There has recently been a great flurry to claim her as a kind of black heroine. And while these efforts are no doubt well intended, they must have been made by people who aren't really familiar with her singing career at all. She first was heard on the Teddy Wilson Brunswick sessions of the mid-thirties. This was the politest jazz imaginable. It was almost dicty in its sweet, modulated, tasteful quality—and that was how she sang the ballads and "torch songs" they gave her, too. All that saved her as a singer was that weird tone of hers—"She sounds like her feet hurt," Ethel Waters once said of her—and her phrasing. She could phrase more subtly and with greater musical imagination than any other singer of her time or since. She was one of the first to come close to what jazz instrumentalists of her era were doing on their horns, and for this she truly deserves the "jazz singer" title that was hung on her. Billie Holiday was also called a "blues singer" in her day by some who should have known better. Although she had a couple of blues in her repertoire, she was never a blues singer. Her whole approach to music was as unlike that of a blues singer as could be. She was simply interested in other things.

There was one big band singer during this era who could, with some degree of accuracy, be called a blues singer—and that was Jimmy Rushing of the Count Basie Orchestra. The short, plump man whom they used to call "Mr. Five-by-Five," had been with the organization even before it was Basie's. In the early thirties, when Bill Basie was just the piano player with those Kansas City terrors, the Blue Devils, Rushing was discovered in an Oklahoma City café owned by his father. He joined the band, and when it began recording, went to New York, and gained national prominence, he was right up there in front of it singing his heart out. It would be a mistake to push him too hard as a bluesman; he was really a band singer—and a good one. He could do songs of all sorts with style, ease, and a certain extra grace—even down to the most banal "hit parade" material. But he could and did sing blues, too, belting out those good sounds above one of the most powerful brass sections in the business; it took a man to do the job, and he was equal to it, as he proved again and again on such big band blues as "Goin' to Chicago," "Sent for You Yesterday," and "Lazy Lady Blues."

As we go on, the relationship of jazz to blues becomes more and more tenuous. The Bebop Era made the music intellectually respectable but cut it loose from the mass audience. Moving from Swing to Bop introduced a kind of cult quality into the sociology of jazz that ultimately would prove nearly fatal to the music. Who were the singers of this period? Sarah Vaughan, certainly, Lambert-Hendricks-and-Ross possibly—but who else? The point is that it was not vocal music at all, and the music suffered when it lost the humanizing quality of the human voice. The blues? Forget it. Nobody in jazz even tried to sing them then. About the only singer who could really belt the blues and worked with jazz backgrounds was Dinah Washington. She was a fine singer, underrated by critics during the forties and fifties and largely forgotten today. She came up through gospel music, sang lead with the Original Sallie Martin Singers, and brought all that fervor and conviction with her into secular music. Her best recording was done with jazzmen, some of them as musically sophisticated as the great trumpeter

Clifford Brown. In these recordings she came about as close as anyone to hammering out a synthesis between the new intellectual music and the old blues.

THINGS HIT BOTTOM in the late fifties. The music became so introspective and inhuman that it was hardly to be listened to outside of the concert context. There remained an audience of sorts for it into the sixties, but soon that vanished, too, when the college kids found their own music—rock-and-roll. They no longer had to be quiet and attentive during Dave Brubeck's forty-five-minute piano solos (complete with quotations from Stravinsky and Bartók); they could just go out and dig the Paul Butterfield Blues Band or maybe Big Brother and the Holding Company with good old Superjanis and just *groove* on it.

Rock is the best thing that ever happened to jazz. It has removed it from the smug climate of intellectual snobbery that had almost overwhelmed it. It has put "black" back into the music (jazzmen like Cannonball Adderly and his brother Nat were working on that years before), given it balls once again, and re-established the link with the blues. The jazz-rock phenomenon—Blood, Sweat & Tears, Chase, and the much quieter Mark-Almond Quintet, as good examples—has worked a very healthy change in mainstream jazz. It is a change that is still taking shape, and so it would be difficult and probably undesirable to attempt to define it too precisely. But jazz is today funkier and more melodic—in short, bluesier than it was even five years ago.

Critics, jazz audiences, and jazzmen alike are less exclusive and less inclined toward snobbishness than before. They are less willing to exclude this bluesman or that young rocker from the jazz company because suddenly people are rather healthily uncertain about what jazz is or ever was. For the last few years, for example, B. B. King has placed highly in both the *Down Beat*'s critics' and readers' polls. That's right, B. B. King, the Beale Street Blues Boy—and not just in the male singer category, but as a guitarist as well.

And that is as it should be, for B.B. is a first-rate guitarist. Does he play blues or jazz? Well, what the readers of *Down Beat* and the critics are saying is that it really doesn't matter so very much *what* you call it, as long as it is improvised and as long as it *feels* right, as long as it is right as *music,* then we will accept it for what it is and worry about labels later. That seems satisfactory to B. B. King, too. He's not going to change to suit anybody, but he's glad for the new acceptance being given his music today. Here is what he told James Powell in a *Down Beat* interview:

> There was a time, when I first started out, when my way of playing was like the old musicians used to play. . . . And you sometimes get a little bit ashamed to play that to certain people. At some time they would look down on it, you understand, but you want to do the thing that you feel they're used to seeing or want to hear, and this is why a lot of the guys will do that. But you come to a certain age—I don't mean you have to be as old as I am (44)—after a while you get to believe that you are *you.* As regards the airs you might put on, it doesn't change the fact that you're still you: So some of us come back to earth.

You don't have to see B. B. King in action and listen to him more than once—and I have seen and heard him many more times than that—to know that he doesn't put on airs. His feet are solidly on the ground. I remember one performance in particular that did more than any other to communicate the particular quality of this remarkable man to me.

It was at Lorton Reformatory, near Washington, D.C. Lorton, located out near Interstate 95 in northern Virginia, is the "state prison" for the District of Columbia. This was the second of a long series of prison concerts that B. B. King had played and continues to play all across the country. As you read this, he has probably played the state prison or big-city jail nearest you. He works the concerts in on off-dates and layovers, brings his band out at his own expense, and plays for the prisoners under whatever conditions are permitted. They weren't ideal the day I saw him. Because there was no auditorium deemed safe, B.B. and his band had set up in midafternoon on a hot July day on the pitcher's mound of the prison baseball diamond. The Lorton inmates filled the bleachers along the first- and third-base lines as B.B. sweated to please them. Nobody sweats like he did that day.

But that doesn't mean they were a tough audience. No, they were hungry for whatever he had to give that day—and he had plenty. The music he and his band played seemed to have an almost therapeutic effect; the boys in the bleachers seemed visibly healthier when things really got swinging. Maybe that was what B.B. meant when he ad-libbed, "If you're sick, the blues will make you well!"

This, along with everything else he said, sang, or played from that point on, met with an enthusiastic response. He and his band played a long set beginning, as he always does, with the Memphis Slim tune that is his theme song, "Every Day I Have the Blues." He went on to sing all his old favorites—"Sweet Little Angel," "Sweet Sixteen," "Three O'Clock Blues," and others—as well as a few of the new tunes he is doing, like Leon Russell's "Hummingbird." And in between he kidded with the inmates like the good showman he is. He presented each member of his eight-piece, jazz-oriented band to the audience, and even introduced his guitar, Lucille.

It's a story he tells at every performance: "Oh," he will say, "you want to know how Lucille got her name? Well, that was one night in the little town of Twist, Arkansas, which is located just seventy-nine miles west of Memphis . . ." It seems there were two fellows who fell into a hell of a fight over a girl at this dance hall about the size of a sardine can where B.B. was playing one night. "One of the two fellows kicked over a kerosene heater in the middle of the floor, and the place went up in flames. Both those boys died in the fire, and all I got out with was my guitar. I asked who that girl was who had caused all that trouble—and they said she was called Lucille. And I thought, 'She must be some girl,' so I named my guitar after her."

B. B. King's history as a performer is crowded with towns like Twist and memories of gigs played in roadhouses and dance halls like that one. No bluesman today is better established than he is, yet none has worked so hard to get where he is. Years and years of one-nighters have taken their toll. In 1956 he set a personal record that few other performers would care to equal, playing 342 one-night stands in a single year. Living on the road broke up a marriage. One auto accident—"You play all night and drive all day"—left him broke; another nearly severed his right arm.

And he is still traveling today—though now in better style

than ever before, it is true. I talked with him after the Lorton concert in his suite at the rather swank Hotel Madison in downtown D. C. His valet-driver was readying his wardrobe for his next concert. B. B. King was in an expansive mood, feeling easy, and I remarked that it must be difficult to relax in odd hours like this.

"Yes," he said, "but it's how you learn to cope with the road —you learn to be yourself wherever you are. My home is usually a hotel room. My manager is up in New York, and my mother and father are on a farm that I own with them outside Memphis. But me? Well, I don't have a home, not really—I've got 300 working days this year, and recording dates on top of that. Where would I live?"

But though B.B. continues to work at just about the same grueling pace as before, the character of his audiences has changed considerably in the last few years. He has been discovered by young audiences around the country. And now, in addition to club dates, he plays colleges and universities, concerts, and festivals. How do the audiences differ? "Well, the attention is better at the concerts, of course," he says. "You take your average club-goer. He's got other things on his mind. He's got a bottle at the table and a lady along. And you may never get his full attention, but he's enjoying himself. He may yell over to his neighbor, 'Hey, Sam, listen at him.' That's his kind of appreciation. I was brought up with people like that."

He smiles. "Playing audiences is like a man planting a crop. If he's done his work right at harvesting time, he's going to get a good crop. They're going to keep coming back again and again."

I remark on the analogy to farming. "Oh, sure," he says, "I'm a country boy. Can't you tell?" Yes, he was born in Itta Bena, Mississippi, and did all the farm-boy jobs for his parents—and for a favorite aunt, too. "She was one of those hip young aunts who would let me play her phonograph. Yeah, I would do her chores and listen to Blind Lemon the rest of the afternoon. Little Riley B. King never goofed with her. He was her good boy."

Whether inspired by Blind Lemon or by the accomplishments of his cousin Bukka White, he went north to Memphis, got a disc jockey job on a black radio station—and that was

when Riley B. became B.B. (short for Blues Boy). He loves the
blues, and that's why it came as a shock to him when, in the
mid-sixties, the taste of young blacks turned against the music
that he himself had been brought up on.

It was at the Royal Theater in Baltimore. He was on the bill
with Sam Cooke, as he recalls, and B.B.'s band was playing the
whole show. What happened? The black kids there booed the
blues—not B.B., but the blues. It shook him up. "Yes," he admits,
"it really hurt in a way. I think maybe they're ashamed of the
blues. They think it's some kind of old-fashioned Uncle Tom
music. Well, it's not. It's the best music there is. And I got mad
and told them so. Well, later I apologized for blowing up, but I
still think what I told them was right."

Why do white kids feel so differently about the music?
"Well," he answers, "they got used to hearing it from their own
white stars, and it sounded good to them then, so they figured
it must be all right. You see, they weren't thinking in terms of
the past and all those associations with the music the way the
black kids were. But no, I think it's changing anyway with the
black kids. They're just beginning to come around to it. And it'll
be good for them when they do."

I ask him the usual questions about his musical development:
Who taught him? Who influenced him? How did he start?

But he's heard them all before. He gives me a wave of his
hand and a wink of his eye. "Look, I learned not in school, but
from the music itself. There are only seven notes of music and
five accidentals—B flat up to F sharp. There's only twelve
choices we've all got to work with—whether it's Beethoven or
B.B. And I just started playing around when I was a youngster
until I found that out, and from then on it was up to me.

"When I got my first electric guitar, though, I did start listening to T-Bone Walker pretty hard. I did love that clear touch of
his, and many of us tried to duplicate it. But finally I started to
move into my own direction when I began recording. But I kept
right on listening to people. If you want to know the people on
guitar who made a difference to me, I'll tell you it's been T-
Bone, Lonnie Johnson—oh? you know him?—Blind Lemon,
Django Reinhardt—yes, well, that makes two of us—and
Charlie Christian. They've all been important to me one way or
another."

Does he play jazz or blues? Is there a difference?

He smiles and shrugs very expressively. "Well, I'll tell you, what I play doesn't worry me, how I play does. The better jazz-men and I play about the same, but the average tries to put too much into it. I just get up there and do my best. I'm not trying to play it the same every time. I take the basic chord progressions and play it as I feel then. It's rarely I play a long, long solo in a song—twenty-four bars is the usual form. In two choruses I can be inventive. I enjoy it, man. I don't know if people know it, the way I screw up my face sometimes, but I do."

CHAPTER THIRTEEN

"PREACHIN' BLUES"

IT WAS one of those temperate January Sundays that only seem to happen in New Orleans. Starched white curtains hanging in the windows that faced on sunny St. Ann Street billowed slightly, lofted by the pleasant breezes that swept the French Quarter. There are no lights on in the living room where I sit, and the woman who is talking is almost hidden from me, her sharp features nearly obscured in the shadows. Her eyes are not, however; they flash at me now as she speaks, emphasizing an uncompromising, angular, even harsh quality that is certainly there in her personality. She's nobody's Aunt Jemima.

"Well, it stands to reason, young man," she says. "When people get together and start making music, they all gets to feeling happy. Any kind of music make you feel good—blues or church music. It's the sincereness of it—that's what make you feel good. It does seem to me, though, that you're bound to feel different when you sing for Jesus than when you sing the blues, because *then*"—she jabs a finger in my direction for emphasis —"then you are inspired by the Holy Spirit."

I nodded and asked if bluesmen weren't inspired, too.

She looked away from me and chose her words carefully:

"Well, being as good a musician as my husband was, that comes from inside, too. There's no doubt it takes a sort of inspiration, though I'm not sure from where."

Her name is Annie Pavageau, and she is the widow of a jazz bassist of some reputation named Alcide Pavageau who bore the nickname "Slow Drag" to the day of his death in 1968. He became best known during the forties and fifties when he played with the Bunk Johnson and George Lewis bands that toured widely in this country and Europe. He had played for years in New Orleans before that, though. Born there in 1888, he taught himself to play guitar and could be heard in dives and street corners around town from 1905 on. It wasn't until later, sometime in the thirties, that he took up bass. By that time he had met and married Annie, and the two of them had teamed up and were playing and singing around town together.

I asked about that time, and she admitted that yes, she used to play and sing the blues some. "I did one time play in a club with my husband. That was at the Autocrat Club on St. Bernard. Actually, my husband and I used to work a lot together. I learned guitar from him. I was a young woman when I was playing and singing the blues. I wasn't a church member at that time, not even a churchgoer."

Don't bluesmen go to church? "Sure they do," she snapped. It was clearly a sore point with her. "A lot of them began there. And my husband, he went when I did. I could tell you others who were church members, too. You know Punch Miller, the trumpet player? He belonged to Reverend Dunne's church. They belong to different churches around town. You know. I mean, they might be going around playing different ragtime songs and blues and all, but they call that just making a living. That's how it is."

But what about herself? Does she still play the blues? She shook her head emphatically. "No," she said, "I just like church music, religious music. I don't like blues and I don't play it any more at all. I quit. I didn't believe I could play all that ragtime music and still serve God in truth and spirit. I give all my time to the church today."

It is time well spent. She plays piano and organ ("Never took no music. All my wisdom comes from the guitar.") and serves as choir director for the Morning Star Baptist Church on Burgundy Street in New Orleans' French Quarter. I had been there earlier that day and stayed through the morning-long church service that seemed to take more than some could give in the way of endurance. They came and went. One white girl in jeans and barefoot darted in from the street and left almost immediately—looking for something but not finding it there. But I stayed on through "Amazing Grace," "Precious Lord," and all the rest—stayed on through the short sermon of the visiting Reverend Eddie Brown, who caused some stir when he said, "If you're going to be righteous, then you got to *be* righteous, If you're going to be a hellhound, then you be the biggest hellhound ever was. God don't like none of that halfway. There's right *righteous,* and there's wrong—and you got to be one or the other."

Through it all, Annie Pavageau presided at the piano; an imposing presence, she seemed as much in command of things there as the Reverend Brown. It was hard, watching her, to imagine her in that good-time life that legend said she had led before she got religion. I was curious about that. So later I asked as tactfully as I knew how if her life had changed completely when she joined the church.

She was emphatic. "It did," she declared. "It did. Of course, I was raised in the church. I sang in the choir ever since I was a girl in Columbus, Mississippi, where I'm from. I had such a strong voice they used to use me for high tenor when I was just a girl. Then I came here to New Orleans, and like any child I started going to various dances and all, and they got me to playing piano for them, and that's how I met my husband."

She half-turned in the sofa she was sitting in and looked at the large poster-sized photograph of Slow Drag that hung above her. "That's him there," she said. "Here, let me get some light on that so you can see him." She turned on a table lamp next to her, then stretched the length of the couch to switch on a floor lamp. I came over for a closer look and commented that he looked very young in the picture. "He did," she agreed, "and that's how he looked right up to the day he died, and he was eighty then."

I asked about her husband's relation to the church. Was he accepted by the congregation?

"Sure," she said, "the congregation would accept a blues

singer or a player as a member of the congregation—*if* he give it up."

And had he given it up? She was clearly annoyed by the question and felt some ambivalence about the whole matter. She seemed to feel a conflict between her loyalty to her husband, on the one hand, and, on the other, her conviction that good-time music and church music simply don't mix. And so instead of giving me a straight answer, she started preaching at me: "You know you can't serve two people. Jesus said that. You can't serve God and mammon, too. Everything that is not right is wrong. Everything that does not pertain to God is sinful. We believe the way Christ did."

She had become personal and very direct in what she was saying. She was demanding a personal response from *me,* but all I did was continue writing down what she was saying. And that annoyed her even more. Finally, she broke off in exasperation and asked, "Are you a believer in Jesus Christ?" I said I was. "Well, you better be! And you better believe in just what the Bible says. You could write all day in that book of yours, but unless you believe in Jesus it won't do you no good." She nodded emphatically and crossed her arms, and that was about all she would say to me that day.

ANNIE PAVAGEAU had made quite plain an attitude among blacks of which many whites are completely ignorant. It is commonly assumed that because blues and gospel sound so much alike many of the same people sing both. They don't. The official attitude of the black church—and I mean under that umbrella to gather the Baptists, the Methodists, and the Pentecostal sects—is that the blues is the Devil's music. It is not just the music alone that they are against. After all, not all blues are profane; not every one treats illicit love; some are simple songs of complaint, fundamental comments on the human condition. But no matter, the blues is roundly and universally condemned by the black church because of the way of life it represents— the milieu of hard drinking, loose sex, and quick violence in the city bars and country juke joints where the music is played. And the black church, as a conservative, stabilizing force in the community, has been fighting hard against this way of life right from the start. The blues is condemned because it is such a vivid reminder to so many in black congregations of the places they had been, the drinks they had drunk, and the lovers they had known, and all that they had left behind when they "crossed over."

Because whites tend to overlook or disregard such feelings, there have been some unhappy moments at concerts and folk festivals. At UCLA in 1965, for instance, blues singer Son House was to appear on the same bill with that unique spiritual group, the Sea Island Singers. When the choir saw that it was to participate in something called a "blues workshop," they got up in a huff and said they would head back to Georgia before they would ever appear on a *blues* program. It was only by renaming it a "black music workshop" that the sponsors persuaded them to stay. Even so, there were problems. During the program, John Fahey, a fine young guitarist who was then a graduate student in the University's Folklore Department, suggested that Son House and the Sea Island Singers do a number together. Fahey should have known better. Son was willing, but the choir said no, they weren't about to share the stage with a man who was a known singer of sinful songs. Son didn't take kindly to that. He called them a pack of hypocrites and told them that when the sun went down they were out dancing to the boogie beat just like everybody else. It developed into a regular shouting match before Fahey managed to calm them all down—and, of course, they never did get together and sing.

This particular incident may have been complicated further by the fact that Son House had himself been a Baptist preacher before he became a blues singer. He left the church to play sinful music and may thus have seemed sort of a pariah to the Sea Island Singers. But many blues singers got their start in church choirs—Muddy Waters among them, and Muddy will tell you straight-faced that what he plays is "sinful music." Although some of the younger bluesmen adopt a more professional attitude about the music they play and don't seem to think much about the church one way or another, many of the older men have accepted this pariah role in which they have been cast. Following the blues trail has in this way taken them beyond their pale. If they are damned men, they say, then let them at least enjoy their damnation. This has led many of them to the sort of excessive, reckless, self-destructive behavior epitomized by Robert Johnson, who sang so eloquently of that life he lived in the blues "Hellhound on My Trail."

Certainly some few bluesmen—among them the late Skip James and Sleepy John Estes—and many of the old songsters have managed to satisfy their own consciences and have sung both blues and sacred music. Nevertheless, the relationship between the two styles (and content aside, they really are only two styles of the same music) has been both complicated and ambiguous. On the one hand, you must note Big Bill Broonzy telling Studs Terkel in an interview that "The blues is a steal from the spirituals," thus acknowledging the debt of his music to the hymns of the nineteenth-century black church. And on the other hand, you must recognize the debt of the black church to the blues in the person of Thomas A. Dorsey, the man who is generally recognized as the father of modern gospel music.

He started out his career as "Georgia Tom," for he was born in Atlanta in 1889. Brought up in the church, Dorsey did not hesitate to join the local Baptist congregation when he emigrated to Gary, Indiana. He soon found, however, that he could make a good living for himself as a blues and jazz pianist around Gary and the South Side of Chicago if he put aside, at least temporarily, the prohibitions of the church against good-timing. And so that was how he happened to become one of the top piano bluesmen of his day. He was asked by Ma Rainey, then a top performer, to organize a band for her and serve as her accompanist. He put together a first-rate group with at least one soloist—trombonist Al Wynn—who went on to make a reputation for himself as a jazzman. Dorsey toured and recorded with the ebullient "Mother of the Blues" for a number of years, and the last band he led for her had in it a guitarist named Hudson Whittaker who doubled on kazoo and called himself Tampa Red. When Georgia Tom split up with Ma Rainey in 1928, he intended to give up the blues and go back to the church and religious song writing. Tampa Red, however, talked him into teaming up with him, and for a couple of years the two played and sang together and collaborated on a number of original blues, including the raunchy "Tight Like That."

Then in 1929, Thomas A. Dorsey gave up the blues life completely. ("If you're righteous, then you got to be righteous.") Plenty of sacred music had been written and recorded before

Dorsey turned his talents in that direction, but what he brought with him were his keen feelings for the blues and his preference for its personal, direct, and unabashedly emotional appeal. He translated all this to the sacred music he began to write and came up with a style so fundamentally different that he even gave it a new name, calling what he wrote gospel songs. During the thirties, when he did most of his work, he wrote scores of these hard-swinging gospel blues-based songs, including "I Surely Know There's Been a Change in Me," "I'm Gonna Live the Life I Sing About in My Song," and "The Day Is Past and Gone." Along with his partner, Sallie Martin, a raw-voiced shouting lady, he began touring black churches around the country, presenting his own material in revival concerts. This was the beginning of the gospel circuit, which so many great performers have traveled successfully since.

As early as 1932, the new style was so well established that Dorsey convened the first Gospel Singers' Convention and was able to attract singers and choir directors from all over the country. And it was also in 1932, under the saddest of circumstances, that he wrote his greatest song. While he was away on tour, his wife and child died in an accident, and he was brought down to a state of despair from which he rose to write his great "Precious Lord."

> *Precious Lord take my hand,*
> *Lead me on, let me stand,*
> *I am tired, I am weak, I am worn,*
> *Through the storm, through the night,*
> *Lead me on to the light,*
> *Take my hand precious Lord, lead me on.*

This one, a favorite of both blacks and Southern whites, is the song Martin Luther King, Jr., had just requested for the evening's service when he was shot down on the balcony of his Memphis motel room.

All gospel singers have at least the feeling of the blues in their songs. Some come by it quite naturally. The late Mahalia Jackson, the only one of them known widely to white audiences, was born in New Orleans in 1911 and grew up there listening to the records of her favorite, Bessie Smith, and absorbing the sounds of jazz and blues in the streets all around her. But she herself sang sanctified right from the start. By the time she moved North, to Chicago, in the thirties, she had a reputation as a sacred singer who could really swing. In contrast to her later appearances on the *Ed Sullivan Show* et al., in which she sang syrupy songs (much of it ersatz material manufactured to order by whites) in moony, doleful, but awfully dignified style, the early Mahalia was a terrifically spirited performer who just might pick up her robes and dance for joy when the feeling was right inside her. You can catch some of the old Mahalia on her recordings from the fifties, but by the time she had become a national celebrity outside the little gospel world, the style had changed completely. Only the voice was the same—and that remained with her until she died in 1972.

Bessie Griffin was also born in New Orleans and grew up hearing the same sounds as Mahalia. You can hear echoes of them in the fine, earthy things she does with her great contralto voice. The Reverend Alex Bradford also cheerfully admits to blues influence on his own singing and composing. He will tell you he used to spend whole days following blues singers around in his native Bessemer, Alabama, and remind you that the lady who taught him to play piano was herself a jazz pianist. Sister Rosetta Tharpe of the Holiness Church is famous—notorious in some circles—as the gospel singer who did more than just introduce blues elements into her sacred music. She kept right on playing them. Sister Rosetta is not only a singer but is a good, primitive electric guitar player, somewhat in the style of Aaron "T-Bone" Walker. The combination brought her a recording contract with Decca as early as 1938. On her records she may have been singing words as pious as you please, but when she let go on that guitar what came out was low-down, dirty blues. Decca began featuring her with the Lucky Millinder big band, and it wasn't long before she had recorded a few blues with them as well, to the great consternation of her gospel fans. Once her secular audience was established, she even began playing night clubs. Through all this, however, her basic material was gospel, with a few secular songs mixed in, so that she felt she had never really left her religion behind but had simply taken it along with her into some pretty curious places. She looked upon herself as a sort of musical missionary, and using this line, managed to talk her way back into the good graces of her church when her fling in the night clubs and on the *Billboard* Race charts was ended. Today, she is back singing her gospel songs to gospel audiences.

Although Sister Rosetta Tharpe was the first to bring sacred songs into the night clubs, she was not the last. One of gospel's finest groups, the Ward Singers, under the direction of Gertrude Ward, worked hard and was respected by all who heard it in churches and auditoriums around the country. It included not only Gertrude's pretty and precocious daughter, Clara Ward, but a girl named Marion Williams, with a powerful and affecting voice, who has since become about the finest soloist in gospel today. At that time, however, Clara was the star of the show. She had great style on the up-tempo stuff, was prettier and younger than Mahalia Jackson, and so she was considered by some to be a logical replacement when Mahalia made her way into the white world. Clara soon began acting like the new queen, swanking imperiously. She dressed up the rest of the Ward Singers like ladies-in-waiting and coiffed them in beehive wigs. This got to be a little much for Marion Williams and the rest of the Ward Singers, and together they all walked out on Clara Ward and her mother in 1958. The Ward Singers never really made a comeback in the gospel field, for Clara went into night clubs with a gospel act in 1961. Today, although Clara Ward and the Ward Singers (as the attraction is now known) continue to play auditoriums in big gospel shows, they do most of their shouting in Las Vegas and Disneyland—and have adjusted their program accordingly.

There is neither time nor space for me to attempt a survey of the huge, rich field of gospel music—and there is really no need, either, for there is already a good survey available, Tony Heilbut's *The Gospel Sound.* It is complete, offering a view of the whole field, written without pretensions but with a lot of love. You may have guessed that it is the source of much of the information that I have presented here—though the opinions have certainly been my own. A sort of minor theme that runs through the Heilbut book is the secularization of performers in gospel—blatantly, as in the case of Sister Rosetta Tharpe and Clara Ward, or somewhat more subtly, as it was with Mahalia Jackson. Then, too, there has been a steady drain of singers from the churches that started way back in the forties when

Dinah Washington left the Original Sallie Martin Singers to become the queen of rhythm-and-blues.

The music has been secularized, too, though in this case the alteration has been so complete, and the secularization so absolute, that a new label has now been applied to this new style, and it is called—soul. Heilbut remarks in passing: "The first things that will strike any newcomer to gospel are its stylistic similarities to soul music and the obvious, if not overwhelming, sexual presence of its performers." Given that sexual presence, which nobody would or could deny, perhaps the development of soul from gospel was inevitable. The important personalities in soul music, those who created the style, have nearly all been graduates of gospel. The late Sam Cooke, who comes as close as anyone to being the man who started it all, dropped out of the Soul Stirrers Quartet to become the top attraction among black male singers in popular music. Lou Rawls began with the Pilgrim Travelers; Wilson Pickett came up with the Violinaires; even Dionne Warwick, who seems to have lost the earthy gospel sound completely, got her start in the churches of Newark.

Soul music's biggest star is, of course, Aretha Franklin, and of them all, she is probably the most firmly grounded in gospel, too. She grew up on the gospel circuit. Her father was the Reverend C. L. Franklin, who for years toured with the Ward Singers and other groups, sermonizing at the song sessions. And Aretha? She traveled right along, making those long car trips and staying up to listen to her idol, Clara Ward, giving her all. With all this it is not surprising that Aretha herself began singing when she was only fourteen—or that in the beginning she sounded a lot like Clara Ward. What did surprise people, though, was that after a good beginning in gospel, she quit the field after only four years and signed with Columbia as a pop singer. She had little success, however, until she switched labels in 1966 and went with Atlantic. Then the hits—"Respect," "I Never Loved a Man the Way I Love You," "Chain of Fools," "Since You've Been Gone," and all the others—began to roll out with really astonishing frequency and precision.

Her gospel background was well known by many, though certainly not all, of her fans. It was partly to satisfy those who did know and to inform those who did not that Atlantic recently followed through on a project that had been in the planning for years. They recorded her in an all-gospel set, live, at a church location. For Aretha's part, she may have felt it was time to repay a debt of long standing to the music that gave her her start. But whatever the motives involved, the two-record album, *Amazing Grace,* which she recorded with the help of the Reverend James Cleveland and the Southern California Community Choir, succeeds beautifully. Atlantic did just right, of course, recording it in a church; all gospel albums should be recorded live before a congregation. It is this that helps make it authentic stuff. Aretha shows she has certainly not forgotten what she learned as a child all those nights on the circuit. But she also reveals what we would never have dreamed from her pop performances—that hers is not nearly as strong a voice as that of some others in gospel. Rhythmically, she cannot be faulted—she rides as few singers can, soul or sacred. Her phrasing is bold and venturesome. All that she lacks is the power and intensity of a Marion Williams—and that she will probably never have.

Her efforts seem to go over very well with the congregation. (Some credit for this must go to the choir, which performs beautifully through the whole set.) They realize who Aretha is and that this is something of an occasion for her, and they seem quite willing to forgive her her trespasses into the pop music field. In fact, they are most enthusiastic when Aretha's father, the Reverend C. L. Franklin, stands up and recalls a time when James Cleveland came to direct the choir and Cleveland and Aretha spent hours in the living room just singing sacred songs. He concludes, "If you want to know the truth, she ain't never left the church!"

BUT NOT EVERY comeback goes as well as Aretha's. The Staple Singers came out of Chicago in the fifties to become for a time just about the top attraction in gospel. Back then, the group was made up of Roebuck "Pop" Staples, the leader, and three of his children, Mavis, Cleotha, and Purvis (who has since been replaced by a third daughter, Yvonne), and they were billed as "the first family of gospel." Pop Staples did some writing, and one of his songs, "Uncloudy Day," comes about as close as anything written recently to being a gospel classic. But as performers, what they had to offer chiefly was Mavis. She has a contralto voice of immense range, one that can sweep down close to baritone, then push well up into high soprano. What she lacks in raw power she makes up in emotional intensity. Mavis was the great favorite of gospel audiences. In the early sixties, when the Staple Singers began playing the folk circuit, white audiences seemed to respond to the intimate "living-room" feeling they projected.

From gospel to "folk gospel," it wasn't far to soul, and that was where they headed next, hooking up with the new black label, Stax, in Memphis. Mavis was soon being pushed into a solo role by the company as a second Aretha Franklin. Yet partly to keep their old fans, and partly, too, because it means a lot to them personally, the Staples have tried hard to hold on to their identification as a gospel group. Toward this end, they went to Philadelphia—Marion Williams' territory—and played an all gospel program on Thanksgiving Day, 1969. What happened there, as described by Tony Heilbut in *The Gospel Sound,* was pretty brutal.

> They went back to the same routine that had sustained them for years; the Staples are probably the only gospel group who still feature the songs they sang in 1956. Mavis shook hands on "Help Me Jesus" and groaned with suffering on "Tell Heaven I'm Coming Home One Day." Philadelphia remained very still. The girls walked off stage shyly and obviously hurt. But Roebuck wouldn't give up. "Listen, church, you have to look out for yourself," he said strumming the guitar. "Don't nobody want to go to heaven more than I do, children, but we got to live down here too." The message was clear, but no "Amens" resounded. Finally Roebuck brought Mavis back to sing "Precious Lord." I've seldom seen her work harder. She was all over the audience, crying, roaring, running. Four ladies screamed, the least such effort deserved, but the rest of the church remained very still. The applause was barely polite as Cleotha led the entranced Mavis out.

Pop Staples insists that at least in intention what they are doing today is not all that different from what they were doing during the fifties in gospel. "We're telling the truth," he says, "and that's gospel."

And is gospel protest? "Sure it is—and that's what we're doing, too. Right now, today, we're trying to sing what Martin

Luther King was preaching on. I'll tell you true, I never changed from gospel. We're still preaching, and we're getting more listeners from the kids and grownups."

And there is certainly something to what he says, too, for the Staple Singers have had their greatest success with "message" songs, of which their best example is their big hit, "Respect Yourself."

> *If you disrepect everybody that you run into,*
> *How in the world do you think anybody 'sposed to*
>   *respect you?*
> *If you don't give a heck about the man with the*
>   *Bible in his hand,*
> *Just get out the way and let the gentleman do his*
>   *thing.*
> *You the kind of gentleman want everything your*
>   *way.*
> *Take the sheet off your face, boy, it's a brand new*
>   *day.*
> Refrain:*Respect yourself, respect yourself, etc.*

This is secular preaching of a sort, and it no doubt has some effect on that vast, secular, record-buying congregation out there in soul-music land. And they make it a point to include some gospel material in all their shows. It works with the audiences. I have seen a theater full of young fans react with the sort of spontaneity and personal enthusiasm you expect only from real gospel congregations.

And the Staples love being loved. Pop Staples remarks in passing on how good the audience at that soul show had made them feel. "We really had them singing along last night, didn't we?" he asks with a sudden ingenuous smile. "I can't express how well that makes me feel. You'll just never know until you've been through the ups and downs we have."

I asked if he were referring to the Staples' changeover from gospel to soul. He nods. "Well, yes. It was really kinda hard. People were so sure we couldn't do it, while in our own minds there never was much doubt. I knew we wanted to give a message in contemporary music—to really tell about what was happening right *now* in our songs. You see, when you're in gospel it's really hard to get through to the public. The radio stations didn't play it then, though it's getting better today.

Being a religious man, I didn't feel it was in no way sinful to give a message out to the public."

And what is that message? He had put it very plainly in his pitch to the audience the night before. After introducing his daughters, he went on in that low-key way of his to tell them that they had come to entertain them with some gospel and some blues that were all about love, freedom, and peace. "The main theme is unity," he admonished, beginning a kind of preaching rhythm. "Don't rip one another off. You with Pop. I want you to go to school now. Because things are changing. Because you might be president." Then, without further notice, the Staples swung into the old hymn "May the Circle Be Unbroken" (the "unity" theme)—and the house went wild with applause.

If this seems a little corny—the sort of quietistic, pietistic hogwash that kept people in their "place" for far too long—there is at least this to be said for Pop Staples' message: He really believes it. And he has a right to, for he has seen it work in his own lifetime. Ask him about how the Staple Singers got started, and he will tell you that it was when he was working in the Chicago Stockyards. "Oh, they were *hard* times, let me tell you. We were down so low we couldn't go from one week to another without borrowing. There just never was enough money back then. So one time somebody asked us would we come and sing at their church for 50 percent of the collection —see, we were known as a singing family, but it was just singing around the living room was all. Anyway, we did go and sing for them then, and we made seventeen dollars—and didn't that come in handy!

"But anyway, that was how we got started. We were just a straight-out gospel group then, but we made international tours and everything. Which is a long way to come for a Drew, Mississippi, boy."

I asked if that was where he was from. "Yes," he said, "that's right. I was born in some little town in the hills, but I grew up in the Delta—in Drew. They're all from the Delta—Big Bill, Son House, all of them. That's what inspired me, listening to all that blues down there. I started playing guitar just by ear, just what I heard around me.

"That's right, I used to listen to a lot of blues. Maybe that was why it always seemed to me there wasn't no real reason we couldn't play both blues and sacred. But there's been a change in this feeling, I think, even down South. It's not quite like it used to be."

ROEBUCK STAPLES may be right. Maybe the old attitudes are changing. The uncompromising rejection of blues and good-time music that Annie Pavageau articulated almost angrily that Sunday in New Orleans may even now seem anachronistic to younger members of the Morning Star Baptist Church. And perhaps it is just as well, too, for the Staples are at least realistc about the secular origins of their sacred music. Gospel was brought forth from the blues by Georgia Tom Dorsey, and those other songwriters and singers who helped shape the swinging sacred style back in the twenties and thirties. And so it is nei-ther surprising nor shocking that gospel, in turn, should have spawned soul. It just reminds us once again of the continuity, the wholeness, of the music.

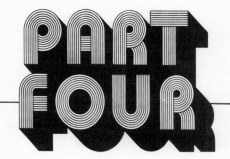

PART FOUR

CHAPTER FOURTEEN

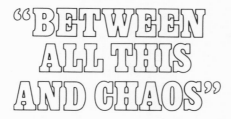

"BETWEEN ALL THIS AND CHAOS"

ONE FACT not widely appreciated by the general public today is that the biggest single market for live entertainment is the college circuit. More acts of all kinds are put before students at American colleges and universities than in night clubs, theaters, public auditoriums, at festivals, or at state and county fairs, or anywhere else. The kids own it all.

Of course, it was not always so. Not so many years ago, about the only contact students had with the big world of professional entertainment was when the prom committee went out timorously, check in hand, to book the big band for the big dance. But gradually television killed off the "adult" entertainment world: except for Las Vegas, Miami, and a few rooms in New York, the idea of the night club with its house band, touring headliners, and supporting acts is a thing of the past. With the single exception of Radio City Music Hall the movie houses show only movies and no stage shows. After a certain age—or perhaps it is after marriage and the first child—people seem content to get all their entertainment free right there in the living room.

During the latter fifties and throughout the sixties, as all this was taking shape, the character of a distinct youth culture was also in formation. In business they began to talk about the "youth market." What this meant was that they had suddenly discovered that kids had money to spend—a lot of it by the end of the fifties, and a lot more by the end of the sixties—and they would spend it most freely on items that gave them a sense of separate identity, of uniqueness, of being distinct from the straight adult world. This meant essentially clothes and entertainment. It was through these two that the youth culture expressed itself and began to make itself known to adult America (which, in a few years' time, it all but subdued). Although ultimately the festivals—such as Monterey Pop, and, of course, Woodstock—would be thought of as the true youth culture events, it was really the weekend concerts that were held at nearly every college in America that paved the way for them, that in a sense made them possible. For college was the place of youth; it fostered the sense of otherness that so obsessed American young people during the last couple of years of the sixties.

It has become an enormous market, no doubt about it. It is so big, in fact, that the entertainment weekly *Billboard* now issues an annual directory of "Campus Attractions." It goes out to sponsoring organizations of all kinds in colleges, and serves as a kind of catalogue to allow them to browse around in ads and listings to find out just what is available in the way of live entertainment. What is available turns out to be everything from comedians to dance troupes, hypnotists, mentalists, magicians, and lecturers. From the Ace Trucking Company to Allen Tate, it's all showbiz as far as *Billboard* is concerned, and *Billboard* is probably right.

Of course, music is what they want most at colleges and universities. And since, with student buying power, they have the wherewithal to book any acts they want, it may be interesting to see what these happen to be. In one of the brief articles in *Billboard*'s ninth annual "Campus Attractions" directory there is this: "Jay Jacobs of the William Morris Agency says that students usually decide on the live entertainment they want on campus by the artists who are on top of the popularity polls. 'For instance, we've got an overwhelming demand for Don McLean since his *American Pie* album was released.'" The title of that little article is "Booking Agent Activity Dominated by the Big Beat." Unimaginative, but it tells the story.

If this were the whole story, it would be more than disappointing; it would be tragic. But, fortunately, there is something more to tell. For many American colleges and universities offer a kind of extracurricular major in the blues. If you could do an instant survey of the boys and girls who are really into the music today you would find that something like 90 percent of them learned to like it while in college. Why should that be? Simply because they get their first exposure to the music there on records and in live concert.

The biggest and best-established of all the college blues events is the one held each year at Ann Arbor, Michigan. It is held on the University of Michigan campus, and the several sponsoring organizations are all affiliated with the University. The weekend-long affair has been held annually since 1968, and one year or another nearly every big name in the blues has appeared there—Big Mama Thornton, Roosevelt Sykes, Junior Wells, Little Brother Montgomery, Victoria Spivey, all of them. A few, such as Son House and Fred McDowell, appeared at all the festivals. Each year they have lost money. They expect to. But nobody was quite prepared for the wipeout they got in 1970, when by some unlucky coincidence the Goose Lake Festival— rock and pop—was held in nearby Jackson, Michigan, the same weekend and attracted 200,000. They were prepared to lose $5,-000 that year, but the sponsors took a bath to the tune of $20,000 —and that's a conservative estimate.

Nevertheless, the Ann Arbor Festival continues. Although they were forced to cut the length of the program and the number of artists drastically in the following years, they have put on representative events. The quantity may not always have been what it was during that glorious 1970 session, but the quality has remained very high indeed. And because the Ann Arbor Festival hung in there and has endured as an annual event, other colleges and universities around the country have begun to sponsor similar events of their own, making it possible for bluesmen to plan their way along a kind of short Festival circuit of their own, which may pay less, but is at least a bit steadier than the pop festivals. (Whoever heard of Woodstock II or the second annual Altamont?)

The Midwest Blues Festival, which has been held for a couple of years running at the University of Notre Dame, South Bend, Indiana, is one of those spawned by the Ann Arbor Festival. Like the rest of them, it is essentially a student enterprise. If it is held there, it is because there is enough student interest in the blues to fill a hall for one, two, or three nights running. Student promoters and their sponsoring organization depend on this interest to put such events over. How can they gauge this interest? What sort of planning goes into such a blues festival? These were things I wanted to know, and so, in advance of the event, I got in touch with the students who were putting it on and got an invitation out to South Bend for my trouble.

Owing to flight difficulties, I got there a little late on Friday, the first night of the three-day festival. Inside the auditorium things were cooking. The first night's session included a set by Mississippi Fred McDowell, another by Chicago blues harpman Carey Bell and his band, and a finale by no less than Howlin' Wolf and his Chicago band. As I listened, I kept edging my way through the half-filled circular auditorium, asking for Perry Aberli and Bill Brinkman, the two who had organized and promoted the event.

I located them at last, not long after the last set had begun, over near the side of the stage where Howlin' Wolf himself sat, legs dangling down off the apron of the stage, waiting to go on. Meanwhile his band tore through its paces, led by Wolf's guitar man Hubert Sumlin, a brilliant and fluent soloist. You could feel the electricity building up as the crowd waited impatiently for the mighty Wolf. Make no mistake—he *is* mighty. Standing a good six-five or six-six, he must weigh close to 260 without giving away much (if anything) in flab. And because he is what he is, it is a bit of a shock when he makes his entrance at last to see him crawl across the stage to the microphone on his hands and knees.

When he gets down like that he seems to be reminding the audience that he's the growling, howling wolf, that he goes about quite naturally on all fours like a beast. If that's the idea, he seems to get it across, for the young crowd loves it. He is greeted by wild cheers as soon as he comes in sight, and they keep right on cheering as he begins roaring through his repertoire—"Wang Dang Doodle," "Shake It for Me," "Little Red Rooster," and so on. He wound up sitting down at the microphone—the old ticker ain't what it used to be, boy—but seemed to lose nothing in power from that position.

But finally the set ended, and with it, the first night of the Midwest Blues Festival. At last Perry Aberli—I had stuck close to him through the Howlin' Wolf set—could tell me a little about the Festival and the way it had been organized—just a few basic questions, I assured him, as the crowd was filing out. He told me this was the second year of blues here at Notre Dame, but that it was the first time they had tried anything "on this level"—a real Festival. "Last year it was more like a two-night concert."

How did they go about lining up the talent? "Oh, well, it was mostly Dick Waterman." He said it with a shrug as if I ought to have known all about that.

But I didn't, so I asked him. It turned out that Dick Waterman managed a number—though not all—of the blues artists that were appearing on the program. Sure, he offered a package, but if they didn't want the whole package, he helped them line up the artists that he *didn't* manage, such as Muddy Waters, Little Brother Montgomery, and Howlin' Wolf. "He helped set up everything," Aberli explained. "It was all done through letters."

Then he's not here now? "Oh, sure, he's here. Would you like to meet him?" I said I would, and he led me backstage, where Wolf's band was busy packing up, getting ready for the long drive to their next date, which happened to be in Toronto. Where was Dick Waterman? Perry Aberli found him over in one corner, engaged in conversation with Wolf's piano player, Sunnyland Slim. He brought him over at the first opportunity —a middling-tall white guy in glasses with a bushy mustache and wearing a jean suit—and introduced us. I told him that I was interested in how blues festivals were put together and just how important they were to the bluesmen who played them. Instead of volunteering answers right away, he suggested that we get together the next day and talk about all this at some length.

That was how it happened that I came by for him about the middle of the next morning and waited in the lobby of his very straight South Bend hotel until the very un-straight Mr. Waterman emerged from the elevator. We found a place down the block to talk, and during breakfast I began feeding questions to him.

I asked him, first of all, whom he managed—and he seemed

to sense I wasn't exactly asking for a client list, for he answered, "I manage those I respect as people. I have a personal feeling for all these men. The only one of them all for whom I've lost any sort of objectivity is Son House. I'm just there to help out with him however I can."

Waterman has managed many, if not most, of the surviving Delta bluesmen. His enterprise, Avalon Productions, is, as a matter of fact, named after the hometown of Mississippi John Hurt, who was with Waterman until his death in 1969. The great Skip James was also with him from about the time of his exciting appearance at the Newport Folk Festival of 1964 until the time of his death in 1969. Among those with him today are Mance Lipscomb, Robert Pete Williams, Arthur Crudup, and, of course, the great Son House. I had heard that Waterman had "discovered" Eddie "Son" House, the surviving king of the Delta bluesmen, long after Son had given up the blues and become a Pullman porter, and persuaded him to take up music again. I asked Waterman if that was true.

He nodded. "Looking at it all from a philosophical viewpoint," he said, "I think that that is what I am most proud of—if that's the word—that is, proud of having brought the music of Son House back to a whole generation of people who would otherwise never have known he was alive. To some extent, this is also true of Skip James and Robert Pete Williams and Arthur Crudup, I guess. I have helped bring their careers to the point where they can be booked to play in person and younger people can talk to them and learn what it was like to be a bluesman in the late 1920s and 1930s in the South."

Son House was not to make an appearance here at Notre Dame this time around. I understood that Waterman kept the schedule of that old blues master down to a manageable minimum of concerts. However, he did have a couple of other blues attractions—the Buddy Guy-Junior Wells Blues Band and that of Otis Rush—that were a long way from the old-time blues that people expected from Son, Mance, Robert Pete, and the rest. These younger Chicago bluesmen were on the program in force.

"Yes," he conceded, "I started in band management in 1966 when Bob Koester, owner of Delmark Records, in Chicago, told me that he had just issued a record by a guy named Junior

Wells and Junior wanted to get out on the road and travel as a touring band. I started with Junior in 1966, added Buddy Guy in 1967, added the late Magic Sam in 1968 and later Luther Allison. Junior and Buddy worked with separate bands for several years until I put them into the same band in 1970 for the Rolling Stones' tour of Europe, and they have been together ever since. I've just added the Otis Rush band after having been a personal friend of his for years."

I could understand how, with all this talent at his disposal, Waterman could book a whole blues festival. And yet there were plenty of others here whom he did not handle. Perry Aberli had said that he had helped bring them all here. How? And why?

"Well, I am good friends with virtually every bluesman, whether I work with him or not. I value my long friendships with B. B. King, Muddy Waters, Howlin' Wolf, James Cotton, and many others that I don't manage or book. Many people in the business will call me for advice about recording contracts, publishing contracts, new offers, and so on. And student promoters call and ask to be put in touch with these people, too. I do what I can. I try to give back to the business this way because it has been pretty good to me over the long haul."

Dick Waterman's name for what he is is ombudsman. You must have come across that curious word of Scandinavian origin. In general, it is a public official who listens to complaints against government agencies, a middleman who helps people cope with the system—and that just about sums up his function for the bluesmen he manages. What does he do for them? Everything. He not only lines up jobs for his clients to play, he makes sure the jobs are clustered within reasonable distances for the older bluesmen to travel. He works out airline schedules and travel arrangements for these men, many of whom had never traveled out of their home states before the blues revival of the 1960s shot them into prominence. And he makes sure that none of the old-timers, all of whom are from the South and are unaccustomed to the rigors of a Northern winter, should have to work in the North between December and March.

He works just as hard for the younger blues bandsmen. He gets jobs for them at the same blues festivals that the older men play, but he has also had some success booking his blues bands on tours headlined by rock supergroups, as he did when he sent the Wells-Guy band to Europe with the Stones. Waterman serves as a maildrop for them while they are on tour and exercises discretion in forwarding letters, making sure that those perfumed envelopes don't get his guys in trouble with their wives at home.

He goes after music and record royalties for them. He reads the fine print in contracts. He handles the myriad of hassles and irritations that may arise to keep these artists away from their music. He is the intermediary between the bluesmen and the big world that frightens and intimidates so many of them.

It was as a man whose integrity is known and respected that Dick Waterman was sought out by a number of the bluesmen of lesser reputation during that weekend at Notre Dame. A couple of them had come as replacements. Others had been booked just to fill out the program. They were not his clients. I remember watching him spend a long time with a couple of them backstage that Saturday night. I made no effort to listen in, but I could tell they were talking about something that mattered. Afterward, I'm afraid I was so obviously curious about what had been discussed that he answered my unasked question: "It's really important to give the smaller-time bluesmen their time to talk and to listen to their pitch. They'll say, 'Look, I've got a truck. Me and my sidemen can make it anyplace. You just get the date for us, and we'll be there. You can count on us.' " At this point, I remember, Waterman sighed sympathetically, as though he suddenly felt burdened by all this imposed upon him.

"The trouble is," he continued, "there's a lot less work out there than they think there is. They think they can get the jobs that Buddy and Junior don't play and live pretty well just off that alone. But Buddy and Junior, and Luther [Allison] and Otis [Rush]—and all the rest of them I manage—take most of the jobs I'm able to get for them. No, it's not an easy life, being a bluesman."

I followed Dick Waterman around most of that weekend at Notre Dame, trying to pick up whatever I could from him, trying to get a fix on the realities of the professional performing side of the bluesman's life today. Around Waterman was a good place to be, for he was always close to the center of the action at the Midwest Blues Festival. He would pop out front and listen hard when somebody interesting came onstage, and the rest of the time he would hang out behind the scenes, talking with the performers and taking part in a long poker game with the boys in the Wells-Guy band. This was his life, and in spite of a kind of professional gloomy-Gus manner, he enjoyed it, you could tell. I even managed to pump him on a few points on the economics of the blues.

Sometime Sunday he came away from a discussion with Perry Aberli that was very clearly about money, and I asked him just how important the colleges were to him and his blues-men-clients as a market for the kind of music they had to offer. "Very," he said simply. "Very important. When I started at this business, there were a few clubs in urban areas, folk music places a lot of them, that booked bluesmen, and there were festivals—maybe just Newport. There was no place else for most of these men to play until colleges started up as the big entertainment spots they are today. Today, of course, all that has changed, because there are colleges and college festivals for them. Some of the urban clubs and those around college towns are still open, but one night on a campus date like this one will bring a performer about as much as a week in a club. Plus, with an older performer, there is the question of the strain on his health. It's much easier on him to come to a place like this, play a set or a whole concert, and then return home, than it is to hang around a place a whole week and wind up playing about four or five hours a night. It's this, I think, that has made me concentrate on college bookings. It's so much easier on the older performers. For some of them it can be rather pleasant, going around talking to the kids and all. They like it.

"My biggest job is convincing these student-union boards, and other student organizations and so on, that they can have a whole two-day blues festival with a lot of really big names and all for just about the same money they would have to pay for one night with one big rock group. Not a supergroup like Creedence—just an ordinary big rock group. A lot of rock groups get $25,000 a night now. You give me $7,500 to $8,000, and I'll give you a hell of a night of blues—with some of the best and most authentic music you ever heard. And the kids might even learn something about where rock came from at a blues concert."

And is it good for the colleges? For the students themselves?

"Sure it is," he said emphatically. "The thing I'm trying to do at colleges is to help promote and present an art form that is really dying out with the men who created and practiced it. I mean, nobody's going to know about this old-time blues thing after people like Son House and Mance [Lipscomb] and Johnny Shines die off. That's why I always encourage *any* kind of filming or videotaping that any university wants to do—if they have the facilities and the inclination. All they have to do is guarantee the film will not be used for commercial use. Film is the most accurate way of keeping a record." Which is another way of saying that what they *are* is almost as important as what they *sing*.

BECAUSE I was interested in Waterman himself, I did a bit of digging and found out as much about him as I could in preparation for a meeting we arranged later. I found out, for instance, that he got into the business almost by accident. Although he had always been interested in music (a self-confessed "Buddy Holly and Bo Diddley freak" as a kid), it was always as a listener. When he started in at Boston University he became a pretty passionate folk fan. It was easy. There was a classmate of Waterman's named Joan Baez who played and sang in a coffeehouse called the Golden Vanity, which was then located next to the University. He came in a couple of nights and listened to her, and that's about all it took. But when graduation time came, he had no intention of going into the business side of music. He wanted to be a writer.

He took a job as a reporter on a small-town Connecticut newspaper for a while, and then tried free-lancing for a long, lean period. When things got too tight, he put in a stint as a publicist-advance man for the legendary Joan Baez-Bob Dylan tour of 1965. This was about as close as he had come to real involvement in the music business except for that trip he took down South in 1964.

By then blues was his music. He had picked up a rumor that the legendary and long-lost Eddie "Son" House, by reputation one of the greatest of the Mississippi Delta blues singers, had popped up briefly in Memphis. That was enough to send him and two fellow fans, Nick Perls and Phil Spiro, there in hope of finding the bluesman. It was a bad time to go. This was the

summer that Chaney, Goodman, and Schwerner were murdered in Mississippi. And this was the year Violet Liuzzo was
gunned down in her car. There were people down there who
didn't much like white boys coming down in cars with Northern license plates making inquiries after black bluesmen.
Their search took them down to Mississippi, where, with the
help of the Reverend Robert Wilkins, a blues singer turned
evangelist, they went from town to town and cotton field to
cotton field, asking after the whereabouts of Son House. The
answer, when it came, surprised them. He was living in
Rochester, New York.

They found him, all right, a retired Pullman porter who had
not played or sung regularly in four years. He was flattered that
they had come all this way to see him, though, and so he gladly
sat down and gave them a concert. As he did, the years seemed
to slip away, and by the end of the afternoon he was playing
well and singing in a full, strong voice. The three who had
found Son House told him he ought to go back to music. Well,
if I do, Son said to them, can you get some work for me? Neither
of his two companions could give that sort of time to the enterprise, and so the job of finding jobs for Son House fell to Dick
Waterman—and that was how he got into the music business.

This led eventually to the founding of his Avalon Productions. "At that time," he told me later, "the blues business was
all messed up. Festivals were able to 'shop around' for their one
token bluesman. They could get one old-time Delta artist for
$250, or somebody else for $200, or somebody else for as little as
$150. Or at least they'd say so, trying to whittle down the asking
price. I stepped in and tried to get them all to come with me. I
told them they would be working less but making more money.
And this is how it has worked out for them."

It was at one of Dick Waterman's blues package shows that
we arranged to meet again. The event would be held in an
auditorium in Burlington, Vermont. Workshop sessions were to
be held the afternoon of the concert at the University of Vermont which is located there right in the heart of town.

I began to get an idea of what the show would be like at the
afternoon workshop sessions, which were held at the student
union at the University. Dick Waterman was there, acting as

master of ceremonies in the little mini-concert he had planned to start the session. This was to give the students an idea of what they would hear that night. He wanted the students to appreciate the sort of blues eminence he had assembled before them. After Robert Pete Williams had played and sung for them, and retired to a good round of applause, Dick Waterman got up and remarked, "I just noticed while Robert was playing that there is over one hundred years of blues-playing experience on this stage right now." And there must have been, all right, for up there with Robert Pete were Arthur Crudup, who is sixty-seven, and Son House—and blues historians only guess at his age!

Later, I asked Waterman how old he thought Son House really is, and he shook his head and said, "It's hard to tell. He doesn't know himself. He talks about living in St. Louis and working in an East St. Louis steel mill when he was in his twenties, and that was probably during World War I, so that would put him in his late seventies today. I'd guess he is about seventy-nine."

As it happens, however, Son did not take up blues or even learn guitar until comparatively late. For one interviewer he fixed the date at 1928, which, by Dick Waterman's reckoning would put Son House in his early thirties. He had stayed clear of the blues until then, for he was a Baptist preacher, and like all the rest he regarded secular music as sinful. But when he gave in, he gave in all the way, left the church, and with his partner, Willie Brown, began playing and singing all around the Clarksdale, Mississippi, area.

He got very good very fast. With barely more than a fundamental knowledge of guitar he began composing songs of his own. His blues had an easy fluent, lyrical quality to them, and an eloquence that probably came from those years in the pulpit. Some, too, were spiced with irony and humor, like his "Preachin' Blues."

> *Yes, I'm gonna get me religion, I'm gonna join the*
> *   Baptish Church*
> *Yes, I'm gonna get me religion I said, I'm gonna join*
> *   the Baptist Church*
> *You know, I want to be a Baptist preacher so I won't*
> *   have to work.*

*You know, one deacon jumped up and he began to
    grin
You know, one deacon jumped up and he began to
    grin
You know he said one thing, elder, I think I'll go
    back to barrelhousin' again.*

And so on for many satirical stanzas more. In a way, this song
is pure bravado, Son's nosethumb at those years he gave to the
Lord. But, as we shall see, he feels a little uneasy about all that
today; he seems to wish he had not shut the door quite so tight
on that part of his life. Significantly, he has now eliminated
"Preachin' Blues" from his performing repertoire, but makes it
a point to do a hymn—"one for the Man upstairs"—whenever
he appears before an audience, usually something like "John,
the Revelator" or "This Little Light of Mine."

After he left the church, his reputation as a bluesman
brought him in contact with the man who was then the reigning king of the Delta singers, Charley Patton. They played a
little together with Son's sideman, Willie Brown, and Patton
was so impressed that he recommended Son to Paramount Records. They went North, to Grafton, Wisconsin, in the summer
of 1930. Son and Willie sat down and recorded nine sides, of
which only four were ever released. For this he got forty dollars
plus expenses, and he was delighted; this was about as much
as he made in a year working in the cotton patch.

He didn't record again for twelve years—and when he finally
did, it was only by accident. He happened to be nearby when,
sometime in 1942, Alan Lomax, then folk curator of the Library
of Congress, came through and set up his recording equipment
at the crossroads which was Robinsonville, Mississippi. Word
was sent to Son, and he came by with his guitar. He played and
sang for him for nearly all of an afternoon thinking this was
another chance to make an easy forty dollars. But then, when
he finished, he was given only a bottle of Coca-Cola as payment
for his day's work.

The following year he went North, to Rochester, New York.
Why Rochester? Because a friend had preceded him there and
said he could get him a job. Son held several, in fact, until he
took one as a Pullman porter with the New York Central and
stayed on until retirement. He gave up playing guitar and sing-

ing in 1948 because people up there in Rochester didn't seem to want to hear the old blues anymore. And that was how things stood in 1964 when he was found by Dick Waterman and his two friends at the end of their long search.

Although he has been performing ever since, the years have taken their toll on Son House. In many ways he is physically robust for his age, but he is quite dependent on alcohol, and this in turn has left him somewhat senile. He is a bit foggy about what did or did not happen in his past. I talked with him for a while in his motel room in Burlington, Vermont, and though he was obliging, polite, and pleasant through it all, he really didn't have much to say. And much of what he did remember for my benefit, he remembered inaccurately.

For instance, he recalled the two men with whom he played down in Mississippi: "Willie Brown and I started playing together after I learned to play guitar. Me and him played together at least twenty years. We traveled to all them places—to Europe and up to Wisconsin. Charley Patton, too. We went to Europe together, just us three—the three of us, playing them blues. Then Willie, well, it wasn't too long after that until he died."

Well, he and Willie Brown weren't together much more than ten years, and while Son eventually got to Europe after his rediscovery, neither Brown nor Charley Patton ever did. But that's the way it's fixed in the mind of Eddie "Son" House today.

In general, he was not much interested in talking, and so I didn't push him. There was only one point on which he spoke with any degree of passion, and that was his decision to leave preaching for the blues. "Oh, yeah," he said when I asked him about "Preachin' Blues." "I preached a long time before ever I get to play the blues. But I got to wanting to play the blues. I had the Bible in one hand and the guitar in the other. I knew I had to turn one loose, because you can't pretend with God. Yes, I knew I had to give up religion. You can't fool God. And it was right on behind that I started playing those old country blues."

But it is only onstage that he comes fully to life and shows live sparks from that old fire that burns within him. I found that out later on at the show. There was a terrific turnout for the Festival. Even the cop at the front door was impressed. "I haven't seen this many people," he told me, "since the last time they had wrestling here." Tickets they had been unable to sell out at the University went quickly at the box office, so that quite unexpectedly there was a sellout crowd waiting for the performers when the show began.

They were a good-natured, appreciative audience, too enthusiastic but not rowdy. They were attentive to Robert Pete Williams' distinctive blend of folk poetry and blues, appreciative of Arthur Crudup, and downright enthusiastic for Bonnie Raitt. Although she is white (records for Warner Bros.) and has a future in pop, she clearly belonged there that night. If not a blues singer, plain and simple, she sure is bluesy, for in addition to songs by Stephen Stills and Paul Siebel, her repertoire includes a lot of authentic blues material, the best of it by a neglected lady named Sippie Wallace. And can Bonnie Raitt play the guitar!

All in all, she was probably the best possible act to precede Son House. She had the crowd up and receptive, expecting something special from the man Waterman calls "Mr. Legend." What happened was special, all right, but not quite what anybody there had bargained for.

After Waterman's introduction—"the standard by which blues singers are measured"—Son swung into his first number, "Louise McGhee," with tremendous passion and enthusiasm. He bellowed forth the words and whopped away at his steel-bodied National guitar so that it whined and sang in his hands.

"You know," Dick Waterman remarked to me then, as we were watching and listening from the wings, "when he starts to sing all the aggravation and misery he gives me is worth it. I've been everywhere with him, and at every performance I'm still tremendously moved by this man as an artist."

Son did a couple of more straight blues and after the last waited for the applause to die down before he began his final number, the hymn "This Little Light of Mine." It went just fine. When he does it he lays down his guitar and does it *a capella,* but this time he got the audience clapping time with him. They continued all through the song and, bursting into a long round of applause, they kept it going after he had finished and was starting for the wings.

And then in response Son House cut a caper, doing a shuffling buck-and-wing step, and looked as if he might return for an encore. But Waterman thought that might be a bit too much for him and motioned him off. Son became momentarily addled, torn between going off and returning to the microphone. He stumbled slightly and looked as if he might fall, but two brightly dressed and bearded young black men suddenly appeared from the other side of the stage and swept him away. Nobody knew who they were or what they were up to.

They were the local militants. In the discussion that followed immediately (with Son sitting placidly outside on a bench), the two angrily accused Dick Waterman of "pushing an old man to the point of exhaustion." One, taller and leaner than his companion, was the spokesman. He asked menacingly if Waterman had a paper that said he was not legally responsible if Son House fell dead onstage.

The atmosphere in that little room was very tense indeed. But when Waterman began to speak I could tell he wasn't rattled in the least. Ordinarily he has a slight stammer that shows up from time to time in conversation, but it wasn't there as he explained that there was no paper at all between him and Son, that he did business with him, as with all other bluesmen, on the basis of a handshake. As for how strong and healthy Son was, every year he is examined by a doctor, and it is on the basis of that examination that they decide whether or not he should make the tour that year. Although he only plays a few dates every spring, Waterman added, the money he makes from these appearances eases things considerably for Son and his wife in their old age.

"Yeah," said the tall black, "and I'll bet you get a hell of a big cut out of that money of theirs."

Waterman shook his head and gave a firm no. "Because it's Son," he said, "and he and I have been together for so many years, I don't take anything. Not a thing. He's the only one I handle this way, but it's true, I take no cut."

They were impressed and began backing down a little. "Well, I'm not prophesizing against you personally. All I know is there was one mighty sick and tired old man up on that stage."

"I'm not denying there's a strain on him. There certainly is. The Mississippi Delta blues style is physically tiring. I mean I'm not being patronizing in explaining this, but it's more exhausting than other styles."

"You don't have to tell us that, man," the spokesman snapped. "We was born there." He hesitated then, wavering perceptibly, then added, "Well, we'll go out and talk to him some more about this—get his side of it."

Dick nodded. That was quite all right with him. "He'll probably make light of it, but it's serious enough. Unfortunately, he's not the best judge of his own condition." He ended by giving the two young men his card and telling them to call or write him if they wanted to discuss this further. They went outside and huddled with Son for some minutes and then left.

Afterward, Dick Waterman and I had resumed our place in the wings. Junior Wells and Buddy Guy, complete with two saxes and rhythm, were laying down some funky, heavy sounds, and the crowd out front was really taking it in. They loved it, as well they should. Waterman even seemed to be enjoying himself, relaxing a little after that encounter in the dressing room. I complimented him on his coolness down there and said he seemed quite unflappable. "I *am* flappable," he replied, "but not in my own element. When I go, everything goes." He gestured out to the stage and the audience, taking everything in. "I'm all that stands between all this and chaos."

CHAPTER FIFTEEN

SOMEBODY in Memphis gave me some advice when I said I was
going to Brownsville, Tennessee, to look for Sleepy John Estes:
"Find a local cop and ask him. These small-town policemen
know where everybody lives." It seemed like a good idea, so
when I pulled up and parked opposite the Haywood County
courthouse, with its gallant-boys-in-gray statue in the front
yard, I took a walk around the surrounding square and looked
for a uniform of some kind.

Something struck me about Brownsville. There seemed to be
a lot more black people than white out on the street, and I
wondered if this reflected an imbalance in the town and in the
rest of the county. Maybe not, for when I realized I was hungry
and ducked into a kind of combination hamburger-joint-pool-
parlor, I found all the good old boys in town, chomping hamburgers and wolfing down bowls of chili in between games of
pool as the jukebox blared forth rockabilly and country and
western. I did a quick check and saw that the only black man
in the place was the ball-racker who worked the pool hall.

Outside again, I met a Brownsville policeman just down the
street and asked him about Sleepy John. He was young and

serious and determined to be helpful. There was no hint in his manner that I, a white man, should have no legitimate business with a black man there. "Well, sir, I'll tell you," he said. "I used to know where he lived, but to tell the truth, he just moved. That's a fact. Now, I know the general area where he lives now, but I don't know the house. Maybe your best bet would be to try the post office." So I took off in the direction he indicated, and as I started across the street, I happened to look down the block and got a surprise.

A car had parked diagonally at the curb and among the four people who got out was a tall blind black man. There was really no mistaking those sharp features and that abstracted manner: It had to be Sleepy John Estes. It was. I came up and introduced myself. He took the interruption in his stride, but a short, plump man named Hammie Nixon interposed himself and told me that John was just on his way to see "Lawyer Reid, up at the bank," and that I could interview him at his place after he finished. He would be happy to lead the way and show me just where John lived. That sounded good. I showed him where I was parked, and Hammie said he would get his own car, and I could follow.

But before we really got started, Hammie came back on foot to my car and told me, acting a little embarrassed, that Lawyer Reid wanted to see me, and would that be okay? He took me to the bank, up in the elevator to a second-floor office that was posh by any standard. The secretary nodded us in, and in a moment I was inside the paneled inner office, shaking hands with Lyle Reid, attorney-at-law, taking the seat opposite Sleepy John, and explaining to him just why I wanted to talk with John Estes, what I hoped to find out from him, and so on.

Lawyer Reid was okay. He just wanted to look me over. If I was going to interview Sleepy John, he just wanted to be sure that I would not be taking advantage of him, as had evidently happened in the past. What seemed to convince him was that I would not be using a tape recorder.

"No sir," I assured him. "Just a notebook. I take pretty accurate notes, and I've been around enough to know that a lot of damage has already been done with tape recorders."

He nodded. "It has," he agreed. "John has suffered some himself, and we don't want that to happen again. We're just now beginning to get his affairs in order. He's come in today to talk to me about a letter from a Mr. Carter in New York about the settlement on some royalties that are due him, and, well, we don't want him to be taken advantage of ever again. That's why I'm helping out."

He gave me his okay then and suggested that I drive out behind Hammie, as I had arranged to do, assuring me that John would be out shortly with his wife and son. I never quite got who the "we" were that Reid was talking about, but I really got the idea that he was speaking for the community, that there was genuine concern in Brownsville that Sleepy John Estes, blind as he was and at the mercy of the outside world, be protected from those who had hurt him in the past.

John Adam Estes was born in 1903 in nearby Ripley, Tennessee, the son of a guitar-playing sharecropper. When he was six, he lost the sight of one eye when he was injured in a baseball game. Not long after that, the family moved to Brownsville and John, who had been given a guitar by his father, first began playing and singing around the biggest town in Haywood County. He attracted the attention of local musicians such as Willie Newbern, who gave the boy some coaching on guitar, and mandolin-playing Yank Rachell, who began gigging around with him at country suppers and parties. Eventually, Hammie Nixon, a twelve-year-old guitar player and jug blower, joined him, and they got as far as Memphis. When Hammie was nineteen he and another Brownsville bluesman went North, to Chicago, and got a chance to record. He sent word to Sleepy John, who hopped a freight and came North and got to do some recording himself. These were his first sessions, recorded for Decca in 1934. He did them every now and again for the next six years running, when he switched to Victor's Bluebird label, recording his last for them in 1941. During the war and after, the recording industry forgot about him. He stayed close to Brownsville, though he made it as far as Memphis—was there, in fact, in 1950, when he finally lost the sight in his other eye, which had been failing gradually. Blind, he stayed close to home, and was right there in Brownsville when he was rediscovered by a documentary-film maker, Ralph Blumenthal, in the late 1950s. What followed was a series of concert, festival, and club dates that eventually took him all the way to Europe. He began recording again, found others were also recording his songs—Taj Mahal, for one, has done his "Diving Duck Blues"—and with the help of Lawyer Reid, who looks after his finances, and Hammie Nixon, who looks after his day-to-day needs, he makes a pretty good living for himself and his family.

Sleepy John Estes is no great shakes as a guitar player. His voice, somewhat thin and very intense, gives a kind of authentic urgency to the songs he sings, though it is not an exceptional voice as, say, Howlin' Wolf's is. His special talent is as a blues composer. He has written hundreds of songs, some of them improvised right on the spot, and has recorded many of them himself. Ultimately, he is the very model of the local bluesman. Although in his most active years he spent a good deal of time in Memphis and traveled as far as Chicago to record, Brownsville remained his home base. And today, since being "rediscovered," he and Hammie travel more widely than ever—to colleges, to Washington, D.C., and even to Europe—but keep coming back to Haywood County. This sort of intense identification with place has been reflected in his music, too. He has written a number of blues about persons, places, and events in the Brownsville area, a kind of blues version of Edgar Lee Masters' *Spoon River Anthology*. The best of these local blues can be heard on his Delmark LP, "Brownsville Blues."

His style of life is about average for Brownsville's black population. Approaching the Estes house from the highway, I followed Hammie Nixon's little Rambler, followed him on a right turn that took me down a dirt road. We did a bit of winding on it—he was right, I would never have found it by myself—and came to a halt at last in front of a white single-story frame house. Sleepy John moved there not long ago from a place outside of town that was pretty run down. Hammie said this place is a lot better, and he hoped John's kids took better care of it.

Hammie did quite a bit of talking that afternoon. A plump, quick man, he worries a lot—about his partner, the condition of the world today, and nearly everything else. As we waited for Sleepy John to arrive, Hammie told me a little about himself. He was born in Lauderdale County, he said, but has lived here since he was twelve. He plays harmonica, jug, tub bass, washboard, and guitar. I asked him how he first got started on the blues. He said, "That would be when Charles Barber and David Campbell of Lauderdale came through my father's yard playing. I caught that sound and I loved it. I told my father, and he said, 'Son, if you work good, I'll buy you a guitar.' He did, and that's how I got going."

John drove up in his own car, his son at the wheel, his wife —a silent, sullen woman who has been in and out of the state asylum a couple of times—in the rear seat. Greetings all around again, and John remained outside to talk with Hammie and me.

I told him that Hammie had just said he had gotten started as a bluesman. How had John Estes begun?

"Oh, I got me a cigar box with just one string, and I started whanging on that and singing along. Got me some change, and then I got a regular guitar, so I could get that real, true sound. But I just played around here until 1929, when I commenced to travel. Hammie was with me then. We was hoboing then."

Was this about the time he began to record?

"Along about this time, yes. There was this man Mel Williams of Decca. He'd give us money to come to Chicago and record, and then we'd hop a freight and save the money."

"Yes," put in Hammie, "we made a lot of trips back there then, for RCA Victor toward the end, but John's eyes started giving him troubles."

That was when people sort of lost track of you for a while?

"Yeah, I guess," said John. "They knowed of us up there because of our records. They say they looked for us for twelve years and couldn't find us. When they did, they said they heard old Hammie was ninety-five, and I was a hundred and five. Memphis Slim told them that. I guess that was his idea of a joke. I don't look no hundred and five, do I? I was born in 1903. That makes me sixty-nine this year. What would you have thought?"

I said I would have taken him for a little younger than that. He was satisfied, and so I changed the subject: What about other bluesmen from Memphis and the Delta? Had he heard them?

"Well, yes," he conceded. "I heard some. You want to remember we played all these parties and dances, and the man would say, 'Keep it up all night.' And that's what we did. The singers and players would come and go, and we'd keep right on. Yeah, for instance, Memphis Slim and Memphis Minnie, we met them before they went to Chicago."

"Robert Johnson, too," said Hammie. "He did pretty good."

John agreed. "He was good in my book. If he'd lived up to now, he'd be awful good."

People they had known. Places they had been. This got them to talking about their tours in Europe. They had liked all that traveling, and both Hammie and John were ready to go again. "Yeah, I really like Europe," said John. "I learned a lot. In London, they got a lot of nice people. We met the Beatles while we was there. We went out to their place—that was in 1964—and spent the night there. Then they had to leave and go to another part of England. Yeah, they just went crazy about our music over there. We were there in 1964 and 1966."

"Tell him about Russia," Hammie urged.

"What about it?"

"How I got lost there. You know. I did get lost. That was behind the Iron Curtain, they call it. But we did every show over there. Never missed one."

John nodded. "Yeah. We been called back several times, but we wouldn't go. Crossing that blue water scares me a little bit."

John Estes *is* sort of sleepy. It was about this time—the suggestion of peril at the crossing of the ocean—that Hammie started preaching pretty hard on when your time comes you have to go, and so on. Sleepy John acted as if he had heard it all from him before and proceeded to prove it by nodding off as Hammie talked on. I had noticed him do something similar as Lawyer Reid talked to me earlier in the office.

But making an effort to bring him back, I asked him just where he got his songs.

"You mean the blues?" he asked.

I nodded, then remembered he couldn't see me and said yes.

"Oh, the blues," he said. "The blues will never be forgotten. The blues is a feeling. You get something happen to you, and then you can sing it off. It's a feeling that comes to you when there's anything you want to do and can't do. And when you can sing it off in a song, that gives you a thrill."

Hammie nodded in agreement. "The words and music come together," he said. "We don't never have to rehearse. We just do it."

"That's right," said John. "When we're going to make records we may not know what it is we're going to do, but we know we'll get it. We could make a record about you, and this talk we're having, and everything. Or we might write a song about Lawyer Reid. He helped us a lot, getting our money for us and all. I wish we had him before. In our younger days they got a hold of us, and we never got anything from them. Now I'm stone blind and we're both sickly. . . ."

He trailed off with that, seeming to doze off once again behind his dark glasses. Hammie took up the line where John had dropped it and said they sure could use some bookings to keep themselves going. There was a pause then, and I said I thought maybe John was tired and I'd better go. He roused to say goodbye. We shook hands all the way around, and I jumped in the car. Turning it around, I had to swerve a couple of times to avoid the yard litter, so that I almost got stuck out there in the January mud.

My point in describing the situation of Sleepy John Estes in such detail is to give you some idea of the quality of life experienced by many of the surviving bluesmen today. His condition is fairly typical. Some are better off than he is. John's blindness restricts his travel somewhat, and his health, as he enters his seventies, is otherwise none too good. But in other ways, he is far more fortunate than others. In Lyle Reid, he has someone to look after his affairs, to go after royalties and fees that are rightfully his. Since he is almost totally dependent on these for his income today, he and his family would find it hard to survive without the attorney's help.

Most bluesmen need such an intermediary—an "ombudsman," to use Dick Waterman's term—to help them get by in the world. Many of these with whom I talked in the course of the research for this book have proved to be illiterate, able to write just enough to sign their names—which is, of course, all that is needed on a contract. Without someone whom they can trust to read that contract for them they cannot be sure they will receive compensation, just or unjust.

For the awful truth is that bluesmen are being cheated, ripped off, and taken advantage of today, just as they were before—or not in quite the same way, for the ground rules have now changed just a little. Let me explain. Before, it was the guys with the big black cigars who did the fleecing. They talked fast, had a score of ploys for holding onto monies that ought to have been paid out for record sales and publishing royalties, and it was all legal, of course, for they had signed contracts to back them up. But some of the more cunning, street-smart bluesmen learned how to deal with them. The Memphis Slims and the Big Bill Broonzys would dispense with contracts, demand cash, and not be put off by promises of money coming to them in the future.

There aren't many of those guys with black cigars around any more. The money to be made cheating superannuated bluesmen is nothing to that which may be picked up from underage rock-and-roll stars. But here we are in the middle of what is at least a modest blues revival, and the men who make the music are still not getting what should be coming to them. Who is?

It is, unfortunately, going to many of the very scholars, critics, and folklorists who are themselves in part responsible for this blues revival. We are not talking about great sums—the amounts involved, in many cases, would be computed in the hundreds rather than the thousands of dollars. Yet it adds up, and there seems something especially pernicious in the fact that those whose motives seem purest, who seem to be rescuing the blues from the crass commercialism that had all but stifled it in the 1930s and 1940s, are actually keeping small sums that should legitimately be passed on to blues artists and composers. There is, I'm sure, a process of rationalization involved here; it is not the sort of direct, cynical thievery that was practiced in the past.

How does it work? The blues scholar has, let us suppose, started a small record label to make available to a small public the work of a bluesman or songster he truly admires. He may even have rescued him from the obscurity of a sharecropper's cabin in Arkansas or the lowest West Side blues dive in Chicago. He pays the artist's expenses and a small advance, as much as he can afford, probably, at the time of the recording session. Although upon issue, the album has no immediate impact, as the bluesman's reputation grows through college concerts and so on, it continues to sell steadily until it has exceeded the modest advance against royalties made at the time—perhaps now a couple of years ago—when it was recorded. Our blues scholar may hardly have noticed at all. He may be plowing all he makes back into the enterprise so that he can cut more records and advance the cause of the blues. Because of his sacrifices he may have become a hero in his own eyes; and heroes put notoriously high demands on others. Without being consulted on the matter, the bluesman makes his sacrifice, too.

This is not to say that all small blues labels are run with this same careless disregard for the artists who record for them. But you cannot assume that because a bluesman has a number of albums available that he is doing well. His entire LP discography may have brought him less than a thousand dollars.

You may recall that the fact that I had no tape recorder along made quite a favorable impression on Sleepy John Estes' attorney, Lyle Reid. The sort of small, cassette voice recorder used by many interviewers was not what he was on the lookout for —most of these cannot even record music. But it takes only a little larger machine to record voice and guitar at commercial quality, if other factors are favorable. Begin an interview with a bluesman, and he will reach for his guitar and start playing to make a point. He is more comfortable singing than talking, anyway, and so with the right equipment, an interviewer may walk away with a fine collection of blues that includes personal introductions, anecdotes, bits of gossip, and so on—just the sort of back-porch concert that blues fans value for its informality and authenticity. These tapes have a mysterious way of appearing, edited, as albums on the European market. In the same way, informal blues jams at concerts, which have been recorded without permission or compensation, show up in Europe or are bootlegged here in America. Some bluesmen hold out their hands for payment whenever they see a tape recorder. They're entitled to.

And there is also the vast and troublesome area of copyright. Admittedly, a good deal of the material in some blues has come from traditional folk material that goes back well into the nineteenth century. Certain images, certain lines and rhymes, and a few whole songs have come down from those days when the laws of copyright would have been quite unknown to the black folk musicians whose work is so important to the origins of the blues. At least one latter-day blues musician has founded his reputation as a composer of traditional material that he has taken the trouble to copyright in his own name, or material that he has borrowed from long-dead blues writers such as Charley Patton, having altered it slightly in order to make it "his." Another blues player has some deserved reputation as a composer, yet he has for some years been practicing an almost childish dodge: He has been republishing his old songs, applying for new copyrights each time, while changing titles only slightly ("Someone" in one title becomes "Some One" in another).

The new breed of blues scholars and folklorists have also been guilty of questionable practices with copyrights. Let me give a specific example. As described earlier, the father-and-son collecting team of John A. and Alan Lomax have been credited with "discovering" Leadbelly, the blues singer Huddie Ledbetter, whom they first recorded in prison in 1933 for the Library of Congress. When he was pardoned in 1935, they took him North, did more recording, and helped him copyright his material (most of it unquestionably his, but some of it—"See, See Rider," for example—more likely of traditional origin). Many, if not most, of Leadbelly's songs, however, are credited in copyright to H. Ledbetter, A. Lomax, and J. Lomax. Why? How does "Death Letter Blues" belong to the Lomaxes as well as to Leadbelly? What lines did they contribute to his great song of tough teenage experiences in Shreveport, Louisiana, "Mister Tom Hughes Town"? These are personal blues that Huddie Ledbetter played and sang most of his life. How could he have divided authorship with white men whom he did not meet until he was well into his forties? And if they did not share authorship, what are their names doing on the copyrights?

There is an organization in New York called the American Guild of Authors and Composers, which exists as an auditing agency to make sure that composer-members receive the one-half of all mechanical royalties from recordings to which their copyrights entitle them. Membership in it is voluntary, of course, and its first members were jazz and popular music writers, but lately, at the urging of "ombudsmen" like Dick Waterman and Lyle Reid, blues composers have been joining the AGAC, as well. Settlements from recording companies or, more commonly, from music publishers (who withhold the composer's share of the royalties when it has been paid), are now beginning to come through. Sleepy John Estes is a member, and the "Mr. Carter" whose letter he was to discuss that afternoon with Lawyer Reid is John Carter, the managing director of the American Guild of Authors and Composers.

I went to visit Carter one day at the Guild's modest offices on

West Fifty-seventh Street, right in midtown Manhattan. We had an affable, though somewhat rushed, conversation right there, for he is one of those harried, work-right-through-lunch guys who gives himself completely to his job. He is a black man with a New York accent.

I asked how, in general terms, he would describe the AGAC and what it does. He explained: "Well, what we do is to represent the composer in an area in which he is very interested, of course—his royalties. We have 3,000 members, and among them are some of the top names, people like Ned Washington and Sammy Fain of the old guard and more modern writers such as Hal David and Bob Dylan. We audit publishers' books on a kind of continuing basis—every four years is standard, but we can go in for a special audit on a special case, of course. We also try to help our members on any contract problems they may have—anything that has to do with the collecting of recording and publishing royalties."

Since I had heard that Sleepy John Estes was an AGAC member, I asked Carter to fill me in a little on his case.

"With John Estes our work has fallen into two categories. There was one song that he had sold outright to Southern Music in New York, and, of course, he was entitled to no royalties on it, but we found out with a little digging that his bill of sale to them did not encompass the copyright-renewal period—that is, anything after the first twenty-eight years, and since it had been recorded since then, we were able to collect for him. There were also three other compositions of his that were not owned by anyone but had been recorded by Taj Mahal. We were able to collect 100 percent on these—with no difficulty at all, I might add, for Taj had credited John and was most cooperative.

"In all, I'd say we've collected about $7,000 on four compositions for him. That gave us a lot of pleasure. I remember that on that first thousand we collected for him, he was down in Washington, D.C., at a blues festival, so I took the check down to him personally."

For a special case like Sleepy John's, which requires copyright research, as well as audits and legal advice, there is a formula of payment worked out between AGAC and its members that seems quite equitable. For its work, the organization keeps 5 percent of the first $20,000 collected for the member, but only ½ percent for any amount over $20,000 up to $100,000. Anything above that goes to the member.

Dick Waterman had urged me to ask Carter about Arthur Crudup and the settlement they were negotiating on the royalties due him. When I did, Carter shook his head and said, "Believe it or not, we still haven't gotten the contract on that. It's going to be terrifically favorable for him when at last it does come through, though, and he's been very patient through all of it. Sometime in the near future he's going to be a very happy man."

The case of Arthur "Big Boy" Crudup is at once one of the most depressing and most heartening of all those with which John Carter has dealt. Probably none of the other bluesmen has been fleeced quite as thoroughly and shamefully as has this genial, relaxed giant of a man. In spite of his considerable talent as a performer and composer, he has had to support himself and his family all his life as a sharecropper and migrant laborer. He was never able to make a living in music. And the Xerox copy of the check that Carter pushed across his desk for my inspection told the story. It was made out to Arthur Crudup by Blanche Melrose, widow of Lester Melrose, and was drawn on an Orlando, Florida, bank. It was a royalty check for $1.06, meant to satisfy his claim for what was due him on his song "Mean Old Frisco." This was typical of his payments from Wabash Music. He had written one song that had become a big Elvis Presley hit—"That's Alright, Mama"—and another—"My Baby Left Me"—that was recorded not only by Presley but also by Elton John, the Grease Band, and Creedence Clearwater Revival. His "Rock Me, Mama" was a big blues hit for B. B. King. But from all these and from the many other songs he wrote and recorded, Crudup made so little that finally in the fifties he gave up music altogether. He knew he was being taken advantage of, and since he could do nothing about it, he simply walked away from a bad situation.

Unlike other Delta bluesmen, Arthur Crudup never really made a name for himself as a performer—that is, until recently, when he was "rediscovered" and his second career began. He worked almost purely as a recording artist. It all goes back to 1940, when he had been traveling around the country singing in a gospel quartet but somehow got stranded in

Chicago. With no money in his pocket, and no job in sight, he did what black musicians have been doing in this country for the past two centuries: He took to the streets with his guitar.

What happened then? Here's how Arthur Crudup remembers it: "Lester Melrose and a man named Dr. Clayton happened to come by where I was and saw me singing on the street with my guitar. They stopped and listened, and Melrose said he wanted me to sing at a party at Tampa Red's."

Melrose was, of course, the head of RCA Victor's Race recording operations on its cheaper subsidiary Bluebird label. He had, as noted earlier, gathered quite an array of talent in Chicago, a stable of steady blues singers and musicians who backed one another up on recording dates and played dates in the meantime at the gin mills on the near South Side. Tampa Red was one of these regulars; so, also, were Memphis Slim, Big Bill Broonzy, and Robert Brown (Washboard Sam).

They were all there at that party to which Lester Melrose took Arthur Crudup. "Yeah, I'd heard some of their things, too—some of Tampa Red's and Big Bill's and some others. But at the time, see, I didn't know but one or two blues myself. I had made up a song that I started out calling "Coal Black Mare" and then took to calling it "Black Pony Blues." I was so embarrassed I could hardly play, but finally I got it out, you know, and they were all very friendly to me—Tampa Red, he was a good old guy. And Melrose, he asked me if I had ever heard my own voice. 'Not more than just when I'm singing,' I told him. So he says, 'Come on up to the studio and cut some wax, and we'll see how you sound.' And that was how I started recording.

"I'll tell you the truth, it was all pretty new to me then. Why, I only learned to play the guitar six months before I started recording. And the one I had had a broken neck that I'd repaired with haywire. But I kind of liked the sound, and to this day I play with a capo on my guitar. Who taught me to play? Nobody taught me. I learned myself. I started out with four strings, added a fifth, and then a sixth when I could handle it."

What happened after that first recording session, on which he cut his "Black Pony Blues" and another, "Death Valley Blues"? "Well, I went back to Mississippi, around Forest, where I'm from, and I started traveling back and forth to make those records for Lester Melrose in Chicago. He'd send me some money, and I'd hop a train and come up and record, and then get a little more money."

But all during this period he continued to work as a farmer. He took his family and moved to Belzoni, Mississippi, and there he worked as a sharecropper. "Had to earn a living some way. I wasn't making money off those records to amount to nothing, and all those kids of mine were little then, so I just kept on recording every time I was asked and working the farm in between times. All this time I never hardly played in front of anybody, as I can remember. Only place back then was the Indiana Theater in Chicago during the war on some big blues show. It didn't amount to much. My first real performance was in Chicago, though—at the University of Chicago just three years ago. Dick Waterman got me that date, and I been at it ever since."

It was Waterman who had put me in touch with Arthur Crudup. As his manager, he had been deeply involved with John Carter of AGAC in working out a settlement for Crudup with Wabash Music, the publishing company of the late Lester Melrose. Wabash held copyrights on all the material written and sung by the bluesman during more than a dozen years of recording for Bluebird. But matters were complicated by Melrose's death. Wabash—and all its rights and obligations—had been sold to another, much larger music publishing house, which had found Arthur Crudup's claim dumped in their laps almost immediately. After their lawyers had taken a look, they admitted their liability in the case, but things were at a temporary standstill at the time I talked with John Carter while the formula for the settlement was being worked out. In any case, Arthur Crudup stands to collect a great deal of money in the near future. As royalties still accrue (Rod Stewart recently recorded "That's Alright, Mama" and made it a hit once again), his fortunes as a composer continue to grow on paper. Before the money stops, he may well get a sum in six figures for those songs he wrote between 1940 and 1955. "Arthur's is that rare case," says Dick Waterman, "where the little guy wins." Let's hope so.

Arthur Crudup has waited for the money that is coming to him for so long, however, that he tends to be a little skeptical about it all. "It's just like an old song I heard," he says, " 'You can't miss what you can't measure.' That's the same with me, see, I won't miss what I never had. I never owned $10,000 in my life at one time. I just want a little, enough to keep me till I die."

I had driven from Washington to see him, across the Chesapeake Bay Bridge, and down the Eastern Shore to the very tip of the Delmarva Peninsula. His home is in Virginia, just inland from the beach resorts where middle-class Baltimore and Washington go to splash the summer away. Take a look around and you would never guess that, though. Here, all is rural and remote and farther south than you would ever suppose from its location on the map. I had found the house with no trouble and discovered Arthur Crudup out in the yard to greet me just as soon as I emerged from my car. He steered me over to a weather-beaten building of no great dimensions removed some distance from the house. This, he explained as we settled down to talk, is where he and his boys play the country dances for the people around here.

"Your boys?" I asked. "You mean your band?"

"No, I mean my sons. They got their own band, but they let me sing with them when they're here around home. We do some pretty good stuff together. They do the playing and I do the singing." The name of the group is the Malibus. They were traveling north that day to play a job in Long Island. A couple of them had already left, but a couple more were still here, and I'd have a chance to meet them in a little while, he told me.

Now that he has been at it these three years, playing dates that have been booked for him at colleges and universities, he has decided he likes performing before audiences pretty well. He wishes he had taken it up long ago and had tried touring as his boys are doing today. "Yeah, I do," he said with a nod. "But a person just concentrates on what he's making a living out of. That's how it was with me back then. The more you do of that, the more it seems there is to do. For me, it was just farming and traveling up to Chicago to record. Now I go all over and play and sing. Why, I went to England even, just got through. They seemed to think a whole lot of me there, and I did of them, too."

I told him I could certainly understand why he had quit, but I wondered just how it had come about.

"Well, the reason I quit playing is that gradually I realized I was making everybody rich, and here I was still poor. You know, Elvis made some number of mine. He gave me credit on his records right from the start and paid money and all, but I never saw any of it."

I nodded and said I had heard that.

"Well, I guess it was that that really did it to me. I started hearing that song of mine, 'That's Alright, Mama,' just all over in Mississippi. It was a big hit, so I wrote to Melrose, who was my manager then, and asked him if I shouldn't be getting some money out of that, and he wrote me back and said he'd look into it." Arthur Crudup repeated the last four words, shaking his head in disgust. "But I never got anything extra for that, so I knew something was funny there. Five hundred dollars was the most I ever got from him, and that was mostly recording fee. No difference between hits and nonhits for me, just get the same old $200 or $110 or $90."

I asked him if he had ever gone to Melrose's office and asked to see the books.

"No, I never even been in Melrose's office once. He'd just write me and send the fare for me to come to Chicago and say to meet him at Tampa Red's, which I'd do, and then we'd go to the studio. Afterward, when the session was all done, I'd go and be paid off at the union hall. When I started, see, you had to belong to the union before you could record. The whole thing would take about five or six days, and I'd stay with a half-sister I had there or maybe with Tampa. He used to live around Thirty-fifth and State then. I think Tampa was in the same boat with Melrose I was. I never heard of him having no hell of a lot of money. He usually worked at a club at Thirty-ninth and State and had a lot of people around him. I learned to know a lot of them up at his place—Big Bill, Lonnie Johnson, Big Maceo, St. Louis Jimmy, and Memphis Minnie. Just all of them."

Just about that time Arthur Crudup's sons, George and James, came over from the house to say goodbye to their father. Their car was loaded up and ready to go, and they were ready to head for their date in Long Island. After introducing them to me, he walked over to the car with them, held a brief conversation that ended in laughter between them. He waved them off. They jumped in the car and were on their way.

He came back smiling. "They're good boys," he said. "James, he's the drummer, he learned to play on washboard or just anything he could beat on. And George, the other boy, he plays bass, only I started him on guitar and taught him chords and stuff. Jonas, the guitar, and Charles, the other brother who plays organ, they went on ahead. They sings anybody's songs, but they got their own material."

"Kind of a rock band?" I asked, and he nodded. *Down Beat* had called him the "daddy of rock"; I wanted to know how that set with him.

"Oh, well. Pretty good. You know." He ended with a shrug that told me it didn't matter to him much one way or the other. "I like what they do with my material. Elvis did a nice job on my songs, kind of a hillbilly version."

I asked if he felt bitter toward Elvis Presley and B. B. King and the rest who had made money from his songs.

"No, it's like down there in Mississippi when I was on a little farm of my own, that's when I wasn't sharecropping. They beat me out of everything I ever owned, so we just picked up and moved to Florida and then up here. I wasn't bitter over that. I'm not bitter over this. Who am I gonna get mad with? At Melrose? He's dead, so I can't hurt him. At Presley? I don't even know him. I can't get mad with a man I don't know. There's nobody around to fight, and there's no sense in getting mad if you can't fight nobody."

We talked a little longer, but nothing he said afterward stuck with me quite like that. I thanked him for the time he had given me and headed back to Washington.

AND THAT WAS IT. That was the end of my trip. Quite literally so, for when I returned from that afternoon with Arthur Crudup I started writing this book. It had begun as a kind of tour, one that would take me—and you—down to the back country of the blues, where there were still a few of the old survivors of that time when the music was first given style and shape, and into some of the back-alley bars and boulevard concert halls where the blues is still being played today. Yet it took me to a few places I had never expected to go—back into my own past, for one, because I found that the more I wrote about this music I had been hearing since I was a kid, the more personally I became involved with it. As a result, what you have read is more subjective than I ever expected it would be when I began writing.

And I have also been taken deeper into the American past than I expected to go. For the story of the blues is so much the record of black and white in America that it has been instructive—though not necessarily pleasant—to go back over that record as I have been doing here. There is a jackleg curriculum called American Studies offered at most of our colleges and universities today. It is about equal parts literature and history, and purports to communicate something to students about the formation of the American character. That sounds skeptical, I know, but my doubts are not about substance but about sources. There is such a thing as the American character, all right, although it is still in rapid metamorphosis, being shaped daily and subtly by influences that are never mentioned in the textbooks. American music is one of them. If you want to find out what America is and would like to be, the good and the bad of it, listen to its music. Listen to the blues.

INDEX

THE LEGAL LIMIT

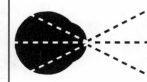

This Large Print Book carries the
Seal of Approval of N.A.V.H.

THE LEGAL LIMIT

MARTIN CLARK

THORNDIKE PRESS
A part of Gale, Cengage Learning

Detroit • New York • San Francisco • New Haven, Conn • Waterville, Maine • London

GALE
CENGAGE Learning™

LIBRARY OF CONGRESS CATALOGING-IN-PUBLICATION DATA

Clark, Martin, 1959–
    The legal limit / by Martin Clark.
        p. cm. — (Thorndike Press large print reviewers' choice)
    ISBN-13: 978-1-4104-1206-5 (hardcover : alk. paper)
    ISBN-10: 1-4104-1206-7 (hardcover : alk. paper)
    1. Public prosecutors—Fiction. 2. Brothers—Fiction.
    3. Murder—Fiction. 4. Patrick County (Va.)—Fiction. 5. Large
    type books. I. Title.
    PS3553.L2865L44 2009
    813'.54—dc22   2008038147

Published in 2009 by arrangement with Alfred A. Knopf, Inc.

Printed in the United States of America
1 2 3 4 5 6 7 12 11 10 09 08

FOR MY WIFE, DEANA

So we look for a message and we search in our souls
As we sift through the wreckage like we're shoveling coal.
— ROBERT EARL KEEN, "Train Trek"

In any prosecution for a violation of driving under the influence, the amount of alcohol in the blood of the accused at the time of the alleged offense as indicated by a chemical analysis of a sample of the accused's blood or breath shall give rise to the following rebuttable presumption: If there was at the time of the alleged offense .08 grams or more per 210 liters of the accused's breath, it shall be presumed that the accused was under the influence of alcohol intoxicants at the time of the alleged offense.
— Section 18.2-269 of the 1950 Code of Virginia, as amended

PART ONE

I became a judge when I was thirty-two years old, and my first novel, *The Many Aspects of Mobile Home Living,* was published when I was forty. Given my interest in both law and writing, people have frequently encouraged me to put together a nonfiction, insider's book about the legal system, a temptation I've always avoided for two main reasons. Most notably, I very much value the business of the courts and the importance of what we do as judges, and I believe that parting our velvet curtains to offer the world a wholesale view of the cogs, cranks, belts, braces, booms and pulleys deep behind the stage is not necessarily a wise idea. Courts need a certain measure of dignity — and, yes, mystique — to function at their best. The Great and Powerful Oz was never the same after the dog embarrassed him, and without his mask the Lone Ranger would be a run-of-the-mill do-gooder, just another guy on a fancy horse.

Moreover, and at the risk of eroding that dignity and mystique, it's fair to say that day-to-day jurisprudence is a numbing, flat, repetitive affair, leavened with occasional spells of predictable farce and eye-rolling nonsense. On probation-violation afternoons, for instance, the officers and clerks usually bet on which criminal with a dirty drug screen will be the first to claim — his right hand raised extra high for emphasis — he's the victim of "some dude" slipping cocaine into his coffee. "Dudes are bad about giving their dope away as a prank," I always respond with a straight face, while a five-dollar bill discreetly switches owners in the periphery. As an author, I've never seen where it would be worth the effort to chronicle such as this for three hundred pages.

My thoughts on not mixing law and literature lasted until 2003, when I changed my mind and decided to write about one of my cases and turn it into this book. At quitting time on a drab Thursday in November of that year, a deputy at the Patrick County jail phoned and informed me there was someone who hoped to speak with me, someone I knew. This call led to three lengthy meetings during which I became privy to a remarkable history, a narrative that was far more compelling than anything I could ever dream up, and it gradually occurred to me there might be a novel in the story I'd been told. I was convinced I'd gotten the truth in these meetings, but I nevertheless spent the next few weeks quietly nosing around and checking the particulars. I talked with a couple of the people involved, read old files, studied transcripts, and took a trip to state police headquarters. Everything jibed.

The Legal Limit, then, is not a literal diary of what I do as a circuit court judge — it's not quite the undertaking that has been suggested to me — but it is at its core a reasonably accurate account of lives and happenings I discovered only because of my job and wouldn't have come across otherwise. In terms of perspective and the angles I see from where I sit, this story should also give folks a taste of how it feels to make hard decisions, stick them in a lonely black robe and situate them so they can understand how the correct answer, the right ruling, sometimes brings along its own tricks and complications.

That having been said, this book is done as fiction. I cut several scenes from whole cloth, portions of dialogue are an educated guess as to the actual conversations and names are tweaked or rearranged in places, although my friends here in Stuart, Virginia, won't have any problem deciphering who's who. A few parts are inverted, sort of written backward. Much of the small detail, however, is reproduced exactly, with only a minimum of writer's gloss. I was amazed by what people could recall two decades removed from events: a missing section of plaster in a room, a sound, a scent, an odd phrase, even the luckless kamikaze bird that introduces the first chapter. Simply put, there are plenty of facts in these pages, but I've definitely retooled them to serve the story I wanted to tell.

Finally, I suspect many people will find my choices in this matter troubling and disagree with how I determined to finish things, since my attempt at an act of conscience arguably doesn't square with the familiar, black-and-white dictates of the law. Perhaps I made a mistake. Still, my predecessor on the bench, Frank

Richardson, once advised me that a smart judge always has a little juju up his sleeve, even if the rules don't contemplate it and the parties don't see it coming. "Every now and then you're entitled to play the wild card" was how he explained it. "Justice can occasionally be a fickle, blind bitch, and somebody has to keep her honest."

PART TWO

CHAPTER ONE

The shooting came in October 1984, abrupt and rash, a quicksilver *bang.*

The day it happened, Mason Hunt had spent most of his morning settled into the afghan-covered recliner at his mother's house, watching a nondescript black and brown and white thrush fly against the big den window again and again as it tried to punch through the glass, the bird evidently sickly or a bona fide lunatic, remaining behind while its kin abandoned Virginia and migrated farther south. Despite the suicidal thumps and flutters that gained it nothing and left it pitifully outside its hope, the misguided bird never learned a lesson or gave up on its headlong, full-steam shortcut to sanctuary, never stopped, kept at the foolishness for hours. Mason was home from his final year of law school, visiting his mother and enjoying her flapjacks and rich casseroles for a weekend, waiting for his older brother, Gates, to arrive so they could saw up a maple

17

tree that had blown over in the front yard and stack it into winter firewood. By the time Gates pulled in the gravel drive at eleven thirty, Mason had finished two cups of coffee, napped, read three issues of the *Stuart Enterprise* and carted the kerosene heater from the basement to its spot near the couch, even though there was no fuel in it and the weather wouldn't turn cold for another month or so. Soon after he heard Gates cut his Corvette's ignition, Mason noticed that the bird had quit its sallies and was stuck in a holly bush next to the window, one wing draped across a run of green, prickly leaves, its beak gapped, its head listing and its feet dangling, unable to take hold of anything.

Gates opened the mudroom door but didn't move too far past the threshold, let out his neck like a terrapin leaving its armor to get a better view of Mason and his mother. "Hello, Mama," he said in a voice a few notches above normal.

"Gates," she said, not looking up from her kitchen work. She was peeling green baking apples, circling off the skin in deft turns and cuts that went from stem to bottom without a hitch.

"What're you cooking?" he asked, leaning against the doorjamb.

"A pie." The two words were absolutely neutral, ciphers. "The phone not workin' where you were at last night?"

18

"I'm sorry; I know I promised I'd call when I can't make it home. You forgive me?"

"It's common courtesy, Gates — if you're living under my roof you could at least let me know where you are. Twenty-seven years old, and it's the only thing I ask from you."

"It won't happen again."

"Perhaps you should ground him or take away TV privileges," Mason joked, trying to lighten the mood.

"There you go," Gates said. "That'll keep me on the straight and narrow."

"You ready to get started?" Mason asked, bending over to retie his shoes.

"Sure. Yep. Ready, ready, ready. Ready as can be." Gates was wearing a Washington Redskins jersey with the name "Hunt" stenciled across the back in gold block letters. Five inches over six feet tall, he didn't fit well into the doorframe. "Mason, man, I need you to run an errand with me before we take care of the tree, and then we're right back here lickety-split." He glanced at their mother. She still didn't look in his direction.

"An errand?" Mason repeated.

"You boys be careful with the saw," Sadie Grace Hunt said from the kitchen. "Chain saws are dangerous, Gates." She finally made eye contact with him.

"Yes, ma'am," Gates answered. "You don't need to worry about us."

"And if you're goin' somewhere with Ma-

19

son" — she held the paring knife in front of her, pointing it at the ceiling — "you let him drive, you hear?"

"If it'll make you happy, then I'd be delighted to have my little brother chauffeur me around." He winked at Mason, promised his mom he'd be back for a piece of warm pie and headed out the door.

Mason was a large man as well, two inches shorter than his brother and not as thick through the shoulders and trunk, but substantial enough that the Corvette's passenger seat was uncomfortable. The shape hit him all wrong, and he had trouble with his knees. He didn't attempt the safety belt. "Damn, Gates, what — you just start distilling the hooch in your car, cut out the middleman? It smells like a speakeasy in here." There was a plastic Star Wars cup — a faded fast-food giveaway — resting on the console; the contents were yellowish green, SunDrop and vodka without any ice to dilute the potency.

"I'll roll the windows down and drive real fast." Gates nudged a cassette with his index finger and a mechanism eased it from sight, inhaling it into the dash. He had recorded a Huey Lewis and the News album onto the tape, and "I Want a New Drug" came on mid-refrain. "While we're on the subject, can I offer you a little nip?" he asked. "I've got vodka and a bottle of Wild Turkey Denny gave me for my birthday."

"I'll pass," Mason said. "Thanks just the same. It's a bit early, isn't it?" The question didn't have any bite in it, wasn't a rebuke. He grinned at his brother.

"I'm grandfathered in for the entire day, a carryover from last night. So long as you don't stop, it's just a continuation, not the same as drinking for breakfast or somethin' pathetic and alcoholic." Remarkably, besides the odor and a few aggravated blood vessels in his eyes, Gates seemed fairly level. An occasional syllable was spit-heavy, but that was about it. "Our pal Robbie Hanes is leavin' for the Navy, so we had a throwdown yesterday for him at the Woolwine Ruritan building. That's why I'm behind schedule — the party took us hostage and wouldn't let us go."

"I'd have never pegged Robbie for duty on the high seas."

Gates reached under his seat and located a Crown Royal bag, a deep-purple felt sack with bold yellow stitching and matching yellow drawstrings. He set the bag in his lap and took out a vial of cocaine and an elaborate spoon, the spoon either silver or pewter, in the shape of a mermaid, her hair serving as a grip, her toes clutching a tiny scoop. "I need to boost my shit, brother. I'm assuming you're still not interested?"

"If I tried it, I'd probably like it way too much. In no time at all, I'd be pissing myself

21

and scavenging butts from ashtrays at the bus terminal. Quoting Timmy Leary at the homeless shelter. Thanks just the same." Mason turned down the music. "Perhaps we'd be wise to get out of Mom's sight before you start doing that."

"Only take a sec." Gates dipped the spoon into the powder, raised it to his nose and snorted — hard — three times.

"By the way, why does everyone I know carry his dope in a Crown Royal bag? Or the cassette cover for an Allman Brothers tape? Can you explain that to me? I think the Supreme Court's decided the cops have probable cause to search whenever they spot either of those in a car, regardless of the circumstances."

"You have a better suggestion?" Gates wiped his nose, then sipped his drink. "The bag's a pretty damn fine creation."

"True. Can't argue with you there."

"You like the album?" Gates asked. "Huey Lewis and the News?"

"Yeah. It's okay, though it's a shame they don't get any more airtime than they do. And I always feel like Huey might be sort of pulling our leg musically."

"Too much schoolin', I'm sorry to say, has made you into a boring smart-ass." Gates fired the engine and they crept down the gravel drive, the car chugging and straining in first gear, the tachometer barely registering because Gates didn't want to risk nicking the paint with kicked-up rocks.

"Where're we going?" Mason asked. "What kind of mischief are you dragging me into?"

"Nothing too tough, I promise. Robbie's leavin' behind a nice dresser, and he said I could have it. You and me are going to meet Claude and him in Woolwine, load the dresser onto Claude's pickup and haul it to Denise's trailer."

"How are you two doing? You and Denise, I mean?"

"Everything's cool. She got a promotion at work — off the floor and into the office — and she finally finished her associate's degree. Looks like a million bucks, still crazy about me." He made a goofy face after the last declaration. "We're thinkin' about maybe considering buying a house together. The old Mabe home is for sale. I love that place — it's on five acres, has a nice pond and a humongous porch for cookouts and warm-weather drinkin'. Man, you could just put the speakers in the windows, grill a steak, invite friends by. Only problem is that I need my luck to improve so I can pull my part, you know? I'm hopin' this insurance job with State Farm comes through, so I can quit living fuckin' hand to mouth."

"Good for you. I think the world of her."

"Me too."

Mason wanted to maneuver more space for

his knees and shins, but the seat was at its limit, had no play in it. "It'll take us two hours to drive to Woolwine, load the dresser, then drive to Denise's and unload, don't you figure?" He wriggled into a new position.

"Close to it. You can call Mom from Robbie's and give her an update." Gates sniffed and touched his nostrils with the back of his hand. "So long as we have the tree done by dark, we should be okay."

"We have all morning tomorrow if we need it," Mason said, flashing his brother a wry smile.

It took them several minutes to cover the half mile of dirt and stone that led to the blacktop, but Gates slammed the accelerator the moment the wheels touched the asphalt, causing the car's tires to spin and the rear end to break traction.

They met their friends and wrapped the piece of furniture in an old quilt and laid it in the bed of Claude's pickup. Before they started to Denise's, Robbie warmed barbecued pig and baked beans, left over from his party. He placed the food on the tailgate of the truck, and they all dug it straight out of tinfoil tubs with plastic forks and wiped their hands and faces on paper towels. Gates poured himself another mixed drink, and the other three men popped cold Miller beers. The truck's doors were open, the radio playing, the hardwood trees in southside Virginia turning crimson, yellow and fire-orange, an occasional dry, brownish leaf sifting through the air on its way to the ground.

Denise's mobile home was in Five Forks on a small parcel of land she was buying from her uncle. She was a hard worker and a smart, solid woman with restraint and sensible tastes uncommon for her circumstances, and she kept her yard and dwelling neat. Mums and azaleas and other flowers and bushes that Mason couldn't identify were planted here and there, the grass was still green and nicely trimmed, and the property was free of birdbaths, kitschy cement animals, busted lawn chairs, junked Monte Carlos and matted cur dogs chained to a rusted post. Gates had helped her build and stain a covered deck; a single dragonfly wind chime hung from the four-by-four that supported the tacked-on roof, a friendly jack-o'-lantern welcomed visitors from the top step. Denise's white Celica was parked in the drive, a Mazda RX-7 behind it, and the moment Gates saw the Mazda he became angry.

"Damn," he snapped.

"What?" Mason peered across the interior at his brother. "What's wrong?"

"That's Wayne Thompson's car."

As Mason understood it, there had been a period when Gates and Denise, romantic since high school, had separated for a number of months. After Gates walked away from

Virginia Tech, and after he failed to catch on with the Redskins, and after he declined a plum job at Masonite — human resources, a gig with dress shoes and a coffee mug, for heaven's sakes — and after he barely squirmed out of a DWI over in North Carolina, and after Denise allowed as to how — six years removed from his graduation — he needed to find work, quit freeloading at his mother's house and stop lollygagging around in the Corvette for hours on end, and after she finally gave him a deadline he spitefully ignored, after all this considerable forbearance, she sent him packing and began dating Wayne Thompson. Gates quickly enrolled in real estate school and signed a lease at the Dorn Williams apartment complex, begrudged measures that lasted just long enough to tamp down Denise's ire but were sufficient to spark their reconciliation. At least he'd *tried,* she told friends who poormouthed her boyfriend and suggested she was making a mistake by offering him yet another chance.

There was also small-town scuttlebutt that Denise had slipped a time or two or three or five since reconciling with Gates, talk that she'd been spotted at the Tanglewood Beach Music Festival with Wayne or gotten hooted with her girlfriends and mentioned him favorably or been seen picking up her car — early in the morning — from the elementary school parking lot not far from his house. And who could blame her, given what Gates had to offer and his headstrong, good-for-nothing nature?

Wayne was a paradoxical fellow, a handsome boy who'd moved from Georgia to Stuart with his parents in the middle of his ninth-grade year and finished Patrick County High School with Gates's class. Quiet but tightly wound, Wayne had been in a vicious, bloody fistfight in the school hallway and tended to turn scarlet around his jawline when a teacher called on him with a math problem he was unable to solve or a treaty date he couldn't remember. Yet he was polite to the point of shyness, a whiz with an arc welder, a volunteer at the old-folks home, the treasurer of the Spanish Club. He'd begun a minimum-wage, part-time job with the highway department while he was still in school, and nine years after earning his diploma, he was employed at the same place, now an assistant foreman with a few night classes at Patrick Henry Community College to his credit, drawing a steady state check, cruising the roads in a bright orange VDOT truck, keeping tabs on bridge repairs, potholes and vandalized traffic signs.

He'd fathered a child out of wedlock but never hemmed and hawed about paternity. He let the lad take the name Wayne Jr., paid for the baby's delivery at the hospital and made arrangements to have child support deducted from his check and forwarded to the mother in Roanoke. By all accounts he generally attempted to do right by his son, keeping him every other weekend and treating him to dirt-track races, Santa photos at the Martinsville Kmart, a Myrtle Beach vacation and trips to the Patrick County fair, even though the boy was too young to ride most of the attractions or win prizes on his own. It was widely known that Wayne had once sucker punched Harley Stevens at the Old Dominion roadhouse and then kicked him in the ribs when he was flat on the floor, but if anyone had it coming, it was Harley, a lout and a loudmouth, so the law was never notified and nothing more came of it.

The brothers were still in the Corvette, the engine idling, Huey and the News playing, when Wayne appeared on the deck. He was wearing a snug leather jacket scarred by asymmetrical silver zippers and black jeans rolled into chunky cuffs. Gates erupted from the car without turning it off. "What the hell do you think you're doin'?" he demanded, striding for the trailer, Mason instinctively falling in beside him. Claude saw the Hunts sail out in a hurry, and he jogged a few steps from his pickup to join them.

"It's a free country, Gates." Wayne was walking guardedly toward his RX-7, careful not to act cowed or to blink too much.

Denise stepped onto the deck and told Gates to calm down. She was a shapely, graceful woman with a striking face, and she pushed her hair back with both hands after she spoke.

Wayne made it to his car, where he opened the door but didn't get in. Gates and Mason halted at the bottom of the wooden deck steps. Their friend Claude, a beanpole of a man with a sketchy mustache, was beside them. "How many times do I have to tell you to stay away from Denise?" Gates shouted. "Huh? Am I just goin' to have to beat your ass to a pulp so you'll understand?"

"This is Denise's property, not yours, Gates. You ain't got any control over how she uses it or who she sees."

Denise didn't hesitate. "Wayne, I've asked you before not to come around. You're a good guy, but right now you're just making things bad for all of us."

Wayne put his hands on his hips and squared off toward Gates. "I'd be embarrassed if I was you, Gates. Damn right I would. A grown man and you don't even have a pot to piss in. Livin' off your mama and your girlfriend."

Mason had a fast grip on his brother's biceps, but surprisingly, Gates didn't attempt to pull free or rush Wayne or ape through a frenetic, piss-and-vinegar, hold-me-back charade in an attempt to impress Denise.

Instead, he half-smiled and chuckled, stared at the closest step and kicked the ground next to a bright yellow mum. "Yeah, Wayne, you're the man," he said in a mocking tone, pausing to look up. "King of the road, ridin' around and shoveling dead possums and dogs off the highway. We all want to be you."

"Nice jacket," Mason chimed in gratuitously, making certain there was no doubt where his allegiance lay. "Part of the *Knight Rider* collection?" He released Gates's arm.

"Opossum Boy," Claude added.

Wayne seemed relieved that this was the extent of the confrontation and that the brothers were keeping their distance, content to insult him from across the yard. "You all can kiss my ass," he said as he was sliding into his car, but the words didn't have much vigor in them. He drove to the main road, stuck his middle finger out the window in their direction, turned left and disappeared on the other side of a severe curve.

Agitated again, Gates stared up at Denise, who was bent over the porch railing, a small crook in her back, her arms stiff and supporting her weight. "What the fuck was he doin' here?" Gates asked, his voice sharp. "In your house?"

"He came by and said he needed to talk to me, claimed it was important and wouldn't wait."

"And you said, 'Sure, come on in and I'll

chill the champagne and put on something low-cut'?"

The Corvette was still running, and Claude scurried toward it, eager to be occupied. He took a seat on the driver's side and switched off the engine, staying put after the car went quiet.

"It's not like that at all, Gates," Denise protested. "I haven't even seen him in months, and he shows up on my porch with no warning, hell-bent and beggin' me for five minutes. I told him you were on the way, but he was bound and determined to speak his piece, so I let him. I can't help it if he shows up out of the blue, now can I? I was as surprised as you."

"So why can't he do his important talkin' on the porch?" Gates asked.

"Listen, Gates," she said, her voice gaining an edge, "if you want to pick a fight about this, fine. But I'm not going to stand here and listen to you cuss me and accuse me of crap I didn't do, okay?" She straightened up from the railing. "He caught me by surprise, and when he asked if he could come in I said yes. Anyone would. I'm sorry if that's a sin. I told him you and me were together, and you and Mason were due any second."

"You heard her, Gates," Mason said, touching his brother's shoulder. "You heard her tell him how things are."

"What'd he say?" Gates demanded. "Why'd

31

he drive out here in such a lather? Why today? All of a sudden?"

"Just stuff, Gates. It's not worth repeatin'." She was looking directly at him. Her hands had shifted to her hips, but her tone was more plaintive now, conciliatory.

"You want me to move the truck closer?" Claude asked from the Corvette. "I think I will."

Gates ignored him. "He was walking on the very deck I built, talkin' shit about me and hittin' on you, right? That pretty well sums it up, doesn't it?"

"Yes, Gates, but like I said, I told him to forget it. You could've knocked me over with a feather when I opened the door and he was standin' there. I don't know what in the world made him come out here all torn up after . . . Well, you know, I haven't said more than hello to him since forever, and the last time we discussed the situation I was crystal clear about me and you, and him not fittin' into the picture."

"Pretty exceptional circumstances," Mason said. "And she handled them with class, as well as could be expected." He focused on Gates, trying to make him see reason.

"He's a piece of shit," Gates said, but he wasn't looking at anyone, instead was staring at the curve where the RX-7 had driven out of sight. "I could snap him in two if I wanted," he muttered, still locked onto the road.

"Just forget it, Gates," Mason encouraged him.

"I think he's gone for good," Denise said. "Come on, Gates, let's not ruin the day."

"If he ever says another word to you or even so much as drives by here, I want you to tell me." Gates twisted his head so he could glare at his girlfriend above him. Two creases met and formed a "V" between his eyebrows. His mouth was a peeved slit. "We understand each other?"

"Yes, Gates," she said.

"I'm heart-attack serious," he warned her.

"*Okay,* Gates. So now can we just put it behind us, please?"

"Fine advice," Mason told him. "Let's see about unloading the dresser."

"Yeah . . . well . . . well, first let's see about a stout drink to celebrate how ol' Wayne tucked tail and ran," Gates suggested, his tone brightening.

"Count me in," Claude said.

"The bottle's under the seat, Claude." Gates started up the steps. "You got any mixer, baby?"

"Probably," Denise answered.

"You gonna have one with us?" He walked to where she was and put his arm around her. "It's the weekend and a pretty day and we have a special guest appearance by Mason, the boy wonder."

"I might," she said.

"How about you, Mason?" Gates asked. "You gotta bend an elbow with me, no more than we see each other."

"Sure, a beer would be great."

Denise spoke almost before he finished the sentence. "I'm fresh out, Mason. I knew you were going to say that's what you wanted. I've only got a few wine coolers and a dab of vodka Gates left in my car. I'll be glad to drive to the store — what kind do you like?"

"Don't worry about it. There's no need to go to any trouble. I'm happy with whatever's here."

"I need to get some cigarettes anyway," she said. "It's not a problem."

"I'll drink a wine cooler or some vodka. No big deal. I'm okay."

Despite his protests, Mason's simple beer request was soon made the mainspring for a slice of the improvised, freewheeling, low-wattage hedonism that Gates could scare up from the barest of surroundings, and just like that the men were checking their wallets and Denise was contributing a ten from her purse, and since Claude and Mason were going to buy beer they might as well grab burgers, buns and charcoal and another bottle of vodka, and while they were taking care of business in town Gates and Denise would pick out some excellent tunes and roll a joint from the reserve she kept hidden in a tampon box, and she would call her friend Shannon to see if she wanted to come to a cookout, and the dresser stayed put, draped in patchwork while the party took root around it.

The quarrel with Wayne Thompson was forgotten by the time Shannon arrived at three o'clock with her cousin Suzi from Florida. The women brought chips and snacks, but it was left to Claude to cook the hamburgers, and it was growing dark before they ate supper, everyone except Mason buzzed off the pot and beer and vodka and peach wine coolers, and even Mason drank four Budweisers, more than normal for him. Goosed by the alcohol, he was probably too long with his explanation when he phoned their mom to let her know they were delayed at Denise's trailer, helping her move heavy furniture. "Don't bother waiting up for us," he sheepishly told Sadie Grace.

After the Blue Ridge Mountains completely stamped out the sun, the six of them sat on the porch wrapped in jackets or blankets, watching the orange briquettes fade to ash, talking nonsense, swapping stories and singing and howling along with "Werewolves of London." They moved on to drinking games with a deck of cards — Mason didn't play — and Claude entertained everyone with his impressions: Nixon, Reagan and John Wayne at a bordello. Gates was stoned, relaxed, happy to be with his girlfriend and delighted to have his brother home for a visit. All afternoon, he'd teased Mason about his prissy diction and tight-ass habits, but encouraged by a shotgunned beer, he finally broke down and encircled Mason in a headlock and told him how proud he was, and there was no doubt he was sincere, meant every word. When he turned loose of his brother, none of the others said anything, just sat there with dopey grins and starched eyes, the women and Claude wholly taken in by the men's affection for each other. A dog barked somewhere close by, a car whooshed past, the cassette finished and the portable stereo clicked off.

Shannon broke the silence, sweetly blurting that she loved Herb Alpert and the Tijuana Brass, having heard them as a kid on an eight-track her folks owned, and her Florida cousin suddenly left for the car and returned with a spiral-bound notebook and volunteered to read some of her poems. Mason politely noted he'd be glad to listen but warned her he didn't much care for poetry: it was a fine trick, but what in the world to do with it. "It's like a party favor or a Matchbox car or those stunted trees and shrubs people carve all tiny and precious, kind of literary bonsai." For several mute moments, they all looked at him as if he'd solved Stonehenge or translated the Dead Sea Scrolls, then Gates began giggling and said, "What the fuck are you talkin' about?" and Claude snorted and snickered and the women began cutting up also, and the lot of them went on a laughing jag that didn't end until Denise announced she needed to pee and wobbled off the porch.

Around ten thirty, after the dope, food, alcohol and cigs had been exhausted, Mason mentioned the firewood tree and his four-hour trip back to Richmond the next day. The men finally carried the dresser from the truck into Denise's bedroom, and when they'd situated it in the space she'd cleared, Gates stood back, folded his arms, cocked his head and said with silly, exaggerated satisfaction, "Now *that,* gentlemen, is an excellent effort. Mission accomplished." He debated staying the night with Denise, especially since Shannon and Suzi were making noises about traveling to the Dutch Inn Lounge in Martinsville for dancing and Fuzzy Navels, but he decided to kiss his girlfriend good night, biting her neck and squeezing her rear before letting her alone. He and Mason thanked Claude for the help, shook his hand and left him talking to the women about what to do next.

Like always, Gates — drunk, stoned — insisted he was going to drive, and Mason — sober, clearheaded — agreed he could, thus avoiding a skirmish over the keys and a point-less, profane give-and-take that would end with Gates even more determined to have his way and result in his speeding and ripping through the gears so as to demonstrate that he and his liquored-up self were beholden to nobody: it was *his* fuckin' car and *he* would drive it and the hell with the police and the rest of them who wanted to tell *him* how to live *his* life. It helped that the rural roads to their mom's house wouldn't be busy, Gates was an old hand at drunk driving and there were ordinarily only two county deputies on duty, most likely lenient sorts who'd know both brothers and Sadie Grace and could be counted on to sigh and make the brothers change seats, or at worst, shake a finger at Gates and swear to him this was his last break.

They'd gotten to the crossroads at Five Forks, and Gates had just fished a cigarette butt from the ashtray and clicked fire to the last hint of tobacco when headlights zoomed in behind them, aggressive high beams, fierce illumination that made the knobs, gauges and numbers in the Corvette starkly apparent and lit the side of Gates's face, his neck, his arm as it angled toward the shifter. They quickly identified the car as Wayne Thompson's — "it's friggin' Wayne," Gates said, his eyes rolled up toward the rearview mirror — and for the rest of their days, neither of them would know whether it was happenstance that Wayne had discovered them or whether he'd come looking, still brooding about his ill treatment at Denise's trailer and determined to prove a point where she was concerned.

For reasons that seemed sound to a drunkard behind the wheel of a Corvette, a drunkard who was also frustrated and at war over a woman, Gates punched the gas, shot across the main highway and barreled down a two-lane side road, Wayne and the RX-7 right on his ass. Mason shouted at him to stop it, told him to quit acting like a moron, but Gates didn't pay him any attention, and for two miles of narrow shoulders, blind curves and spotty, patched blacktop, Gates and Wayne performed reckless, pea-brained stunts, the Corvette accelerating to eighty and then screeching as Gates jammed on the brakes, the RX-7 filling the lane beside the brothers so the two cars were racing down a country road door-to-door, neither of them yielding, neither of them giving the slightest thought to precisely what they were accomplishing.

Mason told Gates to slow down or he would jerk the car out of gear and let him worry with what happened after that. "I mean it, Gates. You better fucking quit it. You two can kill yourselves, but you're sure not taking me with you." He put his hand on Gates's wrist and squeezed. "What the hell do you think this is proving?" Wayne had dropped behind them again but was still giving no quarter.

They zipped past a field of cattle and a lopsided barn. "Asshole," Gates muttered, alternating his gaze between the mirror and the road. The word was slightly slurred, stuck to his tongue.

Mason leaned closer to the driver's side and ratcheted up the pressure on Gates's wrist. "I don't know how you're planning to pay for a blown engine or a new transmission."

"I've had enough of this shit," Gates said, his voice without inflection. He began slowing, gradually, and Wayne mimicked him, sixty to fifty to forty, the RX-7 following suit, its lights continuing to burn on high, thirty, twenty, ten, nothing, and the two cars were stopped dead in the road. A lackadaisical moon and a pasture with large round hay rolls at one corner were to their right, a tangle of woods, mostly pines, was on the left.

Gates turned off the car, set the brake and stretched across to the glove compartment. He was quick, efficient, and Mason could see him clearly, the light pouring in from behind them unnatural and loud. Gates removed a gun. Silver, unholstered, a brief barrel, a .38, and before Mason could utter a word — warn his brother not to do something crazy — Gates was standing in the night, the driver's door swung open, tucking the pistol into his pants at the small of his back.

"Easy now," Mason said, stepping from the passenger seat onto the side of the road, but at least the weapon wasn't pointed at Wayne and with any luck it would stay put, right where it was, no more than a dangerous precaution.

Peering over the car's roof, Mason saw Wayne advance on Gates, closing the distance with uneven, choppy steps, a small club, maybe a foot long, at his hip. He halted at the rear of the Corvette and cursed Gates. "You sonofabitch," he said.

Gates didn't respond, simply stood there with his arms folded across his chest.

"Why were you tryin' to run me off the road? Wreck me?" Wayne demanded, obviously torturing the truth, ginning up a reason to fight. "Huh?"

"That's hardly what happened," Mason said, his forearm resting on the Corvette's top. Wayne was far more boisterous than usual; Mason assumed he'd been drinking. "Why don't you," Mason continued, "just forget this and drive away before Gates hurts you?"

"Fuck the both of you."

"Wayne," Gates said, "that pitiful little stick you're holdin' ain't goin' to help you when I come back there and whip your ass. Either leave right now or take a beatin'."

"Oh, don't worry, you ain't gonna have to come to me." He took a step closer, then another, so that he was almost within Gates's reach. "I damn sure ain't afraid of you."

To Mason, who well knew his brother's moods and inclinations, Gates seemed irritated but not irrational, anxious in the manner of someone who had the upper hand and was eager to use it, like a sixteen-year-old poised above a yellow jacket nest with matches and a gallon of gasoline at twilight. "This has been a long time in the makin'," Gates said.

"You need your baby brother to help you?" It had become clear Wayne wasn't planning to leave without taking on Gates, who was considerably taller and a hundred pounds heavier. "Think you might could handle somethin' by yourself for a change?"

"I won't need any help with a pissant like you," Gates told him.

"You're so worthless, Gates. Sorry as a dog. How's it feel to go downhill every single day after high school? Huh?" Wayne still had the club, but it was at his side, flat against his thigh. His voice was shrill, the words rushed. "Big football star, ready to shake up the world and now you're livin' with your mommy, probably stealin' beer money outta her purse." He bobbed his head up and down in agreement with himself. "Never done nothin' 'cept sponge off your momma and Denise, and never will do nothin'."

Gates licked his lips and started to speak, but the thought was stillborn, arrived dead and gurgled. His mouth remained open, and he took a stride away from Wayne, creating more space between them. The retreat was slightly off kilter, unbalanced, and Mason realized that his brother probably hadn't slept the night before and was chock-full of dope and alcohol, but still figured he would maul Wayne. And if he couldn't, Mason would pitch in to make sure Wayne received a good thrashing, fair or not.

"I want you to think about where I've been whenever you're kissin' her. You think about that, Gates."

"You goin' to drop that billy club?" Gates's voice was empty, dull.

"A loser, that's what you are. Me, I'd take welfare before I hung myself around my mother's neck. It's just a matter of time before Denise sees the truth and dumps your ass. Me and her are goin' to be together — you know that, don't you?" The club didn't stir.

Mason — concerned with the blackjack — never saw his brother take the gun from his pants and aim it, but he heard the shot, saw a whitish-orange burst at the end of the muzzle. He looked directly at Gates . . . and the scene stalled right there for an instant, seized up while the report from the pistol took issue with the trees and hills and anything else the least bit solid and doubled back on them. The Corvette's interior light and the high beams from the Mazda overran

43

Gates's face, made it seem as if he'd been plugged into a socket and flooded with current, his skin electrified chalk, the artificial glow clinging to his features, turning them out eerie and pronounced: an etched, viperish mouth; a raised, crescent-shaped scar near his temple; a brace of violent lines cutting through his forehead. His eyes, though, remained dark, sequestered, two black gouges in the midst of all the shocking white.

When Mason glanced away from his brother, Wayne was gone, shot, out of view on the ground, partially hidden by the tail end of the Corvette. Dumbfounded, Mason hurried around to where Wayne lay on the road, his head split and soggy, the awful damage barely skimmed by the bottom of the RX-7's beams. Mason looked at the dead man, then at his brother, so stunned and unhinged that his first words were trite, lacking, the stale scold of a stick-in-the-mud spinster aunt: "Now you've gone and done it, Gates."

Gates appeared horrified, was actually holding the gun at arm's length, examining it as if it had mysteriously arrived and latched on to him. "I . . . I . . . damn . . . I didn't mean to do it." He continued to puzzle over the .38.

I didn't mean to do it: a peculiar, last-ditch mantra that Mason Hunt would hear many times over the years, from many lips, in many courtrooms, though it rarely, if ever, had any application to the genuine truth of the matter. His brother had stopped the car, reached across to the glove compartment, armed himself, left the vehicle with the pistol, considered his choices, removed the gun from his trousers, aimed, fired — hardly an accident or fluke. No, what he really meant was *I wish I hadn't done it*. Peering at his brother's spooky face and regaining a trace of clarity himself, Mason realized that the violence had issued from Gates in a spasm long in the making, like an accumulation of tinder hit with heat. The shooting was not so much malicious as hardwired and visceral, a copperhead's strike, a third cousin to the impulse that causes an owner to kick a pet at the end of a crummy week, or a spouse to scream wild threats and slam down a receiver. Feckless, thwarted, angry and left behind, his world gone to naught because of his own weaknesses, Gates Hunt shot and killed a man for no good reason.

At first, acting on adrenaline and brute instinct, Mason didn't question what he should do, never really considered anything beyond helping his brother. "Let's go, Gates. Get in the car, and let's go before someone drives by."

"Damn, Mason. Shit. I can't believe this." Gates was anguished, on the verge of tears.

"Go! Go! Drive." Mason was scrambling for the door.

"We . . . wait . . . wait . . . we need to hide him or somethin'." His voice quavered. "We can't leave him here."

"No way. We can't move him — the body will be found sooner or later anyway, and we're in this stupid Corvette with no room, and there'll be blood and hair and all kinds of evidence if we use his car. And we damn sure don't want to be seen driving a dead man's ride."

"Then we should take money or his wallet, right, make it seem like a robbery?"

"Only if you want to get sent to the chair — that would make it a capital crime." Mason was standing beside the door, about to duck down. "I'm the lawyer, okay? Come the hell on. There's nothing to tie you to this. Nothing. The more you try to do now, the more you give the cops later on."

"You mean just leave him here?" he asked, slowly gaining composure, his voice stabilizing.

"Exactly. Now come on. Somebody probably heard the shot. And don't spin the tires when you pull off."

Gates glanced at the dead man bleeding out onto the pavement. "Jeez, I can't believe this." He dashed into the car, cranked the engine and babied the gas. "Lord, Mason, what're we goin' to do? Huh? I didn't mean to shoot him . . . It . . . it just freakin' *happened*."

"Listen to me, Gates. There are two people in the world who know the truth. You and me. Don't ever say anything to anyone about this." Mason was staring right at his brother. His voice was stern. "No matter how drunk or stoned or mad or boastful you become, never, ever say a word. Not a peep. Never. Do you understand me?"

"Yeah, yeah. I wouldn't anyway."

"You know you can trust me, right? I'll take this to my grave for you — you know that. It's always been you and me, Mason and Gates, taking care of each other."

"I'm so sorry to drag you into this," Gates said. "It just came over me. I swear I barely remember shooting him." He shifted gears and was clumsy with the clutch, causing the car to lurch.

"Yeah, well, I only have a toe wet, Gates. You're the one who fucked up and shot the guy. I'm not *into* this at all. This is your albatross, not mine."

"What about self-defense? We could say he was threatenin' me with that blackjack. Tell the police —"

"Sure, great idea. Let's see: there are two of us, he's drunk, you're twice his size, he has a pathetic little stick and you have a gun. Brilliant plan."

"It's better than nothin'."

"No, Gates, it's not," Mason said emphatically. "Nothing, in this case, is the least shitty

47

choice where you're concerned. They'll have a body on the side of the road, no witnesses, no forensic evidence, no leads, no confession. We last saw Wayne hours ago, and you laughed him off, didn't jump him when you had the chance and all grades of provocation. So what we're going to do now," he stated, his voice dropping, "is travel to Martinsville, stop by Peter's Lounge, get lost in the bar, flirt with the girls, act normal and pay for our drinks with my credit card when we leave. If Claude and those two women aren't there — and it's a cinch they won't be — you'll call Denise's collect, to check on them. Short term, you need to find a safe place to stop so I can drive us; it would be nice to get there without wrecking. We'll take the back roads to the gravel pile, then haul ass to Martinsville."

"Claude said they were goin' to the Dutch Inn, not —"

Mason interrupted him. "Exactly, Gates. And on the outside chance they've shaken themselves free of the Doritos and Pink Floyd, we damn sure don't want to run into them, now do we? Arrive there *after* they do?" He shook his head. "I'm positive they said Peter's."

"Yeah. Okay. I'm with you." Gates paused to look at his brother. "Should I go over shit with Denise? Or Claude? Rehearse what happened and so forth when Wayne was there?"

"Absolutely not. Just let it unfold and act surprised. We don't need any of them to have suspicions. You and I left, thought about missing a good time with our friends, went to Peter's Lounge, didn't see anyone, called to check on Claude and what'shername, stayed till closing, then drove home. That's the story. It'll be the truth minus the problem with Wayne. You clear?"

"We left Denise's, you mentioned maybe extendin' the night, I'd been partying right smart, so you drove us to Martinsville, then home."

"Correct. Say I started driving at Town and Country Market." They passed a vehicle, a pickup judging from the lights and silhouette, the first one they'd met since the confrontation with Wayne. They'd traveled four or five miles past the shooting scene. "Maybe it'll turn before it gets there," Mason said anxiously. "Buy you some more time and make it harder to establish when he was shot." He peered over his shoulder, following the truck until it vanished. "Find a pull-off and let's switch. And then we're actually going to have the entire conversation, give it a couple runthroughs so we're consistent about who said what, that sort of thing. Oh — wash your hands and face as soon as we arrive at Peter's, and we'll need to check your clothes before

49

we go in, then burn them after we get back to Mom's, just to be safe."

"Okay. Yeah. I will." Gates seemed distracted.

Mason rubbed his eyes with his thumb and forefinger. "I'll take care of the gun. We'll hide it tonight temporarily, and I'll carry it with me tomorrow and destroy it as best I can and dump it somewhere." He sighed. "I hate to do it, but I'm worried you'll screw it up, and for damn sure it doesn't need to surface around here. Neither of us is going to be well served if the police discover the gun, you especially." Even though it entangled him more than he would have preferred, would make him less than passive in Wayne's killing, Mason concluded that disposing of the pistol himself was his only option if he planned to protect his brother.

Gates nodded but didn't say anything.

"Understood?" Mason demanded.

"Fine with me," Gates said, still distant.

"What's wrong?" Mason asked.

"You know, that prick pretty much got what was comin' to him," Gates remarked, trying to sell himself on the notion, no more than minutes removed from the killing, his fear and conscience already elbowed aside by a scoundrel's brazen denial. "Hell, he chased us down, called me out, pulled a bat on me, attacked Denise's character — what'd he expect?" Gates stopped the car.

The sudden lack of remorse and crude rationalizing pissed Mason off. Before changing seats, he put his hand on Gates's arm and glared at him in the dark. "Shut your frigging mouth, Gates. There's no need to make it worse than it already is — quit acting like a punk." He resisted an urge to punch Gates, to draw back and knock him cockeyed and show him what he thought about his craven, unrepentant behavior, maybe bust his nose or loosen a tooth, punish him for the dreadful mess he'd pinned to them both. Mason formed a fist but kept it in his lap, just squinted and breathed deep, and as he was exiting the Corvette, he took another pass at Gates, spoke with one foot on the floorboard, the other in weeds and unruly grass: "At least he had a job, Gates. And it wouldn't hurt you to shape up, would it? Mom's too old for you to be constantly disappointing her. Don't you dare say another word about how anyone's to blame except you."

He didn't mention it, but he considered reporting Gates to the police — he could call and leave an anonymous tip, and it was manslaughter and not murder so they wouldn't jail him and discard the key forever. Besides, Gates was thoroughly guilty, very much deserving of consequences, if not for the shooting, then for living his life as a wastrel and weighing down so many of the people around him.

"I'm sorry, man," Gates mumbled as they hustled past each other at the front of the car. To Mason's ear, he didn't sound contrite, merely tired, drugged and in a bind, willing to mouth whatever it took.

"A damn tar baby," Mason said, more to himself than his brother, as the deed began to tattoo itself into his mind and gut and he imagined the shape of things to come, the pangs and complications that would always companion the poorly lit image of Wayne Thompson lying there with his head bored through.

CHAPTER TWO

In a certain fashion, Stuart, Virginia, was the same in 1984 as it was in 1994 or 2004, and the same as it will be into perpetuity.

The county seat, Stuart is a village of 971 people, and Patrick County itself contains 19,000 or so residents scattered over a chunk of the Blue Ridge Mountains and the spread of flatlands below. It's a part of the world where people wave as they meet on the highway, take baked goods to a neighbor after a funeral service, organize fire-department fund-raisers for families with unexpected afflictions and call firstborn boys by their daddy's name, always with a "Junior" or "Little" affixed — a five-year-old Harold becomes Little Duane until he grows big enough to make his own mark, a young Terry is Mike Junior until Big Mike passes on and Terry respectfully corrects an elder and asks to be called by his given name. There's a weekly newspaper, the *Enterprise,* and a radio station with a signal that doesn't quite reach the county line. Sixth-generation Rorrers, Heaths, Halls, Beasleys and Turners eat ample portions of fair-priced, straightforward meals at the local cafés and talk about the board of supervisors or the proper mixture for a hummingbird feeder or deer hunting or gospel singings or kids gone away to college, the parents hoping their children won't land too far from home when they finish their studies at Radford or Virginia Tech.

The citizens frequently carry tales and trade rumors, but the gossip is never sneaky or sub rosa in Patrick, instead takes place for all to hear and see at the Coffee Break counter or in the grocery store aisles, as people are fond of blunt speech no matter what the subject. Predictably, the area has always had its fair share of crackpots and mugwumps, the usual naysayers and malcontents who bitch about how LBJ ruined the country and dispatch poorly spelled screeds to the newspaper decrying their high property taxes or the influx of know-it-all newcomers. On balance, though, it is — and has been for decades — a splendid, serene, no-frills spot where the population is satisfied to be on the banks of the mainstream, clear of the current, passed by. Great old customs may have vanished in other communities, but Patrick County merchants still seal agreements with a hand-shake, and local gents politely touch the bills of their hats when a lady approaches on the sidewalk.

In this staid place, Wayne Thompson's murder was extraordinary. His corpse was discovered not long after midnight by a carload of teenagers aimlessly riding the country roads, five kids who stopped simply because they thought the RX-7 might have broken down. WHEO didn't broadcast the incident until its Monday-morning news program, and the *Enterprise* ran it as a headline article on Wednesday, but the convenience stores and breakfast tables were abuzz well before that, and the story picked up distortions and colorful speculation during its race through the area early Sunday morning. A deputy's wife told her Bible study class at Stuart Baptist that marijuana was found in Wayne's car and the police were exploring the possibility of a drug deal turned sour. Before he learned of the shooting, Claude had recounted — and much embellished — the dispute at Denise's to his rabbit-hunting buddies, the four of them sipping coffee laced with moonshine at dawn while their beagles yelped and squalled and gleefully chased smells into the bramble. When he contacted them later and swore them to secrecy, it was too late — word was out and Gates Hunt's name was circulating. Wayne had been drinking at the Old Dominion for several hours on Saturday evening, and he'd raised a ruckus with Allen Roberts about a ten-dollar pool bet, so the cops were knocking on Allen's door early enough after sunrise that he appeared in his undershorts, half-asleep.

Denise received the report from her sister's husband's nephew, who volunteered on the rescue squad and had helped deliver the body to the hospital. When she phoned Sadie Grace's house a few minutes past nine on Sunday morning, Gates answered and did a credible job of acting surprised, foggy. "No shit," he said, his voice freighted with disbelief. "Dead?" He stretched the black spiral cord from the wall phone as far as it would go and leaned against the edge of the kitchen table. "Do they know what happened?" he asked. Then: "Well, I can't say I liked him, but you hate to see anyone wind up killed." Next came a series of grunts and huh's. Finally, he barked an indignant, insulted "No!" He glanced at Mason, who had been standing beside him, eavesdropping. "If I'd wanted to do somethin' to his worthless ass, I could've done it at your place, Denise. Mason and me left your trailer and went straight to Martinsville. That's where we were when I called lookin' for Claude." He told her not to worry, to just tell the truth, exactly what had been said. "Hell, I was with Mason the whole time, and we were at Peter's Lounge. I don't have anything to hide, babe. Here — Mason just came in. Talk to him. He's the lawyer in the family."

Mason took the receiver and asked Denise why Gates was so out of sorts. "I only heard the tail end of the conversation," he fibbed.

She told him Wayne had been murdered. "Don't take this the wrong way, Mason, but I was, you know, worried about Gates because of Wayne bein' here yesterday and the two of them arguing. It was the first thing that went through my mind."

"Well, we left your house and drove straight to Martinsville. Gates said he called you, looking for Claude."

"Yeah. He did."

"I'm sorry to hear about Wayne," Mason told her. "Do you know any details?"

"Just that they found him shot over on Russell Creek Road." Her voice cracked and Mason could tell she was crying. "What should I tell the police if they ask me questions?"

"Everyone needs to tell the truth, okay? Don't try to lie or cover for Gates. There's absolutely no reason to — we were either with you guys or at the bar or at home. We never saw Wayne again. Don't worry."

She sucked a cigarette so hard the sound came over the line. "It's awful close to my house, where it happened. I was scared to death."

"Don't be."

She lowered her voice. "What if they ask me about, well, about me and Wayne? Our relationship?"

"Listen." Mason did his best to sound reassuring. "No one blames you for anything. Gates can be a handful." He looked Gates in the eye and kept talking. "Tell the truth, all the way around."

"This is terrible," she said, her voice trailing off. "So sad."

"You hang in there," Mason offered, continuing his stare.

"Mason, I know how much you think of Gates and what you two have been through with your father and the tons of bad stuff. I mean, you're his brother, and I understand that. Who could pick between helpin' the police and helpin' your family, no matter what they did? The problem is . . . is, to be honest, half the time I don't know what to believe with Gates. But you're different, Mason, okay? Everybody says so — and you're promising me, givin' me your word he was with you and had nothing to do with this?"

"You have my word," he lied. He averted his eyes, quit drilling his brother.

Mason wanted to be present when the police first interviewed Gates, so they paced themselves working on their mother's uprooted tree, taking more rest than they needed. Twice, they practiced their stories again. Sadie Grace returned home from church and, with her apron over her Sunday clothes, prepared a heavy meal for the three of them, topped off by the fresh pie. She mentioned Wayne's death, having heard about it at Sunday school. "That's what happens when you start running the roads drinkin' and druggin'," she pointedly noted, directing the comment at Gates.

"Yes, ma'am," he agreed. "Mason and me were talkin' last night. I really am going to fly right and scale down on my bad habits." He laid his fork across the rim of his mother's old china plate. "I'm sorry to be such a chore for you," he said softly.

Their mother nodded, dabbed her mouth with a paper napkin and didn't linger on the topic. "Another piece of pie?" she asked them. She'd heard apologies and promises before and would wait to see if this one was any different, might actually amount to something.

A uniformed deputy and a sheriff's department investigator arrived in the middle of the afternoon. Gates and Mason were sitting in the den, watching an NFL game, and their mother was napping in the recliner, the *Parade* magazine from the Sunday *Roanoke Times* resting on her lap, turned to a story she'd not finished. The afghan — full of orange squares and red diamonds — was draped over her legs. She woke when the cops knocked on the door, and she went to greet them, fiddling with her hair as she walked across the small room, still in her best clothes. Standing at the entrance to her home, holding the screen door partially open, she was polite and respectful to the officers, even inquired about coffee or a cold soda. She didn't presume to ask what had brought them there, but she had her ideas, and her free hand was fidgety and her smile and hospitality were unnaturally fragile.

Danny Owen had worked with the sheriff's office for twenty-three years, the last eight as an investigator. In his fifties, he was trim and easygoing, a pipe smoker whose one vice had discolored his teeth and yellowed the nail of his index finger. He wore glasses with silver metal frames and was dressed in slacks, a knit tie and a blue sport coat. The second officer was stocky and muscular, younger, his hat in his hand, his surname — Williams — announced on a shiny plate above his shirt pocket. Owen carried the conversation; he was gentle with Sadie Grace, and courteous. She and his sister pulled the same shift at United Elastic, and he mentioned the connection, made pleasant small talk, declined the coffee and eventually asked if Gates happened to be there, although the Corvette was parked in the drive and the answer was obvious. "He and Mason are watchin' the ball game," she said. "You sure you don't want to come in?"

"We appreciate it, Mrs. Hunt, but we'll wait here. Maybe you could ask him to step out and join us." Owen gave her a tight, professional smile. He had brown eyes and black hair weeded with strands of gray.

Gates and Mason could hear the exchange, and they went to the door and met their mother. "Go on inside, Mom," Mason urged, bending near to her when he spoke, hoping his size and closeness would bolster her, not letting on that her resignation and weary expression made him heartsick. She left for the kitchen and started with the dirty lunch dishes, and they all could see her through the window after Mason shut the door and the four men were gathered in the drive. She kept to her work and didn't check on them, never so much as peeked to see how her sons were faring.

"I thought you'd be headed back to law school," Owen said to Mason after they'd shaken hands and talked about the game on TV.

"I'll probably leave around seven. Try to entice one more good meal out of my mom."

Owen and the deputy forced a laugh. "Don't blame you," Owen said. He hesitated and took his pipe from the inside pocket of his jacket. "Mason, you mind if we talk to Gates alone?"

"About what?" Mason asked. He narrowed

his eyes.

"A police matter," Owen answered.

"Why can't you talk to me right here and now?" Gates demanded. He was beside his brother, facing the two policemen.

"We'd rather speak to you in private," Owen said. "We could talk in the car." He motioned with his pipe toward their un-marked Ford.

"Mr. Owen, I don't mean to be rude or interfere with your job," Mason butted in, "but I think we're entitled to know why you're here. And if Gates wants me with him, that's his prerogative."

Owen produced a slick plastic bag of cherry-flavored drugstore tobacco. He dipped the pipe into the bag. "Fair enough, Mason. You don't have to call me 'mister,' by the way."

"Thanks," Mason answered.

"Yeah, I definitely want Mason to stick around," Gates said. "Not often a man gets free legal advice."

"So, you gentlemen have any guess why we're here?" Owen inquired. He'd packed the tobacco and was lighting it, eyeing the two Hunts while he puffed and shook a match dead and teased out sweet smoke.

Mason didn't hesitate. "I assume we do. We've heard Wayne Thompson was killed last night."

"How'd you hear such as that, if you don't

62

mind my asking?" The pipe smoke was wafting toward Officer Williams, who moved to avoid it.

"Mom heard it at church, and Denise called Gates this morning," Mason said.

Owen focused on Gates. "I hear you and Wayne had a little row yesterday."

"Yep," Gates replied. "We sure did. He was at Denise's when Mason and me and Claude stopped by, and I let him know I didn't appreciate it."

"I see," Owen said.

"But that was it," Gates added. "He hit the road and that was the last we had to do with him."

"Disagreement over the girl, right?"

"Yeah, basically."

"Okay." Owen glanced at Mason. "Y'all mind if I take a few notes — help an old man remember things better later on?"

"Be my guest," Mason said.

"So what happened after he left your girlfriend's?" Owen now had a pen and small notebook in hand.

"Well," Gates began, "we, uh, stayed at Denise's, had a couple drinks, grilled burgers and whatnot, listened to music, just an ordinary day." Gates hadn't shaved in a while, and his face was covered with black stubble. He sawed the whiskers on his chin with his thumb, shrugged. "Nothing more than that, Danny."

"How 'bout when you left?" the deputy interrupted, and Mason noticed Danny Owen frown before catching himself.

"We drove to Martinsville — Mason and me. Well, you know, Mason drove. I'd been drinking."

"What time you figure you took off from Denise's?" Owen asked.

Gates scratched his head. "Wow. Ten, maybe ten thirty."

"That's fairly accurate," Mason said, looking thoughtfully upward and twisting his lips.

"No stops? Direct to Martinsville?" Owen was writing something on his pad.

"We stopped once, for a couple minutes, at Town and Country —"

"To change drivers," Gates finished his brother's sentence. "Like I said, I'd had a beer or two." He grinned. "Or fifteen."

"What in the world took you to Martinsville at that hour of the night?" Owen pressed.

"Prime party time," Gates answered, and he proceeded to disgorge the altered, rehearsed version of events in which he and Mason had decided to track down their friends and keep the fun rolling. He stuck to the script, managing to seem carefree and helpful. He finished by admitting he didn't have any use for Wayne Thompson — "there's no need to lie about it," he remarked — but he certainly wouldn't wish this on anyone, even a guy as disagreeable as Wayne.

64

Mason held up his hand and volunteered the name of a girl who'd written her phone number on his palm, then went into the house and returned with a crumpled credit card receipt from Peter's Lounge. "I realize it makes sense for you to interview us, Mr. Owen," he said, still not using the detective's familiar name, "but the bottom line is we didn't see the guy after he left, and Gates could've taken care of his gripe at Denise's if he'd had those kinds of intentions."

"I suppose so," Owen said. He perused his notes. "So you boys see the deceased at Denise Puckett's trailer around one or so, have some hot words and he drives off. Correct?"

"Yes, sir," Mason said.

"Then you two, Denise, Claude Whitlow, Shannon Stone and her cousin, lady by the name of Suzi, are at Denise's until ten or ten thirty? Mason and Gates go to Martinsville, remain till closing at Peter's Lounge. Then straight home." The policeman appeared to be reciting his own notes.

"Yeah," Gates answered. "But write down that the time we left is just approximate. We didn't have any reason to tie it to the second, you know?"

"Oh — Claude and I went to the liquor store not long after Wayne left," Mason volunteered. "Just so you have the full details. We also stopped by Alexander's to buy cookout supplies."

65

"I already talked to Claude." Owen took a drag from his pipe, exhaled the smoke. "He filled me in on who was there and what happened. Anything else I should be aware of?"

"Well, I mean, if you have a doubt that we were at Peter's Lounge in spite of everything we've provided you, I know Gates called Denise's from there trying to locate Claude and the girls." Mason's nerves were beginning to vex him. His saliva felt as if it were thickening, and the tension was pinching his belly. He licked his lips, rearranged his feet.

"If you tell me you were there, I'm takin' it you were. Although Claude told me y'all discussed the Dutch Inn, not this other place." Owen flipped through several pages while holding the pipe clamped in his teeth. "Dutch Inn is what he mentioned to me," he said from the side of his mouth. "Least that's what I wrote."

"Did he also tell you they all were fairly impaired? I was sober, and I recall Peter's, but hey, you know, maybe I'm wrong. I can't see what difference it makes." Mason tacked on an ad-lib to demonstrate how in the dark he was: "Was Wayne at the Dutch Inn or something? Is that why you're asking?"

"Not that we know of. It's a difference in the accounts, so I'm supposed to see about it."

"You have any leads or an idea who did it?" Gates inquired, patting his pockets, searching for his cigarettes. "Damn, left 'em inside. You got me wantin' a smoke," he said good-naturedly to Owen.

"None to speak of," Owen answered, his tone revealing nothing of what he'd actually learned.

"We couldn't discuss it with other people even if we did," Officer Williams informed them. He appeared pleased with himself and his contribution.

"You own a gun?" Owen asked abruptly, addressing Gates.

"A .22 rifle that our sorry dad left here," Gates said. He'd purchased the pistol from a greasy survivalist with a mouthful of dental neglect at a South Carolina flea market, spurning the man's invitation to join the Aryan Brotherhood and declining the opportunity to acquire more lethal weapons, such as grenades, assault rifles and mortars. A cash transaction, definitely no paper trail.

"That it? Only one rifle?"

"That's it." Gates sounded almost cheerful. The pistol was deep in the woods behind their mother's, buried there for the time being. They'd soaked his pants, shirt, socks and shoes with lawn mower gasoline and burned them first thing that morning, when the sun was muscling its way over the horizon line, raking a few leaves and setting them on fire afterward in case someone was curious about the smoke.

Owen shifted his weight. "Would you give us permission to look through the house? Conduct a search? It would protect us all later on if there are any questions." Owen had drawn a bead on Gates and was trying to gauge his reaction.

"Hey, fine with me." Gates didn't miss a beat.

Mason reflexively put his hands on his hips and asserted his chest. "Well, gentlemen, I think we should ask my mom before we make any plans concerning her home, don't you? Show her a little respect? Not to mention the legal issues."

"Absolutely," Owen replied.

"Absolutely," the deputy echoed.

"How about the car?" Owen asked. "Gates, you care if we look in there while y'all talk with your mom?"

"Help yourself," Gates said. "Door's open." At Mason's prompting, they'd removed the velvet contraband sack and scoured the interior for roaches and cocaine detritus, but they'd left the trash, beer cans and empty vodka bottles, lest the Corvette seem suspiciously clean for someone of Gates's notorious habits.

Owen gestured to Officer Williams. "How 'bout gettin' me one of them consent forms from the trunk?"

Gates signed a document granting the police permission to search his vehicle, and

68

the two cops began examining the Corvette. As Mason watched them, it appeared to him the effort was on the desultory side, and he took it as a positive sign that there didn't seem to be much enthusiasm.

Their mother was in the kitchen when they returned, facing away from the police and her sons, preoccupied by a cup of black coffee she was reheating in the balky microwave with its spinning glass carousel. The oven stopped its huffing and rotating and let out an alert, but Sadie Grace didn't remove the coffee. "What is it?" she asked. She had been a beautiful girl and a comely younger woman, but at forty-eight her attractiveness had long ago been swallowed whole, replaced by sags and pallor and veins popped by punch-clock days on unforgiving factory floors. There was still a hint of what once was, but her blue eyes were tapped out, her high spirits gone to seed amidst hard knocks and serial betrayals. She was tall like her boys, battle-tested, resourceful, and had maintained a single vanity since her teenage years — a head full of lustrous, dark hair that seemed impervious to age and disappointment.

"The police want to search the house," Mason announced. "They're here about Wayne Thompson." He paused and took her hand, engulfing it in both of his. "Wayne and Gates had a disagreement yesterday afternoon, so the police are chasing down every possible lead. They're just doing their job."

"Lord, Lord," she said. "Tell me Gates hasn't gone and done somethin'."

"Gates was with me and a bunch of other people. He has an absolute alibi. We were at Denise's, then at a lounge in Martinsville. Gates is fine on this. The police simply have to dot their *i*'s and cross their *t*'s. Their being here is routine. Once Gates is eliminated, they'll move on."

She was looking at the floor, on the verge of tears. "Why would they come if he wasn't in trouble?"

Mason drew her closer, releasing her hand and sliding his arm around her waist. "Mom, they're just checking things. It's nothing serious."

She snapped her head up and nailed Gates with a furious stare. "Gates, certainly you aren't part of a killin'? The drinkin' and lyin' and sorriness I can take — I'm used to them — but you better tell me right now you had nothing to do with what happened."

"Goodness, Mom, you know me better than that. I've done some stupid things and let you down, okay? I sure have. But you know I wouldn't cause you this kind of grief. I —"

"Hush," she said, not allowing him to finish even though she'd demanded an answer. "I don't want to hear your same old pitiful apology again." She turned to Mason. "He was with you?"

70

"All day, Mom. I promise." He was relieved to utter a few literally honest words.

She blinked and brushed her eye with the back of her wrist. "There's some family I would lie for, Mason, 'cause that's what blood does. Some I would lie for even if they don't deserve it. And some I wouldn't no matter what. You're almost free of this place, Mason, so close to bein' a success."

The words pained Gates, causing his mouth to shrink and his posture to lose shape. He didn't speak, though.

"I understand," Mason said. "Gates couldn't have done this. A lot of people besides me will stand up for him. I don't know when Wayne was killed, but we were with a group of people who will vouch for Gates's whereabouts, then at a bar miles away." He continued to keep his arm wrapped around his mother.

"I trust you on what we ought to do," she said to Mason. A tear broke loose on her cheek, but her voice was steady. "You decide."

"I think we should tell them they can search, so long as they don't go into your room. Everywhere else is fine."

"There you go," Gates chimed in. "That's a good solution."

"Whatever you think is best, Mason. I'm puttin' this in your hands."

Mason removed his arm from around her. "Let's go tell the police they're free to search on those terms. I'll stay with you. You don't need to worry. I'll be right here until they're gone."

"If that's how you see it, then that's what we'll do," she said.

The two officers both thanked Sadie Grace for her cooperation, and Owen told her he very much regretted the inconvenience, leaving everyone with the impression he truly felt bad about rummaging through her home and handling her property. They found nothing, and Mason and Gates allowed them to take the .22 rifle with them when they departed, along with a pair of substituted jeans and a shirt Gates dug from a hamper and identified as Saturday's dress. "You can look at my shoes, but I ain't gonna let you have 'em," he informed Owen, helpfully raising a foot.

"Think they'll be back?" Gates asked as he and Mason stood at the threshold to the mudroom, watching the police car and its long, thin antenna tail poke toward the main highway.

"I don't know," Mason replied. "Keep me up to speed if they do. And try to stay sober, huh? It would help the odds of your remaining quiet."

"I'm not stupid, Mason, contrary to what you and Mom might want to think."

"I never suggested you were. That's why I know you recognize it's your ass on the line if there's a slipup. You'll be the one wearing

72

the colorful jumpsuit, pleading for cigs and extra shower privileges, not me, not Mom. Try to remember that."

They ate a somber supper together, silent except for requests to pass a dish and the scrapes and squeaks of silverware on plates as they cut through hamburger steak and arranged bites of vegetables. Sadie Grace packed a full meal for Mason to take with him, and Gates accompanied him to his clunker Chevy Monza. They hugged and backslapped, but Mason was on edge as he drove away with the pistol hidden in his trunk, trained as he was to always anticipate every possibility and worst-case scenario: he could wreck and the damn gun be discovered, or the cops might just have a search warrant ready to go, waiting at the foot of the drive to bust him with the .38 in his possession — pretty difficult to explain, especially since he didn't envision his brother charging in to accept responsibility.

He traveled cautiously, keeping to the right lane on the divided highway, lights dimmed regardless of traffic. In South Boston, he stopped at a Burger King and placed a drive-through order. He parked in a far corner, popped the trunk, pretended to search his suitcase and laundry bag, removed the cylinder they'd separated from the .38, palmed it with a napkin, pulled on his jean jacket, then sat in his car and made a show of eating his chicken sandwich and fries. Every time a vehicle circled past, his pulse would surge and the food would turn to sawdust in his mouth. A teenager in a uniform and paper hat appeared at the rear of the business, taking a cigarette break, another worry. Mason and Gates had cleaned and wiped the gun before burying it, and they'd used needle-nose pliers to damage the firing pin. The barrel had been scratched and pitted with a Phillips-head screwdriver, so that if the weapon did somehow turn up and was reassembled, its firing patterns would be useless to the forensic lab and couldn't be traced to Wayne Thompson's shooting.

When the smoker returned to work, Mason placed the napkin and cylinder in the sandwich carton, bagged the carton and, wearing a baseball cap so low it hit his eyebrows, walked to a Dumpster and tossed in the sack. The remains of the sandwich, fries, and large drink and the lump of metal landed without complaint, didn't strike bottom or clash with anything too solid. Paranoid and jittery, Mason left the parking lot and worried all the way to Richmond that a tramp or Dumpster bum would discover the pistol piece or — his luck — it would turn up miraculously wedged onto a tomcat's nose, the perfect kind of filler for the local news broadcast.

He went out of his way to Petersburg, where he ditched the gun frame, concealed in a *Richmond Times-Dispatch,* at a public green-box site. It was late when he returned to his apartment on Hanover Avenue, and his two roommates were asleep, although they'd left the TV playing and most of the lights burning. Mason lay in his bed with his clothes still on, his shoes, socks, jeans and jacket, unable to rest, his conscience flogging him, his thoughts ragged and horrific. For several nights that followed, his sleep was tenuous, fitful, just beneath a translucent surface, never either completely here or there. He'd done nothing but watch, slack-jawed, as his brother slew another man, and yet the turn of events had left him morally hog-tied, an accessory after the fact, the entire damnable bundle laid at his feet by someone he loved dearly, and that visceral, epic connection to Gates, unfortunately, was the alpha and omega, trumping everything and everybody.

As it happened, Mason had no need to be concerned about Gates incriminating himself — he was far too narcissistic and egotistical to do or say anything that might bring him hardship. He proved to have a rascal's capacity to write off his crime and a gift for absolute self-preservation that kept him from ever mentioning the killing, no matter how drunk or high he became. In early November, he even found a job as a floor supervisor at a textile plant in Martinsville, and he announced to Denise he was cutting back to only beer and pot — no more coke and hard liquor and three-day binges. He lost the job after six weeks, showed up for work with the giggles, sunglasses and rum tainting his breath, then packed off his dismissal on his boss, claiming the guy had it in for him for no legitimate reason. In the months after his firing, there were sporadic trips to church basements for AA meetings, a monstrous blowout with Denise that prompted her to call Mason and hotheaded feuds with his mom followed by the usual fulsome apologies and vows to shape up. In other words, typical Gates.

The police worked diligently to solve Wayne Thompson's murder, but they had no leads, no witnesses and no worthwhile evidence. The shooting had occurred on a rural stretch of road, and the occupants of the closest house a mile away didn't hear a thing, or if they did, it didn't register in an area where most people owned guns and there was frequent hunting and target practice and carrying-on that occasionally included firing a few Jack Daniel's rounds at a stump or the wide-open sky. Danny Owen visited Gates a second time, and Gates frowned and sighed and told the officer he simply didn't know what else to say — they last saw Wayne at Denise's and never saw him again. Owen flew to Florida and interviewed Cousin Suzi, hounded Allen Roberts about his alibi after the pool game, contacted Mason's credit card company and the girl he'd met at Peter's Lounge, took a trip to Charlotte to question a drug dealer who'd been arrested with a .38 and obtained statements from Wayne's co-workers and family as well as the owner of the Old Dominion. According to the laboratory, there was marijuana and a small amount of methamphetamine in Wayne's car, but the RX-7 was devoid of anything helpful in the murder investigation. Toxicology revealed he was legally drunk; the small club next to him suggested a confrontation. Owen and an older deputy returned the .22 rifle to Gates in March and futzed around with a few more questions, but it was apparent they had nothing fresh or important to quiz him about.

The file went from Danny Owen's desk to the very front of a cabinet drawer to a thick collection of papers tucked behind ten or fifteen other baffling problems to a case number on a computer disk of unsolved crimes to a statistic that showed up every year on the report the local office sent to the state. Letters were written to the paper highlighting the sheriff's department's failure to solve a cold-blooded murder, the sheriff himself had to hear about his inability to bring the case to a conclusion when he stood for reelection in 1987, the family offered a reward and there were fits and starts and false leads and flashes of effort until there was eventually nothing left but inertia, lore and a rubber-banded old folder with a battered tab and a case number from an obsolete system. When Danny Owen retired in 1991, he didn't even mention the Thompson murder to his successor, instead spent most of his time briefing him on an undercover drug operation and a theft ring that was targeting vacation homes in Kibler Valley. Even the gossips and busybodies lost interest, as they generally do the moment there's something new to excite their tongues.

While the death of Wayne Thompson would always trouble Mason, the raw, punishing anguish started to recede after a couple months — it became permanent in him but less acute, a submerged shame that would occasionally be roused and set his palms to sweating or cause a bolt of adrenaline to burn across his abdomen. He'd see a cop show or hear the name Wayne or hit some catalyst — an RX-7 always did the trick — that would send him through a rabbit hole of speeding thoughts and blurs and fragments and return him to the side of Russell Creek Road and the sight of his brother holding the gun, his arm fully extended.

Near the end of the year at law school, Mason's guilt and concern were unexpectedly piqued when he received a brass-tacks assessment of his brother's situation during an advanced criminal law seminar. The professor had organized a panel discussion on how to properly defend a murder case, advertising the event throughout the university. With a single exception, the panel contained the usual collection of academics who'd never set foot in a courtroom and habitually filed tedious, sixty-page amicus briefs in high-profile appeals so they could see their names in the newspaper or snag an appearance on a Sunday talk show. For most of the presentation, the guy everyone in the class wanted to hear from had very little to say, and when the moderator solicited student questions, the peacock professors jumped in with clever answers and grand, drawing-room circumlocutions.

Jim "Bulldog" Young was one of the best criminal trial lawyers in Virginia, a charming, robust man whose genuine decency never failed to influence a jury and whose capacity to take a witness apart and not seem like a showboat had served him well for thirty years of practice. He was wearing a brown suede jacket and an ordinary tie, a white shirt. He was quick to smile, listened with a gentleman's interest to what was being said, and seemed satisfied to let his fellow panelists dominate the show while he scribbled notes, sipped water and fingered the point of his tie. At last a questioner called him by name and asked for advice: "Mr. Young, what's the most important thing to consider when you try a murder case? If you had to give us one insight?"

Without any flair or preening or affect, Young rocked back in his chair. "Only thing that matters in a murder case is did the fellow who's dead need to be killed, and did the right sonofabitch do the job."

The class roared and laughed and stood for an ovation, Mason along with everyone else. As he was leaving the lecture, though, he became pensive when he replayed the lawyer's response. If the police ever located enough evidence to take Gates to trial, his prospects were not too sound when judged by Young's standard, and Mason understood there was a chance he could be dragged into the bog right behind his brother. He stopped suddenly in the hallway outside the classroom, causing the woman behind him to veer off and graze him with her backpack. He repeated Young's test, mouthing it quietly while a stream of yapping law students washed through the hall. "Zero for two," he said out loud. "Damn."

CHAPTER THREE

By early 1990, Gates had journeyed around the bend. His mother, with Mason's blessing, had evicted him from her house, the Corvette was a two-hundred-thousand-mile heap of scarred fiberglass, bungee cords, duct tape and leaky gaskets, Denise had served him with a no-trespass notice and was engaged to an algebra teacher at Patrick County High School, and he was residing with a twenty-year-old feckless skank and her illegitimate toddler, living off her food stamps and welfare check and what he could earn peddling small amounts of pot and cocaine. On rare occasions, he'd do some logging or help in a hayfield or get paid under the table for a week of warm-weather construction work. Patrick County being what it was, most people greeted him with a word or two and a stony expression or simply acknowledged him with a stiff nod when they saw him in town. His hair was too long, his clothes unkempt, his conversations laden with hustle and excuses and get-rich-quick schemes. He'd spent a month in jail in 1989, after he busted out the windows of a girlfriend's car and was dumb enough to hang around making threats — an eight ball of coke in his pocket — until the police arrived to arrest him.

To no one's great shock, it was a failed, inept attempt to sell drugs that ultimately did him in. Very few people aspire to a job retailing baggies of marijuana or carefully build toward a career in powdered cocaine, but for Gates, it just seemed to be an inevitable fit as time went by, a hey-why-not vocation that promised easy money, scarcely any labor and a business inventory of his favorite drugs, a layabout's trifecta. He started in the mideighties by selling from his own pot stash, then bought a quarter extra on credit, which he mixed with oregano and sold to his buddies in the Old Dominion's bathroom or at the parking lot of Moody's Funeral Home. A biker from Greensboro who went by the name Kong hooked him up with a steady supply of coke, and at first Gates simply took his payment in kind, distributing in exchange for free dope. Given the size of the community, it didn't take long for the police to get wind of what Gates was up to, though for several years he avoided the authorities by sticking to nickel-and-dime transactions and dealing with the same people, friends he'd known since grade school and the regulars at the roadhouse.

The serious trouble arrived in the summer of 1990. By June, Gates and his girlfriend, Sandra, were beset with difficulties. Their trailer rent was in arrears, and the landlord had seen enough, wanted them gone. The Corvette had completely given up the ghost and was parked at a haphazard angle in the yard, the grass the push mower didn't catch outlining the car in a shaggy fringe. Social services had sent legal papers seeking "custody of the infant known as Jade Bon Jovi Bowman," and Gates and Sandra didn't like that plan one bit, hell no, vowed to fight the state tooth and nail and ranted about the injustice of it all, the *idea* that a bunch of meddling bastards thought they could take Jade away from a parent who loved her so unconditionally. "They're tryin' to claim I'm a bad mother?" Sandra indignantly demanded of the poor deputy who'd delivered the paperwork to her. The fact that they would lose a monthly check, rental assistance, Medicaid and free food wasn't important. It was the principle. The *principle.* Wanting only what was best for sweet Jade, they realized they'd need money for a lawyer, since Gates's uppity brother in Richmond was no help whatsoever.

In an effort to raise cash, Gates agreed to unload the Corvette, which would leave them only a single vehicle, Sandra's ragtag Chevette with its mismatched, primer-colored fender. He'd received the car after graduation from high school, obtained it from a Christiansburg auto dealer who supported Virginia Tech and wanted to do all he could to ensure that the talented freshman linebacker from Patrick County understood just how welcome he was in this new world. Gates was . . . uh . . . employed by the dealership, and he drove the car home for the first time during August of 1975, in an era when the NCAA wasn't so nosy and draconian. His friends in Patrick were proud of him and didn't begrudge him the flashy red reward, believed he'd more than earned it, what with his daddy absent for years and he and his brother struggling to stretch Sadie Grace's meager paycheck from the plant. Right off the bat, Gates took his mom for a joyride, kicking it up to eighty through Spoon Creek bottom, both the windows open so the warm, whipping air could add to the thrill. She squealed at him to stop but was laughing when she called him down, delighted with her boy and what he'd accomplished.

Sandra looked up the number and Gates called Clyde Turner, who bought and sold used cars out near Fairy Stone State Park. Gates invited him to drop by the trailer and price the Corvette, claiming they weren't that anxious to make a deal but really didn't need two vehicles. A day later, Clyde arrived and walked around the car and stuck his head in for a peek at the interior, checked the engine. Chewing on a toothpick, he offered Gates nine hundred dollars.

"No fuckin' way," Gates snapped. "What the hell's wrong with you, Clyde? It's a collector's item."

"Well, it might be if you was Fred or Lamont Sanford," Clyde drawled. "I'm interested in cars I can sell. Cars that run. This one's in awful shape, and it ain't runnin'."

"Nope. Not a chance. I gotta have ten thousand, minimum."

"I ain't here to offend you, Gates. No, sir. I'm just tellin' you what she's worth to me. If we can do business, fine. If not, we'll shake hands and leave with no bad feelings. You might do better to try in the paper or with another person 'sides me."

"Give me eighty-five hundred, Clyde."

"Gates, friend, listen. She's been beat to death. She's old. You're lucky I ain't chargin' you to hook to her and drag her off."

"Hell, Clyde, a coat of paint, a little body work, a few parts, the car's mint again."

Clyde arched his eyebrows. "Friend, I'm gonna take her for salvage. You want to put her in shape and call me back, we'll discuss a higher price. I'm thinkin' of this thing for scrap. You're lookin' at serious jack to restore this car — you know that. And you know a '75 ain't no big deal to a collector these days.

I'll go a hundred more, but that's my limit."

In the end, after ten minutes of haranguing and foot stomping, Gates relented, gave Clyde Turner the title to the Corvette and watched him tow it away to be stripped down and sold piece by piece, a worn-out hulk, its luster diminished, its low-to-the-ground sleek speed crippled, its engine spent and gummed up for good, the hoses dry-rotting, the wires brittle and unpredictable.

For months, Kong had been after Gates to increase his productivity, and he agreed a few weeks after the sad Corvette transfer, accepting an advance of five hundred dollars, which he and Sandra paid to a lawyer — together with two hundred and fifty dollars of the car money — to partially finance the custody battle for Jade. Of course, as soon as Gates walked through the mobile home door with a big ol' bag of Kong's powder, they phoned Sandra's mom to babysit for the night and dove into the coke, drinking beer and listening to "Living on a Prayer" at top decibel until Sandra turned blue and melodramatic and they fell into an argument that ended with her chucking an ashtray at Gates, then threatening to leave him for Jade's daddy, who'd written her from the penitentiary and was eager to reconcile. Gates grabbed her by the collar and slapped the hell out of her, leaving elongated red marks across her cheek. They made up within an hour, had high, wallowing sex that they were unable to finish, and awakened at noon the next day with shredded nostrils and fractured recollections of the prior night.

Not long afterward on a stagnant July evening, Sandra and Gates stopped by the Old Dominion for a cold pitcher of beer and a small cheese pizza. Their pal Barry was already there, playing pinball, leaning into the machine, bumping it with his pelvis, rapid-firing the flipper buttons, a draft beside him on a table. An old friend and reliable client named Hank Lawless, Jr., had introduced Barry to Gates and vouched for his trustworthiness. As Gates understood it, Barry lived in Richmond, making a living as a long-distance truck driver, but he often showed up with Hank at barbecues and fiddlers' conventions in Stuart, a good guy who'd always let folks bum a cig or borrow his music. For nearly a year, Gates had been selling him fifty-dollar dabs of cocaine when he was in town.

Barry shouted hello, and Gates walked over to watch the game and chew the fat. Barry had most of the bonuses lit and a high score, and he earned two extra balls and thousands of points before his run ended. He and Gates talked about Hank and a trip Barry had made to Los Angeles to deliver a load of produce. Barry put another quarter in the machine and started with a new ball. "You able to do anything for me today?" he asked, his tone confidential and hushed.

"Yep," Gates answered. "I'm your man."

Barry pulled back the silver knob, adjusted his stance, then released it. *Chings* and *plunks* and wild caroms and skittering lights commenced again. "Weight?" he asked, watching his shot, not looking at Gates.

"I'm flush. You name it."

"Really?"

Gates checked the bar for Sandra. She was drinking a beer, chatting with another woman. "Oh yeah." He rolled out a braggart's smile.

"I've been thinkin' about tryin' to locate enough to hold me between trips up here." He glanced at Gates and the ball got away from him, clipping a flipper and disappearing. "And maybe get a little volume discount." He gave Gates his full attention.

"I'll work with you. You know that."

"An ounce?"

"Cool," Gates said. "Piece of cake."

Barry returned to the pinball game and hunched over the machine, launching his second shot. "How much?"

"For you, twelve."

"Shit, man, I ain't lookin' for no tourist price." He playfully jabbed Gates with his elbow. "You gotta do better than that."

"I'm giving it to you for what I have in it," Gates lied.

"A grand." This play wasn't productive; the ball was retired after only a handful of ricochets and a single trip through a spinning gate.

"Jeez, Barry. I'm not Goodwill. I'm already offerin' you a discount."

"Best I can do. A thousand." Barry winked at him. "And I'll pick up your tab for the pizza and beer."

"Man, you're torturing me here." Gates paused. "Shit, all right, but don't you tell a soul what you're payin'."

Barry pressed his thumb and forefinger together and drew them lengthwise across his lips. "Zipped, Gates. Not a word from me."

"Good."

"I'm goin' to have to go get the cash. I'm staying at Hank's, so where should I meet you?"

"Moody's?" Gates suggested. "Behind the funeral home?"

"Ouch. That's too creepy for me. Let's try somewhere else."

"How well do you know Stuart?"

"Okay, I guess. Pretty good. I can get Hank to come with me if need be. I'm sure once he hears what's up, he'll be happy to tag along and sponge off my bag."

Gates chuckled. "No doubt."

"What about the fairgrounds, down past the hospital? I'll just slip in next to the cinder-block building where you buy your ticket."

"Sure. Fine with me. How long?"

Barry rotated his wrist and checked his watch. "Hour?"

"Cool. I have to make a stop myself, so that's perfect."

Barry extended his hand for a quick shake, entwining his thumb with Gates's. "Treat me right. I'm expectin' some kick-ass shit from you."

It was twilight when Gates, folded into the Chevette, eased into the entrance road at the fairgrounds, the air still stale and sullen, the day's heat refusing to budge. He was dressed in a tank top and cutoff jeans, barefoot, drinking a Miller beer, the coke — diluted with a generous sprinkling of baby laxative — tucked beneath his seat, a .22 pistol lying on the console, just in case. Barry was already there, exactly where he said he'd be, and the large lot in front of the fairgrounds was empty. Gates liked the location; the exchange would take place in a spot that afforded them a thorough view in every direction, and a vehicle or two in the lot wasn't uncommon since people used the flat field inside the gate for Little League practice and pickup softball. He stopped his car so they were window-to-window, facing in opposite directions. Barry was listening to Metallica's "Enter Sandman," but he turned off the music when Gates pulled up.

"You been here long?" Gates asked.

"Nah. Five minutes, maybe."

"We good to go?" Gates set his beer between his legs. He scanned the lot, the road, the area behind the gate and the small, squat building that housed Rotary Club ticket takers when the fair was in residence.

"I've got the thousand if you're ready with the coke."

"No offense, Barry, but, ah, I need the dollars first."

"None taken. Just business, right?" Barry conducted his own quick, tense survey, then handed Gates ten hundred-dollar bills, thrusting them through the window, the cars so close that his arm stretched into the Chevette.

Gates counted the bills twice. "Awesome," he said. He knocked back the beer, reached under the seat, took another nervous look around, located the dope and passed it to Barry. "A pleasure doing business with you."

"You too, Gates." Barry opened the baggie of coke and studied it. "You're the man."

All hell broke loose.

A spotlight hit the cars. The wooden shutters on the ticket building crashed open. Vehicles with red and white lights strobing from their grills tore into the entrance, accelerating even as they made the sweeping turn toward Gates and Barry. Two men — cops, fucking cops — leapt out of the building, weapons drawn, crouched, screaming, "Your hands, show us your hands, Gates," their badges worn like necklaces, STATE POLICE emblazoned in yellow on the black vests protecting them from gunfire. Another officer was sprinting to the scene with a rifle. Barry surged forward in his Firebird, stopped. Spilling out, he aimed a pistol at Gates from behind the door: "State Police. Don't even think about it."

Gates ran. Bolted. A decision, he would later tell his brother, that was his biggest regret in the whole affair. Shoeless and desperate, he jackrabbited, not man enough to salvage even a speck of dignity by raising his hands and swallowing his medicine. As far as the cops were concerned, the futile escape attempt made him the absolute worst kind of coward, and when they gang-tackled him in the fairgrounds parking lot, skinning his knees and staining his shirt with red clay, a crew-cut special agent called him a pussy and bellowed what they all were thinking: "Where the hell you plan on going? Huh?" Two local deputies yanked him up, steered him to a cruiser and stuffed him inside.

Scared and panicked, with his knees throbbing and trickling blood and his hands cuffed behind him, Gates struggled to balance himself on the rear seat of the police car. He spoke for the first time as he and the cops swung through the serpentine curves that led into Stuart. "Guys, listen. Hey, I'm sorry, okay? Can't we work something out? I don't need this. How about a break, some slack?" The road went from left to right, causing his shoulder to hit the door. "Please. I got a mother to take care of and a little girl I'm raisin'. What about them?"

The officer on the passenger side half turned so that Gates saw him in profile. He was still wearing his bulletproof vest. "It's not up to us, Mr. Hunt. The courts make those decisions." The response sounded rote, practiced.

"Heck, right now, it's your call. You can do whatever you want."

"And we want to take you to the magistrate and charge you with felony distribution." He twisted a few more degrees in Gates's direction. "That's how it is."

"Man, there's no need to be so hard-nosed. Come on. Sir, I'm pleadin' with you."

"Nothing we can do." The cop fixed him with a cold stare, started to add something but didn't.

"This isn't fair. It isn't. Shit." He flicked his dry tongue over his lips. "Maybe I could give you, you know, a little help. Point you to the big fish. I'm not the guy you're after. I'm way down the line, barely even worth the effort."

The officer turned away, ignoring Gates.

"Hey, why are you actin' so rude? You could at least answer me."

The two policemen began talking to each other about how long it would take to process Gates and where they could find a meal on their way home.

"You can't hear me?"

They continued their conversation and didn't respond.

"Hey, okay, you know what, fuck both you guys. I tried to be cool about this, but you can both kiss my ass." He was crossing into irrational, cornered, dead-end rage.

They passed the bank, Main Street and the old brick courthouse. The driver flipped on his blinker, and the vehicle sat motionless for an instant while another car passed in the oncoming lane.

"You assholes will regret this day for the rest of your lives." Gates's words were amped and rabid. He began pulling against his cuffs, herky-jerking his shoulders. "My brother's a lawyer, and you clowns will be lookin' for work soon. That's a promise. You hear me? I'll fuckin' have your jobs for this. I want your badge number." He flopped back violently against the seat. "I know my rights, mother-fuckers, and I want your names and num-bers."

"Sure, yeah, you know your rights," said the driver. "You got us there, Mr. Hunt. I'm

Bruce Wayne, millionaire Bruce Wayne, and this is my sidekick, Dick Grayson. We're badges number one and two. How's that? Anything else we can help you with?"

The response made him that much more incensed, and it took a total of five cops to drag him yelling and flailing into the magistrate's office, where they charged him with disorderly conduct and multiple counts of assaulting a police officer in addition to felony distribution of cocaine. The magistrate, whose house he threatened to burn, denied him bond, and he was incarcerated for the second time in his life, tossed in with the slugs and petty criminals to await his day in court.

"This is total bullshit, Mason," Gates railed as soon as the deputy shut the door to the interview room at the Patrick County jail. "Man, this is all so wrong. I'm innocent." He was wearing an orange canvas jumpsuit but, oddly enough, seemed to have a rekindled interest in his grooming and appearance: he was clean-shaven, his hair was orderly, his nails were trimmed and the short sleeves of his jail outfit were rolled into tight, smart bands at his biceps. It was the afternoon of the day following his arrest; Mason had driven to Stuart from Richmond, briefly visited their mom and then traveled into town to meet with his brother.

"Oh?"

"Absolutely." They were separated by a plain wooden table. Gates leaned forward, closer to Mason, gesturing manically. "This is a mistake." He widened his eyes, rounded his mouth. "I'm just hanging around at the fairgrounds, shootin' the breeze with Hank Lawless's friend Barry, and the damn cops swarm in like the Marines or somethin'. Crazy. They claim they found dope on Barry and they arrest me! How does that make any sense?" He waved his hands frenetically. "You need to set this straight, Mason. Apply some lawyer grease and get me out of here."

Mason put his elbows on the table and deliberately lowered his chin into his palms. "That's what you're telling me?"

"Absolutely. Look, I'm no Boy Scout, I've done stupid things, broken the law, but not this time. This is some messed-up shit. They didn't find any drugs on me. None. I can't help it if Barry's holdin' dope and I happen to be there."

"This is what you've come up with after a night of reflection?" Mason asked impassively.

"Meaning?"

"Meaning I don't know what's worse: the lack of creativity or the unconscionable lying." Mason withdrew his chin and sat back against the slatted support of his chair.

"Mason, I'm your brother, and I'm telling

you the truth. I didn't have anything to do with it. My word on it."

"You were in the wrong place, wrong time?"

"Exactly." He vigorously bounced his head up and down.

Mason folded his arms over his chest and made certain his disdain was obvious when he spoke. "Here's the truth, Gates. Barry is a state police undercover officer who was working with your hopeless friend Hank Lawless. Hank found himself in a jam for buying a bunch of stolen heavy equipment and decided to polish up his junior deputy's badge and cast his lot with the cops. You're on tape demanding money for the dope, and two other cops watched from the ticket building while you sold an ounce of cocaine for profit. The bottom line is you are guilty as homemade sin and they can prove it. Lying only makes it worse. Hell, you have to know this fellow Barry was a cop — he helped arrest you."

"Have you heard this tape they supposedly made?"

"No. The sheriff was kind enough to give me an overview. And even if they didn't have the recording, there're three or four cops standing in line to say they saw you sell cocaine. A thousand dollars' worth. With a frigging gun in the car."

"I got that cash from the Corvette," Gates

declared. "You can check with Clyde Turner."

"Yeah, well, Clyde must have copied down the serial numbers and marked the bills, because the money in your car was the same money Barry handed you for the dope."

"So you think I'm boxed in?"

"Yeah — a very precise box, like a coffin."

"And you believe them?" Gates asked.

"What's not to believe?"

Gates scooted his chair away from the table and stood. "Shit, Mason, it's entrapment then. They set me up." He flung his arms to each side and held them aloft, crucified on an invisible cross. "Pressured me into it. Tricked me, lied to me. That won't fly. The police can't operate like that."

"I thought you just told me you weren't involved? Gave me your word?"

"Well, shit, I guess we got a change of plans if what you say is true. Have to go with what'll work, right?" He dropped his arms. His palms slapped against his hips. "Entrapment. You know what? I asked that prick Barry, asked him if he was a cop, and he lied to me. I'll testify to it. They gotta tell you if you ask — the police can't lie."

Mason shook his head, sighed. "First," he said, nettled and glaring at Gates, "you never did any such thing. Second, even if you did, it doesn't matter — that's a damn urban myth. Nonsense. It's the Dillinger exhibit and bathtub kidney surgeons. They're working *undercover* — they're supposed to convince you they're not cops. They don't have to tell you diddly."

"Well, I've heard —"

"I don't give a damn what you've heard, Gates. It's not true."

"Then you are just goin' to have to come up with some lawyer tricks. You can do that, right? Clever as you are, you can get one over on these hicks any day of the week. 'Lawyers, guns and money,' like the song says. I need your help, Mason. I do. And I swear — I swear to God — I've learned my lesson. After this, I'm a changed man — nine-to-five, no drugs, no drinkin', church, the whole kit and caboodle."

"Peace Corps?"

"Say what?"

"What about the Peace Corps? Signing up to do your bit in impoverished countries?"

"Why're you being a dick, Mason? Huh? I'm facin' a world of hurt and you're crackin' jokes?" He'd started pacing.

"Gates, there comes a day when you've cashed all your chits and flat worn everybody out. You hit that mark a long time ago."

"I'm not arguing with you, okay? I've screwed up again, and I know I've promised to do better before, I know that, but you can't leave me danglin' in the wind. I swear on our mother's health this is it for me. If you'll just pull some legal strings and keep me out of jail, I . . ." He paused, swallowed. "I've truly learned my lesson. With God as my witness, I'll never cause you or anybody else a problem if you can please get me clear of this."

"Most people," Mason said solemnly, "would have learned their lesson years ago." He cut his eyes at his brother. "You catch my drift?"

"Yeah." Gates stood still, his breathing erratic, almost a pant. "At least help me fight it, Mason. Please. You're a lawyer — that's what you guys do, work the system and find loopholes. Twist words to make them different. There has to be a way. Somethin'." Sweat droplets were gathering at his hairline and dribbling down across his forehead.

"Gates, I'm not a criminal lawyer, but this much I can promise you: about the only people who could extricate you from this would be Sherman and Mr. Peabody operating the Wayback Machine. Lawyers aren't wizards or shamans. This isn't Tolkien — there's no spell we can cast to erase your voice from the tape or incantation we can recite to strike these police officers dumb. You need to come to terms with what you've done. The more you lie and caterwaul, the more you'll piss off the police and the commonwealth's attorney. I'll see what I can do, but your best hope is to plead guilty, tell the truth and walk into court meek, humble and hat in hand."

They studied each other for a moment, the room silent and stuffy. Above them was the antiquated county jail, and a thud and whooping curse penetrated the ceiling and dawdled there with them in the thick air. Gates closed his eyes and rocked back against the dingy green wall. A chunk of plaster was missing near his head, a white scab, and the wall's weak hue made him appear pale and watery, like he was dissolving. "How in the world did I wind up here?" he said, his voice faltering, his eyes still shut.

"I'll do my best," Mason offered. He went around the table to his brother and laid his hand on his shoulder, squeezed him through the rough cloth and then left him, didn't turn back even though — striding out of the room — he heard Gates call after him to please, please, please wait a minute.

Mason hadn't spent much time in Stuart since finishing law school and accepting a job in Richmond, and he wandered the roads without any purpose after departing the jail, listening to the local radio station and making a willy-nilly tour of the area: the elementary school, the bridge across the Mayo River where he and Gates usually fished on the opening day of trout season, the Staples house where they'd all — teenagers — smoked cigarettes in the basement and pored over a stolen *Playboy* and played pool until

101

Eddie Staples died of leukemia and his parents moved to Norfolk, the ramshackle Chevrolet dealership, Gypsy Boaz's tobacco fields filled with row upon row of sticky green leaves, a Ford tractor and a flatbed trailer parked catty-corner to the curing barn.

The sights failed to stir Mason or set much loose in him. He was years removed from his hometown, and his recollections of Stuart had been refined into stylized, formal renderings, a scattershot collection of snippets and images without juice or vitality, like a series of petrified butterflies skull-pinned to a collector's board, far more husk than heart. Everything was familiar, nothing intimate. He was at arm's length with his brother as well, distant and low on empathy, and he switched the radio to an NPR broadcast, trying to find a distraction. A second-rate pair of sunglasses was in the glove compartment, and he put them on. He raised the air-conditioning fan a notch. He sprayed the windshield with blue cleaner and watched the wipers beat it away. He loosened his tie, went to work on a pack of gum. Adjusted his seat belt before releasing it altogether.

When he returned to his mother's house, she was sitting in the den, a square electric fan blowing on her, her hair gathered atop her head. A TV show was hopping from scene to scene, but she hadn't turned up the volume. Mason offered to treat her to the whitefish and popcorn shrimp plate at the seafood restaurant, but she claimed to be under the weather, not feeling so great, and said she'd rather slice a garden tomato and warm some corn bread and leftovers.

"Mom, you have to face people sooner or later," Mason encouraged her. "This isn't about you. Everybody understands that. No one could've asked more from a parent. Gates should be ashamed."

"I suppose you're right, honey. Gates is Gates. But I'd just like to take me a day off, you know?" Her lips quivered and she drew them determinedly taut and thin. "Just have one day when I don't feel like I'm drownin'."

Gates sulked and pouted and berated his mother and Mason when they refused to hire a private attorney for him and recommended he take advantage of the public defender's office. "Gates, there's nothing anyone can do," Mason insisted. "I've told you over and over." He and Sadie Grace were visiting on a Sunday, talking to Gates through the bars. "And I'll be with you every step of the way. I promise."

"Yeah, thanks. You and a guy the state's paying. You've never even done a criminal case, Mason. I'm real confident of my chances." Gates had been in jail for three weeks and continued to pretend he was entrapped. He'd called his mother and begged her to approach the commonwealth's attorney about a bond, written Mason a long, rambling letter to posit fantastical legal strategies, sent notes to his buddies asking for canteen cash and done his best to get in touch with Sandra, who'd already abandoned the trailer and wasn't responding to the messages and threats he'd left at her sister's. "Ya'll are just turnin' your backs on me."

Their mother rarely talked much during visitation, normally sat silently after she said hello and asked a question or two, occasionally smiling wanly at one of Mason's corny stories or mumbling a thank-you when Gates complimented her appearance. Every Sunday, after the same nonsensical diatribe, she would agree to help find Sandra so Gates could have his leather jacket and "valuable" personal items returned, although it seemed obvious his girlfriend had skedaddled for good, not at all anxious to be on the margins of a felony drug trial. When Gates accused Mason and Sadie Grace of deserting him, her neck and face flushed, and she aimed a finger at Gates and jabbed him hard in the chest. "I wish I could reach my hands inside those bars and get at you. I do. You need to grow up and act like a man. I'm sick and tired of hearin' you complain. *I'm* the one who ought to be feelin' put upon, not you." Her voice was loud enough that another family halted their conversation to see what was causing the commotion. "You better watch what you say to me. I'm about fed up." She left after saying her piece, the low heels of her church pumps clacking on the concrete floor as she went, and she skipped two Sundays before resuming her visits.

Gates's court-appointed lawyer turned out to be a very capable man named Gary Cardwell. Cardwell was a former prosecutor, middle-aged, who'd quit the commonwealth attorney's office for the other side of the street. The senior public defender, he was bright, experienced in court, jolly, and from all accounts a fierce advocate for his clients. Mason was pleased when they met and reviewed Gates's case. Cardwell seemed both realistic and eager to do what he could, assuring Mason his brother was like a lot of other defendants who were reluctant to accept that they were in a legal bind and on the brink of a nasty prison stretch. "You don't try to force the unpleasant truth down their throats," he told Mason. "Nope. No more than a doctor would stroll in and announce to a patient, 'You're dying, there's nothing we can do and we're not planning to try.' They have to come to it in their own time. You listen to them, take them seriously and explain their prospects. Guys like your brother have to know they've tried every exit and exhausted every option. Most of them will see the light, usually when the trial gets close. It's not immediate enough for some people until they actually sit at the defendant's table or hear the indictment read. I've taken this case apart, and they have him cold. We'll try to swing a deal, and if we can't, we'll plead guilty and put on the dog for his sentencing."

"I told him exactly the same thing," Mason said.

"He'll reach that point. It's the only choice he'll have in the end. If he pleads not guilty, the commonwealth will demand a jury, and he'd be a damn fool to take his chances there. They'd eat him alive."

The jury trial began on a frigid January Tuesday, three days after an insistent snowstorm had pushed over the mountains and covered the county with five white inches that would linger for a week. Mason gripped his mother at the bend of her arm as they climbed the steep stone steps that rose to the courtroom, on guard for ice or a slick spot that hadn't been completely shoveled. The commonwealth's attorney had offered five years on the dope case, ninety days total for assaulting the police officers and a dismissal of the disorderly conduct charge, and after seating Sadie Grace, Mason met with his brother in the interview room and tried yet again to reason with him about his plea. A cig pinched between his thumb and forefinger, Gates sat there beside his lawyer and sneered and snorted and arrogantly, pigheadedly, rejected the deal, which both Mason and Gary Cardwell assured him was fair as could be.

"Fuck the commonwealth's attorney," Gates snarled. "I'll take time served and probation."

"You'll take what they suggest," Mason said. "You have no bargaining power."

"How about I tell them where the stuff came from?"

"They already know," Cardwell said. "They arrested your friend Kong the day after they caught you. We've been through that in detail. You're one slot too low in the pecking order because of it. They had his whole network in their sights. In fact, I'm pretty sure the cops followed you down to Greensboro a couple times when you were, shall we say, visiting him. So it's a no-go for any kind of co-operation arrangement."

"Damn," Gates carped. "There has to be something better than five years."

"I'm sorry," Cardwell told him. "But five and ninety is a pretty good outcome, given what we're facing. And if you plead on this, they're going to forget the other sales to Barry. Those cases are still possibilities."

"I'll take my chances," Gates said.

"Suit yourself," Cardwell replied. He removed his glasses and placed them on a table.

Permanent red impressions from the plastic pads marked each side of his nose. "You're exposing yourself to a lot worse, okay? You understand? I'd take the deal. I wouldn't want to go in front of a Patrick County jury on a drug case."

"I'd accept the offer as well," Mason warned him.

"I can't" was all Gates said.

The jury listened attentively to the lawyers' opening remarks, and it seemed to Mason, watching with his mom from the first row of the gallery, they were an evenhanded group, committed to giving both sides a fair hearing. He saw their moods shift after the undercover cop described how Gates had eagerly sold an ounce of cocaine and another officer played a surveillance tape that ended with Gates hotfooting it away from the Chevette. They went from curious to convinced to angry, and by the time the commonwealth rested its case at two thirty, they were quietly livid, insulted because Gates had brought them to town and wasted their day when he was so remarkably guilty. And while they all had been sincere in taking the oath and declaring themselves objective and willing to decide the case on the courtroom evidence alone, this was Patrick County, and several panel members knew Gates or knew of him, and one man, Otis Cooper, had worked with Sadie Grace before retiring from the plant, and he realized that the clean-cut, coat-and-tie fellow at the defense table was an outright fraud — underneath the fancy suit was a boy who had leeched off his mama forever and was so lazy he wouldn't hit a tap at a snake.

The awakening that Cardwell had predicted never came for Gates. Cardwell did the best he could, chipping and scratching and finessing, but the facts incriminating Gates were powerfully simple. The brothers and the lawyer met in a side room after the commonwealth concluded its case, and Mason once again explained the wisdom of a guilty plea.

"Listen," he said. "I sat there and dispassionately heard the evidence and took stock of the people on the jury. They're going to set your ass on fire. You have to know that, Gates. You've got to plead and allow the judge to sentence you or let Mr. Cardwell see what the commonwealth's willing to offer. I'm telling you, don't do this to yourself."

Cardwell was sitting in a chair by a large window. The room was chilly, heated by a rattling steam radiator that had been painted the same color as the walls. "Gates, son, I did all I knew how to," he remarked, "but I have to side with your brother. This is a calamity waiting to happen."

"Easy for you guys to say," Gates complained. "Easy for you to deal away over five years of my life. I can pull this off. I can. I thought of somethin' when the undercover guy was testifyin'."

"Pardon?" Cardwell asked, incredulous. "I'm not sure I understand what you mean."

"You just follow my lead, okay? Put me on the stand and ask me what happened. I'll take it from there. And don't forget to mention the stuff about football, where I was all-state and my scholarship to Tech. People still respect me because of that, no matter what."

"You'll *take it from there?*" Mason mocked him. "Have you lost your mind? Have you? This isn't workshop day at the community college drama class. What're you planning to say?"

Gates was loud when he answered. "You don't have to be such a prick, Mason. Anyway, I'm old enough to make my own decisions without help from you. You think you can waltz in here from Richmond and tell me how to run my life, but you can't. I don't need you around if all you're gonna do is criticize me, okay? You're either with me or against me, and right now you seem mostly against me." He glanced at the floor for a moment and softened his tone. "Guys, five years or five hundred — it's all the same to me. I can't do it. That's what you two aren't understandin'. There comes a point where you get so screwed up and stir-crazy there's no chance of recoverin'. Any more time in here's gonna ruin me, if it doesn't kill me first. I know you think I'm bein' stubborn, but it's a chance I've got to take, even if it probably won't pan out." Another hesitation. "And I'm sorry I've been so short with you both. I truly am."

Mason drew a bead on him but didn't answer. He finally glanced at Cardwell. "Thanks for your help, Mr. Cardwell. Good luck." He left the room, not bothering to shut the door behind him, and took a seat beside his mother.

Cardwell brought Gates to the judge's office and explained, on the record, that his client wished to testify, against counsel's advice. "Unfortunately, Judge, I'm hearing certain details for the first time today and that puts me and my client at a disadvantage. I've told Mr. Hunt it's a bad idea." Cardwell cleared his throat. "So no one gets the wrong impression, his new statement is consistent with what I've been hearing all along. It's just an amplification, sort of an expansion, and while I believe him, I've warned him against presenting it to this jury."

Worried and nervous as he faced twelve men and women who anticipated he was about to tell them a fanciful lie, Gates still managed a certain amount of cheap charisma on the stand. He was large and handsome and seemed to know, at least initially, what to do with his hands, where to look, how to sit, when to say "sir." Cardwell led him through a series of basic questions and then approached the heart of the case, the cocaine sale at the fairgrounds. One of the jurors, a wiry woman from Meadows of Dan, inched forward and cocked her head. A man who'd been taking notes wrote something on his yellow sheet of paper. The courtroom was cavernously silent, sealed off by double walls of meticulously mortared red and brownish brick.

Cardwell walked to the witness stand and actually turned toward the jury, not Gates, when he asked his first question about the charge. "Mr. Hunt, did you in fact meet a man you knew as Barry at the fairgrounds?"

"Yes, sir, I did."

"How did you know Barry?"

"We were close friends, or so I thought. We were introduced by Hank Lawless, Jr."

"Of course, you realize as you sit here today he's an undercover police officer?" Cardwell was now focusing on Gates. The lawyer had both hands in his pockets, his suit coat open.

"Yes, sir. Obviously I didn't know it at the time." Gates bent the wire neck of the witness stand microphone, positioning it closer to him. "I truly believed he was a friend. Him and Hank both."

"Well, let's get to the question the jury wants answered. Did you give that cocaine to Barry for a thousand dollars, as the commonwealth's attorney is alleging?"

Gates bit his lip, dipped his head, playacted remorse. "I did, sir. Heck, it's on tape. I don't deny it. Everything the police have said is true."

"So you don't dispute that money and drugs changed hands?" Cardwell asked. "The commonwealth's case is accurate?"

"As far as it goes, yeah." Gates's face contracted. The single-syllable "yeah" leaked the first hint of deceit.

Cardwell was a savvy lawyer. He waited, didn't rush, allowed a confident silence before asking the tough, obvious question, and he posed it with a mixture of disbelief and astonishment that perfectly mirrored the sentiments of every juror. "What in the world were you thinking, Mr. Hunt? Can you tell these ladies and gentlemen what caused you to do what we all agree you did? Why were you swapping cocaine for money? Why in tarnation are you fighting this?"

"Sure. Yes, sir. Like I said, I don't dispute what's been proved so far — it's just not the whole story."

"Okay," Cardwell replied. "You tell us the parts that have been omitted."

Gates bored in on the jury, but his set jaw and earnest eyes were too aggressive, too dramatic, and when he spoke, he was antsy, pushy, a grifter with a valise and shiny shoes. "Here's what's not being told. See, Barry, or Agent Simpson — I'm not sure which to call

113

him — gave me the drugs. Gave 'em to me days before the arrest to hold as collateral. We were close friends, and I ran into him one evening at the Old Dominion, and he tells me how he's up against it, in a jam because his kid's sick and needs medical care and begs me to let him borrow a thousand dollars. Well, I'd sold my Corvette to Clyde Turner —"

"Mr. Turner is here and prepared to testify, correct?" Cardwell interjected, helping as much as he was able.

"Right. And he'll confirm what I'm sayin'. So, you know, gee, he's a friend and he's down on his luck, so I loan him the money but, like anybody else, friend or not, I need to make sure I'm protected, so I asked for some collateral."

A juror in a coat and tie, the assistant manager of an oil company, was the first to anticipate the remainder of Gates's defense, and his expression soured. He folded his arms across his chest and tipped back in his seat, began gazing at the ceiling.

"What collateral did you receive?" the lawyer asked.

"I know this sounds horrible, and I know I never should've done it but, well, all he had, or so he claimed, was this cocaine. I mean, I asked about car titles or jewelry or guns or whatever, but he said he was broke and in hock and was plannin' to sell the drugs to help with his situation but needed the cash right then, pronto. So, stupid me, I took his coke and kept it, and a few days later he phoned and said he could repay me. We met at the fairgrounds, and I swear to every single person here today, I thought I was only returning his property and bein' repaid. It was dumb on my part, but I was only tryin' to help a friend. I realize I made a horrible mistake, and I apologize to the court and the citizens of our fine county and the police."

"This was a setup?" Cardwell emphasized.

"Yes, sir. I was entrapped. I wasn't in the habit of selling drugs."

Observing from the front row, Mason saw the commonwealth's attorney smile and whisper something to the detective beside him. Cardwell grimaced — his mouth twitched and his eyes nearly shut — before regaining his composure. He asked a couple more questions and sat down, buttoning his jacket once he'd settled in his chair.

The commonwealth's attorney, a tenacious lawyer named Tony Black, asked for a conference with the judge, and when court was called back into session, the jury soon learned — since Gates had carelessly introduced the subject, opening the evidentiary door — that he was indeed a drug dealer, and a relatively active one to boot. After Gates was eviscerated on cross-examination, and after a comically uncomfortable appearance by Clyde

Turner, the defense rested, and Black was then allowed to present evidence of Gates's several other drug transactions, lining up baggie corners of coke on the railing in front of the jury box as he ticked off dates and places. To make matters worse, he'd managed to provoke Gates with his questions on cross, had gotten him riled and flustered, and Gates sat slumped and glowering during closing arguments, a pissy, ill-tempered churl misbehaving in front of the very people who were deciding his fate.

While they were waiting for the jury to return, the sheriff was kind enough to permit Gates a taste of liberty. He sat — shackled at the ankles — with Mason on the blustery courthouse porch and worked on a cigarette, the smoke reinforced by the winter air when he exhaled, a deputy watching him from a distance. "I know what you're thinking," he said to Mason between drags. "But if there was one lie standin' between you and jail, you'd damn sure tell it."

Mason checked to make sure the policeman wasn't within earshot before he answered. "Yeah, well, I think I'd be more careful in selecting my material. The whole thing had the ring of an eight-year-old's sandbox fantasy, kind of made up on the fly — 'then Superman and the Hulk find a secret potion that makes them invisible and they enlist Batman and his rocket ship so they can travel to outer space to fight the Klingons.' That's how it came off."

Gates laughed, a raucous, unchecked burst of pure amusement that caught Mason by surprise. "Well," he said, giddy and frazzled, nothing left to lose, "I gave it a try. But I'm afraid you're probably right. Thanks for bein' with me and puttin' up with my shit. You take care of Mom." He tossed the cigarette onto the concrete and extinguished it with his heel. "You're okay with me, right? I don't want this to get us sideways with each other — we've been brothers too long for that."

"I'm fine," Mason said. "I just hate that you're in this mess."

"Not your fault, despite what I might've said when I was pissed off. Nobody could ask for a better brother. I appreciate it. And tell your beautiful wife I'm sorry I've kept you so tied up."

"Yeah." Much of Mason's aggravation had lifted. He leaned into his brother so their shoulders touched, bumped his knee with a fist. "Let's hope for the best. Who knows what a jury'll do."

"I'm ready to go inside," Gates hollered to the officer.

The jury sentenced him to a total of forty-four years, and as they filed back in to hear their verdict announced, every last one of them stared right at Gates, determined that he would see their mettle and what they thought of his lying and low behavior. Gates cursed when he heard the number, cursed out loud, and he vowed the men and women responsible for his sentence would most certainly pay a price when he was released, shouted it to them while the bailiff was clicking the cuffs around his wrists.

Gary Shelor raised dairy cattle and lived on a farm that had been in his family for generations. The foreman of the panel, he stepped away from the jury area and stood in front of Gates after they'd been threatened: "I wish you *would* come looking for me. One-oh-seven Harrell Ridge Road's where I'm at. I'll be waitin'." Almost every juror acknowledged Sadie Grace as they walked past her, and Justine Hiatt stopped and knelt and patted her on the arm.

"I'm sorry, honey," she said. "We just done what we thought was right. It isn't your fault your son sold drugs."

"I know," Sadie answered, weeping and gagging breaths, her hands trembling. "But why'd you have to take his whole life? It ain't as if he murdered someone."

CHAPTER FOUR

There's a meanness in certain men that is bestial and set apart. It's not the trite, commonplace variety born of an insult or a mouthy challenge, not the slap or fist or hasty knife that has its genesis in carousing and brown liquor and not the kind found in bullies, boyfriends who puncture their exes' car tires or the boss who trifles with employees for sport. Some men, as they say in Patrick County, are just plumb mean, mean without reason, mean without provocation. Gates and Mason's father, Curt Hunt, was such a man.

Curt was tall and stout like his sons, handsome in a commanding way, black-haired, dark-eyed, rawboned. Three years older than Sadie Grace, he married her the October following her graduation from high school. She was enrolled in college, studying to be a nurse, barely nineteen, away from home for the first time, and she wound up pregnant, steadfastly refusing to accept her condition until she was a full month late, praying and cutting deals with the Good Lord right up to the moment the infirmary doctor gave her the news. It was 1956. Belly-sick and clutching three white carnations, she discovered herself at the courthouse in Dobson, North Carolina, with her parents and a girlfriend, the ceremony, as it were, conducted by a skinny old clerk who switched her names around when he asked if she intended to take Curt as her lawfully wedded husband. They'd dated for over a year, so it wasn't the end of the world, but she confided to her happy-go-lucky aunt that she would miss school and the fun people and the life that was more seasoned and vital than the one she'd catch in Patrick County, a toddler on her jutted hip.

Curt never hit Sadie Grace. Instead, he raved and cursed and destroyed doors, plates and furniture to the point she almost wished he'd go ahead and be done with it, her tiptoeing dread as painful as any beating he could possibly deliver. They'd been married three months when he first showed himself, and the worst of it was how the outbursts would always catch her cold, their sneaky cat's feet. A year into the marriage, sitting at the dinner table, Gates napping in a playpen, eating the beans and weenies she'd prepared prior to leaving for a third-shift night at the plant, Sadie Grace inquired of Curt, who was saturating a slice of loaf bread in his buttermilk, whether he'd remembered to pay the light bill while he was in town. Curt stood and took his chair with both hands and broke it to pieces, first slamming it against the table — glasses shattering, the silverware airborne with each concussion — before finishing it off on the counter. Not content to quit there, he took a leg spindle and whipped it against the fridge until the wood finally splintered, the destruction, from beginning to end, steady and calculated rather than crazed. Then he snatched his coat and the car keys and stayed gone for two incommunicado days, stranding his wife and child since they owned only the single straight-shift Chevrolet.

And yet Sadie Grace stayed. She stayed because she didn't know what else to do, because she was afraid, because she was embarrassed, because she had no money and a dead-end job, because she was responsible for a baby boy, because it was an era before activists, vigils, shelters, Hollywood ribbons and laws worth a damn and because she became conditioned to violence in the same fashion a sideshow freak learns to tolerate the sharp point of a nail or some Holy Rollers become immune, bite by bite, to a rattlesnake's venom. She worked at the plant, tended to Gates, cleaned their shotgun shack of a house and kept her distance from Curt, always on edge, never taking a whole breath.

The best she had day to day was a phone call with her mama on the semiprivate line or a trip to buy groceries, where she might run into a friend and chat for a few moments without worrying about what kind of wrath a word or a pause between sentences could incite. Even her dull job became a sanctuary of sorts, the back and forth of the looms and the clacking of machines a monotonous comfort.

Sex was a forced march. Curt would arrive home from his job as a diesel mechanic, carrying his silver thermos and rounded lunch pail, his shirttail neither tucked nor all the way loose, and tap her away from the stove or washing machine with a blunt "let's go," undoing his trousers as he spoke. For a couple years, she actually found a measure of hope in his demands. When he ordered her to take off her clothes, she understood exactly what he wanted, she felt odd relief he was still interested and she believed she could somehow tame him, screw the mercurial cruelty right out of him and fix their troubles. Nothing changed, though, except that Mason was born in 1960, three years after his brother. Sadie Grace told the doctor to make certain Mason would be the last.

Gates and Mason, even as youngsters, did not enjoy the same safety from Curt's physical side that their mother did. As soon as they were upright, smacks, wallops, kicks, spankings and belt lashings came from their blind sides, helter-skelter. Who knew when or why. Six months would pass quietly, calm — Curt would chuckle at Red Skelton's black-and-white skits, repair a broken bicycle chain, cook venison steaks and quiz the boys about their schooling, rewarding them with a slingshot or Silly Putty or a single-blade pocket-knife if their marks were satisfactory. Then he'd erupt twice in a week. Out of nowhere, Gates received a hellacious beating for taking a SunDrop cola from the fridge, despite getting permission from his mother. Another time, Curt chased him down and flogged him with the butt end of a fishing rod for no discernible reason; Curt just shot him a look and the boy ran and it was innate almost, the tug of feral instinct for the father to catch his son and flail away. Not surprisingly, the boys learned to scatter when Curt would cant his head and curl his lips and demand to know "what you lookin' at?"

It was Gates, growing and gangly, who rebelled first, trying to fight back. Curt would light into him, and Gates would kick and bite and claw and launch impotent punches that his father easily blocked, often catching the boy's wrist and wrenching it until he took a knee. Young Gates became a furious, angry kid whose resistance and wild rushes made Curt that much worse, and Curt would frequently subdue him with a choke-hold and

123

taunt him: "You wanna hit me, boy? Hit me now — come on, let's see you do somethin'." During these melees his voice was always battened down, his words deliberate, pointed. Curt Hunt never took a drink of alcohol, never lost his temper in the sense he simply flew hot after reaching his limit and never seemed shamed by his violence.

For a while, Sadie Grace would stand nearby and beg him to leave the children alone, but it didn't take long before she was jumping in and wrapping herself around an arm or a leg, protecting her sons. Finally, she hit the bastard. It was summer of 1964, and Gates was seven, wearing a bathing suit and no shirt, no shoes, in the yard rolling a beach ball to Mason, and their father arrived home from his job, called hello to both his sons, and as best everyone could tell, grew angry because they weren't inside the instant supper was ready forty-five minutes later.

He stalked through the door and gave the top of Gates's head a good whack, and Gates told him he was a shitpot, kicking him in the calf to underscore the elementary-school profanity. Curt went straight to the choke hold, trapping the boy's windpipe in the crook of his arm and heaving him off the ground. Gates began sputtering and his eyes bulged and his face filled with blood and he pedaled the air with his naked feet. Sadie Grace came up from behind and whopped her husband in the rib cage with a cast-iron skillet, the warm grease splattering her hand and staining his blue shirt. He released Gates, ate his meal alone and warned Sadie Grace he'd kill her in her sleep if she ever got between him and his sons again. Then, pretty as you please, he tinkered in his shed, listened to the radio, ate a molasses biscuit and climbed into bed without washing up, his grimy boots and white socks discarded by the toilet. "Night, y'all" was all he had to say as he passed his family, timid on the sofa.

Sadie Grace took to stashing the boys at her mother's more and more, telling Curt they wanted to spend time with their grandma. The brothers slept in a tiny room on pallets made of quilts and cheap fuzzy blankets, in a house that smelled of analgesic rubs and musty clothes, while Sadie Grace stayed with Curt and made excuses and told lies and fell on her sword and watched the madman she'd married go from Jekyll to Hyde at the drop of a hat. Sex was rape for her by now. Curt would lead her to bed and roll her over and pound away, and it got so intolerable she'd half-puke, the acid burning her throat and seeping into her nose so that she had to cram it back down with a sick swallow and packed-in air.

Gates and Mason pricked their fingers and made pacts and swore all kinds of oaths, and they shuttled between their home and their grandma's and watched their mother do all she could to defend them when the pitched battles were fought, clinging to Curt's waist or leg, hitting him with a double fist, pushing, shoving, whatever it took to free them or keep the torment to a minimum. Curt would just shuck her off or hold her at arm's length and continue punishing his sons. It was Gates who got the brunt of it, and by the time he was ten, he never failed to take a sacrificial stand in front of Mason and suffer a backhand or an ass whipping in an effort to stick the bull's neck with a few lances or give the younger boy a running start. By rights, many of Gates's welts and bruises were not his own.

There came a day when the two brothers together — Gates at fourteen and sinewy, Mason on the cusp of adolescence — could give Curt a run for his money, and whether it was coincidence or not none of them ever knew, but on a glorious day in 1971, Curt Hunt didn't come home from work, simply up and left. He didn't even stop for his clothes or tools or arrowhead collection, hitting the road with a woman who kept the books at the garage. He never returned, and rumor had it they'd moved to South Carolina. No cards, no letters, no child support, no visits, no phone calls, no explanation. Dead gone. Mason's classmates catcalled him and raked him with taunts, and he pummeled the bejesus out of one of the Fain kids after the little snot announced in the school cafeteria that Sadie Grace was now a prostitute, an eleven-year-old's mixed-up dig that was dumb and inaccurate but to-the-marrow hurtful.

Without Curt's check, the family went from making ends meet to free lunches and blocks of gooey government cheese, though Sadie Grace signed up for welfare reluctantly and as a last resort and would drive to Mount Airy when she needed groceries so her friends and people she knew wouldn't see her redeeming food-stamp coupons for canned beets and value packs of hamburger. She took in sewing on the side for extra cash, the boys received used clothes and hand-me-down shoes from the better-off families at the big Baptist church in Stuart, and the county kept a concerned eye on the Hunt boys, watching them with a generosity that was never condescending or meddlesome. When Sadie Grace honestly reported her seamstress earnings to Mrs. Tatum at the welfare office, they weren't recorded for the state, and the family carried a steep tab at the drugstore, toward which Sadie was allowed to pay five dollars a month, an installment schedule that made it possible for her to keep her pride but had a negligible effect on her debt.

She dated on occasion, but a third-shift job and two ragtag boys kept her strung out and frazzled, and she'd seen enough of men for a while anyway, which isn't to say several of her suitors weren't decent and respectful, and one, a retired Army sergeant, actually discussed marriage. She didn't frequent the honky-tonks or doll up and drive to the bars in Greensboro, spurned her married supervisor's advances and promises of a raise and a newer car and, unlike some of her friends, never brought men by the house when the kids were there, "uncles" who would lavish extravagant attention on the children in hopes of bedding their mothers, promises of fishing trips and BB guns forgotten after sex and a free meal.

She stayed wed to Curt for nearly six years after he departed, figuring a divorce was an expensive formality, a luxury that would gain her nothing, and when she finally visited a lawyer and made a down payment, it was Mason who asked her why she'd gotten tangled up with such a bum to begin with. "I suppose I mistook quiet for reliable and solid," she said. "And nice looks for character. Then along comes Gates and I didn't have any choice. You just kinda get your foot caught in a trap, and there's nothin' much you can do."

Gates grew into a community darling, a joker and a football star, his ferocity on the field and violent, freight-train hits almost pitiable at times given that most people recognized the story behind them, and it shouldn't have surprised anyone when it became apparent a huge anger and a sturdy frame were the extent of his talents as a player and a person — by his final year of high school, he couldn't take the slightest bit of coaching or criticism, he couldn't bear not being king of the hill as a freshman at Virginia Tech, and he damn sure couldn't tolerate correction from some sissy English professor, stubbing up and pouting and then skipping class altogether, gone from college by Christmas.

Mason weathered their father differently. He was studious and self-contained, his own redoubt, a reader who appreciated the distraction of science fiction and the promise of *Ragged Dick* and *The Count of Monte Cristo,* a pupil who delighted his teachers, a kid who came from zilch and wore brogans and his brother's ill-fitting winter coat and still was elected student body president, prom king and "most likely to succeed." He occupied himself with every club, field trip, sports camp and school activity available, and he spent many a Saturday cheerfully volunteering at the pound, mopping urine and scooping dog crap, always making it a point to bring the strays and castoffs table scraps, a leftover chunk of biscuit or the burned end of a wiener, whatever he could scrounge, last suppers for most of the animals before Wanda the supervisor pierced them with a lethal needle and they yelped and lost their breathing and she burned them in the incinerator out back. Wanda told her sister you didn't need a Ph.D. to understand why he spoiled the skittish ones — the curs with lumps and cuts and tucked tails — more than the rest.

And while he didn't have his brother's size, swagger or aggressiveness, Mason was a gifted athlete also, a left-handed first baseman who earned a free ride at James Madison University and did well enough on the field to get drafted in the middle rounds by the St. Louis Cardinals. Ever practical, he thanked them for their offer of twenty-five thousand dollars and a minor-league contract, told them he probably didn't possess the skills to make a living as a big leaguer and accepted a substantial scholarship from the University of Richmond's law school. A torts professor gave him a part-time job, his grades were superior, his outlook sanguine, his prospects sound.

No matter how busy he was with classes or work, he never failed to keep his mother in mind, doted on her, surprising her with simple gifts and then the entire first check from his summer job at a Richmond law firm, occasionally returning home to sit with her on the brick steps and eat watermelon slices or plink snap beans into a thick glass bowl, the two of them jawing about local concerns, everything from a neighbor's cancer scare to the big Saturday-night Rook tournament. By

his third year of law school, his break from
Stuart was looking clean as a whistle, his way
clear — clear until he discovered himself on
Russell Creek Road, caught in Gates's slip-
stream, jarred and rattled, shit coming at him
he hadn't bargained for.

At Allison Rand's core was a patent invitation to sex, and there was nothing she could
do about it, even if she'd wanted to: her eyes
were green, honeyed embraces, slightly
languid but permanently in on a very private
joke, her hair blond, her smiles given more to
satisfaction than mirth, her shape, from calves
to breasts, overtly appealing. She was an inch
under six feet but never seemed large or
clumsy or heavyset, moving in fluid, breezy
steps, gliding into a room, reaching for a
cocktail and encircling it with fingers that
suggested caress rather than grip. She was
blessed with a voice perfect for her build,
neither flighty nor leaden, and a quickness in
conversation that was natural and unrehearsed. She had a tender heart and kind
disposition, and to her credit she never lorded
her appearance over other people. Even so,
an occasional acquaintance would keep her
at a distance and flay her name with whispers
and gossip, tut-tutting about her wardrobe or
habits or sports car or trips to Bermuda or
boyfriends or the "arrogant" way she reclined
against the railing during the Foxfield steeple-

131

chase, sipping a mimosa and making nice to everybody's date or husband. To the petty and envious, she was a bitch by beauty, and she'd come to accept the cold shoulders and lukewarm smiles for what they were, deciding the trade-off wasn't so bad, not so bad at all.

Allison met Mason late in the summer of 1985, after he'd graduated from law school. He'd taken the bar examination and been offered a job at McCloud, Flanagan in Richmond, recommended by one of his professors who did freelance consulting for the firm. They were at a bookstore in Shockoe Slip, Allison to hear a popular author read, Mason because he saw the crowd spilling onto the sidewalk and stopped to see what was happening. Allison caught a glimpse of him standing in the overflow near the shop's doorway and made no bones about nudging the woman beside her and turning back for a second, obvious gander, happy to spy the rare man who made her first cut: taller than she, handsome, possibly literate.

The author was reciting from her novel, and Mason hung around for twenty ponderous minutes listening to the story of a maddening husband and wife on a picnic, ants invading their sandwiches, their conversation about a sickly child. When the writer finished, Allison sidestepped to the end of a folding-chair row and turned to leave. Mason was lingering at the threshold of the store, watching her, waiting to find out if they were going to advance any further. He gave her a direct smile as she walked toward him.

"Hello," he said, cocksure. "I'm Mason. Nothing like a stiff shot of prose in the afternoon, huh?"

"Hi," she said, her eyes up and down, not long on his face. "Allison."

"I think we noticed each other during the reading."

"We did, yeah," she answered.

"Did you enjoy the show?"

"Yes. I think she's an excellent writer. How about you?"

"To be honest, I saw the crowd and was curious. I don't read much for pleasure. Wish I did."

"Ah, what a clever opening," she said impishly. "I'll rise to the bait." She moved away briefly to let a pair of chattering ladies pass. "What is it you read — not for pleasure — that you want me to ask about?"

Mason laughed. "I'll try to refine my pitch in the future. I'm a lawyer, a very new one. I took the bar exam in June, and studying for it provided me with all the reading I needed, thank you. I'm starting at McCloud, Flanagan soon."

"Do you think you passed?" she asked, and it hit Mason that everything about her, from the five-word question to her shortish skirt to the way she subtly spread her hands at the end of her sentence, was tinged erotic, the effect like moisture weeping through dam fissures, a puissant promise not quite held in check.

"I studied hard," he said. "Stayed up late, didn't shave, ate bad food, worried myself silly — did all the right things."

"What kind of lawyer are you?"

"I don't know yet, to tell the truth. Are we playing twenty questions?"

"Let's make it ten," she suggested. "Your bar exam for today. We don't really have time for twenty."

"I agree." He put his hands in his pockets, leaned against a bookshelf. "Have at it."

"Okay. Hmmm . . . Favorite lizard?"

"Gila monster." He smiled.

"Me, I'm a chameleon girl myself." She produced a tube of lip balm from her purse and began applying it while she spoke. "Joy buzzers, cigarette loads, rubber snakes or invisible ink?"

"Joy buzzers."

"Good choice, though they all have pizzazz." She dropped the tube into her purse, letting it go near chest level so that it free-fell through the air before landing. "Ever read Gertrude Stein?"

"Lord, no. I guess I don't mind laboring for a payday, but I don't aspire to be in a fistfight for three hundred pages, either." He stood straight, quit resting on the shelf. "She was a lesbian, yes? Of the wool-socks, pomade persuasion?"

"You should give her a whirl. She's amazing."

"We could have a deal breaker there."

"Last one," she said.

"You've got plenty more left."

"I know." She fluffed the side of her hair. "This is important: best painter ever?"

"Huh." He studied her and noticed she really did seem to be putting him to the test. "Well, I'd say either Vermeer or Salvador Dalí. Those were my favorites from the art class I took at JMU to fulfill my elective requirements, and names like Cézanne will land you in trouble when you're not sure how to pronounce the *a*." He hoisted his hands from his pockets, realized a store employee was watching him and definitely not wishing him well.

"I've heard it both ways." She hunted through the contents of her bag without removing anything. "Either's fine with me," she said, not looking at him.

"Where're you headed? I've got enough cash to buy us a drink or two, maybe a cheap dinner if you play your cards right."

"Let me see your driver's license, please." She'd finished with the purse.

"Why?" he asked.

"Well, I like to get an idea of people at their

135

worst, sort of reverse beer goggles. Plus, I can make sure you're not some ogre who lied to me about his name."

Mason gave her his license, and she held it in her palm and finger-read the information with her free hand. "Yikes! You favor Mr. Bentley, the guy who lives above the Jeffersons." Her eyes were lined and painted like a pharaoh's daughter, her hair an eighties Glamour Shot canopy. She smiled, white teeth, nicely sized and spaced and aligned.

"Really? I thought I looked more like Gary Cooper."

"Gary Cooper after a jailbreak or a bender at Studio 54, maybe."

Mason grinned at her.

"You and I were born in the same month," she noted. She finally met him eye to eye, a tiny flirt.

"So how about the drink?"

"I'm with my friend, and I shouldn't leave her," she said, checking her watch.

"Bummer. So am I at least allowed a question or a driver's license inspection?"

"Okay, but the clock's running." Mason noticed she had very little accent, finished off the *g*'s and didn't linger on her vowels.

"Worst song ever?"

She answered immediately. "I'll give you three. This is the kind of important info people need to prepare and have at their fingertips. One: 'Honey,' by Bobby Goldsboro; two: 'You Light Up My Life,' by Debbie Boone; three: 'Stairway to Heaven,' Led Zeppelin. Honorable mentions go to anything by John Cage, 'Convoy' —"

"Whoa now," Mason interrupted. "Hang on there. I'm filing a protest. It's not fair to use obvious novelty tunes."

"And finally, Neil Diamond and Streisand dueting on 'You Don't Bring Me Flowers' — terrible, painful commercial dreck. Being a boy, you will, I'm sure, object to the 'Stairway' inclusion, but I stand by that choice. It's so overwrought and dramatic, a screeching, loud, pompous, white-bread cliché."

"Pretty compelling list," he conceded. "You won't find me defending Robert Plant." He touched her at the elbow, a small come-on, almost a brush, his hand cupped, palm up, not much to it. "You're sure you're going to kneecap me on the drinks? I'd be glad to treat your friend. Bring her along." He glanced at the crowd inside. "By the way, I know who John Cage is. I took a music appreciation class, too."

"You're nice to ask, but I can't. My last name's Rand. It's in the book. A bunch of us are going to a big party tomorrow night on Monument Circle — you'll see the cars if you want to come."

They met that way, and they never embellished it or rearranged the facts or romanticized the circumstances or colored their motives. Years later, with no qualms and her head held high, Allison would tell close friends Mason simply wanted to fuck her from the first second he glimpsed her — no more, no less — and that was a compliment of the highest rank, a comforting connection, because say what you will, relationships, she was convinced, ignite in the eye. The most unassailable marriage has its roots in the quick math, the sine qua non, the base yes or no, the "bedrock issue," she was fond of saying, often pausing to enjoy the pun when she explained her thoughts. There's much more that has to come, many more integral numbers and symbols in the equation, a slew of other calculations, but by golly who wants to spend a lifetime with a sexless buddy, playing Scrabble or bridge, fussing over seating arrangements at a dinner party and sneaking home early from work every now and again to a bottle of Chardonnay and a mail-order vibrator. "Lay the block, *then* worry with the wallpaper and crown molding, you know?" she always remarked when she was on the subject.

They met up at the bash she'd mentioned, and it ran on until dawn. Mason drank sparingly — doing so, he frequently informed his hungover pals, gave him superpowers around midnight, when everyone else was stoned, sloppy and reckless — and Allison switched from white wine to White Russians to white powder, white being her party motif for the evening, she declared. A cab carried them to her town house, where they kissed and rolled and rubbed and tangled up on the floor, the couch, the huge mahogany dining room table and finally her bed. Her skirt got pushed to her waist, her blouse was mostly undone and her bra loose, and Mason shed his shirt in the hallway near her door, but that's where she stopped it, skin on skin, skin on cloth, exquisitely incomplete, a cocked pistol. She made them a breakfast of fried eggs, toast and cold smoked salmon, and they napped till noon, her head on his chest, her knee against his thigh. He left with her phone number, walked to a bus stop and went home happy as a clam, his recovered shirt all the way open, Eddie Grant's garish "Electric Avenue" looping in his skull, unshakable.

Mason was footloose that summer, at the tail end of a catch-as-catch-can romance with a feisty law student named Brenda who'd already packed her bags for a job in Boston, so with a clear conscience he phoned Allison the following morning and, not finding her, tried again that evening and three times the next day. Unable to afford a ritzy florist, he bought a quality bouquet of flowers from a street vendor, took the bus to her neighborhood, attached a note and had the doorman send up the gift, tipped the guy a dollar and then — when he didn't hear from her — fretted that his lilies and daisies and single sweeping gladiolus had been tossed into the trash or forgotten during a shift change, never making it to her. A week passed, and she didn't call.

He next saw her at the Border Café, a raucous bar in the Fan District, where he'd gone with two law school friends to knock around and make a meal of the free "Thirsty Thursday" promotional hors d'oeuvres, mostly overcooked chicken planks and greasy wings with tepid ranch dressing. When Allison arrived, he and his friend Frank Eggleston were chatting up two college girls from VCU, though Mason had left several times to stand in line and fill his small plastic plate and bring Frank and the women fifty-cent cups of draft Natural Light. Allison blew in with a group of noisy people, and as soon as she spotted him, she waved and smiled and didn't hesitate, cut through the crowd, beelining toward him. She kissed his cheek and introduced herself to Frank and the women, who resented the intrusion and coolly said, "Nice to meet you" without offering their names or any sense that she was welcome. "I loved the sweet gift," she said. "Sorry to interrupt, but I wanted to say hello." She focused on the woman beside Frank. "What a gorgeous top," she remarked, sounding sincere.

"Oh, thanks," came the curt reply.

"I'm glad we ran into each other," Allison

140

said to Mason. "Stop by the bar and visit if you have a chance."

"I will if Master Frank and the ladies allow me time off from my manservant duties, fetching fowl and keeping their chalices full of grog."

She briefly bunched her lips, amused. "I've never thought I'd care for a manservant. Now a stableboy, something sort of D. H. Lawrenceish, that might be the ticket."

Frank dipped his head and pushed his tongue into his cheek. He peered sheepishly at Allison, then caught his friend's eye. The two women hammered her with a stare that said, "You may be prettier than we are, but you're still a big classless bitch, D. H. Lawrence or not."

Mason didn't seem to notice. "I think, technically speaking, Wilbur Post was a stable boy. You're setting your sights on Brylcreem and cardigans, are you?"

Frank performed a quick Mister Ed riff, mimicking the horse's speech. He ended by observing that Mister Ed reminded him of Carol Channing for some reason.

"Nothing wrong with a snazzy dresser, Mason," she said. "Nice to meet you ladies," she added. "You too, Frank."

Mason kept track of her for another fifteen minutes or so, then excused himself under the pretext of using the restroom and threaded his way through the crowd to where she was standing at the bar. She was talking to a man and another woman, and from what Mason had observed, the man was making it apparent he had designs on her, leaning in to listen, handing her glass to the bartender for a refill, offering an aside no one else could hear. He pivoted a shoulder toward Mason as soon as he arrived, blocking him from Allison. Mason didn't like him in the least, and wouldn't have even if they weren't interested in the same romance. Allison introduced him — Clement Watkins, Jr. — and he shook Mason's hand a little too vigorously, smiled too aggressively and spoke with too much volume, as if he were pissing a circle around her with words. He was snarky and impatient and didn't bother to conceal it.

"Clement was just saying how crowded it is here," Allison said blandly.

"Cheap beer and free food will bring out the masses," Clement cracked. Despite the swarm of people and stifling heat, a white cotton sweater was tied around his neck. He was wearing snug shorts that halted before they reached mid-thigh.

"Lured me here," Mason said.

The other woman pressed closer to the bar, her drink held above the crowd, out of harm's way. "I'm switching to tequila," she said to Allison.

"We're just back from St. John," Allison mentioned, turning to face Mason, her expression and intent impossible to decipher.

Clement took this as an invitation to slide his arm around her waist.

"Hey, great. Hope you had blue skies." Mason was deflated, a bit embarrassed. His common rearing had never been a concern for him before, but for whatever reason, he suddenly, for a moment, felt like an interloper, smelling of high-dollar cologne — an extravagant birthday gift from his mom — and dressed in slacks he'd ironed himself while eating leftover KFC from the bucket and watching a *Dallas* rerun, a bare mattress and sleeping bag in his bedroom, a single fan blowing through the apartment to lessen the suffocating tenth-floor humidity.

"Thanks again for your kindness," Allison said cryptically.

"Ah . . . oh," Clement said, raising an index finger to his lips. "Are you the Romeo who sent my sweetheart the bouquet?" He was nearly as tall as Mason, with sharp, alert features and long brown hair that made him attractive in the casual fashion of men who are at ease around sailboats and tennis courts and know how to fox-trot at black-tie galas, who rarely wear socks and favor money clips over wallets.

"Pardon?"

Clement didn't flinch. "I asked if you sent flowers to Allison."

"I did, but what is it to you?" Mason

lowered his cup of beer.

"It's a free country, Marlon," he said, unruffled. "Send away. I just like to know where my competition lies." He directed a wolfish smile at Mason. "Though for the short term, not to put too fine a point on it, I can't see any reason for you to hang around here hitting on my girlfriend."

"Mason, not Marlon." He kept his composure. "And I suppose you're right. But things do have a tendency to change. Not many men can get away with wearing a cape over the long haul — you, Underdog, Elvis, French kings. Never know."

"What, pray tell, are you talking about?" Clement asked. "My first beer made me a little incoherent, too."

Mason patted his throat. "Oh damn — my bad. That's a *sweater* tied around your neck. Sorry." He bulled his way forward and kissed Allison's cheek, surprising her, and he peered at Clement, told him he'd enjoyed meeting him, deadpanned it with a wink in every syllable, and what was Clement going to do, quick as it came, in a jammed bar, with a guy as big and audacious as Mason. "Hope you liked the flowers," he said to her. "I delivered them myself."

"Yeah, well, don't forget, Underdog could fly," Clement said. "He was the star of the show."

Later, a friend of Allison's, at her bidding,

144

approached Mason and requested his number, and Allison woke him at three in the morning, inviting him to meet her in twenty minutes for biscuits and gravy at a diner on Cary Street. She poured vodka from a flask into her tomato juice and sprinkled the drink with a lemon squeeze, and they talked for two hours, shared the saturated biscuits, a BLT and a piece of pie with meringue topping, selected from the glass display case near the cash register. At first, Mason was sore about their earlier meeting at the bar, and he sat back against the wooden booth and frowned and tucked his chin and — even though he realized he should've been far more cavalier — wanted to know why she was keeping company with a guy dressed for the local theater troupe's *Chitty Chitty Bang Bang* revival.

"If you didn't think he was impressive, you wouldn't be so curious, now would you?" She took a sip of her doctored juice, looking at him over the glass's rim.

"I'd ask you the same question if you were dating Grendel or Sasquatch — flummoxed doesn't mean I thought he was impressive."

"I don't get the *Chitty Chitty Bang Bang* reference. I don't think it's technically too accurate."

"How about effete and goofy? That's what I was aiming for."

"Clement is neither. If he were, I wouldn't

see him. He's an architect, a published poet and a ranked amateur tennis player. He spent a month in El Salvador, not for the politics, mind you, but just trying to help out. He was stabbed in the arm and arrested once while he was there. I would hope, Mason, if you and I were together in a bar and another man showed an interest in me, you'd give him his walking papers, same as Clem did with you."

Mason mentioned he didn't care for poetry, informed her of his Matchbox car analogy, adding he'd need to see the hospital report before he believed Clement Watkins, Jr., had been wounded in the course of tending to the poor and unfortunate in another country. "Maybe he was nicked by a cricket bat or beaned by a snooker ball — I'd come closer to believing one of those."

She sawed off a chunk of biscuit, loaded it onto her fork and offered it in his direction, stopping near his plate so he'd have to leave his small sulk and move forward to get it. "You're blown up like a toad," she teased. "Jealous as a schoolboy."

He relaxed and took hold of the silverware and food, fed himself. "I'm not anything. I was a little — what's the right word? — *surprised* to discover you had a boyfriend after we spent the night together."

She cocked her head playfully. "So, what, you expected me to sit home arranging my figurines and reading the Brontë sisters, waiting for you to call?" She idly bumped a piece of piecrust with a spoon. "Listen, Mason, it's more complicated than you might think." Her voice changed, her face sobered. "Clement and I have been on and off for a while now, and we'd booked this trip months ago. He's about eighty-five percent for me, if you know what I mean, and that's more than a lot of people ever have, so I've been sorta trying to figure out if I've reached the max. It's like a dress that's flattering but not perfect, the kind you'd wear to work or to an important party but not to your five-year high school reunion. And who knows about you, okay? Or even if it matters long-term, since we've known each other for all of a few days. There's no need to be upset about it, not really. I'm sure you've probably been in the same situation."

"I guess," he answered. "Most everyone has. At any rate, it's decent of you to explain. I had a great night when we met, and — see there — not only did I call, but I sent flowers, too. It'll be my stated goal to move the meter to at least ninety percent."

They began dating the next evening and eight months later decided they'd see only each other, though with the exception of two ill-advised reunions with Brenda and a dizzy weekend of shacking up at Virginia Beach with a girl he met at a poolside bar, Mason didn't take advantage of their open-ended arrangement, and all his wandering came during the first month of their courtship. When they finally had sex it was unhinged and passionate, a celebration that began as she was helping him hang curtains in his austere apartment, and despite her bacchanalian zigs and zags and a bearing that rained down frank allure, she confided to Mason she'd been with only four other men, all of them serious beaus except a professional soccer player in Monte Carlo.

Allison was a painter, and a very talented one as best Mason could tell, and she made her living that way. She had no patience with Reagan but thought Tip O'Neill was a blundering, backroom hack, she never failed to acknowledge the donation hats in front of walleyed saxophone players and street-corner beggars, she attended the Episcopal church most Sundays — a Saturday night of merrymaking notwithstanding — and dragged Mason along and, most important, she seemed to have no malice, no scores to settle with anyone, no bruises, no trigger points, a bright woman whose sunny nature was never mistaken for naïveté. Oddly, she'd been to a series of colleges, but held no degree. She'd studied in Rhode Island, Paris, California, North Carolina and at a diesel school in Nashville, explaining to Mason she learned what she needed to know and left before the superfluous hours of calculus and medieval history.

Her rich, daredevil father had perished in a scuba-diving accident, became lost in an underwater cave and exhausted his air, a horrific death counted down by the needle of an oxygen gauge, and she often told people her mom died later of a broken heart, but the truth was cancer had gnawed up Sophia Rand's pancreas when her only child was twenty and nursing her at home, doling out pills and changing giant diapers, honoring a frightened parent's plea not to be hospitalized and given over to the custody of antiseptic strangers.

On a chilly, wet Thursday in the fall of 1986, she admitted to Mason she was afraid the dope and partying were chain-ganging her, and she asked him to miss work and look after her while she dealt with it. He rented a house at Nags Head, where he took care of her for eleven straight days. They walked on the beach, fired late-night bottle rockets toward the dark-gray ocean, prepared mac and cheese from a kit, cooked seafood spaghetti, carted Whoppers and fried-flounder plates from town to their kitchen and played Monopoly for real money and then sex so that "taking a ride on the Reading" became part of their private lexicon. Without any warning or preface, she woke up at dawn in their second week there and starting filling her suitcase and said she was ready to go home, done. "Thank you," she told him as they were poking down a sand and grass driveway, aiming toward the hardtop. "I love you."

It was on the return trip she revealed something else, that she'd been "fortunate with money," the beneficiary of a grandfather's trust, not enough to make her rich, but enough to make her comfortable, a windfall of close to two hundred thousand dollars every year.

"Shit," Mason joshed, "let's get married."

CHAPTER FIVE

Less than a year later, in April of 1987, that's what they did, got married by a priest at St. Stephen's Episcopal Church, not too far from Allison's town house. Mason was making solid money by now, and Allison had recently sold out a twelve-painting opening, and they set aside three weeks for their honeymoon, first visiting her flighty aunt in Naples, Florida, then stopping to spend time with Sadie Grace, who baked them a lemon chess pie and unpacked photos of Mason, everything from his baby shot naked in the bathroom sink to his blue-tuxedoed prom picture. Without protest, Allison accompanied Mason to a trailer park to meet Gates, and when their visit was finished, the brothers hugged and exchanged sincere good-byes and she covered Gates's hand with her own, told him she was pleased to be his sister-in-law, wrote down his address and sent him a note the next evening, enclosing a quick sketch of the Patrick County mountains, highlighted with

151

a splash of watercolor. From there, they traveled to a rented cottage in Cape Cod, which they scarcely left for two weeks, under each other's spell, slaphappy each morning when they awoke and remembered — oh, wow, damn — they were wed.

Their daughter, Grace Hannah Hunt, was born on September 8, 1988, and she was a delight to her parents, especially her father, who'd occasionally feared during Allison's pregnancy that whatever had haunted Curt might be recessive in him, might somehow bubble in his blood and turn him into a belt-swinging beast where his child was concerned. He grew ever more bumbling and protective as Allison's due date neared, became a sweet, devoted oaf, but at her urging he chose to wait outside the delivery room, elected not to loiter about underfoot mouthing slogans from behind a surgical mask as she ached and strained and tore giving birth. When he held Grace for the first time, he clutched her to his chest and knelt, his knees on the hospital's hard institutional tile, his eyes astonished by a face that jotted down everything superior from her parents. "We did it," he said to Allison, his whole attention on the baby, his voice raspy. True to form, drained and weary after a taxing labor, she blew him a kiss, proud and relieved and over the moon with her infant girl and giddy husband.

For the next several months, Mason took two-hour lunches and frequently worked half days, and despite their lip service about how happy they were for him and how they believed family was paramount, the partners at his firm grew disgruntled with his productivity and office habits. Mason recognized the tension but didn't give a damn, and in the late summer of 1989, he was hauled into a partners' conference and informed by a guy wearing a flamboyant red tie and matching suspenders that the firm respected his commitment to his daughter — and good for him, fine and dandy — but thirty billable hours a week would not be earning him a corner office or a partnership check. "You're a cracker-jack lawyer, Mason," the managing partner chimed in, "by far the best associate we have. But it's like we bought a Porsche that we can only drive at thirty miles per hour. We're telling you now so you won't feel ambushed or mistreated when we make promotion decisions."

Mason wasn't insulted. He'd known what was expected when he signed on — fifty billable hours per week, minimum — and he wasn't pulling his share of the load, plain and simple. "I appreciate the heads-up," he replied, surveying the table and making eye contact with everyone in the room. "Believe me, I'm grateful for the latitude so far, and I understand the economics of this firm. Still, it's altogether possible — assuming it's satisfactory with you ladies and gentlemen — that I've found my niche. I'm happy with my pay, happy with my status and happy with my hours." He stopped and rolled around a smile, signaling he recognized how his response would play with many of the lawyers listening. "Most likely, I'll be content as this firm's first associate-for-life." He paused again. "The understudy without ambition."

Allison was a darling from the get-go, come what may. "You know I can manage this by myself," she informed him that same evening, the family at their kitchen table, Grace shoveling up banana pieces with tiny soaked fingers. "I hate for you to be kept behind because of us." She shrugged. "Or, for all I care, you can quit today. Makes no difference to me."

"I'm okay. Hell, they're paying me close to eighty grand, and I'm around you guys enough to not miss the important parts. I figure I've got it made."

"You realize you don't have to do twice as much, pay off a family debt, prove something . . . because of Curt, because of *your* father." Her heel was tapping a wooden chair leg. She was twisting her wedding ring. "I just wanted to clear the air. To mention it. Once."

The suggestion irritated him. "Curt-fucking-Hunt," he croaked after a deliberate

154

silence, "has nothing to do with me and my daughter."

"Good." She made her voice comically deep, mocking his boss, a man with wavy silver hair and monogrammed cuff links: "We love having you home, in all your goldbricking, underachieving glory."

An interesting by-product of his vocational stall was that Mason appeared in court frequently and tried a number of cases, almost always the dogs, Hail Marys and quagmires no one else wanted attached to their résumés or partnership review files. "I'm the Hamilton Burger of Richmond," he quipped to friends. "Wile E. Coyote, attorney at law." Because he had nothing to lose in most instances, he was free to learn on the fly, and he became confident and adept in the courtroom, discovering how to corral evasive witnesses with cross-examination questions, mastering the tricks and rhythms of a jury proceeding, and sorting through which technicalities were critical and which didn't amount to a hill of beans. He was never unprepared or indifferent, and his clients were well served. Judges and other lawyers respected him.

And so it went, until the clerk of the Patrick County Circuit Court, a gracious, lanky man named David Hanby, phoned Mason at his office in Richmond, and not finding him there, located him at home, watching Grace

155

while her mother touched up a painting that was almost ready for a gallery in Delaware. It was 1993, May, and Grace was closing in on five years old. When the call came, she was alternating between a coloring book and a battered Etch A Sketch her namesake grandmother had purchased at a Stuart flea market. Mason was surprised to hear from Hanby, alarmed at first. "Everything okay there?" he quickly asked the clerk. "Mom? Is something going on with Gates?"

"Oh, no. I saw Sadie Grace at the church potluck last week, and she was fine, fit as a fiddle." He cleared his throat. "I assume Gates is still at Powhatan. I know that's a burden for you and your mother. I'm real sorry for you both."

"Thank goodness," Mason told him. "I'm relieved. It's not every day you receive a call from home, out of the blue."

Hanby chuckled. "Well, I certainly hope I'm not interruptin' you. I'm glad to see you high-powered, big-city lawyers are able to knock off early." His tone made it apparent he was kidding; if anything, he was impressed to find Mason cooling his heels on a Tuesday afternoon.

"As I understand it, the office runs better if I'm absent," Mason replied in the kind of modest give-and-take that was a mainstay in Patrick County, and also had the advantage of leaving Hanby with an impression that was

156

more favorable than the truth of the matter. "What can I do for you, Mr. Hanby?"

"Ah. I'm calling on behalf of Judge Richardson and our bar." Here he was precise, his diction stilted, the syllables flags and trumpets. "I'm going to connect you with the judge, but I wanted you to know our commonwealth's attorney, Tony Black, is leaving to take a job in Roanoke. I think you recall Tony?"

"Sure. A good guy, good lawyer. He prosecuted my brother. I thought he was fair and professional. He wrote my mom a nice letter after the trial. Sent an overly kind and unsolicited recommendation to Richmond when I applied for law school."

"Well, I doubt it was overly kind," Hanby remarked. "We're all very proud of you."

"Thanks," Mason said, his mind jumping ahead, trying to anticipate why the circuit court judge in Stuart had business with him.

"People know how you've taken care of Sadie Grace and how well you've done for yourself in Richmond. And I remember that home run you hit to win us the regionals."

"I had good coaching and talented teammates," Mason demurred. The Patrick County way, he recalled: unhurried, genteel, sidling up to the point without too much haste or urgency. He smiled, for some reason enjoying Hanby's slow, discursive civility. Mason knew the clerk would get there when

157

he got there.

"We'll miss Tony. Big shoes to fill."

"Yeah, he's been in office a long time."

"It's a very, very important job, servin' as the commonwealth's attorney," Hanby said.

"Yes. You hold people's lives and property in your hands. I agree." Grace showed him a jumble of black Etch A Sketch lines and squiggles before shaking them away. "Brilliant," he mouthed to her.

"Judge Richardson has to appoint someone to fill the vacancy, then we'll have an election."

"Okay . . ." The first hint of wariness arose in Mason's voice. Surely this wasn't why Hanby was calling.

"After thinkin' it through, the judge and the lawyers are prepared to offer you the job."

"Me?" Mason sputtered. "The commonwealth's attorney? There? In Stuart?"

Hanby was forceful. "You're what we're lookin' for, Mason. A smart, honest man who's familiar with Patrick and its people."

"Well, you know, I mean . . . I'm flattered to be asked, but I'm very much invested here, and —"

"I realize you'd be leavin' the catbird's seat," Hanby interrupted. "A high-class firm, a big city, excellent pay — but you give it some thought. There's a lot to recommend this part of the state, and oodles of people are behind this. People who want to see you

158

come home." He hurried ahead before Mason could speak. "I'm goin' to put Judge Richardson on the line. Hope to see you soon. I'll pass along your regards to everyone."

Judge Frank "Tunk" Richardson repeated essentially what Hanby had told Mason, formally extending an invitation to serve as the county's appointed prosecutor until the election in November. Richard Rogers was the president of the bar, and he took the phone next, promising he'd polled all the lawyers in town and no one would oppose Mason when he had to stand for the office. Not wanting to seem rude or conceited, Mason thanked them both and told them he would sleep on the generous offer, fully intending to call them back the next day with feigned anguish and a firm rejection, a tough decision, he'd say, but he'd have to remain in Richmond.

Oddly, when he stepped into Allison's studio and mentioned the offer to her, she seemed intrigued — this despite his tone of voice and ironic brow, which conveyed exactly how he sized up the idea. "So what do you think?" she asked. "Lovely, rugged country there. I've always been partial to Stuart."

"It's behind me. Sealed, padlocked, stored in the archives." He took a breath and exhaled it through his mouth. "Sort of a disconnect now, a greatest-hits recollection of the place and that's about it, very bloodless. We've discussed it before, my sentiments."

"I know. But you've never had any animosity. I've never heard you mention you hated Stuart or Patrick County. People were good to you, you had friends, you were a star athlete, your mom was a saint, you had some fun times."

"Good and bad both. Like anyone else. But that's not the point; that's not why we would or wouldn't go." He was standing at the border of a drop cloth. He stooped and took a brush from a bunch in a quart jar. "No movie theater, no airport, no galleries, no plays, no museums, no colleges, no circle of smart, educated friends, no bookstores, no restaurants with tablecloths." As he ticked off each shortcoming, he tapped his palm with the brush. "One public high school. A nosy, gossipy, inbred culture. Turnip greens and corn bread. Coon hunting. Fundamentalist, intolerant churches that frown on makeup, a glass of wine and women in slacks. Moonshiners. Square dances. Squinty-eyed hunchbacks in bibbed overalls who refuse to let their kids receive a free measles vaccination, swearing it's government poison."

Allison laughed. "Is a squinty-eyed hunchback like a gnome? Same as your basic bridge troll? You forget I've been there — it's hardly that primitive."

"I didn't say it was, entirely." He was slowing down, catching himself. "The county's

160

blessed with a lot of positives. Life there has its own proud pace, and the great majority of people are trustworthy and helpful in a pinch."

"And I'm sure, Rex Reed, you'll really miss those movies and plays." She gave him a mischievous look, her lips curled with amusement, her eyes in a caper. "When's the last time you went to either?" She flickered a grin before turning serious. "The Bible-thumpers and busybodies I can do without, but maybe we should at least think about this. You can nitpick any city — Richmond, for example, is too crowded and clogged with traffic and socially stratified and overpriced. You could say that if you were being harsh. Too much crime here, way too much. Too much third-generation money. Too many snooty, pretentious people."

"Are you serious?"

"I'm not — well, I'm not saying one way or the other. I like change and movement. I always have. The idea of a home with land and a view of the mountains sounds okay. I've been in this same town house for who knows how long now, sort of doing the identical things. Why not break the routine? I mean, at least think about breaking the routine."

"I enjoy the routine," he protested.

"You know, a rut's a routine with a little deeper groove."

"Are you insinuating you're restless or stifled here? Bored?" The notion caught him off guard, and it showed in his expression. "I hadn't picked up on that."

She walked to him and took the brush out of his hand. "I'm happy as can be, Mason. I've loved every day we've spent together. But I think we're coming to a spot where if we stay here, we'll be staying here for good. Permanently. Which may be great. I say let's just take a look around. If not Stuart, then let's keep an open mind. There's a lot here for Grace, but she'll probably never have a yard or pet a horse or splash in a stream. I want us all to be in the best possible place. I adored the three years we lived in the country when I was a little girl, our house in Arkansas. It's not totally abstract for me."

Mason tried to suppress a smile. "You make Patrick County sound like a cross between Walden Pond and some fanciful PBS show. As best as I can recall, having lived there for eighteen years, I never splashed in a stream or touched a horse. We did have a yard, and it was a pain in the ass to keep it mowed." He let the smile form. "Hey, if we do it, if we move, I can teach Grace how to skin a bear and live off the land. How to roll her own cigs. Drive a Trans Am. Find water with a divining rod. Plow with a mule. Whittle in a rocking chair. Tell the weather by reading the stars. The whole shebang, all the earthy, mystical, folklore shit only we rustics know."

Allison laughed, bent at the waist and folded her arms across her belly. "Don't forget she'll need to know how to handle a longneck in a bar brawl."

"There we go." He was still smiling.

"So call them back," she urged him.

The playfulness vanished. He was quiet for a moment. "I guess the whole deal with Gates clouds things, too. Not a situation you want to be reminded of every day — your brother the imprisoned drug dealer." He'd never told his wife about Wayne Thompson's shooting, nor did he ever intend to. "But I suppose we can pay my mom a visit and mosey around. It's a good enough place — hell, it's a fine place in a vacuum if you want that kind of life. I'm just not sure I can change gears from what I'm used to."

Allison walked to the big window that framed their avenue. "I know there are some parts you can't really erase, that'll always be stamped on you. But try to take a fresh look. No regrets if we do it this way, right? And I'm going to try to come at it different, too. I've always seen it as your hometown, a quirky little village we spend a day or two in. It may be strange if I think about it, you know, more long-term." She stared out the window, completely turned away from Mason, her shoulders uncovered except for the two fabric straps of her top. "But, jeez, the

163

city is getting monotonous," she said, her voice flat. "I've thought about the West, too. Some new scenery couldn't hurt my painting. Or this nice town I visited in high school, outside of Boston, called Maynard."

"Who woulda thunk it," Mason said. "Jerri Hall wants to park the jet and raise chickens."

On the first day of June, Hanby, along with Richard Rogers, met Mason, Allison and Grace at the courthouse that dominates the sloped, quarter-mile-long Main Street in Stuart, and they were soon washed over by hospitality and goodwill and the enthusiasm of old friends who'd heard the rumor Mason was planning to assume Tony Black's job. There were free plate lunches at the Coffee Break, welcome-homes and recountings of key hits and baseball championships. As they toured the street surveying the stores and businesses, seeing what was available, Mason's old biology teacher, brought low by a stroke and relying on a cane, told him from a mouth that only half worked he was "tickled to death" for him, especially in light of what Mason had overcome. Grace was scared of the wracked, deformed stranger, but Allison didn't flinch, squeezing Mason's hand as the afflicted man struggled to enunciate his words, her eyes switching back and forth between her husband and his former teacher. Dinner with Sadie Grace was at the swanky winery restaurant in Meadows of Dan, and that night Grace was fascinated by a fat, thieving raccoon who sat on his haunches in the midst of Sadie's overturned garbage, filling himself with black, agile paws.

They stayed for two days, spending the night at Sadie Grace's, Mason serving as a tour guide for his wife and daughter, showing them the county's pig paths and obscure beauty, winding their car up Squirrel Spur at dawn to watch the sun saunter out from the Blue Ridge Mountains, then dropping by Barnard's Store in Kibler Valley, where cantankerous Bill Barnard presented Grace with a piece of horehound candy and Mason paid a quarter for a cold Pepsi. Sadie Grace played it close to the vest, waiting until they were about to leave for Richmond to tell them how much it would mean to have her granddaughter nearby. They made two more trips to Stuart, studied the elementary schools, the doctors, the homes for sale, the cost of living. They considered Wrightsville Beach, flew to Boston and tooled around Maynard, and contacted the chambers of commerce in Fairhope, Alabama; Bozeman, Montana; and Charleston, South Carolina. Not yet ready to quit on Richmond altogether, they toured several open houses on its fringes, thought about a home close to the city but not so engulfed by it.

But the more time Mason spent in Patrick

County, the more he warmed to returning, and he confessed to Allison that part of the attraction was tied to a clichéd sense of accomplishment, the validation he would feel as a poor local boy who'd struck it big and was coming home to parades and fanfare, a success story in spite of everything. They decided to move in late July, finally persuaded by three circumstances. They received a call from their Realtor informing them a forty-acre farm was available in Patrick Springs, a spread with a stream, a barn, a view of Bull Mountain and a jaunty porch surrounding the front and flanks of the house. Additionally, that same day's *Richmond Times-Dispatch* reported there'd been yet another shooting on Hull Street, and a frustrated councilman was quoted as saying the city's schools were a failing mess, not likely to improve.

They visited the property with Grace two days later and tried out the place for a night, rocked on the porch and watched the deer slip into the pasture and take up their twitchy grazing, their ears erect, tense, restless, searching. After they sat with Grace and talked her to sleep at her grandmother's house, they ventured to the barn with a bottle of mediocre Merlot the owners had left for them, and they drank straight from the bottle and had sex that was far more carnal than poetic, finishing with Allison gripping the rough-hewn oak board of a stall front, naked, and Mason behind her, his hands tight on each side of her waist, his bare feet digging in the dirt.

The next morning they signed the paperwork agreeing to purchase the farm. The Realtor presented them with a country ham in a coarse cloth sack, and they held hands as they left his office, a copy of the contract folded in half and sticking out of Mason's hip pocket. They kissed next to their white Volvo, for everyone to see. Strangely, though, during the return ride to Richmond, Allison seemed distressed — she was fidgety, unhappy with any of their music, unable to get comfortable in her seat, squirming, impatient with Mason's chatter. "I hope we're doing the right thing," she said at a stoplight in Danville, but she didn't have any more to add when Mason attempted to draw her out.

"We can always call them and try to cancel," he said when she revisited the subject fifty miles later. "Forfeit the escrow payment and forget about it." He peeked at her, hoping to get a read. "I don't understand the change of heart."

"I'm not saying there *is* a change of heart, okay? This is just such a major step. It's pretty damn overwhelming when you actually do it. Talking about it and looking at brochures is one thing, but . . . now . . . it's happening." She was sitting with both feet pulled up on the seat, her knees encircled and gathered

167

against her chest. "I'm really excited," she insisted. "It's just I can't help thinking, looking back, about how much I've changed. I hope I don't miss, you know, the glamour — well, that's not the right word — the sort of cutting edge or whatever. I mean, I don't miss it now. I love you and I'd die for Grace — but I don't want to wind up faded and drab, a fishwife or something. That's a huge part of what I'm saying."

"I can't believe you'd feel that way." Mason looked across at her, lifted slightly from the gas. "You're as brilliant and sexy and talented as the day I met you, and where we live isn't going to change any of that." He glanced at the highway, then checked her again. "There's not a more irresistible woman on the planet — Picasso crossed with Bridget Bardot. Margaret Thatcher's brass. Men will always drop what they're doing and fall in line, no doubt about it."

"It's hard to explain."

"What's hard to explain?" he asked.

"I don't know." She sighed. "I'm trying to make sense of stuff. I hope I'm doing this for the right reasons."

"Well, I thought we'd talked about the reasons. You wanted to leave Richmond more than I did."

"We've talked about it," she said, peeved.

"So what's the matter?"

"Nothing," she answered dully.

"There has to be something bothering you."

"It's okay."

"Is there a message I'm supposed to be able to decipher from your clues and heavy hints? Last night we're on cloud nine, we just bought a new house, and now you're weird for reasons you can't explain to me. Your neck's starting to splotch, so it must be pretty serious."

"Can we get Twizzlers at the store?" Grace interrupted from the rear of the car.

"Maybe, honey," Mason said, pegging her in the mirror when he answered.

"The next place," she said.

"Okay," Mason answered, distracted.

"The next place."

"Yes."

"I've tried to tell you as best I can," Allison said. "There's no reason to beat me up about it."

"We're making the right choice," he said. "And I'm hardly beating you up."

"Yes you are."

"No I'm not. I'm simply trying to understand your problem."

"Well, I suppose there is more to it, but I don't want to talk about it with you in this mood."

"What mood?" he demanded, tossing his hands so they slapped against the steering wheel.

"The mood you're in." She was almost to tears.

"This is stupid. What's wrong with you? Why're you so emotional all of a sudden?"

"You wouldn't understand anyway."

"Not unless I'm Mandrake the Magician and can read your mind."

"Stop! My Twizzlers!" Grace wailed.

"I'm sorry, honey. I didn't see the store."

"You promised."

"The next one. You watch and tell me when it's coming."

"You told me a story," Grace said sullenly, feeding on the discontent in the car, sensing her mother's withdrawal.

"It wasn't on purpose," he assured the child. "I'm sorry if I've pissed you off," he said, returning to Allison. "I was only trying to get at what's plaguing you. I suppose I'd have been better off simply ignoring you and the method acting you've been doing for two hours, all the bottled-up angst over there." He barely waited before continuing. "Of course, then I get blasted for *not* asking, for being inconsiderate and self-centered."

She was composing herself. The red splotch on her neck had stopped its attack. "I'll remember this the next time you're in a bad way. I will."

"Whatever," he said, defeated. "You'd think we'd be celebrating." He was almost to another store but couldn't stop in time to make the turn. "Oh damn."

"Stop! You said you would." Grace was instantly bawling, revving up on big gulps of air and loosing them with all the shrieking disappointment she could muster.

Mason pressed the brake more abruptly than was called for and veered to the shoulder of the road. He jammed the Volvo's shifter into Park, turned off the ignition, exited in a huff and trudged back down the side of the highway to a gas station, cars whizzing by, their warm whooshes butting into him as they passed. He bought a pack of Twizzlers, a liter of orange drink, a giant bag of M&M's and a box of cookies. "Go to it," he said to Grace, handing her the cache of goodies as soon as he reached the car. "Knock yourself out."

"Pick one, please," Allison said to her while Mason was jerking on his safety belt and clicking it secure.

The child studied the bag's contents, reached in and removed the M&M's. "These," she said.

"Hand them to me," Allison calmly directed her.

Grace complied, and Allison poured out a handful of colored chocolate and returned it to the girl, then took the rest of the treats, rolled down the window, and tossed them onto the ground, still in the bag.

Grace didn't bat an eye, didn't protest, and she started in on the candy, content and mute. Before accelerating onto the highway, Mason checked his daughter, swiveling so he could see her. She held a single red M&M pinched between her thumb and first finger and bit into it with her front teeth, peering at her father, church-mouse silent, too canny even at age four to utter a word.

"So you're not going to tell me what it is?" he asked again as they drove off, but Allison completely ignored him.

A conscientious wife, she apologized two days later, made him a nice meal and wore her pricey perfume, promising him her bad patch was nothing more than stress from the decision and certainly had nothing to do with him. "I can't wait for us to get there," she said. "I'm ready."

Chapter Six

"We was wonderin' if you could help pay for your daddy's funeral," asked the woman whose voice Mason heard for the first time ever when she said hello. Johnette was her name, and she requested the money before she told him Curt was dead, a cart-before-the-horse rush that left Mason — blinking, jolted — to inquire if his father was in fact deceased.

" 'Course he's dead. Why else would we be wantin' you to help bury him?" The response was a cocktail of bitchiness, impatience and entitlement. She was calling from Marion, South Carolina.

"I haven't seen him in years," Mason said. He was in his Richmond office, the James River viewable if he maneuvered his chair close to the window and strained his neck. "Why're you calling me?" Flabbergasted, he heard his voice change registers. "So he's gone, huh?" he said before Johnette was able to respond.

"You still his son, ain't you?" she answered.

"And who, exactly, are you?" he demanded. "How do you know Curt?"

"I'm his wife."

"His wife?" This wasn't the woman with whom he'd hightailed it out of Stuart. "You were married to Curt?"

"Common law," she said dourly. "We was common-law husband and wife."

"Ah, I see. So you and Curt shacked up for a while."

"We was together for nearly three years, thank you."

"Well, last time I checked, there's no such thing as common-law marriage in this part of the world."

"Call it what you want, he was my husband. So are you goin' to pitch in?"

"Tell you what, Mrs. Common-Law Curt Hunt. Put me down for a thousand, and we'll just knock it off the six-figure unpaid child support tab he ran up with my mother. How's that?"

"It's a damn sorry son who wouldn't want to see his own daddy properly laid to rest."

"It's a damn sorry daddy who'd walk out on his family and abandon them. And that's not the worst of it."

"Well, he left you somethin', but you can bet you ain't goin' to be gettin' it with that kinda bad attitude."

Mason snorted into the receiver. "There's

nothing he could leave me I'd be interested in." He snapped back his desk chair so he was looking at the ceiling. "Thank you for calling. Lots of luck finding anyone who'd pay for Curt's funeral. Good-bye." He gave the phone a rude toss onto the carpet, where it lay bleeding long-distance rants and threats and profanity until Johnette ran out of steam and ended the call.

He allowed what he'd heard to steep and spread until it had his whole mind. He remained reclined in his seat waiting to see how it would strike him, sitting there as if he'd chugged some mysterious potion and was tensely awaiting the results, but nothing came, nothing moved or stirred or broke or changed, nothing big or small, not so much as a nibble of melancholy because he'd lost his father for good. Allison was at their town house packing for the move to Stuart, and he called her with the news, and she was soft and comforting on the phone, her words cushioned. She offered to drive to his office; he told her there was no need.

After a few minutes, he stood and gazed through the window at the city's ragged backside — bridges, warehouses and construction cranes — and he became angrier and angrier precisely because he felt so little. His dad had passed away, and instead of a grief born of bottomless love and a blood bond, nothing was registering, and that missing hurt was the final of Curt Hunt's thefts, the capstone of his selfish, ill-tempered life. Mason laid his head on the cold, air-conditioned glass, then let his weight follow and closed his eyes, twenty-one stories high, pitched forward.

Gates phoned collect while Mason was still at the window. Mason never refused his calls, which came at least three times per week on a direct line, and he sent cash to keep his brother's canteen account solvent, listened to his carping and plans and schemes when prison was grinding on him, rounded up a firm secretary to type the wacky jailbird pleadings Gates sent along for comment and correction and did whatever else he could to make Gates's meager confines tolerable.

"You hear the news?" Gates asked after the operator had finished with her questions and Mason had accepted the charges.

"Yeah, just now."

"So the devil is dead," Gates said, the sentence almost singsong.

"So I'm told. How'd you find out?"

"A lady from South Carolina called and left a message with the warden."

"I forgot to ask what killed him." Mason could hear the prison hubbub on his brother's end, jeers and shrill hostility, the occasional echo of metal against metal.

"I'd like to think the Good Lord hunted his ass down and hung him up by his heels and beat the holy shit out of him."

"I doubt the Lord has that much time to devote to individual cases."

"So we're attendin' the funeral, right?" Gates asked. "You're going to spring me for a day?"

"Hell no. I'm not about to go to his funeral. Have you lost your mind?"

"Listen, Mason, no one hates Curt more than me, but it's my one chance to get free of this shithole, okay? If you pay for an off-duty cop, they'll let me out for the service. I consider it a mini-vacation. Hell, it'll be about the only thing our sorry dad has ever done for me. If you don't want to make the drive, hey, cool, that's fine, but please loan me the cash so I can spend a few hours in civilization, maybe eat a Big Mac and some fries and smell air that doesn't stink."

"I'll make the arrangements. Sure."

"Thanks, Mason. I don't know what I'd do without you." A man in the background screamed at another inmate, cursing furiously.

"I suppose I should call Mom," Mason said, dreading the chore. "Let her know."

"Yeah, I guess."

"I'll have my secretary contact the prison." Mason paused. "When's the funeral? I didn't even think to ask."

"Day after tomorrow. Hell, Mason, just come and visit me. You don't have to sit through the service or take part in anything. After everybody's cleared out, maybe you and me will have the pleasure of pissin' on old Curt's loose dirt."

"We'll see."

Almost on impulse, Mason left for South Carolina the morning of the funeral, unable to rest, setting out at four thirty, dark and muggy, a Styrofoam cup of black convenience-store coffee his companion, the radio neglected, a map in the passenger's seat, the headlights forlorn on the interstate, eating into the distance. He'd left Allison a note: "Gone to the funeral. See you tonight." He was grateful when the sun brightened the sky and more cars joined him on the highway, felt better in traffic and color.

He located the funeral home and was greeted by a professionally solemn young man with a gold bracelet and a droopy boutonniere. Mason was early, and the lad sympathized with him about his "loss," then ushered him into a small chapel for some private time with his father, stepping dramatically backward through the double doors and pulling them closed as he withdrew, bowing slightly all through his departure. Mason caught the scent of funeral flowers, and the full-throttle air-conditioning braced him, shocked his skin. Curt's casket was in the front of the room, a gaudy floral heart atop spindly metal legs posted beside the body. A sash with gold glitter words bisected the arrangement, but Mason couldn't make out the letters from a distance.

He walked to the casket, aware of how many steps he took, counting them in his head as he went. He heard the air blowing from vents, tasted a sour current in his spit, noticed the sway in the floor when he stopped a few paces short of his dead father. GONE TO GOD, that's what was written on the sash. He didn't hesitate or reflect or ready himself before looking down at Curt. The mortician's best art couldn't conceal how diminished the body was, wizened and faint, as if a considerable portion of him had left the earth ahead of the remainder. It struck Mason that he was staring at painted-up dregs, sediment in an ugly blue suit, dross prettified by rouge, powder and a belly full of sawdust. He was relieved in a certain sense that the remains were so different from the dreadful man he remembered, so diluted they were unable to summon Curt in any meaningful way.

He stood there for several minutes, taking a long look at his father, finally touching one of his entwined hands — clay cold — before turning away, recalling how powerful they had seemed to him as a boy. He took a seat on the first pew, bowing his head and dabbing at his eyes with his sleeve, emotional because of what he'd never had, crying-mad because of such a fundamental disappointment, gypped and betrayed by his own damn daddy.

Johnette arrived with her three sisters and two grown sons, wearing sunglasses and solicitously attended by this flock of relatives, woozy and weak-kneed until she learned Mason was present. She recovered from her grief and regained her strength long enough to dicker with him about payment for the funeral, smoking a cig and exhaling from one side of her mouth, wagging a finger at Mason and leaning forward in her chair when she spoke. She tapped the ashes on the floor of the business office, where they were meeting by themselves.

"You don't jest get to come here and enjoy all this for free," she informed him. "No more than you'd expect to walk into Dollywood or the demolition derby or whatever without payin' for a ticket. Especially since you're his son and rich as Midas." She was in her fifties, fleshy, with an abundance of dyed-black hair and a round, attractive, gentle face that gave no warning of the harridan underneath.

"So how much is my ticket to the Curt Hunt farewell tour?"

"I don't see why you shouldn't pay it all, especially bein' such a smart-ass. The whole six thousand and change." She expelled a stream of smoke. "And you better believe you ain't gettin' the stuff he left you with your present attitude."

Rank curiosity got the better of him, and they negotiated a payment of five hundred dollars to Johnette Flippin for "reimbursement," and she sent one of her sons to fetch Mason's legacy. The boy returned twenty minutes later with two large toolboxes and a letter, belligerently announcing to Mason he'd taken the socket set for himself, because that's what Curt would've wanted. "I'm sure," Mason said sarcastically. He put the letter in his suit pocket, saving it for a less hectic setting.

There were maybe twenty-five people at the service, and Gates arrived immediately before it got under way. "Hope they hired a Primitive Baptist," he said, laughing, as he and Mason and an off-duty cop sat outside in the swampy South Carolina air, flying, humming pests occasionally lighting on their necks or hovering around their ears, their *zzzzzz* sounds like tiny drills. "The longer the better." Gates was sausage-wrapped in a suffocating black suit, a wool monstrosity that had him sweating all over himself, even with the coat removed. It was the suit he'd been wearing the day of his conviction in Patrick County. He'd gained fifteen or so pounds, and his skin was eerily white, as if he'd been bleached, colorless except for dark, concave sinkholes beneath his eyes. Yet he seemed fairly chipper, fairly upbeat.

"You not going in?" Gates's keeper asked.

"Hell no." He laughed. "I'm plannin' to sit right here and visit with my brother." He was in leg irons, but his hands were free. "Enjoy bein' outside and the fresh air."

"Nothing to me, one way or the other," the man said, then introduced himself to Mason. He moved to another bench to allow the brothers some privacy, and a funeral home employee brought them all cold sodas.

"You recognize anyone here?" Gates asked. "Who the fuck would come to Curt's funeral?"

"I'm pretty sure I saw a representative from the Joan Crawford Foundation," Mason cracked. "Then there was the ambassador from Dante's innermost circle. The guy with the fur hat was Rasputin, I think." He sipped his drink. "Seriously, I ran into our cousin, the redheaded kid who used to come by with Curt's sister. He works for the railroad. Seems nice enough. Mostly it appears to be the high-white-trash clan of his last squeeze, this Johnette bitch."

Gates lowered his head and aimed for Mason's ear. "So you're headed back to Stuart," he said confidentially. "It's a done deal."

"Yeah. Pretty strange, huh?"

"Strange, maybe, but good for me, I'm hopin'."

"In what way?" Mason tensed, set his drink on the bench but didn't release it.

"Shit, Mason, you'll be the man, the commonwealth's attorney." His face grew animated, his voice quieter. "I didn't want to mention anything on the phone, but for damn sure you can pull some strings for me now. Get me out on probation or find a loophole or have 'em lose my file. We both realize how this shit works. You can help me, get me out from under this. You know I got a raw deal anyway. You'd just be putting things right."

Mason frowned. Shook his head. "I couldn't do anything if I wanted to, okay? Are we clear on that? More important, you need to understand that while I will continue to help you in any legal way possible, there is no frigging chance I'd even think about doing something that would leave me or my family at risk." He locked on to his brother, eye to eye. "Don't ever ask me again. You hear? Forget it."

Gates ducked his head. "Hey, cool. I know what's what. I understand. Just keep me in mind. If the chance ever comes up, I know you'll go to bat for me."

"I'll do my job, pure and simple."

"Man, I'm proud of you," Gates said, changing his tack. "No matter what happens."

"Yeah."

He thought about sharing his father's letter with Gates, but decided against it, unsettled as he was by his brother's desperation and convict's wheedling. They made small talk until the funeral concluded, the deepest notes of an organ's closing hymn vibrating outside to where they sat. Mason had no interest in attending the graveside service, so he wished Gates well and slipped the cop two twenties and told him to make sure they enjoyed a good meal on their return, steaks if possible. Before leaving, he phoned his office in Richmond and instructed his secretary to contact the bank and stop payment on Johnette Flippin's check.

He opened the letter sitting in his car, the engine cranked, the air on high, battling the trapped South Carolina heat in the interior. The letter was in his father's hand, the script unlearned and shaky:

To Mason,
So I hope you are find. Me I'm not to good. They tell me I have some Cancer. I am in the hospitel. I wanted you to have all my tool's when I am gone. Johnette will give them you. I'm sorry I haven't been there allways. I don't no why you an your brother and Sadie had it in for me. Why you hated me and done me like you did but I wonted you to have my tools cause there's no bad feelings from me. I for give you. An your mom and Gates to. I hope you for give me. Take care, your dad.

love, Curt S. Hunt

Mason read the note three times, and when he finished, he was left with a weak, sad grin. "Perfect," he said out loud. "What else did you expect?"

CHAPTER SEVEN

"It's not like I have a periodic table of the elements nailed to my wall."

Those were the first words Mason ever heard from Custis Norman in person. Mason had gently rapped on Custis's office door and poked his head — cautiously, politely — through a small crack without violating the threshold. Custis was at his topsy-turvy desk, facing away from the door, his feet plopped on a credenza, a phone receiver jammed between his cheek and formidable shoulder, a newspaper folded down into a fourth of its size held aloft, the crossword puzzle visible from where Mason stood, peeking into the room.

" 'Symbol for tin,' and it's not *t-i* or *t-n*. What kind of feebleminded vice president are you, anyway? Shouldn't you know this, being's how you guys make metal?" He twisted toward Mason, then slid his wing tips off the furniture one at a time. "Gotta fly," he said, hanging up the phone.

Custis was impossible to miss in small-town Stuart, and during visits home from college and law school, Mason had seen him on occasion, collecting his mail from the post office or inflating his tires at the old Gulf station, but they'd never crossed paths close enough to actually meet. Robust, imposing, hefty, bigger than Mason in every respect, over six and a half feet tall, Custis was a force of nature with quick brown eyes, blunt features and black, black skin. A thicket of dreadlocks, carefully barbered and groomed, corkscrewed out of his leonine head. "My brother in Memphis," he explained, glancing at the phone. "You must be Mason Hunt." He came around the desk, covering the distance in two nimble strides. He wore a wrinkled seersucker coat above khaki pants, and the idiot faces of Larry, Curly and Mo spilled down his tie. "Welcome."

"Tin is *s-n,* if I'm not mistaken," Mason said good-naturedly. "Strange what kind of junk sticks in your mind. Maybe that'll help break the stalemate." They shook hands. It was late in the summer of 1993, Mason's first day at his new job.

Custis was the assistant commonwealth's attorney in Patrick County, a position he'd held for twelve years, and Mason had twice talked to him on the phone, wanting to make sure he wasn't stepping on toes or leapfrogging Tony Black's legitimate successor. "I have no desire to be the man," Custis had assured him. "I catch enough grief as it is. You can handle the complaints, midnight calls and tongue-lashings from the guy who says he controls a hundred votes and is guaranteeing your defeat next term 'cause you won't fix his wife's reckless driving ticket. And yes, they did ask me about movin' up. Judge Richardson checked with me before they began looking elsewhere."

Forty-one the day he met Mason, a graduate of Tulane and William and Mary's law school, Custis had landed in Stuart after an unsatisfying stint in northern Virginia, where he'd loopholed policyholders out of their insurance proceeds and spent twelve-hour days defending his firm's most important client, a pharmaceutical company, against a class-action suit brought by a gazillion plaintiffs with kidney damage. Wanting to do his bit and actually take some genuine wrongdoers to task, he'd responded to an advertisement Tony Black had posted in *Lawyers Weekly* and decided to give Stuart a whirl. At the very least, he figured the bush-league credentials would serve as a solid stepping-stone to a larger city and better work, his apprentice's dues fully paid. In the meantime, how bad could it be?

On his second evening in town, he'd sat for twenty minutes at the Kountry Kitchen Diner without so much as a glass of water or a menu, and when he located the owner, Luther Beasley, a spindly, red-nosed man wearing a cook's apron, the skinny hick took a drag from an unfiltered cig and — not fazed by Custis's size — told him, calm as you please, his tone dry and weary, his demeanor creeping up on exasperation, like a parent reminding a child about a winter coat or a hot stove, "We don't serve niggers here. Everybody knows that. Sorry."

But despite all the predictions and speculation that followed Custis's dismal treatment, the new black lawyer didn't file suit against the peckerwood owner of the Kountry Kitchen or invite the NAACP to investigate or raise a ruckus in the media. Custis simply avoided the bigot and his deep-fried business and kept the wrong to himself. As luck would have it, the Kountry Kitchen was robbed eighteen months later, and it fell to Custis to prosecute the case, which he did professionally and successfully, accepting Luther Beasley's mumbled, embarrassed " 'preciate it" and shaking his tentative hand outside the courthouse, thinking to himself how pitiful and dog-dumb the scrawny man was, a creature cast by the tools of a retarded deity, a brute who'd dropped his tail and learned to clothe himself like a human.

Surprisingly, though, Custis gradually discovered that most people in the area — Luther Beasley and his ilk notwithstanding

— didn't care one whit about his race so long as he let them alone and told the truth and met his obligations. Seven years after arriving, Custis was elected to the town council (against a leash law, for a stoplight at the intersection of Routes 8 and 58), his 126 votes the second-highest total among eleven candidates, and every year the daffy old matrons from the DAR Society invited him to speak on Dr. King's birthday, where he told them about discrimination and they innocently used the term "colored," as they had since they were children. There were no bruised feelings — any correction seemed pointless to Custis, and the ladies knew they weren't prejudiced, most of them having supported Custis in his campaigns — and the hostesses and their guest sipped Russian tea and enjoyed finger sandwiches and from-scratch cake, good humor the order of the day.

Asked at a black lawyers' conference in Detroit how he could stomach Stuart, Custis chuckled, clasped his hands and gave a practiced reply: "Archie Bunker lived in Queens, Andy and Barney in Mayberry. Take your pick. I prefer the odd hillbilly in a sheet and cornpone slurs to white lip service and worrying whether or not I've strayed past Checkpoint Zulu into a neighborhood where I don't need to be." So instead of leaving, he bought a house on Chestnut Avenue, tilled and planted his own vegetable garden, kept company with a pretty widow by the name of Inez Rucker and took to the place and its people, frequently traveling to Richmond and Washington for long weekends but rarely missing Ted Martin's Wednesday-night poker game and always showing up to stir apple butter at the Woolwine Fall Festival. He even joined the local theater troupe, where the other members agreed he did the best Sky Masterson ever.

He and Mason became fast friends, and their size put a goodly fear in defendants on those days they entered the courtroom together, "a whole lotta justice rollin' at you," as Custis liked to say. "The Yin-Yang Towers" was Judge Greenwalt's admiring tag upon initially seeing them in district court. When their paychecks arrived from the state, Mason, without any fanfare, directed Sheila Shough, their secretary, to put them both in the office account and split them equally, despite his being much larger than his assistant's. "Only fair," he told Custis. "As soon as I get up to speed and can pull my weight, we'll see about changing things." They never did, even though it took Mason only six months to become acclimated; he began racking up convictions and commanding the courtroom, always articulate and prepared, his many hours in the Richmond trenches paying off. Still, he wasn't a tyrant or a prick, and the defense lawyers and the community knew you could count on him and Custis to offer a break or compromise if it was warranted.

Mason first became indebted to Custis during the Brett "Shug" Cassidy drug trial. Fourteen months into Mason's tenure as commonwealth's attorney, he indicted Shug for ten counts of cocaine distribution and a variety of other crimes. Wild, erratic and unpredictable, Shug Cassidy was rumored to have shot and killed a client from West Virginia who was slow to pay his coke debt, and he lived in a compound of trailers surrounded by mongrel dogs, chain-link fence and jackleg surveillance cameras. Lived at the end of a dirt road that led into Whitlow Hollow, scores of store-bought orange-and-black NO TRESPASSING signs tacked to the trees. In case the signs didn't make the point, he'd located a piece of warped, propped-up plywood at the foot of the driveway and covered it with hand-painted threats and "bewares" vowing violence to anyone who came snooping around the Cassidy property.

Soon after the indictment, Mason began receiving notes composed of pasted magazine letters that warned him to steer clear of "Mister Cassidy" and drop the charges or bad things would certainly happen. One afternoon, Allison called Mason and reported a car kept easing down the road to their house, slow and deliberate, halting in front of the porch, then crawling away, the driver and passenger cloaked in hats and sunglasses, the license plate obscured. Of course, the cops couldn't prove anything or locate anyone when they hurried out with Mason to check on her, and it certainly wasn't a crime to meander down to someone's house a time or two. A week later, a quick strike came at three in the morning, a roaring engine and yelling and cursing and spinning tires and a gun discharged into the air, a doll with a severed head and fake blood and another anonymous note tossed onto the doorstep, poor Grace scared to death by the noise and disruption, and Mason — who was, after all, Curt Hunt's son — had seen enough.

The next day at work, still fuming, he informed Custis what had happened and told him he planned a thoroughly personal visit to Shug Cassidy's.

"Let's go drop by the sonofabitch's right now," Custis declared, standing up as he spoke. "No reason I can see to wait."

"I didn't tell you so you'd go with me."

"I know." Custis opened his desk drawer, removed a nickel-plated .38 and dropped it into his coat pocket. "I'll drive."

It was early fall, cool and crisp, the leaves perishing in color, the summer's humidity gone so the air wasn't noticeable unless a wind kicked up or a field of orchard grass shimmered and yielded to weather arriving late in the afternoon. The season and the gun caused Mason a flash of uneasiness and put him in mind of his brother. Still, as they were making plans to confront an armed drug dealer, it seemed wise to anticipate the worst.

Custis's El Dorado bottomed out twice as they approached Shug's fortified home, and they were escorted in by a pack of barking, frothing, snarling dogs of all colors, builds and sizes, fifteen or twenty of them, Mason estimated, the more aggressive ones leaping against the side of the car, their muzzles and teeth and pumping claws right beside his face, slobber and dirt fouling the window glass.

"Shit, Mace, I do hate them damn dogs." Custis looked directly at Mason.

"Can't swim either, can you?" he said, laughing.

"Nope."

"Hand me the gun," Mason said.

"Oh, so you're gonna tell me those Cujo-lookin' hounds don't cause the hair on your neck to raise up, too? Don't act like you're not fazed by this, Mr. Racial Stereotype. Mr. Bull Connor. You know they fired Jimmy the Greek for that kinda attitude. 'Can't swim either,' " he mimicked. "Hey, here's a thought — why don't you just dive in and use your aquatic skills on 'em?" He handed Mason the .38. "Bullet comes out the small end," he

194

said, screwing on a smile. "Maybe I can kill a couple with the car. They've already managed to destroy my paint."

Shug and another man were standing outside a cinder-block garage, staring at the Cadillac, doing nothing about the dogs, sneers on their faces, a holstered pistol strapped to Shug's hip. Mason forced open the door, and a dog that was predominantly German shepherd lunged toward him, grabbing his pants at the thigh, the animal's top and bottom teeth sinking into his flesh. He shot the dog, then another. Then a third one even though they'd all turned tail. He popped a final cur as it was scampering off but didn't kill it; it yelped and squeaked and dragged its wounded, bleeding hindquarters underneath a ratty trailer skirt and started whimpering and manically licking at its injury. Mason trained the gun on Shug. Custis was out of the car, in the mix, beside his friend, step for step.

"Ain't got no right to do what you jest done," Shug announced. "Nosir. I'll have your job for sure, Mason Hunt. You and your pal Kunta Kinte both. Got it on tape." He pointed at a camera dangling from a power pole. "My Uncle Jacob's rightchere as a witness, too." He appeared only marginally disturbed by the death of his dogs, and he and his uncle seemed smug, pleased to have goaded the commonwealth's attorney into a sticky situation. "Don't know why you got such a hard-on for me, Mason. First them unfair charges, now this. I recken this proves what I been sayin' all along." His mouth was creased into an obnoxious, taunting smile.

Mason stopped in front of Shug, very close to him. "Take the gun out and give it to me."

Shug complied, then took a step away and raised his hands to shoulder height, palms showing. "This is gonna look awful bad on your part," he said, the words spoken slowly and laced with spite. A confident grin revealed yellowish teeth, one chipped. A tatty beard framed his mouth.

Mason gave both Shug's gun and his own to Custis. "You and I know you're guilty, Mr. Cassidy, guilty as can be. You sold a bunch of dope to an undercover cop and, speaking of video, we have a fine little film of you, starring as Shug Cassidy, dumb-ass drug dealer."

Shug lowered his hands. "Maybe you're confusin' me with your brother. Your family's got right smart sperience in the area of sellin' shit on tape, right?"

The uncle cackled at his nephew's reference to Gates, and Custis popped him with a meaningful stare and asked what the hell was so funny. "Nothing, I guess" was the reply.

"Excellent answer," Custis told him.

"Here's the point of my visit, Mr. Cassidy," Mason said, crowding in closer. "Don't you ever even *think* about bothering my family

196

again. Don't send me any more notes, don't have your punk-ass henchmen drive by my house, don't so much as look at our property or come near any of us. Clear?"

Shug didn't give any ground. "Don't know what you're talkin' about." Squinting, he pointed his chin up at Mason. "Sure don't. But I figure a man like you controls that kinda thing hisself, dependin' on who he treats fair and who he treats not fair."

"I will make your life a living hell, Mr. Cassidy. You have my promise."

"Like I say," Shug answered, "I ain't never been involved with none of whatever it is that's eatin' at you. But a man like you, for his own sake, concernin' not me but other peoples, a man with a pretty wife and a fine daughter — Grace, right? Goes to Patrick Springs Elementary? — a man like that oughta be darn careful to always do what's best and fair." He finished with another hateful smile.

Mason jerked him up by the collar, pushed him away to arm's reach, then lit into him, and when Shug's potbellied uncle brought out a section of pipe he'd hidden underneath his shirt, Custis just about wrenched his arm off and rammed his bald head into the cinder-block wall of the garage three times for good measure before hauling him to the ground and planting a foot in his spine. As he was busting up Shug, any number of thoughts tumbled through Mason's mind, his rage unchecked, the sensation of knuckle finding bone and the surge of adrenaline and his choppy breaths all familiar and queerly agreeable, like the wicked taste of nicotine after a long absence. Custis had to yell at Mason to make him stop the beating, but he had to shout only once, and he didn't have to lay hands on Mason or pull him off. At the end of the fight, two buttons were missing from the front of Mason's shirt, and there was blood on the cuffs and sleeves, as well as his coat and pants, all of it from Shug Cassidy, who was drawn up on the ground, a red, battered lump, finally quiet.

Mason looked at the camera above them and traced its black cord into the side of a double-wide. He walked past Custis and entered the trailer. A window-unit air conditioner was lying on the den floor, an expensive TV was wedged into a corner, a matchbook collection was cased and displayed on the wall. Mason located a VCR in a rear bedroom where the line entered from outside, removed a cassette tape and returned to Custis, who still had Shug's uncle subdued, a pistol in each hand.

"Give me the gun again," Mason said.

Custis didn't waver. He offered the .38, butt first. Mason walked toward Shug, who'd sat up from the dirt and was patting his face with both shirtsleeves, his legs splayed in front of him.

"You ain't got the balls," he dared Mason, his voice ruptured, the words full of phlegm and saliva.

"Careful, Hoss," Custis said.

Mason made a show of squaring himself to the man on the ground. Mason's hair was pushed to one side, his navel visible through the gap in his shirt, his suit coat jacked too high on his neck, his trousers dog-bitten, his tie cockeyed. He raised the gun. Extended his arm to its full length. Custis was mutely committed, trusting Mason, crossing the line with him. Mason set the trigger. Closed an eye. Sighted. Shot. Twice. Shug Cassidy fell forward, his fingers digging into the dirt and sparse grass, his mouth rounded, his eyes bugged. Behind him at the edge of the trailer, the wounded dog whined, then collapsed onto its side, dead, shot through the head and neck. "Put the bitch out of her misery for you," Mason said as he was pivoting to leave and Shug lay belly-flat in his yard, scared and manhandled and speechless, at least for the short term.

"Quite a predicament I've gotten us into," Mason remarked as they were bumping over Shug's driveway, several of the dogs baying and barking behind them but keeping their distance, not chasing after the car. "Sorry." His tone was collected, and he was watching the rutted road, staring out the windshield.

"There's no way I'm going to mention your involvement in this, Custis. It was completely my problem, completely my doing. As far as I'm concerned, you weren't here." He sighed, looked at the guns beside him on the seat. "Shit."

Custis smiled so broadly that Mason could see an arc of gold dentistry at the rear of his teeth. "Kind of you to offer, Mason, but impossible to pull off. I'm in this up to my ass. And I'm a grown man, you know? I came with you full well aware we weren't making a Welcome Wagon visit." They reached the state road and the tires took traction against the pavement.

"This could cost us our law licenses," Mason said. "Not to mention a criminal charge or two."

"No doubt." Custis hadn't accelerated yet; the Cadillac was coasting along, barely doing twenty. He looked across at Mason. "Which is why we take the offensive on this shit, Mace. I've already started formulating our plan." He slowed even more and a car raced past them.

"Really?"

"Does Pastor Odell from the Samaritan Apostolic Holy Temple of the Rugged Cross drive a brand-new Lincoln?" A habit of Custis's, answering with rhetorical questions, some of which were child's play, some of which were arcane and puzzling.

"I assume he does, given the context."

"We need to come out swinging."

"I have to admit the thought crossed my mind, but I hate to pull you into my mess."

"I'm already in your mess," Custis replied. "I signed on for your mess. We're past that debate." He drove the car off the highway into the lot of a vacant convenience store. The gas pumps had been removed, leaving a cement island occupied by a few weed sprigs and crimped pipe ends, and the windows were patched with silver duct tape and weathered cardboard. "No need for us to take the fall for a piece of shit like Shug Cassidy. Being noble isn't the same as doing right."

"You're sure?" Mason asked.

"Yep."

"I mean —"

"Damn, Mason — don't wear me out on this. I'm gonna stand with you."

"The only other thing . . . I . . . I hate the hypocrisy of it. We're about to become the same as they are, no damn different."

"Hardly. This guy is a lowlife drug dealer who never so much as earned an honest dime and was harassing your family. You took care of business. He'll still receive his fair trial and all that jazz, still have his day in court beyond a reasonable doubt." His voice rose, almost squeaked. "And if you want to couch it in legal terms, you acted in self-defense. Is there any doubt you had a right to intervene on behalf of your family? Bastard was threatening your little girl." He rested his forearm on the steering wheel, twisted sideways. His tone returned to normal. "I've told you before and I'll tell you again: Justice ought to be a bottom-line proposition. I've been doin' this a lot longer than you, and I've decided it's misguided when we worship musty old words in a text at the expense of innocent people's suffering. Thomas Jefferson and Learned Hand and hearsay rules ought to come into play if we don't know the truth or if it's a close call, not when we have the guy on tape, Technicolor friggin' guilty. We should be concerned with how the soup tastes and not so damn worried about the particulars of the chef's hat."

"I'm not in much of a position to argue with you. I'm only hesitating because I don't want to put you in a jam. If you're okay with rearranging this, then so am I. I can't see much reason to ruin our lives over a little self-help and the niceties of how to deal with a criminal who endangered my wife and kid."

"Exactly. So here's the scenario as I see it." He clicked the car into Drive and gassed it back onto the road. "I catch a call from a guy who claims to be Shug's uncle and says he wants to talk to us about his nephew."

"Has to be the uncle — I've done the same math."

"Says he'll only talk to us, wants to see us.

We meet him at the top of Shug's drive, we're —"

"Skeptical and cautious," Mason interjected. "He lets on to us that Shug's still in the trade, still selling drugs, and he's worried his nephew's sinking fast, running with some dangerous people and will wind up dead or in more trouble."

"After some chitchat, he invites us to follow him, claims he wants to show us something." Custis was nodding his head as he spoke.

"The weakest part of our story," Mason added, "but the best we can do."

"We arrive at Shug's, next thing we know, they've let a bunch of dogs loose on us."

"A trap," Mason said. "The scoundrels jumped us."

"Dog bites you, we have to kill a few and defend ourselves." Custis's nods became more involved.

"We get the drop —"

"On Shug and the uncle."

"Even though they attacked us first. And we have —"

"Shug's pistol and the pipe and fingerprints on 'em both to prove what we're saying."

"As well as the bite on my leg." Mason almost spoke over his friend.

"Who knows he's been threatenin' you?" Custis asked.

203

"You, me, my wife, the sheriff, my daughter."

"I'll speak to the sheriff," Custis volunteered.

"The big picture is that Shug started this," Mason said.

"And we finished it." Custis paused, remembering something. "Make sure you lose the video."

"Really? You think I should?"

They looked at each other and laughed, the giddy, crazy, guilty, fevered laughs of two adolescent boys who'd just vandalized a mean teacher's car and vowed never to tell.

"Done deal," Mason declared at the end of their tear.

"Amen," Custis said.

"It's weird," Mason said after they'd quieted down and Custis was searching for a cassette tape, "how life's full of so many overlays and echoes. Small stones in your shoes you can't get rid of, riddles . . ."

"Ain't any stones in your shoes, and you aren't your brother and you damn sure aren't Aristotle, nope, so don't start wallowing around in any jibber-jabber."

"I'm just saying this was strange for me," Mason replied, perking up. "I'm fine." He cocked an ear, frowned. "What the hell are we listening to?"

"Luther V., my man."

"Ah, yes. The warriors return from battle to

the smooth, overproduced sounds of soulful R&B." He grinned. "Wouldn't Wagner or AC/DC be more appropriate?"

"No reason for you to go philistine on me — Luther's always the man."

"Maybe if you're gay or really ancient."

"Never know. Could be my lady Inez is only for show." Custis gave him an over-the-top wink, and they both laughed some more.

They drove directly to the magistrate's office and swore out all manner of warrants, leaving behind the pipe and Shug's pistol as evidence before traveling to the ER for treatment and photographs of Mason's bite. Shug arrived forty minutes later with his uncle, wheeling down Main Street in a slick-as-a-button 1982 Ford pickup, the tailgate dropped, a clump of dead dogs in the bed, a few flies circling after he parked and limped into the courthouse. He was soon joined by his hotshot lawyer from Rocky Mount, but the magistrate, a beefy man with a clubfoot and a stubborn temperament, steadfastly refused to issue warrants for the commonwealth's attorney and his assistant. "No way on God's green earth am I gonna have Mason Hunt arrested on the word of a snake like Shug Cassidy" was how he stated it to Shug's apoplectic lawyer.

Allison knew immediately what had happened, and she nursed Mason's wound and laid her head against his shoulder and took

Grace by the hand and sat her on her father's tender lap and told the child Mason had punished the dreadful men who'd scared her in the middle of the night. The state police interviewed Mason and Custis, left them together while they were questioned and barely took notes, a pro forma visit if there ever was one. "I mean, why in the world would we go to this guy's house unless they'd invited us?" Mason asked them. "What — for no reason I wake up and recruit Custis and say let's ride to Shug Cassidy's and shoot his dogs and start a fight and while we're at it take his pistol and a piece of pipe with his uncle's prints on it? How much sense does that make?"

"Exactly," said the state police investigator. "We see it the same way."

Months later, a special prosecutor from Harrisonburg tried Shug, and Judge Richardson sent him to the penitentiary for a long stretch and the state seized the vehicles and land he'd purchased with the dirty profits of a decade in the dope business. Most everyone in the county had a version of the truth concerning the dispute between Mason and Shug, but no matter how it was understood, no matter who went looking for whom, Mason Hunt had kicked an ass that needed kicking, and people were well pleased with their commonwealth's attorney, impressed by his grit.

After Shug's drug trial, Mason and Custis requested the charges they'd lodged against him be dropped — he'd already been stiffly sentenced, they suggested — and they never so much as uttered another syllable about what they'd done in the years that followed, this irregular lawlessness that kept them tethered and bound, and sometimes when the one would finish the other's sentence or there was a mention of the Shug Cassidy case, there'd be an extra blink or a look-away, perhaps even a faint grin, and they'd both know why and take a peculiar satisfaction in the contours of their friendship.

It rained the morning after the melee at Shug's, *plinks* and *splats* sounding off the new aluminum gutters on the Hunt house, the sky a dull gray monochrome when it finally got a dose of light in it, and Mason was up early, drinking black coffee at the kitchen table, content with the somber, shrouded day. Allison came into the kitchen wearing long pajama bottoms and a tank top, barefoot, her hair gathered away from her face. She helped herself to the coffee and flooded it with skim milk, then added a sprinkle of sugar straight from the bowl.

"You know I love you," she said, sitting down opposite him at the table, clutching her mug with both hands. "More than anything in this world."

Mason keened his head and let out a wary breath, realized he was being forewarned. There was no "good morning" or disjointed account of a dream or yawning, stretching transition from sleep to composure — she was bursting to turn loose some unwelcome fact, and this was the balm that preceded the sting. "So what's up?" he asked, sitting straighter in his chair, rubbing his stubble against the grain.

"I need to talk to you."

"I gathered as much," he said, inspecting her face. "I know the drill."

The mug was still in her hands, held above the table. She hadn't tasted the coffee. "I expect you're going to be angry."

"It only makes it worse when you dillydally and give me thousands of disclaimers."

"I was so taken by what you did to that Cassidy man."

Without thinking, Mason glanced at his bandage. A dark red stain had soaked through the gauze, and the white tape had separated from his skin on one side. He was sitting there in a robe and boxer shorts and cheap black flip-flops. "Yeah, well, I hope my conflict with Mr. Cassidy doesn't cause me trouble down the line."

"It won't." She seemed to have forgotten about her mug. "So, well, so . . . do you remember how, uh, pissy, I guess you'd say . . . how pissy I was when we were coming back from buying the house? We were driving to Richmond and you pulled over and got Grace a bagful of candy?"

"Yeah. You've already made amends for that." He noticed the loose knot in the robe's belt, wasn't looking at Allison while he spoke.

She finally lowered her cup. "I was upset because — and please don't take this and lawyer-twist it — I wanted to make sure I wasn't leaving Richmond for the wrong reasons. Wasn't running away."

"I thought we discussed the reasons," he said.

"We did." She folded her arms, then unfolded them. "There was a man there, in Richmond, who was interested in me. Romantically interested."

Mason immediately focused his full attention on her. "What the fuck does that mean?" He gripped the edge of the table and pushed his chair away, started to stand but didn't. "So what did you do about it, Allison? Huh?"

"Nothing. I mean nothing serious."

"We wouldn't be having this conversation if you weren't feeling guilty, now would we?" He was still attached to the table, holding on.

"I —"

"Who the hell was it?" he asked.

"It doesn't matter."

"Of course it matters."

"Why?" she asked. "If I didn't act on it, what difference does it make?"

"I'd like to know who's trying to cut my throat and steal my wife so I don't end up at some party shaking his hand and wishing him well and trading stock tips. 'Situational irony' is the term, I think. Plus, since I seem to be in fighting trim this week, I guess I need to know who to beat the shit out of — lots of men in Richmond."

"It doesn't —"

"And why the hell am I just now hearing about this? Tell me that." Mason released the table.

"Listen. It was Norris Deaver, and I didn't do anything, okay?"

"The greasy little cretin with the colored glasses? The art gallery pussy who sniffed his wine at the restaurant and then wouldn't drink it, made such a frigging scene? *Him?*"

"Mason, calm down." She raised her voice, trying to shift the battle. "He came on to me, and I put a stop to it."

"Did you have sex with him?" He stood and glared down at her. The robe was open, his hands were on his hips.

"Absolutely not. No." She looked at him square. "I didn't."

"So what *did* you do?"

"Could you please not wake Grace?" she asked.

"If you answer me."

"Maybe I *should've* kept this to myself." Her voice was firm.

"Yeah, and choke on your own conscience."

"I was at a point where, I guess, I doubted myself. No one wants to be a thick-ankled babushka cooking potatoes and cabbage and suckling babies on floppy tits, okay? My painting was stalled, I'd started questioning —"

"This is going to be a bad cliché, isn't it? 'I needed my worth affirmed, needed to know I'm attractive, so I screwed another man.' Nice. Profound. Very original." He sat in the chair again, scowling.

"I even sort of tried to broach the subject with you."

"Funny, I don't recall your ever asking me if you could have an affair, but it might've slipped my mind."

"I was flattered by the attention and it came at a time when I needed it, but the sum total, Mason, all I ever did was have too much to drink at lunch and let him kiss me once, and I'm sorry and it was wrong and I'm telling you now, and yes, I'd probably kill you if you did the same thing." She dropped her head, and all the defense and resistance drained from her. In an instant she went to pieces, a collapse that started in her lips and undermined her whole face, tears welling and spilling over red rims. "Mason, I swear on our child that was it." She sucked a breath and took a napkin from the wooden holder and wiped her eyes. "You are such a wonderful husband . . ." She stopped, the words hoarse and drowning. "I've always known I love you. It was more . . . I just considered it, thought about it, and I wanted to tell you so our slate would be clean. Nothing bad between us."

"You promise that's it? You thought about having sex with this dick-head and he kissed you?"

"Yes," she said, the word delicate, almost sough.

"Anything else?"

"No. I needed to tell you. I love it here, and there's not an inch of doubt anywhere. Everything is perfect. I wanted this gone, this single, stupid little mistake."

"Okay," he said. "I believe you." He thought for a moment. "I appreciate your being honest."

"But you're mad at me." The squall was leaving, her eyes clearing.

"You bet I'm mad. Who wouldn't be?"

"I'm sorry, but I had to deal with this. For my own sake. In the long run, I think having the temptation and not giving in should tell you tons about how committed I am. This was a tough period for me, and our marriage and our sweet girl had such a pull that I barely even broke faith. It's a good test, a good challenge. It was wrong and I'm apologizing, but there's an upside."

"Yeah — that'd make for a splendid Rikki Lake segment. I think you're being a little too self-congratulatory there, Saint Allison. The image I have is of this greasy, pretentious asshole pawing all over you and you deciding whether or not you plan on sleeping with him, picturing what it would be like."

"You don't need to be so rude about it. I'm sorry, and I love you and I will work to be a great wife because you deserve it and it's what I want to do. I don't know what else I can say."

Two weeks later, when Mason had passed through his mope and forgiven his wife, she invited him to skip work, and they rolled around in bed all morning and got up to speed again, watching TV game shows and snacking on Swiss Cake Rolls and dry chocolate cereal. They sent Grace to a babysitter after school and visited their neighbor's farm pond, where they took out the johnboat and cast plastic worms for the last of the warm-weather bass, cutting up and playing around until the boat tipped and they both tumbled into the water, Mason first, grabbing Allison as he went. Groping, kissing and laughing, they rode home with Allison perched on the car's console, wrapped in a scratchy picnic blanket, goose bumps on her arms and legs, naked except for her underwear, her hair stringy and damp, her hand in her husband's wet jeans all during the trip to their house. They had sex in the driveway, and afterward they went upstairs and she lit a lone, well-used candle and they squeezed into a hot bath together, still careful of the four punctures in Mason's thigh, the hurt.

To his surprise, he did seem more attached to his wife following her admission, and she to him, and they rocked along in the bull's-eye for several years, hit the jackpot, raising their daughter on forty bucolic acres and painting and practicing law and reveling in what was happening to them, time, place and desire aligned and serendipitous, so much so they'd occasionally just sit on their porch — the air chilly or hot, it didn't matter — and not say the first thing, tuned in to every newborn moment, the sensation so sublime and penetrating that Mason, alone one night after Allison had left for bed, actually lifted his hand to see if he could feel the spell and pull it down and make it tangible.

The fulcrum that would rearrange everything arrived in 2001, and like so many other momentous beginnings, it slipped in plain and middling, the kind of commonplace intrusion that goes unnoticed until someone realizes — too late, of course — where the pox was birthed and says, *Oh shit, oh my, why didn't I realize it way back then, when it was nothing, when I could have fixed it, before the briar scratch raged into gangrene?*

CHAPTER EIGHT

"What'd he blow?" Mason asked Custis. They were sitting in Mason's office, both of them in chairs on the client side, files stacked indiscriminately near the edge of the desk. It was March 2001, early, before the office opened for business. Custis had brewed them a potent pot of coffee, and they were eating slices of sweet breakfast cake with brittle plastic forks. Although Custis generally had carte blanche to dispose of cases as he pleased, he and Mason met each Monday and shot the breeze and talked about sports and discussed the week's dockets, especially any trials that might prove difficult or unusual.

"Point-oh-eight." The legal limit for blood alcohol content in a driving-under-the-influence case.

"What's the kid's name again? Doesn't ring a bell with me."

"Lonnie. Lonnie Gammons. He's twenty-one."

"Who're his parents?" Mason took a bite of cake.

"His dad's long gone. His mother raised him by herself." Custis checked a file. "Her name is April. April Gammons."

"Good folks?" Mason asked through a mouthful of cake.

"Definitely."

"Connected or rich or high-profile relatives? Too much prominence always makes it harder to cut 'em a break."

"Nope. And not trash nouveau, I'm happy to confirm."

Mason wrinkled his brow. " 'Trash nouveau'? Haven't heard the term before. Did I sleep through a seminar at the convention?"

"Minted it myself, Mace." Custis grinned. "It refers to the newest breed of white-trash royalty, the haughty third-generation simps who inherit the last of a little coin and hang around the family business thinking they're the cocks of the walk. Get the picture?"

"I'm beginning to."

"Their grandfathers wore the narrow ties and dress hats with those tiny curlicue feathers sticking out of the felt band. Lived frugally and made buckets of money sawmilling or manufacturing furniture or truckin' freight. Fine men. Their fathers took over the business and the profit margins sagged — couple wives, aborted plant expansions,

216

expensive condo at Myrtle Beach, too many bourbon nips before quittin' time — and now you've got these saltine kids with an attitude and the damn *Internet,* shoppin' at Banana Republic online and drivin' the roads in a hocked-to-the-gills BMW even though they fucked up freshman year at two different colleges. The first in their clan to write a bad check. Lie on a credit card application. Buy a case of Natty Ice at Wal-Mart because of the buzz it packs for cheap — trash nouveau. I toyed with 'uber-neck,' but it doesn't carry quite the same wallop."

Mason chuckled. "Very apt, Custis. I think you've outdone yourself. Sociologist that you are, why don't you hip-hop on over to the Old Dominion and field-test your new nomenclature on the leather-vest crowd at the counter and see how they take to it. 'Axe' them for their reaction. Run it by a focus group." He ended with a big, broad smile.

"Yeah, there you go — I'll get my clipboards and the number-two pencils."

From the start, Custis and Mason had enjoyed a comfortable, free-wheeling give-and-take where race was concerned, clashing only once, when Custis returned from court with a strut and Mason called him George Jefferson and sang the chorus of "Movin' on Up" in front of Sheila and a lady from the clerk's office, injuring Custis's feelings for reasons that seemed thin to Mason. Mason

217

had apologized but was puzzled because the ribbing was far less raw and point-blank than some they'd both delivered in the past.

"So the Gammons kid is okay?" Mason asked, back on topic.

"Yeah. An honor student who was valedictorian of his class here at the high school. Scholarship to Virginia Tech. Works a job at college. Even the sheriff's wife called on his behalf."

Mason swallowed the remainder of his coffee. "Was he cooperative with the cop?"

"Nice as could be. Very apologetic. Didn't do badly with the field-sobriety tests, speech was normal, mild smell of alcohol. They caught him at a road check — luck of the draw."

Mason thought for a moment. "A DUI will break his mother's back paying for insurance. Pretty much ruin his opportunities after college. Probably wouldn't hurt to find him a little breathing room."

"We're usually flexible with point-oh-eight. I mean, it's the lowest rung of the ladder, just barely there, and the simulator came up an eleven instead of a ten, so his lawyer can argue the machine's off a fraction. I know a few months ago we reduced that Arrington guy's case when he had an eight and no record. Gammons told the cops he'd been drinkin' champagne at a weddin'. Claimed he'd never tried alcohol before and didn't realize how much he could or couldn't drink. From all reports, he's probably bein' truthful. His lawyer's Charles Aaron — claims the DUI will cost the kid his scholarship. I've got some sympathy for him."

"So what do you want to do?"

"Reduce it to reckless driving and a fine, send him to liquor school, stick him with a hundred hours of community service, make him walk for thirty days or so."

"Sounds good to me," Mason agreed. "You certainly have my blessing. Make sure you let him know we're doing him a favor. Aaron, too."

The same day, while Mason was eating lunch at his desk and reading the *Roanoke Times,* Gates called from the penitentiary, collect as always, and Sheila announced he was on the line. For the first time since he'd been sentenced, he was surly with Mason, combative and bitter. "I have a question for you, Mason" was how he started the conversation.

"What?" Mason asked. "What's up?" He assumed Gates was calling to unspool yet another harebrained defense theory, the most recent prison wisdom that would provide him the keys to his cell. Mason's tone was terse and prickly, betraying his annoyance.

"What exactly are you doing to help me beat this charge and get outta this place?" He didn't pause for an answer, plowed ahead. "I mean, actual positive steps you've taken. I've been here for ten fuckin' years, Mason. Ten years in this hole, and I don't think you or Mom or anyone else gives a damn."

Mason's hackles rose. "You mean beyond sending you weekly care packages and money twice a month and typing your thirty-page habeas pleadings free of charge and intervening so you could be transferred closer to home and driving Mom to visit you and accepting every collect call you've ever placed? I'm sorry if that's inadequate by your standards. I'll see what I can do about a personal chef and a water bed complete with a hooker."

"Crumbs, Mason. Crumbs and window dressing that don't move me one inch closer to leavin' here."

"What exactly is it you have in mind, Gates? Huh?" Mason was angry, his voice loud. Custis opened the door between their offices and looked in. "You cool?" he asked quietly, and Mason nodded, waving him away.

"Listen, Mason, you and I both know you can pull a string or two for me, okay?"

"We've had this conversation before — there's nothing I can do. I might as well be an astronaut for all the influence I have in your case. I'm not a judge, I'm not the governor and I'm not the parole board. And I'm not going to arrange something unethical, even if I could."

"Exactly. No shit." Gates was shrill, belligerent. "You're king of the hill in your big house, everybody's darling, callin' the shots, and you really don't care what becomes of me. There's no reason in the world you can't take five minutes to walk up and see the judge and put in a word for me. Or call somebody in the system. You're the commonwealth's attorney, for fuck's sake. Why won't you even try?"

"You know, Gates, you are absolutely an unappreciative dick."

"Yeah, well, you just try and remember how many times I saved your ass. Runnin' and cryin' when Curt was on your tail — and this is how you repay me. How you take care of your big brother. Shit, Mason, there're guys in here whose court-appointed lawyers fight harder for them than you do for me."

"This is the last time I'm going to tell you: there is no magic bullet, no escape hatch, no error in your trial. No attorney can help you. You were guilty and your trial was clean and the law was followed. Every court you've appealed to has affirmed your convictions. Why? Because you were selling dope and then elected to lie on the stand. End of story." Mason exhaled a rough, abrupt breath. "While we're on the subject, let me remind you how *you,* Gates Hunt, stubborn asshole, refused to take a plea agreement that would've had you free by now. But —"

"Yeah," Gates interrupted, almost yelling, "which shows what the correct sentence was, the five years they offered, and now I've pulled more than that and I'm still here. How can anyone say I'm being treated fairly?"

Mason laughed sarcastically. "You know, Gates, when some dumb shit falls for Carol Merrill's lovely arm sweep and sparkly evening gown and trades his new washer-dryer combo for a donkey because he picked the wrong curtain, Monte doesn't allow him a do-over. You had your chance."

"Fuck you, Mason."

"Drop dead," Mason snapped and slammed down the phone.

Gates called back immediately, but Mason told Sheila to refuse the charges, left him hanging.

Two months later, in May, Mason and Allison hosted a costume party at their house to mark Allison's birthday, her fortieth, and it was a hoot and a success. The big day fell on a Wednesday, and Allison was determined to celebrate accurately, deciding not to move the party to the weekend. Loads of people came, and Mason dressed like Captain Hook with a plastic sword and buccaneer's striped shirt, and there was only one glitch, only one uncomfortable moment, which occurred early in the evening when Mason greeted a friend's husband — a man he'd never met —

and offered him a fake dime-store pirate's hook only to discover the poor fellow had in fact really lost a hand and was extending the genuine article, a stainless-steel pincer attached to a prosthetic forearm. Later on, after a round of drinks, the man joked about the awkwardness and told Mason not to worry. Allison was a knockout vampire, and Grace, who was allowed to stay up late and enjoy the party, was a twelve-year-old hobo, a getup she insisted on no matter what, declining more conventional choices like a princess or genie or rock star or Simba's lioness wife.

After the last of the guests left, at close to one in the morning, Mason brushed his teeth and drank a glass of water and called for Allison to come to bed and she didn't answer. He called again and then walked through the living room and the kitchen, plates stacked in the sink, trash bags filled and cinched. He went all the way to the opposite end of the house, to Allison's studio. The door was pulled shut but not completely closed. He pushed it open and saw her, without the long black wig but still in her ghoulish makeup, wearing loose green army pants instead of her costume bottom, her Gothic, pale vampire blouse above the pants, listening to music, a brush in her hand, painting.

She turned when she sensed him there, stopped her work. The canvas was part of a suite she was preparing for a New York gallery, her best ever as far as Mason was concerned: a rhino peered over a man's shoulder, contemplating a table of cheese, crackers and wine, the hues piercing, the details painstakingly precise. She smiled at him, the both of them happy, rapt. Neither said anything. She returned to her easel, and Mason left her alone, checked on their daughter and went to bed. A whip-poor-will switched on in a front-yard tree, and the bird's three-beat racket kept Mason from falling asleep right away despite how tired he felt.

Allison was beside him, conked out, when he woke at seven; he'd not heard her join him, didn't know how long she'd been there. He had to shake and poke and cajole Grace to get her going and dressed for the school bus, but they did enjoy a nice breakfast together, French toast and scrambled eggs, a bit more than usual since Mason didn't have to be at his office until ten, a precaution he'd taken in light of the party. He tidied the kitchen, filled the dishwasher, hiked the trash to the top of the drive, showered and dressed for work, kissing Allison's cheek as he left the room. She didn't respond, only moved her feet slightly under the covers.

That same afternoon, Sheila Shough was at her desk chatting with her friend Vicki about the Hunts' party when the phone rang. It was one thirty. Mason was in his office talking to a family about a trespass problem, and Custis was upstairs in the office's small law library, doing research. Sheila listened for less than a minute and dropped the receiver, which hit her desk, then the carpet. She abandoned her friend without an explanation, just said "Oh God" and lost her color and headed for the stairs to fetch Custis, the cord catching her shin as she left, nearly pulling the base of the phone onto the floor.

Custis was seated at a rectangular wooden table, surrounded by law books, and Sheila was crying by the time he saw her. Frantic. He stood, and before he could speak or ask why she was upset, she said, "Mason's wife. It's Allison. The police called . . . Terrible." She walked to the closest chair and collapsed there, cried and cried and wasn't much good to anyone for several hours.

Downstairs, Custis found the phone disconnected and bleating, and upon discovering that Sheila's friend Vicki had no answers or information, he hustled out the door and spotted a state trooper, Darrell Bowling, striding toward the office. They met under the office's awning, and Darrell stood close to him, gripped Custis's biceps and spoke in a voice that knew how to modulate dreadful news. "Mason's wife was in an accident in Patrick Springs," he said, his eyes tracking Custis's. "The intersection at Charlie Mar-

225

tin's old store. Vehicle come through the Stop sign and T-boned her. She was dead when the rescue squad got there." Darrell shook his head and removed his hat. "Impact was as bad as I've ever seen." He'd released Custis's arm. "Tough," he said. A tear appeared, but he didn't bother with it. It didn't affect his posture or the clarity in his voice. "Me or you?" he asked. "You want me to give him the news? I was on my way to do it."

Custis had both hands on top of his head, his elbows angled. He kicked the ground and bowed at the waist, stomped a half circle before twisting back to face the trooper. "You're sure? It was her?"

"We're sure. T. J. Meade and Bryant Pruitt were first on the scene."

"How?" Custis asked, his face pained, his hands still raised. "I mean, what happened?"

"From what we can tell, this driver in a Ford, a full-size pickup, didn't see the sign — happens all the time — and tore right into her. How many accidents we had there, Custis? Fifty? Sixty? Lord only knows."

"Who was drivin' the truck? Is he hurt?"

"Boy by the name of Lonnie Gammons, a college kid. Home for a long weekend before exams or some such. He's got a few cuts and scrapes, but that's about it. Always happens like that, huh?" Darrell hesitated and cleared his throat. "Bryant says this Gammons fellow was in court not so long ago with a DUI. We

226

checked, though, and he was okay to drive. Wound up with a reckless driving and a thirty-day suspension, so he was perfectly legal."

Custis lowered his hands and arms. He stared at Darrell. "Oh shit. How about this time? Was he drinkin'?"

"Nosir. Straight as an arrow. Not a drop. Zero on the alka-sensor, nothing in the car. He's all to pieces over it, cryin' and whatnot. He's at the ER. You hate it for him, too. It'll stick to him the rest of his life."

"Well, maybe it should," Custis said, frowning. "Damn."

"Just one of those things," Darrell said. "An accident nobody intended."

"I'm gonna let you break it to Mace." Custis loosened his tie and unbuttoned his collar. "I need to check on somethin'. You stay with him, Darrell, don't leave him alone till I get there, you hear?"

Darrell knocked on Mason's office door and asked the group of elderly men and women inside if they could excuse themselves. He told them in a quiet voice there was an emergency, and it was important that he speak with the commonwealth's attorney. He stood formal and erect, his dark blue hat in hand, his gaze downward, as they filed from the room.

Mason rose as Darrell was closing the door. "What is it, Darrell?"

The trooper made it a point to be near Mason, went to where he was standing, within easy reach. He didn't beat around the bush. "There's been a bad wreck, Mason. Allison was in it." He waited a moment, swallowed. "I wish I wasn't the one tellin' you, but she didn't make it. I'm so sorry."

And that was how Mason heard the news, how he discovered his wife was dead. He was silent for an instant, folding in his arms to his chest, his hands gripped together underneath his chin. Everything seemed to lag and warp, then his legs lost their resolve, tumbling him down into his chair. "Allison's dead?" he asked the trooper. "My Allison?"

"Yes."

"Oh God." Mason left his arms pressed against his chest and cocked his head toward the ceiling and sealed his eyes, clenching his whole face as if he were trying to fend off Darrell's words. "You have to be wrong."

"I'm gonna sit here with you," Darrell said. "For a while, anyway." He took a seat and tugged a folded white handkerchief from his uniform pocket, did his own grieving. They'd known each other since elementary school, two local boys who'd grown up together.

"Where is she?" Mason asked after a few seconds. "What happened?" He paused, balling his hair inside a fist. "What am I going to do?" Tear on top of tear sliced down both cheeks. Several kept going and wet his lap, his sleeves.

"I reckon she's still at the hospital. You'll need to make some arrangements, but there's plenty of time for that. I'll drive you when you're ready. Whatever I can do."

The phones were ringing and not being answered. Sheila wobbled into the office sobbing and Darrell allowed her a brief stay before helping her leave, steering her away with a gentle hand on her shoulder.

"The wreck was at Charlie Martin's intersection," Darrell said when they were alone again. "Pickup come through and didn't slow down."

"Did . . . ? The car . . . How did it happen? I mean . . ." Mason slumped forward. "Did she . . . ?"

"It was over in a second," Darrell promised him. Two decades of dealing with covered gurneys and disemboweled automobiles had taught him what needed to be heard. "She never knew."

Mason just stared at him, shell-shocked, slowly throttling down, his vitality leaking from every pore, like a child's mechanical toy sucking the last juice from weak batteries, wallowing to a harsh, metallic stop. They could hear voices in the waiting room, the phones were still noisy but not being attended to, and through the window, Sadie Grace was visible, hurrying from her car, the door left open behind her.

"There's one other thing about the wreck I, uh, need to tell you," Darrell said.

Custis had jogged to the *Enterprise* office and found Gail Harding, the paper's editor. Because it was Stuart, she'd already heard the miserable report and didn't seem altogether surprised to see him. She told Custis she was heartbroken and asked after Mason and reached out and squeezed Custis's huge hand, got mostly fingers. They walked to a corner and Custis leaned against the wall. "Here's the deal," he said. "It's gonna surface that this Gammons boy was in court for DUI not so long ago. He was a good kid, Gail. College, job, scholarship, raised by a single mom. No record. Everybody and his brother callin' to support him. I reduced the charge. If I'd left it alone, he would've been suspended for a year and not drivin' today. Instead, I gave him his license back after thirty days. Shit."

Gail's face registered the news. She shook her head from side to side. "It's not your fault." She peered up at him. "And I'm not just saying that. You did the right thing for the right reasons. Don't beat yourself up over it. Heck, the way kids are, even if you'd taken his license, he might've still been driving. Suspended or not, people get behind the wheel. Who can say, Custis? And who could've known?"

"Well, people are gonna start gossipin' about it, and I'm sure it's a story with some appeal in certain quarters, so I just wanted to put it on the table, here and now. Mason had nothin' to do with the decision, never even knew about it. It was my case, my call. Now I gotta drag up there and tell him."

"I'm so sorry for all of it," Gail said. "But the kind of man Mason is, he won't hold it against you."

"Doesn't make it any easier." Custis sighed and pushed off from the wall. "At any rate, how 'bout you printin' the whole ball of wax, let the radio know and maybe the *Roanoke Times.* I'll get my ashes and sackcloth and wait for the MADD pickets and the minions from the cable networks." He smiled but didn't mean it.

"So Mason wasn't involved?" Gail asked, though the answer probably wouldn't have made any difference in terms of her story.

"Nope. Completely me. He's always trusted me to manage my cases. You're welcome to check the paperwork."

"No reason to."

There were several people in Mason's office when Custis arrived, and he went directly to his friend and they wrapped each other up, embracing and holding tight. They were emotional and unguarded, but neither was crying or overwrought. Custis's mouth was so close to Mason's ear it almost touched:

"This is totally on me, brother. My fault. I hope you'll forgive me." The room was quiet except for sniffles and the gentle, padded sound of a woman's steady weeping, and most of the visitors heard what Custis said.

"It couldn't be helped. Not your fault. No one could ask for a better friend or partner." Mason had recovered somewhat, was operating on adrenaline and numb instinct, his world pared down to the very next noun and verb, the person immediately in front of him, the effort to blink and breathe. The rest was nothing, scrambled — gray, grainy static beyond shrunken margins. He made space between them so he could see Custis. "I was right there with you, and —"

"I wish I could have it to do again," Custis interrupted, talking over Mason. He took a step away. "I can't tell you how . . . how . . ." He gave up, hung his head, wiped a wrist across both eyes. "I can't believe it."

"I know," Mason assured him.

"It's God's will," said a lady from the Baptist church standing beside Sadie Grace. She meant well, had come to see what she could do to comfort the family. "As hard as it is to understand, we know Allison's in a far better place."

"Yeah, and so is our daughter," Mason snapped. "Maybe the Good Lord should have his spectacles checked before he goes down the list again. Or get better information from his agents on the ground. I don't want to hear that shit right now." He was allowed the breach of faith by everyone there, even his churchgoing mother, and the Christian lady who'd made the suggestion understood why he was so distraught and didn't think poorly of him or take umbrage. "How about riding with me and Darrell to the hospital?" he said to Custis after the room fell silent, and the three men started to leave the office, the trooper leading the way. Mason stopped at the threshold and addressed his mother. "I'd appreciate it if you could go by the house. I expect I'll need some help."

"Of course," Sadie Grace told him. She crossed the room and touched him on the arm, sixty-four years old, her knee not completely reliable, the joint sabotaged by arthritis.

The family night was held at the high school auditorium because so many people wanted to pay their respects. The wait stretched into the parking lot, some in the line straight from work and still wearing their blue shirts and steel-toes, others in coats and ties, overalls, sport jackets and Sunday best for many of the ladies. A few visitors barely knew Mason but came because they'd received a fair shake in court or a kind hearing of a past problem, and even reclusive old Hazel Overby, a widow with a dip of snuff rolling around her dentures, stood for hours waiting to see the Hunts. No telling how much food was brought to Mason's house, plate upon plate, chicken, cakes, casseroles, pies, baked beans, cold-cut trays, country hams and Crock-Pots filled with stew. The local arts co-op collected nearly five thousand dollars in memorials. All the Patrick County attorneys wrote checks to fund an Allison Hunt scholarship. There was not enough room in the funeral home's chapel for the flowers.

After a simple, two-hymn service, several hundred people drove from the chapel and encircled Mason and Grace at the Stuart Cemetery, virtually every one of them nicked or saddened by the death. Standing there graveside and wearing a dark suit, Mason was struck by the thought that spring was not the season in which to die. A burial was incongruous and wrong during a time of dogwoods and blithe perennials, stories of empty tombs and rolled-away rocks, and frenetic children combing fields full of poorly concealed, brightly dyed eggs, one always golden. With the world being rebirthed all around him, Mason mourned underneath a tent on a mat of artificial grass, holding his child's hand, occupied by his own concerns, the preacher's words disintegrating into the air, too frail and slight for the huge outdoors, pulverized by the vault of sky and the hard, ancient mountains. He returned to the grave twice that day, knelt and touched the turned dirt, red clay flecked with mica, trying to make sense of what was happening to him.

Grace was devastated. Gutted. Mason had collected her from school and sat her down in her grandma's kitchen and slow-walked her into the tragedy, the worst experience in his forty-plus years, bar none. For five nights, he made a pallet and slept on the floor beside her. He allowed her to miss school for two days, doing what he could to answer her questions, comforting her when she cried and indulging her with movies and rich desserts. The child took a stab at making breakfast for her dad the day following the accident, and once he had to hustle after her when she set out with her pink and yellow backpack and a claw hammer, planning to find Lonnie Gammons and put a beating on him. They did the best they could, the both of them staggered.

Gates, meanwhile, remained in the pen, didn't make the trip to Stuart — he and Mason were still at odds, their communications more and more infrequent and often by letter. "I've got enough to put up with," Mason had told Sadie Grace when she broached the subject of bringing him home for the funeral. "I don't need that monkey on my back, more to vex me." To his credit, Gates did call Mason on his own dime — glibly promising to keep his brother in his "thoughts and prayers" — and he had a peace lily dispatched to the funeral home. "I know it's a bad time to ask," Gates said before his last pay-phone minutes expired, "but did you have a chance to look over the motion I sent you? I mean, I'm not askin' you to do it now or anything, that wouldn't be decent, no it wouldn't, but just when you get past all this. In the next day or two. I've got a deadline." Mason was so enraged that he went barreling to his office, found the envelope full of ponderous longhand on notebook paper and burned it. He shook the ashes into a box and sealed it, leaving instructions for Sheila to return the package to the penitentiary.

Not long after the service, Mason discovered the lie Custis had told for him, and he immediately wanted the truth to be known, thanked Custis but refused to let him be blamed for something not wholly of his making.

"Why you wanna go and do that?" Custis asked him. They were sitting on the porch at Mason's. Sadie Grace was inside molding hamburger into a meat loaf, supper for her son and granddaughter. "What good will it do you or Grace or Allison? The fact of the matter is I'm the one who really pushed the issue with the Gammons kid. My case, my call. It's a wrinkle you shouldn't have to deal with. You know how people can be."

"Our case, our call. I'm not going to be a

coward and hide behind your skirts, Custis, much as I appreciate the gesture. I could've stopped it." He sighed and stared at the pasture, the grass greening and uneven. "Can you believe this? What a damn mess. What an unfair, one-in-a-million, Greek tragedy cluster fuck. The day after her birthday. We were set, too. Perfect with each other — I loved her and she loved me." He watched a line of ants curving across the porch boards. "But I'll make sure everyone knows what's what. I'm as much at fault as you. Hell, more at fault — I'm the boss."

"Which assumes both of us did somethin' wrong. In our minds, at least, we have to realize maybe we didn't, Mason. We didn't cause this. You could argue we're no more to blame than Gammons's driver's ed teacher or the guy who sets the exam schedule at Tech. For any number of reasons, you don't have to carry this bag, and you shouldn't. You couldn't see around the corner. You damn sure didn't mean for it to happen."

Mason dipped his head. He wasn't looking at Custis when he spoke. "So why're you scrambling all over the county flogging this lie?" He grinned slightly but didn't lift his eyes.

" 'Cause I knew what you'd think, and I knew it would come up even though it shouldn't. It's a tiny bit of aggravation I wanted to take off you."

Mason looked at his friend but didn't answer. He proceeded to walk inside and tell Sadie Grace about his involvement, and he called Inez Rucker, Custis's lady friend. He wrote a letter to the editor, which Gail Harding returned to him unpublished. The community didn't know precisely what to believe, and ultimately only the most moronic of the jackasses and dolts viewed the collision as anything but a Byzantine fluke, simply horrid bad luck. Still, Custis and Mason both suffered their decision like a millstone, and sometimes when he thought about Lonnie Gammons and the crash at Charlie Martin's intersection, Mason would curse out loud or bang his fist against a wall or a counter, seething.

After nearly a month, at night he took to sitting on the sofa in her studio, the stuffing pressing through tears and slits, a rough blanket from a Mexican vacation partially covering the cushions. He would gaze at the spot where he last saw her awake and wonder if the rhino was finished, if it would suit her. At dusk one warm evening, his doctor buddy Vince Castillo dropped by to check on him, and he told Vince he was out of whack, felt like he'd become saturated and was sinking, a dreamy, suspended free fall, aimless and soupy, breaking up and dropping at the same time, destined for the muck. Vince gave him a prescription for Valium, but Mason didn't

fill it, couldn't see where it would change his
circumstances.

CHAPTER NINE

For Mason, loss played to form: he was bewildered, then furious as a wet hen — frustrated and quick-tempered — and finally, depressed, swamped by sadness.

Early on, Sadie Grace spent most of her nights with him and her granddaughter, pitching in with the cooking and the household demands, and friends frequently stopped by to say hello or coax him over for a meal or mention a fishing trip or invite him to a Saturday-evening movie. Midway through June, his old pal Claude arrived unannounced with wild rabbits he'd killed and skinned, and he and Mason visited in the den, telling high school tales and recounting Gates's antics, marveling at how popular he'd been. "Nobody could charm 'em like your crazy brother," Claude said. They'd gotten comfortable, the conversation oiled and rolling. "Ol' Heaven's Gates. Remember that? How he'd say to the girls, 'I'd be delighted to let you enter and take you on a tour you'll never forget.' " Claude laughed and clapped his hands. "What a lady-killer, huh? Always . . ." He caught himself and took a furtive, self-conscious peek at Mason. "Aw, shit, man. Here I am supposed to be cheerin' you up and I go and put my foot in my big mouth. My bad."

Mason shook his head, forced Claude to look at him. "Don't fret about it. Every reference to a woman or wife won't cause me to fall apart. I'm not that hopeless, okay?"

But, in truth, he *was* floundering, and eventually he yielded to his mother's nudges and encouragement and started attending church regularly, eager to find some solace in religion, some tonic that would set him right. He and Allison had occasionally gone to the Presbyterian church on Staples Avenue, hitting the high spots like Christmas, Mother's Day and Easter, and they'd sent Grace to Vacation Bible School there, where she learned snippets of scripture and fashioned crafts from Popsicle sticks and pipe cleaners. Mason shopped around a bit, even tried his mother's True Gospel House of the Risen Lord, an Independent Baptist affair, but the service was too long, too hardscrabble, too strident, too tent-revival, electric-bass theatrical. He finally decided to pin his hopes on the Presbyterians. So, perplexed and sucker punched, seeking a hint as to why his wife had been killed for no discernible reason, he

241

spent the summer in Sunday worship and Wednesday-night Bible studies.

He found the congregation to be generous and sincere, the minister thoughtful, the denomination's doctrines worthwhile, the charity laudable and the entire enterprise a wrenching waste of his time — before hearing the organ and beholding the stained glass, he already knew sin was wicked, tithes were a necessary burden and his neighbors deserved better treatment and more attention. What he couldn't discover was why in blue blazes his wife was no longer with him. The sermons and messages were simply not on topic for him, missing his needs with a defiant regularity, and the frequent suggestion that he and the others occupying the pews were not meant to solve the majesty of a grander scheme — the trite fallback "The Lord works in mysterious ways" — seemed like a sophist's crooked masterpiece, a squishy dodge requiring a much bigger buy-in than he was willing to make. After three months, he felt as if he were an ignored schoolboy, raised high off his seat, his arm shot straight up, straining to catch the teacher's eye, never called on or acknowledged.

One morning late in September, disturbed by a rocky, sleepless night, he appeared at his preacher's study, demanding more than the clergyman could give.

"Why did my wife get killed in a car wreck?"

Mason asked, agitated and unshaven, having rushed through their pleasantries. Reverend Hunsicker had offered decaf coffee, which Mason declined. It was morning, the air outside brisk but not bitter.

Using his index finger, the preacher slid his reading glasses farther up his nose. "Pardon me?" The men were separated by a desk, alone in a modest basement room, books spilling from cardboard boxes and red plastic milk crates.

"Why is my sweet, talented Allison dead, when the fools and criminals and drunks, the flotsam and jetsam who fill the courtrooms, can't be killed with a sledgehammer? Why does my daughter not have a mother? How can this be authored — or allowed — by a benevolent God? And if your answer is 'sometimes we can't understand His purpose,' I don't want to hear it. That's not an answer, it's an excuse."

The preacher looked at him with sympathy, an earnest cast to his features. "I wish I had an explanation, Mason. I do. I don't think it's fair either, to use the term generally, as it relates to the here and now. Her death was tragic. Difficult." He ducked his head, emotional. "But you've got to hold fast to your faith. Continue to pray." His voice was low, on the verge of a whisper. "Continue to humbly petition the Lord and ask for peace of mind. The Lord answers prayers."

Mason considered what he was about to say. Ran through it silently. A space heater kicked on, humming and glowing orange. "No offense, Reverend, but the whole prayer routine seems like a parlor trick to me, an elegant variation on the Amazing Randi's act or the Magic Eight Ball game. Let me see if I understand: We're supposed to pray, but the request only comes to fruition if it's God's will, correct? So if we don't get our cancer cure or new job or marriage saved or rent money or spouse to quit drinking, it wasn't His will, and we're okay with the rejection, but we're still positive we're blessed by our Almighty. He simply knew better than we did." Mason hesitated. He gestured with both his hands, tossing them out disgustedly. "And if we win the prayer lotto, well there you go: We sing hymns and give thanks and rejoice, praise be, because the Lord delivered a new car or jammed the coffers of the building fund. Who could doubt the connection? Our prayers were answered. It's a can't-lose gimmick, a damn shell game — I hate to say it, but it is. I mean, how far are we removed from the days when we bowed to Zeus because we burned a goat and chanted his name and the thunder quit?"

"I understand why you're so disappointed —"

Mason interrupted. "The prayer thing is a side issue for me anyway; I've got a bigger bone to pick. No matter how you cut it, either your God allowed my innocent, undeserving wife to get killed — omnipotent neglect, I guess you'd call it — or He intended for it to happen, and that's clearly screwed up given the world's infinitely more deserving choices." Mason sighed and bit his lip. "This isn't . . ." He slouched in his chair. "This isn't working for me, Reverend. I appreciate your decency, I appreciate the good hearts in this church, I appreciate the fine deeds everyone does for the community, but my wife is dead, and it's cruel and random and there's nothing here to change any of those painful facts. No hard feelings, and for what it's worth, I think you're a good man. Very considerate. Problem is, your employer needs to do a better job stocking your store — can't sell what you don't have."

Reverend Hunsicker trailed Mason to his car, and he phoned and visited in the weeks that followed, and he listened to Mason's vehement complaints, absorbed his criticism, struggled to brace Mason's faith, did all he could to transfer a certitude he possessed but Mason didn't. Mason, though, had made up his mind, and the preacher's many efforts and devout entreaties bounced off a man who was too angry to listen and too far gone to care.

For the next several months, into the onset of winter, Mason was a bear in court, brutal to the chronics and petty criminals, the wastrels who stole small items from unlocked sheds or forged a check lifted from their very own mama's purse, the worthless recidivists who whined and whimpered and boohooed, always begging for *one more chance,* another trip to rehab or a suspended sentence, clutching their prison-ministry tracts on the stand, swearing fealty to a new way of life for the sixth or seventh time. But nothing riled him more than shiftlessness, flagrant sorriness, and pity the stupid crook who made the mistake of dragging his aged mom or crippled grandmother in to testify how she knew her boy had learned his lesson this go-round, was sure to shape up if he could come live with her. "Nice," Mason would sneer at these defendants when he questioned them. "How proud you must make your family."

Also, the county's habits, quaint bent, erratic pace and unpredictable characters — its offbeat country charm, if you were in the mood for it — began to prick him, weighing on his patience, like a medicine that had been splendid and effective, then suddenly went toxic. "It's a *wharf* rat, not a *wolf* rat," he declared to Mo Jenkins, the humble hired man who helped with the yard, cleaned the gutters and mowed the pasture. "And while we're at it, the dog is a *Rott*weiler, not a *Rock*weiler." Rustic became irksome — the slow-ass pickups that never gave a turn signal, the

246

farm tractors, hay wagons and old people in muddy Buicks that clogged the main highway, the stores that didn't sell a respectable dress shirt, the endless chatter about nothing, the same-old, same-old all along every route. Then there was the sort who got everyone's goat, the snaggle-toothed clods who drew a government check they didn't deserve, slurping their bowls of pinto beans bombarded with chunks of corn bread, green feed-store hats still on their heads while they ate in a restaurant, no manners whatsoever. "It's all I can do," Mason told Custis, "not to knock the piss out of someone. I used to like this shit. Now it drives me crazy."

Unable to stay still for very long, he skipped meals, ran extra miles at the high school track and added reps to his gym routine. Always fit and athletic, he lost eleven pounds he shouldn't have lost, the majority of it through his face, or so it appeared to the people around him. "Mason really looks like he's bad off," Sadie Grace's cousin mentioned at an elementary school fund-raiser. "He ain't hisself, is he?"

There was one mild, interesting deviation. When the special prosecutor consulted Mason about offering Lonnie Gammons a reckless-driving plea, he didn't object, insisting only that Gammons lose his license for a year and be required to volunteer at the hospital ER. "His punishment's really not my main issue," Mason said obscurely. "He's a dumb kid with no daddy." After court concluded, Gammons, scared and remorseful, standing beside his plain, threadbare mother, choked out an apology, and while Mason only frowned and grunted, he didn't curse the kid or lunge at him or threaten retribution, allowed him his say, a tiny forgiveness.

Coal-fed ire takes its toll, of course. The bile and twenty-four-seven, high-end fury couldn't last forever, and gradually Mason wore down into the last phase of his suffering. After the searching and confusion, and after the rants, anger and days of looking to pick a fight for no real reason, he grew weary, blue. Gloomy. He realized what had happened to him, his sad state, standing at a convenience-store counter on the first day of the year 2002, gazing at a Peg-Board on the wall behind the clerk, caught up in the hairbrushes, rubber bands, fingernail clippers, combs, playing cards, off-brand condoms and colorfully wrapped patent medicines, unaware he'd been asked three times, very politely, if he was ready to pay for the gas he'd pumped. He was so distracted he never responded until the clerk touched him on the sleeve and said, "Are you okay, Mr. Hunt?"

Most everything in the world had become a detour or trapdoor for him, sucking him away into chutes and sluices of the past, leaving him distant and dumbstruck. A court reporter's painted fingernails as she adjusted a microphone summoned Allison's hand around the green throat of a wine bottle, pouring herself a glass for breakfast soon after they'd met. A sloppy Hardee's restroom took him to his father's sink in the old shed and the dried, dirty webs of black grease that fanned from a bar of Curt's Lava soap. A glimpse at a DMV transcript in juvenile court and he was drinking sloe gin fizzes with Gates, underage but ready with a fake Wisconsin operator's license when the Myrtle Beach bartender asked. Passing the Stuart hospital carried him to the day the nurse handed Grace to her mother, thirteen years ago. And an ordinary convenience-store hairbrush had ended up in Allison's hand, gliding through her hair while she sat before an antique mahogany vanity, the strokes rhythmic, music without sound. "I'm fine," Mason assured the clerk. "Didn't mean to ignore you."

Worsening his dislocation, he would dwell on change and what had gone missing. Nothing seemed to be nailed down. Nothing could hold. Driving around Stuart one morning, he passed the spot where Smokey's Restaurant and Motor Court used to be, and he coasted to the side of the road, staring at a flat patch of grass and the yellow lines that marked the blacktop. First the motel rooms were razed, then Smokey's became the Lumberyard Grill, next it was Skip's Seafood, and forty years later there wasn't anything left, only a curve in the new four-lane, the Mayo River rechanneled to accommodate the expanded highway, the building bulldozed and the debris hauled away in dump trucks, the kitchen equipment sold to a junk dealer, the old site buried under asphalt and steamrolled earth, Smokey and Ada Fulton and their homey café thoroughly vanished save for a few photos at the county historical society.

Following the holidays, in January of 2002, an unexpected ice storm encased the county, bejeweling branches and power lines and broom-straw fields, and Custis marched into Mason's office for their usual Monday-morning meeting wearing galoshes and a wool scarf, his coat still buttoned to the neck. He tossed a large yellow envelope onto Mason's desk.

"What do we have here?" Mason asked, glancing up from a Code of Virginia volume.

"Important business." Custis sat down. "Inside you will find both your *Allman Brothers at Fillmore East* CD and your Jimmy Cliff CD. I got one from your car, the other from the stereo at your house. I took the liberty of defacin' them with a screwdriver before smashing 'em to pieces. I'm tired of walking into this office or your house and hearin'

'Whipping Post' and 'Many Rivers to Cross.' Enough of that shit, Mace. It's time for the handkerchiefs to go. Time to rejoin the rest of us." He smiled, hoping to get a rise.

"I'm sorry, Custis," Mason said without conviction. "I know I haven't been much good to anyone."

"Listen. You gotta rally. It's awful what happened, but let's draw a line and look at what's left, what comes next. It can't be all bad. Plus, your daughter deserves better."

"I've never, ever neglected my daughter. In fact —"

"Yeah," Custis jumped in, "in fact you've been too damn nice, like a Stepford father or something. Grace thinks she's taking care of *you*. Kids can tell when the train's jumped the tracks, Mace. You ain't foolin' her." He finally loosened his scarf and undid his coat.

Mason put his elbows on the desk, his chin in his hands. "I suppose you're right. Hell, I know you're right. But I can't change how much this punishes me, every moment of every day."

"Well, amigo, Uncle Custis has a plan." He reached inside his suit jacket and produced another envelope, this one white, letter-size and thick. "For you." He stretched the envelope across the desk and Mason took it.

Mason lifted the flap and removed the contents. "Puerto Rico?" he asked, befuddled. "A ticket to San Juan?"

251

"Me and you, Mason and Custis, sampling the high life come next week. We're gonna forget our troubles and jet to hot weather and drink. We'll sit by the pool, and if the opportunity presents itself, roll up on the fine tourist women. Start the new calendar with a bang. Turn the page in style. Your mom's taking care of Grace, the docket's clear and you'll notice those aren't just any tickets, nope, they're two first-class rides across the ocean. We're gonna fly away from winter for a while and find you a party. Gamble, drink, carouse, burn the midnight oil. The brochures should tell you all you need to know."

Mason laughed. "I'm not a big drinker, Custis. You know that. I've never gambled in my life."

"All the better. It's healthy to explore new vices."

"How much is this costing you? I can't let you buy me a trip."

"Not costin' me a penny, Chief. I had Sheila write the check from your personal account." He grinned at Mason. "I paid for my own, naturally." He leaned back in his chair. "This is a done deal, Mason. Pack your bags."

Mason studied the ticket. He flicked his eyes up at Custis. "Why the hell not? I've got to do something. A break might be what I need."

"Make no mistake — this isn't going to be a break, okay? This isn't a change of venue so

252

you can be unhappy by the pool instead of in the woods. This is about a crushed-velvet, seven-day, groove-on, roof-off, Mayor Marion Barry party. And I'm drivin' the bus."

"I'll be sure to bring my festive clothes." He grinned a little, cheered by his friend. "Thanks."

Two days later, Gates phoned Mason at the farm, around ten at night. It was the first call since November, as their relationship had continued to decline at a steady clip, especially after Mason had burned Gates's legal papers and returned them with a short, hostile note.

"It's me," Gates said. "Callin' to check in." He sounded tense.

"I know it's you. Collect call tipped me off."

"Right, yeah." It seemed unusually quiet at the penitentiary, no shouting or clamor coming through the receiver from Gates's end. "So are you makin' any progress, you or Mom, on getting me some help? Thought of anything?"

Mason resisted the impulse to hang up. "No" was all he said.

"How come? How come you've forgotten about me? I don't understand."

"Anything else I can do for you, Gates? Any new business before the secretary adopts the minutes and we close the meeting?" He actually looked at his watch, even though he was standing in his den, wearing sweatpants, nowhere to go, Grace bumping around upstairs preparing for bed.

"I just wanted to give you one last chance." Every word was coiled and deliberate.

"Or what?" Mason quickly asked.

"Or else. I've been patient long enough."

"Excuse me, Gates? Are you . . . are you threatening me from there in the pen, miles away? Are you? Have you lost your fucking mind? Let me guess: you've met a guy who belongs to a motorcycle gang or some hood with ties in New Jersey and this new buddy owes you a favor. You're a damn joke these days, Gates. A joke. You ought to be grateful for everything we've done, but that wouldn't be your style, would it?"

"Don't say I didn't warn you or give you a million chances."

"Whatever, Gates. You —"

The line went dead.

When Mason woke up at the Wyndham El San Juan, the sun was jitterbugging about on the ocean, his room was bright, the balcony doors were wide open and a set of long, translucent drapes was hanging free and swaying with the breeze. Custis was missing; it was 10:16 according to the red digits of the clock next to the bed. Mason walked out onto the balcony and surveyed the blue-green water, the buildings ringing the beach and

254

the hotel pool, already filling with tourists. He located ESPN on the TV and unzipped his suitcase to start putting away his clothes. Not long after he began, he heard a card slip into the lock and looked up, saw Custis holding the door against his hip, boxes and bottles on the ground, grocery bags cradled in his arms.

"How 'bout givin' me a hand?" he said to Mason. "The bellhop got me this far."

Mason helped him carry in two cases of beer, half gallons of rum and vodka, a bottle of Courvoisier, champagne, mixers, food, napkins and plastic cups. The small fridge was overwhelmed, so they filled a sink with ice, dumped in several beers and the champagne and covered them with a bath towel.

"You were serious about the big vacation," Mason said. He was sitting at the foot of his bed, still wearing his boxers.

"This is just a down payment, my man. No more than the pre-party appetizer." Custis was occupied with a boom box, searching for an electrical outlet.

Mason laughed. "The minibar would have lasted me a month. I don't know who's going to help you slay this dragon."

"Never want to get caught short."

"No worry there." Mason yawned.

"Let's see about improving our situation and headin' to the pool. It's eighty degrees, and I'm already feelin' a very promising, platinum kinda vibe take shape." Custis had the box operating. He was piling chips, nuts and snacks onto a table, next to the liquor.

"Jeez, Custis. What is that? Rap? It's bad music generally, even worse before noon."

"A little old-school to get your blood pumpin'. Wu-Tang Clan. Come on, Mason. Dentists listen to this shit." He was nodding to the beat. "And I don't have any Conway Twitty, so it'll have to do."

"Now I discover this wicked flaw, stuck here with you for a week." Mason stood, took his swim trunks from a drawer, dropped his boxers and changed into the trunks and a button-front cotton shirt. He talked as he was dressing, naked for an instant. "Some tone-deaf turd carves the sweet spot out of a real talent's song — steals it, to be blunt — then litters it with studio tricks and seventh-grade rhymes while his cousins and lowlife friends yelp in the background. Awful. The worst of it, Custis, is you have to know the chump with the gold teeth and Fatty Arbuckle pants, the brother with the mike, has about as much talent as a block of wood."

Unfazed, Custis was pouring a beer, taking care not to let the foam get away from him. "By the end of the trip, you'll be sold on Wu-Tang. I'll bet you fifty bucks, confident you'll be such a fan you won't lie just to win the cash."

"Done. Bet."

"I got another little treat for you," Custis announced.

"I hope it's an improvement."

Custis reached into his pocket and came out with a clear bag, dark across the bottom portion. He held it up with his thumb and first finger, letting it dangle. "A little smoke to boost our spirits."

"Well, now." A few fine lines formed at the corners of Mason's eyes. He extended his chin a tick forward. "Where in the world did you get that?" he asked, more amused than surprised.

"People sell it, you know." Custis tossed the bag to Mason, who caught it with cupped hands.

"Damn, I mean, here — you bought it here, I hope?"

"Of course."

"What if you'd gotten caught or —"

"Not to worry — it's all taken care of."

"How'd you find it?"

"I bought it from the concierge. But, hey, I charged it to your credit card, so I'm in the clear when the DEA arrives with the black helicopters and night goggles."

"You what? You —"

"I'm just fuckin' with you," Custis said, laughing so hard he snorted.

Mason relaxed, a grin twisting into his lips. "Smart-ass."

"I paid a kid on the beach fifty bucks; he

seemed enterprisin'. Runs a Jet Ski rental right below the hotel." Custis sipped his beer. "So you gonna take advantage of my acquisition?"

"We'll see, I guess. I've told you before I've never tried it. No lie, I never have, not even with Gates. Allison used to dabble a bit. I mean, I don't have a major problem with it. It's not a moral thing or whatever. Just never had the urge, especially when I was playing baseball and trying to stay in shape. Hell, it's no worse than alcohol, right?" He was distracted, concerned with the bag. "Don't see too many potheads beating their wives or holding up the liquor store, all jacked up on grass. Hmmm." He fingered the dope through the plastic. "You do this much, Custis? At home, in Stuart?"

"Never shit where you eat, Mace. And it wouldn't be quite righteous for me to prosecute people and then burn one during the drive home from work. I might party a bit when I'm visitin' out of town, with friends in D.C. or Atlanta. It's all politics anyway — reefer madness, you know? One toke, you'll become wild-eyed riffraff, playin' the jazz piano and kickin' in doors to support your Mary Jane habit. Comes down to it, the moonshine and apple brandy we laugh off and wink at is probably far more harmful."

"I'm not saying I disagree."

"Since we're on the subject, I appreciate

258

the fact you've never pressured me 'bout my, uh, what should I say, my appearance and libertarian streak. Don't ask, don't tell has been a good policy for us."

"Sure," Mason said solemnly. "But now that I've learned the truth, I'll be firing you. Can't have a druggie on the state payroll, can we?"

"Damn, what a bitch. You'll probably give me bad references, too. 'Course, you the man holdin' the reefer. I don't have the first idea how it got in our room." Custis grinned.

"You know, why not? Let's smoke some. You're absolutely right — I need to loosen up. We're on vacation in a foreign country, miles away from everything and everybody, and I've been through a hellacious year. Who'd begrudge me a simple misdemeanor? Fix us a joint."

"It's not quite a foreign country, Secretary Albright. Last I checked, Puerto Rico is a U.S. commonwealth, but —"

"They speak Spanish — close enough for me."

"Comin' right up," Custis said. "Attaboy. Grab yourself a cold Corona to wash it down." He gestured toward the bathroom. "I knew this was gonna work out. Damn straight." He took the pot from Mason. "There's an opener on the back of the door — say what you will, that's takin' care of your guests, yes indeed. A fine omen, Mace. Your accommodating hotels know to hook you up with some convenient hardware on the door or right under the sink. What would you prefer — French-milled soap or a place to open your malt liquor?"

"So this stuff is going to make me high, correct? Giddy and fun? Carefree?" Mason was on his way to the beer.

"Do electric razors and Chia Pets command the stage at Christmastime?"

"That would be a definite yes." Mason opened a beer. The metal cap hit the floor and rolled toward the tub. He chuckled. "It's not even eleven o'clock, and we've got seven days of this in front of us."

"Wake and bake," Custis said.

"I don't feel anything," Mason declared. They were standing in the hallway, waiting for the elevator to arrive. "What's it supposed to be doing?" He took a drink of beer. "Maybe we need to go back to the room. Or maybe your merchant on the beach took you for a ride without the Jet Ski. Sold you a bag of nothing."

"From the smell of the goods, we're okay on that account. Perhaps if your tight ass would relax and slide into it, we wouldn't have to smoke a bail to get you buzzed." Custis was wearing a shirt and swimsuit that matched, green, red and black, a "gay Jamaican's pajama ensemble" Mason had teased.

He'd added some beads and bright bands to his hair. The shirt was mostly unbuttoned, and he'd purchased a new pair of leather sandals for the trip. Mason could smell cologne.

"This is the worst elevator I've ever seen. We've been here for decades."

"It does seem slow," Custis agreed. "Any idea where the stairs are?"

A mother and her small son approached and stood beside them. The woman was holding the boy by the wrist, and he was twisting and squirming, his shoulders and nose red from the sun.

"The elevator's not too swift," Mason informed her. He switched his beer to the hand on the other side, away from the kid. "We've been waiting forever." He smiled at her, then her son. She zipped him a stern look.

A moment later, she took a step forward and pressed the call button. It illuminated, turning white around a black arrow. Her boy peered up at Custis and Mason, and the elevator arrived almost immediately. *Ding.*

"Oh, wow," Mason said. "Good thing you came along, ma'am."

Custis was struggling not to laugh, his huge hands covering his face, looking out through spread fingers. He gestured for the woman and her son to go ahead. "We'll take the next one," he said, avoiding eye contact.

The doors shut, erasing the woman and child, and it was on, oh was it ever, the two men giggling and high-fiving, happy almost to the point of tears. Mason hadn't felt so good in months, and by the time they found chairs at the pool, he was enraptured with the number pi, punching Custis's arm and saying, "I'm serious, think about it, it's this aberrant number, one of a kind, that goes forever, that never terminates or repeats. It can't be stopped or finished, not by anyone. What an amazing fucking phenomenon — infinite, invincible. Damn." He asked the waitress to bring him something "sweet and lethal," and he and Custis enjoyed the sun, the warmth, the new scenery, the separation from home, both of them stoned as cats, their world rendered in concentrated colors and heavy outlines.

They ate plates of French fries for lunch and visited the room to smoke another joint. When they returned to the pool, a DJ was playing music and people were dancing and drinking, the resort afternoon starting to hit its stride. The DJ selected "Electric Slide," and a rush of people, mostly women, popped up and started dancing. More vacationers trickled onto the pool deck as the song progressed, some with drinks still in their hands. Swaying, clapping, spinning, the group moved together, side to side, up and back, one large woman flamboyantly adding extra shakes and gyrations to every turn in the choreography, her giant rear and huge breasts jiggling like nobody's business.

"Shit, Custis, here's our chance," Mason said, high and half-serious. He was propped up in a chaise longue, a fresh piña colada balanced on his stomach. "Though I have to admit I don't know how to do the dance."

"Well, that's a plus. Here's a little secret for you since you've been on the shelf a while: no man who does the electric slide is ever going to get laid. It's a universal truth. Take a look at the pigeons and goofs you got out there. Ain't a woman alive who's gonna be impressed by a bunch of stiff-kneed, upright, counted-out cracker moves — it's barely above a hoedown. Barkin' up your do-si-do and checkered-shirts tree. This shit is for the jesters and the wannabes on the undercard who don't know any better. Don't embarrass me."

Mason set his piña colada on the ground. "I knew that," he said, laughing until he began coughing. "So when do we make our move? We listening for Luther? The Bruce Lee Clan or whatever it was?"

"Wait for your pitch, Mace. Don't need to be swingin' at the slider in the dirt. Your man Custis will give you the assist. Try not to screw it up."

As good as his promise, an hour later Custis had corralled three women at the pool bar, and they were traveling with two affable couples, all of them from a North Carolina doctor's office, sent to Puerto Rico and the Wyndham every year courtesy of their plastic surgeon boss.

Custis beckoned Mason to the bar and introduced him to everyone there. Two golfers from Ohio, still in their long pants and knit shirts, joined the group, and Custis somehow recruited an attractive older lady who had been reading a paperback book by herself the entire day. He ordered a round for everyone, and Mason commandeered a waitress's tray and served the drinks, a mock bow and a request for a tip following each delivery. By four thirty, after shots, ribald jokes and several slapstick dives off the board — predominantly cannonballs and jackknives — the celebration had moved to Custis and Mason's room, more people along for the ride, twenty or so in all, strangers mixing free drinks and chugging beers, music blaring, the women in bathing suits and skimpy cover-ups, sticky with coconut-scented oil.

Custis and two of the North Carolina women found their way to Mason, who was pouring rum into orange juice and eating from a bag of corn chips. One of the women was named Liz; the other's name he couldn't remember, but he'd taken to calling her "the Contessa" because of the way she handled her Cosmopolitan at the pool, sipping it daintily with her pinky pointed away from the plastic cup. The women were tipsy and loud, very flirty, both attractive, and Liz hadn't changed from her two-piece, was flitting around the room in flip-flops, a tattoo decorating her ankle, smoking cigarettes.

"Reggie says you guys know tons of celebrities," the Contessa said to Mason. Custis had introduced himself as Reggie, and Mason was Holden, though Mason kept forgetting to use the aliases and caused everyone confusion. Having misunderstood him at one point, the golfers were addressing Custis as Festus, and naturally Mason became Marshal Dillon.

"You could say so. Yep." Mason raised his drink. "Cheers. Everybody okay alcohol-wise?" His speech had started to slip, *s*'s and *d*'s affected the most.

"I told your skeptical self twice," Custis retorted with feigned offense. "Now you gotta come and ask my partner. Being sports agents, you tend to encounter a few folks with a profile."

"I thought you were lawyers," Liz said. She was a blonde with short hair and slender legs and arms.

"We are," Custis told her.

"You want a milkman doing your important sports-agent business?" Mason added. "Of course we're lawyers. Ask me a legal question." He took a swig of his drink and shuddered. "Whoa — little too strong there,

265

bartender." He scrunched his face. "Oh shit, I *am* the bartender."

"So who do you know famous?" the Contessa demanded. She was blond also, taller than Liz, with longer hair. It might've been the dope, but it appeared to Mason that she'd had her lips and breasts altered. Probably a job perk.

"What we do is confidential," Custis told her. "I can't be chattin' 'bout our clients to strangers at a cocktail party."

"So we have to take your word, huh?" Liz pressed him. She was smiling, impaired, bullshitting and enjoying it.

"Reggie says you played baseball." The Contessa was addressing Mason.

"I did."

"College All-American, three years with the Mets," Custis said, clueing his friend.

"True, true. Swing for the fences. That's my motto."

"I think you two are makin' this up." The Contessa pouted her exaggerated lips.

Custis shook his head. "My, my, my. Ye of so little faith. Wait right here." He left, rummaged through his suitcase and located his cell phone. "You've heard of Deion Sanders, haven't you?" he asked when he'd rejoined them, phone in hand.

"Sure," said the Contessa.

"The football player," Liz noted. She shook out a cigarette and touched Mason on the

266

arm to ask if he had a light. He didn't, apologized. One of the golfers tossed them a plastic Bic. She lit her cig and touched him again, seemed very close. "Do you guys have any tequila?"

"Afraid not," Mason replied. "It's one of those tastes you acquire as you get older. Like onions. Or black coffee. Or rare meat. We're not that mature yet." He laughed at what he'd said, his own rambling. Slightly dizzy and too warm, he set down his rum and orange juice, aware he needed to take a break. He opened a Coke and drank it from the can.

"So just to satisfy you ladies, I'm gonna put Deion on the line and let you say hello," Custis announced. "Try not to say somethin' stupid, and don't mention Tim McCarver. Not a word about Tim."

One of the golfers overheard the conversation and sidled up beside the Contessa. "Sweet," he said. "You know Neon Deion?"

Custis made a show of holding the phone in front of him and pushing two buttons. "Motherfucker's on speed-dial — you could say I know him." He placed the phone against his ear, waited. "Where Deion?" he said, his voice high, the tone purposefully aggressive. "Tell him his man Reggie's callin' from San Juan." A knot of people had now gathered around Custis; the music had been switched off. "Deion, man, this is Reggie," he said, evidently to someone on the other end. They bantered for several minutes, the exchange about a Porsche and a barbecue restaurant in Memphis. "Listen, 'PT,' I got a lady here wants to shout at you — it might raise Reggie's stock if you say a word or two, if you take my meanin'. And don't forget to call me about the variety show with CBS — it's gonna happen." He transferred the phone to the Contessa, and she talked awhile, laughing and sipping a beer, before telling the man on the line he could be anyone — how did she know he was really Deion? The golfers suggested a football question, which he correctly answered, and finally Mason heard her say, "Okay, I will," and she disconnected the call and handed the phone to Custis.

"What? What'd he say?" Liz asked her. "Why'd you hang up?"

Mason was as ensnared as everyone else, buzzed and tripping, wondering about the conversation. He caught Custis's eye but couldn't read him.

The phone rang, and Custis turned it so the Contessa and Liz could view the screen. Mason craned to see as well. "Saunders, Deion" appeared on the caller ID. He answered the call after one ring, thanked Deion for the effort and said good-bye. "Deion says to tell you hey," he told Mason. "You can check the area code, too, ladies — Atlanta."

"Holy shit," said the Contessa. "It really was him. Did you see that?"

"Impressive," said one of the golfers. He slapped a high five with Custis, then Mason.

"I suppose now you'll want me to call Columbine and prove to you we were *there* for two weeks, tryin' to lift spirits and contributing free legal services to the families. Some sad, tragic shit," Custis said somberly.

"You've convinced me," Liz told him.

"Me, too," Mason agreed, and everybody laughed.

As soon as he could, Mason pulled Custis aside and asked about the call. "So you know Deion? Really? How come you've never brought it up before now?" He dropped a chip on the floor and stooped to retrieve it. "How'd you do that?" he asked, tossing the chip toward an ashtray and missing.

Custis's eyes were red. "I know my cousin in Atlanta, Deion *Saunders,*" he chuckled. " 'Course drunk white folks at a party usually don't catch the *u,* now do they? People go straight for the 'Deion' and hell, if they did pay attention, how many people know the difference? Sanders or Saunders. Deion and me, we've had that play for years, bread-and-butter, my man." He bumped his Corona against Mason's soft-drink can, a toast. "Custis has traveled all the routes before. Consider me your personal cartographer."

"Shit," Mason said. "Damn." He toasted again. "Slick, slick, slick." He laughed. "The

269

maestro." He swallowed some Coke. "Reggie."

Before too long, Custis, Mason, Liz and the Contessa were in the bathroom with the pot, the women hell-yeah good to go when the dope was offered. Mason took only a small toke this time, not wanting to tumble off the revelry cliff and end up passed out before sunset. They made plans to eat dinner together, and Mason and Custis, with handshakes and promises to do it again tomorrow, shooed the party away, switching the CD to jazz, declining the golfers' invitation to catch a cab into the city and hunt for a strip club. They showered and dressed and met the women at a hotel restaurant, ordering wine and Bailey's with dessert. Together, they were the kind of voluble, high-flying foursome — large men, one black, with short-skirted blond women — that caused people to look twice or cheat their eyes over a menu and follow them to their table.

The hotel lobby was bygone elegant, in the vein of Batista's Cuba: marble, chandeliers, polished wood, three energetic bars, live music, well-dressed people dancing with dramatic dips and cha-cha-cha feet and a dark-skinned man with a full mustache rolling cigars beside the casino entrance. Liz wrapped her arm inside Mason's, and he escorted her to the center bar, the busiest of the three, where she ordered a martini that was impeccably made and served with a flourish. They tried the casino, roulette and blackjack, Custis doing his best to explain the smart strategies and Mason, sloshed and reckless, betting whatever felt good in his gut, somehow not losing his shirt.

Another trip to the room for pot and the night became spotty for Mason. He and Liz made it to the beach, a bedspread on the sand along a seawall, and he kissed a woman other than Allison, remembered it had been years and years, and it felt oddly good, the breeze and her mouth, the lights around them dots, low-hung bogus stars. They had sex, in the shadows, tucked into a hitch in the wall, close and restrained, the bedspread pulled over parts of them, people walking next to the ocean below where they were, the tame waves repeating the same sound over and over.

Mason passed out and woke up to several people quarreling by the pool, and he was lost, spinning, didn't know where he was, stoned and drunk, and he guessed maybe he was in his front yard, near the barn. Allison was there with him, he could feel her, and he closed his eyes. "Oh shit," he said, realizing it wasn't his wife, his stomach stinging, his thoughts haywire. The woman with him was different, and it wasn't the right neck or shoulder. The way she lay against him was foreign, too low on his chest. He dozed off again, sick and not sure of much.

The next time he came to life, a hotel security guard was crouching beside him, amused and kindly. "Hola, amigo. Good morning." The guard had a flashlight but was merciful with the beam, keeping it away from Mason's eyes. Liz was gone.

He revived enough to tell the man he was a guest at the hotel. He didn't seem to have a key or all his clothes, and he wasn't certain of his room number but knew how to get there. He recalled his own name and his wallet was still in his pants pocket, enough information to have him returned to their room after a walkie-talkie contact with the front desk. He slept until noon on gritty, sticky sheets, finally shaken awake by Custis.

"Rise and shine, Party King." The Wu-Tang Clan was on the box, harsh as ever. "Nice to have you conscious." Custis grinned.

"I feel awful. Uhhhh. Damn." He dragged a pillow across his face. "How're you so chipper?" he asked, the question muffled.

"Plenty of water, no hard liquor after midnight, food before bed. I'd suggest you consider dialing your party back to a steady six or seven instead of red-lining it at ten."

"Try zero. I'm done." He removed the pillow. "You're the fucker who kept at me. Kept pouring the poison down my throat and egging me on. Big of you to worry now."

"I apologize." Custis took a seat and began strapping on his sandals. "So'd you do okay

272

with the lovely Liz?"

"As best as I remember, yeah." Mason sat up against the headboard. "You?"

"Not as fortunate, I'm afraid. It's one thing if you're a white woman to dance and kiss and talk shit, bump and grind; it's a different story to close the deal with Mr. Johnson. Black man's got two battles to fight with a white girl — it's tough enough to get any woman to sign up for a one-night stand, much less jump races."

"Really? Huh. Seemed to me, Mr. Mandela, the only fight you had was keeping the Contessa from screwing you in public. Hell, Custis, she was grabbing your crotch in the lobby."

"Trust me, it's not as easy as you might think. 'Course, I've still got six days to make my case." He finished with the sandals and stood. "But I'm happy for my buddy. Glad to see you catchin' fire again. Not standin' against the wall moping."

"Yeah." Mason swung his feet out of bed, sat on the edge with his head thumping. "It goes without saying it was bittersweet. And now I wish I hadn't fucked her." He put the heels of his hands against his temples and rubbed small circles. "I shouldn't have done it." He flopped back onto the mattress.

"You've been in the monastery for eight months," Custis said. "It's okay."

"To top it off, I didn't even think about

birth control or AIDS or whatever."

Custis folded his arms. "I swear, it's like lookin' after a child. A handicapped child."

Mason didn't leave the room until almost five o'clock. Custis, Liz and the Contessa checked on him twice during the afternoon, Liz explaining she'd hated to leave him alone on the beach and had tried to wake him several times before she stumbled off, afraid of what might happen to her. Worried, she'd sent a man from the hotel to check on him. He ate some pasta and a bowl of soup for dinner and went to sleep early. He told the maid she could skip their room. He never showered.

A day's rest helped. Mason recovered, and they finished out the week with the remainder of the marijuana and more moderate amounts of alcohol. They took the women to watch the cocks fight but stayed for only one raw, to-the-death battle, all of them put off by the loser's missing eye and limp neck. Relying on Custis's recommendation — "trust me on this," he promised them — everyone agreed to stay in for an evening and watch *Cannonball Run.* Custis had discovered the movie at a video store in town, and he rented a VCR from the hotel. They closed the drapes, started the movie, smoked dope and ate a box of Whitman's candy, the sampler, high as Georgia pines, selecting a piece of chocolate on the lid diagram and then tracking it down in the maze of brown wrappers and yellow cardboard. "Hell, that's Sammy and Dean Martin," Mason exclaimed, walleyed and chewing the solid square with the messenger boy's image. "I hope they win. This is great, Custis. Excellent choice as always."

Mason had sex he could remember with Liz the night before she was due to fly home to North Carolina, and they walked on the beach afterward. His conscience hurt him as they were having an early breakfast the next morning, seated outside on a restaurant's veranda, and he told her his real name and what he did for a living. Solid black birds with yellow eyes and black legs and feet were flying around, hopping from table to table, diving into abandoned plates, skittering and flapping, extracting scraps and the crumbs of pastry sweets whenever they had the chance. The waiters would shout at the birds in Spanish and wave at them with white cloth napkins. There was only one other couple at the restaurant, older, sharing a newspaper.

"I hope you aren't cross with me," he said. "It was fun meeting you. I didn't think we'd be seeing each other as often as we did, or I would've been honest when we met. Or at least corrected Custis and told you my name."

"Not at all — it means a lot to me you wanted to tell me the truth and so forth." She tossed a toast corner to a bird and seven or eight others swooped in, screeching, fighting for a bite. Two waiters gave her an unhappy look. "So how much better or worse is the rest of the story? You know, are you married or engaged or like, I don't know, serious with someone?" She'd told him she was twice divorced — but amicable with both her former husbands. She had an eight-year-old son.

"My wife was killed in a car wreck last May. This is the first . . . you're the first woman I've given any thought since then. I have a daughter named Grace. She's the center of my universe. I probably ran up a two-hundred-dollar phone bill calling her."

"Oh my, I'm so sorry," she said. "Bless your heart." She was absently twisting an empty Sweet'N Low packet around her finger. "How terrible for you."

"Yeah." He watched the birds, kept his eyes off Liz. "Yeah, it is. But being here was nice. Thanks for taking such fine care of me. I've been really struggling."

He carried her heavy blue pleather suitcase to a cab at the hotel's entrance, and they exchanged numbers, kissed and hugged and talked about seeing each other down the road, although Mason wasn't sure he'd be up for it. Custis hit him with an empty beer can when he confessed he'd ratted them out to Liz, laughing and shaking his head and screaming "Judas" while Mason tried to justify breaking ranks.

"So you feelin' better?" Custis asked after he'd finished the needling. "You off the skids?"

"Not really. I'm improved, I guess. The problem is, I mean, well, spending time with these women, who were okay in their own way, pleasant and entertaining for sure, makes me realize how I'll never replace Allison. But I'm going to quit feeling sorry for myself — that's the important thing. Getting some perspective, stepping away from Stuart and a place so . . . so . . . saturated with Allison and me, yeah, that's been helpful. I'd like to think I can miss her and not have it ruin me." He blinked and looked away, gazed at the carpet. "I appreciate your going to all this trouble," he said. "It's great to know you can count on someone, a friend. I'm grateful, Cus. Thanks."

"My pleasure," Custis said quietly. He emptied potato chip crumbs from a bag straight into his mouth. "Let's hope our new girlfriends don't go broadcastin' everything they know, huh, Mason? I still can't believe you gave her the real goods."

"You owe me fifty bucks — I still hate the Wu-Tang Clan." He didn't look up.

CHAPTER TEN

When he returned to the farm, Mason set about anchoring his life again. He apologized to Sheila, the other lawyers in Stuart, his mom and his friends, telling them he was sorry he'd been so moody and unbearable. They all claimed to understand, assured him that grieving came with the territory, charitably lied and said they really hadn't noticed anything out of the way. He talked to Grace at the kitchen table and promised her they were over the worst of it and suggested they'd now just take care of each other double and enjoy what they were fortunate enough to still have. She took in his words, listening with her head slanted up at him, her mother blooded into her looks and mannerisms, her gangly legs. "Triple," she answered him, and seemed relieved, smiling and wiggly, happy to have her father reformed, done with his hangdog stares and late-night pacing.

A week later, he cashed a sick day and stayed home to pack Allison's clothes in cardboard boxes and haul them to the Martinsville Goodwill, keeping only her wedding gown, his favorite cocktail dress and several blouses Grace fancied. He gave her perfume and cosmetics to Grace, who wrapped the bottles, tubes and compacts elaborately and tucked them away in her dresser.

Following a cordial negotiation with the owner of the New York gallery that had dibs on her last piece, he drove the rhino to a Winston-Salem shop and had it framed, holding on to it for himself. He sorted through Allison's studio, carefully storing her books, sketches, paints, brushes, easel and canvases in the attic. He cried on and off while he did it, but he didn't flag or let himself become sidetracked. He and Grace invited about thirty neighbors and friends to stop by for a get-together, where they unveiled the framed painting along with the room's new pool table and a big-screen TV. They decided to leave the ratty sofa as it was and didn't disturb the hodgepodge of drops and smears on the floor where the easel had stood. Custis christened the table, taking the first shot.

Mason placed a photograph of Allison on his bureau, secured her jewelry in a box at the bank so it would be safe for their daughter, filed the estate paperwork at the clerk's office, and finally returned the calls of the lawyer who managed her trust. She'd left the stipend to him, now close to $275,000 a year, the change of beneficiary instruction dated three days before they'd wed. He took steps to transfer it to their daughter at his death, signing the forms and faxing the documents from his office the same morning he received them.

He dutifully sent Liz several photos from Puerto Rico and phoned her a time or two so he wouldn't feel like a cad, and they met for a meal in Greensboro, but removed from the perfect hothouse of a weeklong island romp — all pool drinks and pot and blank slates — their romance withered. He was relieved when she allowed in an e-mail as to how she'd begun seeing someone from Durham and it would be difficult for her to keep in contact. "Dumped your timid ass, didn't she?" Custis razzed him.

He visited Reverend Hunsicker and mended fences, told him he was still miffed and couldn't make sense of his predicament, but at least had come around to a general notion of deism, was back to Jefferson's armchair creator, a god who fashioned the universe and occasionally ventured from his lair long enough to add another ring to Saturn or adjust the thermostat a few degrees in the Amazon.

"That's a beginning," the preacher beamed. "Something's better than nothing."

"Yeah — I think I'm pointed in the right direction," Mason replied.

In the months ahead, he gradually became a man who learned to crutch his loss, compensating until the dreadful became routine, *his* normal, shit he just incorporated and dealt with, same as diabetics with their insulin or a car you always have to park on an incline so it can be push-started, making do.

Chapter Eleven

"Remember, we're probably only gonna have one crack at this," Jay Lane said before he walked through the door to the Patrick County Commonwealth's Attorney's Office. "Our first pitch needs to be a winner, Gerald. It'd be nice to snag this guy."

"Yep," Gerald Hooper said. It was the spring of 2003, the countryside starting to bloom in Stuart, the sun finally sticking around past suppertime.

The two men introduced themselves to Sheila, mentioned their appointment and were ushered in to see Mason without having to wait. Mason met them and shook hands and welcomed them. Custis was there too, perusing the *Enterprise,* and he made it a point to cross the room and greet both men, calling them "Mr. Lane" and "Mr. Hooper" even though they were younger than he. Everyone took a seat.

"Mr. Hunt, I'm here in my capacity as the governor's assistant chief of staff," Lane said without any arrogance or pretension. "Gerald works with me in Richmond."

"That's what Sheila told me when you phoned last week. You didn't need to drive four hours to speak to me. Can't imagine what's so important."

Lane shifted in his chair. "Glad to do it; we felt our business was serious enough we should visit you personally."

"Okay," Mason said.

"As you know, this region is really hurting, your county in particular. You have the second-highest unemployment in the state, the textile and furniture industries are absolutely kaput, jobs are scarce, the economy's dead as a horseshoe nail. You've lost Tultex, DuPont, Spencer's, J.P. Stevens, Fieldcrest Mills — the list goes on forever."

"I hear they're plannin' layoffs at United Elastic," Custis added.

"It's bad, yeah," Mason said. "Truth be told, I don't know how people are going to make it. Ten years ago, I'd never have believed it. The shame is most people here will give you a good day's effort for their paycheck."

"Well, I'd like to cut to the chase," Lane said. "Are you familiar with the Tobacco Commission?"

"Generally. What I've read in the papers."

Hooper spoke up. "The Tobacco Commission, Mr. Hunt, is the entity tasked with disbursing the commonwealth's share of proceeds from the federal litigation with various cigarette manufacturers." His recitation was crisply delivered, no doubt polished before scores of newspaper reporters and subcommittee muckety-mucks. He sat erect in his chair. "The stated goal of the commission is to promote growth and development in communities such as yours. Over the next two decades, the commission will distribute four-point-one billion dollars to localities." He lingered on the "billion" part.

"I'm all for it," Mason said. "We can use it."

Lane looked at Hooper, then back at Mason. "We're here on behalf of the governor to ask you to serve as a board member. We feel you would be an excellent representative."

"Really?" Mason picked up a yellow pencil from his desk. "I wondered why you gentlemen were driving down here; we assumed it was about an extradition or something sensitive with the attorney general's office." He started tapping the pencil's eraser end against his thigh. "Huh. Why me? It's no secret I hate politics and politicians."

Lane laughed politely. "Your senator, Roscoe Reynolds, recommended you. You're extremely well thought of in this area, and the people here need a voice, an advocate, someone to honestly take care of them where this money is concerned. You have a fine record as a prosecutor, plus you've had a

284

taste of Richmond. And it's precisely because this isn't a political job that we think you'd be a great asset."

"Listen — if there's big money, there'll be politics." Mason laid the pencil on his desk blotter. "In fact, in my opinion, they're one and the same."

"Sad but true to some extent," Lane agreed.

"What would I have to do?" Mason asked.

"Obviously, this isn't the local library board or the Lion's Club parade committee. It's a serious, heavy-duty commitment. It would involve twelve to fifteen meetings a year, the thorough review of hundreds of grant requests and frequent consultations with other members and staff. It's no picnic, and we can't pay you, but it would be a huge service to Patrick County and all of Southside."

"Essentially, you would be on the board of a multibillion-dollar corporation," Hooper explained. "A board that would make critical decisions affecting you and your community."

"Pretty cool gig," Custis remarked.

"You think?" Mason glanced at him.

"Maybe you could score us money for the office revitalization project we been discussin' — the Jacuzzi and wet bar for the law library and matching sharkskin suits for key jury trials." Custis grinned at the two bureaucrats.

Lane didn't seem upset by the joke. "If you'd like, Mr. Hunt, the governor would be willing to speak to you directly about this.

285

Your participation is a priority for him."

"Why not, Mace?" Custis had turned serious. "You might do some good. Might help pull us out of the ditch."

Mason was quiet. He pursed his lips. "I'll sleep on it, if that's okay with everyone. I'll speak to my daughter, too. How about I give you an answer tomorrow?"

"I'll leave my card and my cell number," Lane said. "We appreciate your time and your allowing us to interrupt you."

"Jeez — they make it sound like you're Lee Iacocca or Commodore Vanderbilt or somethin'," Custis kidded him after the Richmonders were gone. "Evidently, the whole enterprise will collapse unless you sign on."

"It's their job to make people feel important. They're professional sycophants, a level above your common jester with bells on his shoes. Apparatchiks minus the vodka and tiny dacha."

"At least they seemed like good sports."

"Yes, they did," Mason answered.

The following afternoon, Mason phoned and accepted the governor's offer, became a board member of the Tobacco Indemnification and Community Revitalization Commission. He agreed to the appointment because his community was broke and suffering and on the brink of ruin, and he figured he could do as well as the next fellow when it came to showing up at a meeting to wrestle for pork-barrel dollars. He also took the job because he needed something to keep him sharp, a challenge. The business of a rural commonwealth's attorney's office tended to turn routine after a while, stale, and Mason was determined he would never fade into the ways of a sad-sack country lawyer, like the ham-and-eggers doing basic wills for seventy-five bucks a pop or poor old Wally Walters, Jr., harrumphing and hooking his suspenders, a blowhard with a fat tie and brown shoes who last opened a proper legal text during law school, waving his hands and spouting moldy truisms in court, his arguments so obvious an imbecile could see them coming. Mason didn't want to stagnate and peter out at the county line, and this would allow him to stay in circulation.

"Seems like it'll help me and could help the area," he informed Custis. "I'm making the right call, don't you think?"

"Does the ambitious local weatherman, angling for a network promotion, don his slicker and broadcast live from the eye of the hurricane?"

Twelve days later, on a Tuesday, Ray Bass was standing beneath the metal awning at the Patrick County Commonwealth's Attorney's Office. "As much as I hate doin' this, we take it seriously," he cautioned his companion. "We've got one chance. We're gonna get one

287

read, and that'll be it. Quick and sudden —
that's the plan."

"Absolutely," replied Rick Minter. Out of
habit, he pushed back his blazer and checked
his holstered gun. Spring was sailing along by
now, the yellow forsythia bushes past their
peak, the hardwoods awakening, the bugs
hatching from the dirt and beginning to grow
active in the evenings. The crickets and
cicadas were the most noticeable, shrill and
steady, their sounds everywhere and always
at a distance, encircling the outdoors like
sheets of noise tacked to hilltops and high,
sturdy limbs.

Bass and Minter introduced themselves to
Sheila, and because they weren't expected,
didn't have an appointment, they had to wait
in the lobby for nearly an hour before Mason
returned from district court. Mason buzzed
Sheila at her desk, and she walked with them
to his office and showed them in. Mason
stood and the men reached across his desk to
shake hands. He'd met Minter before, but
didn't know Ray Bass. Mason sat down first,
then the two visitors, almost in unison. Bass
didn't waste time addressing what was on his
mind. "We appreciate your seein' us on such
short notice. Agent Minter and I realize you
have a busy schedule."

"Always happy to help when I can," Mason
said. Minter and Bass were state police
investigators; Mason had worked with Minter

on a 1998 homicide, the stabbing of a man by his live-in girlfriend.

"We have some good news. A break on a case, an old one."

"Great, let's hear it." Mason noticed both men seemed uneasy and stiff, their shoulders squared off toward him.

"Remember a shooting years ago, back in the eighties, a boy by the name Wayne Thompson was murdered?"

Mason felt his skin tingle, juiced with adrenaline. "Yeah. Uh, yeah, I do." He crossed his legs.

"Well, we've turned up a witness — a Frederick Wright — who says the killer confessed to him. He says a man named Allen Roberts is the shooter. We checked, and this Roberts was a suspect originally, but nothing came of it. Roberts and the deceased were in an argument earlier in the evening, a dispute about a pool game as best we can tell."

Without meaning to, Mason gripped the edge of his desk. His collar and cuffs suddenly felt scratchy, binding him. "So this witness, this Wright fellow, so, uh, you believe he's reliable?"

"Passed a polygraph," Minter assured him. "I can send you a copy if you want it."

"Yeah. Please." Mason stopped pinching his desk. He put his hands in his pockets. "Is that it? A witness? And why, pray tell, does Mr. Roberts confess after all these years?

What's his relationship with Wright?"

"They used to work together. Drinkin' buddies. Wright tells us they were sharin' a bottle and Roberts says he needs to get it off his chest. Admits he shot Wayne Thompson. Wright didn't know what he should do, so he told his brother-in-law, who's a deputy in Floyd. The brother-in-law contacted us."

"I'm not sure how strong a case we can build from a drunk's ramblings. Hell, maybe he did say it, just flapping his gums. Or maybe your witness misunderstood or has some grudge. Polygraph or not, I'd need more. Over and above all that, I know Allen Roberts pretty well — it's going to be a tough sell for you to convince me he's a killer."

"I agree," Minter said. "A good lawyer'd clean our clocks." He barely paused, but changed the set of his head. " 'Course, we got the gun. We have the murder weapon. A thirty-eight. Lab is positive on the match. Found it at Roberts's house." Minter was short and skinny. His hands were interlocked at his belt buckle, his black shoes were planted on the floor. He seemed stock-still.

Mason eased his chair backward, rolling on brass casters and speaking at the same time. "That's impossible . . . impossible to, uh, imagine, but lucky, I guess. A real break, it being so many years ago. The shooting. Incredible you'd find the gun after so long."

Reaching inside his coat, Bass produced a

report from the Division of Forensic Science, placed it on the desk and gave it a small push. "No doubt we have the pistol," he said. The paper hung on the wood and didn't slide very far.

Mason left the report alone. "So you want me to indict Allen Roberts?"

"Well, we think we're pretty close — a confession to a disinterested witness and the gun."

"What's Allen say about this?" Mason asked. "Have you interviewed him?"

"Denies it. We talked to him yesterday. Won't give an inch." The way Bass was sitting, Mason could see his silver badge. It was attached to his belt, above the hip. "Says what he said in 1984 — claims he ain't involved."

"I see," Mason mumbled. He was thinking of the Burger King Dumpster, the muted, unremarkable sound the cylinder and bag made when they landed, the kid taking a smoke break.

"Not to step on toes," Minter said, "but your brother was a suspect, too, wasn't he? I saw where Danny Owen had questioned him."

A flatbed truck passed by the window and took Mason's attention. After it cleared, he saw Roy Lee McAlexander hobbling from the grocery store to his house, a translucent plastic sack in each hand. Probably toting beer home to get snockered. "He was. But he was with me and lots of other people. For what it's worth, I was there for his interview. He —" Mason was seized by a thought that caused him to break off and bring a finger to his temple and fisheye both cops. "He didn't have anything to do with it." Every word stuck on the roof of his mouth as if it were coated in flour. He hoped his face and neck weren't mottled.

Bass and Minter didn't reply right away. They reminded Mason of the summer toads at the farm, always biding their time beneath a floodlight or brightened transom, vigilant brown lumps watching . . . watching . . . watching . . . watching, waiting for a gnat or moth to dip too deep and become food for a sticky, darting tongue. The three men sat there in a fierce silence — at least a full minute — until Minter spoke. "You okay takin' on the case — any conflicts or doubts?" His voice was carefully formal. Stilted.

"I'll do just fine. Thanks for asking. I might talk to Allen myself. Have the sheriff bring him in."

"I don't think he'll give you anything new."

Mason shrugged. "Just the same, it wouldn't hurt to see if he'll talk to us. Never know what might come of it." He glanced out his window again. Roy Lee was gone. "So what did Allen say after you told him you'd located the gun there? Was he present when you found it?"

"Claimed he'd never seen it," Bass answered. "He wasn't at home when we arrived and executed the warrant, so we served it on his wife." Bass was tracing the bright outline of his badge with his index finger as he spoke.

"Where exactly was this gun?" Mason asked.

"Buried beside an oak tree."

"Allen lives on ten, fifteen acres, right? And you knew to dig at exactly this spot because . . . ?"

"Because that's what Roberts told our witness," Minter said. "Roberts told Frederick Wright where the gun was located and, lo and behold, that's where we found it. Pretty powerful stuff, huh?"

"Why would anyone bury a murder weapon in their own backyard and then tell a drinking buddy where it was?" Mason asked. "There's something screwy here."

"Well, like I said, we have ourselves a believable witness, a lie-detector test, the weapon which done the shootin' and a confession. You're the lawyer, but I like our odds." Minter rocked forward. "Why *wouldn't* you hide the gun on your own place, where nobody but you has access and you can keep watch?"

"Why wouldn't you throw it in Smith Mountain Lake or bury it on someone else's property?" Mason asked.

"Who's to say, huh?" Bass stuck Mason

with a tight, prickly smile.

Mason picked up a legal pad and wrote Roberts's name across the top along with the words "gun" and "confession." He stared at the pad and pretended to consider the facts he'd been given. He faked concentration and made a whistling sound, almost a hiss, air pushed through his teeth and dry lips. "Definitely worth taking a look at," he said, still focusing on the pad. "Definitely." He mustered enough grit and composure to raise his eyes and face the cops. "I didn't mean to harangue you guys — just playing the devil's advocate. Better to find the problem here than at trial. I need to have all the bases covered before I charge someone with murder, but it seems like you've done your homework."

"I understand," Minter said.

"Send me everything you've got. I'll have the sheriff take another pass, and we'll go from there."

"Affirmative," Bass said, already rising. "Thanks for seein' us."

"Fuck," Mason muttered after he heard the men speak to Sheila and knew they'd departed. "Damn." He ran his hands through his hair, stopping at his crown, and sank into his seat with his palms pressing against his skull. "Damn." He was utterly rattled, feverish, sick all over, poisoned by the ambush, dizzy, his lungs choked with pitch, snakes squirming in his guts. He took his hands down, noticed they were trembling. "Thank you, Gates," he said aloud. "You piece of shit."

Outside, as they were striding toward their gray Ford, Bass caught Rick Minter with a sidelong glance. "Gee," he said, his mouth pointed at the ground, acting nonchalant for the benefit of anyone watching. "Maybe there's somethin' to this. He looked like we'd slapped him upside the head, and then it took dynamite to get him to move on a slam-dunk case." Bass kept walking, his partner close by. "Let's have the tape transcribed soon as we can." He patted his blazer's breast pocket. "Man, I hope we got everything, especially the 'impossible' part."

The following morning, Sheriff David Hubbard and Investigator Roger Wilson met with Mason in the sheriff's private office. Across the hall, Allen Roberts was by himself in a sparsely furnished room, the door shut, a half-empty soft drink beside him. At Mason's request, Wilson had telephoned Agent Bass and received several faxed pages and an overview of the murder case against Roberts.

"He ain't admitting to it," the sheriff informed Mason. "We've been at it for an hour. He claims he doesn't know anything about the gun and didn't shoot nobody.

Roger's given him a pretty thorough talkin'-to."

"He's not gonna change his story," Wilson said, frowning. "I mean, you know, it is what it is." He was gray-headed, wearing a maroon windbreaker. Above him, on the wall, was a framed picture of the entire police force and staff from the year 1999, taken on the courthouse portico. "I gotta say, Mason, I'm a little surprised, what with the kinda person Allen is. We were in school together; I've known him all my life. He just don't seem like the type."

"You and the state police been on this for a while?" the sheriff inquired. He was a tall, strong man with a black mustache, a cattle farmer from off the Meadows of Dan mountain. Shrewd and unflappable, he rarely raised his voice and was popular with his employees.

"I heard about it yesterday for the first time," Mason said.

"Kinda strange they didn't include us or give us a courtesy call," the sheriff mused.

"Yeah," Mason agreed. "You guys mind if I talk to him?"

"Be my guest," Wilson said. "You want us to be with you?"

"No need."

"Tape recorder's in there — on the table — and we Mirandized him soon as he got here."

"Can't say I ever recall you questionin' a suspect," the sheriff remarked. "Isn't that a little tricky — what if he admits somethin' to you? You'd be in a fix, wouldn't you? You couldn't prosecute him if you were a witness, right?"

"We'll cross that bridge if we come to it," Mason told him. "Roger's probably correct — he's not going to change his story. I just want to get a feel for this, see how he's reacting."

When Mason opened the door, Allen Roberts was smoking a cigarette and his knee was firing up and down like a sewing-machine needle, rapid and kinetic. He was dressed in bibbed overalls and a blue shirt, weathered boots splattered with specks of white. He'd worked at the same job for over twenty years, hanging Sheetrock for Clark Brothers Construction. Seeing Mason, he stubbed out his cigarette in a thick glass ashtray already filled with butts. "Hey, Mason," he said.

"Allen," Mason said quietly. He checked to make sure the recorder wasn't running. "Sorry to see you under these circumstances." As a precaution, he removed the cassette from the machine and laid it on the table.

"Mason, I swear to you on my mama's grave I didn't do this," he blurted. He took a fresh Camel from a pack in the chest pocket of his bibs. He couldn't get the first paper match to strike and had to use a second one to light his cigarette. He inhaled and blew out shaky smoke. "I know it looks bad, but damn, Mason, you know me. This is some kinda crazy nightmare."

"It would have to be," Mason said. He bent forward so both his palms were flat on the table, his arms rigid and bearing his weight. "Look at me." He said it gently, without any suggestion of malice or command.

Roberts tried, but his eyes were waterbugging all over the place.

"I know you didn't do this, okay? Don't worry. Go home and kiss your wife and drive to the store and punch the clock. As long as I'm the commonwealth's attorney, you will never be charged. Do all you can not to worry. You're innocent. You have my word nothing will happen to you. My firm oath." Mason pinned the man with a stare, honed, intense, sincere. "You hear me, Allen?"

"I don't . . . This ain't some kinda confusion, is it, you tryin' to get over on me?"

"Nope. You need to walk out of here and keep your mouth shut." Mason straightened up.

"I don't understand, Mason. This don't make sense. That ain't my gun, and I damn sure didn't bury it under no tree and I didn't kill Wayne. I never seen him after he left the Old Dominion. As for this Fred Wright, he showed up for a few days on a job we was doin' over in Ararat, and I had one beer with him in Mount Airy. He was gone the next week, and I sure as hell didn't tell him I killed a man." Roberts was flying through the words, the cig wasting in the ashtray, forgotten. "Back when this first happened, my ex–old lady done told the cops I was with her, but now I'm afraid she'll switch her story 'cause she's pissed at me over the divorce. There goes my alibi. Have ya'll found her yet? Last I heard, she was stayin' with her mom in Yanceyville. Did they keep a copy of her statement — maybe you can find it. Danny Owen was the police who talked to us."

"There's no need. I believe you. This is a terrible mistake." Mason smiled. "Come on — I'll walk you to your car."

"You sure? I . . . I . . . I don't know how the pistol —"

Mason shoved out an upturned hand — final, suffocating, brooking nothing — to cut him off. "Judge Richardson used to tell people you don't need to run to catch a streetcar you're already riding. You're on the streetcar, Allen. This is finished for you. I'm sorry we've scared you to death, sorry the system has failed you. Forget about this and put it behind you."

"Honest? You're positive?"

"Positive." Mason kept his hand in the air. "One other point: don't speak to the police anymore. If they come to see you again, you simply say, 'I don't want to talk to you. I want a lawyer.' That's the rule, no matter what they promise or what they threaten." He took down his hand. "Don't even get started with them. Slam the door. Hang up the phone. You'll only get burned by answering their questions. That includes the cops here in Stuart as well."

"Believe me, I've learned my lesson. I ain't makin' a peep next time they come around."

"You understand you don't have to talk with them about anything. Not the crime, not the gun, not even our conversation right now. Just refuse and request a lawyer. We clear?"

"Yeah. Keep my mouth shut and right off the bat say I want me a lawyer."

"Exactly."

"So I can go?" Roberts asked tentatively. "Me and you's okay with each other?"

"You're free to leave. We're done."

Roberts came around the table, a burly man with a full beard and hands damaged by decades of hammers and drywall compound, and he hugged Mason, crying and sobbing and wiping his eyes and nose with a balled red bandanna he pulled from his back pocket. "Thank you, Mason. Thank you. Lord in heaven, thank you. I got me two kids to feed. Two boys. I thought I was a goner. You're a good man."

"Not really," Mason said. "But I appreciate your saying so."

That night, Mason made a mess of dinner,

scorching the mashed potatoes so they tasted like he'd mixed in the bottom of the metal pot, and he and Grace had a round about her school dance and her sixteen-year-old "boyfriend." She called her dad Hitler and barricaded herself in her room and was still sullen the next morning, muling through breakfast, barely deigning to speak. After she'd stalked off to the bus, Mason called his mother for advice, and she promised to drop by and lend a hand. "It's only a phase," she assured him.

Before leaving home, he sat on the porch and gazed out over the pasture, watching the newborn sun scale the sky, listening to the seasonal birds celebrate their return, but he missed his wife and was pained by his loneliness, the magic spooked from his sanctuary. Forty acres and not another soul to be found. He fretted about how much he'd given away, how much truth the cops had assayed from his surprise and stumbling and clumsy playacting. Somehow, without tipping his intentions, he needed to communicate with Gates, and he had to do it quickly. Feeling claustrophobic and cramped, he drove to Stuart with the car windows rolled down, already fatigued, running on four hours of fitful, sketchy sleep and three cups of coffee, the last one black with grounds in almost every swallow.

301

■ ■ ■

When he arrived at work, Mason discovered Custis was busy in juvenile court, already gone. Around noon, after three impatient, wasted hours, Mason finally heard him next door and went into his office. John Coltrane was on the wall, along with framed degrees and a picture of Custis wielding a gavel at a town council meeting. He was still carrying his files under an arm, standing beside his desk, reading pink phone slips.

"Mace, hey. Check this out: Judge gave our boy Benny Watson twelve months for assault-in' his wife. If a man ever had it comin', it was Benny. You shoulda seen the fucker when they dropped the twelve on him. Priceless. It's why I love my job."

"I'm glad it —"

"I was thinkin' maybe we could implement some kind of recognition system for kick-ass victories, something along the lines of the Ohio State football team, you know, where you get a sticker for your helmet, a buckeye for every exceptional game. We'd give each other rewards to wear on our lapels — gold stars or justice scales or a set of miniature cell bars or perhaps exclamation points. Might help morale. I know I'd go the extra mile." Custis did his best to appear sincere.

"As successful as we are, I'm sure we'd use

302

up our lapels in no time at all and have to go with auxiliary sashes or chevrons."

"Killjoy," Custis said with mock disappointment.

"I need to talk to you about grand jury," Mason stated with a new, different voice, pared down and serious. He folded his arms into his chest. "How come there's a first-degree murder indictment for Allen Roberts on my desk?"

" 'Cause I put it there," Custis answered.

"Since when did you start preparing indictments in my cases?" Mason was testy.

"Since always. I was only tryin' to help. The state police called while you were gone yesterday, about four thirty, and asked me to draft it for you so we could have it done for June term. Agent Bass was the dude's name. Said to check with you, but you were up to speed. Sounds like it's a pretty righteous case from what he told —"

Mason interrupted. "So now we're taking our marching orders from the state police?"

Custis clenched his face. "Damn, Mace, what's in your craw? Huh? The cops called and asked, and seein' as how we're the good guys and they're the good guys and we work together I attempted to be accommodating. It's not like I tried to hide it or sneak it in — the cop said you were ready to go, and I did it so you wouldn't have to. Assistin', like my job title suggests. I don't give a damn if you submit it or toss it in the trash." He glared at Mason.

"Exactly what did Bass tell you?"

Custis set down his files. "Said we have a confession and the gun and a motive. From what I gathered it was Law School 101, ripe fruit ready for the pickin'. He led me to believe you were on board."

"Well, I'm not. There's more to it." Mason dropped his arms.

"Hey, cool, whatever. I just work here." Custis was still perturbed.

"So we won't be taking it to the grand jury. Not in June. Not ever. We on the same page?"

"Same page, same chapter, same book, same library, same universe," Custis answered.

"Good."

"No need to be so damn hateful about it," Custis said, more hurt than angry.

"Sorry." Mason pivoted and left the room, returned to his own office and shut the door. A few minutes later he went back and apologized to Custis again. "I shouldn't have snapped at you," he told his friend.

"No problem." Custis's suit jacket was draped over the highest peg of a wooden hat rack. His cuffs were unbuttoned, his sleeves rolled up. "What's goin' on? Why're you so torn outta the frame 'bout this?"

"No reason in particular — bad couple days, that's all. It's not really connected to the murder case. Things in general could be better, I guess. I'm fine."

"You sure? You seem awfully tense."

Mason flicked his hands, grimaced. "You know, trying to deal with an eighth-grade girl, not sleeping worth a darn, worrying about work."

"Can't be easy rearin' a chap by yourself. Especially when they start thinkin' they know more than you."

"True."

"Hey, here's an idea." Custis maneuvered a foot onto the corner of his desk. "I've got ten pounds of top-notch ribs — I'm talkin' primo eatin', first-class — I brought home from Memphis last weekend. I was savin' them for me and Inez, planning a big event, but I'm sure she wouldn't mind if we sampled a few early. I'll chop some slaw, cook my special baked beans, have you come by and fill you up. Nothing like a good meal and cold beer to float your spirits."

Mason smiled. "I appreciate it, but —"

"Before you blow me off, let me also mention I have a little Puerto Rican panacea I imported from Tennessee as well. Follow what I'm sayin'? Seemed to cure your woes last time you were in the dumps."

"Ah. Well, that was a singular experience for me." Mason checked behind him to make certain no one was listening. "I'm afraid Rasta Mason has retired his dreads."

305

Custis chuckled. His other foot joined the one already on his desk. "Your choice to make. It'd be strictly a medicinal use, my man. A remedy for what ails you. I got the major entertainment goods ready, too. My own mix CD, with War's "Spill the Wine" and Renaissance man William Shatner lettin' it loose on "Lucy in the Sky with Diamonds." A gem of a Cypress Hill cut. Plus I found *Bride of Frankenstein* for a dollar at the video store. I'll bet the ranch ninety or so minutes of under-the-influence, black-and-white mad science will put you in a far different mood — can't beat sparks flying in the lab and all those crazy sets."

"Nope. Not for me, although I will have to admit San Juan was big fun. Still, I'd just as soon you don't ever mention the topic again." Mason was firm but there was no scold in his words. "I'm grateful for the food offer. Thanks."

"You don't need to be backsliding on me. You're done with the blues, okay? I can't afford another trip to resurrect you."

"I'm fine," Mason promised him. "I shouldn't have jumped down your throat about the case."

"Yeah." Custis smiled. "Don't do it again."

Mason made it to Sheila's desk before he stopped and headed back to Custis's office for the third time in ten minutes. He tapped on the door and invited him to lunch, offering to pay. They ate at the Coffee Break, underneath the antique posters for Flatt and Scruggs and Chet Atkins and the auto-graphed fender of Michael Waltrip's race car, suspended from the ceiling. Custis ordered three hot dogs, double potatoes and a diet soda. Mason had a chicken salad sandwich he didn't finish. When the booth behind them emptied and the customers were at the cash register, Mason removed a blank check from his wallet and wrote it to the order of Custis Norman in the amount of fifty dollars. On the memo line, he printed "Retainer." He placed the check beside Custis's napkin.

"What are you doin'?" Custis stopped chewing and tucked his chin. "Why did you write me a check for fifty bucks? We bein' charged off the tourist menu or something?"

"Pick it up, please."

Custis took the check. "Okay."

"That's a retainer. I'm hiring you to be my lawyer —"

"You don't have to pay me to do legal work for you," Custis interrupted. He was of-fended. "What's wrong with you? *Hiring* me? What could you possibly want me to do?"

Mason hunched over the Formica table and squeezed Custis's wrist. "Listen to me. For once, be quiet and listen. I'm hiring you as my lawyer. I'm in the middle of a nasty legal situation, and I think you might've just inadvertently become a witness against me."

Custis pulled his wrist free. He pushed his plate to the side and cocked his ear. "Sorry. I'm lost."

"Here's everything you need to know and everything I can tell you: this Allen Roberts case isn't about Allen. It's a smoke screen. I know for a fact Allen didn't shoot Wayne. There are people, most notably these pricks Bass and Minter, who have it in for me. I'm ninety-nine percent sure this whole Roberts investigation is a sham, a test. A trap of sorts." Mason was whispering, hoarse. "So now you're my lawyer, okay? You and I are going to walk up the street and cash your check at the bank and from here on out we'll have attorney-client privilege."

"I don't need no check to go to the mat for you, Mace. You oughta know that by now. We've been in too many foxholes too many times. Been through too much."

"I understand. And I believe you. Just the same, this will make it easier for us both if push comes to shove down the road."

"Your call. If you think we need to, then off we go to the bank." Custis cupped his hand over his mouth. A gold ring cut into his dark skin. "But I'm not up to speed here. I'm still fuzzy. Why would the state police be fuckin' with you? Have you done somethin'?" He removed his hand and located his water glass. He thumped free an ice cube and began crunching it, the bulge switching from cheek to cheek.

"I didn't shoot Wayne Thompson, if that's what you're asking. Obviously that's not the problem." Lois the waitress breezed by with a coffee-pot and Mason hesitated. "Neither did Allen Roberts. He's totally innocent."

"Okay."

"You know my worthless brother was a suspect in the Thompson shooting," Mason said cryptically. He stopped talking and mashed his sandwich with the flat side of a butter knife. "My brother is now very angry with me." He fussed with the knife and sandwich some more. "I was his alibi for certain parts of the evening." Another emphatic, pointed pause, the dull tip of the knife piercing the bread and all the way to the plate by now. "I'm not able to say much more, but I hope the fog's lifting a bit."

"Shit." Custis was rubbing and squeezing his chin between his thumb and forefinger. He appeared distressed. "Yeah, I'm gettin' closer, but I'm not sure I'm there yet."

"I've given this a lot of thought, and here's the plan if you're agreeable. You need to call Agent Bass, tell him you've drafted the indictment, conferred with me and we're ready to charge Allen. Also inform him he'll have to be here for June grand jury to present the bill and testify. We'll run our own little experiment. You watch and see — there's not a chance he'll go in front of that jury and recite his bullshit under oath. You watch. We'll call his bluff."

"You told me no less than an hour ago we weren't gonna go after Roberts. Not ever."

"I said we wouldn't indict him," Mason replied. "I still don't think we will. I'll give you the script for the call while we're walking to the bank."

As soon as Mason and Custis returned to work, they went into Mason's office, closed the door and had Sheila ring Agent Bass. They were squeezed side by side between a desk and a credenza, the receiver not flush against Custis's ear so Mason could eavesdrop on the conversation.

"Agent Bass," Custis said when he picked up, "Custis Norman here, from Stuart. Afternoon to you. We spoke the other day about an indictment in the Roberts case. First-degree murder of Wayne Thompson."

"Yessir," Bass said, his voice bland, professional.

"I spoke to Mason and he's good to go, very much invested in your case. We both agree we should move on it next grand jury, in June."

"Okay. So you talked to Mr. Hunt and he definitely wants to proceed?" He labored on the last word, unable to hide his astonishment.

"Absolutely. Mason and I went over it together and we had the sheriff bring Roberts by for tea and crumpets and a little visit. Mason's convinced you guys have the right man."

"Okay, well, I'm glad he's come around. He seemed a little iffy when we saw him earlier in the week. So he personally approved this?"

"Yeah. Mason can be cautious. That's his style. He'll prod and poke and put you on the spot, but once he's sold on the facts and has analyzed every speck of evidence, he's like a junkyard dog."

"So, what, you guys are going to indict? June?"

"Yeah, just like you wanted — that's why I'm calling. We need you or your partner to present this to the grand jury. How about you be here around nine thirty on the fifth, and we'll send you in first and have you back to Salem before they even miss you." Custis widened the gap between the receiver and his ear.

"Well, uh, I guess, yeah, I think we can be there. Let me check and call you right back. I'm thinking we might already be scheduled to be somewhere else . . . already subpoenaed."

"Can you let me know kinda quick?" Custis asked. "I realize it's just April, but we don't need anyone fumblin' the ball in a murder case."

"Sure. We'll do our best."

Custis hung up the phone. "No way he's coming, Mason. Fucker was crawfishin' on me to beat the band."

"He certainly doesn't seem so enthusiastic all of a sudden." Mason leaned against the credenza.

"So where does this leave you? I'm not likin' the vibe I'm gettin', and the way I'm thinking this thing is traveling."

Mason was preoccupied, gazing down at the bottom of a rickety file cabinet, the last drawer of which was pitted and dinged, marred by the first hints of rust. "Still in a jam," he said distantly, "but at least I know who my enemies are and how this was supposed to operate."

Two hours later, Bass's supervisor called and requested that Custis delay the indictment and not submit it, told him neither of the agents would be available and, more important, there had been a "reevaluation" of several critical factors in the investigation. "So let us know," Custis told him. "Far as we can tell on this end, we're on solid ground and eager to take this one to trial."

CHAPTER TWELVE

The Saturday morning after the cops came to Stuart, Mason cornered Grace and attempted to make her answer him with more than a grunt or sarcastic frown or sullen, dismissive snort. Having wandered out of bed around ten thirty, she was watching the big-screen in the room where her mother used to paint and was still wearing pajama bottoms and a man's plaid flannel shirt that evidently had some connection to her be-all-and-end-all sweetheart.

"What?" she said irritably when Mason straight-armed the control at the TV and the sound fell off incrementally. "There's a mute button, you know," she remarked. "So you don't have to readjust it to where you want it."

"I appreciate the tip — been feeling the first twinges of carpal tunnel lately." He managed to sound jovial. "I've come to brighten your life," he said, silly and clownish, keeping several days of temper under rein.

"Wow."

"I thought, given the gorgeous weather, you might like to spend the morning with me. We could go to Dobyns and try a little trout fishing, then visit your grandmother's for a late lunch. I could use the break, too. Work's been merciless." He made a cast with an imaginary rod and cranked an invisible reel handle. "I haven't so much as wet a line since we moved here, and your uncle and I used to love the streams in the spring of the year. Any interest?"

"Ick. No. Why would I want to be stuck in the middle of nowhere and catch slimy fish?"

"Next plan: let's drive to Stuart and buy a cool kite and take it to DeHart Park. Pack a picnic."

She didn't even answer. She watched silent TV.

"Okay, last option: I'll take you and a girlfriend of your choosing, anyone but the obnoxious Wray kid whose parents I can't stand, to Hanes Mall in Winston and you can buy overpriced, faddish clothes and act like you're older and hipper than you actually are. Maybe a movie, maybe Chili's for dinner."

"Really?"

"Yep. A reward for your good nature and delightful attitude as of late." He smiled crookedly, ironically. "I prefer the fishing or kite flying, of course, since at the end of the day we'd have this huge PAX channel moment, a touching father-daughter understanding where everything would be heartwarming and shot through a colored filter. We'd be beside a fantastic yellow stream or a shimmering red lake and soothing classical music would be playing as the camera panned in. I'd tell you how much I love you, and you'd puckishly punch me on the shoulder. Drop some cuddly line while we're frying the fish over a campfire."

"If we go, will you not hover and not be totally nosy and *promise* not to embarrass me?" She was growing excited.

"I'll do my absolute best."

She wound up inviting two of her friends, and Mason drove the three chattering teenagers to the mall. The girls all rode together in the backseat and huddled and giggled and tried on clothes at the Gap and Abercrombie & Fitch and did all they could to keep Mason at a leper's distance. Outside the discount cinema, they begged, wheedled and whined and repeated "pleeeez, Mr. Hunt" and "pleeeez, Dad" like it was some powerful, sacred chant when he considered whether he ought to allow them to see *Queen of the Damned.* He didn't yield, however, and they bought tickets to *Ice Age.* Mason sat in the last row and the girls in a far right corner close to the screen.

He was pleased to have the respite and the dark, and he sipped a fountain cola and picked at a tub of oily popcorn, concentrating on his complications with the police. Midway through the movie, he looked over the rows of rounded seat tops toward the front of the theater and found his child's silhouette, and it made him mad as hell, livid, thinking about what was happening to him and what a weak, craven brother he was tethered to. The dim theater put him in mind of Richmond and tending to Grace during the early-morning hours, when her nursery was illuminated only by a gentle night-light and the streets and city were peaceful, particles of the baby's sweet powder glinting in the gray glow after he changed her. "I will kill Gates Hunt before I let my daughter lose another parent," he vowed, mouthing the words as Sid the Sloth hammed it up on the screen.

When Mason called Sadie Grace early Sunday and pitched a trip to visit Gates, she protested that she didn't want to miss church and drive four hours to Powhatan. "Preacher Logan from Greensboro is coming, and he always has a good message. I just hate to miss it, and I saw Gates a week ago."

"Well, I haven't been in a while. Grace is spending the day with the Anderson kids, and I'd certainly appreciate the company."

"Oh, Mason," she sighed.

"I'll buy you lunch and you can smoke in

the car," he offered.

"Honey, you know I'd love to spend time with you, and you know I love your brother as much as a mother can, but to tell the truth, I'm not up for listenin' to him fuss and say ugly things about us. It's the same old song, same old accusations, same old crazy junk. I go see him faithfully, but it's kinda like the way I go to the doctor for my flu shot. He sits there all puffed up, and he's got more gripes than Carter's got liver pills. I'm right tired of it."

"I'm not disagreeing with you, but maybe if we both go it would be better."

"I know y'all are feudin', so why now? Can't we wait till next Sunday? Give me a little more warnin'?"

"Next week is tough for me, and I've got Grace situated today. I want you to go *because* Gates and I haven't been on the best of terms lately. Your being there will help, I think."

Sadie Grace relented, of course, her mother's conscience captured twice, first by Mason's hopeful entreaty and then by the guilt of avoiding a trip to see her imprisoned son, no matter how rude and undeserving he was. "I can't say no" was how she phrased it, none too thrilled about the prospect.

During the trip to the penitentiary, they listened to an oldies station and a full hour of a preacher on the FM band, a man whose

317

purified, dulcet voice was tinged with accessibility and soft-pedaled seduction. Mason's relationship with his mother was unassailable and deeply rooted but starting to blur. They'd cycled through the stark divisions between parent and child and begun the pivot at which Mason would watch over *her* and remind her she shouldn't do this or that and telephone to make sure she'd remembered the dead bolt at night and slip her cash she was far too proud to request regardless of her needs. Driving together, they didn't have very much conversation, but that was okay with Mason, a point of pride actually, how well he and his mother could abide silence, their comfort during the lags and frequent quiet spells. They felt at ease when nothing was being said, trusted each other's nature, and didn't prattle on for the sake of talking or chigger from topic to topic because they thought it necessary to always keep balls in the air. They'd ridden without a word for fifty miles when Mason pulled into the prison lot and said, "Thanks so much for doing this."

Not surprisingly, it took longer than usual for the guards to produce Gates in the visiting area, the delay, Mason surmised, the result of a scramble to get him wired, cue his handlers and reiterate his instructions. He was fraudulently upbeat when he appeared, smiling and pumping Mason's hand, acting delighted to see his brother. Mason noticed he twisted his torso before he embraced their mother, gave her mostly shoulder and ribs, not risking a complete hug.

"What a super surprise," he gushed. "My two favorite people. You didn't have to drive down here on such a pretty Sunday."

Sadie Grace was immediately suspicious, and it showed in her posture and how she arranged herself in her chair, quickly on guard, her purse deep in her lap, her hands defensively clutching its strap. "I'm glad you're so chipper, Gates," she said. "It's nice to see you happy."

"Oh yeah. Hey, why not, huh? I can't believe you brought Mason, too. How long's it been, brother?"

"Several months," Mason replied. "I'm relieved you're not still angry with me. I was a little afraid to come after you were so mad at me and threatened to . . . to . . . you know, do whatever it took to cause me problems because I couldn't get your sentence reduced or help you with court."

"I'm not sure I remember exactly what you're talkin' about but, heck, whatever it was, it's behind us. We'll always be brothers, me and you. Sometimes I probably say crap I shouldn't to you and Mom both. It's bad here, difficult to keep your head screwed on." Gates was prison-pallid, underbelly white, and he was near enough for Mason to smell him; Mason well knew the scent, a dank, vinegary, rotting odor that infested the convicts' skin and came from inside them, couldn't be washed off by the occasional communal shower and two-bit soap.

"How're your classes?" Sadie Grace asked. Gates was a credit or two shy of a community college degree.

"Almost there, almost done," he told her. He'd taken a seat. An institutional metal table that ran the length of the room separated him from Sadie Grace and Mason. Other families visited nearby.

"Good for you," she said, still wary, still awaiting the inevitable ambush.

Prison cooks down time for its inhabitants, boils it away to concentrate, so the long-termers always seem hyper and rushed, their speech and habits accelerated, jumbled, telltale. They can't wait. Can't wait. Hurry. Press. Squirm. Even out of the joint, they eat and talk and live like a clock's about to expire, the curtain drop. Jumpy, scrambled, hasty, anxious. Gates couldn't curb his convict's instincts, couldn't stick with the drill, had to make his pitch *now* no matter what, no matter how forced or clumsy. "Mom, uh, you mind if I speak to Mason in private for a sec? It's good to see you, sure is, but man, it's been so long since I saw my favorite little brother. I'm just so tickled he's here, and, well, maybe, uh, we could talk about some personal stuff if we were alone.

Not that I don't appreciate you and your sacrifices. You are one more wonderful mom."

Sadie Grace didn't bother to quiz him or attempt to unravel his motives. She patted his hand, stood, smoothed the front of her blouse and said — without inflection — "Bye, son." She showed Mason a chilly look and tersely informed him she'd be in the car.

Before she'd even reached the officer at the steel door to the visiting area, Gates ducked in toward his brother. "Damn, Mason, I'm glad you came." He dropped his voice confidentially. "Listen, the, uh, the cops were here like last week and they were askin' about that thing back in the eighties, you know, the deal on Russell Creek Road." He bored in closer, almost touching Mason's face.

"Huh? Say what? What're you talking about?" Mason gestured broadly with his hands for the benefit of any video surveillance. "Russell Creek?" He leaned away from his brother's smell.

Gates remained hunched over the table, his voice almost a hiss. "Russell Creek, in Stuart. 1984, Mason. You and me."

"I'm lost," Mason said calmly. "Slow down and just tell me what it is you want me to know."

"The initials 'W.T.' mean anything to you?"

"Uh, Wu-Tang Clan?" It was the first usable match that popped into his mind. He was taking a devilish pleasure in watching

Gates grope and scheme, becoming more frenetic as each obvious snare failed to do the trick. Soon they would exchange a hard, mean glare and Gates would realize the jig was up, but he wasn't there yet, was still trying to dupe Mason and give the police a taped admission to improve their case. "Why are you speaking in code? I have no idea who or what you're referring to."

Gates had grown itchy and flustered. "Wayne Thompson. 1984. You and me. Him bein' shot." He wiped the back of his hand across his mouth. "That clear enough for you?"

"I guess. Why would the police be interviewing you about Wayne? You didn't have anything to do with his death. I know that better than anyone. You're innocent. You were with me or our friends the whole day. We never saw him after he left Denise's place. I wouldn't worry if I were you."

"Well, I am worried," Gates screeched. "Somehow they know, Mason. They know it was me and you." He grasped Mason's wrist, squeezed.

"What're you talking about, Gates?" Mason asked. "Have you lost your mind? Are you all right?"

"I didn't admit anything, but they're on to us."

Mason pried away his brother's grip. "I'm going to call the prison first thing tomorrow and have the doc take a look at you. I have no earthly idea why you're freaking out, and you sound paranoid. Are you taking medicine? Some kind of prescription they have you on?"

"Hell no."

"I'm sorry I can't help you, Gates. I have no clue why you're so upset. Wayne Thompson died years ago, and you and I had nothing to do with it. You sure you're not on something? You okay?"

"Damn it, yes, I'm fine. Me and you —" His mouth opened but the next words stalled and he was momentarily lockjawed and popeyed, dumb as a post, and then he began a slow, deflated retreat into his chair, part slink, part crumple, like the stopper had been yanked from a blowup valve in his middle and air was wheezing out. "Me and you need to decide what we're gonna say about Wayne's shooting. Unless you're plannin' on sittin' there and pretendin' you don't have any idea what happened and leave me holdin' the bag." He kept at it, but he was losing his fire, knew he'd been discovered and had no chance. His last few words trailed off and blended into the other conversations around them.

"Gates, as best I can tell, you and I are on different planets. No one's going to cause you or me any grief over Wayne Thompson. How could they? We didn't do anything. You need to take a breath. Who's been to see you? The cops, you said? Maybe you're overreacting to something routine. I'm worried about you — this isn't normal."

"Right. Yeah." The hate and stench were so strong they almost translated visibly. He was a corpse in a baggy orange jumpsuit, seething, haunted, beaten. "I can't believe you, Mason. You're gonna fuck me again."

Mason feigned hurt. He worked his hands some more. "I'm not aware of ever having done anything to you. I've always tried to go the extra mile, no matter how much dope you sold or how many times you came to me needing a loan or a favor. No matter how many times you lied to me or our friends or our mom. No matter how many jobs you pissed away. We've always stood by you." Any court or jury that listened to the recording of this conversation was going to receive Gates's entire despicable résumé, from soup to nuts.

"Thanks so much." Gates was buried in his seat.

"I'm sorry I've upset you. I don't know what else to do. This is why it's so damn difficult to visit. I really am going to have them send a doctor by." Mason stood and peered down at Gates. For a second or two, he burned his brother with an incensed, blistering stare that belied his charity and pleasant demeanor and spoke what he'd come to speak, and there was no doubt Gates took his meaning, understood they were now enemies rather than kin, understood Mason was aware he'd gone Judas.

"I'll leave a twenty for your canteen account," Mason promised, his voice honeyed and sympathetic. He offered his hand, an effort requiring considerable discipline, but Gates childishly refused it. "Good-bye, brother," Mason said, the syllables so loaded and somber that Gates dipped his head and knew he'd been cut loose forever, cleaved and kissed on each cheek and dismissed into the desert.

As they exited the parking area, Sadie Grace kept her focus on the highway and said in a stern voice, "Trouble has a way of rubbin' off to the people around it."

The sun had warmed the car's interior, and Mason switched on the air-conditioning, the first use since last year. "I know. Better than most people, I know."

"I don't have any idea what you two have goin' or why we came today, and I don't care to find out. But Gates is trouble. It pains me to say it, but he is. You need to steer clear. You've made a life for yourself. You've got a daughter to raise. Gates has too much of his daddy in him." She touched her eye, though there was no tear apparent. "I take my share of the blame, too. I could've made different choices."

Mason looked at her, but she kept to herself. "We were lucky to have had you," he said to comfort her. "You did everything anyone could have. More, in fact. No telling what would have happened if you weren't around. You are a saint and a godsend." He patted her knee. "I can handle Gates."

"You remember the story of Joseph?" she asked.

"I seem to recall he had a fine coat. And a good run on Broadway." Mason smiled.

She finally faced him and recited from memory: " 'So when the Midianite merchants came by, his brothers pulled Joseph up out of the cistern and sold him for twenty shekels of silver.' I've read that verse a thousand times. Brothers who would sell a brother 'cause they're jealous and petty. Selfish. Tradin' their own flesh and blood. It can happen, Mason. It happened in the Bible."

"I doubt we could get the full twenty shekels for Gates," he joked.

"Oh, no. It'd be the other way around, believe me."

"I understand — I was only kidding."

"Watch yourself," she said. "You've been good to Gates. You should have a clear conscience. You don't owe him. Don't risk your good name on him."

"I wish it were that simple." He decreased the car's fan. "Along those lines, let me say I was glad to drive you to see him after you asked."

"Huh? I asked? You called me. I'd rather been at Sunday service."

"Maybe I'm mistaken, but I think you wanted to go, and I volunteered to take you."

Their roles briefly reverted, and his mother eyed him as if he were sixteen and seeking a white lie about his homework or where he'd been when a girl called the house asking for him. "You're a good son," she said. "Always there if I need something. It was nice of you to take me. As best as I can remember, I asked you to." It came out almost primly, and she seemed curiously gratified, eager to be maternal and help her boy, even if she didn't know the specifics and even if it required her to discount the truth, her church teachings and the Ten Commandments crowded to the rear where her son was concerned.

The world seemed to swap ends the next morning. Early rather than late, the sky looked like a sketch pad full up with doodles, scribbles, crosshatches and blots of bold lavender and flaming orange, as if evening had arrived hours and hours prematurely. Clouds imprinted the hills and swales with slow-moving shadows. The light lacked power. The day seemed to have ripened at birth. Mason drank from a cup of coffee on the porch and figured the strange doings augured poorly for him, assumed he was receiving some sort of supernatural tip-off that his woes would only increase as time went by. He scanned the farm, half expecting to catch a glimpse of a mad owl beating its wings or an apocalyptic horse rearing in the pasture.

Grace trudged down the drive to await the "crappy old bus" her father made her ride. She continued to dwell in a province that excluded Mason, but at least after the peace-offering mall trip, the malice seemed to have vanished from the gulf between them — now he was simply out of her loop, irrelevant rather than loathed. Soon the bus lumbered to a stop with a swinging red sign and blinking lights, the doors folded in on themselves, and Grace mounted two big steps and was swallowed up, the doors' black rubber strips reuniting and sealing shut. Betty Smith, the driver, waved at Mason and pulled away, taking the bus through its gears. Mason's coffee had gone cold, and he left the cup sitting on a railing, walked through the dew-damp grass to his car.

Sure enough, Custis was in a tizzy, pacing around his office when Mason located him at work. He had neglected to brew their coffee, and there were no donuts or bakery sweets or honey buns to eat while they talked about the coming week's cases. His attention snapped to Mason the instant he entered the room. "I can't fuckin' believe this," Custis brayed.

"I had a feeling," Mason said, resigned, ready for the bad news.

Custis shook his head. His dreads flipped and flopped. "Seventeen pounds. I've gained seventeen pounds since San Juan, Mace. I'm the damn affirmative-action Michelin Man." He parted his suit coat and turned sideways. "Why didn't you tell me how fat I've become?"

"I didn't notice."

"Well, part of the problem is this damn confab we have every Monday. We sit here and eat trash — no telling how many calories I'm crammin' in because of this little ritual. But no more." He faced Mason and jerked open his belt with a frustrated tug to the right. "Look. Can you believe this? I can't even hook my damn britches." With the belt loosened, a gap was apparent at the top of the zipper where the pants should have fastened. "Man, I gotta take steps."

"So that's why you're so wound up? You think you've put on weight?"

"Ain't no *think* to it," Custis replied, refitting his belt.

"Sorry. I honestly hadn't seen a difference. You carry it well, big as you are."

"Damn. No more bread, I can promise you that. No more desserts."

Despite his own difficulties, Mason laughed out loud. "Well, why don't you try the LA

329

Weight Loss program?" he said sincerely, after the amusement passed. "I've heard several people say it's effective. They opened, what, a month ago? In the building next to Hudson's Drug. We walk past there five times a day. Art Anthony claims he's already dropped nine or ten pounds."

"It's like every other small-town business. It isn't anything but Frieda Compton in a flashy smock surrounded by a bunch of dumpy posters and silk plants, just tryin' to scrounge a buck. She bought the starter kit and went to three training sessions in Greensboro and that's the high-water mark of her expertise. I'll bet you she's smokin' cigarettes in the back and feasting on Little Debbie, and we both know her husband's fat as hell and basically a slob. She doesn't know nutrition from a hole in the ground."

"My, my. No need to be so cynical."

"Yeah, well, it's true." He adjusted his pants. Centered his belt buckle.

"You're welcome to go with me to the gym. I exercise three or four times a week, and it's the best cure there is. I'll show you the ropes. You'd enjoy it, and it'd be a treat to have someone to talk with. Break the monotony."

"I might. Thanks. Maybe I'll sign up. I know I really should."

"Heck, I'll buy you a three-month membership."

"I'll give it serious thought. Kind of you to

330

offer." Custis turned and walked behind his desk. His chair was of the standard office variety, four legs with rollers and a lever on the side that adjusted the height. He settled in and reached for a file. Mason stayed where he was. "I'll at least make the coffee," he told Custis.

"Okay," Custis said. And then, boom, a pin gave way and his seat collapsed and slid down its metal support and lost all its altitude and hit bottom so that Custis's chin was about level with his desk drawer, his startled eyes alligatoring over a *Michie's Jurisprudence* volume.

Mason couldn't help himself and tore out of the room laughing. "I'll find the workers' comp forms," he shouted over his shoulder. "It's slapstick hour at the commonwealth's attorney's office," he quipped to Sheila as he approached her desk, still in stitches over his friend's misfortune.

CHAPTER THIRTEEN

"A Mr. Carson from Richmond is on your line," Sheila announced to Mason. It was Tuesday, two days after Mason's visit to the penitentiary.

"What's he want?" Mason asked, not recognizing the name.

"Said it was personal." Sheila was coming through over the phone's speaker, but she was close enough to his wall that Mason could also hear her in the room next to his. Each of her words sounded doubled, the muted voice on the other side of the wall piggybacking the clear version on the phone.

Mason felt a hitch in his stomach. He wet his lips and picked up the receiver. "Mason Hunt," he said.

"Mr. Hunt, good morning to you and thanks for taking my call. My name is Carter Carson."

The man was too courteous and too affable to be a cop. Mason swelled his cheeks and quickly sighed out a breath, relieved. "No problem. What can I do for you?"

"I'm the executive director of the Tobacco Commission, and for starters let me welcome you aboard and thank you for your service."

"Oh. Right. I'm looking forward to it."

"Great," Carson said. "Your first meeting is June thirtieth, and I'll be sending you a packet of information in the next day or so. More to the point, there's one grant proposal that impacts your area, a request for a public-private partnership with a company called Chip-Tech. They're basically a computer component manufacturer wholly owned by Caldwell-Dylan."

"Ah — there's a name I've heard. Caldwell-Dylan is none other than Herman Dylan, correct?"

"Exactly, Mr. Hunt."

"The Iceman. I've read about him. Got rich in frozen foods."

"It would be fair to say he's somewhat controversial, but there are people in business and government who swear by him."

Mason found a paper clip and began bending it straight, trapping the phone between his chin and shoulder. "From everything I've seen, he's definitely a mixed bag. What concerns does he have in our neck of the woods?"

"According to his application, he's interested in bringing Chip-Tech to Patrick."

"Huh. Well, more power to him."

Carson's tone dampened. "Of course, he wants us to kick in a healthy six mil, he wants your county to waive taxes for five years and lease him a shell building for cheap, and he wants discounted water and sewer."

"How many jobs do we get for our largesse?"

"Seventy. But bear in mind that number is 'an aspiration' as per his application. If you read the fine print, the commitment is for fifty-five positions with an average wage of nine dollars an hour."

"I guess that's fifty-five more than we have now."

"True."

"I appreciate the call and information. Thanks for the warning."

"My pleasure. It's what I do." Carson chuckled. "And if I were you, I'd brace myself for a little cold weather. Keep the down jacket handy."

The police, meanwhile, had decided they were best served by making a formal appointment with Mason, trading away surprise for the grind of dread and worry. Late Wednesday, Ray Bass called Sheila to schedule a meeting, and she assumed he and his partner were coming to see the commonwealth's attorney just like every other cop who requested an hour to review a case or ask advice or prepare for trial. She booked Bass and Rick

Minter for Friday morning, and Mason learned of the visit Thursday afternoon when Sheila handed him his schedule for the next day.

"Shit," he said, staring at the photocopy of her calendar page.

"I'm sorry. Is something wrong?"

"No. No. I didn't mean to curse. Seems . . . seems like a lot to do, that's all."

"I can switch stuff if you want me to," she offered.

"Nah. It's actually not so bad." He almost asked her about the appointment with Bass and Minter but immediately swallowed the impulse, realizing there was nothing she could add and that the inquiry would only draw attention to a subject he preferred to keep off everyone's radar.

Convinced that the cops would sooner or later be on his tail, Mason had devoted a fair amount of thought to what he should tell Custis when the pincers began closing and the state police arrived in their unmarked Crown Vic for an interview, ready with Gates's accusations. Custis had left earlier in the day, and Mason drove directly from their office to his friend's home on Chestnut Avenue. He parked behind Custis's new Caddy, left his suit coat in the car and knocked on the front door. There was no answer, but Mason was able to hear loud music and dull thumps, and he could sense a vibration in the wooden porch, movement that began inside and traced out along joists and planks and registered in his feet. He knocked again, and when Custis didn't respond, Mason eased the door open and shouted hello. The music dropped. "Who is it?" Custis yelled from another part of the house.

"It's me. Mason."

"Damn. Maybe you should knock."

"I did." He spoke louder than normal.

Custis stuck his head around a doorframe on the opposite side of the room. "Who's with you?"

"Nobody. Why? You smoking crack back there?"

Custis came through the door. He was wearing tennis shoes, white tube socks, gray athletic shorts and a red T-shirt that didn't make it all the way to the elastic band at the top of the shorts. A strip of brown belly skin wallowed in the space between the shorts and shirt. "I'm workin' out, smart-ass." He was sweating and breathing hard.

"To what? The sound track for *American Graffiti*?"

"It's a Richard Simmons tape. It was all they had at the library, okay?"

Mason smiled and put his hands on his hips. "Richard Simmons is a category-one flame, and the routine is for fossils and ancient women with canes and artificial joints."

"Actually, Mace, it's pretty damn rigorous, and even if it wasn't, what exactly would you suggest for me?" He glanced at his stomach. "I mean, you know, right now, old fat women would be about my speed."

"I told you I'd buy you a gym membership and we'd go together."

"You think I'm gonna stroll my lardass into a public gym lookin' like this?"

Mason sat on a sofa arm. "That's why you go, Custis. To get in shape."

"When I can go and people aren't thinkin' I'm 'Rerun' Berry, I'll go."

"Your choice," Mason said. "It's good you're exercising. Wherever you do it, it's a positive."

"Yeah. I can't believe how this shit creeps up on you."

Mason faked a wince. "Friend to friend, seeing your baby-doll shirt and kneesocks, I've got to say lifestyle changes are definitely in order."

Custis balled a fist in Mason's direction and raised his middle finger. "Fat or not, I can still beat you down. You'd be smart to not forget it."

"Amen."

As Mason balanced there on the leather arm of Custis's couch, about to confess his involvement in a murder, it occurred to him how frequently settings fail to match important moments, how critical, wrenching events that deserve the dignity of a hearth or respectable office or church altar wind up poorly staged, jammed into the first empty space available, willy-nilly, revelations loosed and souls bared at gas pumps, bowling alleys, carnivals, bus stops, department-store toilets, the surroundings be damned. Mason took stock of the revved-up oldies and Richard Simmons's exhortations and the comical red shirt, but he decided they probably didn't mean anything or make much difference. Perhaps the absurdities might even make his burden more tolerable, draw off some of the poison. "Have a seat," he said to Custis. "We need to talk."

"Uh-oh. That doesn't sound cool." He pointed at Mason with his index finger. "Hang tight." He left and returned wearing a bulky sweatshirt that kept his middle concealed. "Problems with the situation we discussed at lunch?" he asked, twisting the top off a bottled water.

Mason heard the plastic seal break. "Afraid so."

Custis perched himself on the edge of a recliner. "I hope you know I haven't forgotten you or ignored anything we discussed. I took it to heart, but I figured you'd get back to me when you needed to. It's been weighing on me, though. Sure has."

"Thanks. Well, the time is here, I'm sorry to say."

"I got a fair idea of your troubles, but I'm hopin' I'm wrong." Custis lifted the hem of his shirt and patted his face.

"We're in confidence here, right? Attorney-client?"

"Yeah, Mace." The question obviously annoyed him. "We cashed the check. If my word and my friendship won't hold, we can always count on the technicalities."

"I wouldn't be telling you this unless I trusted you. I've never had a better friend. The check may end up keeping *you* off the griddle — it's more for you than me."

"Whatever," Custis groused.

Mason moved from the arm onto the sofa proper. "I apologize for dragging us both into such a mess. I'm particularly sorry that over the long haul this affects you, too." He stared at the oak floor, noticed a dark, swirling knot in the wood. He thought of his wife, how he never told her he'd protected his brother and allowed a killing to remain unsolved, for years aiding and abetting a criminal. He stopped studying the floor, jacked up his posture and met Custis eye to eye.

Mason told him the story. He omitted nothing and included every detail, from the number of Budweiser beers he'd drunk before the shooting to Gates's clumsy embrace of their mother at the prison.

Custis listened without interrupting.

"It's been a shackle for nearly twenty years," Mason said at the end. "To this day, I don't know what the answer is, what I should've done. I mean, there I was, sucked into it, surprised as hell. Of course, if I'd had a crystal ball and could've seen what a prick Gates would prove to be, I'd have reported him to the cops. But in 1984, Custis, we were both young and he was my *brother.* You've probably heard what a beast our dad was, and I owed Gates for taking care of me. We were really a pair in those days, close. We wouldn't have made it otherwise." Mason sank into the cushions. "Still, I broke the law. There's the plain old moral issue, too. Law or not, I probably had an obligation to tell the truth." He turned silent, pensive. The upbeat music continued in the background. "I've often wondered," he said after the pause, "and I've never said this to anyone before . . . I've wondered about Allison. Maybe in the big scheme of things her wreck was my payback. My punishment. Sort of to teach me a lesson about loss. Karma. You could find a certain divine symmetry if you wanted to."

"Nah. No. I doubt it's anything punitive. You're readin' passages that don't exist. Anyway, your theory wouldn't be tit for tat. It'd have to be Gates's wife for the score to be even."

"Maybe there's a penalty and interest. The toll goes up. Who knows?"

"It was bad luck," Custis said. "No more, no less."

"So you won't think I'm a moron, this isn't a staggering turn of events for me, what Gates is doing. Hell, it's almost predictable. It's nagged me for years and years, like a damn open sore, and I guess I've always understood it was a possibility. A cutthroat brother with leverage will definitely make you lose sleep. A year and a half ago he actually called and threatened me, and even though neither of us mentioned it, I couldn't help but wonder if he was finally desperate enough or pissed enough to sell us both down the river. It was like he was ready to launch the missiles. But I thought I was okay, or at least reasonably safe, because I didn't see how he could use this to his advantage or hurt me without screwing himself worse."

"Well, I had this close to puzzled through. From your big ol' hints at lunch, I figured you knew Gates was guilty or involved in the Thompson guy's death. I didn't realize you were there while it went down. Dumped the gun. Bald-face lied for him." Custis took a slug of water. " 'Course I damn sure didn't guess he was tryin' to lay his crime at your doorstep." He screwed the cap onto the bottle. "Some dilemmas can't be solved. Yours is murky. Tough. I can't say what I'd have done in your shoes. Me, I'd pimp the truth for either one of my brothers or my parents. No doubt. Family trumps the Code of Virginia. Plus, it wasn't clear-cut murder — this dumb-ass evidently was lying in wait, and then decides to chase you two down, curse Gates, call him out and threaten him with a stick. A good lawyer could generate a lot of smoke with those facts."

"A club. It's accurate and it makes our case a bit more presentable."

"Yeah. Exactly." Custis concentrated for a second. "Hell, it's probably the low end of voluntary manslaughter. In hindsight, it might've been wise for you to have leaned on Gates, maybe persuaded him to fess up. This is Patrick County, after all. You go huntin' for trouble and find it, even if you find it in spades, people usually are pretty understandin' of the person who dished it out. He'd have had a strong case with a lot of mitigation. Seven or eight years, that's what I'd do with it if it were mine. Can't imagine a jury callin' it much different."

"Fat fucking chance Gates would've pled to anything. And who can say what Tony Black would've offered or a jury would've done. Let's not forget Wayne Thompson was drunk and there were two of us and my star-athlete brother had a good hundred pounds on him and a car to drive away in — it's not as if Gates was cornered and had no option except to shoot the guy."

Custis stood. "Yeah, well, be that as it may, the big concern is your situation now." He folded his arms. "Let's game this thing out."

Mason recovered his posture and sat more erect. "Okay. Thanks."

"How 'bout you drop it truthful? Tell the gospel." Custis walked across the room and settled into a different chair. "Come clean. By my math, you're guilty of, at most, accessory after the fact. Misdemeanor. The statute of limitations is a year, so you're good to go. Can't be prosecuted. With this scenario, there's the added advantage of your punk-ass brother receivin' his due."

"Far too risky," Mason replied. "Huge downside. Believe me, it's the first permutation I went through, too. But here's the problem: I really think all it would do is guarantee me a murder trial. See, if I tell the truth, Gates's story suddenly has credibility. I was in fact there, I did dispose of the gun, I did lie, I did help construct the alibi. Any prosecutor or cop worth his salt is bound to ask why I did those things if I'm not the shooter or at least a willing participant from the get-go. Moreover, the second I choose the honesty option, the best I can hope for is a damn swearing contest with Gates in front of a jury, and even if they kind of believe I'm being straight, you and I both know it's human nature for them to be angry and find some way to nail me. Why should a guy who helped hide a murder walk away scot-free? Or they pop me with a nice stiff sentence for being a hypocrite and sending people to jail for all these years despite my own dirty laundry." Mason bowed his head. "God, it sounds awful, doesn't it? When you put voice to it — when I hear it out loud — I can't help but feel I *have* done wrong."

"Well, you did break the law. But you didn't shoot anybody, and you tried to honor your brother as best you could. Let's not forget who's the polecat in this piece."

Mason looked up. "Yeah — I guess that makes me like a flunky or henchman. So I'm Renfield. The captain of the Wicked Witch's winged monkeys. Great."

Custis hinted at a grin. "So the only other option is balls to the wall. We play it like you've been playin' it, and when the cops come tomorrow, we find the props and costumes and act our asses off. Big surprise. We're stunned. We're the Prefect of Police in Casablanca. We pound away at Gates. Who the hell would believe Gates Hunt, a drug-dealin' felon? You're gonna go to trial against a well-respected commonwealth's attorney based on the word of his felonious, vindictive, piece-of-shit brother? We do all we can to convince them they got a loser."

"I agree." Mason shifted his weight. "But like I told you, my worry is I can't exactly recall what I said to Bass and Minter in our discussions about the gun. They knew I was flustered, and now I'm betting my slip is on tape. I was so rattled I said something close to 'that's impossible' or 'that can't be,' and they really flagged it."

"But you covered yourself, right? Muddied the water? If there is a tape, it's bound to be ambiguous. It's not like you confessed. We pass it off as professional skepticism."

"Yeah, but it's one more little brick for their house."

"No way a judge or jury would convict you if that's the whole case, everything in their satchel. No chance, Mace." Custis stood again. "I can't imagine they'd be dumb enough to even indict you if that's all they have."

"Well, you know what we say about close cases: too good to ignore, probably not good enough to win. Some you simply have to take to trial, no matter the probabilities. It's tricky for them, too, just like it is for us from time to time. If the press discovers the state police have credible evidence that a commonwealth's attorney committed a crime and they refuse to file charges, they'll get skinned alive in the newspapers — along with the attorney general, and I don't need to remind you they're political animals in that particular office."

Custis scowled. "The more I'm in this busi-

345

ness, the more I dislike it. Hell, about half the crap we do is either boondoggle or placating people who don't deserve it. All these rituals and fictions that absolutely shit on common sense. The worst of it is, the rest of the world's come down with the same disease: The chumps at airport security harass wheelchair granny so we can justify askin' the guy with the sword and prayer rug to let us search his suitcase. Clerks have to see an ID from the BMW lady in the pink sweater and three-carat diamond so they can press Lawanda when she breaks off the first starter check from her new account to buy her strawberry blunts. Fewer and fewer folks have the guts to do what's obviously right if it means catching a little abuse in the process. Everything's a damn referendum or a jury trial or left to the rabble in the name of egalitarianism." Custis was agitated when he finished, his mouth strict. He returned to the recliner but kept standing.

"We can't do much about all that except deal with it," Mason replied. "Besides, I've got my own dragon to slay. You and town council can fix the country's shortcomings, okay? The bottom line is it'd be a difficult decision for any prosecutor to make, especially if I sound like a crook on the tape, assuming there is a tape." Mason smiled. He crossed his legs. "Better not let the officers in the Urban League hear you spouting such heresy. If they discover you've signed on with the fascists and plantation owners, you'll be banned for life. Lose your Stokely Carmichael card."

"It's just wrong to indict someone because you want to pass the buck and don't have the courage to tell the papers and whoever else to kiss your ass. That's all I'm sayin'." He was still disturbed. "As for my bona fides, when brothers run the planet and we fuck it up, you can take me to task on it. Till then, this is your show and you guys are the ones who've allowed it to fall apart. Most of the time, democracy ain't really been the black man's friend, now has it?" He strafed Mason with a look. "So you'll know and not embarrass your bumpkin self, it's Kwame Toure. He changed his name."

"I was only kidding," Mason said. "Ranting and tilting at windmills and soapboxing isn't really doing much for the problem at hand. My problem."

"It pisses me off. Sorry."

Mason cleared his throat. "For me, the big issue is not jamming you up. I'm here for advice, but this is my mess and I don't want to take advantage of our friendship or pull you over the cliff with me. I guess we've sort of been down this road before, years ago when my family was threatened. I appreciate your help, but you need to take care of Custis first."

"If my situation changes, I'll tell you," he said, the passion ebbing in his voice.

"I mean, you know, tomorrow I'm basically going to mislead the cops."

Custis nodded. "You're not under oath, and I'm not plannin' on sayin' too awful much. I'll be there listenin' and learnin'. In the end, no matter which way you come at this, it seems pointless and wrong for you to be charged and have your life ruined. Who benefits from that? You're a good man, a good father and a good son. Not to mention a good friend." Custis sat again. He rubbed his hands over his face. "Whatever punishment is fair, I'd say you've served your sentence, carryin' this cross around as long as you have."

Mason walked toward him and Custis stood and they met chest to chest and slapped each other on the back, and Mason left without either of them saying anything else, Richard Simmons still counting to the beat and chanting encouragement.

That night, from his table at the seafood restaurant, Mason saw Jasper Griffith's pickup circle the parking lot and take a space near the end of a row. He had a dog cage in the truck bed, stuffed full of rowdy bluetick coonhounds. Mason and Grace were eating dinner, two popcorn shrimp and whitefish specials, and for reasons that were impossible to pin down or articulate, she was in a good humor, her fickle sulk suspended for the moment, lightning caught in a jar. She was talkative and agreeable, chatting with her dad about school, cheerleading, friends, boys and whatever else struck her fancy, eating one tiny shrimp at a time after spearing it on a fork and twirling it in cocktail sauce. Already dreading his morning appointment with the cops, Mason had no appetite, but he was enjoying his daughter's generous mood, and he sipped his tea and ate a hush puppy and a few bites of broiled fish. Jasper came through the door, by himself, dressed in Carhartt coveralls and new brown boots, and while the hostess was collecting a menu and scouting out an empty booth for him, he noticed Mason and tramped across the restaurant to where he and Grace were eating.

Jasper was a bossy, opinionated man with a big yap who thought highly of himself and his place in the community. He'd inherited land and a few dollars from his crotchety dad, and he sold used cars and did excavation work and swapped and traded odds and ends, especially antique furniture and Depression glass. He approached Mason's table, said hello and, remarkably, slid into the empty chair beside Grace without being invited, announcing in a determined voice he wanted to take care of a legal matter that wouldn't keep.

A large part of Mason's job was listening to

the oafs and dolts who tugged on his sleeve at the high school play or cornered him at the grocery store to tell him their bullshit, convoluted legal woes and ask him to do the impossible, to snap his fingers and settle a decades-old boundary-line dispute, force a landlord to repair a mobile home's grievous plumbing or persuade a deadbeat dad to ante up his child support. It was the bane of every small-town lawyer, the thoughtless boors who swooped in with no respect for place or privacy and invariably began the intrusion by declaring, "I need to ask you a legal question," as if they were entitled to put any attorney to work on the spot, wherever and whenever, for free, for as long as they wished. Now here was Jasper Griffith, a grating, self-important man, sitting beside Mason's daughter, interrupting their meal and the first decent conversation they'd had in weeks.

Mason raised his eyebrows and cocked his head. He'd said a curt hi, but that was the extent of it.

Both elbows on the table, Jasper remarked he'd "thought about visitin' during business hours but hadn't had a chance," then launched into a diatribe about a hundred eighty dollars he was owed by Oneal Pack for a used transmission and set of rims.

Mason interrupted him while he was indignantly rambling on. "Jasper, my daughter and I are in the middle of our food, and I was enjoying our time together."

"This ain't gonna take long," Jasper remarked, oblivious.

"No, it's not. If you have a problem, call Sheila, set up an appointment and we'll discuss it."

"No need to get snotty about it, Mason."

"I'm not. I'm simply telling you I don't appreciate you busting in on us."

"Really?" Jasper was a short, wiry man with ruddy skin, always clean-shaven and fussily neat. He usually smelled of sweet hair tonic.

"I'm simply asking for a little common courtesy."

"Unlike all you hotshots up there in Stuart with bankers' hours, I have to actually work, so it ain't always real convenient for me to call your secretary and sacrifice my entire day so I can suit your schedule."

"Then your problem must not be too urgent. Certainly not urgent enough to warrant discussing now. My daughter and I are going to finish our supper. By ourselves."

Jasper smirked. He jerked his chair away from the table and shot to his feet in a huff. "You need an attitude adjustment, Mason. I've known you and your family all your life, and you're gettin' too big for your britches. You're Curt Hunt's boy, not some king. On top of that, you're a public servant, son. You work for us, not the other way around. It's a shame when a taxpayer, the man payin' your salary, can't have two minutes of your precious time. You better hope nobody runs against you next election, I can promise you that much. I can swing a bunch of votes."

Mason set his fork on the table, took hold of the napkin in his lap. Already frazzled and close to the margins because of his police stress, he considered whether he ought to stand and put his finger in Jasper's stupid face and light into him. Very quickly, he was thinking "why the hell not," even though he ordinarily would've dismissed the likes of Jasper Griffith with silence and a stern stare and returned to his seafood and tea, aware that a public spat with an imbecile was the worst kind of quicksand.

Before he could speak or act, Grace twisted forty-five degrees and said to the man who'd challenged her father, "It wouldn't make any difference who ran against my dad. My dad would win." She sounded mad, defensive and slightly scared. She glared at Griffith. "I think you are a rude idiot. You suck."

Mason glanced at Griffith, then switched to his daughter. "Grace, I don't . . ." He hesitated, felt his shoulders go soft, his breathing decline. "You know, come to think of it, you're right, Grace. I agree." He reached into his hip pocket, took out his billfold, removed a five-dollar bill and held it in Griffith's direction. "Here's fair reimbursement for your part of my salary, your share of all the whopping taxes I'm sure you pay." He waved the five in the air. "Go on, take it, Jasper. Take it so I can be rid of you and won't have to listen to your nonsense from now on."

Several other diners were watching, and a waitress with a tray of refill pitchers and extra hush puppies had halted her path to the Hunts' table.

"This little display is gonna cost you more than any five dollars, you mark my words." Jasper didn't lower his voice. "And if I was you, I'd think about teachin' my youngun a lesson on respect." He looked sideways at Grace.

"Good-bye, Jasper," Mason said coolly. "Tell Mr. Griffith good-bye, you uncouth heathen girl," he said to his daughter. "And please don't tell him he's an idiot or that he sucks."

"Good-bye, Mr. Griffith," she singsonged through a huge, insincere smile.

"Comb your hair next time you leave home so you'll look like somebody," Griffith said to Mason before he turned to walk away, one of his four or five stock lines and his attempt at a parting shot. He stomped toward the metal and glass double doors at the front of the restaurant, waving off the teenage hostess and her single menu as he passed her on his way to his truck.

When the waitress arrived with more water and tea, she congratulated Mason and Grace for laying into Jasper. "He talks and talks and talks and just worries you to death. The same old dumb sayings again and again about 'comb your hair so you'll look like somebody' and how he's always 'fine as frog hair split three ways.' Ugggghhh. He was achin' for a comeuppance, Mr. Hunt — good for you. And you too, sweetie," she said as she was tending to Grace's glass. "He runs us to death and tips you two quarters or some pocket change, which ain't even worth the effort. I'm glad he's gone."

After the waitress moved to the next table, Mason addressed Grace in his paternal voice. He leaned closer to her as he spoke. "I appreciate your pluck, and I'm tickled you wanted to defend me, yes I am, but let's not make that kind of language a habit."

"Okay," she said, intuitively understanding he couldn't let on how pleased he was with her, how gratified. "But he did suck," she said.

"Enough. Hush." He raised a finger across his mouth. Her hair was as light as her mother's and she was already tall and blessed with Allison's slender, elegant hands, but she favored him, too, most noticeably through the mouth and chin, and he loved her fully, adored how he and her spectacular mom were etched into her in so many ways. "Finish your plate," he said gently, gesturing with his fork. He prayed he wouldn't soon shame

354

her, leave her with scars and clipped wings, and for the first time since his travails began, he considered the possibility of jail and the prospect of his unlucky mother raising another kid.

CHAPTER FOURTEEN

The next morning, Mason made Ray Bass wait in the lobby for thirty minutes, and when Sheila knocked on the door and showed him into Mason's office, not only was Minter with him, but to Mason's surprise his friend Ed Hoffman was there as well, the last of the three to enter the room. Hoffman had been employed by the state police for over two decades, and he was a perfect cop — honest, fair, deliberate, smart and reliable. He and Mason had worked together on several cases in the past, and Hoffman had invited Mason to his car on the last occasion he'd been in Stuart for a trial and they'd sipped top-shelf bourbon from paper cups to celebrate a favorable verdict. Hoffman was paunchy and bald but utterly average in every other physical regard, an ordinary guy given to plain dress and brief, direct sentences.

Mason was sad to see him there, hated to disappoint a man he respected. He spoke to Hoffman first, striding out from behind his

356

desk to greet him. "Well, well, what a fine surprise," he said. "A visit from Kojak himself." He was nervous, juiced, struggling not to muff his lines. He shook Hoffman's hand. "Hope you're okay."

"I'm good," Hoffman said unenthusiastically.

Mason welcomed the other policemen and returned to his desk. "Sorry to keep you waiting. I apologize. We're swamped today."

"No problem," Minter told him. They were all silent while he and the other officers took their seats. Something metal — a ring or watchband — dinged a chair arm. Coins jangled in a pocket.

"What's on the agenda, gentlemen? I assume you're here about Allen Roberts. The old murder from eighty-four?"

"You could say that," Bass replied.

Mason pretended not to pick up on the pointed answer. "I think Custis told you we were prepared to go. Last I heard, you guys wanted us to hold off, so we did. It seemed like a solid case to me — what happened? I was planning to track you down and go over things again, and Sheila told me you gents were coming today. Thanks for making the trip."

Minter was fingering a gold button on his blazer. "Mr. Hunt, we, uh, we're here because we have information we need to discuss with you. You personally. Believe me, we don't take any pleasure in this. No sir."

"I'm not following you," Mason said. "You've already told me the facts and given me the evidence we have for trial. I'm satisfied and ready to indict, but obviously there's some sudden reluctance on your end. How about you guys just tell me what's on your minds? I'm lost."

Minter buttoned his jacket. "Mr. Hunt, we have a report — credible — that you was heavily involved in this shooting."

"Huh?" All at once, the lines and creases in Mason's face deepened. "Pardon me? Involved? Involved how?"

"The truth is you're a suspect," Bass said somberly. "We're here to question you based on everything we've learned. I'm sorry."

"Question *me?* Question me about what? You're telling me you think I know something about Wayne Thompson's shooting?" Mason glowered at Bass. "You can't be serious."

"Serious as a heart attack," Bass answered, holding his ground.

"So you're a part of this?" Mason asked Hoffman. "You're here with these two because you believe I'm involved in a murder? Am I understanding this right?"

"You're my friend, Mason," Hoffman said sincerely. "I go where my job takes me."

"That's helpful," Mason snorted. "So what is it — this is fucking insane — what is it I'm accused of doing? And who the hell is accusing me?"

"Your brother," Bass said.

"Beautiful. There you go." Mason rocked back in his chair. "You're here in my office, all full-tilt *Dragnet,* because my dumb-ass, drug-dealing brother said I somehow had a hand in a twenty-year-old unsolved murder? Come on." He sat forward and brought his heels down hard. "That's rich, guys. You should be embarrassed. Credible? Gates Hunt?"

"Well, we think he —"

"Hold on a minute — I'm going to bring Custis in here. I want him to hear this, so when everybody has to account for themselves down the road, there'll be no mistaking who said what."

"We'd prefer you —"

"I don't give a damn what you'd prefer, Mr. Bass," Mason snapped. "If you don't like it, you can pack up and leave for all I care."

None of the three police officers responded. Mason used the phone to summon Custis, who rolled into the room a few seconds later and playfully punched Hoffman on the shoulder as soon as he recognized him. "It's my boy Ed Hoffman, fashion-plate and slickster extraordinaire — the hip quotient in Stuart just went off the charts." The razzing was harmless; Custis also admired Hoffman. "Nice to see you." He approached Bass and Minter and shook hands, calling them both by their first names. "What's cookin'?" he asked. "Everyone seems a little grim." He was standing beside Minter, facing Mason.

"You know, Custis, I think I'll let Officer Minter tell you. Or his partner. I'm not sure I can actually spit the words out of my mouth."

Minter peered up at Custis, who was big enough and near enough that the cop had difficulty fitting all of him into his vision. "Well, to be blunt, to, uh, not sugarcoat nothin', and I don't take any joy in doing this, well, we have information Mr. Hunt, Mason, was involved in the death of Wayne Thompson. The 1984 shootin'." He quit straining to see Custis and refocused on Mason.

"You're shittin' me," Custis whooped. "Say what?"

"Nosir," Bass said gravely. "This is for real."

"You tryin' to tell me you think Mace is mixed up in a crime, this deal you two were so hot to trot on a week ago? Wanted me to indict Allen Roberts?" Custis smiled. "You're pullin' my chain, aren't you? Let me guess — it's practical joke week down at the station house and you get bonus points for dupin' a lawyer."

"They're serious, Custis," Mason said. "They think I'm complicit in this murder because none other than the oracle of truth himself, my righteous, holy brother, has

360

evidently told them something or other."

"Ya'll ever spent any time with Gates?" Custis asked. "Huh? Everybody in this town can tell you he ain't to be believed. Good Lord. Hell, I was workin' with Tony Black when we prosecuted him — you shoulda heard his version of events on the stand. This is crazy." Custis was very convincing. Several of the words were squeaky high; he expanded the *a* in "crazy."

"It's not just Gates," Minter said.

Custis walked behind Mason's desk and sat on the corner of the credenza, close to Mason, opposite the three policemen across the room. "So what else could it possibly be?" he demanded.

"This makes perfect sense," Mason interjected before anyone could answer. "Now I see. Sunday, when I visited Gates, he was raving about how people were trying to blame us for the Thompson murder. He was loony. Berserk. Hell, I called the prison doc the next day to have him examined. I thought he was losing his mind. But you geniuses put him up to that, didn't you? You wired him and had him try to snake his own damn brother."

"Gates was wired," Ed Hoffman said. "Sounded like maybe you were speechifying right smart when you were talkin' to him. Making your argument."

"What the hell is that supposed to mean, Ed?" Mason asked.

"Funny you'd all a sudden decide to drive to the pen for a visit," Bass said. "How long was it between trips? Months?" There was no deference left in his tone. "You two been on the outs for who knows how long and then — snap, crackle, pop — there you are about the time you get wind of this investigation."

"My mother asked me to drive her. Why don't you check with her? While you're at it, ask her if she has even a jot of faith in her older son's word."

Bass theatrically scratched his head. "Strange how the logs show she went regular as you please every other week till you and her made your trip last Sunday. She hadn't been back-to-back since the Pilgrims landed. Maybe things had started to click and you needed a chance to eyeball your brother."

"This is some powerful evidence you guys have. I drove my mom to see my brother. Shit, Ray, you got me. Wow. I surrender." He extended his arms. "I'm done. Cuff me now."

"Returnin' to my question," Custis said, "tell us why you think Mason's wound up in this shooting? I'm hearin' you represent that his brother's makin' claims."

Bass reached inside a file and produced several typewritten pages joined by a single staple. He didn't read from them or offer them to Custis. He rolled the papers into a tube and clutched them with both hands. "Gates Hunt has give us a statement which

362

says Mason and him were stopped by Wayne Thompson after they left the home of Denise Puckett, who was Gates's girlfriend. Mason had been drinkin'." He caught Mason's eye and spoke in his direction, holding the gaze. "Accordin' to your brother, you and him and Mr. Thompson had a disagreement on the side of Russell Creek Road. Gates says he and Thompson were arguing over Denise; she'd been datin' both of 'em. Gates and Thompson have a scuffle, a fight, but Gates whips him pretty easy, just kind of pushes him away. Then Thompson sets in on you, Mason, sayin' unpleasant things about your father and how you guys — you and Gates — have ganged up on him. He starts at you with a club." Bass slapped the papers against his thigh. "Gates says you were mad and scared and shot him when he was cursin' you and comin' at you. Favorable to you, he says you claimed you only meant to nick the deceased, not kill him." He hit his thigh again. "What's the old saying? You're the guy who brought a gun to a knife fight. Except with you and Mr. Thompson, it was a little blackjack, not even a knife."

"That is a fucking complete and absolute stone-solid lie. Totally untrue and made up by a damn worthless coward." Mason was so livid, so indignant, so rabid, so furiously unrehearsed that Minter ducked his head and Bass shrank back against his chair as if they'd been flogged by fierce weather, wind and thunder. Mason pushed out of his seat, stood and slammed his fist into his desk. *Whump.* While the noise from the first blow was still lingering, he hit it a second time. *Whump.* "And you motherfuckers treat it like it's from the pope." His face pinched and red, Mason yanked at the knot in his tie, loosening it. "And what did my brother want in exchange for this valuable information? Wait — let me guess. He wants to get out of jail." Mason was yelling.

Ed Hoffman watched impassively, his hands idle on his bump of a belly. "Nada. Nothing. He knows we can't help him." Hoffman shrugged. "Don't want a thing. Made me think there was less chance of him lyin'. Why would he? He did ask about a pardon. I told him we'd be happy to write the governor on his behalf. Also informed him the governor will say no."

Custis put his hand on Mason's shoulder, but Mason kept standing.

"He'll want more," Mason sputtered. "You mark my words. Gates never does anything unless it's calculated to help him." He wasn't as fiery, had quit shouting. "Even if he realizes there's no benefit, I wouldn't put it past him to do this because he's a jealous, petty, mean, common punk who blames everybody but himself for his problems. He's mad at me because I won't bend the rules to help him.

Envious because I've worked hard and have a life and he's squandered his."

"Actually, he ain't got that long left to pull," Minter said. "He tells us he only wants to clear his conscience. Wants to start with a clean slate."

"You guys are loadin' up on Mason because of a convict's uncorroborated song and dance?" Custis was calmly fishing, attempting to extract as much as he could from Minter, Bass and Hoffman.

"The boy pretty well passed a polygraph," Hoffman said casually. "Two of 'em. Two different examiners."

"Pretty much?" Custis asked. "Pretty much doesn't cut the mustard, does it, Ed?"

"We know Gates was there when it happened. He knows who done it. Mason was with him. Mason hid the gun. Mason did the alibi. He's twice truthful on those points, Custis. Passed with flyin' colors. I don't like it either."

"He's a sociopath," Mason said. "He probably believes his own cock-and-bull fantasies."

Custis removed his hand from Mason. "He flunked the only one that counts, didn't he, Ed? You asked the sorry turd if Mason shot Wayne Thompson, and your boy Gates went south, didn't he? Even a practiced liar like Gates Hunt couldn't trick the box on the grand-prize question."

"We don't have to tell you our case, Mr. Norman," Bass chimed in. "But let's just say we wouldn't be here unless we were fairly confident of his version of events and had verified it."

"He failed on one and the other was inconclusive," Hoffman said. "I don't mind tellin' you. You're entitled to know. Get the results for trial anyway."

"What a huge surprise," Mason said sarcastically.

"But damn, the men with the voodoo say he's Abe Lincoln on everything else." Hoffman wasn't combative, wasn't gloating.

"They can say he's Malcom X," Custis replied, "and they can confirm it till the cows come home, and we all understand it's not admissible in court. It's worthless to you at trial."

"True," Hoffman agreed. "You asked. I told you. You know me well enough to know I'm not goin' off half-baked. There's a reason I'm investigating. Another small nugget: Gates knows details. Information which wasn't made public. Knows about the club. How the car was positioned. Location of the body. Lights were on high. Details."

"Hell, Ed," Custis scoffed, "everybody knows everything in Stuart — people are all up in their neighbors' business. Rescue squad guy tells his wife what he saw at the scene, she tells her mom, the cat's outta the bag.

Can't say I'm impressed."

"I'm just addin' the numbers, Custis," Hoffman said. "Same as you'd do."

"So it's still only my brother's wild accusations," Mason said. "As I'm understanding you, you've confirmed by a polygraph I didn't shoot the victim, and my brother was there and knows who did. Seems to me you're talking to the wrong guy."

"Nice lawyer trick, but that ain't exactly what the results was." Bass was firm, dogged. "If his version is true, then you've been lying 'bout every kind of thing, whether you shot the boy or not."

"So it's his brother's word and a lie-detector test you can't use?" Custis wanted to see how much more Hoffman was willing to give.

"Nope. Bass and Minter recorded Mason. Their first trip to talk to him." Hoffman's hands hadn't moved, and his head hung slightly too far forward, as if it were oddly weighted and straining his neck. "Mason spooks bad when they tell him they got the gun. The gun from the shootin'." He was trained on Custis, speaking as if Mason weren't present. "Sounds guilty. Says it ain't possible we could have the weapon. They jumped him with a little setup. You listen to it, Custis. See what you think. You can tell."

Mason flew hot. "Wait. Hold on. Wait a minute. So you sons of bitches faked a whole damn criminal investigation attempting to

367

get a rise out of me?" He decided to glare at Minter. He jabbed a finger at him. "You tried to . . . to . . . test me by making up an entire fucking case?" He was surprised at how angry he actually was.

"Man, that's some bad shit there," Custis remarked. "Crooked shit. Is that true? You fellows were scammin' Mason and me?"

Minter and Bass seemed momentarily cowed. Hoffman didn't hesitate: "Yep. The Roberts case wasn't real. We ran it by the AG's office. We were extremely careful what we told Roberts. We never accused him of anything. Never arrested him. Asked him a few questions. Played around in his yard and came up with a gun. Let him know we had it. We've explained to him since we were at his house that he's not a suspect. 'Course, we had to tell his wife and write him a letter since he lawyered up on us. Slammed the door. Wanted nothing to do with us. Mad."

"That's the type of police manipulation that should land you fuckers in a world of hurt," Custis said, frowning as he spoke. "I hope Allen Roberts sticks a stake through somebody's heart. You're out of line, Ed. I'm surprised."

"It's frigging illegal to lie to obtain a search warrant last time I checked," Mason said disgustedly. "And serve it on Allen's wife."

"Never happened," Hoffman replied. "They walked onto his land, made a show for everybody to watch and flashed the fake gun. No more. Asked Mr. Roberts about the shooting and about the gun. Two or three questions. No accusations. They gave his wife their business cards and a paper with our addresses and phone numbers. There was never no warrant. We told you it was served on his wife so you wouldn't be askin' Mr. Roberts about it. We created the rest. The witness Frederick Wright was a Salem cop we sent to Roberts's job site. Posed as a carpenter, a subcontractor. Him passin' the lie-detector test was baloney. We had to be sly. Do it different. You're a smart man and a lawyer. If Mr. Roberts has a gripe with us, we'll deal with it. His situation don't help you none, though, Mason. Whether we was right or wrong with how we treated him. Not as I can see."

Mason wasn't finished. "Cat got your tongue, Officer Minter? Don't have the guts to admit how you tried to have me indict an innocent man, scared the shit out of him and abused the system? Broke every rule in the book and fabricated evidence to deceive me? You can go to sleep tonight knowing — *knowing* — that your ass will be investigated the second you walk out of here. You and your dipshit partner both. Hope you weren't counting on a pension. You guys are totally off the rez."

"Do what you have to do," Minter replied.

"See if I care. If I was you, I'd be more worried about my statements on the tape than how we got 'em. Remember, you're the fool who pulled Roberts in and grilled him, not us."

"I didn't say shit on your tape. You three are acting like I confessed or something."

"Help me here, but didn't your sting prove Mason's innocence?" Custis surveyed all three cops. "Huh?" He bunched his lips and pretended to be piecing the facts together for the first time. "Man, I gotta tell you, as the assistant commonwealth's attorney for this county and the brother with over twenty years' experience in this office, Mason reviewed the file with me and green-lighted it. I mean, come on, he told me to call you and agree to indict."

"Never would've happened," Bass said. "Misdirection."

"Hell, it did happen," Custis insisted. "I'll show you the damn paperwork. We were ready." He stood. "In fact, seein' how you guys are playin' this, I'm gonna have Sheila go fetch the actual document and give you a copy for your file, so you'll know we were on the up-and-up and ready to take it to the grand jury."

"Appreciate it," Hoffman said.

"I'm not impressed," Custis remarked. "This isn't like you, Ed."

"I'm trying to be as fair as I can," the officer replied.

"Anything else we should know?" Custis probed.

Hoffman smiled, a grin without any happiness. "Sorry. Have to turn off the spigot. You'd be entitled to this stuff anyway before trial. But it ain't our ace. I'm not at liberty to divulge any more. I would if it was possible."

"Your ace?" Mason asked, trying to sound sure of himself. "Sounds like you'll need it, because so far you've shown us a two and three of clubs."

"I wouldn't be so cocky if I was you," Bass said smugly.

"I will tell you," Hoffman added, "that Judge Williams down in Henry County has already appointed a special prosecutor. He's calling the shots now. The attorney general's office is basically through."

"So who's the turncoat prosecuting a fellow commonwealth's attorney?" Custis asked. "Based on this bullshit evidence."

"Went through nineteen people to find somebody," Hoffman replied. "Least that's what I'm informed. You should take that as a compliment, Mason. Recognition of your good reputation. The guy they finally got is a reckless little shrimp from Waynesboro, name of Leonard Stallings. Ink addict this one, with big plans for himself. This would be a hide for his trophy wall. I wish for everybody's sake we'd done better in that area."

"You want to talk about the shooting?" Bass asked. "Tell us your side? We've somehow managed to jump off track, but we're here to interview you. It'd probably be helpful to us all if you cooperate. Help you and us."

"Yeah. Take out your pad and pen. Listen carefully to my cooperation. Write this down. My brother is a liar. I didn't shoot Wayne Thompson. I have an absolute alibi which you can confirm from the old files. End of story, end of our interview."

"It only makes it worse if you —"

"Mr. Bass, I'm afraid I'm not going to be swayed by the Dick Tracy strategies they taught you in the three-hour interrogation class at the academy. What — next you're supposed to offer me a cigarette or a free soda? I'm not a junkie or a dim-witted thief. We're done. I'm innocent, so there's nothing to discuss."

"I was only trying to give you a chance —"

"You heard Mr. Hunt," Hoffman interrupted forcefully, respectfully. "He said we're done, and so we're done." He shot Mason a frank look. "This is bad for the both of us. Ugly business. I'm not happy with none of it. But the truth is, as much as it hurts, unless things change, come this fall, Stallings is gonna insist on an indictment. He'll skip June grand jury. Too rushed. Case still needs our report from today and a little more prep. But it's comin'. Let me know if anything occurs to you between now and then." He finally disturbed his hands, lifting them to chest level. He matched fingertip to fingertip but kept his palms spread apart. Head bowed, speaking almost inaudibly, he said, "It would be awful to try and help a man and have it switched around on you. A brother. Your favor used against you."

Mason could feel Custis beside him. He smelled the chemicals in Custis's dry-cleaned suit and a pungent edge on his breath. He waited for Hoffman to set the hook with his eyes, to invite him into an easy, compromised door, but Hoffman cut it off there, never showed anything more than the top of his shiny head. Mason avoided the temptation to answer, and the police filed out, gone.

Cautious and rattled, Mason and Custis remained tight-lipped after the cops exited the room, their positions unchanged, Custis propped against the credenza, Mason listless in front of his high-backed leather chair, the seams outlined by decorative brass nailheads. Eventually, Custis shuffled to the door and closed it, first checking outside the office to make certain no one was within earshot. He flopped into the seat Minter had just left, his huge, thick legs stretched and splayed.

"Damn," Mason said.

"No shit," Custis replied.

"Damn."

"Man-oh-man, this saga all of a sudden got ill. Severe."

"What else do you think they have?" Mason asked. "I mean, hell, what else *could* they have? Huh?" He picked up the phone and had Sheila confirm that the cops were no longer in the building. "They're bluffing, aren't they?" he said when he'd finished speaking to her.

"I don't know, Chief. It wouldn't be Ed Hoffman's style to threaten cards he's not actually holdin'. I'm worried sick. He's shrewd, too — you hear him talking about how awful it'd be for your own brother to take advantage of you? Ed's no chump. 'Course, I figure he's doin' all he can to benefit us, revealing as much as possible."

"Damn."

"I know. I'm hard-pressed to see how we're gonna beat the odds on this, Mace. Sounds as if they're waiting for the grand jury, and ain't much we're able to do. I swear I think this Stallings motherfucker's going to drop papers on you." Custis shook his head, stopped, then shook it even more vigorously. "You talk about this and think about it and it's all abstract and just like that they show up with the badges and bullets and pepper spray and it grabs you by the collar and completely mugs you, whales on you, real as can be. I gotta admit it kinda caught me off guard."

"Maybe they're bluffing," Mason repeated without much conviction. "They ran an elaborate sting to start this, right? Gates simply can't give them a shred of hard evidence. He can't. It's impossible." Mason's color had seeped away — his skin was blanched, mushy, the hue of lima beans left simmering too long on the stove. For the moment, there was no fight in him, no resistance. He was limp, squashed, passive, bobbing in the undertow. "Mystery to me," he mumbled. "A few months from now, though, unless there's a hellacious change, I'm going to be arrested."

"We'll figure something out," Custis promised. "And if we don't, we'll coldcock the bastards at trial."

"This is unbelievable, Cus."

"Damn."

Mason recovered some, firmed up. "If you need to, feel free to hop off the bus right now. I mean it. I appreciate your being here today and everything you've done, but —"

"Hey," Custis butted in, "fuck that. I'm your lawyer, right? I'm not about to take a dive on you, nosir, not a chance. I'm not goin' anywhere."

"Thanks. So I guess we just wait for the other shoe to fall, huh? Unless we can magically turn my shitbird brother around, and I don't think we've got too many options where he's concerned."

"Well, let's concentrate on that for a minute," Custis said. "Perhaps we can —"

Sheila knocked and opened the door without waiting for a response. "Sorry, guys, but we're already way behind, and Mr. Gunter has to be at the dentist's and Mr. Stovall has a load of cows to take to the stockyard and everybody's getting impatient. Can I send them in?"

"Yep. Go ahead," Mason told her. He glanced at Custis. "We'll keep thinking and see if we can come up with a solution."

"Definitely," Custis said. He thumped Sheila on the top of her head as they were leaving Mason's office, a silly, playful pop with his forefinger that caused her to laugh and freeze where she stood and ask him if he thought other professionals acted like second graders, childishly harassing staff members. "I don't know why they wouldn't," he kidded her. "Especially if their staff's all grumpy and wound tight and it's not even noon yet."

Walter Gunter, Hubert Stovall, Avery Wood, Marvin Stanley, Lucas Barnette and James Staples were all businessmen of one sort or another, and they were almost the entire membership of Patrick County's economic development commission. They were ebullient when they paraded into Mason's office, beside themselves with grand news, almost squirming, reminiscent of schoolboys waiting in line for their first ride on the Tilt-A-Whirl at the county fair. "Have you heard Caldwell-Dylan is probably comin' to Stuart?" Gunter asked Mason when everyone had crowded into the room.

"Bits and pieces," Mason answered. He was distracted, irritable, his mind elsewhere. He wasn't in the mood for the men's panting enthusiasm, nor did he give a damn — right then — who was planning to locate in Stuart. Still, he attempted to be polite, aware that he might need to call his current visitors as witnesses at his trial to testify how composed he was, hardly acting like a criminal who'd been caught and exposed only minutes before. "I understand Herman Dylan is interested."

"Aw, no, Mason, he's more than interested," Stovall drawled. "So you don't know the latest?" he asked, pleased to be an insider, giddy with his secrets.

"I guess not, Hubert. Why don't you enlighten me?" Despite his best efforts, Mason sounded nettled, and the men noticed and dialed back their smiles and high-octane exuberance.

"Yeah, well, Mr. Dylan isn't just interested. He's as good as here. We got it from the horse's mouth."

"Oh?" Mason raised his eyebrows.

"Yeah. We was guests of Mr. Dylan's at the Homestead last weekend. He put us up and bought us dinner, the royal treatment."

"My wife got a massage," Lucas Barnette

volunteered. He was wearing a short-sleeve shirt and striped tie, khaki Dockers. He owned several Laundromats and car washes. "I played golf."

"The point of it all," Stovall continued, "was for us to meet with his top man, this gentleman by the name of Ian Hudgens. Mr. Hudgens showed us a presentation, and he's given us his promise that their company Chip-Tech will come to Stuart if you can lock 'em into a grant from the tobacco people."

"There're a few other strings as well," James Staples noted. "But we can make it happen. Water, sewer, tax exemptions. A shell building."

"The thing is, Mason," Stovall said, "we need you to get on your hind legs and make them give us the grant. It's the key. You need to hang tough and really fight for us in Richmond at the next meetin'."

"I understand," Mason told him. "But I'm still not as sold on this as you guys are. Maybe missing out on the canapés and lush fairways has left me poorly educated, but from my research so far, Herman Dylan has a spotty record, most notably in terms of staying put after the free money expires. This grant is going to be critical for us — let's make certain we don't trade our birthright for a cup of porridge."

"These are new-paradigm jobs, Mason," Barnette announced. "We're comin' in on the ground floor with an industry that will have a long life. Textiles and furniture are gone to places overseas. Dead and dying. Here's a new beginning for us. Seventy jobs, great jobs, and a chance for many more. Expansion's almost a given. I don't see the downside."

Mason cracked a smile. " 'New-paradigm jobs,' Lucas? That term must have appeared early in the dog-and-pony show. Listen, all I'm saying is let's not rush into an arrangement and waste our money. Four or five years from now, we don't want to see the moving trucks and padlocks on the factory gates. Mr. Dylan has hit the highway far too frequently for me to be completely comfortable. For starters, it might be wise to extract some tighter guarantees from our prosperous suitor and not just hand him the combination to the vault. I agree it's a business with significant potential for us all, but we have an obligation to negotiate the best deal possible for the county."

Marvin Stanley spoke for the first time. "I'm with you, Mason. No need to burn our resources and wind up screwed. It may be to our advantage, it may not. You ride herd on it and find out."

"Well," Gunter snipped, "I hope we don't dicker and dither and lose the best chance this area's had in years. There are other localities champing at the bit for this factory. I think I speak for the rest of us, and we're convinced it's a sound project. We've seen the numbers and met the head honcho personally. Let's hope you can arrange the tobacco money. We're ready to take care of the other incentives we can control, the local issues."

"I'll consider your opinions," Mason said tersely. "Then I'll do what I think is right. No more and no less. Thanks for stopping by."

At lunchtime, Mason informed Sheila he needed "to see a man about a dog" and wouldn't be returning, and she'd have to cancel his afternoon appointments or transfer them to Custis. Sorry, but she'd just have to do it. He drove to his house, changed clothes and collected his fishing gear, stopping by the Panda #2 to buy a tub of live night crawlers on his route home. Like most county stores, they kept the big worms in their cooler during the warm months, on the bottom rack beside the eggs, bologna and Jesse Jones sausage, next-door neighbors to the beer and wine. Mason removed a container, took off a lid that was pricked with tiny pinholes and shook the dark dirt to get a peek at the bait, made sure the crawlers were fresh before taking them to be rung up.

He went to Kibler Valley and planted a lawn chair on a skinny sandbar that connected with the bank and fingered into the Dan

River. He cut a branch from a maple tree and pared it down to a "Y" shape, sharpened the end and twisted it into the ground, cast and set his rod in the stick's fork. Above him the river was fast and truculent, a series of choppy falls and swift rushes, but it gradually relaxed into a deep, calm pool that joined the sandbar, no bottom in sight, the water good for fishing. The river was noisy where it shot quick and white, the sound penned in by trees and steep hills on both sides. An occasional car or truck would pass on the dirt road ribboning through the valley, none of the vehicles making much speed.

Mason sat there in his chair and let the May sun coat his skin. He studied the eddies and swirls, finding leaves, twigs, foam bubbles or an unfortunate bug, then watched them ride and bounce and dip along, carried off downstream. He felt better, braced, unencumbered. Finally let alone. He'd purchased a six-pack of Budweiser at the Panda, but he left the beer cooling in the shallows next to his chair, untouched. Despite his laziness with the rod, he caught a trout, a decent-size rainbow, hooked through the lip. Pulled to land, the fish's gills fanned open and shut — red and silver, red and silver — and it had a stunted fin in the front, a translucent nub, probably worn to nothing on the hatchery concrete before it was stocked. Mason removed the hook and lowered the trout back into the water. He watched its silhouette dart for the heart of the hole, and he hoped, somehow, he would receive the same courtesy when — and if — his day came.

Chapter Fifteen

The following Monday, Route 58 to Stuart was blocked by a paving crew, ten or twelve dump trucks lined up in one lane, waiting to spread their asphalt, a steamroller idling behind them, flagmen with two-way radios posted at both ends of the project, slouching against their traffic signs, flipping STOP or SLOW depending on which side was needed. "Brownout season," Curt Hunt had always called it. "You know it's hot weather for damn sure when the Mexicans and coloreds finally start their five months of yearly road work." He'd say it snidely every spring, usually at supper, perturbed for whatever reason, chewing while he spoke, then licking his fingers, dirty grease-monkey nails and all.

Stalled in the highway with the radio mute and the windows partially lowered, Mason listened to the diesel engines clatter and rehashed what he'd decided on the riverbank: there was nothing — *nothing* — to be gained by wringing his hands, fretting, anticipating

Armageddon or collapsing into fear and spoiling the days and weeks to come. A trial was the absolute worst possibility, and as wretched and embarrassing as it would be, he was at home in a courtroom and he'd win and be free to raise his magnificent daughter. Afterward, people might whisper or gawk or think less of him, but he'd manage, just as he always had. He'd grown up with a violent madman on his heels, every moment a tight-rope walk across an infernal pit, and he was fiercely resilient because of it, impervious, whet-leather tough and able to wall himself off and stand his ground. Custis would help him prepare for a trial if it came to that, and he'd hire a crackerjack lawyer and they'd all go to battle. Fuck it — he'd lived with bigger problems and not knuckled under.

He received the SLOW command and touched the gas. Homer Amos was operating the steamroller, perched in its tiny round seat, wearing a hard hat and a fluorescent safety vest, and he waved at Mason, shouted hello and called him by name. "Lock 'em all up, Mr. Commonwealth," he said as Mason pulled away, "and keep that ol' assistant of yours straight."

Mason and Custis arrived at the parking lot within seconds of each other, and Custis beckoned him over to the Cadillac and invited him inside. Tucked into the passenger seat, Mason noticed the car smelled of drive-through breakfast biscuits and a splash of top-drawer cologne. He twisted toward the rear, pretending to search the interior.

"What?" Custis asked. "What're you lookin' for?"

"The source of the nice smell. Since there's nothing dangling from the mirror, I thought maybe you were riding high with one of those classy air-freshener crowns in the back window."

"Yeah, well, they were sold slam-out at the dealership when I checked. It's aftershave balm, a skin-care product. It's why I look like I'm thirty and you remind people of Granny Clampett."

Mason laughed.

"So I've been at the grindstone all weekend, Mace, tryin' to crack this. I couldn't sleep."

Mason focused on his friend, barely blinking. "Listen — I'm not going to cave, not going to cower, not going to let it dominate my life. I've made it through rougher times. Hell, this is only a blip on the Curt Hunt scale of discomfort."

"Somehow, we need to yank the switch on your brother and shut him down. He's the key."

"No doubt," Mason agreed.

"It's gonna be impossible for you or me to get a clean shot at him; cops are bound to be watchin' him like a hawk. In fact, he probably wouldn't even speak to us."

"True," Mason said. Leon, the dog warden, walked past the car and wagged two fingers, grinned. Two of a kind, it meant in Stuart. Quite a pair.

"I hate to even bring it up, but you think Sadie Grace could —"

"Nope. No, no, no, no. No. It'll ruin her when this breaks. It'll be bad enough then. More to the point, I'm not about to rely on my mama's apron strings."

"I guessed as much," Custis said somberly. "Don't blame you."

"I can't phone him, and I damn sure can't write. I'm guessing he doesn't have access to the Internet, huh?"

"A whore like Gates, if we can offer him a more attractive prize, he'll change his tune. Feeble as it is, that's gotta be our strategy until we can shake something else loose."

"I've done the same calculations," Mason said. "Gates is their whole case."

"I'll keep at it," Custis vowed.

"Thanks."

"You're positive there's no way they have the gun? Or a witness? Or evidence you've forgotten about? Surprises are cool at birthdays and Christmas, a bitch at trial."

"Like I said, I hid the gun myself and we scraped the barrel. Can't be any other witnesses, or they'd have surfaced years ago. I've been through it with a fine-tooth comb, Custis, and it's a mystery to me."

"Another thing: You know I'm with you — every step I'm right there — but if this goes to trial, you're goin' to need a lawyer besides me. I appreciate what the retainer does, the protection and so forth, and you understand I'd be glad to do the time behind bars for you if it came to that, but number one, you'll need me to testify, and number two, we both realize I can't represent you while I'm an active commonwealth's attorney. The state and the bar would probably take a dim view."

"I know. I've been thinking about who to hire."

"I'll work like the Godfather of Soul for as long as I can, and I'll raise my right hand and be the sweetest witness you've ever seen — you can take that to the savings and loan."

"I appreciate it. I owe you. Someday, somehow, I'll return the favor."

"But if this doesn't disappear soon, you'd better be linin' up a lawyer."

"No need to retain somebody now and have the world gossiping about my problems and telling tales. You and I can do whatever needs to be done until an indictment. Let's keep the situation under our hats for the time being. Maybe we'll get lucky and the lawyer question will be moot."

"I'm committed to beatin' it for you," Custis said. "I won't quit."

"Do I also smell biscuits in here? The bacon, egg and cheese from Hardee's part of your new diet? You sign up for the long-haul-trucker weight-management plan?"

"I've lost seven pounds, thank you. Ain't a man alive who can go total cold turkey."

At his desk there was a pink message slip in Sheila's flowery script informing him a Mr. Ian Hudgens had phoned and wanted Mason to return his call. Mason had her ring him while he checked through her other notes and reminders. Hudgens was in Manhattan, and he spoke with a cosmopolitan's studied lack of accent — his diction to the tee, his vowels neutral and sterile — as if he'd grown up in Saginaw or Butte or Gainesville and taken a postgraduate class somewhere along the line to master the details of hip ennui and white-washed intonation. He juggled sounding cordial and blandly superior, no small task. "I had hopes we could meet and discuss our Chip-Tech endeavor," he explained after they'd run through their formalities and chitchat about Patrick County's splendid weather. Mason imagined the word "en-deavor" leaving Hudgens's lips with its af-fected British spelling: *endeavour* was the way he heard Hudgens fashioning it.

"I'm not sure we need to meet," Mason said politely. "You can just tell me over the phone what's on your mind."

"Ah. Yes. Exactly. I'd thought perhaps I could be even more informative face-to-face, but I understand you are a busy man with a full schedule."

"I don't know how busy I am, but I'll be glad to hear you out. We could use a solid employer."

"I'm grateful," Hudgens said. "Though we would be pleased to invite you to New York as our guest and let you have a closer, more intimate look at who we are and how we operate. Mr. Dylan will see to it you are well received — a Yankees game, Broadway, a restaurant of your choosing, whatever engages you."

"Very kind of you and Mr. Dylan, but I'm not sure I'd be entirely comfortable accepting hospitality from folks I'm considering for a multimillion-dollar contract. Might be a little sticky ethically."

"I respect your sensitivity," Hudgens replied. "Of course, the trip would be purely educational."

"So what exactly is it you want me to know?" Mason asked, impatiently enough that Hudgens knew to move on.

"To be candid, some of your fellow citizens there in Stuart tell me you have questions about us and our intentions. Our viability and good faith. I'd like to dispel any reluctance you have along those lines. Cure any misgivings. As your region's Tobacco Commission representative, you will have great influence on our plans to locate in Patrick

County. We want to convince you we're an asset for your area."

Mason tried to put a face to the voice — he envisioned slicked-back dark hair, clear skin, slippery eyes, trendy spectacles, a slightly beaked nose. "Feel free to tell me anything or send me information or come to Stuart and make your pitch. To be honest, I've spent a fair amount of time investigating your company's track record, and the big problem for me is your staying power. You gentlemen have a tendency to spend the free money and hit the door."

"I applaud you for safeguarding your community and its investment. Sincerely, I do. But I trust you'll also note our long presence in many, many locales after the grants and incentives have disappeared, often to our detriment. Given your research, you must know our plants have long tenures in Columbia, South Carolina, in Bangor, Maine, and in the modest city of Fremont, Ohio. We understand our obligation to the communities who have welcomed us and dedicated their resources to our arrival."

"True enough. But since 1998, you've shut down five plants in four different states, every one in a smaller locale like ours, and the closings always come, as best I can tell, soon after the freebies expire."

"In many instances, we find ourselves at the mercy of marketplace conditions we can't

390

manage. Taking a manufacturing unit off-line is also very costly for us. It's certainly not part of our business model or a systematic component in our integrated strategy. I would invite you to contact Mr. Clay Austin, the city manager for Hopkinsville, Kentucky; he will tell you we struggled mightily to remain intact in his small town, but we simply could not fill the job slots with competent, qualified people. In fact, he will tell you that, if anything, we — Caldwell-Dylan — were sold a bill of goods in terms of the quality of their available workforce. I can only trust you will look at the big picture and not a few isolated realignments."

"I haven't come to a decision yet," Mason said. "And hearing your perspective is helpful. I don't have any agenda except to do the best I can for Patrick County. Once we receive our grant, we're not going to be able to return to the well for a second dip. I'm taking this seriously. I want to ensure we don't wind up in the hands of confidence men and highfliers, our only stake down the tubes."

"And we want to partner with you to make this a worthwhile, profitable relationship for all involved. We are proud of this company's commitment to our workers and their communities. In fact, I'll overnight you a copy of our charitable giving."

"Really? Huh. Excellent," Mason said, his

tone suddenly positive, accommodating. "I think charity's critical. I'm pleased to hear you feel it's important to lend a hand."

"We do everything from Little League to fire departments."

"Our fire departments and rescue squads are all volunteer, so any contribution means a lot. They work hard for free and squeak by on fund-raisers and donations. A real shoe-string budget."

"A crying shame," Hudgens remarked.

"Recognizing their dedication carries quite a bit of weight with me," Mason added.

"I'm sure we will be eager to make a generous commitment if we set up shop in Patrick. I'm delighted we have this as a common denominator. Whether we're awarded our grant or not, I would certainly be honored to cut a check immediately as a token of our goodwill. As an employer, we also value fire and rescue personnel — they are vital to what we do. How does two thousand dollars sound?"

"Great. But five sounds better."

"Five it is," Hudgens agreed.

"Thanks. Make it payable to the Patrick Springs Volunteer Fire Department. They cover the district where I live, and they can use the cash."

"Consider it done. I'll have it forwarded to your office."

"So I take it you're the man to contact

about any changes in the terms of your deal?" Mason's voice remained upbeat.

"Changes?"

"Yes. I'm happy to have established this channel," Mason said, smiling to himself, "so we can streamline our negotiations."

"Uh, yes, I'm always available to discuss any issues," Hudgens answered after a moment's hesitation, caught off guard because he hadn't sweet-talked Mason into submission and bribed him with shiny beads and a pittance for the natives.

"Excellent. We can start by adding some assurances in your contract with the county, guaranteed by Mr. Dylan personally or a corporate surety, that you will remain here for a minimum of ten years and provide seventy jobs with a pay scale forty percent above minimum wage. If you fail to do so, depending on when you breach, you refund a pro-rata share of the local tax forgiveness and the tobacco grant. Gives us security, gives you your free money, and we both have every incentive to make your stay in Patrick profitable and lengthy." By the end of his proposal, it was evident the earlier aw-shucks acquiescence in Mason's voice had been feint and flypaper, a snare.

"I see. Of course, we believe the document as written is extremely fair. We find it difficult to be economically bound to situations we have little or no control over. Speaking for

Mr. Dylan, I can honestly say we'd thought our reputation, integrity and global success would be sufficient to warrant your county's acceptance of our terms without change." Hudgens sharpened his words: "While it is theoretically possible we could encounter events which require your facility to become superfluous, it is equally possible we could expand threefold wherein you receive more than you bargained for. As we see it, this is classic risk allocation."

"So's a dice game in an alley," Mason said. "Doesn't mean I want to play."

"I mention this as background and for no other reason: as you might guess, there's quite a queue for this plant. While Patrick County is near the top of our wish list, we have other attractive alternatives."

"So you won't give us any guarantees or structure a repayment if you fold your tents?"

"I will bring it to Mr. Dylan's attention, but I'm not optimistic. I doubt he'll want to purchase a sea of monetary uncertainty, and any underwriting via insurance would not be cost-effective for us. There may be a degree of tweaking or a very limited guarantee we can provide, but, much as I despair in saying it, your demands could be a barrier to consummating the deal."

"Hmmm," Mason grunted. "Consummating and getting screwed are close kin in this part of the world."

"Pardon?"

"The commission is meeting soon. I'll let you know what I decide."

"Thank you," Hudgens said. "I appreciate the consideration. I truly believe if you reflect on the offer, you'll conclude it's beneficial to you, your county and Caldwell-Dylan. As best I can discern, you are the only fence-sitter, the only obstacle holding up this transaction. Your various boards and any number of prominent citizens have embraced us and are eager to make this happen. As is. Without change. Perhaps I might send them in your direction?"

"Jeez, no. Thanks. I've already had an earful." Mason chuckled to let Hudgens know there were no hard feelings. "Believe it or not, I have an open mind. See what Mr. Dylan will do. Please at least ask him about my suggestion. I want this to come together, too."

"I will. I look forward to wrapping this up to everyone's satisfaction."

The following afternoon the fire department check arrived, FedExed overnight, and included in the envelope were four third-row-center seats to see *The Lion King* and a number to call for "courtesy round-trip air to New York, plus hotel and transportation." Mason had Sheila return the tickets the very same day, but when he foolishly mentioned the lost opportunity to Grace, she pitched a hissy fit and howled and pouted because she wouldn't get to go and had to live her life in the sticks, set on a dead-end trek to the white-trash backwoods. "Don't blame me," she griped, "if I wind up stuck in Branscomb's Trailer Court with tube tops and purple Maybelline eye shadow."

Mason allowed a parent's amused, wiser-than-thou expression to form, drawing and rolling his mouth, pretending he was trying to derail a smile but — this was the infuriating part — letting on he really wasn't taking her seriously, and she became madder and madder and madder, to the point of tears. Twenty minutes later he knocked on her bedroom door and conveyed through the wood he'd called his cousin Sean in New York, and they now had two *Lion King* tickets for July, as well as a fancy hotel room to boot, a suite at the Waldorf. Within seconds she was in the hall, bouncing, excited, squealing and proclaiming him the best dad in the world. "I'm sorry I was such a baby. Wait till I tell Evette and Monica — they'll die," she said, and off she went to call her girlfriends, her door once again closed to him.

On the anniversary of Allison's death, her daughter and husband rode together to the Stuart Cemetery in the late afternoon and visited her gravesite. Mason knelt and plucked away a few grass sprigs that had trespassed over the boundary of her foot-marker, and he stared down at the dates cut in granite, but, for Grace's sake, he strangled his emotions, refusing to tear up or cry. When she wasn't watching, he shut his eyes and recalled the blind, splendid times before he'd been force-fed forbidden fruit and schooled in what could indeed *happen,* the dandy years before he feared that every tractor-trailer might veer across the center line and worried that every muscle cramp was multiple sclerosis, every belch a stomach cancer's calling card. There'd been a day when he and Allison set their clocks by cocktail parties and the future was simply the next weekend, the next thirty ticks of a second hand, the lazy minutes it took him, sprawled naked on a sagging couch, to recover and have another go at sex. Now, like it or not, his horizon line had evaporated and there was a long view, and it was full of chicanes, perils, hazards and pit traps, enough inevitable bad news to make anyone jittery. He opened his eyes. He caught sight of a man unloading a push mower from a pickup bed, a red and yellow gas can already on the ground beside him.

After they'd been there a while, silent and keeping to themselves, Grace asked Mason if he was planning to stay forever.

"Huh?" he mumbled, distracted. "Stay, uh, where?"

"Here," she answered, childishly put out

397

with him. "Looming. Invading my privacy."

"Oh. Okay. I see. Yeah. Sorry." He was standing by then, and he pawed at the ground with the toe of his black dress shoe. He jingled the coins in his pocket. He blew a kiss toward the dirt and said "Bye, Love," to his wife, said it aloud. Finally, he bent over and moved the flowers he'd brought — red roses, a frivolous gift that would soon wilt in the sun — to a spot a few inches away from where they already were and rotated the vase half a turn, leaving everything just so for Allison, doing all he could for her, even if it was only bustle and fuss and not a soul would notice the difference in the big graveyard, monotonous with its headstones and chiseled names. "No hurry," he told Grace. "I'll be in the car."

She stayed for fifteen minutes more, and checking on her in the mirror, Mason could see she was speaking occasionally, and as she was leaving she removed a rose from his arrangement and dropped it onto the grass. Her cheeks were damp and her breathing knotty when she returned to the car. Mason met her, and she allowed him to drape her shoulder and walk her to the passenger side, help her with the door. He cooked them a better meal than normal, and after supper they unboxed snapshots and photo albums, but neither of them mourned or strayed into sadness, and Grace smiled at one picture of her mother, beheld it as if she were viewing a movie-poster stranger, and she remarked on how gorgeous Allison was, how perfectly she wore her dress.

On a stale, humdrum morning in the middle of June, Mason was crossing the town's public parking lot, returning to his office after a short docket in general district court, and he thought he heard someone say his name. He checked behind him but didn't break stride until he heard the voice again. He followed it to his left where he spotted a man rising out of a green Honda. It was Ed Hoffman, and seeing him startled Mason so much he quit walking and, like a dope, allowed one of his files to get loose and fall to the ground. Papers went everywhere, but thank God there was no wind.

"Sorry," Hoffman said, approaching Mason. He gestured at the spilled file. "Need me to help you?"

"Hey, Ed." Mason was gathering his papers, trying not to rush or appear discombobulated. "Well, I suppose if you're here to arrest me, you can hold off on the cuffs long enough for me to pick up everything. I need both hands free."

"Nah. Personal visit."

Mason finished collecting the file's contents. Page corners were sticking from the top, bottom and side, slapdash. "Personal in what sense?" he asked.

"Buy you coffee or a cold drink?"

"Do I need my lawyer?" Mason wanted to know.

"Personal, Mason. Off the record." As usual, Hoffman spoke in abbreviated bursts, stinting with his words.

"There's a new coffee shop on Main Street — Stuart's climbing the ladder. You willing to spring for a two-buck cup of decaf?"

"Good coffee's worth two dollars. My opinion it is. I drink it by the bucket." He was gripping a rolled-up magazine, popping it against his palm.

"I'm surprised, tight as you are," Mason needled him.

"I also spend extra for sheets. Third of your life, you're in bed. No place to skimp. Me, I'm a thread-count man. I'll pay top dollar for quality linens."

"Are you serious?"

"I am. Why wouldn't I be?" He continued a beat with the magazine that had no relation to their conversation.

"Any other extravagances?" Mason asked.

"Nope. Not on what the state pays me."

At Firebaugh's Coffee they took a corner table away from the counter and its traffic. Mason asked for lemonade, fresh-made by the owner, and Hoffman ordered a specialty blend that had to be started from scratch, the beans scooped from a canister and ground.

"So what's the 'personal' concern that brings you to my neck of the woods?" Mason asked soon after they'd been served.

"We're friends, Mason. I hate where we're at right now. With your brother. Me and you know you didn't shoot nobody. Least I don't think you did." He stopped stirring his coffee and peered up at Mason, then returned to his spoon and sugar packets. "But it's hinky. Gates is too close to the bull's-eye. Me, I got my idea of what happened. You already know that." He bounced another glance off Mason, who remained impassive.

"I'm listening, Ed."

"Gates Hunt is a dung beetle. Truth be told, I'd bet he done it. Hell, the dead boy wasn't screwing your gal, now was he?"

Mason hadn't touched his drink. Water beads were forming on the plastic glass, on the cusp of trickling. "I'm happy to hear whatever you have to say, Ed, but, uh, help me here, this hardly seems like a personal visit. Sounds to me like this is part two of my interrogation."

"I ain't on duty. I promised you we're off the record. Gave you my word."

"No notes, no wires? You're not recording me?"

"No," Hoffman snarled. "Hell no. We know each other better than that. You want, we'll step in the toilet and you can shine a light up my ass. I'm not in Stuart, never was."

"I didn't know cops were ever off duty. Exactly how does that operate? I suppose if I were to confess right now, you'd act like it never happened, huh?" Mason took a swallow of lemonade. He kept the glass in the air so it came between him and Hoffman. "So, anyhow, you were saying?" He lowered the drink.

"If I'm readin' this right, you're between a rock and a hard place. For another man's crime. Brass tacks, my friend, I'm assuming you covered for him. Not legal by the book, but understandable between brothers. Don't have to be a genius to solve the puzzle. Unless you're Minter. Minter's fuckin' Sherlock Holmes. He's after you, believes what he wants to believe. You're in Minter's sights."

"I'm still listening, Ed. Let me just say again, I had no involvement in Wayne's death, before, during or after, but I'm happy to listen."

"Gotcha. I understand. My proposal: a polygraph. I'll bind the commonwealth, put it in writing. You pass, you walk. You fail, we throw it away. Can't use it at trial."

"Can't use it anyway, Ed. We've already traveled this road. I'm not about to take a polygraph." Mason put his elbows on the table and laced his fingers.

"Difference being, you pass it and everything ends. That's new. It's a bonus not many receive. Satisfy the examiner, you're done.

You fail, we can't hurt you with it. Stallings'll never catch wind of it. He'll never know if you bomb. Also, I'll see to it you only have to answer two questions. One: Did you shoot Wayne Thompson? Two —"

"I didn't," Mason interjected.

"Two: Do you know who did?"

"Lee Harvey Oswald, maybe? Woody Harrelson's dad? Raoul, this international guy with sunglasses I met in a bar?" Mason unlocked his hands. "I don't have any idea who shot Wayne Thompson, and as much as I trust you, I don't trust the lie-box, and more important, I have to question whether you can legally bind our pal Mr. Stallings, even if you wanted to."

"Already thought of that. I'll sign off on it, and Mike Madison in the attorney general's office will, too. We'll write it down. I'll play dumb. Pretend I didn't know we were operating through Stallings. Mike has high regard for you. You were in law school together?"

"Yeah. We were friends in school, then we kept in touch while Allison and I were living in Richmond."

"You can't lose. I'm offering a free spin at the big wheel."

Mason jabbed at the ice in his glass with the wrong end of a butter knife. He spoke while he was stabbing the ice, his head down, Hoffman completely missing from his vision. "I appreciate it, Ed. I realize you don't have

403

too many days off, and it's kind of you to burn your gas and waste one on me. I understand you're trying to help me and respect your job at the same time." He adjusted his gaze to take in the detective. "Sitting here, right this moment, the answer is maybe. I'll give it some more thought, and if I decide to do it, I'll contact you. If I decline, it doesn't mean I'm not grateful. Why don't you see if you and Madison can have something typed up and finalized for me to review?"

"Already done." Hoffman opened the magazine and withdrew two sheets of paper held together with a single corner staple. "Mr. Madison signed. I signed. Place for you to sign."

"Huh." Mason could see the heading of the document: FULL IMMUNITY AGREEMENT. "You're way ahead of me." He laid the knife on a paper napkin, and the lemonade began to spread and dissolve the area around the handle. "Of course, a court might rule the AG's office has no standing and I receive zilch. I'd wind up screwed, jumping through hoops for nothing. Let me sleep on it. I'll probably discuss it with Custis, too." The papers were bowed from their stay in the rolled-up magazine, didn't rest flat on the table. Mason took them and turned them facedown. He pressed them with both hands, trying to mash away the hump. "If I don't accept your offer, Ed, it has nothing to do with

404

my guilt or innocence," Mason dissembled, already building an excuse for his friend. "From here to trial, it's just about strategy, whatever works best."

"No problem. Unless it's cheatin' or illegal, I'll do everything I can for you."

They spent a few more minutes talking about Grace and the professional baseball standings, and as they were heading for the door, Mason noticed Hoffman had left his magazine on the table. Mason reminded him he'd forgotten it, and Hoffman immediately said, "Yeah. Meant to leave it. It's not an accident."

"Oh."

"Good merchandise in there," Hoffman said with odd vigor and enthusiasm.

"Okay," Mason replied uncertainly.

"I'm done with it. Don't need it."

"Maybe I should go retrieve it," Mason said.

"Free country, Mason. You're welcome to. Might learn a lot." Hoffman extended his hand. "I'm goin' home. Treatin' my granddaughter to the zoo. She loves the tigers. Enjoyed the coffee with you. It was worth the price."

Mason accepted his hand. "Take care," he said, and he watched Hoffman leave and never turn around to see what was happening behind him. He had a quick, upright walk, almost ceremonial, like a palace guard or a drum major.

The magazine, Mason discovered, was actually a trade catalog for a company called Tactical Technologies, and one color page was conspicuously dog-eared. It displayed an "audio listening device," model CST 702V, and described its transmitting distance, power requirements, number of channels, size, cost and warranty period. It was endorsed by a police chief from Delaware. The remainder of the catalog was more of the same.

Mason sat back down, took the knife by the proper end and began poking at his lemonade again. He ran through the possibilities, picking apart his clue: It could be no more than Hoffman warning him generally to watch his step and keep his yap shut, simply a friend reiterating the basics, a reminder that the state is omnipresent, the walls have ears. More likely, though, it meant Mason was being monitored, his office bugged, perhaps his home or car. Because he had a lawyer's perpetual fear of eavesdroppers and intercepts, he would never discuss his predicament over the phone, but maybe that was it, a warning not to forget how easily the authorities could obtain a wiretap. He knew they'd miked Gates at the prison, but this was too much song and dance for old news, so he discarded that theory. It was a listening *device,* not a hidden wire or small camera, so it seemed most likely Hoffman was tipping him about a problem in his house or office. And, of course, it was possible that he — nervous, apprehensive, paranoid — was misreading the policeman's intent, seeing haunts and shadows where there were none, and the forgotten catalog was merely a forgotten catalog. No question, he'd run it past Custis.

"What the fuck you think it means, Gilligan?" Custis railed when Mason showed him the picture and informed him of Hoffman's courtesy trip to Stuart. "Mr. Orwell's probably at your house and listenin' to your daughter on the phone tellin' her friends about crushes and math grades. It's no piece of cake to invade a lawyer's business, but who knows, maybe they talked some nimrod judge into a warrant for our office as well." Mason had left the coffee shop, buttonholed Custis at the end of an arson trial and dragged him into a vacant jury room in the old Main Street courthouse. "From now on," Custis continued, "no conversations unless we're positive they can't bug us."

"Well, so far we've not discussed anything harmful in the office — it's been the Coffee Break, your house, your car."

"Unfortunately," Custis said, "come to think of it, maybe we have. We were pretty damn loose with our talk after Hoffman and the Righteous Brothers lit the fuse in your office and left. Can't say I recall the specifics, but we might've been a little too careless."

"Oh shit. Yeah. I'd forgotten. Jeez. Like I need something else to worry about."

Custis concentrated. "Best I remember, it was more along the lines of how inevitable the indictment was. How they were bluffing. Gates's lying. We're probably okay."

"I'm pretty hazy on it. The promise of a murder indictment will do that."

Custis closed his eyes. "Yeah, goin' over it again in my mind, I'm not hittin' on anything they could use to snag you." He opened his eyes, focusing on Mason.

"Believe it or not, I actually think Ed's sort of trying to help."

"It's the best of both worlds for him, Mace, the best of both worlds. He can offer you a sweetheart escape as a friend, and if you pass the test, he did right by you and the system. If you turn him down, he's got himself a little better feel for the case, another reason as a straight-arrow cop to think you're guilty."

"His charity does put me in a jam, doesn't it?" Mason smiled. "The instant he made the offer, it occurred to me what a porcupine he'd handed me. But you have to give the devil his due — Ed's smooth as they come."

"Can't help but like him."

"I'd never say squat on the phone about anything, but this is a wrinkle I didn't anticipate. So I guess it's fair to assume I'm under surveillance — you see it the same way?"

"Is it a rookie error to buy an entire CD after you hear the one good song on the radio?" Custis broke with habit and answered his own rhetoric: "Yes. A big yes. Hell yes."

CHAPTER SIXTEEN

Asshole Bingo was the game, and the students had played it in the larger lecture classes when Mason was enrolled at James Madison University. Without fail, the same suck-ups and brown-nosers would — *every single class* — raise their hands and ask some rehearsed question designed to get them noticed and show the professor how much they cared about the subject, how deeply they'd delved into the assignment. How smart they were. The trick for these grandstanders was to humbly pose what they perceived to be a profound question while seeming simultaneously confused and consumed by learning's narcotic majesty. First would come the brilliant soliloquy, next the squinched face, then a calculated pause and, finally, the Socratic payoff. You could always count on a tortured inquiry from Gertrude London, José Perez, Steve Ackerman, Joe Fowles, Eddie Nicholson, Walter Post III, Julie Warriner and the king of the assholes, Roger Patel, whom the students called "Hadji" after the character in the Jonny Quest cartoon.

It was Emmett Montgomery who invented the game, selling bingo cards with the assholes' names arranged in squares for two bucks and a chance to win a pot that occasionally went as high as a hundred dollars. Any student could buy a card, and Emmett held the cash and collected a ten percent skim as compensation for serving as czar and commissioner. When an asshole spoke, the corresponding block was marked on the card. Once a player scored an asshole line, he or she had to finish off the win by joining the class discussion and using the word "bingo" in a sentence. As in: "So, like, they find Gatsby dead in a pool and, bingo, all his wealth means nothing," or "MacArthur fights to the Yalu River and, bingo, he's done." The games usually required two or three classes to complete, and the professors had to have known the deal, but they detested Hadji and his gang as much as anybody and never interfered or sought to shut down Emmett's entertainment.

He and Mason roomed together their last year at college, and they remained close after graduation, visiting and phoning and showing up for each other's weddings. Using thirty thousand dollars he'd inherited from his grandmother, Emmett was one of the first people to discover that, hey, wow, there really might be something to this Internet thing and one of the first to also discover that there wasn't quite as much to this Internet thing as everybody thought. "Pigs get fat, hogs get slaughtered" was his investment mantra, so he dumped his go-go start-up stocks and cyber tulip bulbs well before they crashed, becoming rich enough that he didn't have a regular job and was able to play tons of golf at pricey courses.

Not long after Hoffman's visit, Emmett made the trip from his home in Charlotte to Mason's farm, bringing with him a month's worth of research on Caldwell-Dylan. He hugged Grace and made her blush by announcing how gorgeous she was, this despite the "foul, medieval genes" she'd suffered from her father. Emmett was around five eight or nine, and it registered with Mason that his child was almost as tall as his college roommate, a realization that caused him to feel displaced, the victim of a velocity he couldn't arrest or curtail. The three of them ate together, and after Grace — on her best behavior — cleared the table and loaded the dishwasher, Mason and Emmett moved to the den and went directly to business.

"Looks like a bunch of research," Mason said, eyeing the thick sheaf of papers on his friend's lap.

"Yeah. But I can cut to the chase for you. It's far more likely than not Mr. Dylan will put on his walking shoes once the grants are exhausted."

"Not the news I wanted to hear," Mason said, truly disappointed. "Damn it."

"See, here's the story. To begin with, even the *name* of this outfit is candy-coated. Chip-Tech has such a current-sounding ring, suggesting technology and computers and all the bells and whistles designed to make small towns wag their tongues. Truth be told, they will be sort of involved with high-tech operations and basic component assembly. But here's the rub: guess what they make?"

"I give up," Mason said. "I've read everything I can lay my hands on, and it seems they make chips and other parts for larger distributors. They claim to have contracts with GE, Whirlpool, two British companies. KitchenAid, I think. I remember sales to twenty or so different countries."

"True. Correct. But what they'll really be doing in Stuart is manufacturing freezer and cooling components, some circuitry, some simple technical guts to run and regulate various industrial merchandise. Hardly Microsoft."

"No surprise there, Emmett. Even I knew the basics from perusing the Internet. This is how you got so rich? Mastering the obvious?" Mason grinned.

"Here's what's not obvious to rookies like you, Slugger. Caldwell-Dylan routinely sets up shop in smaller, distressed towns. Places aching for business, with giant aspirations and whopping grants to spend. The secret is, Caldwell-Dylan's most noteworthy client is a corporation called Aegis Integrated Systems."

"I hope your reservations aren't political, Emmett. The county needs the jobs, and I'm not interested in taking a quixotic ethical stand. Sorry."

Emmett chuckled. "Why am I not shocked? Nope, no worries there. The problem for you guys is simple. Aegis is wholly owned by Caldwell-Dylan. He sells to himself."

"So?"

"So, he sells to himself cheap. Extremely cheap. He'll design your plant to manufacture what he needs for his major-market products at the parent company, use your grant money to subsidize the loss at Chip-Tech and run as fast as he can once you're bled dry. As a result, Caldwell-Dylan can undersell its rivals. For window dressing, he'll engage in small-potatoes contracts with other firms — probably break even on those deals. Five years from now, one of his minions will appear before your town fathers, invite them to audit the books and whine about losing money. Tough business environment, he'll say. The numbers will confirm the loss. Then you're in a bind, Slugger. He's hooked you. Give him more money, more incentives, or he leaves and the bubble bursts. The employees, now accustomed to decent wages and maybe even basic health insurance, will raise hell with the politicians and the local panjandrums. Can't blame people for wanting to keep a good job."

"So he doesn't care if we fold?"

"Not really. Think of it like this: you may as well hand him half the grant in cash and let him pocket it."

"Pretty damn clever," Mason said.

"Clever, legal, aggressive. After spending a little time with your friend Mr. Dylan, I bought his stock. Thanks for the tip." Emmett smiled and tossed his papers onto the floor. "By the way, I'll wager he's expecting cash from other sources, too. I doubt he's stopped his panhandling with just the Tobacco Commission request. There's so much of this money floating around these days. It's a racket, especially if your training costs and start-up expenses are minimal. Watch the news, Mason. The minute the ink dries on this deal, he'll padlock an identical plant either in Florida or in South Carolina, truck it here and bring his managers along with it. They're like a traveling carnival troupe."

"So we're a temporary stop?"

"Definitely," Emmett declared. "His plants with long histories in the same place are the terminal producers, much farther down the line. You're not. The Stuart location will be expendable."

"But we'd at least have the jobs for several years?"

"Oh yeah. He'll hire your people and pay them okay until the government's not under-writing him any longer. He wants a competent labor force, which he'll find here, especially since people are so anxious to have a job. They'll bust their asses for him. Another reason he selects locales with tons of unemployment. He likes the Loretta Lynn, Pentecostal poor because of their eagerness." Emmett leaned over and tidied the pack of papers. "Hope I've been helpful," he said when he finished. "Sorry I can't be any more optimistic."

"Thanks. I appreciate all the insight. I doubt I would've seen behind the wide-angle shots on the glossy brochure."

"The upside, though, is this visit with my home-run-hitting roommate and his daughter. How're you doing? You seem a little, I don't know, faded."

"Hunky-dory, Emmett. Top of the world."

CHAPTER SEVENTEEN

It was near midnight, June, in the middle of the week, and Custis had driven the Caddy to Mason's farm and knocked-knocked-knocked-knocked on the front door until the porch lit and Mason appeared, disheveled and shoeless, his shirt's buttons out of sequence and the collar folded inside itself. Custis was wearing a Panama hat, a Grambling football jersey, loose jeans and sneakers. "Sorry to disturb you, Mace," he announced the instant the door opened. "But I found a major snag in our case tomorrow. Needs your immediate attention, so I brought the file with me. You mind takin' a look and see if you can offer some advice? It's in the car, or I can lug it to your kitchen — it's a gigantic file." He puckered his mouth and pointed toward the vehicle with a subtle finger laid against his chest.

"I'll walk with you to the car. No need to wake Grace. School tomorrow, you know." Mason rubbed his eyes.

"Who's there?" Grace yelled from upstairs. "Everything okay?"

"It's Custis," he told her, gaining on his senses. "A work question. Go back to sleep." He leaned close to his friend. "Excellent timing, huh?" he whispered, a hand partitioning off his mouth. "We should be in espionage, quick as I am on my feet."

They settled into the car, shut the doors and sealed the windows. Custis cranked the engine and tuned the radio to an AM talk show. He was excited. "I wanna hear you say it," he instructed Mason, the volume in his voice held underneath the gabbing from the radio program. "Say, 'Custis Norman is Superfly.' "

"Custis Norman is Superfly," Mason repeated dully.

"A little call-and-response before I dazzle you with my wisdom. Shout it righteous. Let me hear you proclaim it. Say, 'Custis Norman *is* Superfly.' "

"Custis Norman *is* Superfly," Mason intoned.

"Say, 'He's a genius, smarter than Dr. Carver, slicker than Clinton, more mojoed than Miles.' "

"Could we do that one in segments, Reverend?" Mason asked, playing along. "You're asking me to remember a whole lot of new material."

"I've conquered the Gates issue," Custis

informed him, his tone enthusiastic, straining at the seams but still contained within the sound of the radio conversation.

"No shit? Really? How?" Mason wiggled himself higher in the leather seat.

"Okay. Here we go. This would be me earnin' that heavy-duty fifty-buck fee you paid me. Remember Otis Jernigan, the dumb cracker we sent to the joint for all those burglaries?"

"Yeah. Mean, worthless, lazy. Been in jail most of his life. Always claims to be cheated by the system and never accepts responsibility no matter how guilty he is."

"Exactly," Custis said. "And remember what he promised you last he was in court? How he'd never rest till he got even with you for prosecutin' him?"

Mason grinned. "He says that every time. Does the same diatribe as they drag him away kicking and screaming."

"This afternoon I received a call from an assistant in the Powhatan Commonwealth's Attorney's Office. Seems our boy Otis decided to make good on his threat. About a month ago he discovered your brother was servin' time with him, and he — dumb shit that he is — sticks Gates with a plastic fork and bashes him with a lunch tray."

"Shame we didn't know in advance. We could've upgraded his arsenal."

"Obviously, Otis isn't aware you and your

brother despise each other. This was his big payback."

"I thought they took steps to keep Gates away from our convicts."

"Generally they do, Mason. I asked the very same question. But let's not forget we're dealin' with the Department of Corrections, and he's been there for years. Shit happens. I mean, hell's bells, Corrections ain't much more than DMV with Tasers and riot batons. How huge a surprise is it they make a mistake?"

"So why's this helping me?"

"Patience, my man. They're tryin' Otis soon for the assault. Gates will be a witness. They called here to confirm the threat. Naturally, they want to show Otis's motive, why he selected your brother. They've agreed you and I can do an affidavit so we won't have to trudge to Powhatan."

"Even if we volunteered to go in person," Mason said, anticipating Custis's plan, "I doubt we'd have a chance at Gates without setting off every alarm and trip wire known to man. I suppose there's a slim possibility they might sequester the witnesses and we'd all end up together, but most likely they'll keep him in a holding cell, have him testify and return him to the pen. Not to mention there'll be other people around — cops, inmates, lawyers."

"Here's the Norman stroke: My cousin's

husband is a deputy in Henrico County. They're next door with business in Powhatan several times a month, no big thing. Regularly in and out of both the courtroom and the jail. He slips Gates a cell phone. Maybe in the holding area, maybe as he's visitin' the john, maybe as he's standin' around waitin' for the prison van. Gates hits redial and you're on the other end. You probably won't have too long, but at least you can take his temperature."

"Phone records?" Mason asked.

"We use Inez's phone and my brother's. I'll arrange it."

"Can we trust your in-law?"

"Yes, we can. And supposin' we can't, the worst he can do is say he handed your brother a phone at my request."

"Hmmm." Mason extended his arms toward the roof, stretching as much as he could in the interior. "Maybe."

"It's not all the way uptown, but it's not Baltic Avenue either. He won't be wired, I doubt he'll have a minder and we'll catch him by surprise. Even if Minter or Hoffman should somehow learn where he's goin' to be, they won't be hangin' around in the holding cells."

"Why're you so confident of a distant in-law's loyalty? A cousin's husband?"

"Perry's his name. First off, he's a reliable dude. Solid. I've known him for years. Sec-

421

ond, he borrowed a grand from me after a bad trip to Atlantic City. His wife has no idea, and he's still on the hook for part of it to the Bank of Custis."

"Excellent," Mason scoffed. "A gambler with secrets from his wife: the optimum ally."

"I'll vouch for Perry. Like I say, if it blows up on us, so what? We admit it: 'Yeah, damn right we wanted to talk to him to see why he was hawkin' wicked reports to the police.' There's a risk, but it's not like we're buyin' Louis Vuitton from the trunk of Street-Corner Harold's Maxima. You *could* argue this seems heaven-sent. Providence's gift. I'm afraid we won't do any better."

"It's your girlfriend's phone —"

"And my brother's," Custis interjected.

"So the records would be difficult to locate," Mason mused. "Gates won't be miked, and he won't be expecting me. The only weak link is your cop buddy, and we can't get burned too badly if he fucks us over."

"So we're clear, Mace, your name won't ever be mentioned. Perry doesn't know the who's or why's or anything else."

"Good enough," Mason said. "Yeah, let's give it a shot."

"I'll take care of it."

"Custis Norman is Superfly. Thanks."

Rich — real-McCoy rich — when Mason was a lad growing up in Stuart, consisted of a genuine winter suntan and perfectly adequate teeth that had nonetheless been topped off by a few caps and washed bright by bleaches, or even better, a cat's-pajama luxury along the lines of a Piper Cub at the Spencer airport or a T-Bird convertible straight from the showroom floor at Blue Ridge Ford. In college, he'd been wowed by Southern boys whose families owned third homes on Yankee beaches and hired illegals to plant their flowers, dust their shelves and bathe their infants, the help always dressed in uniforms of one sort or another and careful about direct eye contact. Then there was Mason's high school friend Darrell Haney, who'd moved to Orlando and shot the moon in the landscape business before he turned thirty — he'd built a movie theater smack-dab in his own house, started a bank and purchased more heavy equipment than he could possibly use, some of it just so he could rumble around on a dozer devouring whatever he pleased when he returned home to Patrick County for a summer vacation. But upon meeting Herman Dylan for the first time, Mason soon realized that the updated incarnation of the filthy, Rockefeller rich possessed far bigger ambitions than silk stockings, fancy automobiles or even big-ass bulldozers. Dylan, it seemed, had somehow managed to buy off decay and age and the laws of nature, in effect striking a priceless bargain.

After informing a flustered Ian Hudgens that he'd decided Patrick County's grant would be more wisely invested elsewhere, Mason received a call from Dylan himself, an event that prompted Sheila to appear in his office, practically on her tiptoes, and whisper — even though they were alone — the remarkable news: "Mr. Herman Dylan's on the phone. For you. I recognize his voice from an interview I saw on TV." Mr. Herman Dylan noted he had a real estate closing in Winston-Salem, fifty minutes away from Stuart, and he invited Mason to join him for dinner so he could take a final stab at selling the Chip-Tech project. Mason agreed to the meeting but cautioned him not to be too optimistic; they'd arrived at an impasse, and there wasn't much left to discuss. In fact, he'd already told his fellow commissioners he had serious reservations and didn't support the application.

Curiously, Dylan arranged their meal at a Japanese steak house, not a country club or private home or hoity-toity restaurant. Arigato, it was called, and a black limo was already parked by the entrance when Mason arrived. The interior was crowded with people seated eight to a table, and the sounds of knives, spatulas and metal seasoning canisters clanging on hot grills were all around. As Mason was being led to Dylan's table, one of the chefs squirted oil onto the center of a grill and a blaze jumped and then quickly died in a sizzle, and the diners laughed and clapped, entertained. Dylan was seated alone, in a recessed section of the main room that was empty except for him but wasn't blocked or cordoned off. From his private area, he could see most of the other patrons and they could see him. It was apparent that several people recognized Dylan and were attempting to study him without being altogether obvious, especially a group of younger, raucous men who were enjoying beers and mixed drinks with their food, probably a year or two into their first jobs.

When Mason reached the table, a stocky man in a dark suit and sedate blue tie appeared from nowhere and greeted him, and, after the hostess had departed, the man casually asked him if he minded a search and quick "wanding." "Don't take it personally," he told Mason, "but with an individual like Mr. Dylan, we can't be too careful." Mason didn't want to seem overly meek or submissive, so he didn't answer, instead unbuttoned his blazer and slightly raised his arms away from his trunk. Mr. Blue Tie rapidly did his job, so efficiently and discreetly it was likely no one noticed.

Dylan rose and came to where Mason was standing, and they shook hands. "Pleasure, Mr. Hunt. Thanks for coming." He gestured toward Blue Tie, acknowledging him. "This is Matt Strong. Aptly named, I'm fond of saying."

It was then Mason noticed Dylan's appearance: Pushing seventy, he had the hair, skin, countenance and manner of a man two decades younger, and if Mason hadn't known his age from magazine articles and a lightweight, ghostwritten autobiography, he would have been utterly fooled. The scalpel and conjurer's arts had been spectacularly generous to Dylan, so much so that Mason caught himself searching the man's neck and forehead for missteps, scanning his hands to see if the work matched all over. Everyone in Stuart knew Loni Akers had flown to Atlanta so she could have her breasts improved, and the occasional second wife or industrialist's pampered daughter would have her wrinkles and sags banished by a physician, but *plastic* surgery summed it up quite nicely — the results in the provinces were invariably jarring and fraudulent, an incomplete and checkered grab at reclamation akin to a chunk of flashy chrome slapped on a gray, washed-out jalopy. But with enough money to buy and sell Dr. Faustus himself, Herman Dylan was sublimely altered to the point of seeming remade, wealth incarnate, and Mason had never in his life seen anything so beautifully unnatural. Courtesy of Dylan's warlock doctor, Mason now had a new take on what it meant to be well and truly loaded.

He sat beside Dylan and they ordered and the chef began his full routine, flipping a shrimp tail into his hat and juggling the salt and pepper shakers, even coming at Mason with a joke squirt-bottle that shot red string, not sauce.

"I love the whole shtick," Dylan told Mason. "And if you take it easy on the rice, this is some of the healthiest food around."

"It's certainly tasty."

Matt Strong kept his distance, and while Dylan was civil and courteous, there were stretches of silence when he simply ate and had nothing to say. At the end of several quiet minutes, he turned to Chip-Tech without a warning or preface, wiping his lips with a crimson cloth napkin before he spoke. "So you're against Caldwell-Dylan setting up shop in your county?" he said, and returned to his dinner, collecting a piece of chicken with chopsticks.

"I'm not against you or your company, Mr. Dylan," Mason replied. "I want the absolute best for Patrick County. I'm trying to do due diligence as a board member, and part of that was to ask you for a guarantee you weren't comfortable giving. I truly wish matters were different."

"Me, too. Promising to return money already in my pocket isn't going to happen, though, especially since the business world can turn on a dime. One day you're king of the hill, the next day you're obsolete. Gotta be nimble, Mr. Hunt. Flexible and fast."

"I'm not arguing with you."

"So," Dylan asked, pausing to sip his hot tea, "tell me again why it is you aren't in favor of us receiving the grant? Why you're not interested in our jobs?"

"Sure. It's simple — I think you'll take the money and run. I'd rather invest in something a little less likely to be transient. No offense."

"None taken. Where exactly is it you intend on spending your money, if I might ask?" Dylan had stopped eating.

"Well, there are some local businesses which could really become more competitive with a small boost. Nothing on your scale, of course, but half a million might allow Kreager Woodworking to expand and upgrade their health-care choices, maybe grow by ten or twelve jobs. Same with Mechanical Design and Hutchens Petroleum. They're not going anywhere, and I've never understood why we ignore our own — the local people who've busted their butts and we see every day — in order to fawn all over strangers. I'd also thought of offering financial aid to kids if they'd come back to Stuart as a teacher or lawyer. Believe it or not, we don't have enough lawyers. We definitely don't have enough teachers. The county would have to submit a grant proposal, but I think there are more productive options for us."

"Nothing wrong with that, I guess, if you believe it's as simple as handing these businesses cash and watching them all magically prosper and create jobs. Money, even well-intentioned money, dropped into the wrong sector or spent at the wrong time is money wasted. Like throwing seeds on concrete."

"So's money spent at the carnival." Mason twisted his chair so he could have a full view of Dylan. "They come to your town, everybody's thrilled for a week, and they leave you with empty pockets, Taiwanese teddy bears and a feeling the rides weren't as fun as the year before."

Dylan chuckled. "Besides your guarantee idea, what will it take to earn your support?"

"I don't know," Mason said. "I suppose I'm open to suggestion." He cocked his head. "We've been waltzing around it, but how about you tell me you're not planning to hit and run, that you'll make a good-faith effort to ensure we stay viable?"

"I could tell you most anything I wanted to, but I doubt it'd mean much. I'm not a fan of fools' errands." Dylan smiled, but there was a strain of malevolence in his expression, like the silver edge of a razor blade visible in tainted Halloween chocolate. "Truth is," he said casually, "we'll probably leave in five or six years. I'm not going to sit here and blow smoke up your ass. You've got a handle on the situation. Bully for you — you saw past the fairy dust and slide shows."

"So why am I here?"

Dylan smiled again, allowing more menace to slice through. There were barely any creases at the corners of his mouth. He slid his plate away and rested his hands on the table, one stacked on top of the other. "To see if we can do business."

"How come this one plant in a tiny Virginia town is so important to you?" Mason asked.

"Six million in grants from the Tobacco Commission, a million from the Governor's Opportunity Fund, no local taxes, free water and sewer, a shell building there in your industrial park and about another million and a half from the federal government. Of course, you're the first domino — no local support and no tobacco money screws me everywhere else. Those kind of dollars certainly warrant taking you to dinner and asking for your confidence a second or third time."

"I'm sorry I can't be more helpful." Mason shrugged and flipped up his palms. "I don't know what to say."

"You're convinced, are you, that six years of excellent jobs is something you want to sneeze at? The grant money'll go somewhere, so why not to your citizens? Hell, if I was to tell you, 'Mr. Hunt, I'm a philanthropist and hope to give forty or fifty people health-care insurance and thirty-five thousand dollars a

430

year for five or six years,' explain to me again the reason you'd say no? And that's all this is, subsidies and socialism packaged so people can feel good about taking it and politicians can thump their pimply chests and claim they've delivered the bacon. It's all a shell game, and I'm telling you which shell's got the pea under it."

Mason looked out into the restaurant. "If you wanted to write us a check, a donation from *your* account, we'd be tickled pink." He kept his focus on the people in the adjacent room. "Probably even present you with a key to the city and name you grand marshal of the Christmas parade. The bottom line is I think we can do better. I realize there are people who would grab the short-term benefit and be happy, but I'm not one of them. Maybe I'm wrong — maybe we'll lose your plant, my ideas won't hold water, the tobacco money will go elsewhere and we'll wind up left behind. Still, I've decided. For what it's worth, I appreciate you being candid with me." Only when he finished did he face Dylan.

"Lying's difficult when the other side knows they're being lied to. You need a level playing field if you're going to get anywhere with dishonesty." He removed his hands from the table. The chef was gone and the waitress appeared and poured his tea from a small ceramic pot. "I'll offer this also," Dylan said once they were by themselves again. "I can always use smart, tough people in my business. I'd be pleased to hire you on as a consultant. Of course, we'd have to be cautious about how the arrangements were made."

Mason stiffened. He noticed a piece of rice on the table, and he mashed it — soft, tiny, cold — with his thumb, pressing it into paste. "I'm not interested in a bribe," he said icily.

"I didn't offer you one," Dylan replied, not flinching. "I mentioned a business possibility. I'm disappointed you read something corrupt into it. I understand you have no money needs, or at least you shouldn't in light of your late wife's assets."

"I think we're done here," Mason declared. "I appreciate the invitation and the dinner."

"Yes, we are. I'm sorry we didn't make any progress." Dylan finished the last of his tea and clinked his cup into its indentation on the saucer. "I'd hoped we would. Now we leave set against each other. At odds. I regret it, Mason. Damn, I do. You're a likeable fellow."

"Is this your stick since I didn't go for the carrot?"

"I'm not sure I take your meaning," Dylan said with an inflection that made clear he understood exactly what Mason was suggesting.

They left together, Matt Strong at Dylan's

elbow, and a bold young man from the drinking group approached Dylan and asked him to autograph a dollar bill. Strong produced a pen and Dylan wrote his name on the currency and wished his admirer well. Dylan paid with a credit card and the three of them walked through the door into the summer air, Mason in the lead, Strong tending to the door for his boss.

Outside, it was more night than day. Cars on the highway had their headlights burning, and the afternoon's weighted heat had lifted. Dylan and Strong didn't hold up at the limo, instead stayed with Mason, following him across the parking lot, not speaking. Mason wondered about Dylan's intent — their tailing him seemed ominous, and neither of them gave any hint as to why they were tagging along. Mason took stock of Strong, and the brute saw him doing it, didn't seem to care. Strong would thrash him, Mason immediately concluded. He looked like the sort who knew about pressure points and vulnerable bones — but certainly Herman Dylan had better instincts than to have a commonwealth's attorney attacked in a public place lousy with witnesses. This was probably just Dylan's method of intimidating him, a silent, unexplained smothering that would end with some elliptical reference and a sinister goodbye.

Mason stopped suddenly. "You don't have

to escort me to my car," he said to Dylan. "I appreciate the thought, but I'll be fine." He was firm, bordering on confrontational.

"Oh. Well, okay," Dylan answered, and from his tone, Mason gathered he'd misconstrued the man's purpose. "I didn't know we were going to anyway, but it's . . . it's . . . good to be relieved of the duty."

Mason hadn't moved. "Then why are you following me? You and Mr. Strong? Quiet as mice?"

Having swiftly sized up the source of Mason's anxiousness, Dylan was amused. Glib. "Uh, because we just ate together, finished at the same time and we need to get our car so Matt and I can drive to the airport? As for the 'quiet' part, you'll find I don't talk unless I have something to say."

"You're a long way from your limo," Mason said, but the alarm and accusation had almost left his voice.

"Ha. Now I see," Dylan chortled, although he'd guessed what was coming, wasn't surprised in the least. "Now I see," he repeated, relishing his advantage. He glanced at Strong, who took it as a cue to crack merry as well. "Sorry to disappoint you, Mr. Hunt, but the limo's not mine. I'd bet it's being rented by kids headed to a club or girlfriends painting the town or maybe our buddies who sent their leader for an autograph — the young hotshots could split the cost into very reason-

434

able shares."

"Oh, um," Mason grunted.

"Sorry to disappoint you."

"My mistake. Bad assumption. I thought it was yours and didn't want you to feel, to feel, you know . . . obligated to keep me company." He hoped he wasn't red-faced. "So it belongs to somebody else?" he rambled.

"Yes, it does. Matt and I are Town Car men."

"I'll be damned," Mason said. "I mean this in a complimentary sense, but you seem like a man who'd travel large."

Dylan turned to Strong. "Tell Mr. Hunt our story, Matt."

"So," Matt Strong began as if he'd been waiting in the wings, expecting the request, "one day in the jungle this mouse discovers an elephant up to his neck in quicksand, sinking fast. 'Please, please help me, Mr. Mouse,' cries the elephant. The mouse leaves and comes back with his Porsche and hooks a cable to the elephant and drags him to dry land. The elephant is eternally grateful, and lo and behold, months later the elephant is strolling through the jungle and finds the mouse stuck in the same quicksand, about to go under. 'Remember me, Mr. Elephant?' squeaks the mouse. 'I saved your life. Please help me.' The big ol' elephant steps close as he can to the danger, unrolls his huge penis and tosses it out to the mouse, who grabs it

435

and is pulled to safety."

"And do you know the moral of the story?" Dylan chimed in.

"Be kind to animals?" Mason offered, still off balance.

"If you have a big dick, you don't need a Porsche." Dylan delivered the punch line stylishly, with a raconteur's polish.

"Or a limo," added Strong.

"Or," Dylan said more plainly, "to muscle your fellow man in a parking lot because he won't help you get your important deal done. That would be tiny. Coarse." He held his index finger millimeters away from his thumb. "Not my style."

The phone played a grating, electronic, tinny, accelerated version of the "William Tell Overture," *datta-dut, datta-dut, datta-dot-dot-dah,* and Mason snatched it from the table and pushed the green talk button. He was in the jury room at the courthouse and Custis was with him, the door shut and locked, a handwritten DO NOT DISTURB sign taped to the outside, although it was unlikely anyone would happen by, as circuit court was not in session and there was no reason for people to be in the building. Mason and Custis had been waiting for over an hour, trading sections of the *Roanoke Times,* and when they'd finished with the paper, they began speculating about what Gates and Perry might be up

436

to, the possibilities and pitfalls in Powhatan, two hundred miles distant.

"I'll wager this is my famous brother, the commonwealth's attorney," Gates said as soon as Mason clicked on, before he'd so much as said hello.

"It is."

"Amazin' what you can accomplish when you're motivated, huh, Mason? When you have a vested interest." He laughed sarcastically. "I was about to take a dump, a real pleasure for me, you see, the luxury of a private stall and a bit of dignity, and not only do I get to relieve myself without an audience, but holy cow, a big black deputy gives me a cell phone and free minutes. He's probably not supposed to do that. Kinda like it would be bending the rules to help me have my sentence reduced. Depends on whose ox is bein' gored as to how hard you work on things, doesn't it?"

"What is it you want, Gates?" Mason asked. "Plain and simple, name your price. Why in the world are you doing this? You damn well know I didn't shoot Wayne Thompson."

"Yesterday was July Fourth. I'd like for you to describe your holiday."

"Why? We don't have much time."

"Oh, I doubt your lackey's gonna rush in here and pull me off the crapper. So humor me, make me happy, tell me about your Fourth."

Mason spoke mechanically: "Mom came over and two friends of Grace's, and I grilled hamburgers for them. The kids had some sparklers. Mom made a pound cake."

"And me, Mason, I sat here, like I have year after miserable year, eatin' shitty food and listening to crazy motherfuckers rant and rave. No pound cake, no fresh air, no fireworks, only the same horrible day repeated." Gates paused to let his complaints sink in. "There's your answer, Mason, the key to your legal woes. Nothing new. Same as it's always been. I think if you spent as much effort on gettin' me free as you did settin' up this call, I'd be munching pound cake and lighting sparklers, too. You need to put your shoulder to the task, boy."

"You have less than two years left. We both know you were sentenced before the state abolished parole. You're virtually through anyway."

"Less than two fuckin' years, huh? If it's so minor, how about you come down here and serve it for me?"

"It must make you feel great, whoring yourself for a handful of months and slitting your brother's throat. Selling your conscience for next to nothing. Maybe I can scrounge up thirty pieces of silver for you."

"Hell," Gates spat, "what really bothers me is you shootin' a boy and walkin' free while I'm locked up for half my life. I'm only tryin' to see justice done."

"I'm not taping this. You don't have to recite your bullshit for the record."

"The truth's the truth, Mason."

"But if I somehow get you released," Mason probed, "the truth might change?"

"I'm just lookin' for some brotherly love, you understand? I'm sorry I had to come forward on this Thompson deal, but I've acquired a profound respect for our legal system. I'm into truth and honor now. The flag and our great American country. You do what's right, and it'll all pan out. Even if you did pull the trigger."

"I understand," Mason said.

"Excellent," Gates replied. "You think your cop buddy will mind if I call my lady pen pal? I'm in high cotton here for a little long-distance sex."

"I have no idea why a policeman would offer you a phone, and I certainly didn't put him up to it. I was surprised as heck to hear from you."

"Better go heavy on those law books, Mason. Find that special case."

"Good-bye," Mason said dryly. He folded the phone shut and handed it to Custis. "Major surprise. He wants out of the slammer. He's such a piece of trash, he'll destroy me and my daughter and our mother to save himself the last year and few months of his sentence. Naturally, he'll forget the murder

439

accusation if I spring him. Or so he says —
you can never be too certain with a jackal
like Gates."

"Well, we got two months till September
term," Custis remarked. "Maybe the fucker'll
drop dead."

"Superb legal strategy, my friend. Congratulations. Why didn't I think of that?"

A week later, Mason caught sight of Gail
Harding, the *Enterprise* editor, as she was
leaving her basement office under Stuart
Drug and locking up, finished for the day.
Mason was swinging by the pharmacy to fill
a prescription for Grace, medicine for a mild
sinus infection, and Gail waved him over and
said she was glad to see him and had been
meaning to pay him a visit at the farm. "I
have a question for you," she announced
mischievously. She withdrew her key and
checked the door, grabbing the knob and
simultaneously pulling and twisting.

"I have one for you first," Mason replied.
"What's with that crazy story about the rac-
coon? The 'Man Bitten by Raccoon on Main
Street' piece? Was it satire or something?"

"If it were satire, Mason, you'd know. It's
true. Hard news, as we say in the biz." She
was spirited, ironic, her glasses dangling from
her neck on a beaded chain.

"You want me to believe a man or woman,
whose name you won't print, is strolling

440

down Main Street — right here — and a rabid coon materializes from the vapors and bites him? Or her? The story wasn't a lark or goof? Heaven forbid — you didn't get snookered, did you?"

"I doubt anyone would go through those excruciating rabies shots as a joke. It's just a quirky, weird story, accurate to the last period."

"So why not print the name? Preachers with dope charges, politicians with ugly secrets, information you know will decimate people — you've never sanitized a story before."

"Yeah, a watershed edition for us. It was such dreadfully poor luck, I felt sorry for the guy. I figured everybody and his brother would make fun of him. He'd be a laughingstock for the rest of his life, don't you think? The story works without revealing his identity."

"Only in Stuart." Mason smiled, a smile that expanded into a laugh. "Pulitzer-grade stuff on your end. Invite me to the ceremony."

"I will. Now, on to more important topics." She opened her purse and deposited the office key, which was attached to a plastic Wonder Woman figure. "If this isn't appropriate, you stop me, but, well, I have a friend who's interested in meeting you, a lady. I don't have any idea about your personal life, and she doesn't want to seem brash or

441

intrude or stick her nose where it doesn't belong."

"So who is it?" Mason asked. "This friend?"

Gail giggled, suddenly flighty and girlish. "I'm not supposed to tell."

"Then how would I know if I'm interested?"

"So you might be okay with it?"

Mason shifted his weight. An elderly man in bib overalls walked between them, leaving the store with his pills. The old man said "hey" but didn't linger, and Mason waited for him to shuffle out of range before he continued. "Who knows? Maybe. I'd have to think about it. I've been pretty much a hermit since Allison's accident."

"Yeah, jeez. And everybody's different. We want to absolutely respect your situation."

"So who is it?"

"Well, a teacher at the high school. A teacher you see at the gym."

"Huh. A teacher . . . I see at the gym. I'm thinking . . . I'm stumped, Gail. Sorry."

"Shoni. Shoni McClean."

Mason did a double take so pronounced it was almost slapstick. "She's married, Gail. Damn fine-looking, but damn well married."

"She and her husband are separated. They have been for several months."

"Last time I checked, she was wearing a wedding ring."

"So you noticed," Gail teased him. "Yeah, she still does occasionally, mainly to keep men from hounding her, but she and Mark are history. He moved to Detroit, and they've signed all the legal papers. You'd know more about those matters than I, what has to be done for it to be official. Their split is old hat. You haven't heard?"

"Nope."

"So?" Gail dragged out the *o*.

"I'll mull it over. She seems nice enough from our conversations in the gym. How old is she?"

"Thirty-eight."

"Yikes." Mason widened his eyes, then shrank them back to normal. "Kinda young for me."

"Not really."

"Well, I'll give it some thought." He flicked a piece of lint off his lapel. "Yeah, thanks. I'll probably run it by my daughter, too, if I get that far."

"She's a sweetie," Gail said warmly. "It'd be good for you."

"Since you're not available, I'll have to settle for second best, huh?"

"Another little thing I need to check with you about, Mason." Gail's stance changed, and her voice became less vibrant, the upper register disappearing. "What's this I hear about the old Wayne Thompson murder? I was going through the court orders last month, and there's been a special prosecutor appointed, some guy I've never heard of. The sheriff's no help, claims it's being managed elsewhere and swears he's as much in the dark as I am. I contacted this Stallings, the new prosecutor, and he's like talking to a rock, but he did say you might be involved — that's the word he used, 'involved' — so you weren't able to handle the case. He also sent me a photo of himself for the article, by the way. A lot of smoke, wouldn't you agree?"

She'd taken long enough building the question that Mason was able to keep his poise and answer her coherently. "Beats me. I've had a visit or two from the state police, but you're as informed as I am. Years ago when it happened, they interviewed Gates, and I was part of his alibi for the night, so I obviously have to be careful if there's a charge. Could be a conflict."

"They wouldn't be gearing up like this unless there was something to it, would they?"

Mason brushed his suit jacket again. "The cops who talked to me seemed kind of desperate and scattershot, if you want to know the truth. Left-field, snipe-hunt stuff."

"I heard a rumor Allen Roberts might have some worries."

"Allen's a hundred percent safe. That much I can tell you."

"I'm getting the impression you're not as uninformed as you let on," Gail challenged him.

"Let's leave it like this: I'm giving you all I

can, and if the case takes off, I'll be more than happy to fill in whatever blanks need attention."

"They're after Gates, aren't they? Aren't they? He's tangled up in this, isn't he?"

"Come on," Mason said jocularly. "Put away the bamboo shoots and I'll walk you to your car — wouldn't want you left alone with the rabid street animals."

Chapter Eighteen

The following Monday morning there was an onslaught of rain, the kind that came companioned by thunder and capricious gusts, the downpour so strong windshield wipers couldn't clear a view, even on the highest setting, and umbrellas snapped inverted toward the sky, breaking their metal ribs. Arriving in Mason's office, Custis was grumpy and incommunicative, and there was no coffee, nothing to eat.

"I take it the diet's kicking into a new gear," Mason tweaked him. "Tap water and conversation the whole menu for us?"

"If you're hungry, I'd suggest you hoof it across the street and place an order," Custis responded. "Or visit the vendin' machine at the sheriff's department." He was humorless, the comments tart, defensive. "I'm not your toady."

"Ah, but today you are. I was *your* toady last Monday, and I went so far as to bow and scrape to your low-cal demands and had my mom fix that fruit concoction; plus I paid a pretty penny for the fat-free muffins at Food Lion. It's your turn."

"It's raining like hell, Mason, and I didn't stop for anything. Sorry. We got any business to discuss?"

"Not really," Mason said cautiously. "No." He began swiveling his desk chair from side to side, pointless motion. "The diet seems to be going great, huh? What is it now, fifteen pounds?"

"Thereabouts."

"You do anything entertaining over the weekend?" Mason inquired. "Travel anywhere?"

"No. Why're you askin'?"

"Just making conversation."

"I hung around here," Custis said.

"What's up your ass?" Mason demanded. "You think you could possibly be any more surly?"

"I'm not surly. Fact bein', I'm the duke of good cheer. But we don't have any cases to discuss, I didn't bring breakfast and I'm not in the mood to rehash the details of our weekends like we're a couple teenage girls at our lockers. That okay with you?"

Mason dramatically raised his hands and wheeled away from the desk, as if he were at the point of a weapon. "Sorry I asked. Jeez."

"I've got a case in circuit court," Custis declared. "I'll see you later." The wind shifted, and rain sheeted the office window. Thunder boomed and the lights dimmed, struggling and flickering before they healed. "Shit," Custis groused. "Why is it I always catch court on the friggin' nastiest days — I'll be soaked and have to sit there dog-wet for three hours, listenin' to losers and crackheads."

"Oh — you don't know by now? I signed up for the weather hotline, this deal with Zeus and Willard Scott. I buy the forecast a year in advance and use it to make your life miserable."

"Hysterical," Custis said.

"You sure you're okay?" Mason asked. "I mean, obviously something's on your mind. Anything I can do or help you with? I'd be glad to."

"I'm fine. Besides, you have your own cross to bear." He stood and turned to leave, his full back to Mason.

"Hey," Mason said awkwardly, Custis's mood beyond his reach, "you want me to cover for you? It's not a problem, not in the least. I'll be happy to take your docket. Sheila can postpone my appointments, and I'll fight the storm and crackheads for you. It'd be my pleasure."

"No, thanks." He was walking as he said it.

Mason didn't see him for the remainder of the day, and he called in sick on Tuesday, instructing Sheila to continue his cases and reschedule a meeting. "He seem all right to you yesterday?" Mason asked her after she gave him the news of Custis's illness. "Normal?"

"Well, he was kinda quiet. I really didn't have much to do with him. He went to court and went directly home. He wasn't actin' himself, though, now that I think about it."

"Yeah. Guess it was already bothering him. There's a nasty bug making the rounds."

Mason was lonely; there was no avoiding it, no putting it aside. He was lonely partly because he lacked a marriage, the joy of his wife and the salts, spices and flavors of living with a woman, needs as fundamental as water or winter heat and as damnable and visceral in their absence as a punch to the stomach. He *felt* the empty breakfast table and solitary cup of coffee every single morning, *felt* the dead rocking chair beside his own on the porch, *felt* the hours that were simply stock replications, chapters and verses without promise or spontaneity: the clock radio, work, bench presses, a rental video, Grace's school assignments, TV sports, the king bed suspending him in the dark, the twenty-watt hall night-light, the silhouettes of furniture as he dozed off. Still, the bigger portion of his loneliness was self-imposed, a barefoot pilgrimage to a shrine that wasn't yet visible and likely never would be, the monotonous march the best he could do to honor Allison, his way of keeping her with him, a slog of his own creation. He chose to mourn, to assume the habits of a widower, to withdraw into sackcloth and the sanctuary of his forty acres.

Complicating matters, he grew concerned he was doing wrong by his daughter, turning her into his sidekick and best friend by default, steadily dragging her into his own predilections, the two of them Ralph Kramden and Ed Norton, or Sinatra and Deano tearing up the Strip. "Pretty soon," his mother had recently scolded him, "I'm goin' to find you and Grace drinking beer on the sofa together and watchin' the monster trucks. Peanut hulls on the ground. Or you'll have her dealin' cards at a poker game. She's too pretty and too smart to waste. You have to be her daddy, not her barstool buddy. You need your life, she needs hers."

"I know" was all he could muster. "I'm trying. I enjoy spending time with her, though . . . in those rare moments when she'll actually have something to do with me."

Tuesday night, after supper and an unanswered call to check on Custis, he tracked down Grace in her room where she was busy on the computer, sending e-mail. He knocked and entered and sat on the corner of her bed. "Hey," he said.

"Hi." She didn't stop typing or look in his

direction. Typical.

"Question for you." His hands were flat on her comforter, at right angles to his hips, pressing craters into the billowy fabric.

She continued with the keyboard.

"Are you listening?"

"Um-hmm," she said.

"I've been thinking . . . been considering the possibility of having lunch with a lady." He'd taken the sentence through several permutations, shaping it, careful to omit the words "date," "dinner" and "another woman." "I'll never do better than your mother, and I'll never stop loving her, but I wanted to ask how you'd feel if I went to eat with someone. A meal. Nothing serious."

She whipped around toward him, and her face reacted as if a bee had found her bare foot in clover: first came a half breath of startled, steel-trap surprise that erased everything and reset her features to zero, then the spasm from the sting hit — damn, ouch — and ran roughshod over her. The cursor was abandoned on the screen, blinking in mid-word: *tho.* "A date? You mean you have a date?"

"No, no, no. I don't *have* anything, and if I did, it wouldn't be a date. I'd thought about getting out of the den for a change and spending time with people my own age."

"Custis is your age."

"True."

"So it has to be a date," she said. She was practically bug-eyed.

"Not really."

"It's just weird. Icky. Gross." She folded her legs into the chair, knees against her chest, flip-flops on the seat. "Sorta awful, you and somebody different."

"Listen, I realize none of this is simple. That's why I'm talking to you. I'm not even sure I want to do it, but it's been over two years, and . . . well . . . here I sit, probably depending on you too much, teaching you how to do a box score and pitch a softball and inviting you to kung fu movies, repeating the identical day again and again like I'm knitting Laertes's shroud or channeling Ben Cartwright, and I assume I need to try to balance myself, inhale some fresh air, not become a hermit and pull you along with me. Plus, the truth is I'm lonely. Not every day or anything," he added immediately, "and I love you and it has nothing to do with you." He looked at the hardwood floor, the throw rug, the yellow walls, the truncated word on the computer screen. "You're a blessing as a daughter. Yes, you are. I wish things were different and we didn't even have to discuss this, but . . ."

"So who is it?" she asked. "And how come you're trying to mention stuff you think I won't understand?"

"Shoni McClean."

"Ohmygod. Are you serious? I'll be humiliated."

"Why? I see her at the gym and she seems pleasant enough."

Grace buried her head into her knees and grabbed hold of her hair with both hands. "She's a slut. Everybody knows it. All the guys in my class call her 'Sexy Shoni.' " She was speaking into her pants legs, but she was loud enough that Mason had no difficulty hearing her. "Why don't you just date Pamela Anderson and get it over with?"

"From what I've heard, she has an excellent reputation. The fact she's attractive doesn't make her a slut."

"You don't know; I do."

"I see."

"Why are you even askin' me if you've already decided?" She popped up and stared at him.

"I haven't decided. I wouldn't do anything unless I checked with you."

"If you think you have to check, it must be somethin' huge, so that means it's a date, like you and her are . . . are . . . a couple." Her chin crumbled and the first mad, wounded tears wet her cheeks. The tears dropped fast, straight. "I can't believe you're doing this to me. I'm not even fifteen. Don't you think I've been punished enough without you making it worse?"

"I'm not trying to hurt you or make it

worse. I'm only trying to recover and have a tolerable life. Normal. Happy. The both of us." He slid off the bed. Still crouching, he attempted to take her hands, but she wasn't about to let him, jerked away, slapping and pawing at the air before hunkering down behind her shins. "I love you," he told her, supplicant there as she bawled and thrashed and retreated into her chair, and he understood how she felt, what it was like to be screwed out of a parent, rooked and shortchanged. "Don't worry," he assured her. "We'll be fine."

Don Wiggington wore his soul on display — hooded eyes, fleshy oblong cheeks, a dash of gargoyle running through his wide nose and rubbery lips. His were the sluggishly corrupt features you'd expect to mark a Renaissance cardinal on the take, one robe pocket full of dispensations, the other stuffed with bribes and Medici kickbacks. Unfortunately, what you saw with Wiggington was exactly what you got, and Stuart people kept their distance where he was concerned. He was a big talker, a glad-hander, a regular at the café counters and lunch tables, but everybody knew he couldn't be trusted, knew the story of how, in the eighties, he'd pled guilty to misdemeanor disorderly conduct, a charitable legal arrangement that blurred the true nature of his crime, a sexual overture to a first-grade girl fresh off the bus from Red Bank Elementary School.

Wednesday at lunch, Mason passed Wiggington on the chipped concrete steps of the Coffee Break. Mason was heading in for the cheeseburger and orangeade special, and Wiggington was leaving, three white to-go bags clamped together in his chubby hand, grease outlines already penetrating the paper, turning it slick and translucent.

"Mr. Commonwealth," Wiggington said cheerfully. "Everything goin' to suit you?"

"No complaints," Mason said, slowing between the top step and the landing but not intending to visit.

"I tell you who has no complaints: your assistant, Custis. I seen him in the tall timber this weekend, down at Richmond. How's he gettin' along?"

Mason stopped, straddling the riser from the last step. He ducked his head, not certain he'd understood. "Custis Norman?"

"Yeah." The sun was bright, and Wiggington shaded his eyes with his free hand. "Me and my wife was in Richmond to see our granddaughter at a dance recital, and Saturday a bunch of us went to the Tobacco Company, the nice restaurant, and there was ol' Custis with a steak in front of him as huge as a mountain." Wiggington laughed.

"Last weekend? Four days ago?"

"Yeah." Wiggington situated himself so the

sun wasn't as fierce, dropped his hand.

"Huh," Mason murmured. "You positive it was Custis and it was last Saturday?"

"I'm downright positive. Robbie Unger, a big wheel with Farm Bureau Insurance, took several of us out for dinner. Robbie's close with my boy Louis. Custis was talking to a police officer and a sorta average-lookin' bald guy. Not that I should say anything about another fellow's hair." Wiggington chuckled — false modesty — and raked a clump of comb-over strands off his forehead.

"A cop? How would you know?"

"He was a state man, Mason. Had on a blue uniform and a badge — pretty easy to identify. They was at a corner table, the three of them." Wiggington shielded his eyes again. "How come you're so surprised?"

"Oh, well, Custis, you know how he is. Tight as a tick. I'm stunned to hear he was in a fancy restaurant. Burger King, yeah. Wendy's. Subway. But not an expensive place, not Custis Norman. It's a cinch the other guys were paying." Mason counterfeited a grin. "You should've walked over and handed him your check or something." He was trolling, sussing out as much as he could. "Given him a hard time, cheap as he is."

"Nah, we didn't have a chance to speak. They was totally on the other side of the dining room." Wiggington glanced at the sidewalk, then back at Mason. "And Custis, he's never really warmed up to me. He's polite, speaks and whatnot, but we've never completely gee-hawed." He gestured with the sacks, lifting and dropping them. "I'm not saying anything against him, you understand. Me and him just aren't as friendly as you and me are. I like Custis a lot. Appreciate all he does."

"I'm sure he thinks highly of you, too, Don. I wouldn't take it personally."

"I don't," Wiggington replied. "See you later." He arranged his hair again and waddled off.

"Later," Mason muttered. He made it no farther than the edge of the landing before veering away, straggling down the steps and crossing Main Street, retreating to his office, his appetite squashed, his skin so hopped up with distress and adrenaline it ached. "Sonofabitch," he said aloud, cloistered by himself and pacing the floor, doing his best to decipher why Custis would lie to him, why his attitude had grown so foul, why he was meeting in Richmond with a state cop and a man who sure might be Ed Hoffman.

Maybe Wiggington was mistaken on the date.

Maybe it was simply a man who looked like Custis, and the cop being there reinforced Wiggington's perception — it would make sense for Custis to be breaking bread with a policeman.

457

Maybe Custis was in such a vile humor he gave a pat answer about the weekend to escape having a longer conversation, an innocent fib.

Maybe it wasn't Hoffman.

Mason couldn't quit pacing, thinking, stewing.

Maybe Wiggington was lying. Who knew with a guy who'd offer up his pecker to a little girl?

Maybe it *was* a cop and Hoffman and the meeting had nothing to do with the Wayne Thompson murder.

Maybe Custis was trying to help, had a plan cooking.

Maybe —

Sheila opened the door so violently it bounced off the stiff-spring stop and nearly ricocheted back into her. The *thwack* from the door surprised Mason, and Sheila was right on top of him, busting in just as he was circling past the threshold, staring at the plaster walls but not actually noticing them, his arms pinned behind him like bony wings and his hands clasped. She was all to pieces, sobbing and snubbing and mad, her nostrils yo-yoing snot when she breathed through her nose, spit threads running from lip to lip when she fish-gulped air with her mouth. Her neck was red. Her blouse wasn't right. She was an angry house afire.

"Damn," he exclaimed. "What? What's

wrong?" He instinctively stepped away from her.

"Custis," she fumed. "He —"

"Is he okay?"

"Yes," she shrieked, "he's okay, but I don't have to put up with his treating me like dirt."

"Here," Mason said, offering her a cotton handkerchief. "Take it easy."

"He called me a moron." She wiped at her nose with her blouse sleeve. "And stupid. He said I was stupid."

"Okay, okay, okay. Okay. Sit down." Mason positioned a chair for her. "I'm sure it's a misunderstanding."

"I don't want to sit down." She stomped her foot and became even more emotional. "I work as hard as I can, Mason. I stay late, I miss opportunities with my kids, I —"

"No one doubts that, Sheila. You're the best in the business, and this place would collapse without you. What exactly has happened? Tell me what's wrong. Try to relax."

"He had no right," she said.

"No right to what? You need to tell me."

"Custis came in last week after circuit court and gave me a discovery motion in that Jack Morris case, the guy with the nineteen larceny charges." She dabbed at her eyes with the handkerchief, and the crying and sniffling lessened. "He said, and I quote, 'Send them all the statements in the file.' I said, '*Every* statement?' and he told me a second time to send everything. So today he claims I've ruined the case because I sent a *witness* statement we didn't have to reveal and he was intending to use as an ambush." She picked up steam again, growing louder: "I'm not a lawyer, Mason. Send 'em all, he told me, and I did what he wanted."

"Wow. Huh. You sure he's not picking on you, just kidding around? You know how he is, especially with you. The rubber mouse, the stuffed skunk in your drawer, the exploding pen, the props and gags. The guy's practically Gallagher. He's always teasing you or thumping your head. Nailing you with paper wads. Acting silly."

She sucked a breath through the flow of mucus in her nose. "He was mean as a rattlesnake and he meant it. He said I was stupid. He said I was a moron."

"Well, I'll talk to him. I'm sure you guys just have your wires crossed. He thinks the world of you. So do I."

"I'm entitled to an apology," she said. "Especially since the whole thing is his fault for not being more definite. He's blamin' me for his mistake."

"I'll check with Custis. You go in the restroom and calm down. Take a few hours off, go home, eat a long lunch, whatever. I'll get this resolved. I promise."

"I'm not goin' anywhere," she said determinedly. "I'm not gonna let him run me out of this office or think he can bully me. No, thank you, nosirree. I have as much right to be here as he does. I'll fix my makeup and be at my desk expectin' him to be a man and say he's sorry."

"Fair enough," Mason said. He slid around her and eased the door completely open and solicitously waited, lightly, briefly, gently touching her shoulder as she went past, making her way to the ladies' room.

As soon as she disappeared, Mason paid Custis a visit. He was speaking to someone on the telephone, and he spied Mason in the doorway, smiled, and motioned for him to come in. A Tupperware tub loaded with carrots, broccoli and cauliflower was on his desk along with a napkin and dressing packet. "Not good," he was saying into the receiver. "It's never promisin' when you order a kitchen table and it comes in a flat box. Mail order's a bitch like that. I'm predictin' obscure directions, pre-drilled holes we can't quite line up and a need for Allen wrenches and pliers. I'll take a stab at it, though. See what I can do. I'll be by tonight 'round seven. Hey, Mason's here — I gotta roll." He said good-bye, hung up the phone. "Inez," he explained. "She ordered this damn table from Williams-Sonoma and — greetings from the factory — it's not assembled, despite the fact it cost a king's ransom. Sweet, huh?" He seemed serene, normal, very

461

much his affable self.

"Never buy grills, bikes, dollhouses or furniture unless they're already put together," Mason said. He shut the door and took a seat across from Custis. "What kind of skirmish did you and Sheila have?"

"Nothing, really. She screwed up a case and I called her on it." He shrugged. "We had a discovery motion, and instead of sendin' the other side only the defendant's statements, she, for reasons known only to her, decided to provide them witness statements as well, a gift you and I both realize they aren't entitled to, and an error that took away my chance to do serious impeachment damage at trial. Why's it an issue?"

"She's crying and bent out of the frame," Mason said softly. "She claims you insulted her, called her a moron and stupid."

"I told her it was a stupid mistake. I didn't say she was stupid. There's a considerable difference. She's the one who then got all up on me and wanted to argue about how I'd authorized it, which is nonsense. I don't need that kind of static, not from her, not from my secretary, not from anyone, so, yeah, I cut her down to size a little bit and called her a moron. She deserved to hear it."

Mason grimaced. "Damn, Custis. Man . . . um, um, um, um. She says you told her to send every statement in the file, not just the defendant's stuff."

"I did no such thing," Custis said, his tone formal. "And supposin' I did, how long's she been doin' this gig, Mace, huh? We're too damn lax around here. This was basic and she was careless and now she's runnin' to you and actin' like a child. I don't have time for this. It's petty."

"Petty or not, do you think you might help me make her happy again?"

"Meaning what?" Custis growled. He glared at Mason, tugging and twisting a dreadlock. Gray had begun to stain his hair and side-burns.

"How about we write it off as a misunderstanding, a bad moment, pressure, whatever, and you jolly her up and assure her you didn't intend to insult her?"

"So she's at fault, and you want me to apologize to her? She's insubordinate, and your reaction is for Custis to dive into his Stepin Fetchit routine, hat in hand, and shuck and jive and grovel? She crosses the line with me first, and I'm the villain?"

"Christ, Custis, give me a break. What's with you the last few days? I only suggested we try to mend fences with the best secretary in the state — who also happens to be our friend — and yeah, for what it's worth, you were wrong to say she was a moron. You should address that with her."

"Right," Custis snarled, his voice larded with disdain. "Here we go. Custis gonna crawl up to the manor house and ask the missus for forgiveness. Well, maybe I'm tired of bein' the house nigger. Maybe I'm tired of bein' Sammy Davis, Jr., and keepin' everybody happy, the song-and-dance man. How 'bout we have her come in here and apologize to *me?*"

Mason wouldn't allow Custis any purchase. "This isn't about race," Mason said, not flinching, making it a point to stand from his chair. "And you know it. It's chickenshit to hide there. This is about you treating another person the way you'd expect to be treated. End of story."

"Everything's about race," Custis said. "You try bein' a black man in Patrick County. You try always bein' the oddity. See how chickenshit you think it is." He rose, too.

"Sort of like the drawing of me in court last month — the 'Supercracker' caricature you sketched because I didn't recognize some ridiculous hip-hop term. The flying redneck with the Saltine shield and banjo death ray." Mason hoped mentioning the scene, funny as it was, would diffuse their quarrel and nudge Custis toward civility.

"If the shoe fits, brother."

"You're making a mistake, Custis."

"You're entitled to your opinion."

"So you're going to hide behind your skin color and play the victim and refuse to even speak to your employee? The lady sitting out

464

there at her desk, your friend of over twenty years? Let's assume you're right and she's wrong. You think the correct thing to do is blow her off and declare a race foul? She's doing this because you're black — that's your position?"

"Tell you what. Since you're the philosopher king and have a corner on the morality market and know everything there is to know, I'm gonna glide on through the front door and let you and Sheila take this ship over and sail it however you wanna. I'm gone. You can kiss her ass for me if you'd like. Tell her how sorry I am. I don't care." Custis snatched his suit coat from the rack and hurried past Mason, brushing against him as he went by because Mason wouldn't grant him a wider path, wasn't about to yield or show him the courtesy of a step to the side.

Custis was missing the next morning, nowhere to be found, forcing Mason to hustle between two courts and beg indulgences from the judges while Sheila did her best to placate miffed victims and impatient cops, a disaster of a day that had Mason tired and cranky by three o'clock. He twice sent a deputy to Custis's home and he called Inez Rucker, but it didn't do any good; Custis had disappeared. To make matters worse, Ed Hoffman phoned while Mason was huddled in his office with a pair of investigators, attempting to learn —

from scratch — one of Custis's cases during a fifteen-minute recess he'd cajoled from Judge Greenwalt despite a docket that was over an hour behind. Already harried, Mason had to excuse himself and bound up the stairs and answer the call in the library.

"Afternoon, Mason," Hoffman said.

"Ed." Mason was slightly winded. He held the receiver away from his mouth while he recovered, didn't want Hoffman to hear him panting.

"Sheila says you're busy. I won't dillydally. You decided on the polygraph? My offer still stands."

"I'm considering it, Ed."

"This bugger's comin', Mason. Stallings has made up his mind. Sent me to re-interview your brother. Don't care for him, your brother. Sorry sack of shit, if I can say so."

"I'll let you know, and I'm grateful to you, Ed." Mason's breathing was quickly regular. "We'll see, huh?"

"This ain't fair," Hoffman said, and he struck Mason as concerned and earnest. "It's upside down."

"The fair left town in September, right?" An old courtroom saw they'd both used before.

"So I've heard."

"I'm aware this is difficult for you, and I appreciate how generous you've been with

466

me." Mason checked his watch. "I think I told you as much at the coffee shop."

"Keep in touch."

"So Ed . . . so when're you going to tell me more about your secret evidence? The nail for my coffin." The question was clumsy, more desperate than Mason would've preferred.

"Can't. Wouldn't be ethical. Can't tell you jack that I'm not supposed to."

"I know."

"Can't tell you. You might guess it. On your own. Readin' magazines, studying, you might piece it together."

"Yeah, thanks," Mason said. They were both silent. Mason noticed the rows of tan Virginia Reporters on the shelves, numbered law books containing decades of disputes and rulings. "Is it reasonable to assume, if I were speculating, that I need to watch people close to me?" He shut his eyes. Clenched his teeth. Swallowed. The window-unit air conditioner was humming, its control cover sprung open and three knobs visible.

"Always wise in any situation," the cop replied. "Especially them who *was* close to you in the past."

"You're a prince, Ed." But Mason was sick when he said it, numb, and the injury, the wound, was obvious in his voice, a weight so pronounced he slurred the words.

"Don't know why you'd think so. The box

is the only route you got, seems to me. Bus is leavin' the station. Call anytime, twenty-four-seven."

Mason used the handrail as he descended the stairs from the library, kicked-in-the-groin pained, his pace a single step and a pause, both feet together on each worn oak board, and he made it halfway to the bottom before he surrendered and sat down and bent at the belly, his hands catching his face, the hell with the cops and their shoplifting file, they could wait forever. He remained in the stairway until he'd squandered most of his fifteen minutes, accomplishing nothing, stymied, wondering, half-ass contemplating disguises and fake passports. He finally collected the waiting policemen and went to court and muddled through the rest of his docket, distracted and indifferent, losing most of the cases or giving away the store in lenient plea agreements.

No Custis on Friday, either. As soon as he had a break, Mason hustled to the clerk's office, scanned the index and found a lawsuit filed by Art Anthony, a boundary-line fight between bullheaded neighbors quarreling over fifty feet of worthless dirt. At the end of the complaint was Art's address, phone number and Bar ID number. Mason copied the ID number onto a scrap of paper. He walked across the street to Art's law office and asked the secretary if he could use their library, a request that was fairly routine, given that Art had more legal volumes than anyone else in town, an inheritance from his former partner, Howard Pilson. Mason had been there three weeks ago to find a criminal precedent from 1903, and today the secretary smiled and inquired about Grace, then told him to make himself at home. "Where's Art?" Mason asked, and discovered he was in Martinsville, involved in a deposition.

Mason shut the door to the library, removed two books at random and placed them on a table. There was a phone in the room's corner, near the edge of a small, junky desk, and he picked up the receiver and depressed the clear, square button for line two. The button lit red. He checked the room, considered locking the door but didn't. He dialed the number for the state bar, got a receptionist and was put through to a lady named Marie Reilly, who was assistant bar counsel. He told her he was Art Anthony, and she confirmed his ID number.

"So how can I help you, Mr. Anthony?" she asked after they'd finished the preliminaries.

"I have a question about attorney-client privilege," he informed her. "I think I know the answer, but I wanted to discuss it with the experts."

"I'm not sure if I'm an expert, but I'll try to help."

"Here's my scenario: Let's say I'm standing

on the street and I see my best friend running from the bank. As he passes me, he says something like, 'Can't talk, I robbed the bank and the cops are hot on my trail.' "

Marie Reilly chuckled. "Now, there's an original one."

"Right. So the next day, my friend is arrested, and he retains me to represent him. The trick is, he claims the commonwealth can't call me to testify about his earlier statement, wants to assert the privilege to prevent me from revealing what I saw and heard before I was hired. How do we stand under those facts?"

"First off," Reilly noted, "I'd have serious reservations about taking the case when I was a potential —"

"I understand," Mason interrupted. "Sure. You're correct, no doubt. That's really not my issue, though. I need to know if the attorney-client privilege reaches back to insulate information gained before representation, info or facts that were obtained completely independent of the client's communications and prior to any formal, legally recognizable relationship."

"The answer would be no. Pretty easy one there, Mr. Anthony. As a policy matter, it only makes sense — you're not betraying any client secret or improperly revealing any unique or special insight gained via the representation. For example, a murderer couldn't hire you months after the crime and then bar you from testifying how you observed him shoot his victim. Pretty straightforward, but again, I'd be extremely hesitant to accept such a case if I had critical knowledge I'd discovered earlier, totally apart from the representation."

"Yeah, thanks," Mason said, attempting to sound chipper. "I'd pretty much come to the same conclusion." *There's more to it,* he remembered shouting at Custis. *We won't be taking Allen Roberts to the grand jury. Not in June. Not ever.* Lord only knew what else he'd said before he wrote the check. Great.

Brooding on his porch that night, still wearing his suit and tie, waiting for Grace to arrive home from a friend's pool party, the outside light swarmed by gnats, moths and hardshell bugs, the toads lying in wait beneath the azalea shadows, Mason recalled watching, years ago, a deer leap the pasture fence, chased by dogs. Not long relocated from Richmond, he and Allison had been planting perennials when they heard baying and barking and saw a fawn, still spotted, no larger than its pursuers, jump the top rail, and it was momentarily a gorgeous sight, graceful and elegant, but the baby was tired, evidently drained by the run, and its rear legs clipped the fence, causing it to go crooked in the air and stagger its landing. The dogs, a pack of them, feral, ugly and wolfish, came into view, wild brutes breakneck charging, but Mason was certain they'd never catch their prey, never have the stamina or speed regardless of how weary the deer was. Its head start seemed enough.

Then another group of mongrels emerged from the woods below, coming at an angle, and together with the first pack they had the deer cut off, trapped. It stopped and tried to flee to the right but was boxed in, and it leapt straight to the sky and squealed and shuddered as the first cur chewed into his thin hind leg. It was mangled and as good as dead by the time Allison reached it, shouting and waving a garden hoe and not thinking about the danger, Mason beside her clapping his hands and yelling curses. The dogs trotted to the edge of the pasture, all together now. They wouldn't leave, just stayed at a distance, some moiling, some on their haunches, ears up. Determined not to let them reap benefit from their bloodletting, Mason and Allison wrapped the dying animal in a sheet and paid the vet a hundred dollars to put it down. Whispering comfort, Allison stood witness to its pitiful fading and vowed to kill every one of the motherfucking strays on her property.

Surrounded and abjectly isolated, barricaded against his own particular hounds, Mason rocked in his chair, the night humid and the pasture under patches of fog. It made no sense for Custis to betray him, no sense whatsoever, and that plain inconsistency, along with his belief in Custis's ironclad decency, gave him a dribble of optimism, kept him thinking. There was nothing to be gained, no advantage, no reason for Custis to help the cops and decimate a friend, no grounds for retribution or punishment. Perhaps Custis felt he couldn't lie, felt he was beholden to some rule of paramount integrity that required him to honor the law and hew to the truth no matter the consequences, especially with a murder involved. But why does the guy who invents rough justice with Shug Cassidy suddenly change his stripes and decide to worship at the altar of abstract notions? And why be so suddenly, transparently hostile? Custis would've had to have been in cahoots with Bass and Minter from the beginning, part of their ploy with the prop gun and fake lab reports, the law office wired so he could spin webs and tease out information. But Custis Norman wasn't a tattle or a stool pigeon, hell no, far from it, and they were as close as kin, each other's favorite.

Mason heard the Gregorys' minivan bringing Grace home, and the headlights spoked through the driveway poplars and then into the pasture, animating the fog and coloring three sets of eyes red-orange. A buck and two mature does, briefly revealed from the dark, evaluated the vehicle and returned to their grazing, not alarmed or frightened, unaware of any history there in those fields.

CHAPTER NINETEEN

Violet, yellow, orange, white, crimson and many of their shades and variants stacked at least five feet tall — an arrangement of flowers the likes of which Mason had never seen before was waiting on Sheila's desk when he arrived early Monday morning, a magnificent mea culpa from Custis. There was a Mylar balloon fastened to her chair, floating the words I'M SORRY, the apology issuing from the jowls of a contrite cartoon basset hound. A box of Godiva chocolates was beside her computer, a present wrapped in metallic paper was in her chair, but there was no sign of either her or Custis. Driving to work, Mason hadn't known what to expect, but since it was his turn to supply food and snacks, he'd optimistically brought along a bag of fruit, reduced-fat cereal bars, pecan twirls, and two pint-size containers of orange juice, hoping for the best.

He flipped on the light behind Sheila's desk, took another gander at the flowers and the gift and noticed, topping a neat pile of messages for Custis, a slip marked "Urgent": "Call Ed Hoffman ASAP." Hoffman had phoned on Friday, right after nine. Mason picked up the small piece of paper, held it between his thumb and index finger, read it aloud to the empty room in his normal voice, then laid it down; he felt no more or less disturbed than he had before finding it. He snooped through the rest of the messages and didn't discover anything else of interest.

Custis had also left a gift on Mason's desk, along with a note instructing him not to open it until they were together. Settling in to wait for his partner's arrival, Mason pried apart the juice's waxy spout, drank from the carton and bit into a pear. He separated the sports section from the *Roanoke Times* and checked the baseball scores. Several bites into the fruit, nearing the stringy core, he saw a sleek black limo pass by his window — an odd sight in Stuart — and make the turn onto Main Street. Almost immediately he heard a horn honk and keep honking. He walked into the lobby, carrying his juice with him, and found the limo parked in front of the office. The driver went briskly to the rear door and out stepped Custis and Sheila, laughing and goofy, their argument apparently behind them, both in fine fettle.

They strolled into the building and greeted Mason, and Sheila gasped at the flowers and teared up because of the balloon. "Custis came and got me in a limousine," she said. "You coulda knocked me over with a feather. Roger saw it and ran screamin' from the bathroom to the kitchen 'cause he thought we'd won the Ed McMahon sweepstakes or somethin'." Her hands were excited while she spoke, embellishing her words. "And I don't think I've ever seen such gorgeous flowers." She smiled at Custis. "Thank you."

"The production's not done, Mrs. Shough. Act two moves to your desk." Custis was beaming, and as Mason saw him there, so sincere, generous and humble, making amends in high style, it was difficult to imagine him as a serpent with a hidden agenda, lying to his friend and sleeping with the cops, Ed Hoffman's recent message notwithstanding.

Sheila oohed and ahhed over the candy, and when she opened the present — bam! — a spring snake uncoiled and rocketed from the box, startling her and causing her to shriek and then wag her finger and promise revenge. They hugged and the rift was repaired, the first good sign for Mason in many a month.

Later, seated in his office, Custis devouring a cereal bar and leaning against the wall, Mason asked if he could unwrap his gift as well.

"Soon, my man. Soon." Custis crossed his legs at the ankles, set a toe against the floor.

He was wearing a tan poplin suit and novelty socks with vibrant Dr. Seuss rings. "Listen, Mace, I'm to-the-bone sorry 'bout my conduct last week, okay? Embarrassed. It wasn't professional, it wasn't justified and it wasn't the way a friend should respect a friend. So you got my apology, straight up and no strings. I shouldn't have broken on you like I did, and I hope you can wipe the slate and me and you go back where we were."

"Absolutely, Custis. And if I did or said something or offended you, whatever, you know I'm sorry, too. Basically, you're the best friend I have, and I'd wrestle the devil for you. Last week never happened. I'm relieved you're okay now. It worried me to death, you being so unhappy."

"Thanks. I was goin' through things, and I should've never carried it to work or let it get between us. My fault."

"It's nobody's fault, Custis. I was a pain in your ass after Allison's wreck, completely useless and glum, and I probably still would be if you hadn't helped cure me. I figure you have plenty left in the bank where I'm concerned."

"Kind of you to say."

"I don't want to be a nuisance, but is there anything I can do for you? All you have to do is ask."

"Nah, I'm clear of it." He dabbed at his mouth with a paper napkin, wiped his hands and tossed the wadded napkin into the trash. "I need to give you a heads-up on a situation, though. I hate to do it, hate to have to tell you, but it is what it is."

"Okay." Mason tensed. "Sure." He chain-blinked. He made fists and jammed them partway into his pockets.

"Man, this is a bitch. Man . . ." Custis tilted his head and spoke toward the ceiling. "It has nothin' to do with you or our friendship, but I'm guessin' you'll probably see it differently. Some events, Mace, some events just kinda shake out naturally." He leveled his gaze and studied Mason. "They're what comes next."

"Okay."

"This ain't about you."

"Okay," Mason mumbled again, stuck on the response.

"So, well, uh . . . damn . . . I'm probably gonna be leavin', Mason. Movin' on. New job, new town, new Custis." He shut his eyes and pinched the bridge of his nose. "Not immediately, mind you, and you know I won't put you in a hole. But it's most likely gonna happen, and you should be gettin' ready, lining up my replacement. Takin' measures."

"Why would you leave?" Mason was incredulous. "You've been here forever. I can't . . . I mean . . . shit, Custis. Why? Is there a problem — you certainly don't seem to be too thrilled about your decision. Is it money? I realize we aren't getting rich, but we split what there is to split."

"Nah, it ain't about the cash. Money's cool. But no doubt in my mind I'm takin' the route I need to take. A bigger city, more black folks to hang with, more for me to do. These days, I'm travelin' to D.C. or Atlanta twice a month, and that program gets tedious. I came here planning to stay a year, and I made it with plenty to spare. Truth is, if it weren't for you and Inez, I'd have flown this coop long ago."

"There's nothing else behind this? No undercurrent? You're simply moving to another place because you want to?"

"Amen. Precisely. You and everyone else have treated me like family for the most part. It's time to vacate, though. A man can leave and not be pissed or angry or disappointed. School superintendents and college coaches do it every day and nobody wonders why. Better gig at the next stop."

"So, Councilman Norman, the king of small-town life, is suddenly eager for traffic, crime, pollution, four-figure rent and five-dollar specialty coffee? How do the sly white editorial writers put it? What's the code? You're leaving us for the 'urban' side of the street? Why am I skeptical?"

"You shouldn't be."

"I damn sure can't speak to being a minority — I've only been poor, and you can fix that — but forgive me if I'm not sold when

479

you tell me you're moving so you can be around people in dashikis and go to the jazz club. Better ribs and the Maya Angelou Festival. Nope, not your style, and I should know. Especially when your announcement follows on the heels of your week as Captain Queeg. Hell, you're more content in Stuart than *I* am. Why do I think you're not giving me the whole story?"

" 'Hip-hop culture' is big, too, when George Will opines about us. And the ribs around here are tasty, no complaints." Custis grinned. He took his weight off the wall, stood on his own. "Listen, Mace, no one harangued you when you decided to stay in Richmond after law school. Made sense for a bright lad to want the city. People switch and relocate, okay? You and Allison did. Skipped Richmond for Stuart. It doesn't necessarily mean you've got a secret motive." The last touch of light-heartedness vanished from his expression. "No matter how good of friends we are, you can't be another person. You *don't* know what it's like to be me or to be black in the sticks. You don't. Plain truth. You have no idea how narrow and convoluted the path between Uncle Remus and uppity Negro is. I'm always calculatin'. Always ridin' shotgun. Always wary of the booby traps."

"You've never let on it was a concern. Seems to me maybe you're reading in senti-ments that don't exist. Or making false

480

excuses. You've said yourself how much better it is living here with the random Klansman and impotent, obvious bigot than having to cope with a more sophisticated breed of redneck."

"I'm not sayin' there aren't good people here, and lots of 'em. It's just time for me to move on down the highway. Take in new scenery elsewhere."

"Inez?"

"Probably not a long-term proposition once I leave. But we'll see. We'll just play it by ear."

"Wow. Does she know this?"

"Yeah," Custis said. "She does. She's okay with it so far."

"Where're you going, by the way?"

"Atlanta. I already have three job offers. One's with the district attorney's office."

"Seriously?" Mason asked.

"I used Judge Greenwalt as a reference, if you're wonderin' why you haven't been contacted."

"I'll be damned."

"But I'm gonna stay as long as you need me to. Wouldn't think of leavin' you in a jam, though it would suit nicely if I could be relocated by October."

"Thanks," Mason said.

"It's been a pure pleasure practicin' law with you. You're like a brother. Custis and Mason. The Yin-Yang Towers, as Judge Greenwalt tagged us all those years ago.

481

That's what makes this situation so friggin' tough, not where I'm headed. I hate it 'cause of me and you." He was suddenly emotional, and he paused to stare at the ceiling again. "Me and you, we've had a helluva run."

"I don't know what I would do without you," Mason said pensively, almost as if Custis weren't there. "I can't believe it."

"Me either."

"I never saw this coming. Never. I wish I could change your mind. I'll miss you."

"On this end, too."

Mason peered up at his friend. "If you tell me there's no concealed motive hiding in the bushes and give me your word you're not being pushed or forced, if you can shake on those terms, then you and I are square and I'll be satisfied. I'll help you pack and throw you a party. More power to you if this is truly what you want."

"My word, Mace." Custis stepped closer and they shook hands across the desk.

"Done," Mason said hoarsely, but he held the connection a few seconds after Custis relaxed his grip, continuing to focus on his friend, still not altogether convinced, mining for a telltale flinch or twitch.

"So open your gift," Custis said.

Mason tore off the paper and removed the lid from a rectangular box. "A shoehorn?" He grinned. "I mean, it's a superb shoehorn.

Don't think I'm not grateful. On cloud nine, even."

"The handle's ivory, carved in Africa, the horn's stainless steel, so smooth sandpaper would slide down it like silk. Top of the line. An inexpensive luxury in your life, and trust me, you'll become addicted. Keep it in your closet and every morning, instead of fightin' with your shoes and squeezin' and stompin', you can be a gentleman on the cheap. Find a comfortable chair, take a little extra time and slip your feet into your wing tips easy as you please — it's a sweet feelin', Mace. Butler and castle kinda shit." Custis was sincerely enthusiastic. "If you really wanna go uptown, locate yourself one of those old-fashioned electric buffers with the red and black whirling brushes and hit that baby before you leave. A few seconds on each shoe, *zzzzzzt, zzzzzzt,* and you've set a tone for the day, highbrow right outta the gate. On top of everything else, your shoes will be stylin' and last forever."

"This, Custis, is why I'll miss you so much. Thanks. I'll give it a try tomorrow."

"You won't regret it. You'll be surprised what a major difference it makes." Custis backed away from Mason's desk and nodded at his feet. "Check out these puppies, smart and fly as you'll ever see. Says somethin' about the man wearin' 'em, too."

"Why've you been keeping this a secret,

Cus? All these years I could've used a boost to my day, and only now are you inviting me to the club."

"My bad, I admit it. But better late than never."

Mason put the top on the box. "You didn't have to buy me a gift, but thanks."

"You're welcome."

"You want the other cereal bar?"

"I'm good," Custis said.

"You can have it," Mason offered.

"Not worth the calories."

"Fruit?" Mason was stalling, fretting, deciding. He'd forgotten about his own pear, and its white meat was starting to brown.

"Appreciate it, but no."

"Okay."

"I'm gatherin' from the long faces at the council meeting Chip-Tech's DOA in Patrick County," Custis remarked. "You for certain against it?"

"Yep," Mason said distractedly.

"You see it as a rip-off? Hit and run?"

"It's not end-of-the-world bad, but we can do better."

"Stick to your guns," Custis encouraged him. "People enjoy the hell out of crack over the short term, too. I'm with you. Don't let a mean-spirited prick like Herman Dylan boss you around, you hear?"

"Uh-huh." Mason drummed his desk with all ten fingers. "Listen, since we're clearing the air, I need to ask you a question." It seemed to Mason his blood was too heavy for his veins, taxing everything inside him. He was on the brink of dizziness.

"Yeah?"

"Yeah. Were you in Richmond last weekend — not this weekend, but last weekend — with a cop and Ed Hoffman? At the Tobacco Company?"

Custis emphatically shook his head before answering. "No, I wasn't. Haven't you already asked me? The Monday it was pourin' rain? Sittin' here in this very same office?"

"I didn't really ask you directly, and it wasn't much of a conversation."

Custis finally sat, his knees splayed in opposite directions. "I didn't lie to you then, and I'm not lying now. Why're you so curious? Whoa. Wait. Hold on. You think me and Ed got something percolatin' to your disadvantage? *Do* you? That's a pretty rude accusation from the guy who claims we're so damn tight, such major pals." Custis stretched his neck forward, leading with his chin, defiant. "Especially shitty seein' as how I've busted my ass to protect you, and I'm still willin' to do my bit — by any means necessary, as brother Malcolm would put it."

"I didn't accuse you of anything. For all I know, you could've met with him trying to help me." The surge of nerves was waning, the threat of dizziness passing.

"No, you're suggesting I'm lying about bein' in Richmond with Ed. Don't try to sugarcoat it."

"So you weren't?"

"Fuck no, Mason, I didn't meet with Ed. Not in Richmond, not in Area 51, not in Timbuktu, not any-freakin'-where. Suddenly, I'm not regretting my decision to leave quite as bad. Who's spreadin' this nonsense, huh? Where you hearin' this rumor?"

"Don Wiggington said he saw you and a man who could've been Hoffman and a uniformed cop at the Tobacco Company restaurant. He was positive."

"And I'm positive he's a pervert, a liar and a troublemaker. I wouldn't believe that seedy SOB if he told me the sun rises in the east. You're in my business because of Don Wiggington? The child molester? I need to slap myself, cause I know this has to be a dream."

"Why's Hoffman calling you? He called last Friday — you didn't mention it."

"I oughta leap over there and knock the shit outta you." Custis was furious. Strident. "I should. You think — you have the balls to challenge my . . ." He was tongue-tied mad, spluttering, so angry he couldn't continue.

"I had to ask, Custis. Wouldn't you?"

"You're not asking," he snapped. "You're accusing me of lying and plottin' against you. That's what's at the bottom of your question, and I resent it."

"If you tell me I'm off base, we won't mention it again. You say you weren't in Richmond, you weren't in Richmond. You tell me you didn't have dinner with Ed Hoffman, you didn't have dinner with Ed Hoffman."

"I shouldn't have to say it three times, but I'm gonna, just so I won't undo the dab of goodwill I've tried to spread this morning." His voice was still heated, but he wasn't as confrontational. "I've never talked to Ed in Richmond or anywhere else on this planet about your case unless you were there. I don't have some secret plan, good or bad, goin' with Ed or the cops. Despite your lack of faith and appreciation, I've stuck with you and will continue to do so come what may, even though reasonable people might say I shouldn't. Understand?" He glared at Mason. "Ed, who is a policeman with cases other than yours, phoned Friday to tell me the forensics weren't ready for the trial we have tomorrow, the Arlen Spencer credit card forgeries. He needed a continuance. I saw the message when I brought the flowers and called him Sunday night at his home." Custis rose from his chair. "Here's the gospel, Mason Hunt: like the song says, paranoia will destroy you. You better chill and quit actin' the fool. Remember who's your friend, who's your enemy."

Mason believed him. "Far as I'm concerned, the book's closed, then."

"Far as I'm concerned," Custis huffed, "there never shoulda been a damn book."

Mason managed a weak smile. "You want your shoehorn returned?"

"I'm not playin', Mason. I admit I shouldn't have jumped on you last week, and I came in here today and apologized like a man. But I've never questioned your character, never sunk so low as you did just now. Never would. Like I'm gonna pretend to be your friend and . . . shit, we probably shouldn't be discussin' your personal affairs in here, anyhow. Too many potential ears."

"You're right."

"Shame on you," Custis rebuked him.

"I regret it, Custis. I'm sorry. I don't blame you for being pissed at me. Seems to be the day for apologies around here, huh?"

"Well, you're not finished with yours yet. This insult's got some legs. Your restitution's just beginning."

They didn't have any desire to be Ling-Ling and Hsing-Hsing, eating their meal while a hoard of gawkers scrambled for a peek at the town's newest curiosity, so Mason and Shoni McClean drove to Mount Airy on an August Saturday to have their first lunch together. School had begun, and even though it was still plenty hot, the air was crisper at night and the grass dew-soaked when the sun rose. Yellow leaves were starting in the poplars, maybe five bright inserts in a tree a hundred feet high, the changes still lost among all the green, insignificant.

Mason hadn't told his daughter where he was going or what he was doing. She and a group of friends were rehearsing a play at a teacher's house, and Mason had instructed her to call his cell if she needed him. He was pleasantly excited as he showered and shaved and dressed, and he debated which shirt he should wear and looked at himself in the mirror, gauging his appearance. He decided against cologne and settled on flip-flops with his chinos. It felt good to have a trickle of juice flowing, to finally register something besides dread at the same gray, stifling loop he toured every day, but as he was leaving, he saw Allison's picture, prominent on his dresser, and the lovely reminder caused him to sit on the bed in his silent house and ponder how out of whack this was, how flukish and screwy.

Before calling Shoni and asking her to lunch, he'd parked himself in the room with the rhino painting and scoured his conscience, trying to get a handle on what Allison would have expected of him. He concluded he'd be the jealous, childish ghost rattling his chains and shouting boo at his wife's new suitors, rearranging furniture and shorting light fixtures, a selfish spirit who'd rather see Allison in brown, droopy sweaters and drowning in cats than content with another man. Conversely, she probably loved him more than that, would ultimately wish him whole and attached to life, and he imagined her elegant hand raising a wineglass in a toast, subtle and sorrowful, of course, but still offering her blessing. She'd say something like, "So long as she's not as pretty as I am . . ." because she had always been confident and complete in herself, more assured and more generous than he could ever be.

Mason and Shoni had lunch at a Main Street restaurant called Pandowdy's, and despite his looming legal problems and the undeniable weirdness of a first date, the phenomenon of being both buyer and seller, performer and audience, Mason enjoyed the meal and he was impressed by Shoni, who had the grace and good sense not to discuss her estranged husband and was interested in all manner of things from kayaking to Ingmar Bergman. They discussed law and teaching and mutual friends and the new treadmill at the gym. They chattered past dessert and coffee, staying until two o'clock, even finishing the hard peppermints that came with the bill.

Returning to Stuart on Route 103, they commented on the cement dinosaur, polka-dot elephant and giant pink amphora at the entrance to Slick's Pottery, and they passed an old coot in a metal folding chair, a flyswatter resting across his lap, peddling his wares from a roadside shack, mostly hubcaps and lawn mower motors and dusty glass bottles. They turned around at a white clapboard church and went back to the man's junky stand, where they bought a pair of hubcaps, one shiny prize for Mason, one for Shoni, matching first-date mementos, the kind of calculated craziness that's funny and loosey-goosey and vaguely romantic but would have a veteran husband fussing at his wife and braying, "Why the hell would I want to drop twenty bucks on hubcaps we can't ever use?" Mason kissed Shoni on the cheek at her door, told her he'd see her again soon, he hoped.

At the end of August, now firmly convinced he would be indicted by Leonard Stallings in the September term of Patrick County Circuit Court, Mason traveled to Martinsville and hired a pair of lawyers, Pat Sharpe and Jim Haskins, to represent him. Sharpe was the younger of the two, around six feet, thin, fair-skinned and impossible to rattle in the courtroom, deft at developing his case with thoughtful, compact questions that left witnesses no space to hedge or lie. Haskins was in his sixties, a warrior from the first pleading to the last post-trial motion, savvy and persistent, and he was famous for his impeccable manners, natty suits and cheap black-plastic comb, which he would unabashedly produce, anywhere, anytime, and carefully groom his hair, whether in the middle of a trial or while talking to a friend on a street corner, it didn't matter to Gentleman Jim, and the idiosyncrasy had become a trademark of sorts for him, to the extent that other attorneys and court personnel often cued on it, figuring the comb's appearance likely signaled a turn in a case, big doings, a sign the hammer was about to fall.

After mulling it over, Mason decided to include Custis in their initial meeting, and the four of them gathered in Haskins's conference room, late in the afternoon. Mason explained he was soon going to be charged with the 1984 murder of Wayne Thompson. Saying it, sitting there in Haskins's conference room amid the black leather chairs and fox-hunt prints, saying it caused Mason to come to a dead halt, his own voice repeating in his brain, the awful gravity binding him for several seconds. Finally continuing, he also informed them the commonwealth's case was based on three items: his brother's testimony, an incriminating statement he'd allegedly made during a police sting and some mysterious evidence he and Custis hadn't unearthed but believed to exist, since Ed Hoffman was an honest cop and wouldn't bluff if he didn't have the goods. Mason declared his innocence, repeating the false account of where he and Gates had been on the night of the killing. "He's doing this because he's angry with me," Mason said in a steady voice, "and because he wants me to help him get out of jail. Since I won't do his bidding, I'm sure he'll try to trade his testimony for some sentence reduction or an advantage in the system."

True to his temperament, Haskins was enraged. "What a bastard!" he exclaimed, bellicose and combative, immediately spinning out no-holds-barred legal strategies. Sharpe listened intently with his index fingers steepled in front of his face and said, "I'm sorry this is happening to you, Mason."

They discussed options and speculated and debated strategy for over an hour, and at the conclusion of the meeting they were in agreement on all issues save one: the question of the polygraph. Sharpe and Custis thought there was nothing to lose and everything to gain, but Haskins was against the idea, arguing the tests were unreliable, he wasn't sure the agreement was enforceable and it was beneath Mason to participate in a "damn witch hunt." "Those tests are wrong too often for my taste," Haskins said. "You catch an erroneous reading or an inconclusive, and you better believe this Stallings or the cops will leak it to the court, slip it in, and while the jury might not hear it as evidence, you'll wind up with a judge who thinks you're guilty and that'll color every ruling he makes. Besides, your sympathetic chum Ed Hoffman, who's helping and feeding you under the table right now, might switch teams if he thinks you're lying."

"I'll sleep on it," Mason said. "Grand jury meets on the eighth — I'd need to do it before then. How about you guys helping me with the research, see if Ed and the AG's office can tie Stallings's hands once he's appointed as special prosecutor? I've spent several hours on the computer reading every case I could find, and I think we can rely on the agreement, but I'd rather have a more objective opinion."

"I'll have your answer by tomorrow," Sharpe promised.

"Every case I found references commitments made by the *commonwealth*," Sharpe explained in a call Mason took at his mother's house the next day. "The rulings don't necessarily focus on individual prosecutors except in the sense that they're agents for the state and can therefore make agreements on its behalf. Who better than the heaviest hitter of them all, the attorney general and his authorized staff, to conduct the commonwealth's affairs? Do we really think a judge is going to ignore an immunity offer made by the cop in charge of the case *and* the office of the commonwealth's chief prosecutor? You could very

494

legitimately argue that the attorney general is Stallings's boss and can trump him. Legally, my opinion is the same as yours — we've got the horses on immunity if you want to have a go at the polygraph. Tactically, of course, it's up to you. Jim has raised a number of very valid points contrary to mine."

Ultimately, Mason sided with Custis and Sharpe, concluding that there was a strong possibility of enforcing the deal and defeating any prosecution *if* he could beat the test. Mason himself phoned Ed Hoffman, and they rearranged several schedules so Mason could drive to state police headquarters in Salem and undergo the examination before the grand jury convened. "Who you want on the box?" Hoffman asked.

"I get to pick?" Mason replied.

"So long as it's one of our guys. Or one of the feds."

"Huh." Mason thought about the possibilities. "I'll take Morgan Witmer."

"I would, too. Good luck, my friend. I'm rootin' for you."

Mason spent hours preparing for the test. He would ask himself the money questions out loud and practice saying no, attempting to repeat the deception again and again and again and again until he was immune to it, desensitized. He concentrated on his breathing, the pace of his heart, the adrenaline bumps in his stomach. He rehearsed with a thumbtack positioned in his shoe, pressing it into his middle toe before he began each series of questions to himself, hoping to elevate his breathing and heartbeat so there would be less room for deviation from the recorded baseline, no peaks and valleys. To dull his responses, he washed down a Valium with his breakfast orange juice before leaving for the exam.

Aware the cops might search him or require him to remove his shoes and discover the tack, he parked at a Hardee's in Salem, slit the underside of his middle toe with a razor blade, placed a slender, flesh-colored Band-Aid on the cut and experimented with the pain level. He was satisfied — the fresh slash hurt more than the tack he'd used as an approximation. Pat Sharpe met him at the entrance to the state police building, wished him the best and accompanied him down a long hall with fluorescent lights and dingy white ceiling tiles, several discolored by water stains.

Morgan Witmer was careful not to grant any advantages or favorable treatment. He spent forty minutes asking questions and explaining the test and ground rules before he hooked Mason to the machine with wires, a chest strap and a blood pressure cuff and asked the first question: "Is your name Mason Hunt?"

Mason mashed his cut toe into the floor

and monitored his breathing. "Yes." He was still wearing his shoes, perhaps a concession from Hoffman, or maybe the experts weren't concerned with countermeasures gleaned from the Internet, confident they could see through a layperson's most disciplined subterfuge, barefoot or not. The control question was "Have you ever lied about anything to keep from getting in trouble?" and Mason answered yes, aware this wasn't the key inquiry, nor was it really directed at his case. "Did you kill Wayne Thompson?" and "Do you know who killed Wayne Thompson?" were sandwiched between innocuous softballs about the color of his shirt and Mason's home mailing address.

Witmer then repeated the questions word for word, this time in a different order. "You can relax," he said at the end of the second round, and the device's skittering, darting needles went calm over their paper.

Hoffman and Witmer left the room after the exam was concluded, and Mason made an effort to appear relaxed and assured, given that he was most likely being recorded by a concealed camera. Having ambled in to join his client, Pat Sharpe was calm also, a pro, and he projected confidence, chatting about deer season and his son's roster of teachers at elementary school. Ten minutes later, Hoffman returned alone. Dispensing with the customary song and dance and post-interrogation razzmatazz, he stood in front of Mason, his arms against his rib cage, a soldier's posture almost. "So, you want Mr. Sharpe to stay here?"

"Absolutely," Mason said, his mouth dry, his stomach suddenly hollow, realizing from Hoffman's question that the results were not going to be favorable. He saw Sharpe quickly remedy a dejected mouth, masking his own disappointment.

"Well, you got fifty percent. Passed on whether you killed the boy. No surprise there. Showed deception on knowledge of who killed him." He glanced at Sharpe, not Mason. "For me, no surprise there either."

"The test is wrong," Mason protested. He struck the right tone, too: firm, astonished, aggrieved.

"This isn't a police trap is it, Ed?" Sharpe inquired. "The Hail Mary where your polygraph guy actually has no idea, but you claim Mason failed so you can pressure him into admitting something? Hope he'll collapse because you tell him he failed a test we both know is on a par with tarot cards and Ouija boards?"

"Witmer says he's lying. I don't like it either. At least give me credit for not underestimatin' you gents. I'm not interested in screwin' Mason."

"Thanks," Mason said. "You've been completely fair. It's not your fault. I was probably too nervous or overanalyzed the questions."

"I told Witmer to make you a copy," Hoffman said. "You're welcome to have an independent take a look at it. But you and me know Morgan Witmer's a straight arrow." He peered at Sharpe. "Hell, I wanted Mason to pass. This investigation's off track. Wrong."

"So this stays between us?" Mason asked.

"Me, you, Mr. Sharpe, Witmer, your classmate at the AG's office." He reached inside his coat pocket and handed Mason a sheet of paper. "You have the only other copy of the agreement. Morgan can't destroy the test, but you have my word we won't mention it. He's filin' it under my name, not yours. This is deep-sixed."

"So what if an independent examiner will certify he passed?" Sharpe asked.

"If he's credible, we'll talk." Hoffman pulled one side of his mouth taut. "See, Mr. Sharpe, I'm not a man who wants to convict the wrong guy. For the sake of lookin' good. The big bust. Make my bones in the papers. Another pretty letter in my permanent file." His arms were still slack, against his sides. "Here's what I know. What I've known for a while. Gates Hunt killed this guy Thompson. Gates is a dogshit criminal. He has reasons to lie — thinks it'll help him with us. Or maybe he's only bein' spiteful. Years ago, Gates's brother helped him with the cover-up. Brother takin' care of a brother. Young boys, immature. Tough upbringing. I don't know how deep Mason's in, but I figure it's enough to make it bad legally."

"If that's your theory of the case," Sharpe said, "then why are you planning to indict Mason?"

" 'Cause we have the evidence to do it. Sad to say. Mason's gettin' hosed because he lied and continues to lie. Now he's so tangled up, if he tells the truth, it potentially makes matters worse. Gives his jailbird brother credibility." He caught Mason's eye. "Right, Mason?"

"I didn't kill Wayne Thompson," Mason said, the reply rote. "I'm not lying."

"Minter and Bass, good men. They see it different. They believe you did. Truly believe it. There's another thorn for you."

"Any suggestions?" Sharpe asked.

"Me, I'd try to cut a deal for Mason. I'd come clean, toss this grenade back to Gates. Where it belongs. Maybe lock in a misdemeanor, plead guilty, no jail, community service, go after the man who actually pulled the trigger. Probably over the girl. There's your motive. I personally will do everything I can to sell it to Stallings. People would understand. Brother and brother. I'd recommend an obstruction or the like for Mason. If he quits lyin', damn it. He'd have to testify."

"You can recommend it," Sharpe said, "but Stallings has to go along."

"True. Truth is, he might not. Sense I have, he won't."

"How strong is your case?" Sharpe asked. "How do you evaluate it?"

"As it stands now, I'd lay my bet on us."

Mason smiled. "Are you giving odds, Ed?"

"Nah." For the first time, he appeared perturbed. "By the way, Mason. Morgan said to inform you bitin' your tongue wouldn't skew the test. They can tell."

"Huh? Bite my tongue? I didn't bite my tongue. What a bizarre thing to say."

"I'm just repeatin' what he told me." Hoffman gestured slightly with his hands.

"I've read that you can use thumbtacks or pins or, yeah, bite your tongue, but you and Morgan can look at mine if it makes any difference."

"Doesn't matter to me," Hoffman replied, still irked. "Sorry this went south on you. Wish we coulda done better."

CHAPTER TWENTY

The night before he was due to be charged with first-degree murder, Mason brought Grace to their kitchen table and told her about his likely grand jury indictment and what she could expect because of it: the arrest, the media attention, the gossipy stares and smirks, the uncertainty, the pressure, the whole ball of wax that accompanied a high-profile homicide case, especially one in which the defendant is the county's commonwealth's attorney and a local boy who'd overcome a hardscrabble past. The tale would be terrific fodder for the newspaper writers and ravenous local TV reporters, rags to riches to ruin, the tragic cycle, capped off with neon irony, a prosecutor in danger of a trip to the hoosegow.

Grace went from bored to alarmed to hysterical, her eyes paralyzed in horror, her mouth drawbridged open, mutely pleading with her father: *Oh God this can't be real, can't be happening.* She seemed stricken, spastic, as if her windpipe were clamped shut and no air was reaching her lungs. Her neck filled with pink, saw-toothed splotches, and before Mason could say more or attempt to comfort her, she dumped herself forward, collapsing onto the floor, her knees hitting first with full force. She clutched her stomach and lowered her forehead, rested it against the Spanish tile her mother had bought and set and grouted, every beautiful square aligned, every joint quarter-of-an-inch perfection. Blond hair spilled across the tan hues like pick-up sticks.

Mason joined his daughter on the floor, sitting beside her with his legs folded, his tentative hand rubbing patterns between her shoulder blades. He didn't force the issue, speaking only occasionally to reassure her, and she stayed hunkered down and withdrawn for what must have been half an hour. When she finally was ready to talk, she rocked onto her butt and rested her jaw on the bony point of her knee; she was facing the cabinets beneath the sink, her view slanted sideways, still not directed at her father. Sobbing, she wanted to know if Mason could be "sent to the electric chair."

"It's not possible. No chance. None. I'll be charged with first-degree murder, not capital murder. There's a difference. You don't have to be concerned."

"You swear? You're not just saying it to

baby me?"

"I swear," Mason said. "Plus, there's no way I'll be found guilty. This will be terrible, but in the end, I didn't shoot anyone or break the law and I'll be acquitted and we'll be normal around here again. I can't honestly tell you it'll be easy, but we'll be okay."

"Would I automatically go live with Grandma Sadie? At her house?"

"Yes. But I'm not going to prison. If we have a trial, I'll win."

"It's possible, though, isn't it?" She turned and met his eyes, switching cheeks on her knee. The crying wasn't as bad.

"Anything's possible. True. It's possible the oceans will disappear in the next five seconds, but it's not something to worry yourself with, is it? You're becoming too much of a lawyer."

"Why is Uncle Gates doing this? Why?" She dropped her head again, fitting it between her knees. "Why?"

"Because he's petty and selfish and he thinks this will help get him out of prison early. He's trying to trade this lie for a break in the judicial system. Sometimes people who help the authorities, even if they are rotten to the core, are given special consideration."

"I hope he dies."

"Can't argue with you."

"Why is this happening to me?" she asked, and it was the moment that weakened Mason the most, bludgeoned his resolve and pierced his heart.

"It's a big burden. You've had lots to carry, sweetie, too much for a girl your age, none of it your fault." His voice clotted in his throat. "I can't tell you why, much as I wish I could. I'll always do my best for you, though. Always protect you, always love you." He bucked up, determined not to cry and dilute the snake-oil palliative he was trying to sell her. He hugged her with both arms and tipped her toward him, and they remained stuck together on Allison's tile floor, the kitchen quiet except for the soft, soft hum of the refrigerator and the surprising clunk of the ice-maker birthing cubes into its plastic bin. Mason ended the silence when Grace separated from him. "I don't want you to think this is another I-walked-ten-miles-to-school-in-the-snow story from the prehistoric days, another tiresome reminder of how difficult it was for me, but my daddy, your grandfather Curt, was the nastiest, craziest, most worthless parent who ever lived. A complete sonofabitch who gave me nothing but grief. It was hard, but I got through it. Unfortunately, Gates didn't. No matter what, Grace, you have a father who adores you and will never, ever abandon you. Right now, maybe that doesn't seem like so much, but trust me, it'll mean a lot in the future. You always have a safe place with me. I'm an absolute for you. You understand?"

She nodded that she did.

"He ain't my son anymore," Sadie Grace announced, spitting mad, when Mason stopped by her house early the next morning and gave her the news. "After all we've done for him, this is the thanks we get." She was in a housecoat and bedroom slippers, and she appeared older without her makeup, the cigarette wrinkles around her mouth more obvious, her lips pale.

"I'm sorry I have to tell you. I'd like to think you've earned the right to enjoy retirement and take bus trips with your friends and spoil your granddaughter."

"Shut up, Mason," she barked. "You brought some of this on yourself, now didn't you? I've told you a million times to keep your distance with Gates. But you wouldn't listen. Nope. Ignored my warnin'." She was standing, and she jammed her hands against her hips. "I knew when it happened, like a mother always knows, somethin' was fishy. The day Danny Owen come by here askin' questions about that dead boy, I knew Gates was in the wrong. I shoulda grabbed you up right then and gotten to the bottom of this so we wouldn't be having this discussion now."

"Well, I'm sorry you'll have to suffer all the scrutiny and embarrassment." He paused, chose his next words. "I'm to blame to some extent, you're right. But Gates would've done

506

this no matter what, whether I'd been in contact with him or not. It's his last straw. I realize it's awful for you."

"How can he say all this and not drag himself into deeper trouble?" Sadie Grace asked.

"He claims I shot the Thompson boy. A damn lie. Claims he was just there, a by-stander. Didn't see it coming, didn't partici-pate. Who exactly can contradict him? It's just me versus him. Pretty cunning on his part — I have to give him credit."

"He's his daddy's son, no doubt. It's in his genes, Mason. Has to be. Curt was a man — if you can call him that — who hit his own baby boys and turned my every hour into hell on earth, and it never caused him so much as a second thought. It's a kind of ugliness you can't understand or explain or remedy."

"I'm optimistic we'll win this, but I wanted you to hear it from me. I hate it more for you and Grace than I do for myself. We both know I've survived worse. I'm more worried about you two than anything else."

Sadie Grace momentarily avoided Mason, seemed occupied by a framed scene on the wall, a reproduction of *The Last Supper.*

"I'll let you know this evening how the grand jury went," Mason promised, "though it's pretty much a done deal."

"Okay."

"I'm sorry to have upset you."

"Well, I shouldn't have gotten ill with you. It's . . . it's just you're all I have, Mason. You and my granddaughter. Sixty-six years on this earth, and my only joy is you and Gracie. Now the single good thing in my life is bein' threatened." She shifted her eyes, stood taller. The crinkles in her face intensified. "I'll tell you this, and me and you will never speak on it again: whatever I need to say or do to keep you out of trouble, I will. We're goin' to fight fire with fire. We've made it this far, me and you, through thick and thin, and we ain't backing down now, not to a coward like your brother. If this jury decides the way you think it's gonna, I'll be there by your side. With my chin up. You fight as strong as you can, and you don't worry about me."

"Thanks," Mason said humbly. "I love you. Lucky for me, I got your genes and grit, huh?"

Sadie Grace was too wily to alert Mason, but she left soon after their conversation, before lunch, and she showed up at the prison wearing tennis shoes and old-lady dungarees, her thick hair pulled tight into a ponytail, a dab of lipstick her only preparation, and since she'd been coming for years and years and knew the guards, they allowed her to see her son, bent the rules when she told them she had an emergency. Gates sauntered into the visitation area — empty and cavernous on a Monday — and he spread his arms and smiled and said how happy he was to see his mother, but underneath the goodwill Sadie Grace could sense, almost immediately, that he realized why she was there and his great welcome was a sham, fake as fake could be.

She never took a chair. She marched directly to Gates and asked him if he'd told the police Mason had killed the Thompson boy in 1984. For whatever reason, she recited the year. He began his answer, hedging and dissembling, Cheshire cat grinning the whole time, like he was talking to some damn fool instead of his mother, but she soon cut him off — "You are disowned by me," she snapped — and busted him in the face with a fistful of rings she'd added before leaving Stuart. The blow wasn't a slap, wasn't symbolic or a maternal correction, but was thrown with bad intentions, calculated to do as much damage as possible, most of it meant for Gates, maybe a little left over for Curt. Gates yelped and ducked and jumped to the side, and when he looked up his mother was walking toward the exit. He shouted, "Wait, Mama!" and even though it pained her to no end, she kept right on going, holding her tears until she reached her car, where she sat weeping with the engine running for so long that a kindly guard came to check on her and offered his handkerchief.

Realizing his mother was done with him, Gates touched the jagged cuts on his mouth

509

and jaw, then aimed his middle finger at the room's locked door and laughed through the ache, a lunatic's cackle, pronounced and malicious, like Vincent Price or Idi Amin, and the noise tangled up in itself, echoing off the cement and metal.

CHAPTER
TWENTY-ONE

Mason glanced at the photograph he'd been handed. "Uhggg . . . nasty. Why the hell are you showing me this trash? Huh? What's the matter with you?" Disgusted, he quickly tossed the picture onto a polished, rectangular table and went through a pantomime with his fingers, vigorously wiping them on his suit coat to remove an imaginary taint. "Today of all days, why're you plaguing me with this? You know I don't have any stomach for homo porn." He and Custis were tucked away in Art Anthony's law library, under the radar and safe from possible police eavesdropping, killing several hours, waiting for the grand jury to return and Mason's life to be recast. Custis had delivered 116 indictments for the jury, stayed until the four men and three women were sequestered and then left, on standby across the street if he was needed. Special prosecutor Leonard Stallings was there with a single count to present, dressed to the hilt, his secretary along for the momentous event.

"Look closer," Custis said solemnly. He was crammed into a wobbly metal chair, diagonal to Mason, at an angle that allowed him to see only Mason's profile.

"No, thanks," Mason replied. "Gay sex isn't my bag. I'm not a fan of costumed queers caught in the act. Butt pirates, my neighbor calls them."

Custis took the photo and held it toward Mason. "You should look closer."

"Is this about a case? Or some stupid Internet gag? I'm not in the mood, Cus, okay? I have bigger fish to fry. Maybe it slipped your mind, but I'm being indicted for murder as we sit here twiddling our thumbs and passing around your faggot nonsense."

"Humor me," Custis said, his tone constrained, purposeful.

Mason was frazzled, pins-and-needles restless. He snatched the photo and gave it a longer inspection. "Oh damn." Squinting and befuddled, he drew the picture so near that his nose almost touched the glossy paper. "This shit is libelous, Custis." He positioned his chair so they were able to see each other full on. "You realize that, don't you? What — is someone circulating this? I'd be pissed off, too. Bastards used a computer to superimpose your head on a porn guy's body. Pretty respectable job, but you can tell it's a gimmick. Who did this? Where'd you find it?"

"I found it in my mail."

"Say what?"

"It ain't no mistake or trick, no Photoshop, no cut-and-paste." Custis hurried, speaking rapidly. "That would be me in the picture, boss. Sorry to be the one droppin' the bomb on you."

"Huh?" Mason shook his head like he'd been roused from a nap, trying to compose himself. "You?"

"Me. Custis Norman. 'The faggot nonsense,' as you so diplomatically labeled it, occurred at a private residence in D.C., couple years ago."

"So that's you in the picture having sex with another guy? You wearing a cowboy hat and vest and a hard-on?"

"Head 'em up, move 'em out, rawhide," Custis said dryly. "I'm not necessarily proud of it. It's not representative of how I conduct my personal life."

"Damn . . . I'll be damned. So . . . ?"

"Yeah," Custis answered.

"Really?"

"Really."

"Gay?" Mason still wasn't convinced. "No shit?"

"Yes," Custis replied, and he was deliberately formal, no retreat in the word, no shame, no quibble. "You got it."

"Like, *gay* gay? How long . . . I mean, how long have you known? How long has it been?"

Custis chuckled, but there was a bitterness to it. "Quite a while, Mace. I didn't simply sample the buffet, study my options and decide before the deadline came and went. You don't read the brochures, list the pros and cons and select the gold lamé package."

"I mean, hey, whatever. Your business, not mine. Live and let live, right?"

"Even faggots and butt pirates?" Custis pressed.

"I'm not going to lie, okay? This is a shock, not really a revelation I was expecting, especially today, of all days. And yeah, the thought of two men kissing and having sex, well, it's not my cup of tea. Viscerally, it's awfully tough for me to accept. I can't help it." Mason couldn't keep his eyes trained on Custis. "And Inez," he blurted. "You've been dating her for years."

"For years. There you go, Mr. Wizard, a big whoppin' signpost for you. Make no mistake, Inez Rucker is one of the finest, most remarkable women to ever leave the Good Lord's mansion, and I love her dearly. But she's devoted to her dead husband and is waiting for the day they'll be together in heaven — you can laugh and joke and make fun of her, but she believes she's still married. When her Harrison died, she was finished. She has no interest in sex; hell, she sees it as adultery. To her credit, I don't think she's ever tempted, either. It's not like she's fightin' the urge to

514

get laid and have a man in her bed. There are folks who're like whoopin' cranes — one and done."

"So she knows?"

"Duh, Mason. Yeah, she does. It's been a blessin' for us both, a perfect relationship for her and for me. Our interests match like gin and juice, we keep each other from bein' lonely, and our friendship prevents people such as you from pesterin' us about our personal affairs."

"All these years, she's protected your secret?"

"Yeah. She has, despite hatin' the gay lifestyle on principle. Her religion, you know. Your churchgoin' sisters take a dim view of sodomites. She's forever prayin' up a storm for me, but unlike a lot of your hypocrites recitin' scripture, her heart's pure. She truly does love the sinner, just doesn't care for the sin."

"Why're you telling me this now? No offense — I'm happy to listen — but I'd say we already have a full plate. Sort of odd timing." Mason rubbed his temples. "Wow."

"Two reasons," Custis said, sounding rehearsed and prepared, like he was presenting a closing argument. "First, misery loves company, and though that proverb doesn't exactly hit the nail, I thought you might be more understandin', more sympathetic in light of your present circumstances and

515

troubles. Struck me you'd have a good idea how it feels to be up against it. There's —"

"I'm sorry," Mason interrupted, smirking, "but virtually everything you say seems Broadway funny now, like gay double entendre."

"If you're fifteen in the locker room, it probably does."

Mason flickered a smile. He felt slightly less uncomfortable.

"Anyway, here's reason number two. The payoff. I wanted to come completely clean with you. See, I gotta figure maybe you're still questionin' my bona fides, what with this Richmond sighting, me leavin' so soon after you're popped by the grand jury, me cutting a shine with you and Sheila, this whole streak of weirdness we've had lately. You need a clear mind to take care of your predicament, and you deserve to have the entire picture — so to speak — and I'm gonna do my damnedest to be an ally you can count on one hundred percent. Truth is, I *was* in Richmond like the pervert Wiggington claims, and I was with a cop."

"You lied to me?" Mason exclaimed.

"Not really. As we say in court, check the transcript, my man, recall exactly what I represented. I've never had any sneaky dealings with Ed Hoffman, and I didn't meet with him in Richmond. I gave you the bare-bones facts on the subject. 'Course, you never asked me if I was visitin' with our mutual friend Ian Hudgens."

"Hudgens? You mean Herman Dylan's minion?"

"Yep."

"Huh. He's a nondescript bald guy? I imagined him very differently."

"He's a bald weasel," Custis said. "An average Joe with a serious facial tic. Probably the stress and long hours."

"Okay. I assume he was chewing your ear about Chip-Tech, but you'll have to help me with the particulars. Why are you and Hudgens eating steak in Richmond?"

"Simple. They're aware you and I are ultra-tight. He and his taskmaster Dylan wanted me to lean on you."

"To vote for their grant?"

"Aren't you clever," Custis said, stretching every syllable. "We're *Perry* Mason today, aren't we?" He grinned. The sarcasm was genial. "And guess what he used as a stick, once I didn't do the carrot dance?"

"It's starting to make sense," Mason said. He was finally able to settle his eyes on his friend. "The faggot nonsense. They're blackmailing you. You didn't want me to find out." There was a peculiar enthusiasm in Mason's voice, a skip in his cadence. "So you really don't want to leave, do you? Your whole big-city-Black-Panther speech was bullshit."

"They prefer the term *quid pro quo.* A bit

slicker, don't you think? I can't stand for my personal details to be broadcast all over our fine Victorian county. I can't. Hell, you're supposed to be my friend, and you're actin' like I'm a leper. Can you imagine everybody else's reaction? The shitstorm I'd suffer?" Custis shot Mason a frank look. "It's a comprehensive slash and burn, too. See, Hudgens had gotten wind of your jam as well and threatened to release the photos right before your trial, thinking — at worst — maybe some of the gay will rub off on you and influence the jury and — at best — we'll have another distraction, two fronts to defend. A bit of lagniappe, as the Cajuns say, a bonus to make me more inclined to persuade you."

"I'm not treating you like a leper. This is sudden — sky-falling sudden — and I grew up fishing, hunting, playing baseball and listening to my mom's Old Testament piety in rural Patrick County, Virginia, the unreconstructed South, and I'm sorry, it's just ingrained, the . . . the distaste I have. I can separate our friendship, and I will, I swear I will, but seeing the photo gives me the heebie-jeebies. It's no different than getting the heaves from rancid meat or retching at the dead-mouse-in-a-heat-duct smell. It's hardwired. Instinct. You know I'm as libertarian as they come, and it's fine with me, do whatever the hell you want, and intellectually

I can accept it, but if I saw you cuddling with some man I'd probably puke. I value our friendship, I'm not making moral judgments, but I can't change how I am."

"The term *faggot* is as offensive as the term *nigger.*"

"I suppose it is."

"It's great to know you're so tolerant and broad-minded," Custis said. "Magnanimous of you to overlook the rat stench, or at least hold your nose for me."

"Actually it is, if you think about it. My friendship with you, my respect and affection, trump everything else. I don't care who you sleep with; I'm just giving you fair warning how it affects me."

"Ah. I'm grateful, too."

"I'll try to do better with my language," Mason said. "But how about a grace period if I forget? Maybe for the first three months you don't take away rainbow points or report me to Queer Nation?"

"It's wonderful you can be so glib," Custis remarked. "I'm delighted you're friggin' Richard Pryor when I have to leave my home and my world's toiletized because I refuse to trade on our friendship and compromise my values by dragging you into Herman Dylan's mud. You have any clue how difficult this has been for me? Do you? I didn't have to tell you any of this. I could've packed my bags and left your homophobic cracker ass in a sling, wonderin' which direction was up."

"I apologize. I'm just trying to . . . to . . . lighten the conversation. Jeez. So I can fuck with you about being black, but gay pride is off limits?"

Custis was growing irate. "Problem bein' the gay stuff is serious and true, the race stuff is just for sport."

"It's not my fault you're gay and embarrassed to tell anyone. Nor is it a shortcoming I'm not keen on humping other men."

"Kiss my black ass, Mason."

"You're my best friend, Custis. I can't put it any plainer. I doubt we'll be roomies again in San Juan, but other than that, you and I are still good to go. Still Custis and Mason, all right? Seriously, I want to put this aside and not dwell on it. I try to take people as I find them, and I try to treat them exactly like they treat me. By that standard, nothing's changed — we've got too deep a history, too much goodwill, and you've done so much for me I could never repay the debt."

"It'll be different, believe me. Your attitude's already adjusted."

"Don't be stupid and paranoid," Mason said.

"Answer me this: What do Elton John, George Michael and Boy George have in common?"

"They're all gay." Mason caught himself. Chagrined, he exhaled and stared down and traced his thumb along a scratch on the table. "And British . . . and musicians, very good ones. Whose friends and fans have stuck by them and made them successful and don't notice their sexual orientation."

"Proves my point, doesn't it? Grammys, Oscars, gold records, knighthood. Hell, Elton could discover a cure for sickle cell and it wouldn't matter — the first thought everyone has is they're homosexual. Nothing can overshadow it. Your whole identity is tied to bein' queer. Everything kicks off there, and it will with you and me from this minute forward. Used to be, if you heard my name, you'd think, 'my best friend, my law partner, my six-foot-seven wingman,' and now it'll be 'the butt pirate.' "

"You may be right in some sense, Custis. It was a very effective parlor trick and I took the bait, but I swear to you I will do everything I can to be a reliable and admirable friend, just like I always have. At least I'm honest about how it affects me."

"I appreciate it, too," Custis answered in a hopeful tone that left room for compromise. "You've certainly been good as gold up till now. Treated me like kin. I hope we can stay solid."

"Thanks. You are kin."

"So we're cool, you and me? Cool as can be expected with your affliction?"

"We are."

Mason turned the picture facedown and slid it toward Custis. He waited for Custis to collect it before speaking. "So Dylan threatens to let the cat out of the bag unless you persuade me to vote for his grant. How'd they discover the photo? Your, uh, stint as Roy Rogers?"

"Hudgens came up with *Le*Roy Rogers when he was tryin' to humiliate me. You're a beat behind the rest of the orchestra. Need to keep your material fresher."

"Not a bad line, I have to admit."

"I've been around the gay scene in D.C. forever," Custis said. "A few whispers here, even."

"No kidding? I've never heard a peep."

"Best bet is they followed me for a week or two, and I led them where they needed to go. Herman Dylan is rich and powerful, and this is pretty basic detective work. I want you to understand I've been with the same partner for almost a decade, Mason. Monogamous except for an unfortunate split a few years ago. While we were apart, I fell in with some unsavory people, didn't protect my interests like I should've, and this guy I was with for maybe a month — a mistake — took some shots while we were together. I'm responsible for my own idiocy — it was a time in the wilderness for yours truly, too much alcohol, too many clubs."

"Happens," Mason said sympathetically,

battling to keep the visuals suppressed.

"After Hudgens threatened me, I called my D.C. friend and he's basically a crack whore these days, blubberin' how sorry he is, sniffin' and cryin' like a schoolgirl. Sold 'em for five hundred pathetic dollars. Who knew, huh? I never thought the pics would surface like this. Never. Hudgens blindsided my ass."

"So that's why you were so hateful around here?"

"Yeah, I was mad at myself for the compromisin' mess I'd cooked up. Mad 'cause I was in a spot and resigning seemed the only option. Rather than come beggin' you to save me and vote against your best judgment, rather than attemptin' to persuade you for the wrong reasons, I called my boy Hudgens's bluff and told him to let it rip, make 'em into posters and billboards for all I care, won't hurt me 'cause I'm leavin' anyhow. And, yeah, sure, it wasn't totally noble. Part of it was I didn't want you or anybody else to discover my adventures in other venues. 'Course, bein' the prince he is, Hudgens says he'll send his package to Atlanta *and* embarrass me here for good measure — Godfather shit — so the next Herman Dylan extortion victim will understand they play for keeps. 'Have to follow through,' Hudgens tells me, 'unless we receive our grant.' Leaves me in a bad way, huh? Shit outta luck both comin' and goin'. I'm Peewee Herman if I stay in

Stuart, and I'll be rollin' into snicker-city wherever I go, assuming my new employer doesn't fire me the second he opens the morning mail."

"Who was the cop with you in Richmond?"

"Aw, hell, it was Drew O'Connor, our favorite state trooper. I had him wear the crime-crusher uniform and stop by and say cryptic, boogeyman things to Hudgens, 'cause I anticipated they were goin' to put the arm on me. Figured I'd show a little muscle myself, have Drew tail the dumb shit back to the airport, ride his bumper, flash the blue lights, get under his skin. Problem is, I didn't know I was gonna be flexin' on Godzilla. Turns out I was far too puny. I came with Schlitz; Hudgens was stockin' Hennessy. Thank heavens Drew wasn't there for the main course, if you catch my drift. He'd definitely freak."

"I guess a lawsuit and extortion charges are not on the horizon?"

"My word against his, he was careful how he phrased it, and do I really want a jury and the papers gettin' hold of this? I don't see myself pursuing any legal remedies."

"Well, the upside is now I know, and the leverage from that is gone. We'll put this in the hopper with my problem and sort through it. Stall Hudgens, string him along, give him the rope-a-dope, delay Atlanta but don't burn the bridge in case you need a Plan B. You belong here, Custis, and if push comes to shove, I'll give the people what they want and Herman Dylan can have his cash. I'll tell the commission I've reconsidered. Chip-Tech isn't completely awful, it's just not the best we can do, and you're more important than a thousand grants. I wish we could fuck Dylan and not have you crucified, and I hate to see us get hustled, but no matter what I'll take care of your interests first, absolutely I will. At least we can solve your dilemma and you're not staring at life in prison — be thankful for the bright side." Mason hesitated, unable to resist, straying past tolerance, a juvenile with spitballs and rubber bands: "Of course, for you, life in prison . . ."

The grand jury foreman, Dewey Lankford, had sent a note asking the judge if the indictment for the county's commonwealth's attorney was "allowable," whatever that meant, and two jury members refused to vote, claiming any evidence against Mason Hunt had to be crooked, but ultimately Leonard Stallings got his wish and on September 8, 2003, Mason was charged with the first-degree murder of Wayne Thompson. Sheila called to tell Mason and Custis the jury had returned, and Custis was in the courtroom when the clerk read the indictments, Mason's last, number 117.

Stallings was a tiny man, not more than five

and a half feet tall. He had a mop of red-orange hair, a prizefighter's strut and skin marred by pimples and raw, vulgar bumps. He also was a dandy dresser, always wore a vest and watch chain, French cuffs with his initials embroidered in block letters. A pocket square. After the jury had been discharged, he boldly crossed the courtroom and introduced himself to Custis, offering to shake hands. Custis rebuffed the courtesy, then crouched down like he was addressing a child, hiking his pants at the knees as he lowered himself, his head tilted and framed by a spill of wooly dreadlocks. He glared at Stallings and said, loud enough so everyone could hear, "You better bring your bazooka, you carrot-topped little leprechaun. Better come big. You have Custis Norman's vow you'll be regrettin' this."

Stallings wasn't intimidated. "Leprechaun or not, Mr. Norman, you have my vow Mason Hunt will be found guilty and go to jail."

Stallings had tipped the newspapers and TV stations, and he preened and pontificated for them on the courthouse steps, serving up clichés about justice being blind to office and power. He directed his secretary to distribute a press kit that included his résumé and a color eight-by-ten of himself, his heinous skin retouched in the photo, the blemishes washed away. He claimed to have an airtight case. A slam dunk. Pat Sharpe and Jim Haskins responded the next morning, releasing a nine-page rebuttal document, which included a quote from Sadie Grace Hunt, stating her son Gates was a convicted drug dealer, a serial liar and utterly unworthy of belief, much as she hated to say it. The trial had already begun in earnest, months ahead of its proper arrival before a judge and jury.

People quickly chose sides, and Mason was surprised and heartened by how thoroughly the county supported him. Stallings received his first taste of Mason's popularity when the clerk of court, Susan Gasperini, pretended she couldn't hear him after he politely asked if the order appointing him as special prosecutor had been filed with her and was on record. Sheriff Hubbard and every officer in his employ refused to serve the capias on Mason and take him into custody. "We're too busy," he gruffly informed Stallings, then proceeded to ignore the prosecutor's many telephone calls and a directive from the attorney general himself.

Stallings finally had to recruit a state police sergeant from Charlottesville to enforce the indictment and escort Mason to a magistrate. The officer phoned and declared his business, and Mason agreed to meet him at his law office — noon, sharp — and walk with him to be fingerprinted and processed, and so four days after the grand jury acted,

Sergeant Max Lawrence arrived in Stuart prepared to formally arrest Mason, the paperwork in an ordinary off-white folder, the words *Hunt Case* scrawled in Magic Marker letters across the folder's middle.

Lawrence was professional, removing his hat at the threshold and asking Mason if he needed to call anyone or make preparations for bond before seeing the magistrate. "I do have to inform you, sir, you are now under arrest for first-degree murder," he said as he presented Mason with a copy of the indictment. "Commonwealth of Virginia v. Mason L. Hunt" was typed across the top. The policeman had promised Pat Sharpe he wouldn't use cuffs, but he did briefly take hold of Mason's arm and steer him through the door and outside. When the cop released him, the two of them were alone in the bright sun, and Mason, his focus scattershot, nervously noticed the NO PARKING AFTER BUSINESS HOURS sign was missing a fastener and starting to droop from the wall.

When they rounded the corner from the parking lot and began the climb to the ancient courthouse, Mason saw the throng of people, probably four hundred of them, and he initially was petrified, under the impression they were there to witness his shame, rubberneckers and busybodies eager to watch the spectacle of his misfortune, but he soon spotted Sheila and her husband, Roger, and there was Custis and Inez, and Sadie Grace, and he realized they were all assembled, on both sides of the street, occasionally three-deep, to wish him luck and embrace their own. Unsure of the crowd's mood, poor Sergeant Lawrence reflexively groped for his pepper spray and spread his hand over his gun. "It's okay," Mason assured him. "Shouldn't be any problem."

His mother and Custis flanked him, and the sheriff and several deputies fell in behind, and Mason shook hands and took every uphill step with modesty and thanked people for turning out and missing work. Custis informed him that Sheila and Susan Gasperini had called folks and asked them to come, and there would've been a larger group if they'd had more notice. Cecil Priddy was the last in line, and he promised to bring Mason by a bushel of peaches, saying he would've done it earlier but his foot had been stove-up and his wife had been feeling poorly. Like so many others, he never mentioned why he was there or the murder case, carried on like it was any other day and laughed when Mason good-naturedly warned him to keep the peaches away from his uncle's still over in Woolwine.

Mysteriously, three TV crews were waiting near the entrance to the magistrate's office, and the cameramen scampered down the street to videotape the warm send-off. "Not exactly the perp walk our boy Stallings had in mind," Custis said before Mason went inside.

With the sheriff watching and Haskins and Sharpe hovering near the doorway, Sergeant Lawrence inked Mason's fingertips and rolled them across a card, took his picture in front of a height chart and questioned him about his full name, address and Social Security information. It was a degrading state ritual that had greeted every thug, hoodlum, criminal and sociopath for decades, designed to isolate them with a string of numbers and drain their piss and vinegar, flagging them as at least *probably* guilty, giving them a taste of the state's boot heel, and now Mason was an initiate, mug-shotted and listed as a defendant in thousands of police computers, on a par with every thief and rapist he'd prosecuted, never the same no matter the result of his trial, stained. Reduced. He seethed and thought of Gates, how much he despised him.

Next came the magistrate, a lady named Peggy Taylor, and she was apologetic and flustered, but Mason told her not to worry and do her job like he was any other defendant, he understood. She set his bond at five thousand dollars and didn't require any surety, basically freeing him on his signature and bare promise to be in court for his next hearing. As she was completing her forms, Taylor quit typing and peered at Mason and told him again she was so sorry, remarking how terrible it must be to have a brother like Gates. "The worst ever," she suggested.

"Well, he's probably not as bad as Frank Stallone or Billy Carter," Mason cracked, trying to take her off the spot, but she later told her husband she could see the strain in Mason, the weight already aging him.

The trial was scheduled to last three days, beginning February 9, 2004. At the end of September, Jim Haskins and Pat Sharpe visited with Mason at his house on a Saturday morning, and told him they had both good news and bad. "Which you want first?" Sharpe inquired.

"The good, please."

"We have a superb judge. The Supreme Court appointed Andre Melesco from over in Rocky Mount. You acquainted with him?"

"Not really," Mason replied. "I think I ran into him once at a commonwealth's attorneys conference. He was a speaker."

Haskins produced his black comb and whipped it through his hair. He was dressed in corduroy and tweed and was silent, content to let his colleague carry the conversation.

"I've been in his court," Sharpe continued, "and he's top-notch. Smart as a whip, prepared, fair and he understands reasonable doubt. He'll make the right call, even if it's unpopular. We're fortunate."

"Great," Mason said. "I'm relieved I didn't draw a dud."

"He's a nice guy off the bench, too," Sharpe noted. "A pleasure to work with. We couldn't ask for better. Oh — I know you've already checked — but I did talk with the state bar rep, and he confirmed there's no reason you can't continue to serve as commonwealth's attorney. Like any other accused, you're presumed innocent. He did suggest you might want to obtain some sort of written waiver from everyone concerned if you're prosecuting a crime of violence or a very high-profile case. Or assign it to Custis until we get your matter resolved."

"So what's the bad news?" Mason asked. They were in the kitchen, the breakfast dishes still in the sink, toast crumbs and a streak of Grace's strawberry jelly waiting to be wiped off the table.

"Two items," Sharpe said. "I contacted several lawyers who practice with Stallings, and they all say he's very competent. We shouldn't underestimate him just because he looks like the dwarf spawn of Pippi Long-stocking and Alfred E. Newman. Consensus is the midget can try a case, and he relishes the spotlight. He's no pushover."

"Okay. I wish we had a pigeon, but we don't." Mason was leaning against the counter. "What else?"

Haskins spoke up. "Pat and I filed our

discovery motion the day you were indicted and Stallings replied the next week and, to borrow a phrase, there's no smoking gun, Mason. For the life of me, I can't figure what he's holding that's making him so smug. I faxed him and called him and so did Pat, and he simply says he's complied with discovery. Sent me a letter, sort of snide, and told us he knew the law and he'd produced everything we're entitled to. I'm buffaloed. Are we positive he's not posturing?"

"Custis and I have thought and thought and thought, and we're stumped, too," Mason said. "No clue."

"Nothing worse than getting your tail caught in a trap at trial," Sharpe remarked.

"Well," Haskins said, "since he gave us transcripts of your interviews with Bass and Minter, we know it can't be a statement you've made to the cops, and it can't be DNA or fingerprints or blood or other forensics. He'd have to produce it."

"So we're left with a witness, maybe?" Sharpe mused. "You mentioned this hint from Ed Hoffman, maybe surveillance? A bug?"

"There are no witnesses," Mason declared. "It's impossible. Unless someone's lying. It didn't happen, so no one could've seen it. Hell, any witness would've come forward years ago anyway. As for the other, I haven't discussed the case with anyone but you, Jim and Custis."

"We'll stay on it," Haskins promised. "If this is their entire case — Gates Hunt and your ambiguous, perfectly innocent statement to the cops — we'll blow their doors off."

"I'm not counting on it being so simple," Mason said.

In October, the assistant principal at Patrick County High School phoned Mason at work and told him a teacher had discovered Grace smoking cigarettes in the girls' bathroom.

"Grace? Smoking?" Mason was flabbergasted. "My daughter?"

"Yes. She was also giving them to other kids."

"You're sure?"

"Sorry to say, I am. Mrs. Rakes caught her with the butt in her hand and smoke comin' from her nose. Pretty cut and dried unless she's part dragon," he said amiably and gently laughed.

"Well, yeah, thanks for telling me," Mason said. "She's under a lot of stress. I'm not making excuses for her, but with this crazy case against me and her mother passing away, it's been difficult for her. She's a great kid — you and I hear that every day, but it's no exaggeration with her."

"I agree," the principal assured him. "We're going to do an in-house suspension, but we can't give her too much more latitude. In our world, this is fairly serious."

"I understand. I'll sit her down this afternoon and read her the riot act and discipline her at home, too."

"So you're aware, I checked with her teachers, and her grades are falling. She's always been one of our best, but lately, according to her teachers, she's not trying. Very withdrawn, they report. We've also noticed her . . . her appearance is changing, her clothes, makeup, kind of darker than before. We understand how fragile she must be, so we want to be proactive and deal with this before it worsens."

"Definitely. I feel like a fool for not noticing the clothes and whatnot myself. I see her every day, and I try the best I can to parent her correctly. We get together religiously, without fail, and review her assignments and discuss her, you know, her friends and school and whatever else. It . . . I don't know. It must have been incremental. She seemed, how would I put it? Sloppier? Quieter? Tense? But I wasn't aware it was so drastic."

"It's probably only temporary, and I'm not sure I'd call it drastic. She's a wonderful girl, and her small detour is completely understandable. We have counselors here and several other effective options. I'm positive we can nip this in the bud. We'll partner with you and Grace to turn this around. Don't worry, it's what we're here for."

"Yeah. I'm grateful. Thanks." Mason had a thought and rushed to speak before the principal left the line: "Let's not send her to a counselor or cross that line yet. I'd hate to . . . to overreact. I'll try to handle it at home, and you keep me posted on her attitude at school. I'll check back with you in a week or so."

"Absolutely. We'll talk again soon."

Overwhelmed, Mason piled up his arms on his desk and laid his forehead on top of them and shut his eyes. His mind was quarantined, curtained off, a dim, bare stage with scant illumination, and he imagined two words, done in scorching yellow against the black, suspended by taut wires, silently screaming: IF ONLY . . .

Grace was cigarette Gandhi — quiet, level, passive, detached, civil. Mason went to the school and summoned her from her last class ten minutes before the bell. Still in the parking area, yanking on his safety belt, he demanded to know why she was smoking at school and breaking the law by giving tobacco to other underage students.

She shrugged. She wasn't looking at him. He noticed her jeans were ripped and her shirt black. Her mascara did appear different, too pronounced, too vivid.

"Were you smoking?"

"Uh-huh."

"Why? It's dumb and harmful for so many reasons I can't even begin to list them. You want lung cancer? Lizard skin and wrinkles? Want to get expelled from school and have colleges think you're a disaster? Want a crappy job and no future?"

"No," she said, dully, submissively. "I'm sorry." She rolled a strand of hair around her finger, then unrolled it. She was slouching.

"Sorry? That's it?"

"I guess," she said.

"Were you giving cigarettes to other kids?" He left the school and accelerated onto the main highway. A window wasn't completely closed and air whistled through the interior. Mason sealed the glass and ended the noise.

"Just my friends. They wanted them. I didn't sell them or anything."

"I'm very disappointed in you, Grace."

She didn't respond.

"Anything you want to say?"

"No sir."

"So here's the deal: no computer, no phone, no TV, no movies for two weeks. Additionally, you're totally grounded. School and our house will be your entire universe. Understand?"

She nodded.

"Voice, please."

"Yeah," she said, so softly the word evaporated the moment it hit air.

"Okay." He glanced across the seat at her,

but she ignored him. "I'm not trying to be an ogre. I realize it's tough for you right now because of bad breaks you can't control. It's wrong you lost your mom, it's wrong you have to fret about me, it's wrong you've been embarrassed by seeing your father falsely accused of murder in the newspaper and it's wrong you have to worry about things most people your age take for granted. You've been a champ so far, and I'm proud of you. Not many fifteen-year-olds could've done as well as you have. You're exceptional, and I love you. But I will not let you use this trumped-up, ridiculous murder charge as a crutch or an excuse or a reason to do as you choose." He relocated his hands on the wheel, brought them both closer to the top of its arc. "I'll admit ninety-nine percent of this is not your fault, but if you quit on yourself, if you think nothing counts anymore, if you fail classes and dress like Morticia Addams and hide in a shell, you're hurting me, too, and hurting people who love you is also wrong. I need you to hold on to yourself. I promise we will lick Leonard Stallings, and nothing will change."

She unspooled a finger full of hair. She slumped against the door, didn't answer, and Mason was scared, stuck, afraid he wouldn't be able to retrieve her. He was distressed, pondering what he could do, and he allowed a tire to drop from the pavement onto the loose gravel shoulder, and the car fishtailed and nearly swapped ends and when he finally steered them back straight on the road, Grace might as well have been asleep, didn't appear alarmed or bothered. She didn't seem to care one way or the other.

CHAPTER
TWENTY-TWO

Three days into Grace's Marlboro Light punishment, Jim Haskins was on the phone, inflamed, Gatling-gunning his sentences, *tat-tat-tat-tat-tat-tat*. "The sonofabitch has the polygraph," he announced to Mason. "I don't know how, but Stallings got hold of the test, and the despicable troll has sent chapter and verse to Judge Melesco. He wants to schedule a damn hearing, so, just as I feared, our well's gonna be poisoned when it comes to the judge. Not to mention the press. It'll be splashed all over the news."

"Whoa, whoa, whoa," Mason stammered. "Say what?" He was leaning on the corner of Custis's desk, Custis standing next to him. They'd been almost to lunch at the Coffee Break, crossing Main Street, and Sheila had come tearing after them, told them it was urgent. "Custis is with me; I'm putting you on speaker so he can hear, too."

"Stallings has the lie-detector results, and he's filed them with the court," Haskins repeated, his voice staccato, crackling from the phone.

"How did he find out?" Custis asked.

"No idea. But it's not too difficult to narrow it down — take you guys, Pat and me from the equation, and it's an extremely limited field."

"I can't believe it," Mason said. "You think Ed Hoffman shanghaied us?"

Custis shook his head. "It'd be off the chart for him. New territory."

Mason sank deeper onto the desk. "Why in the world is Stallings filing the polygraph with the court, Jim? How can he do that? He knows it's absolutely not admissible at trial, completely barred. He's obviously trying to gain a tactical advantage and influence potential jurors. It's blatantly unethical. Clearly misconduct. We need to bust his chops and ask for sanctions or even a dismissal."

"He's clever, Mason, clever. See, he took all the letters we've been whipsawing him with, our inquiries about discovery, and included them with his motion to the court. He's asking the judge to decide whether or not he has to hand over the lie-detector documents." Haskins finally began to brake his speech. "It's angels on pinheads, a ruse, but it gives him perfect cover. He claims he doesn't want his case hamstrung by a technicality, says he's afraid we're setting him up, that we'll appear at trial and complain he didn't release information we were entitled to. In a nutshell, he's asking Judge Melesco for guidance: 'Do I have to give Mr. Hunt the results even though there's an agreement this thing would be buried and can't be used at trial? Does the parties' deal trump the law? Or, if I release the test am I violating the commonwealth's commitment to confidentiality?' Of course, it goes without saying he's manufactured the whole brouhaha and doesn't give a tinker's damn how the judge rules — he simply wants to score points by alerting everyone to the unfavorable results. Melesco will see through the smoke and mirrors and realize the motion's a sham, but now he knows more than we'd like for him to. So will your jurors who watch TV and read the paper."

"Wicked," Custis said. "Gotta admit the midget's on his game."

"So who the fuck leaked it?" Mason asked angrily. "It has to be Ed, the AG's office or the examiner. Damn."

"Don't know," Haskins replied.

"Well, I owe you an apology," Mason said. "You were right: I should've avoided the frigging test. I wish I'd taken your advice."

"Could've gone either way," Haskins said graciously. "Let's not dwell on the past. You don't owe me anything. We'll file and ask for sanctions and a dismissal, and Pat and I'll prepare a response for the media. Hell, the polygraph proves you didn't commit the crime you're charged with. Keep your spirits up, Mason. We're still in fine shape. I'll see to it Mr. Stallings has plenty to occupy him for the next few weeks."

After finishing the call, Mason opened the door and flashed his head from Custis's office. "Get Ed Hoffman on the phone," he yelled at Sheila.

The following morning, Mason and Hoffman met at a Hardee's in Bassett Forks, roughly halfway for them both. Hoffman arrived first and was drinking coffee and eating a breakfast biscuit, egg and cheese, its wrapper tucked underneath as a makeshift plate. Mason stalked across the restaurant and stormed into the booth with him. As he hurtled in, Mason bumped his kneecap against a metal support, and a hot tingle rode a nerve up and down his leg. "Hi, Ed," he said sarcastically. "So why the hell does Leonard Stallings have my polygraph test? The test you vowed to take to your grave?" Mason was loud. His neck and cheeks thumped red. His hands were twitchy. He flexed and bounced his leg, trying to jigger away the pain.

"Hello to you, too. I gave it to him. Three days ago." Hoffman gingerly raised the wrapper and its biscuit and moved them to the side, closer to the window. He set his coffee near the food so there was nothing between him and Mason, only empty table. "Sorry. No choice. I was meanin' to call. Soon. I regret you didn't hear it from me."

"Why would you sell me out, Ed? Because you think I failed the test? Is that it? Or did you just mislead me from day one and plan to backstab me regardless?"

"Stallings put the screws to me, Mason. I held with you like I promised until I couldn't hold with you any further. I submitted my written report to Stallings — your test wasn't mentioned. He's interviewed me several times — kept my mouth shut. So did everyone else. The polygraph had vanished. Here's how he works, though. He has a checklist. Thorough as can be. Gives it to me to complete. I've learned he does it with every officer. Very effective device. Catches info and evidence you might've forgotten, and if the case tanks 'cause a cop neglects or forgets and it ain't on the sheet, Stallings can wash his hands. This sheet he gave me specifically asked if there'd been a polygraph. So I don't turn it in. Delayed. Tell him I've given him the whole schmear, maybe he needs to talk to Bass and Minter. Nope, he says. Do the form. So, Mason, I'm not gonna lie, not me, especially to the players on my own team. I leave several boxes empty or put a question mark. He drags me in and drills me on every single blank. I advise him to call the attorney general's office, say this is too complicated for me. I'm a grunt, this needs chain-of-command input. Didn't take him long then. He's filed a complaint against me with the state police. I'll be okay, but he's not happy, no he's not."

Mason didn't respond. Cashiers were shouting orders to the cooks, an older man and woman behind Mason were discussing a recent trip to Niagara Falls and a lanky black kid with flour smudges on his brown company shirt was sweeping the floor, banging and scraping his wooden broom handle whenever he reached beneath a table or booth bench.

"I'm sorry," Hoffman continued. "Unintended consequences. I wish I hadn't offered the deal. I knew the truth before you were hooked up. Hoped I was wrong or you could end-run the exam. Hate it for you. Don't blame you for bein' pissed."

"Not much I can do about it now, huh, Ed? My stock took quite a hit thanks to your not keeping your bargain."

"Didn't see it comin'. Didn't plan to make your situation worse." He reached for his coffee, took several sips and placed it on the table in front of him, keeping both hands around the cup.

"You're not bullshitting me, Ed? You truly concealed this as long as you could? Really?"

"Absolutely. But I can't totally lie for you

or anyone else. Not my style. And if you want to be a stickler, I didn't actually tell him. He found out from the higher-ups in Richmond. But I'm acceptin' responsibility."

"Lot of good it does me," Mason complained. "Thanks so much for the late, worthless, facile lip service. I'll recommend you for an ambassador's post at the UN — you'd excel there."

"Appreciate it. Maybe I could do it part-time when I retire from this racket. Get paid to wear those earphones and carry on 'bout embargoes and such." Hoffman gazed at the coffee cup and rotated it a full turn but didn't lift it from the tabletop. "So I'm thinkin' last night, been thinkin' ever since Stallings put the squeeze on me — and, hey, he's a man doing his job, I don't have any gripe with him — been thinkin' how to repair this with you. It's nowise simple. Me, I'm in a bind. Too many masters."

"I'm in a bit of a bind myself, Ed, partially because you promised me something you didn't — or couldn't — deliver." Mason jutted forward and rested both forearms on the table, his stomach flush against its rounded orange edge.

"I'm gonna return what I took as best I can. Put us level."

"How?" Mason asked skeptically. "The damage is done. In spades."

"You pay attention to the magazine I left in

Stuart?" Hoffman asked.

"Yeah. I gathered I was under surveillance. Or had been. We've been careful. Thanks." Mason cocked his head. "I hope you're not taping me now, Ed."

Hoffman didn't change his expression. He plowed ahead. "Remember you asked me 'bout people close to you? Remember?"

"Sure."

"You solved it yet? Seemed you was on target."

Mason relaxed, settling into the slope of the bench. "I thought I did, but . . . well, no, I'm not positive. I had some suspicions . . . Nothing's turned up in discovery, so to be honest, we're still confounded."

"Huh."

"In fact, I was probably chasing shadows and too suspicious and obsessing about it — this shit has a way of disorienting you. And this peekaboo show you're doing now isn't helping much. How about you just jump to the nitty-gritty?"

"You spent seven minutes and eleven seconds interviewing a man who'd admitted to a murder. Including the time you spent with your sheriff and Roger Wilson." Hoffman sipped his coffee, peering at Mason over the rim.

"Huh? You mean Allen Roberts? The sting you guys engineered?"

"Yep. I had a watch on it."

"So? Who cares? An experienced detective had spent hours with him and gotten zilch. I'm not a cop, and it's not my job to interrogate people. The fact I went at all speaks volumes. I took the case seriously and had him questioned and did everything I could."

"How many other suspects you, yourself, actually interviewed?"

"I've never given it any thought," Mason dodged.

"I'd bet the ranch the answer is none." Hoffman wasn't cocky, wasn't combative.

"This is meaningless, Ed. Hot air and gibberish. I told Bass and Minter I knew the guy's reputation and had my doubts, serious doubts, but nevertheless I instructed the sheriff to bring him in immediately, and I personally followed through to make certain the case was properly investigated. I've gone over this in my mind and with my lawyers and it merely demonstrates I was doing everything humanly possible to prepare for trial."

"I knew when you wanted to speak to him you was involved," Hoffman said. He sounded almost apologetic.

"Then you need to buy a turban and crystals and mystical bones and set up shop in Atlantic City, because you must have supernatural powers."

Hoffman smiled. He took a folded sheet of paper from his shirt pocket, spread it open on the table and pressed the creases flat with both palms. "Maybe the magazine was too confusing. Instead of hintin', I probably should've had the balls to go full-scale and spell it out clear. Didn't figure I was at liberty to just spill it, but I hated for you to be bushwhacked. Torn between a man I respect and my job and how I felt the case should wind up." Hoffman patted and smoothed out the paper. "Room was wired, Mason. Your sheriff didn't know. We sent an agent with the state computer tech and bugged the place. Days before. Assumed you'd probably interview the suspect. Two reasons: you had to make it look good, plus you could have a gander at what was transpirin'. Try to see where the strings were. You made sure you didn't tape it, too. Left the recorder off."

Mason didn't respond.

"Then you instruct this Roberts boy to dummy up. Tell him not to speak to the police. He's done it, too. Has he ever. Odd you'd give a suspect advice that hinders the investigation."

"I don't remember what I said or didn't say, but knowing Allen like I do, I wasn't convinced. My believing in his integrity and innocence hardly suggests my criminal brother is telling the truth. And if I made him aware he didn't have to incriminate himself, so what? I've been a friend of the guy all my life and had some sympathy for him."

Hoffman put on glasses and bent down over the paper. "Here's what you said. I was listenin'. Wrote it down word for word: 'I know you didn't do this, okay? Don't worry.'" Hoffman stopped and briefly studied Mason. "I'm skippin' a few parts that don't matter." He resumed his reading: "'As long as I'm the commonwealth's attorney, you will never be charged. You're innocent. You have my word nothin' will happen to you.'" He paused again and fixed Mason with a cop's deadeye, hammerlock stare. "You didn't ask the boy a single question. You're too decent for your own good, Mason. Got busted by your own conscience. Couldn't let Roberts suffer and worry. Sent him home to kiss his wife despite the murder weapon we'd found at his house *and* his confession. Then informed Agent Bass you were prepared to indict — a deceit."

"Roberts didn't confess, and there was never a murder weapon."

"'Course you was unaware of those niceties when you cut him free." Hoffman refolded his notes and returned them to his pocket.

"I've been doing this for years, Ed, and sometimes you rely on your gut," Mason protested. "We all do. So I sensed the case wasn't up to snuff, and hey, guess what? I was right."

"Ain't here to debate with you, Mason."

"Wait a minute." Mason slapped the table with an open hand, suddenly incensed. "Hang on. Wait. How come Stallings hasn't given us this? He's under an obligation to produce it. It's discoverable as can be."

"Accordin' to Rule 3A:11, it isn't," Hoffman said, his tone self-satisfied for the first time. "Figured this out for myself. Took me twenty-three years. It's held up for me, too, least in other courts, Judge Weckstein's included. Everybody knows how smart he is. Commonwealth has to give you any statement *you* wrote or we recorded. We didn't record you and Allen Roberts, just listened and took notes. Me, Bass and Minter. Three cops heard you. We have to produce any statement or confession you made to the police. Not the situation here. You didn't make the statement *to* us. Little glitch in the rule. A loophole for the good guys. If we're careful, the Hoffman method allows us to keep a surprise sometimes. A derringer in our socks. Ran it by Stallings, he agreed. He was delighted."

"I've *never* read the law to say that. You can't be right."

"Go study it for yourself."

"What nonsense, Ed. The discovery rules are designed to ensure no one is surprised. They're about disclosure and —"

"Listen," Hoffman interrupted. "You guys with the law degrees and English majors truck in this shit, not me. I did two years of night school at Roanoke College. Barely made it through. But as for this one itty-bitty speck of the system which affects me and my job, I'll match my understandin' up against yours or anybody else's."

"I've seen the language a million times," Mason said. "Maybe after so long you start assuming too much or glossing over it, but I'm still convinced you're wrong."

"Don't matter, not really. We have the statements. You're aware now. If your lawyers raise a stink and I'm mistaken, the judge orders us to tell you what you already know. No help to your case in the long term. The evidence is the evidence. I'm gonna let Stallings know, too. Inform him I've spoiled our big finale. Receive my tongue-lashing from him and have another complaint filed with my lieutenant."

"Pretty sinister shit, Ed. You went all out on this, didn't you? The elaborate sting, the rule bending."

"My responsibility to do the best I can toward findin' the truth. Didn't figure you'd just confess to Bass and Minter if they showed their badges and asked politely. Or threatened to haul you into the station for questioning like they do on TV. It'd be wrong if I'd gone half-ass. I've been fair to you, too.

Now I've made amends. Don't want to hear no cryin' the blues."

"So· Custis and I can remove the cone of silence and stop talking in code? We're not being monitored or listened to? I misunderstood the magazine clue?"

"Our only bug was at the sheriff's office. Nothing else. I thought you might add it up."

"What if Allen Roberts and I have a different recollection?" Mason challenged Hoffman.

"You mean what if you lie and you tamper with a witness? Hard to say. Can't predict who a jury'd believe. Three cops, or you and Mr. Roberts. One thing's set in stone — you went in to see him and you kept the recorder dead. Why?" Hoffman finally broke off a chunk of biscuit and put it in his mouth, began chewing. "It's no foolproof case for us," he remarked through the bread, "but like I told you, if you ask me to handicap it, I'm comfortable the commonwealth will win. You gotta smell trouble, too. With Gates's testimony alone, we're down the tubes. But add the tape of you soundin' so surprised. Blurting to Bass and Minter it's not possible they found the gun at Roberts's house. Jury takes notice. Then stir this last ingredient into the recipe: a commonwealth's attorney who's sittin' on the lab-identified murder weapon and a confession to a polygraphed witness bebops in and tells the suspect he'll *never* be charged.

553

I'd be losin' sleep if I was you, Mason."

"Who wouldn't?" Mason asked. "Guilty or innocent."

"At any rate, I've done what I came to do. I've salvaged my promise. Actually, there's plenty good in this for you. A trade. You're wounded by the judge and media discoverin' you're not lily-white, but now you'll see Stallings's punch coming. No trapdoors when it counts the most. Good luck, Mason." Hoffman slid to the end of the bench. "I can't cut any slack for you when we go to trial," he said as he was rising. "I'll lay it out true. Have to. Chips probably aren't gonna fall completely the way they should, but you've brought a portion of this hurt on yourself. Brother or not, you were over eighteen and made a choice. Been lyin' ever since, too."

Around the close of October, after the first hard frost had faded the pasture and yard, suffocating the last briar flowers and streaks of clover, Mason was in the barn replacing a lightbulb and he stumbled into an ashtray and butts and matches and a pack of cigs hidden inside a dented metal bucket. His curiosity piqued, he also discovered two wine coolers in the tack room, buried at the bottom of a box of rags. The bottles were clear with snazzy foil labels, the rags were sweatshirt strips, culls from the mill that were ripped lengthwise by a machine and sold in red, yellow, black and green bundles at the downtown outlet store. He put the cigs and ashtray in with the wine coolers and rags and deposited the whole damning collection on Grace's bedroom desk. When he confronted her she lied to him and blamed the hired help, Mo Jenkins, who wore Carhartt, dipped Skoal and drank whatever beer was on sale at the grocery store. He referred to his spouse as "the wife." "I'm sure Mo's a huge fan of room-temperature strawberry wine coolers," Mason said, and she quickly switched the subject, attacking him for not respecting her privacy and entering her room when she wasn't there.

"You forfeit your privacy by breaking rules and lying to me," he told her.

"None of it matters anyway," she replied. "I don't care what you do."

"You are grounded indefinitely," he said firmly. "More for not telling the truth than for the smoking and alcohol."

"It can be forever," she sassed him. "Ground me till I'm a hundred. Might as well." She was snide and flippant in the fashion of someone who felt there was nothing at stake, no jeopardy, no fall past supreme bottom, no state worse than the worst. She lay down on her bed, blue-jeaned legs together, toes rigid toward the ceiling, arms against her sides, her hair fanned on a pastel pillow, her lips thinned and stitched, funereal except for her furious, blinking eyes, the lashes pounding "I hate you" over and over and over.

At the beginning of November, Mason and Custis met again in Martinsville with Jim Haskins and Pat Sharpe. They were at Sharpe's office, on the fourth floor of a bank building, the view of the parking lot and a low-slung, ramshackle furniture store. Sharpe showed them a photo of a twelve-point buck he'd killed with a bow and arrow, and they all briefly talked about Virginia Tech football, and Haskins mentioned an antique trunk he'd purchased at an estate sale. Finally, Sharpe opened a file on his desk to signal the preliminaries were through. "I've received an offer from Stallings," he said, "and we need to discuss it."

It was apparent from Haskins's demeanor that he and Sharpe had already conferred. Resting one leg on top of the other, he casually adjusted his sock to do away with a slight exposure of flesh at the end of his pants cuff.

"Fuck Leonard Stallings and his offer," Custis snorted.

Haskins and Sharpe both smiled.

"Easy for you to say," Mason remarked. "Let's hear it."

"Here's the background," Sharpe said. "I took a chance, just got in my car and drove to Waynesboro and stopped by Stallings's office. Cold. Surprisingly enough, he invited me right in and was reasonably cordial."

"I'm trying to visualize the scene — does he use a booster seat?" Custis cracked. "Fisher-Price desk? Dr. Miguelito Lovelace shrine in the corner?"

The room stayed somber; no one laughed.

"The man's a crusader," Sharpe continued. "A true believer. Craves the spotlight as we all know. But he's no dummy. I told him we're aware the cops listened to the conversation with Allen Roberts and warned him we'll be prepared. He's lost the advantage there, although I'm assuming Ed Hoffman had already given him the news."

"Stallings had to realize we were on to him," Haskins interjected. "And for what it's worth, crazy ol' Hoffman might be right about the discovery issue. Funny how we take things for granted because it's the way we've always done it."

"The rule's ambiguous," Mason said. "I checked, too." He was anxious to reach the payoff, tapping a foot on the carpet. "It's academic now, anyway."

"Stallings is also bright enough to know what we all understand: you didn't shoot anyone, and your brother's an asshole."

"Amen," said Custis.

"But — and I want to phrase this as neutrally as I can — he thinks you were involved. I'm not saying Jim and I do, but because of the polygraph and your interaction with Allen Roberts, Stallings is convinced either you helped your brother or you're covering for him. Unfortunately for us, Stallings is a black-and-white guy, and he feels you committed a crime. Broke the law — years ago and in a minor way, perhaps — but broke it all the same. From high on his soapbox, he also feels it's . . . it's hypocritical of you to prosecute people when your own house isn't in order, so he's not willing simply to let bygones be bygones." Sharpe paused, shifting in his seat. He glanced at the papers in his file, then at Haskins and finally honed in on Mason. An overhead light pinpointed in the centers of his glasses, a tiny bright distraction. "He'll accept a plea to involuntary manslaughter, five years with nine months to serve, a thousand-dollar fine and three years' probation. Additionally, he wants to explore a charge against your brother. You'd be required to assist."

Everyone was silent. Mason could hear, barely, a phone in the adjacent office, more of a pulse than a ring or buzz. "A felony conviction and nine months in prison? I'd lose my law license, too. I mean, hell, I'd be ruined. My daughter, my mom . . . Grace is fifteen years old."

"It's a diabolical offer," Haskins said. "The kind you don't want to take, but you're afraid not to."

"We have a week to decide," Sharpe said. He moved and the reflection was gone from his lenses. "After that, the offer's withdrawn and we go to trial on murder one and take our chances. Could be a not-guilty verdict; theoretically could be life in prison. Or anything in between. I don't have to tell you, of all people, how it works."

"We're ready to fight if we need to," Haskins added. "There won't be any stone unturned, my friend."

Distress in its purest state occasionally cooks up to something approximating sickness, apes the first push of a fever or the raw creep of nausea, and Mason felt his skin spike hot, his stomach pucker, his spine sting and quiver and buckle, and he dipped his head close to his knees and clutched handfuls of hair. His circumstances had finally penetrated him, found a foothold, and for the first time he let down in front of other people. Custis started to attend to his friend, raised from his chair, and then he thought better of it and eased back down, very slow-motion as he sat. Several seconds later, Mason stanched his despair and righted himself. His mouth was dry, his thoughts soupy. "Sorry," he said. "It just hits home after a while. Damn."

"Perfectly normal," Gentleman Jim assured him. "I'd be a wreck myself. It's different if you're on the other side of the table. You're handling it better than I would."

"Truthfully, Pat, how do you see it?" Mason asked. "We all know the best thing you can do for me is give me an honest appraisal."

Sharpe nodded, understood. "You never can tell with a jury, but I rate it fifty-fifty. It's one of those cases where the whole's better than the parts. Ed Hoffman's a strong witness, and your comments to Allen Roberts are difficult to explain away, given what you'd been told by Bass and Minter. There's risk, Mason. Wish I didn't have to say it."

Mason turned to Haskins. "Jim?"

"I don't think it's quite fifty-fifty. I feel we're in better shape than that, but dammit, Mason, it'll go to a jury. Melesco can't help us if your brother sticks to his story, can't strike the commonwealth's case, and once twelve random people start deliberating your future, well, it gets iffy. I'm not telling you anything new, but there's always the possibility of a bad result."

"Okay," Mason said. "Thanks."

"Call me here or at the house as soon as you make up your mind," Sharpe told Mason. "And if you have a counteroffer, I'll certainly communicate it. I sense Stallings has given us his bottom line, but you never know."

As Mason and Custis rode home in the Cadillac, their conversation sporadic, Mason noticed Custis was missing a tooth, had a dark stub at the corner of his mouth. "You break a tooth?" he asked.

"No. Hell no. Damn thousand-dollar veneer popped loose last night."

"No kidding? Huh. Can the dentist glue it on again?"

"Yeah. I called him this morning and told him the news. Problem is, I swallowed the little fucker. I was eating and felt it go down my throat before I figured out what was happening."

"Not good," Mason said.

"Dentist tells me I need to 'recover it.' Right, I tell him. Ain't enough Clorox on the planet for that program to work. It's only been a year since he did the job, so I inform him we'll be starting from scratch, his expense."

"Only fair," Mason agreed.

"He doesn't see it quite the same. Things get tense on the phone. He finally says he'll knock off two hundred dollars, and I advise him he'd better be dustin' off his malpractice policy. Lawsuit's good as filed. Can you believe it? Like we need another headache. What else can happen?"

"We're done, aren't we?" Mason asked, his voice floating, dim.

"Done? Meaning what?"

"There're no more doors to try, no escape routes, no buttons to push. I'm going to wind up tried for murder with beaucoup exposure and my daughter's welfare on the line, and the world's soon going to learn you fancy men instead of women unless I bend a knee to Herman Dylan. Brick walls on every side."

"You could put it like that, I guess," Custis said ruefully. "But there's always hope. I try to stay positive."

"How do you rate my chances?"

"Me? Me, I'd speculate there're definitely some wolves between you and the ginger-bread cottage. The kicker is this polygraph in the papers. Popular as you are, a Patrick County jury has been a major mack-daddy advantage for us, and now we might be in a fix."

"Aren't you confusing your stories?"

"Could be. But you get the picture." Custis grinned, revealing his stumpy flaw. "Don't say nothing 'bout my expertise with fairy tales, either. I'll set you and your bad attitude out on the side of the road."

"Amazing," Mason said, and it was apparent he was distracted by his own thoughts, temporarily deaf to what his friend had said. "Amazing." The word was salted with disgust. "How symbolic, huh? Sums it up. Our teeth knocked so far down our throats we're left to pick them out of our own shit. Unbelievable."

"It's a dental problem, Mace. I wouldn't make it into a prophecy or take it as a rooster crowing or burning bush or ring around the moon."

Mason was quiet for the remainder of the trip. The stereo played Teddy Pendergrass songs, and Custis hummed along, joining in on a few refrains. Nearly to Stuart, he asked Mason if he wanted to have a cocktail to soothe their spirits. "Why not?" Mason said. "But first I need you to take me by the office so I can check and see if my mom will watch Grace for me."

"Use my cell," Custis suggested.

"Nah, I need to sign a couple letters, too. Only take a minute."

It was around six o'clock when Custis pulled the Cadillac parallel to the awning at the front of their office, and he waited in the car while Mason went inside, kept the engine running. Mason phoned his mother, who was happy to have supper with her granddaughter, and then he hunted through his desk drawer until he found Ian Hudgens's business card. He dialed Hudgens's number and left a message: "Please have Mr. Dylan get in touch immediately. Not you, but him personally." When he returned to the vehicle, it was growing dark fast, the sun all but exhausted, the fall evenings curtailed, and they traveled through the thickening black to Custis's house and set to drinking.

A few hours later, Mason — for the first time since Allison's death — sidestepped his responsibilities and made arrangements with his mother to keep Grace overnight, and by nine thirty he and Custis were both blitzed off a bottle of good bourbon Custis had been hoarding. Theirs was a happy, sloppy, obliter-ating revelry, a soldiers-off-to-battle drunk, a stopgap and artificial joy that had them slosh-ing toasts to important cases they'd won and Mason's best home run swing ever and the Wu-Tang Clan and San Juan and Custis's several elections to town council. Mason had taken Shoni McClean out several times since their Mount Airy lunch, the last occasion a dinner and visit to a jazz club in Winston-Salem, and it seemed only liquor-appropriate to phone her late on a weeknight and include her in the party, and she was a good sport and came by Custis's at eleven o'clock and pretended to be interested in a bourbon and Sprite, then danced with Mason to an Etta James standard in the living room so he'd quit pestering her about it.

The bourbon finished — killed by Custis and Mason standing shoulder to shoulder and gunning the last shots straight from the bottle — Shoni drove Mason to his farm at two in the morning. She allowed him an inept kiss, but when he slid his hand over her belly and started up for more, she laughed and spun him toward the house and said, "Not tonight, cowboy." Until then, he hadn't tried.

"Why not?" he asked, and before she could answer he apologized, confiding he was smashed.

"Aw, really?" she said playfully.

"Listen," he slurred, facing the house, not

her. "Tell Cus I got an idea. Something that might rescue us."

"I definitely will." She was humoring him.

"And don't mention anything to Grace," he said, and staggered around so he could see her. He slapped a weaving index finger across his lips.

"You have my promise," she replied. Earlier that night, he had admitted to her he'd yet to tell his daughter about their friendship, and she'd replied that she understood and wasn't offended. She took his arm and guided him to the door but didn't go inside with him, watching through the window as he stripped off his shirt and stumbled to a couch, collapsing facedown, thank God, so she wouldn't worry over him strangling on his own vomit.

Mason had experienced very few hangovers since college — it occurred to him the following day that Custis seemed to somehow midwife most of them — and he awakened displaced on his sofa, still clad in his suit pants and socks and shoes, his shirt on the floor, his tie missing, his jacket, with any luck, left behind at his buddy's house. He stood up but was so drained and dizzy he crashed back onto the couch, got to his feet again and wobbled toward the kitchen. He checked the clock, flipped on the radio, started coffee and phoned his mom, who was about to leave with Grace for school. "We're fine, Gates," she said when he asked if they were okay.

"This is Mason," he replied, still woozy.

"Oh. I'm sorry," she said coolly. "Not easy to tell the difference this morning."

"Sorry," he mumbled. "Thanks for helping on such short notice."

As Mason poured a glass of orange juice, Jasper Griffith's hick voice issued from the radio; he was a stalwart on the local call-in show, and he was giving Mason the dickens, citing newspaper accounts of the upcoming murder trial and the failed polygraph and recalling how Mason had high-hatted him at the seafood restaurant. But the final straw was the next yapper, a rational, relatively well-spoken lady from Goose Point Road, who agreed with Jasper, and Mason realized the sea change had begun: He was losing favor in his own county, and in some quarters the disdain would become especially brutal once people began to feel gullible and horn-swoggled, their trust perverted. Even worse, Mason understood that in Patrick the heat of the torches and quality of the tar were usually in direct proportion to the size of the pedestal.

He called Sheila at her house and told her he was ill, unplugged the phone, went to bed and never left the farm until late in the day, shaving and showering and hugging a limp, resistant Grace before driving to the court-house in Stuart.

Order now at:
newyorker.com/go/fiveissues2

Offer valid in the U.S. only. First issue mails
within 3 weeks. Please add applicable sales tax.

NO POSTAGE
NECESSARY
IF MAILED
IN THE
UNITED STATES

BUSINESS REPLY MAIL

FIRST-CLASS MAIL   PERMIT NO. 107   BOONE IA

POSTAGE WILL BE PAID BY ADDRESSEE

THE
NEW YORKER

PO BOX 37617
BOONE, IA 50037-2617

CHAPTER
TWENTY-THREE

"I need your help, Judge," Mason said straight off, no fooling around, no building up to it, no putting on airs. The request was stark and naked. "I'm in a bad fix. My family and I." He took a seat, but he was restless and the chair seemed small and not to scale with him in it. He looked dreadfully wan and tired, but he was wearing a suit and a jaunty striped tie and his hair was still damp from a shower, full of combed rows. He'd rubbed off a streak of his daughter's makeup onto his lapel when he hugged her at the farm, a foundation smear vivid against deep navy wool. Evidently, he'd failed to notice it during the ride into Stuart.

The man he was addressing, Phil Moore, was a steady, conscientious fellow who'd been blessed with quite the judge's gimmick: Moore absorbed the world through eyeballs that were slightly out of whack with his head, a pair of owlish hazel ovals easily a size or so too big for their confines. His gift in the courtroom was a knack for taming his temper and patiently scrutinizing the daily parade of lies he received from the witness stand — some rank and some intricately wrought — and in most instances arriving pretty close to where the truth was lodged, his curious, active, expansive eyes often appearing to assay and filter the bullshit as it came his way. "If I can, I will," he promised Mason, not knowing what to expect. It was almost quitting time, and he'd had to unlock the security doors when a deputy from the jail's reception desk called to say Mason Hunt was there and hoped to come upstairs for a talk.

"Here's a hypothetical," Mason said. One of the fluorescent overheads in Moore's chambers was beginning to hum and quiver, becoming more noticeable as the forgettable November day expired outside, cold and drab.

"A hypothetical?" Moore replied, his tentative tone indicating he had no idea where the conversation was going. Like Mason, he was a Patrick County boy, born and raised, and although they weren't the best of pals, they shared the kinship of people who'd been stamped by a place's peculiar ink. Judge Moore could recall the playground's red clay dust staining the canvas uppers of his PF Flyers, the smell of woodsmoke infecting shirts and trousers on the drafty school bus and the sight of a skinny seventeen-year-old country girl hoeing a tobacco field in summer weather, clad in cut-off Levi's and a bikini top, sunned dark as a hickory nut, her hair caught by a red bandanna. The two men had seen each other countless times, exchanged thousands of casual words dating as far back as a Cub Scout meeting in the Baptist church's basement.

"Yeah," Mason began doggedly, his features determined but a tick off-beam, "hypothetically a guy has a brother who shoots another man in 1984 . . ." And from there, he confessed everything that had happened, the story of Gates and Wayne Thompson and the echoing .38 shot on Russell Creek Road. It took him fifteen minutes, and twice he backtracked to add details and for a while he tugged and shaped a rubber band he found in his pocket and when he mentioned his daughter's decline and the barn cigarettes, he sort of hunched his shoulders and misfired with his blinking, couldn't keep his voice from rupturing. After he finished, he got up and leaned against the wall.

The judge asked him what anyone would: "Why are you telling me?"

"Because you're the only person who can resolve this."

"Me? How? I don't have anything to do with your case. I recused myself the same day the grand jury handed down its indictment."

"What's the key, Judge?" Mason asked

rhetorically. "What stops Stallings?"

"I hate to sound dense, but I'm not following you."

"Gates," he said. "My brother. There's no real evidence against me . . . hypothetically . . . without him. Just some bits and pieces and statements with no context. You agree?"

"I do. Absolutely. If there's no testimony from Gates, the case doesn't even see a jury. It wouldn't survive a motion to strike. And if Stallings is as vainglorious as you're suggesting, I doubt he'd want to be humiliated and would probably dismiss the indictment. A no-brainer."

"So I need to take Gates out of the equation."

"True."

"And you're the only person who can do that." Mason grabbed a chair, dragged it closer to the desk and sat down with purpose.

"I'm still lost."

"Judge Richardson sentenced Gates, but it remains a Patrick County case, and you're the circuit court judge here."

"Yep. Last I checked."

"Gates will tell the truth — or, to state it more accurately, stop lying against me — only if he can get out of the pen."

"Even if I wanted to help him," Moore said, anticipating Mason's pitch, "I don't have any jurisdiction. Twenty-one days came and went years ago. Case is final."

"He can file a writ of *coram vobis* at any time in the sentencing court," Mason said. "You would have jurisdiction to decide the issue."

"Jeez — there's a gem from the archives. I haven't heard *coram vobis* mentioned since law school. It's the king's writ or something, if I'm recalling correctly. To be honest, I don't remember much about it. Never seen one filed."

"It's still on the books, Section 8.01-677. Basically, a prisoner presents new facts to the court that were unknowable at the time of trial and could've affected the verdict."

Moore held up his hand, traffic-cop style. "I don't want to wander too far into a tricky place. If your brother has a legitimate claim, I'll hear it and decide it according to the statute. I'll give him every fairness. But you and I aren't allowed to discuss it here in private. I wish it were different, but I can't ignore the rules."

"Yeah, well, no need to worry about Gates having any legitimate basis for his writ or granting him a fair hearing for that matter. By necessity, any ruling in his favor would have to be . . . extraordinary."

The judge rocked forward in his chair, listening. Like everyone else, he'd suffered right along with the Hunts when Allison died, had gripped Mason's arm at the funeral

571

service and tried to salve the wound they all felt, whispering in a pained, sincere voice, "If I can ever do anything, Mace, anything at all . . ."

Mason drummed his fingers on his side of the desk, a fast, arrhythmic thumping that ended before he spoke again. "You and I both realize there's occasionally a separation, an ugly sulk, between the law and justice. On rare instances, they're at odds. Here's the long view: If I'm convicted, my daughter will suffer profoundly for the second time in her life. She's lost her mother to a damn ridiculous fluke, and now she'll be punished by the loss of her dad. She's had no control over either, and it's eating her alive. Even the prospect of a trial — the *possibility* — is traumatizing for her, regardless of the eventual verdict. She's slipping, giving up, and who can blame her?"

"I can't imagine," the judge said, and meant it.

"My innocent mother, who lived a life of misery not of her own making with Curt Hunt and has since endured the embarrassment and heartache of Gates, gets a second dose of disappointment and the pleasure, at age seventy or so, of raising a buck-wild, heathen granddaughter and probably an illegitimate great-grandkid —"

"Mason," Moore interrupted, "isn't this simply a variant of the defense you and I listen to every day, the type of reasoning I've heard you condemn over and over? You've become the guilty criminal propping up his bawling child or feeble mom as a pity shield. Hell, anytime we send someone to jail, there're ripples and consequences that reach past the courtroom. Nearly every man or woman in prison has a mom or dad or kids or a spouse."

"This is unique," Mason argued. "Here, two innocent people are about to be decimated based on a lie. Three if you count me. A lie — how's that any credit to the system? How's it commendable or appropriate?" Sweat beads were dotting his forehead. He was ashen.

"You okay, Mason?"

"Hungover," he said frankly. "Custis and I last night."

"Can't say I blame you much, given your problems." The judge smiled as best he could.

"Thanks." Mason wiped his brow with his coat sleeve. "At any rate, I admit — hypothetically — I broke the law. But what would you or anyone else have done? Huh? I was twenty-four years old, and I wouldn't have survived my father but for Gates's protection and encouragement. I owed him a debt. There was no real opportunity to think or deliberate. It's not as if I planned and schemed and devoted hours to an elaborate getaway. Plus, that night on Russell Creek

Road, I couldn't have possibly predicted the future — I had no idea Gates would become a worthless dope dealer."

"In a certain sense, you're more culpable than most. You were in law school. I'd say you had a better than average feel for right and wrong. You realized what you were doing was corrupt, not to mention illegal." The judge looked at Mason, and Mason held with him, didn't shy from the gaze. "I'd have more sympathy if you'd just kept quiet and refused to tattle on your brother. But you got your hands dirty and helped make it impossible for the police to solve the crime. Wayne Thompson's kid and family have been left in limbo for years. That's not some theoretical, textbook fiddle-faddle; it's a genuine injury you caused. In a certain fashion, it's fair to say Thompson's son has suffered identically to your daughter. *Hypothetically,* of course." The "hypothetically" had plenty of sting in it.

"I don't dispute my guilt. I screwed up. I was wrong. I'm responsible. But please give some thought to any difference it makes. No matter what I decide in 1984, Wayne is dead and Gates shot him. I can't change it or correct it or undo it. I —"

"By the way, how do I know you're telling me the truth?" Moore asked, though he didn't have any doubt Mason was. "Maybe you did shoot Thompson. Maybe Gates is innocent."

"Because you've known me since we were both knee-high to a grasshopper, and because you also know my brother. Because I had no reason or motive to shoot Wayne. Because I passed a polygraph on the money question and Gates didn't. Because Gates has every reason to lie. Because, for a decade, you've seen my character on display in the courtroom. I can probably give you a longer list if you'd care for it."

"Thought I should ask. Go ahead." The jail served dinner at five o'clock, and the heavy smell of cooking oil and fried food began working through the walls and floor, a hint to start, then the room full up. "I'm guessing hamburger steak," the judge remarked. "Can I have them wrap you a plate to take home? It's usually not too bad."

"No, thanks." Mason was anxious to make his point and hardly considered the offer. "So no matter my choice, the crime is done and Wayne is dead. If I'd reported it to the police, what happens? The huge difference is the Thompson family has some peace of mind. I concede as much. As for Gates, he would've actually been better off than he is now. I would've had to testify Wayne was the aggressor. He'd been drinking, and there was dope in his car. He provoked Gates. He had a weapon. Gates catches a manslaughter conviction, a *maximum* of twenty years, though we both know he'd never draw a full sentence. Depending on the timing and who does what later on, perhaps he's not even around to sell drugs at the fairgrounds and earn the forty-four years he's currently pulling."

"You've taken this apart pretty well, haven't you? I've always said if I was facing the very red devil and could pick one person to do my closing argument, it'd be you or Jim Young."

"Here's the shorter version: The coke-distribution charge was worth five years — Tony Black, who's no friend of defendants, no softie — offered it in a plea. The killing's worth ten or so, twenty tops if the commonwealth had miraculously managed to ring the bell. Gates has already satisfied the time he should've received."

"Unfortunately, a jury decided he deserved forty-four years. He elected to not accept Tony's very reasonable offer. We don't get to make this stuff up as we go along. We either have consistency or we have anarchy and star chambers. Law du jour is no law at all."

"Ninety-five percent of the time, I would agree with you. But if that were the case exclusively, we'd hire bean counters, clerks and pointy-heads with computers to run the show. We'd find a drone with a chart and mandatory guidelines to occupy the big chair where you sit. You're the guy who can sign his name to a piece of paper and have a man executed — you didn't get the job to simply pound the rubber stamp."

"I'm always pleased to exercise my discretion," Moore said, "but if I skirt the law, if I cheat or deviate or ignore the rules, then everything I do — and everything I've done — becomes suspect, its legitimacy lost. I go seat-of-the-pants, and I'm just a hack, a fraud with a robe and a pocketful of whims and a sheriff and bailiff to make them come to pass. It's a slippery slope, as they say."

Mason sawed his teeth back and forth across his lower lip.

"I have a bad feeling we're on the verge of your asking me to break the law myself," the judge somberly told him.

Mason was silent. His forehead was glistening. The office smelled of the convicts' dinner.

"I'm sorry," Moore said. "I wish I could be more helpful."

"Here's my take, for what it's worth. Judge Hooker sat in this same office in that same seat and looked out the window, watched the same mountains change seasons, gazed at the same schoolhouse on the knoll, saw the people milling around in front of the drugstore and insurance agency. Then Judge Richardson did the exact same thing. Now they're both dead and gone." Mason stopped making eye contact and bowed his head slightly. "No offense to you, my friend, nothing smart intended, but in a sense it doesn't

577

really matter. See, none of us can gouge too deeply. Calculate for the long haul. Lay the surefire pattern for the distant domino. Either the world is too tightly and infinitesimally tuned for us to crack the code and have any effect, or it's so damn random and disjointed we're spitting in the wind. Point-oh-eight, and I let the kid go who kills my wife. Decimals. One one-hundredth higher, I make a different decision and my life isn't trashed. She sleeps five seconds longer, she clears the intersection. Believe what you will, there're simply too many moving parts."

"So we wish the murders and rapists well and send them on their merry way? We do nothing because we can't do everything? I'm not as pessimistic as you."

"The opposite actually," Mason insisted. "Sometimes we need to choose whatever will cover the most spots on the board — throw a blanket over as much good as we can and quit fretting about the horizon. We have this whole formidable legal apparatus, this dense set of rules and a twenty-nine-volume Virginia Code, and the truth is we can't accomplish any more than right-now justice. You can sit there and talk about this abstract ideal, the integrity of our *system,* worship an idol that's supposed to contemplate the big picture even though we ourselves can't, figure you're keeping the train on the tracks because you have this map that came from the Magna Carta and piles of ancient books, and you can stick to it and never deviate and think you're safe and this will go *A* to *B* to *C,* and I'm here to tell you — I should know better than anyone, huh? — you're mistaken. Allowing my brother to manipulate the courts and damage lives proves nothing. You're in a position to help three people and put an end to a self-serving lie, or you can kowtow to letters on a page at our expense." Mason spoke humbly, was rueful rather than hostile.

Before answering, the judge waited for Mason to raise up and acknowledge him. "So I'll take a stab at it," he said. "Gates is going to file a bogus pleading and you want me to piss on the law and rule in his favor. Set him free before your trial in hopes he'll amend his story. Throw the blanket, as you put it, over you and your mom and Grace?"

"It's what I'm down to, yeah," Mason admitted. "Crumbs and slim reeds. But I've got several pot-sweeteners for you, not the least of which is my own penance." His face pinched with disgust. "Of course, the worst punishment is I'm here helping my brother, a man I hate."

"Lex ex machina," the judge mused, shaking his head. "It'll have to be awfully compelling. Let's hear it." He was skeptical, still far from sold.

Mason visited twice more to encourage the

judge's intervention, and the Wednesday court closed at noon for the Thanksgiving holiday, Gates's typewritten *coram vobis* pleading arrived postmarked from Stuart, not the penitentiary. It was adequately written and decently argued and totally without merit, basically legal bunk, sophistry. The name "Gates Hunt" was typed rather than hand-signed at the conclusion of the paperwork, and there were a few misspellings and a grammatical blunder tossed in for camouflage.

The judge swiveled his chair and peered out the window at the Swails Insurance sign and the austere winter hills and the red-brick elementary school, stuck the pleadings in his briefcase, walked into the empty courtroom and sat there in the gallery, behind the old oak railing, thinking. Struggling. Taking stock of his own empty spot on the bench, built high above everything else. Judge Richardson's portrait hung on the far wall, an oil painting that showed its brushstrokes when the window light hit late in the afternoon. Richardson was holding a law book, and there was a gavel nearby — all the honorable props — and Phil Moore indulged a fanciful thought: he wished he could ask his framed predecessor for advice, quiz him on how the hell to cut the baby.

CHAPTER TWENTY-FOUR

Awakened at midnight by a prison guard and a third-shift deputy from the Patrick County Sheriff's Office, Gates initially was inclined to demand he be allowed to call Bass or Minter or Leonard Stallings, but he thought better of it when the county deputy told him he was being taken to Stuart for a bond determination and a decision on the recent motion to have his sentence set aside, and, heck, it must be pretty darned serious, the cop said, because here he was with a transportation order signed by the circuit judge instead of the clerk and the case was scheduled to be heard in just a few hours. By the time the warden arrived at nine o'clock and notified Bass and Minter, Gates was long gone, so there was nothing they could do except hotfoot it to Stuart and try to discover what was happening with their star witness.

Heeding instructions from Custis Norman to treat the prisoner "liberally," the deputy allowed Gates to ride in the passenger seat without cuffs or restraints, switched the bluegrass station to classic rock, visited a truck stop for three a.m. cheeseburgers and fries, and meandered through the heart of every city and town instead of using the bypasses so Gates could enjoy the storefronts and window displays and the trip would be stretched by several miles. An occasional home already had Christmas decorations burning, roadside Santas and sleighs and candy canes lit by extension cords. "Been almost thirteen years for me," Gates informed the officer.

They arrived in Stuart at four thirty, two hours prior to daybreak, and Gates was placed in the drunk tank alone. Moments later, the lock clunked and in came Custis Norman, a large, flat jail key dangling from a metal ring in his hand. He snugged the door to the frame but didn't allow the lock to catch. The room contained a concrete bench for sleeping and sitting, a metal toilet and a small sink and was fierce with the odor of urine, vomit, underarms and pine-scented disinfectant. Gates was already seated, which left Custis no choice but to stand. There was barely enough space for the two of them.

"Well, well, well," Gates said sarcastically, "if it isn't my little brother's loyal sidekick, Robin. Nice of you to drop by so early in the mornin'. You walkin' the dog and hear I was visiting?"

"Yeah. My pit bull."

"You done your Christmas shoppin' yet? Bought my present?"

"So listen, Gates, here's the deal. You —"

"No, I'm afraid *you* need to listen, my friend." Gates ratcheted a mean-spirited smile. "First, I'm not saying a fuckin' word to you. I don't need Mason sending his lackey to do his bidding. I'll talk to him and him only — you'd think he'd at least have the guts to see me man to man. Second, I'm not stupid. I'm on strike until I'm sure you're not buggin' me, which I figure is occurring right this minute. So you need to make some arrangements." He flicked his wrist several times in Custis's direction. "Hop to it, Boy Wonder. Chop-chop."

"We're not being recorded," Custis said, keeping his anger in check. "And the deal's the deal, whether I tell you or your brother tells you."

"Nope. I'm done." He made a production of reclining on the concrete ledge and refusing to look at Custis.

"Hey, Gates, what kinda bird don't fly?"

Gates yawned.

"Motherfuckin' jailbird, chump, and your wings always gonna be clipped." He left and noisily secured the door, went across the street to their office and fetched Mason. "Has to be you," Custis said. "I tried."

Gates was still in full lounge when Mason

entered the cell, the pose an insolent, cocky, infuriating show, like he was a damn emperor receiving his subjects. "Ah," he said, "the hero of Patrick County. I knew you'd somehow find it in your busy schedule to welcome me home."

Nothing would have satisfied Mason more than lifting his leg and stomping the ever-loving shit out of his brother, but he disciplined himself, considered his child and his mother and how this was part of his own punishment, same as a tablespoon of castor oil. "Gates," he said, subdued. "I'd hoped you and Custis could handle this."

"Oh, I'll bet you did. But it ain't goin' to be so easy, whatever it is that brought me here. How's it feel to have your ass in a sling, by the way? For people to learn the truth about you and your crimes? Get knocked off your high horse?"

"We're not being monitored, Gates. You don't have to perform for a tape recorder."

Gates sat upright, picked at his fingernails. "You'll forgive me if I don't believe you. See, I'm gonna be forced to demand we hold our brotherly reunion elsewhere, or I'll be unable to participate." He sliced the final word into four taunting syllables: *par-tic-i-pate.*

"Since you're a convict, our options are limited. Where'd you have in mind?"

"Well, let's see," Gates said. "What wouldn't you think of?"

"This is truly stupid. Why won't you just listen to me? You can keep quiet, and I'll do all the talking."

"Nah." Gates cranked an insincere grin. "I vote for the restroom at W & W Produce. They're open twenty-four-seven, right? Maybe I could snag a cold beer while we're there."

"You can vote until hell freezes over. It's not happening for you. You're a prisoner. Prisoners don't go on field trips. I'm not about to put Sheriff Hubbard at risk, even if I could."

"How fuckin' noble, Mason." Gates stroked his chin. He was growing a goatee, but it was coming in tatty, needed trimming and thicker whiskers. "Okay. We hike upstairs to the courtroom, the ladies' bathroom, and you find us a radio to hide our discussion."

The jailer was reluctant to relocate Gates, protesting he didn't want to get in the middle of a murder trial; he knew Gates was supposed to testify against his brother and he'd only gone this far because it was Custis doing the asking and the sheriff himself had okayed it before he'd signed off for the day. Custis returned and browbeat him, and they finally phoned the sheriff at home — he was up, dressing to feed his cattle — and he said there wasn't any problem so long as the prisoner remained in custody, instructed the jailer to take him on to the courtroom toilet and sit there next to the door until Gates and Mason finished. "If he wants to see his brother or our assistant commonwealth's attorney, it's his business," the sheriff stated and brusquely ended the connection.

Mason trotted to his office and borrowed Sheila's small black radio while the jailer accompanied Gates to the ladies' bathroom. He stayed with Gates, aimlessly chatting until Mason arrived, then searched the radio, shut the door and left the brothers to themselves.

Gates also gave the radio a good going-over and spent several minutes combing through the bathroom, pouring out the syrupy blue soap from its dispenser, unrolling toilet tissue, upending the trash can, poking and shifting ceiling tiles. "Never can be too careful, huh?" he told Mason. He tuned the radio to mostly loud static, opened both spigots full blast and ran water into the basin. The water struck bottom and splattered up drops onto the cloudy old mirror and the dingy plaster around the sink.

"Satisfied?" Mason asked.

"Well, almost. Never know about you, do I?"

"Feel free to pat me down," Mason said.

Gates laughed. "Don't think so. You feel free to undress, and we'll proceed from there."

Mason glared at his brother, who'd flipped down the commode lid and was sitting on it with his legs arrogantly crossed, one foot on the floor, the other dangling off his knee.

"You too high and mighty for that, Mason?"

"I'm not wired," Mason told him, but he knew it wouldn't matter.

"You can strip, or we can talk about sports and current events. How 'bout them Redskins?"

Mason began with his belt, handing each clothing item to Gates for inspection until he was completely naked, a bare ceiling bulb illuminating him, cold air bleeding into the room. "See? Nothing. Hope you're happy."

"Almost," Gates answered. He discarded the clothes into a haphazard heap on the floor. "Now you can lift your nuts and finish by turnin' around and spreadin' your lovely butt cheeks. Kinda like we do in prison. Kinda like what they did to me before I left this morning and then again when I got here."

"No."

"Have it your way. I don't care. You can save up till you're able to do it for real, after you're convicted. With a prison guard and a larger audience." Gates smirked.

"And you can finish your forty-four-year sentence. Every second of it."

"I'd say you have more to lose than me. Like you've said before, I'll hit mandatory parole in several months, anyway. Thank heaven I was tried before they monkeyed with the rules, huh?"

"You're pathetic, Gates. You truly are."

Gates unfolded his leg and lowered his foot to the tile. "You can do the nut juggle, or I'll call ol' Barney Fife out there and we'll stroll back to my personal suite without you and me ever talkin' brass tacks. Take your pick, big fella."

"Shit like this causes you to seem even more the punk."

"Barney?" Gates yelled, all dare and challenge. "Deputy Fife?"

Mason complied. He cupped and raised his testicles and then turned and spread his legs and reached around and pulled his butt apart.

Gates responded with mock applause. "You'll make somebody a fine bitch. Yessir."

"Can we cut to the chase now, Gates? The less time I spend with you, the happier I am."

"No reason to be so rude."

"May I have my clothes?"

"May I have my clothes, *please,*" Gates chided him.

"Please," Mason said, boiling.

"No, you may not. Let's see how you enjoy bein' humiliated and denied even basic necessities." Gates rested against the commode tank. "So why am I here? What are you plannin' to do for me? And don't waste your breath on any bullshit that doesn't have me waving bye to the penitentiary."

"I could come over there and take them," Mason declared.

"You could, but you won't because you can't afford to upset me."

"At nine sharp, the judge will hold a bond hearing on your writ of *coram vobis*. You stand there and keep your smart mouth shut, and you'll be okay. If anyone asks, you and your jailhouse advisors wrote the motion."

"I didn't file anything, not here, not lately."

"Correct. I did, on your behalf."

Gates cackled, bitter as hell. "I *knew* havin' to save your own precious hide would focus your mind." He cackled again. "So what kind of legal rabbit have you yanked outta your hat for me? The *Koran*? How'd you say it?"

"The specifics don't concern you. Basically, the motion argues your lab report was suspect because they only tested a small sample of the whole cocaine bag. The commonwealth could only prove — beyond a reasonable doubt — a tiny portion was actually dope. Who can say about the remainder? It wasn't analyzed, just weighed. The jury should've only been allowed to consider a penny-ante drug deal and not stick you with the entire ounce."

"Damn, there you go. Now we're cookin' with gas!"

"Today, the judge is very likely to grant you bond pending the final hearing on your motion. I expect you'll be turned loose well before lunch. I have this on excellent authority. Mom is waiting to post your bail with

589

money I've provided her, but she doesn't want you living there. We've made arrangements for an apartment above the flower shop. Rent's paid for six months."

"No walking 'round money, Mason? You probably know this, being a trained, professional lawyer, but the state really doesn't give you a new suit and a crisp hundred when they're done with you."

"It's negotiable," Mason said.

"I don't come cheap."

"I'll toss in a hundred bucks and the new suit," Mason said sarcastically. "As a bonus, you can keep my jeans and sweater."

"Let me guess — all I have to do is change my testimony. Sing a new tune?"

"All you have to do is tell the damn truth, Gates. We'll have you sign a statement and video you reading it."

Gates gathered his face. "Yeah. Hmmm. And the moment the ink's dry and you have the statement, you bastards revoke my bond and my motion is dismissed and off I go to pull the rest of my forty-four years. You must think I'm a total dumb-ass."

"Yeah, I do think you're a total dumb-ass, but that's not the issue. You need to evaluate what the other side's offering you. Compare your options. They can't save you a single second or pay you one thin dime. There's no reward for being spiteful, other than how great you must feel about yourself."

"They're gonna write the governor and try for a pardon."

"Oh, I'd count on the governor — a politician, mind you — releasing a dope dealer early. You're right: you've got better odds selecting that plan. Yeah, my bad. Hell, Gates, my trial's not till February, and we both realize you're stuck at least that long."

Gates appeared frustrated. "It's worth servin' my whole sentence if it means you'll have to suffer and squirm and get a taste of what you and everybody else has put me through. Fuck it."

"I doubt the judge would grant bond unless he felt your motion had a strong probability of success."

"You're trying to scam me, Mason. Play me for a fool. Look at you standing there with your dick all shriveled up like a bait minnow." Gates snorted. "Well, I'm not fallin' for your bullshit. My testimony changes only if I'm set free and stay free and I have it guaranteed and you drop fifty thousand cash on me. Otherwise, you and Mr. Stallings can settle this."

"I predict you will make bond, I predict the judge will take your motion seriously and strong-arm your court-appointed lawyer and the attorney general's office into a compromise. Moreover, I predict that if you look in the freezer at your new digs, you'll discover five thousand in cash. I'll see to it you receive fifteen more." The radio was popping and cracking and a wispy snatch of an announcer's voice came and went.

"Compromise?" Gates asked.

"I believe the judge will indicate he feels your motion is sound and he plans to grant you a new trial, and he'll note it would be a significant waste of effort and resources to appeal his decision to the Supreme Court or incur the expense of another trial when the dispute concerns the last few crumbs of a forty-four-year sentence. He'll encourage both sides to allow you to serve the remainder of your time by enrolling in the day-reporting center. Basically you'll stop by a couple times a week and attend some classes and piss in a cup. A four- to six-month program. He'll push for that resolution, and I have a friend in the AG's office who'll be sympathetic as well."

"How do I know you won't cut my throat?" Gates asked. He was closer to the edge of the toilet, his hands together and churning, busy, excited, a ball of worms. "I want it in writing."

"Afraid not. Listen. I'm telling you how this will happen for you if you don't screw me. No one is stupid enough to write it down. But you're protected because we want you to disappear. It makes no sense to double-cross you and have you raising hell and whining to the press and returning to Stallings ready to recite your lie again. My goal is to completely put this to rest."

"Once I change, I'm history," Gates said. "My testimony's dead meat after I switch to your side. A moron could see that."

"True, but do you think I want the headache? I'm anxious to tie this off, not have another round with you and Stallings and whoever else." Mason stepped forward and the movement startled his brother, causing him to separate his hands and stand up from the toilet. Mason reached past him and began collecting his clothes, dressing. "Think of it this way, Gates: even if I do swindle you, you're no worse off than you were in terms of how long you have to pull, and you'll be twenty thousand richer and the beneficiary of this nice sabbatical."

"You cocksuckers are as rotten as maggots on roadkill. Funny you couldn't make this possible ten years ago."

"My lawyer, Pat Sharpe, will meet you at nine forty-five, before Bass, Minter and Stallings have their shot at you. I've told Pat we anticipate you're prepared to offer a different version of events, but he has no idea your act of conscience is being purchased, so don't spill the beans and cause complications. I'll give you the balance of the money as soon as you recant and we have it on film." Mason pulled his sweater on. His head stuck at the neck opening, then popped through. "Today's the day, Gates. This will come unglued if you don't cooperate right now."

"I want fifty."

"Twenty's the market price. Take the cash and be sprung from jail, or lie and leave empty-handed. We're finished negotiating. Pat will be at your new address. Key's with Marilyn at the register."

"Apologize," Gates demanded.

"Apologize?" Mason repeated, incredulous. "To you? For what? You . . ." He couldn't help himself, couldn't resist the rage, and he grabbed Gates by the throat with both hands and drove him against the wall, but Gates was ready, fought back, clamped down on Mason's wrists and tried to kick him in the groin. Mason twisted and blocked the blow with his shin, and he slammed Gates's head hard as he could into the wall and Gates let loose of his wrist and swung roundhouse, hitting Mason solid on the jaw, and the deputy came busting in and wrapped Mason around the waist and wrestled the two men apart. They stood there panting and glaring at each other, on fire with hate. Above the commode, an unframed cardboard landscape had been jarred crooked.

"Your choice, Gates," Mason said as the jailer was removing his brother from the john.

"Should've said you were sorry," Gates snarled. "Given me my due."

■ ■ ■ ■

"I lost my temper," Mason admitted to Custis upon returning to their office, Sheila's radio in his hand, the cord unwound and dragging on the floor. "I promised myself I'd kiss his ass for Grace's sake, and I couldn't do it. It's probably irretrievable now. Totally my fault — we knew what was coming, and I let everyone down."

"Can't blame yourself," Custis said. "We're lucky I didn't go off on him, and I was only in the cell a few minutes."

They sat together and marked time, Mason sipping coffee. There was no sunrise to speak of, only a waxing, uniform gray light that blended in with the mountains and rendered the town sluggish and lackluster, and around nine the sky began to spit snow and plump raindrops, causing Sheila to scurry from the parking lot on the balls of her feet and shake off her umbrella underneath the awning. By nine thirty, Mason and Custis didn't even bother with small talk. Custis took several phone calls and Sheila brought the mail, and at ten fifteen there was still no report from Sharpe. Mason and Custis debated whether Gates had actually made bond, and Custis suggested maybe they should check with Pat's office or try his cell, and they spun their wheels and agonized, Custis twice leaving for the upstairs toilet, mumbling "my stomach" over his shoulder. Mason finally lay back his chair and closed his eyes, a pen-and-ink illustration from a childhood magic primer hogging his thoughts, a sketch of a playing card balanced on its teeny edge, a well-drawn finger coaxing it erect, the king of clubs paralyzed by thin air.

A few minutes before eleven, they heard the phone ring at Sheila's desk, and she quickly appeared to tell them Mr. Sharpe was on the line. All Pat said was "You need to come over here, Mason. Your brother wants to see you." Forgetting his coat, Mason asked Custis to please stay put and watch for the cops and then bolted out of the office, jogging through the raw morning, pelted by rain and sloppy, incomplete snowflakes. He climbed the narrow stairs beside the florist's two at a time and banged on the door, and Sharpe and Gates both shouted for him to come in. Gates was sitting on a sofa, Sharpe standing near a window, the view of an alley and the high brick side of another building. There was a grocery-store fruit basket on a table, a gift from the landlord. The apartment was murky, corners and seams obscure.

"We have some unfinished business, Mason," his brother declared. "You were about to admit how you were sorry for repeatedly fuckin' me over when the deputy interrupted us. We need to tend to that before I go

Hollywood with your lawyer." He feigned confusion. "You seem wet. Didn't wear your jacket? Leave suddenly from the office?"

The door wasn't completely closed. A draft pushed in from the stairwell, and Mason heard a tractor-trailer change gears on the steep Main Street grade, the sound of snow chains beating the pavement. He didn't respond.

"Two magic little words: I'm sorry." Gates had his arms spread across the ridge of the sofa. He'd changed into clothes his mother had left at the jail, the pants too small in the waist.

Mason focused on him. "Do you really think I've caused you harm? Wronged you? Seriously?"

"Hell fuckin' yeah," Gates spat. He glanced at Sharpe. "Can you believe this clown?" he asked the lawyer.

Mason went through the same calculus he'd done before, considered his mother and his daughter and how unconditionally he loved them both, but it infuriated him that he'd just been stripped and humiliated and taunted at the restroom. He looked toward Sharpe, who dipped his eyes, wanting no part of this. Gates scooted farther forward, taking down his arms as he moved to the last of the cushion, and the table lamp's sixty watts now illustrated much of his face, white on white, a clear bulb joining mushroom skin. The new light pried him from the dim winter room and sloughed off a warped, elongated shadow onto the wall, and he was suddenly and ferociously every inch his father's sullen son, Curt Hunt writ large in his flesh, reclaimed.

"They say always give the bandit your wallet," Mason sighed. "Don't put up a fight. Not worth your life." He checked on Sharpe again. Felt another chilly draft from behind him. Built the apology in his mind and got ready to pull the lever, let it go. He thought of his father, the rough mechanic's hands, the missing finger joint, the lube and grime in the creases of his palms. He recalled Curt mashing his face into the grass and soil, a grown man's knee set against his nine-year-old spine, and he remembered deciding it didn't matter what he said or how much he begged, because his father would never be satisfied, never relent. "You know what, Gates?" Mason paused, noticing the wet floor around his shoes. "You won't receive another lie from me. I'll leave with my pride and my decency, thank you, two items that must be very foreign to you. You can tell Mr. Sharpe the truth, or you can continue as you are, a cipher and an ingrate, Curt Hunt's only child. His heir. Your account with me is empty."

Mason broke off the words forcefully, briskly, like kindling sticks snapped over a knee, momentarily lingering on his brother when he'd finished. He acknowledged Sharpe with a nod and turned and went into the hall, but he didn't rush or hurry, faced his brother and the room's interior as he was shutting the door, Gates and Sharpe vanishing bit by bit as he pulled the knob, neither of them speaking, a shiny metal *2* swinging into sight, the number glued to the wood. He took the handrail and headed down the steps to his office, never once considered changing direction.

"More of the same," he reported to an anxious Custis when he returned to their building. "It's a hard balance to strike. I'd die for Grace, wouldn't matter how much it hurt or how long it lasted, but I can't — *won't* — let him shit on me like our daddy did. I'll go to trial and take my chances if it comes to that. We'll just have to wait and see if Pat can persuade him."

"Mmmm, damn. I had hopes."

"Yeah."

"Well," Custis said, "a man can't stay down on his knees but for so long."

Thirty minutes later, they heard whooping and hollering in the reception area and jumped to their feet and Pat Sharpe didn't slow up at Sheila's desk or hesitate at Mason's door, entered the room with a resounding "Yes!" his arms raised, a signed statement in one hand, a video in the other. Custis hugged him and hoisted him off the ground, knocking Sharpe's glasses sideways, and they all slapped high fives and yelled and cheered. "Thank you so much," Mason said. "I can have a life again." Sheila came to see what the hubbub was about, and Mason grabbed her by the wrists and flew into a silly jig all around the office, and while they were dancing daft as Dorothy and the Scarecrow, for the first time he could ever recall, Mason felt delivered and altogether loose, finally shed of his loads, no claims against him, no drag, his daddy buried, his brother gelded and behind him, his daughter rescued. He leapt onto the damn desk, yanking Sheila with him, and they bopped, shimmied, reeled and funky-chickened until papers and files covered the floor. There was never a single musical note, only Custis and Sharpe egging them on, but even the expensive pen set engraved with Mason's name was kicked off. "Coming home!" Mason screamed, his arms and legs in a whirlwind. "At last."

"How'd you sell him?" Custis asked Sharpe after Mason and Sheila had finished their gyrations and stepped down, Custis and Sharpe each taking one of Sheila's arms to brace her as she left the desk, her shoes lost from each other on the floor. "Give us the report."

"Oh, man," he said. "I thought we were shit outta luck. Mason comes in and they have a bit of a standoff, and after he leaves, I put on my panhandling rags, and Gates is sittin' there zoning, a million miles away, blowing me off. He keeps checking the freezer and then without any warning he becomes all pleasant and compliant, tells me he's ready to tape. Like someone threw a switch. He skims the statement, signs it, reads it for the camera. I had my secretary waiting in the car, and she notarized it. He admits he made up the murder story, states Mason is innocent, concedes he did it to try and buy himself an early release. Complete exoneration for us."

"The truth, finally," Mason said, his breath quick from the dancing and excitement.

"He made me promise to tell Mason he forgave him. Kept reiterating it. 'You see who the better brother is,' is how he phrased it. 'Who can forgive who. Who's a child and who's a real man.' "

"A real man in the tradition of Ike Turner and Bobby Brown, maybe," Custis muttered. "Or the Boston Strangler."

"As I'm leaving," Sharpe continued, "after I've recorded him and we're through, he pipes up and says, very cryptically, 'Yeah, so Mason didn't kill anyone, but he's still no Boy Scout, not the man you fools think he is. Mason and me will always know.' He let on like he was doing you a big favor. He's lied and brought you an indictment, and he's acting like he's drinking the hemlock for you. It was bizarre."

"Had to be," Mason remarked, standing on a file folder, its contents scattered. "But you can rest assured Gates Hunt never helps anyone except Gates Hunt. Period."

"You guys figure he's really got a chance at a new trial?" Sharpe asked. "I couldn't believe he was free on bond."

"Not our concern," Custis said emphatically.

"I'm inclined to agree," Sharpe replied. "I've never been a guy to analyze good fortune too scrupulously."

"Before I forget — thanks again, Pat," Mason told his lawyer. "I'm so grateful for everything." The tone of his voice, the sincerity, changed the atmosphere, and the party receded. Sheila stopped in the middle of a shoe strap and peered at the men.

"My pleasure," Sharpe replied.

"Couldn't have done it without you."

"No problem," Sharpe said. "I'm relieved, glad it's over. Whew."

Mason pivoted toward Custis, wanting to confess how appreciative he was, how he valued their ties and connections and years together, how *they* were brothers, how he regretted doubting his partner's allegiance, but he became emotional and got nowhere, his chin and lips in a tremulous kink, his voice tamped down into his throat.

Custis helped him through it, waving him

off with a huge brown hand. "No need for all that, Mr. Bojangles."

"I can't even begin to tell you . . ." was all Mason was able to utter.

"You ain't seen my bill yet," Custis kidded him, and the tired old lawyer crack gave everyone an excuse to laugh and be done with the awkwardness, Mason especially.

Custis phoned Jim Haskins. Sharpe hustled to the *Enterprise* office with a press release he'd prepared in advance. Sheila zipped to the courthouse to spread the news. Mason called his mom, who shrieked, "Praise you, Lord!" and drove to inform her minister in person. The instant Grace arrived home from school, Mason explained the video and announced they were redeemed. He was safe.

From the rickety sofa, she watched the tape with her head canted, her neck slightly extended and her lips parted in guileless teenage wonderment, soaking in this man she shared blood with but couldn't recollect meeting, a pale dude with a skuzzy goatee wearing a plain gray sweatshirt, echoes and dribs and drabs of her father in his appearance and mannerisms, the camera jittery in a couple of spots. When Gates admitted lying, she squeaked a soft, satisfied sound and clapped her hands together and left them clenched, then beat the floor with exuberant, girlish feet, running in place, her reaction not so different from her father's. "I love you, baby," Mason exclaimed, and he hooked an arm around her and yanked her closer, her feet still in high gear.

True to form, Gates pointlessly lied to Bass and Minter, promising them nothing had changed. He advised them he'd filed a motion and the judge had released him on bond and scheduled a hearing, but so what, there was no need for them to panic and show up with their panties in a wad. The cops went to the clerk's office and read the *coram vobis* file, called Stallings and warned him there could be a complication. "Awfully suspicious," Minter grumbled to the special prosecutor. "I smell a rat."

Stallings didn't reach Stuart until mid-afternoon, and he also visited the courthouse to review the *coram vobis* pleading. "This is a farce," he complained to the clerk, who could only shrug and state the obvious, that she wasn't a lawyer. "It's procedurally barred," he fumed. "And nonsense to boot." He called the judge's administrative assistant to request an explanation or a meeting, and was primly rebuked.

"The judge says it's not your case," she drawled, "and even if it was, he can't talk to you about it ex parte. Meanin' only one side bein' heard."

"I know what it means," he barked.

Custis had convinced Pat Sharpe to let him personally deliver the news of Gates's defec-

604

tion to the special prosecutor, and tipped off by an assistant clerk, he was waiting at the bottom of the courthouse steps when Stallings stalked out of the building, a cell phone jammed against his ear. "Yo, Stallings," he yelled. "Over here, my man." Custis was underneath an umbrella, wearing an elegant black wool overcoat. The weather continued to be fussy, with sprinkles of rain and snow. "Got a treat for you."

Stallings folded his cell phone shut and walked to where he was, stood beside Custis instead of in front of him, both of them facing Main Street. Stallings was wet, didn't have a hat or umbrella, and Custis didn't offer him any relief. Stallings put his hands in his pants pockets, hunched forward. "I've been home-cooked, haven't I?"

"Your canary just lost his chirp. Here's his statement." Custis handed him a sheet of paper. "We also videoed him for your viewing pleasure. I'd estimate you now have what we in the trade call a credibility problem."

"Shit."

"Yeah, it's a cruel blow, Leonard."

"He could always change again." Still sideways to Custis, Stallings was watching a pickup loaded with firewood crawl down the street, a layer of slush on its hood and roof.

"I doubt he will, but supposin' he does, he's damaged goods for you. The case is junk."

"Your boss was involved in a murder, Mr. Norman. A criminal sitting in judgment of other criminals. You proud to be a part of such?" The smaller man's clothes were wet, his orange hair damp, limp. A snowflake hit his cheek, melted.

"I'm proud of Mason Hunt, yeah." Custis turned and looked down on Stallings. "I'm guessing some turd granted Gates immunity — he's gonna skate, isn't he?"

"Yep," Stallings said tersely. "A man gets shot, we know who was involved, and the guilty go free, unscathed. We didn't lose anything by giving Gates a pass for his co-operation — it's not like he'd ever implicate himself, and there was never a realistic possibility of Mason coming clean and confessing his role, whatever it might've been. I did the best I could with the case I had."

"No," Custis replied, "you didn't. You were too busy puttin' on your pith helmet and scramblin' to bag your trophy to consider anything else. Mason Hunt's no murderer, and you knew that, but you still wanted to bust his ass and hang the trophy on your wall."

"I truly can't believe you guys talked your judge into springing him. The *coram vobis* is total bullshit. Pretty easy to win if the field's tilted and the ref's on your payroll."

"Maybe folks in Patrick tend to look after their own. And maybe around here we're actually willing to make adjustments if need be. Any stupid motherfucker can paint by numbers; it's your freehand work that counts." Custis shifted his weight. " 'Course, as I understand it, this is all righteous. No favors, no skulduggery, no nothing. Just a con finally confessin' his scam."

"Tell that to the Thompson family — they're certainly being well served."

"No need to be a sore loser, Leonard. No need to blame the judge and Mason and me because you coupled your wagon to the word of a rogue and a liar and — big surprise — you wound up in a ditch."

"Every dog has his day, Mr. Norman. You've had yours. Believe you me, I'll be waiting for mine where you and Mason Hunt are concerned."

"Some mighty powerful wisdom, there. I'll write it down so I don't forget: 'Every dog has his day.' Man, that's Oprah-caliber wise. You invent it yourself?"

CHAPTER
TWENTY-FIVE

The Saturday following Gates's payoff, there was a party in the rhino room at Mason's farm, a celebration attended by friends and family and Shoni McClean, who kept her distance and left early so as not to seem forward or tacky. Afterward, Mason sat down next to Grace in front of the big-screen TV, and they gabbed and rambled until the wee hours, and she said, yeah, yeah, yeah, oh yeah, it was a humongous relief to be done with the murder trial. As she flitted from topic to topic — boys and school and clothes and people at the party — he noticed her makeup looked less morbidly dark, and in a somber moment, she conceded she actually enjoyed her sessions with the school counselor, Miss Liesfeld, because, no offense, it was nice to have somebody to talk to other than him and Grandma.

Over the next month, she was allowed to rewrite a term paper and do an extra-credit project in world history, rehabilitating her grades so successfully that her report card revealed nothing worse than a solitary B. There was no sign of smoking, no evidence of drinking and far fewer fights, blowups and pouting spells. She and her friend Mary Anne went with Mason and Shoni to the movies, and although it was tense for the four of them during the drive to Mount Airy, at the start of the feature Shoni offered a tub of popcorn in Grace's direction, and she reached in and took some, volunteering a polite thank-you. Standing around the lobby after the picture was finished, waiting for Mary Anne to return from the restroom, Grace inquired about Shoni's bracelet, told the older woman she thought it was cool, and on the way home they all agreed the movie had been entertaining, prompting the teenagers to enthusiastically recount their favorite scenes.

Naturally, Gates held fast to his nature, remained a loafer and a hoodlum, and within a week of his release he'd moved a druggie welfare mom and her twelve-year-old son into his one-bedroom apartment, where the kid slept on the sofa and lived off candy and cheese sandwiches. Gates clocked just enough temp-agency hours to keep his day-reporting supervisor satisfied, guzzled beer and boasted about prison at the Old Dominion and blew through his twenty grand in less than a month, a used Chrysler ragtop, a state-of-the-art stereo and a trip to Daytona Beach his main investments. Drunk and stoned one frigid night in December, he called his mother and woke her up, pleading to be allowed back into her good graces. Quickly alert, she told him he was a corpse as far as she was concerned, gone. "Quit your whimpering," she rebuked him. Days later, the three hundred dollars in tens and twenties she kept hidden in her bedroom — stashed in the same place since Gates and Mason were boys — disappeared, and although she and Mason and the police all damn well knew Gates had stolen it, there was no proof, nothing they could do.

The year before, a Christmas tree had seemed like too much trouble for Sadie Grace, but this season — in much better cheer despite Gates's intrusion — she found herself a hacksaw in the basement and trekked to the field below her house and cut down a handsome white pine and dragged it trunk-first back to her house, smoking a cig as she went. She baked a ham and cooked sweet-potato casserole and even traveled out of town to buy presents: a pocketknife key chain for Mason, an Abercrombie gift certificate for her granddaughter. Christmas morning, as Mason and Grace were stuffing ribbons and wrapping paper into a trash bag and tidying the den, they heard a blunt thump against the window and they turned in unison and a robin — in December, a robin — had flown into the glass, *splat*. The bird had bounced into the holly bush and lay spread there, addled and scared. Grace hurried outside and scooped it up, placed it in a cardboard box with an old pillowcase for a nest and nursed it with bread crumbs and a medicine dropper, but it never recovered, dying two days later, stiff and dry and its eyes filmy, the full-throttle collision simply too much to overcome.

Honoring his end of the *coram vobis* deal, Mason stepped down as commonwealth's attorney. So the resignation wouldn't appear forced or *too* terribly suspicious, he waited until January to inform everyone he'd had a bellyful of public life and needed a respite and was missing his daughter's best years. "Enough is enough," he would say whenever kindly people encouraged him to stay on. The most difficult part of the arrangement was persuading Custis to take over the gig — he steadfastly claimed he was "happy to be Kevin Eubanks forever." Eventually Mason told him a pointed truth, told him he calculated a portion of the reluctance was tied to a fear of being exposed, a desire to stay modest and gray and removed from the spotlight. "I've capitulated to Herman Dylan to save your queer ass," he pushed, "and you're going to repay me by taking the job and making

611

Judge Moore happy. Step up to the plate, or I'll spread the cowboy pics myself. If you're planning to be gay, you need to do it with a little less timidity."

Custis relented and accepted the appointment from the court, became the commonwealth's attorney on March 1, 2004, and one early April weekend at the Château Morrisette wine and jazz festival, Mason and Shoni saw him with a stranger, a slim black man with chic, trendy spectacles and a navy turtleneck. Custis introduced him as Alton, and they visited for a while and Mason invited them to stop by the farm for a nightcap if they were inclined. Not long afterward, Custis's friend appeared to watch him in a local production of *A Funny Thing Happened on the Way to the Forum,* and everyone was thrilled with the play and several people got the sense of who this new fellow was, especially with Custis bounding around in his stage makeup. "I'll be damned," some remarked, while others confided it was no surprise.

Custis began to relax, quit sawing himself in half and driving away from his home so frequently, and he brought his partner to Stuart more often, but there were some places they knew to skip, some boundaries they didn't chance, and they never so much as dared to sit too close in public, were always just two guys together, the rest left to your imagination. They even persuaded Inez to travel with them to D.C. for an Al Green concert, and she had three glasses of wine and became tipsy before the show, stood between the men and bumped her hips against theirs in rhythm to the up-tempo numbers.

Mason, meanwhile, hired Larry Cowley, the finest carpenter in the county, to refurbish an old barbershop with hardwood floors and intricate crown molding, and he hung out a shingle there and started a private practice. "From one kinda clip joint to another," Larry ribbed him. The first time he had to appear opposite Custis in general district court, Mason woke up early and slipped on his wing tips using the elaborate shoehorn his friend had given him, sitting in an old Windsor chair and grinning like an idiot as each stocking foot eased down the steel. He completed the routine by buffing the leather with the whirling black cone of a chrome-plated machine he'd purchased on eBay, and his shiny, spiffy shoes set a tone right off, just as Custis had promised they would.

That morning, when Judge Greenwalt commented he didn't know who looked the more uncomfortable in the courtroom, Custis winked and said, "I taught the boy everything he knows, but you don't really think I showed him my whole bag of tricks, do you?" And then they had at it, taking almost an hour to try a shoplifting case. "Don't let my sharp-as-hell, machine-buffed, pimping shoes blind you," Mason whispered as they were walking toward the bench to argue over an exhibit.

By May, the effects of Leonard Stallings and his indictment were waning, and Mason was back to enjoying his porch and rocking chair in the evenings, briefly joined by Grace on the first truly seasonable night of spring, the weather now mild enough that the oil furnace barely fired at all, another cyclical rebirth pouring into the countryside, leaves and bushes and flowers arriving as promised, the dead, scarred world perking up and gaining pace.

CHAPTER
TWENTY-SIX

"Why the hell not?" Custis declared. "Might as well put in an appearance — I'm sure they'll be sportin' free punch and peanuts and the sampler platter from Sam's Club." So both Custis and Mason attended the spring groundbreaking for Chip-Tech at the Patrick County Industrial Park, and all grades of politicians and pooh-bahs showed up to claim credit for the coup and the jobs and the boon to the local economy, and one naïve, self-important speaker lauded Herman Dylan and foolishly proclaimed how much he looked forward to a long and prosperous relationship between the county and the company. "Yeah," Mason whispered to Custis, "a long and prosperous five or six years."

"Reminds me of a celebrity wedding," Custis said. "Where a 'lifetime of devotion' lasts about as long as a mediocre sitcom."

Ian Hudgens was there, and he couldn't resist a zinger, a private joke, and in his dull prepared remarks, he noted he wanted to recognize not only Mason Hunt from the Tobacco Commission, but also someone else whose behind-the-scenes involvement had been invaluable, and the smug little weasel asked Custis to stand and the unwitting audience clapped and cheered, the loudest applause of the event, and when all the speeches were done, people crowded around and thanked Custis. Finally, men in suits and women in dresses and heels grabbed brand-spanking-new shovels and posed in a semi-circle and Gail Harding snapped a bunch of pictures for the paper.

Herman Dylan had his grant money, Patrick County had its plant, Custis Norman had his reputation and Mason Hunt had his friendship. Yielding to Dylan had been a simple choice for Mason, though he told "The Iceman," after they'd struck a bargain, that by Patrick County standards, his embalmed, blackmailing ass did in fact need a Porsche. A whole damn fleet of them.

CHAPTER
TWENTY-SEVEN

"Grace?" Mason shouted her name, and he shouted it louder when he spied the breakfast dishes still in the sink and a black fly buzzing the festering scraps and the cranberry juice sitting on the counter, the lid off. Home from work on a June evening, he dropped his briefcase beside the kitchen table, went to the pantry and shook out a handful of almonds, still irritated. He could see Mo Jenkins out in the pasture, burning brush at the far end. Grace's music was playing, something folky and ethereal he didn't recognize. There were two messages on the machine: a call from his mother about her balky oven and a stream of badly mumbled gibberish from a boy looking for Grace who didn't leave his name. Mason yelled for her again at the top of the stairs and obediently knocked prior to entering her room, always careful of her privacy, though the knock was sharp and he barely waited before pushing open the door.

She was lying there flat on her back underneath a comforter she'd pulled nearly to her chin, pale throughout her face and neck, crying, so limp her arm tumbled off the mattress and bent unnaturally, contrary to the muscles and tendons. Mason hurried in and slid onto the bed and took her hand, correcting the bowed arm. He asked her what was wrong. "Tell me," he said. "It's okay. Did something happen at school? Why're you so upset?"

She sobbed and sniffed and then the bawling spread and jerked her shoulders and convulsed her belly like she was on the verge of vomiting. Mason touched her cheek and smoothed her hair. Acoustic music played, a flute prominent. Her screen saver flashed a head shot of her and her girlfriends, smiles and braces and goofy delight. "It's okay," he said. She caught her breath for an instant and, red-eyed and trembling, told him she was pregnant.

"You?" Mason asked, waylaid. "Seriously? You?"

"Please, please, please, a million pleases, please don't be mad. And please don't tell Grandma Sadie." She wiped snot on her bare arm. "I don't know what I'm going to do," she wailed.

"You're not even sixteen, not till September," Mason blurted. He stood and rubbed his temples with the heels of his hands. He walked in an erratic circle. He thought about Allison, wishing once more she were there to help him. "So who's the father?" he suddenly asked, the moment the question formed in his mind.

She rolled onto her stomach and burrowed up in a pillow, continued crying.

"How in Christ's name did you let this happen? Is there just no end with you, Grace? Do you have any idea how hard I've struggled to take care of you? Worried myself sick? And this is the thanks I get." He kicked a stuffed animal that had spilled from the bed, sending it against the wall. "Dammit." He pressed his temples again. "So who's the father? At least I hope it's not some Goth creep or that Burton kid with the earring."

"You promised me I could tell you anything," she wept, the words curbed by the pillow.

"I did, yeah. I sure did. But as best I can remember, I didn't tell you to get pregnant. Being able to talk to me doesn't give you immunity from irresponsible behavior. You can't do as you want and then tell me about it and expect me to . . . to . . . simply forget it." He sat on the corner of the mattress. "Stop stalling," he said.

She turned sideways so she was able to see him. "Are you gonna tell Grandma?"

"I don't know."

"You're the only person I have to help me

619

and you're just bein' hateful."

Mason couldn't keep still. He stood and snatched her desk chair, turned it backward, straddled it and sat with his forearms balanced on the top wooden slat. "I'm not being hateful."

"I'm so, so sorry," she said.

"I'm sure you are."

"I know you must hate me," she sobbed.

"I don't hate you. You're my daughter and the center of my world. I love you, and that's not easy to say right this moment." He stood. "And I'm going to help you figure this out, and yes, I'm glad you told me. You can count on me. But you can also count on living in a gulag for the rest of the year." He stared down at her. "So who's the father, Grace?"

"Alex," she said meekly.

"The Spanish kid? The boy who did the math project with you?"

"He's not Spanish," she said, suddenly more composed. "He's Filipino. Why do you have to be such an awful redneck?"

"Me? How am I a redneck? I'm not the one fifteen and pregnant, looking at welfare checks and GED classes."

"He's smart and sweet. I suppose you'd rather me be with some dumb jock."

"I'd rather you be worried about the prom and learning to drive a car," he said, "instead of all this." He sighed. "I swear, no matter how you sweat and calculate and bust your butt, it's impossible . . . impossible to . . ." He quit on the thought and became distracted, pensive. He sat on her bed again, but his movements were different, gentle and accommodating, the lathered, bootless energy missing. The three pixilated girls held their smiles, declining sunlight silvered the dust and a cobweb strand in the windowsill, an upturned twig with its solitary shriveled leaf rested in a gutter, a ribbon of smoke from Mo Jenkins's fire curled past the window and dissolved as it went skyward. Thousands of pieces, thousands of arrangements and combinations. "But okay," he said, the words mild, tame.

"Okay what?" she asked, sensing the shift in him.

A series of images strung themselves together in his mind: a frail man standing behind a storm door, his gaze off-kilter, the door's metal scrolls, loops and curlicues running the length of his body like a strange exoskeleton; a roach squirting across a drawer bottom when he was a boy, still living with Curt; the weighted nose of a balsa-wood plane he and Gates had put together and sent sailing across their yard; baby Grace fascinated by her mother's painting, mesmerized by the colors and shapes filling in the canvas; trotting around third base at James Madison, Sadie Grace glowing in the stands. There was a gap in the music and the room fell silent

621

between tracks, and a sliver of reasoning took root: then and there he accepted that pell-mell came in infinite variety, from grim to sublime, wrecking ball to salvation, and while he'd always understood he couldn't resist either a sovereign with a Calvinist compass or a gale of random bumps and dips, sitting alone with his pregnant daughter, he recognized — damn — he wasn't even wise enough to distinguish blessing from curse, sweets from poison, gold from flashy pyrite.

"I'm fairly confident," he said in a humbled voice, "that we never understand as much as we think we do." He held her hand in both of his. "You and I will stick together. Come what may."

She looked at him, anxious now, unnerved how he'd so suddenly gone sci-fi on her, all hushed and restrained, like there was a monster in him or a zombie's power gaining sway, and he caught her expression and deciphered it, read her doubt exactly. He assured her he was just fine, and still plenty angry, adding that her punishment was beginning immediately. Then he ceremoniously unplugged her computer monitor and hauled it with him as he left to underscore the point.

Later, hunkered down in his wooden rocker, the porch dark except for some inside light filtering through the windows, contemplating the blank computer screen he'd stupidly deposited on the fieldstone, nothing but empty, inert glass framed by plastic, he phoned Custis on the cordless. "I have a question," he announced, assuming Custis would recognize his voice and probably had caller ID anyway.

"Yeah? Really? 'Bout what?"

"I'm thinking . . . well, maybe, I'm convinced . . . Do you believe it's difficult to be sure, early on, about the true nature of things? The repercussions . . ." He stopped. Froze.

"Mace?"

"Sorry." He was silent again. A moth, mostly silhouette, fluttered against the disconnected monitor. A TV or radio was chattering on Custis's side of the conversation.

"Hello?"

"I need to, uh, tell you something. In confidence."

"Absolutely," Custis said.

"But not now, I guess. Probably some other time."

"What the hell's wrong with you, huh? You been samplin' the methadone clinic? Watchin' *Cannonball Run*? You gonna make me drive over there?"

"Nah. I'm okay. Just learning new shit, Custis. Getting schooled. Again. Sorry to bother you."

CHAPTER
TWENTY-EIGHT

The man in his mid-twenties was sitting at a food-court table on the second floor of Tanglewood Mall in Roanoke, Virginia, an hour's distance from Patrick County. He was wearing Wrangler jeans, tennis shoes, no belt and a long-sleeve shirt. He'd shaved, but his hair could've used attention. He was compact, intense, fit, and he was eating a slice of cheese pizza, using a plastic fork at first, then his fingers. He was gruff when the dandified man in a suit — a young guy with creases and starch and a peculiar accent — approached him.

"I'm sorry to interrupt your meal," the stranger said. "But I wondered if I might have a few minutes with you?"

"Don't need no credit card. Don't need a time-share. Don't need my family's picture taken. Don't need any more religion."

The stranger laughed, a deep, husky, robust ha-ha-ha. "Good for you. Me either. I agree." He offered to shake. "I'm Dallas Ackerman," he announced, though it was a lie, the name an alias he'd created weeks ago. "And you're Mr. Thompson, correct? Mr. Wayne Thompson, Jr.?"

Thompson slowly, skeptically accepted his hand. "Yeah. Do I know you?"

The man took a seat. He and Ian Hudgens had arrived in Roanoke the day before and followed Thompson until he was alone. Hudgens was keeping watch from another table, dressed casually, piddling around with a plate of lo mein. "You don't, but you'll soon be glad you do."

"How'd you get my name?" Thompson demanded. By trade he was a welder, and the kind of man who had little tolerance for nonsense and tomfoolery, especially today. He pushed away the pizza remains and greasy paper plate. The question he'd just put to Dallas Ackerman translated as "you better not be fucking with me."

"Great, yes, I'd have the same response," Ackerman said confidently. "We got your name from a life insurance policy."

"Oh, damn. I left that off my list. No need for you to waste your breath. I ain't interested in the slightest."

"I'm not a salesman, Mr. Thompson. No, no, not at all. I'm here to give *you* money."

"Sure," Thompson said sarcastically. "There's a first."

"Seriously, Mr. Thompson, I represent

Apex-Continental Insurance. Your father, the late Mr. Wayne Thompson, Sr., purchased one of our products years ago. A delayed-benefit, whole-life policy that recently matured. You're the beneficiary."

"Let me guess — he left the cash in a Nigerian bank, and all I have to do is give you a grand so some evil king will release my money. I mean, come on, man, me and you are in a mall and outta the blue you hit me up and expect me to think you're the real deal? What kinda company hunts you down on Saturday afternoon and . . . Hey, how would you even know what I look like?"

"We very much believe in the personal touch, Mr. Thompson. A company hallmark. We phoned your house and your wife said you were here" — this much was true, although they were staring right at him when they dialed the number — "and we obtained your photo from the division of motor vehicles. We have a plane to catch, so we decided to see if we could locate you and save time. Three hundred thousand dollars is a lot of money — you can best bet we do our homework before turning it over."

"Say again? You're gonna give me three hundred thousand dollars?"

"We already have. It was wired into an account yesterday morning. I'm merely here to carry the good news."

"You're kiddin'?" Thompson began to

believe there might be something to this. He unconsciously bit a nail.

Dallas Ackerman opened a small briefcase and presented Thompson with a sealed manila envelope. "Here's the paperwork, Mr. Thompson. The money is in the Cayman Islands. We're an international conglomerate, and we try to keep tax consequences at a minimum. I'd probably leave the money there or take it in small cash withdrawals, under ten thousand. The IRS can be very unfair, especially if people become flashy, no matter how legitimate the transaction. If you or your accountant have any inquiries, there's a company card enclosed with my number. It's a switchboard, but they'll connect you immediately or take a message."

"Is this like a TV show? Hidden camera or microphones in the potted plants?" Thompson scanned the mall, flinging his head every which way, his eyes keen.

"Nope."

"So I just got rich?"

"Well, *rich* is a relative term. You just received three hundred thousand dollars."

"No catch?" Thompson asked, his tone more amicable.

"You'll need to sign a receipt."

"Whoa. So . . . wait . . . how do I know the money's where you say it is? I might be signing for somethin' I don't have."

Ackerman nodded. "I'll leave the document

with you, and when you're satisfied, you can have it notarized and return it to me. One of our principals is anxious to make certain you've been compensated. He knew your father years ago."

"Knew my dad? How?"

"I'm uncertain, Mr. Thompson. Perhaps he sold him the policy. I'm not in that particular loop. It's not my concern."

"So it's done?" Thompson asked.

"Absolutely. Congratulations."

"This is all legal?"

"I wouldn't be giving you my contact information if it weren't," Ackerman assured him.

"So I can go take out five thousand dollars right now?"

"Yes."

"My daddy fixed this up for me?"

"Indeed," Ackerman smoothly answered, unaware of the irony.

"This is amazing." Thompson beamed. "Last month, after five years at the same job, my factory was closed and I was laid off. Jobs are scarce here. I been lookin' for work and gettin' turned down and we were scrapin' bottom. I got bills to pay. You have no idea what this means to us."

"I'm glad we could help."

"I mean, damn, what did I do to deserve this?"

Ackerman thought for a moment and allowed himself to step briefly out of character. "Nothing, Mr. Thompson. You didn't do anything. It simply came your way. How about that? Blind luck."

"I'm still confused," Ackerman said as he and Hudgens were walking to their rental car. "Who is this Thompson character to Mason Hunt? He's certainly not an intermediary or a shield or a bagman. Definitely not the type. Why's Mr. Dylan giving Hunt's consultant's fee to a welder with no connections or clout?"

"Not for us to understand, Henry," Hudgens replied, using his subordinate's correct name. Hudgens, of course, understood very well the tie between Mason and the Thompsons, and though he and his boss generally kept information very much under wraps, he couldn't resist showing off for Henry, revealing a secret. "The really amazing thing is we only contributed two hundred. Frigging *Hunt* kicked in the other hundred thou. I made the arrangements myself, transferred the cash from his personal account. On his instructions."

"No shit?"

"No shit. It's why I love my job. And why Herman Dylan's flying on his private jet and you and I are coaching it back to the city with no legroom."

"Hell, maybe the welder's working for us."

"Maybe," Hudgens said, toying with Henry.

"All I know is it took me forever to scrub the money clean and hide this corporately and conceal our involvement. Let me know if Thompson calls the service with any questions."

"So Hunt lost money on the deal. Go figure."

"Lot of chutes and ladders in our business," Hudgens said gravely. "Always have to watch your step or you might wind up in a rabbit hole."

CHAPTER
TWENTY-NINE

From his office window, more than two years after Gates's release, Judge Moore spied Mason Hunt trickling up the sidewalk, this large, athletic man wearing a pin-striped suit, and he was moving in dainty half steps, a child at his hip, a little girl, beautiful and exotic and already a spitfire, her skin tinted brown, rangy like the Hunts, set off by Allison Rand's blond hair, a genetic long shot if there ever was one. The tiny girl stopped, tired of walking, and she stretched out her arms for her grandfather to collect her, and she must have said something, because he squatted and laughed and grabbed her with both hands, and right there on Main Street, still laughing, he leaned back and held her aloft and tossed her above his head in the fashion that has caused mothers to scold fathers since the beginning of history, and the girl loved it, her expression close to rapture. "Yeah," the judge said softly to an empty room. "Maybe so."

"Life jigsaws on," Mason had told Moore shortly after Grace gave birth, "but it's okay because the odds are fifty-fifty the very next piece will be my deliverance, just as likely good as bad. The secret is — and here's the sweet part — often we don't really know which is which, especially early in the game. I've added that to the formula — makes it easier to be optimistic even when you've been knocked around a bit. My limitations keep me sane these days. Nearsightedness is my own personal lottery ticket." He smiled the smile of a man who'd learned to offset hardship. "We did pretty well, you and me. Sandbagged the flood. It's certainly not according to our exact design, not the domino I would've tripped, but where would Grace and my grandbaby be if I were in jail?"

"A fine thought," Moore had said, "but I guess I believe in the occasional unpolluted cruelty or dyed-in-the-wool tragedy."

"You can still afford to," Mason quickly replied.

"And reasonable people might disagree on how well we did, given all the laws we chiseled." They'd never mentioned the judge's help with the *coram vobis* decision before then, and they would never speak of it again.

The conversation came while they were eating a late breakfast at the café, and Mary, the owner, had loaded up Mason's meal with extra ham and a second gravy biscuit, free of charge, as she always did for him, and after he left, she allowed as to how the new baby really had changed him, how he was his old self again, the way he used to be when Allison was still with them. Through a rectangle of plate glass, above the stenciled red letters spelling COFFEE BREAK, Judge Moore caught a glimpse of Mason crossing the street to his office, mostly his top half, Atlas's shoulders and flecks of gray hair, and in a sense Moore envied him, a man forged and tempered, all the clay and filler and alloy burned away, someone with tales to recite, advice to give, a place that fit him.

Patrick County being Patrick County, Mary began stacking the dirty dishes from the table and wondered aloud, no malice intended, none at all, "Now is that child Spanish or black? I've heard both."

"Swedish, I think," the judge deadpanned.

Oddly enough, a few minutes later that same day, within a stone's throw of the restaurant, Moore met Wayne Thompson's elderly parents on the sidewalk, in town for errands and to pay their insurance premiums. Mrs. Thompson was carrying two new patterns from the sewing shop and several yards of cloth, her husband a cotter key for the deck of his riding mower. As was the custom, the judge lifted his hand to the bill of an imaginary hat and nodded in Mrs. Thompson's direction, and they passed greetings and commented on how darn dry it was, agreeing a good soaking rain was very much needed. Their exchange was brief and they pushed on in different directions, but the judge soon slowed his pace and peeked over his shoulder as they stepped within inches of the door Mason had recently exited, the shards and fragments from 1984 as close to alignment as they might ever be. The judge tested the scene through his big ol' eyes and registered no regrets, no guilt, no second thoughts. He stopped completely, quarter-turned toward the Thompsons and the Coffee Break and doffed the invisible hat again, this time took it all the way off and brought it to his waist, ending with a tiny bow that would've seemed pure lunacy to anyone watching.

PART THREE

My office at the Patrick County courthouse has two curiosities. First, my name is spelled wrong on the fancy brass doorplate the bar association gave me when I began work. *Martin Filmore Clark, Jr.,* it reads. My middle name is actually spelled *Fillmore,* with two *l*'s, but the lawyers' gesture was so generous and heartfelt I've never complained or asked for a replacement. Better yet is the possum. I'm honestly not certain who gave it to me or when or why, but a stuffed possum sits grinning atop the bookcase in my chambers, guarding the law books and craning its neck so it's visible from the defendant's table all the way out in the courtroom. The creature is a novelty, a child's toy, not a real animal skinned and preserved by a taxidermist, and it has white whiskers and a plastic nose that rattles.

Early one fall morning in 2006, I found it lying on the floor with its polyester paws pointed toward the ceiling, its synthetic gray belly turned skyward. As I was about to pick it up and return it to its spot on the bookcase, Sandra, the newest hire from the clerk's office, knocked on my door and asked if she could come in. Seeing what had happened, she laughed and inquired if the critter was dead.

"Looks like he's been poisoned," I joshed.

"Oh," she replied, playing along. "Think he'll make it?"

"I believe so. He's a tough old cuss. Been through a lot."

"Good," she answered. "Wouldn't want to lose him." She glanced down at an open steno pad. "Susan wanted me to check with you about a file we can't locate. She thinks it might be up here." Sandra ticked off a series of numbers and letters. "It's from 2003, kinda old. Do you have it?"

"I do." I wasn't particularly surprised by the request, neither bothered nor agitated.

"Is it okay if I carry it downstairs? The computer shows the case is concluded. We're just trying to tie off a few loose ends. Locate some strays."

By now I had the possum in my hand, and for a moment I let it dangle, holding it by the tail. "Yeah," I told her. "I'll get it for you. It sort of wound up here and never made it back into the system. More inertia than anything else. One minute a case is as hot as a two-dollar pistol, the next it's collecting dust."

"The index says it's a *'coram vobis,'*" she noted, emphasizing the second syllable of each Latin word. "A new term for me. Of course, a lot of this is new for me."

"We don't see very many," I said. "They're definitely rare, thank goodness." I took the file from my drawer and handed it to her, then replaced the possum.

"I sure don't envy you your job," she said sincerely. "I can't believe how much you have to learn and keep up with."

"Can't really argue with you there."

Sandra wished me well and left, carrying the blue cardboard folder with her, a single skinny file about to take its place among thousands of others. I went in the empty court-room, to where the defendants sit with their lawyers, checking to make sure I'd returned the stuffed animal to plain view. I could see it clearly, no problem. Twelve vacant jury chairs faced in my direction, six in front, six behind, the leather worn and cracked on their arms. Plaster walls, thirty-foot ceilings and dark polished wood vouched that this was a solemn place and not to be trifled with. I considered Sandra's visit and decided, after mulling over the law's majestically stubborn ways and limits, that when they unscrew my misspelled name from the door's ancient panels, I'd tell the new occupant what Judge Richardson told me the day he took me into his confidence back in 1992 — I'll offer his wisdom about not being neutered by notions and bloodless stat-utes, and I'll add a little extra, throw in a men-tion of how life jigsaws on. Standing by myself, waiting for the attorneys and bailiff and wit-nesses to arrive for the nine o'clock case, my desk drawers clean and my decision on an obscure writ finally put to rest in a metal cabinet, I was content, convinced it was just fine for me to look through the window at my small town's doings and to walk underneath the line of portraits on the wall, men who'd sat in judg-ment before I knew much about anything, all of us trying to romance the same haughty, impossible will-o'-the-wisp.

ACKNOWLEDGMENTS

Thanks to: My friend and agent Joe Regal, Liz Van Hoose, the magnificent Gabrielle Brooks, S. Edward Flanagan, Charles Wright, Frank Beverly, Julia Bard, Mrs. Ann Belcher, David "Hollywood" Williams, Edd Martin, Eddie Turner, Nancy Turner, Jan McInroy, Barnie Day and Chris Corbett.

Also, a big tip of the hat to my dad, the venerable Martin F. "Fill" Clark, who — in one way or another — is responsible for just about every page of this book.

As always, I am hugely indebted to Gary Fisketjon, the finest editor on the planet.

Finally, I'm grateful to my sweet wife, Deana, for her help, love, corrections and many trips through the manuscript.

ABOUT THE AUTHOR

Martin Clark's first novel, *The Many Aspects of Mobile Home Living,* was a New York Times Notable Book and a finalist for the Stephen Crane First Fiction Award. His second novel, *Plain Heathen Mischief,* prompted *The Charlotte Observer* to call him "a rising star in American Letters." A circuit court judge, he lives in Stuart, Virginia with his wife Deana.

The employees of Thorndike Press hope you have enjoyed this Large Print book. All our Thorndike and Wheeler Large Print titles are designed for easy reading, and all our books are made to last. Other Thorndike Press Large Print books are available at your library, through selected bookstores, or directly from us.

For information about titles, please call:

(800) 223-1244

or visit our Web site at:

http://gale.cengage.com/thorndike

To share your comments, please write:

Publisher
Thorndike Press
295 Kennedy Memorial Drive
Waterville, ME 04901